INSIDE

LEAVING CERTIFICATE

DAVIN KIELTHY • LISA O'BYRNE

The Educational Company of Ireland

First publishe_ _0.9,
The Educational Company
Ballymount Road
Walkinstown
Dublin 12
www.edco.ie

A member of the Smurfit Kappa Group plc

ISBN: 978-1-84536-843-2

Book design: EMC Design (www.emcdesign.org.uk)
Layout: Carole Lynch
Project management: Barrett Editing (www.barrettediting.ie)
Editor: Jane Rogers
Editorial Assistant: Alison Bryan

While every care has been taken to trace and acknowledge copyright, the
publishers tender their apologies for any accidental infringement where
copyright has proved untraceable. They would be pleased to come to a suitable
arrangement with the rightful owner in each case.

Disclaimer: Web references in this textbook are intended as a guide for students
and teachers. At the time of going to press, all web addresses were active and
contained information relevant to the topics in this textbook. However, The
Educational Company of Ireland and the authors do not accept responsibility for
the views or information contained on these websites. Content and addresses
may change beyond our control and students should be supervised when
investigating websites.

05M23

CONTENTS

IMAGE CREDITS

The authors and publisher would like to thank the following for permission to reproduce images:
iStockphoto.com: p.1 bernardbodo; p.2 Marc Dufresne, monkeybusinessimages, filo; p.3 Rathke; p.4 gilaxia; p.5 Bartosz Hadyniak; p.7 courtneyk, doodlemachine; p.8 Deagreez; p.9 MachineHeadz; p.10 DGLimages; p.11 Boris25; p.14 gpointstudio; p.16 zoff-photo, PIKSEL; p.17 kubkoo, HearttoHeart0225; p.18 clean_fotos; p.21 ibusca; p.22 Szepy; p.24 JohnnyGreig; p.26 WebSubstance; p.27 123ducu; p.28 supersizer; p.29 hroe; p.31 Dasiy-Daisy; p.33 Antonio_Diaz; p.37 Images by Trista; p.38 SolStock; p.39 sturti; p.41 izusek; p.44 g-stockstudio; p.49 visual space, sturti; p.52 fizkes, Fatcamera; p.55 pixelfit; p.58 gradyreese; p.60 andresr; p.62 LightFieldStudios; p.63 Pekic; p.65 Manuel-F-O; p.69 stockstudioX; p.72 JohnnyGreig, alvarez; p.73 haru_natsu_kobo; p.75 shironosov, DGL images; p.77 SolStock, monkeybusinessimages; p.78 Rawpixel, julief514; p.81 monkeybusinessimages; p.82 Bojan89; p.84 Rockfinder; p.85 sturti; p.86 raksyBH; p.87 gorodonkoff; p.89 anyaberkut, bluegame; p.92 FangXiaNuo; p.95 nd300; p.96 3DCharacter; p.97 gpointstudio, fizkes; p.98 skynesher, Geber86; p.101 andresr; p.105 UberImages; p.106 Wavebreakmedia; p.108 monkeybusinessimages; p.109 fizkes; p.110 ferlistockphoto; P.113 Katsapura; p.115 fizkes; p.118 beats3, ALLEKO, OksanaKiian; p.119 NicoElNino; p.121 PeopleImages; p.123 fizkes; p.126 filadendron; p.127 Ndul; p.129 gorodenkoff; p.130 AndreyPopov; p.131 Rawpixel; p.132 Rinelle, Wachiwit; p.133 jacoblund; p.136 dolgachov; p.138 Yuri_Arcurs, Pere_Rubi; p.139 DNY59; p.140 PeopleImages; p.143 sturti; p.146 macniak; p.148 Ridofranz, Peter Chernaev; p.151 Wavebreakmedia; p.152 NoDerog; p.153 Tong Baggett; p.154 mathisworks; p.155 alvarez; p.156 PeopleImages; p.160 andreasr; p.162 StockRocket, tzahiV; p.164 zelijkosantrac; p.166 ti-ja; p.168 milanvirijevic; p.169 yoh4nn; p.170 EmirMemedovski; p.172 Machine Headz; p.174 fizkes, Bojan89; p.175 monkeybusinessimages; p.176 PeopleImages; p.177 Image Source; p.178 svetikd; p.180 PeopleImages; p.181 pixelfit; p.182 track5; p.184 pepifoto; p.185 Roger Utting photography; p.186 joel-t; p.187 tommaso79; p.190 AndreyPopov; p.193 SolStock, gorodenkoff; p.194 danchooalex; p.195 sturti; p.196 artvea; p.198 DGLimages; p.199 vm; p.201 M_a_y_a; p.202 Devrimb; p.203 AndreyPopov; p.206 izusek; p.208 MachineHeadz; p.210 vm; p.211 Undefined undefined, GreenTana; p.212 Banks Photo; p.214 sykono; p.217 cosmin4000; p.220 nilimage; p.223 jacoblund; p.226 PeopleImages, Jecapix; p.228 kali9; p.230 Khrizmo; p.233 PeopleImages; p.234 Minerva Studio; p.235 nilimage, Neustockimages; p.236 Stephen Barnes, Andresr; p.240 Wavebreakmedia; p.243 NicoElNino, vale_t; p.245 uptonpark; p.247 Steve Debenport; p.248 Highwaystarz-Photography; p.251 dima_sidelnikov; p.254 Fatcamera; p.258 Ridofranz, fizkes, BrianAJackson; p.260 AntonioGuillem; p.261 skynesher; p.263 fotostorm; p.266 triloks; p.267 gradyreese; p.268 metamorworks, kali9; p.271 Rawpixel; p.275 Imageegaml; p.276 Rawpixel; p.279 fatihhoca; p.286 Popartic; p.288 tolgart; p.295 Steve Debenport; p.305 Scar1984; p.307 lechatnoir; p.309 RyanKing999; p.313 R_Type; p.317 ti-ja; p.326 TkKurikawa; p.329 gerenme; p.332 Steve Debenport; p.335 shironosov; p.336 Gelia; p.337 Credit Mailson Pignata; p.341 Tramino; p.342 Lumina Stock; p.345 milindri; p.347 Lacheev; p.348 max-kegfire; p.351 PeopleImages, ilbusca; p.352 Andrei Stanescu; p.353 hadynyah; p.355 TracyHornbrook; p.356 flavjus, tupungato; p.361 EmirMemedovski; p.363 Wachiwit; p.366 gerenme; p.370 David Hagerman, serts; p.378 urbanbuzz; p.379 monkeybusinessimages; p.383 abadonian; p.389 Credit knape, DanijelaKuzmanov; p.392 pixelfit; p.393 RossHelen; p.395 powerofforever; p.400 jremes84; p.403 urbancow; p.405 andresr; p.408 Kulicki; p.413 sturti; p.417 dima_sidelnikov; p.422 DenisTangneyJr; p.423 rawpixel; p.427 FatCamera; p.429 4x6; p.431 Bojan89; p.433 ohmygouche; p.435 gerenme; p.435 8vFanl; p.437 Liuser; p.438 pagadesign; p.439 servet yigit, luoman; p.440 Jack F; p.443 stevecoleimages; p.445 kulicki; p.447 OcusFocus; p.451 Wavebreakmedia; p.453 Aitormmfoto, Purdue9394; p.434 powerofforever, monkeybusinessimages; p.455 aloha_17; p.458 Halfpoint; p.460 thitivong; p.461 tomasworks, bergserg, Alexey Morozov, Derek Brumby, Ismailciydem, artisteer; p.463 bergserg; p.466 Alvinge; p.472 Alvarez; p.476 Franky DeMeyer, romma; p.477 Jorisvo; p.480 fuchs-photography; p.481 chirs-mueller; p.483 SWInsider; p.484 ictor; p.485 Mirrorimage-NL; p.487 Joe Dunckley, twildlife; p.489 Rawpixel; p.490 andylid, claudiodiv, rusm, Andrey-KZ, niccolay; p.491 Portra; p.493 hanohiki; p.497 lisegagne, danchooalex, levers2007; p.500 metamorworks, Stefonlinton; p.501 Tryaging, Alexey Morozov; p.503 ollo; p.505 nd300; p.506 Sjo; p.507 Onur Hazar Altindag; p.508 undefined undefined; p.510 filadendron; p.512 Yuri_Arcurs. **Alamy.com**: p.4 Jackie Ellis; p.11 Ian Davidson; p.42 Brendan Donnelly; p.59 Pictorial Press Ltd, Fancois Pauletto, Wenn.com, Erik Pendzich; p.74 Trevor Benbrook; p.82 ZUMA Press Inc; p.83 dpa picture alliance; p.88 Kristoffer Tripplaar; p.95 Everett Collection Inc; p.105 dpa picture alliance; p.165 ZUMA Press Inc.; p.208 John Gollop; p.310 UrbanImages; p.311 Desintegrator; p.312 Robert Convery; p.315 AM Stock (*top left*); p.332 Stephen Barnes; p.336 incamerastock; p.340 ManuelGonzalezOlaecheaFranco; p.345 incamerastock; p.354 Bax Walker; p.358 dpa picture alliance; p.375 Sunshine; p.387 Mint Images Limited, Ian Gibson, p.395 Barry Mason; p.405 Stephen Barnes; p.408 Tom Corban; p.411 Cultura Creative (RF); p.420 Keith Shuttlewood; p.422 Ian Dagnall; p.424 Gareth McCormack; p.436 Anne-Marie Palmer; p.438 Everett Collection Inc; p.461 David Burton; p.464 dpa picture alliance; p.468 Ros Drinkwater. **Shutterstock.com**: p.28 vivat; p.83 MicroOne; p.132 dennizn; p.219 Twocoms; p.285 Rawpixel.com, Jenson; p.286 fizkes; p.291 rvlsoft (*top*); p.289 BaanTaksinStudio; p.293 Grzegorz Czapski; p.298 Estrada Anton; p.301 wavebreakmedia; p.304 Dima Sidelnikov, AS photo studio; p.309 monticello, aswadie, Robcartorres; p.310 MDogan; p.315 AirP72; p.320 robert_s; p.324 pcruciatti, dotshock; p.328 Microgen; p.329 Senoldo; p.342 Nigel Stripe; p.369 Happy_stocker's; p.370 Atiwat Witthayanuru, Marcin Balcerzak; p.374 Rgtimeline; p.376 Photographee.eu; p.399 James W Copeland; p.408 Everett Historical; p.422 Stephen Barnes; p.431 BoJack; p.437 LightField Studios. **Getty**: p.363 Richard Cummins, p.397 NurPhoto. **Additional images:** p.45 Mandate workers courtesy of Mandate Trade Union; p.47 Terry Gorry & Co. Solrs; p.201 Created by Freepik (www.freepik.com); p. 208 Simon Smith/Beehive Illustration; p.380 Leo Byrne; p.479 Infographic courtesy of the European Commission.

INTRODUCTION

Welcome to *Inside Business*, a new, dynamic textbook that partners with students and teachers as they navigate through the Senior Cycle Business syllabus in preparation for the Leaving Certificate examination. This book provides a platform to stimulate interest and curiosity among students about the world of business. It provides students with the opportunity to develop key skills, such as critical thinking, that will enable them to apply their knowledge to the business environment, both now and in the future.

Critically, this book places the **student** at the centre of their journey of knowledge exploration, with student-centred features in each chapter, including:

- Case Studies based on Irish and international businesses
- A range of activities to encourage co-operative learning and teamwork between students
- Cross-curricular links
- Numeracy and literacy links
- Use of ICT to enhance student learning
- Interesting 'Did You Know?' facts
- Exam tips for answering both Ordinary Level and Higher Level exam questions
- A variety of Applied Business Questions
- Exam-style questions and a range of relevant past Leaving Certificate examination questions.

The strategies used throughout this textbook encourage students to take responsibility for their own learning as well as ensuring that students are confident in engaging with the business environment and wider society.

For the **teacher**, a range of materials, including a **Teacher's Resource Book** and **online digital resources**, as well as a **student activity book**, support this textbook. These provide a comprehensive resource pack to facilitate students' motivation, enabling them to apply their learning and to develop their ability to learn throughout their lives.

Digital Resources

The *Inside Business* digital resources will enhance classroom learning by encouraging student participation and engagement.

To provide guidance for the integration of digital resources in the classroom and to aid lesson planning, they are **referenced throughout the textbook** using the following icons:

 PowerPoint presentations provide a summary of every section of the student textbook, highlighting key themes and topics.

 Solutions to the end-of-chapter textbook questions.

Teachers can access the *Inside Business* digital resources and weblinks via the *Inside Business* interactive e-book, which is available online at **www.edcolearning.ie**.

ABOUT THE AUTHORS

Davin Kielthy is an Accounting and Business teacher in Templeogue College, Dublin. He has over twenty years' experience teaching Leaving Certificate Business and Accounting and he is also the author of the Leaving Certificate textbook *Accounting for Senior Cycle*.

Lisa O'Byrne teaches both Junior Cycle and Leaving Certificate Business at Templeogue College, Dublin. She has fourteen years' teaching experience and has previously worked as an Assistant State Examiner for the State Examinations Commission. Lisa has recently completed the Professional Certificate for Entrepreneurial Educators with the Innovation Academy at UCD.

ACKNOWLEDGEMENTS

We wish to express our sincere thanks to all those who helped us to complete this book. We are grateful to all at Edco and Barrett Editing, in particular: Emer Ryan, Declan Dempsey and Aoife Barrett.

We wish to acknowledge the help and inspiration of our colleagues who reviewed and tested the materials for us. Special thanks to our families and friends who were exceptionally patient and understanding during the writing and review process.

CHAPTER 1 — PEOPLE IN BUSINESS

🎯 Learning Outcomes

When you have completed this chapter, you will be able to:

1. Define the term *business*
2. Distinguish between commercial and non-commercial businesses
3. Identify and describe the various stakeholders in business
4. Explain the role of interest groups in business
5. Describe the different relationships that can exist between stakeholders in business, i.e. co-operative, competitive, dynamic and dependent relationships.

 Literacy Link

Commercial business, non-commercial business, stakeholder, interest group, relationships: co-operative, competitive, dependent, dynamic

 Numeracy Link

Division, percentages

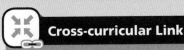 **Cross-curricular Link**

Home Economics – work and consumer studies

CASE STUDY — *Innocent Drinks*

Richard Reed, Adam Balon and Jon Wright were friends from college who spent their early careers working long hours. They realised that there were lots of other young people like them who wanted to be healthy but whose lifestyle made that difficult. They decided to develop a range of fruit smoothies that would provide people with high levels of nutrition for the day ahead.

They conducted some basic **market research** and identified a gap in the market for smoothies using only fresh ingredients. To test their idea they went to a little jazz festival in London and used yes and no bins for feedback. They found a **supplier** in Wales who agreed to supply them with the fresh fruits needed for their smoothies.

The brand name and logo were developed by the three founders and the head of creative, Dan Germain. The **entrepreneurs** used the **services** of an advertising agency to develop the packaging.

The three entrepreneurs had immense difficulty convincing **investors** to invest in their business. More than twenty banks rejected their **loan** applications and a potential investor gave them very harsh feedback: 'You score zero out of five in the investor's handbook – it's a dreadful investment opportunity.' They eventually received **equity capital** of over €280,000 from a private investor, Maurice Pinto, which they used to begin large-scale production.

They decided to outsource the production of the juices and smoothies, which meant that the company was able to adapt more quickly to **consumer** feedback.

As the company grew they needed to recruit **employees** to fill a variety of roles in the business in areas such as marketing and product development.

Innocent also wanted to give back to the **community**, so it established the Big Knit Campaign. Members of the public knit miniature woolly hats, which are placed on smoothie bottles. In Ireland, the company donates a portion of the profits made on these bottles to the charity Age Action. To date over 490,000 hats have been knitted, earning over €150,000 for charity. (see www.innocentfoundation.org)

INTRODUCTION TO BUSINESS

A business is an organisation that buys and sells goods and services.

Types of business

Food Donations

A **commercial** business provides goods and services to consumers and aims to make a profit. Examples of commercial businesses include Apple, SuperValu, Bank of Ireland, FBD insurance, and Arnotts.

A **non-commercial** business puts people and the community first, ahead of profit. They tend to provide a service for people and are run like a business. Examples are Trócaire, the GAA and Amnesty International.

Activity 1.1

Working in pairs, make a list of businesses in your local area. Categorise the list into commercial and non-commercial businesses. Compare your list of businesses with those made by your classmates.

STAKEHOLDERS IN BUSINESS

Stakeholders are individuals and organisations that are affected by the actions, objectives and policies of a business.

The main stakeholders in a business are:

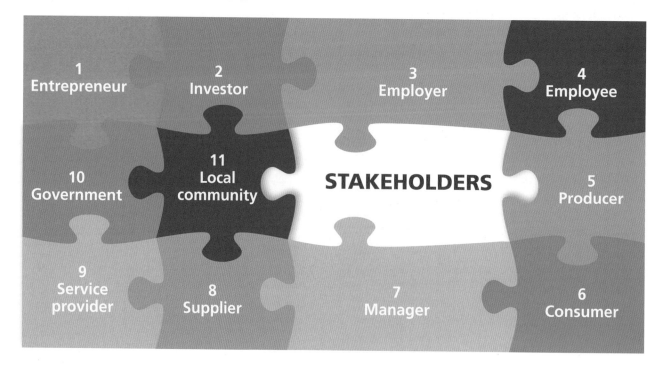

1 Entrepreneur
2 Investor
3 Employer
4 Employee
11 Local community
STAKEHOLDERS
10 Government
5 Producer
9 Service provider
8 Supplier
7 Manager
6 Consumer

1 Entrepreneur

An entrepreneur is a person who spots a gap in the market and comes up with an idea that they can turn into a business. An entrepreneur takes financial and personal risks when setting up a business. They hope to earn a profit from their successful business idea.

Activity 1.2

Search on the internet for the video called 'The Story of Fulfil' and answer the following questions.
- What gap in the market did the entrepreneurs spot?
- How long did it take the entrepreneurs to develop the idea?

2 Investor

Investors are the people or organisations that provide the entrepreneur with the capital (money) needed to establish and operate the business.

The types of capital provided by investors include:

Types of Capital	
Loan Capital	→ The entrepreneur takes out a loan from a lender such as a bank. The amount of money borrowed must be repaid with interest within an agreed period of time.
Grant	→ Money given to a business by state agencies such as the Local Enterprise Office (LEO). The grant does not have to be repaid, as long as the receiver meets certain conditions, e.g. creating a certain number of jobs.
Equity Capital	→ Money invested in the business by individuals or other businesses. These investors become part-owners of the firm and are entitled to a share of the firm's profits, known as dividends.

Example
The founders of Innocent Drinks received over €280,000 from a private investor to establish the company.

You will learn more about the Local Enterprise Office in Chapter 26.

3 Employer

An employer recruits staff to enable the organisation to carry out its business. They are responsible for providing safe working conditions for employees and paying the agreed wage/salary for work done.

Definition: Wage vs Salary
A **wage** is money earned by an employee based on the number of hours worked.
A **salary** is a fixed payment to an employee regardless of hours worked.

Example
- Aer Lingus employs pilots to fly planes. The pilots receive a salary for their work.
- Centra employs staff to operate the checkouts and stack shelves. These employees usually receive a wage for their work.

4 Employee

Employees are recruited by the employer to work in the business in return for a wage/salary. Employees have the skills and qualifications needed to operate the business successfully.

Example
Google has many different types of employee, including administrative staff, engineers and software programmers.

DID YOU KNOW?

If a Google employee dies, their partner receives 50% of their pay for the next ten years.

5 Producer

A producer takes raw materials and transforms them during the manufacturing process into finished products.

Example
Butlers Chocolates uses milk, cocoa, sugar and other ingredients and turns them into chocolates.

6 Consumer

Consumers are people who buy goods and services (see number 9) for their personal use.
The entrepreneur uses market research to find out consumers' likes and dislikes. This ensures that consumers can buy goods and services that satisfy their needs.

Example
- People who buy package holidays are consumers.
- People who purchase cinema or concert tickets are consumers.
- People who buy biscuits are consumers.

7 Manager

A manager is responsible for the day-to-day running of the business and ensures that the firm achieves its goals. Managers use skills such as leading and communicating to manage employees and interact with other stakeholders.

Example
The Virgin Group operates in a number of industries including travel and telecommunications. Experienced managers run these companies and ensure that the Virgin Group's objectives are achieved.

You will learn more about management skills in Chapters 5–8.

8 Supplier

Suppliers are firms that provide raw materials to the business. The supplier provides raw materials needed by the business to fulfil its orders.

Example

Suppliers from countries such as Honduras and Costa Rica provide Innocent Drinks with the fruits needed to make their juices and smoothies.

9 Service Provider

A service provider provides services needed by the business to operate successfully. Service providers tend to operate in the services/tertiary sector of the economy, e.g. banks and insurance firms.

Example

Commercial banks such as AIB provide financial services to individuals and businesses, including loans and 24-hour banking.

10 Government

The government is the body of people that govern the country. It imposes taxes on businesses, e.g. corporation tax. These taxes are used to invest in infrastructure, e.g. schools and healthcare.

Some government agencies provide financial support to entrepreneurs, e.g. Enterprise Ireland and the Local Enterprise Offices (LEOs).

Example

Enterprise Ireland provided support to Mercury Engineering, which is constructing the world's first solar-powered, climate-controlled football stadium for the football World Cup in Qatar in 2022.

> You will learn more about corporation tax in Chapter 16.

11 Local Community

The local community consists of individuals, households and organisations that are located close to the business. Many firms have developed a CSR (corporate and social responsibility) strategy to ensure that they behave in a responsible manner towards the local community.

Example

Kenco Coffee provided a training programme to young people at risk of joining gangs in Honduras. They were trained to become coffee farmers and helped to build coffee businesses with financial support from Kenco.

> You will learn more about CSR in Chapter 27.

Activity 1.3

Each student writes the job titles of three stakeholders on a sticky note and places it on the back of another student. You then move around the room and ask each other questions to try to identify the stakeholder, e.g. 'Do I work in the business?' Questions must be answered Yes or No.

INTEREST GROUPS

An interest group (pressure group) is a group of people who meet and campaign for a common goal. They have more power, skills and capital when they work together and are more likely to be listened to by decision-makers.

Interest groups use a variety of techniques when campaigning to influence decision-makers. These approaches can include boycotting, negative publicity campaigns and lobbying.

> **Definition: Boycotting**
> Consumers refuse to buy goods or services from a firm to show their dissatisfaction with the business, e.g. because it has exploited workers.

> **Definition: Lobbying**
> This involves trying to persuade decision-makers to support laws or rules that give an advantage to your industry or organisation.

There are many types of interest group, including the following.

1 Business Interest Groups

These interest groups represent the interests of business owners.

Ibec (Irish Business and Employers Confederation)

Ibec aims to influence decision-makers such as the government, society and the European Union on issues that affect its members, e.g. taxation and transport. It also provides advice and support to its members in areas such as industrial relations.

ISME (Irish Small and Medium Enterprises Association)

ISME represents the views of small and medium-sized business owners in Ireland. It lobbies on issues that affect its members, e.g. the impact on business if the government raises the minimum wage. It also provides advice to its members, e.g. on employment law.

2 Trade Associations

These interest groups represent the interests of businesses involved in the same industry.

SIMI (Society of the Irish Motor Industry)

This interest group represents the views of the motor industry – dealerships, retailers and vehicle testers. It campaigns to the government, media and the public on issues affecting the motor industry.

3 Other Interest Groups

Trade Unions

Trade unions, e.g. SIPTU (Services, Industrial Professional & Technical Union), represent the views and interests of employees in particular industries. They aim to protect and improve their members' pay and working conditions.

> **Activity 1.4**
>
> There are approximately 2,200,000 people employed in Ireland, of whom 29% are trade union members. Calculate the number of people who are trade union members in Ireland.

IFA (Irish Farmers' Association)

The IFA represents the interests of Irish farmers in Ireland and Europe. It lobbies and campaigns to improve farm incomes and conditions for farming families.

> **Activity 1.5**
>
> There are many other interest groups in operation in Ireland and around the world. In pairs, research other interest groups and their activities. Present your findings to your classmates in a visual format, e.g. a poster or infographic.

RELATIONSHIPS BETWEEN STAKEHOLDERS

The relationship between the various stakeholders in the business can be:

1 Co-operative   **2 Competitive**   **3 Dependent**   **4 Dynamic**

1 Co-operative Relationship

The stakeholders **work together towards a common goal**. This helps to ensure better results than if the stakeholders worked independently or against each other. This creates a **win–win** scenario for both parties.

2 Competitive Relationship

Stakeholders **work towards different goals**. Each stakeholder wants to achieve a particular objective at the expense of the other. A competitive relationship creates a **win–lose** scenario between the parties.

3 Dependent Relationship

The stakeholders **need each other** for success. One stakeholder is not able to achieve their goals without the help of another stakeholder.

4 Dynamic Relationship

The relationship between the stakeholders is **constantly changing**. At times the relationship can be co-operative or dependent and at other times it is competitive.

Activity 1.6

In pairs, create a cloze test (fill in the blanks) to explain the different relationships that can exist between stakeholders. Swap the cloze test with another pair of students to see if they can fill in all the blanks correctly.

Exam Tip!
Provide information about both sides of the relationship when
answering questions about relationships between stakeholders.

UNDERSTANDING THE RELATIONSHIPS BETWEEN STAKEHOLDERS

A Co-operative and Competitive Relationships

There are many different co-operative and competitive relationships between business stakeholders. Some examples of these relationships are outlined below.

1 Entrepreneur and Investor

Co-operative Relationship

The entrepreneur comes up with a good idea for a business and prepares a detailed business plan with future profit projections.

The investor decides to invest their money in the business. The investor now owns shares in the business and hopes that the firm will make a profit on which they will earn dividends.

Example

Levi Roots took part in the television programme *Dragons' Den* and presented the dragons with his Reggae Reggae sauce. Two dragons invested €55,000 in return for a 40% stake in his business. The brand was recently valued at €40 million.

Competitive Relationship

The chief executive officer (CEO) of a business runs it in a way that they believe brings most benefits to the business. Shareholders may be unhappy with the CEO's approach and want to remove them from the position of CEO.

Example

Some Facebook shareholders wanted to remove Mark Zuckerberg as CEO following a number of high-profile scandals. They were unhappy with the fall in company value and believed that a new CEO should be appointed.

2 Consumer and Producer

Co-operative Relationship

The producer conducts market research to find out what consumers like and dislike about products. This co-operation results in consumers getting products that satisfy their needs and helps to increase sales and profits for the producer.

Example

KitKat launched the 'Choose a Chunky Champion' campaign to get consumers to choose a new Chunky KitKat flavour. Eleven million bars were sold and over 60,000 people voted for KitKat Chunky Mint as the winner.

Competitive Relationship

The producer makes a poor-quality product or gives the consumer a poor-quality after-sales service in order to save the business money. The consumer is unhappy and decides to make future purchases from a competitor. This leads to a loss of sales, profits and reputation for the producer.

Example

Cadbury was fined over €1 million when salmonella found in its products made a number of consumers unwell. The company recalled one million bars and launched a PR campaign to apologise to the public.

3 Employer and Employee

Co-operative Relationship

The employer provides financial rewards such as fair basic pay, and non-financial rewards such as private health insurance cover. In return, employees work hard for the business in order to help to increase sales and profits.

Example
Google's headquarters in California offers its employees a range of perks, including free healthy food and drinks, volleyball courts and pool tables. This makes working at Google an enjoyable experience for employees and helps to increase productivity.

Competitive Relationship

The employer may reduce the number of employees in the workplace in order to lower business costs. Remaining employees fear that they might lose their jobs in the future and may become demotivated and less productive.

Example
Multinational computer company Dell cut 1,900 jobs at its plant in Limerick. The company moved its production of computer systems to Poland, which has lower business costs than Ireland.

4 Producer and Producer

Co-operative Relationship

A co-operative relationship exists when two producers in the same line of business combine their resources, e.g. capital and marketing, to increase awareness of their goods or services. This helps to increase sales and profits for both producers.

Example
Food producers in Tipperary, including James Whelan Butchers and Crossogue Preserves, combined their resources and organised the Totally Tipperary Food Festival. This event helped the producers to increase awareness of their product range and boost their sales and profits.

Competitive Relationship

Two producers in the same line of business may compete with each other on some or all of the following areas: price, sales, distribution, market share.

Example
Häagen-Dazs wanted to prevent Ben & Jerry's ice cream gaining market share in the USA. It insisted that stores that stocked its brand could not also carry Ben & Jerry's ice cream. Ben & Jerry's began a media campaign accusing Häagen-Dazs of bullying smaller competitors. The campaign caused such negative publicity that Häagen-Dazs stopped pressurising stores, which enabled Ben & Jerry's to increase its market share.

5 Business and Government

Co-operative Relationship

The government uses state agencies such as Enterprise Ireland to provide advice and financial support to businesses. In return, the business provides employment for people in the local community and pays taxes to the government, e.g. corporation tax.

Example
Enterprise Ireland has provided support to Multihog, which manufactures vehicles that help keep airport runways open in severe weather conditions. The company currently employs over 50 skilled workers in marketing, production and research and development (R&D).

Competitive Relationship

A competitive relationship occurs when a business deliberately underpays taxes owed to the government. This results in less government revenue to fund services for citizens in Ireland, e.g. healthcare.

Example

The head of Begley Bros Ltd was sentenced to six years in prison for failing to pay €1.1 million in customs duty. The company had deliberately mislabelled garlic imports as apples, which carry a lower rate of customs duty.

6 Business and the Local Community

Co-operative Relationship

Businesses and the local community work together to improve the economic and social environment in the local area. Businesses sponsor local youth groups and community events, thus providing activities for young people in the area that help to reduce anti-social behaviour.

Example

SuperValu has donated 50,000 footballs to schools and clubs around Ireland as part of its #behindtheball campaign to encourage families and children to become more active.

Competitive Relationship

A business can damage the health of people in the local community, e.g. through air pollution and illegal dumping of waste. The local community might organise protests or petitions against the business, which can damage the firm's reputation.

Example

There have been high-profile protests against Coca-Cola in India. The company has been accused of causing water shortages in local areas due to the intense water usage in the manufacturing process.

7 Business and Business

Co-operative Relationship

Two or more businesses work together to develop a product that is too expensive or complex for one business to develop on its own. By combining their resources, the businesses create a better product that benefits them all.

Example

Citroën, Peugeot and Mitsubishi combined their R&D departments to develop an engine for electric cars. The companies worked together to create engines for each company's own line of electric cars.

Competitive Relationship

Businesses may compete on price, as they know that consumers shop around for the best price available for goods and services. The firms may enter into a price war to make their products cheaper than competitors' products.

Definition: Price war

This occurs when competitors in the same line of business cut prices in order to increase their market share.

Example

Each week Irish supermarkets compete on price with special offers on fruit and vegetables, e.g. the campaigns Aldi's Super 6 and Lidl's Super Savers.

8 Producer and Interest Group

Co-operative Relationship

The producer and interest group work together to increase awareness of the producers' products or to influence key decision-makers by lobbying, boycotting and using high-profile media campaigns.

Example
Ibec undertakes media campaigns to ensure that the government is aware of the negative impact that some of its decisions may have on producers, e.g. an increase in corporation tax would reduce producer profits.

Competitive Relationship

Producers may make products using raw materials that could be viewed as unethical, e.g. fur. Interest groups may want the producer to stop selling these items but the producer wants to continue with production, as they are profitable.

Example
PETA (People for the Ethical Treatment of Animals) has run many high-profile media campaigns using celebrities to discourage consumers buying from companies that use fur in their products.

Activity 1.7

In groups of three or four, create a mind map to summarise the co-operative and competitive relationships that can exist between stakeholders in a business. You can draw it by hand or use online mind mapping tools such as Coggle (https://coggle.it).

B Dynamic Relationships

1 Employer and Employee

In a co-operative relationship, the employer offers good pay and working conditions to employees and in return the employees work hard for the business.

This relationship can become competitive if the employer decides to reduce employees' pay. The employees may become demotivated and fear for their job security and this may reduce their productivity.

2 Business and Investor

The business borrows money from a bank using their business premises as security for the loan. In return the business makes regular loan repayments in full and on time.

The relationship can become competitive if the business cannot make the loan repayments and the bank may be forced to repossess the premises to recoup the loan.

C Dependent Relationships

1 Entrepreneur and Government

In order to set up or expand their business, the entrepreneur may get a grant from a government organisation, e.g. a Local Enterprise Office. The government needs entrepreneurs to provide employment, as this reduces the number of people claiming social welfare payments.

2 Business and Service Provider

Businesses need the services provided by service providers, e.g. banking and insurance, to run their firms successfully. The service provider needs the business as a customer in order to run its firm profitably.

For example, if a business needs to purchase insurance for motor vehicles, it takes out insurance cover from an insurance firm. The insurance firm needs the business to buy insurance policies in order to increase its sales and profits.

Unit 1

KEY TERMS

Now you have completed this chapter, you should understand and be able to explain the following terms. In your copybook, write a definition of each term to build up your own glossary of terms.

- business
- commercial business
- non-commercial business
- entrepreneur
- investor
- employer
- employee
- producer
- consumer
- manager
- supplier
- service provider
- government
- local community
- co-operative relationship
- competitive relationship
- dynamic relationship
- dependent relationship

PowerPoint Summary

EXAM-STYLE QUESTIONS

Ordinary Level

Section 1 – Short Questions (10 marks each)

1 Outline the difference between a commercial business and a non-commercial business.

2 Steve Jobs was an entrepreneur who was one of the co-founders of the technology company Apple. Explain what is meant by the term *entrepreneur*. Name **two** Irish entrepreneurs.

3 Loan capital, grants and equity capital are types of capital available to businesses. Explain any **two** of the underlined terms.

4 Describe the role of the consumer as a stakeholder in a business.

5 Distinguish between a supplier and a producer.

6 Outline the role played by service providers as stakeholders in a business.

7 Column 1 is a list of business terms. Column 2 is a list of possible explanations for these terms. In your copybook, match the numbers with the correct letters (e.g. 1 = C).

Terms		Explanations	
1 Investor	**A**	A person who works for a business and earns a wage/salary
2 Producer	**B**	A person who spots a gap in the market and sets up a business to exploit the gap
3 Service Provider	**C**	A person who provides money to the entrepreneur to establish and operate a business
4 Employee	**D**	A person who transforms raw materials into finished goods
5 Entrepreneur	**E**	An organisation that provides services needed for the successful operation of a business

8 Explain what is meant by the term *interest group*. Name **one** business interest group.

9 Indicate whether each of these statements is true or false.

	Statements	True or False
A	Greenpeace is an interest group that protects the rights of consumers.	
B	A manufacturing firm is an example of a service provider.	
C	A manager is responsible for the day-to-day running of the business.	
D	Flexitime is an example of a financial reward given to employees by an employer.	
E	An example of a co-operative relationship in business is when employees work hard and receive a good wage/salary.	

10 In business, what is meant by the term *dependent relationship*?

Section 2 – Long Questions

1 Describe the roles of employees and managers in a business. **(20 marks)**

2 Outline what is meant by the term *interest group*. Give **one** example to illustrate your answer. **(15 marks)**

3 Outline the difference between a co-operative and a competitive relationship in business. **(15 marks)**

4 Explain the term *co-operative relationship* and outline **two** examples of a co-operative relationship in business. **(20 marks)**

5 Competitive relationships have always existed between business stakeholders. Choose **two** stakeholders and describe the competitive relationship that exists between them. **(20 marks)**

6 Describe the relationship that exists between entrepreneurs and investors. **(15 marks)**

7 Describe the relationship that exists between producers and consumers. **(15 marks)**

8 What is meant by the term *dynamic relationship*? Outline a dynamic relationship that can exist between stakeholders in a business. **(20 marks)**

Higher Level

Section 1 – Short Questions (10 marks each)

1 List **four** stakeholders in a business and describe the role played by any **two** of them.

2 Write the following sentences in your copybook and fill in the blanks.

(i) _____ provide the entrepreneur with the money they need to establish/expand their business.

(ii) _____ campaign for the rights of employees.

(iii) _____ provides goods/services to consumers with the aim of making a profit.

(iv) The _____ is an example of a non-commercial business that aims to promote and develop Gaelic games.

3 Distinguish between a producer and a service provider.

4 Distinguish between loan capital and equity capital.

5 Column 1 is a list of business terms. Column 2 is a list of possible explanations for these terms. In your copybook, match the numbers with the correct letters (e.g. 1 = C).

Terms			Explanations
1	Interest Group	A	Creates and enforces legislation to ensure businesses behave in a legal manner
2	Stakeholders	B	Recruit and select employees with the required skills to operate the business effectively
3	Government	C	Greenpeace and SIPTU are examples of this type of organisation
4	Employers	D	Purchase goods and services for their own use
5	Consumers	E	Groups who are directly affected by how a business is operated

6 Complete this sentence in your copybook:
   The role of the consumer is to: ...

7 Describe the role of an investor as a business stakeholder.

8 Outline the roles of service providers and suppliers in a business.

9 Distinguish between a co-operative relationship and a competitive relationship in a business.

10 Describe what is meant by a dependent relationship between business stakeholders.

Section 2 – Applied Business Question (80 marks)

Passion for Fashion Ltd

Maria Gabbott noticed that there was a gap in the market for high-quality Irish fashion and decided to establish her own business called Passion for Fashion Ltd.

Maria needed money to purchase equipment and rent a premises. She obtained a grant from her Local Enterprise Office, who were eager to encourage employment in the local area. She also approached a friend who agreed to invest in her business in return for a 20% ownership share. Maria promised her friend a regular dividend in return for the investment.

Over the years the business has grown and Maria has many loyal customers who love her modern designs and use of Irish fabrics. To cope with the increased demand for her designs, Maria employed 15 full-time employees. However, in recent months, the relationship between Maria and her employees has changed. Her staff have complained about their low pay and long working hours. Maria has told her employees that if they are not happy in her firm, they can find employment elsewhere.

Maria has started to experience some manufacturing problems. The machinery she uses is breaking down on a regular basis. She has also noticed that she is receiving lower-quality materials from suppliers. Customers have complained that the clothes shrink when they wash them and that the courier delivery of their orders has been delayed. Maria is also under pressure from cheaper imports from Asia, as businesses there can supply good-quality clothing at cheaper prices.

Maria realises that she needs to make some big changes to ensure the success of her business. She needs to recruit a manager to run the business and help her achieve her business goals. Maria needs to upgrade her machinery and source new suppliers. She has decided to reinvest all profits back into the business to pay for the machinery upgrade. This means that she will not be paying a dividend to shareholders for the foreseeable future.

A Identify and describe the main stakeholders in Passion for Fashion Ltd. Refer to the text to support your answer. **(30 marks)**

B Describe **two** competitive relationships that are present between Passion for Fashion Ltd and its stakeholders. **(25 marks)**

C (i) Distinguish between a dynamic relationship and a dependent relationship in business.
(ii) Outline how a dynamic relationship and a dependent relationship can impact on Maria's business. **(25 marks)**

Section 3 – Long Questions

1 Ibec, SIPTU and the IFA are examples of interest groups that represent the views of different groups of people. Choose any **two** of these interest groups and describe how they represent the views of their members. **(15 marks)**

2 Outline what is meant by co-operative, competitive and dependent relationships between business stakeholders. **(15 marks)**

3 Analyse **one** co-operative and **one** competitive relationship in a business. **(15 marks)**

4 Outline, using examples, the relationship that can exist between producers and consumers. **(15 marks)**

5 Describe the sources of conflict that can exist between:
(i) Entrepreneurs and investors
(ii) Employers and employees. **(15 marks)**

6 Discuss the dependent and dynamic relationships that can exist between a business and its stakeholders. **(20 marks)**

7 Describe, using examples, **one** co-operative and **one** competitive relationship between the government and business. **(20 marks)**

8 Describe a co-operative relationship and a competitive relationship that exists between a business and the local community. **(20 marks)**

PREVIOUS LEAVING CERTIFICATE EXAM QUESTIONS

Ordinary Level

Section 1 – Short Questions (10 marks each)

1 Explain the term *stakeholder* and list **two** examples of stakeholders in a business. [LC OL 2014]
2 Explain the term *employer*. Outline **two** responsibilities of an employer. [LC OL 2012]
3 Explain the term *investor* and give **two** examples of investors. [LC OL 2011]

Section B

1

> Kate has just started working in her first full-time job in a factory in her town. The shop steward met with her and discussed the benefits of joining the trade union.

Describe the relationship which exists between an employer and an employee. **(15 marks)** [LC OL 2004]

2

> **Stakeholders and Relationships**
> Stakeholders refer to different groups of people who are directly affected by the decisions that a business makes. A stakeholder has an interest in the success of a business.

A   In relation to the following stakeholders of a business:
  (i)   Explain the term **employee**
  (ii) Explain the term **manager**. **(15 marks)**
B   Describe the relationship that the following stakeholders may have with a business: (i) an investor and (ii) a supplier. **(15 marks)** [LC OL 2018]

Higher Level

Section A – Short Questions (10 marks each)

1 Identify **two** parties in business and describe a competitive relationship between them. [LC HL 2007]

Section B

1 Describe the role of any **two** interest groups in business. **(15 marks)** [LC HL 2014]
2 (i)   Explain the term *co-operative relationship* between stakeholders in a business.
  (ii) Describe **one** example of a co-operative relationship which could arise between each of the following pairs of stakeholders:
    • Employer and employee
    • Investor and manager of a business
    • Producer and consumer. **(20 marks)** [LC HL 2017]
3 Describe **one** example of a co-operative relationship and **one** example of a source of conflict that could arise between the following stakeholders:
  (i)   Investor and Entrepreneur
  (ii) Supplier and Purchasing Manager. **(20 marks)** [LC HL 2015]
4 The quality of the relationship between stakeholders determines the success of any enterprise. Describe a competitive relationship and a co-operative relationship between **two** producers in the same line of business. Use appropriate examples to support your answer. **(15 marks)** [LC HL 2008]

 Solutions

CHAPTER 2
RESOLVING CONFLICT IN THE MARKETPLACE

🎯 Learning Outcomes

When you have completed this chapter, you will be able to:

1. Identify and explain the elements of a valid contract
2. Outline the ways in which a contract can be terminated
3. Describe the ways in which a breach of contract can be resolved
4. Identify and describe non-legislative methods of resolving consumer conflict
5. Outline the legislative methods of resolving consumer conflict.

 Literacy Link

Contract, capacity, consent, consideration, breach of contract, guarantee, Competition and Consumer Protection Commission (CCPC), Ombudsman

 Numeracy Link

Multiplication

 Cross-curricular Link

Home Economics – consumer protection, consumer rights and responsibilities, seeking and evaluating information to make wise consumer choices

CASE STUDY *Etaoin's Mobile Phone Contract*

Etaoin has recently started working in her first full-time job and wants to purchase the latest smartphone. She has consulted a copy of the magazine *Consumer Choice*, published by the **Consumers' Association of Ireland**. Based on their independent testing, Etaoin has decided that she will purchase the Apple X Max.

Etaoin visits a local phone shop and signs a 24-month **written contract** to purchase the Apple X Max. As Etaoin is over eighteen she has the **capacity** to enter into a contract. There is **consideration** between Etaoin and the network provider. The network provider gives Etaoin the phone and mobile phone service. In return she pays €800 upfront for the device and will make a monthly payment of €40.

Etaoin carefully reads the section on the **termination of contract**. She sees that if she tries to end her contract before 24 months has passed,

she may face an additional fee for early cancellation.

Etaoin is excited about the delivery of her new phone. However, when she opens the box, she realises that the screen is damaged. She knows her rights under the **Sale of Goods and Supply of Services Act 1980**. The product isn't of **merchantable quality**, so she contacts the store to arrange for a replacement phone. The retailer immediately replaces the phone and Etaoin is happy with the level of customer service she received.

PART 1: LAW OF CONTRACT

Many deals agreed between the different stakeholders in a business involve contracts, e.g. the contract between an employer and an employee. The Irish legal system uses the law of contract to establish when a contract exists and when it ends.

> **Definition: Contract**
> A legally binding agreement between two or more parties, which is enforceable by law.

The following elements must be present for a contract to be valid:

ELEMENTS OF A VALID CONTRACT

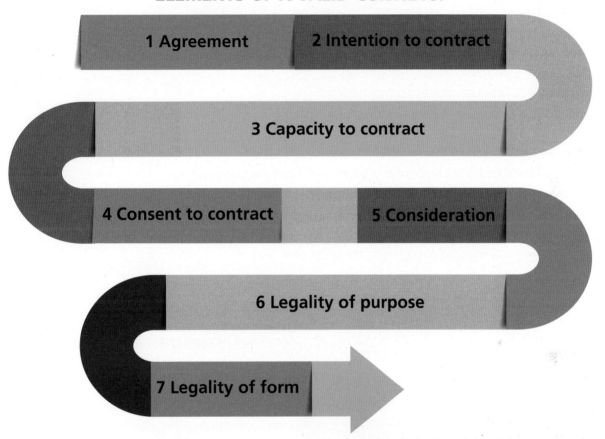

1 Agreement

2 Intention to contract

3 Capacity to contract

4 Consent to contract

5 Consideration

6 Legality of purpose

7 Legality of form

Example

Jill Kelly has just turned eighteen and wants to purchase a new car. She visits a number of dealerships in her local area and decides to buy a blue Hyundai i10. Jill knows that she will have to sign a contract to purchase the car and wants to ensure that she understands all the elements needed for a valid contract.

1 Agreement

For agreement to exist, there must be a clear, unconditional and complete offer made by one party and accepted by the other party to a contract.

An agreement consists of two parts:

- Offer
- Acceptance.

> **Note!**
>
> *The word 'party' can refer to individuals or organisations.*

Offer

An offer is made when one party asks another to enter into a contract. The party making the offer must include all details and communicate the offer clearly. The offer must also be unconditional, i.e. there should be no strings attached to the offer.

An offer can be made in a number of ways:

- **Orally:** 'I will give you €200 for that bicycle.'
- **In writing:** A written contract to purchase a house.
- **By conduct:** A consumer handing a newspaper and money to the sales assistant at the checkout in a shop.

An offer can be **terminated** in a number of ways:

- **Revoked:** The offer is withdrawn before the other party accepts it.
- **Rejected:** The offer is rejected by the other party.
- **Lapse of time:** The party making the offer may impose a time limit on accepting the offer, e.g. special offers last for a limited time.
- **Death:** If the party making or receiving the offer dies.

> **Example**
>
> Jill decides to purchase a blue Hyundai i10 from McHugh Motors. The vehicle is for sale at €26,000 and Jill offers to pay the owner of the dealership, Martin McHugh, €26,000 for the car.

Acceptance

The person receiving the offer accepts all terms of the offer. An offer can be accepted orally, in writing or by conduct, e.g. a retail assistant takes the customer's money in exchange for a newspaper.

> **Example**
>
> The dealership owner, Martin McHugh, accepts Jill's offer of €26,000 for the Hyundai car.

> **Definition: Invitation to treat**
>
> An invitation to another person to make an offer. The offer can be accepted or rejected. Price tags placed on cars in a dealership are an example of an invitation to treat. The price tags indicate that the retailer is willing to receive an offer on the vehicles. The consumer can make an offer to purchase a car at the advertised price, but the retailer can decide to accept or reject the offer.

2 Intention to Contract

Both parties intend to create a legally binding contract. Irish contract law assumes that:

- All business agreements (oral and written) are intended to be legally binding.
- All social and private agreements are not intended to be legally binding, e.g. if Kevin promises to tidy his bedroom and then doesn't tidy it, his parents cannot sue him for failing to complete the task.

> **Example**
>
> Both Jill and McHugh Motors intend to enter into a contract that is legally binding.

3 Capacity to Contract

All people and businesses have the legal ability to enter into a contract except for the following:

- Any person under the age of 18, except for necessities, e.g. food and clothes.
- People who are mentally incapacitated, e.g. under the influence of alcohol or drugs, or of unsound mind.

Example

Jill Kelly is over 18 years old and has the capacity to enter into a contract to purchase a car from the business McHugh Motors.

4 Consent to Contract

The parties entering into a contract must do so voluntarily. A contract is **invalid** if:

- A party is put under physical pressure or threatened to enter into a contract
- A genuine mistake is made by either party to the contract
- Either party is dishonest and gives false information
  that may encourage the other party to enter into the contract (for example, if Jill wanted to buy an electric car and the salesperson from McHugh Motors told Jill that the model was electric, even though it was petrol-powered, in order to close the sale).

Example

If the salesperson in McHugh Motors threatened Jill to force her to buy the car, this would mean that Jill had not entered the contract voluntarily.

5 Consideration

Consideration means that each party in the contract must give something of value to the other party, i.e. both parties must gain from the contract. Consideration can refer to money or goods exchanged between the parties.

Example

Jill will give €26,000 to McHugh Motors. In return, McHugh Motors will give Jill the car.

6 Legality of Purpose

A legally binding contract must be created for a legal purpose. For example, a valid contract cannot exist to buy illegal fireworks.

Example

The contract between Jill and McHugh Motors has been set up for a legal purpose, i.e. for McHugh Motors to sell a car and for Jill to purchase it.

7 Legality of Form

Contracts must be drawn up in the correct legal format. This can be done orally, in writing or by conduct, e.g. a contract to purchase property or an insurance policy must be in writing.

Example

There is a written contract between Jill and McHugh Motors, which was signed by both parties.

Activity 2.1

Work in pairs to summarise the elements of a legal contract using a fishbone graphic organiser.

Termination of a Contract

A contract can be completed/ended in the following ways:

1 Performance
2 Agreement
3 Frustration
4 Breach of contract.

Termination	Description	Example
1 Performance	→ A contract ends by performance when both parties complete their side of the contract exactly as set out in the contract.	→ The contract between Jill and McHugh Motors ends when Jill receives the blue Hyundai i10 car and McHugh Motors receives a payment of €26,000.
2 Agreement	→ A contract ends by agreement when both parties mutually agree to end the contract even if the purpose of the contract has not been completed.	→ After signing the contract to purchase a blue car, McHugh Motors informs Jill that the car can only be delivered in the colour red. Jill is unhappy about this and both parties decide to end the contract by mutual agreement.
3 Frustration	→ A contract ends when an unforeseen event arises that prevents the contract from being completed. Examples include: extreme weather conditions, bankruptcy or death of one of the parties.	→ Storms damage the Hyundai factory and vehicles can no longer be manufactured. This ends the contract, as the car cannot be delivered to Jill.
4 Breach of Contract	→ A contract ends when one party breaks their side of the contract. If a party breaks a **condition** of the contract (an **essential element**), the contract ends immediately. → If a **warranty** (a **non-essential element**) of a contract is breached, the contract does not end. The party that broke the warranty may have to pay compensation to the innocent party.	→ If McHugh Motors delivered the wrong model car to Jill, this would be considered a **breach of a condition** of the contract. This would **end the contract**. → If the car was delivered to Jill without a spare wheel in the vehicle as per the contract, this would be regarded as a **breach of warranty**. This would **not end the contract**. McHugh Motors would source an appropriate wheel and the contract could be completed.

Example

Breach of a Condition of a Contract

While working as a Chelsea Football Club goalkeeper, Mark Bosnich failed a random drugs test. This was a breach of a condition of Bosnich's contract and the club ended his contract.

Breach of a Warranty of a Contract

Soccer player Nicklas Bendtner turned up 45 minutes late to club training. This was a breach of warranty of his contract. His contract was not terminated but his club fined him €50 for every minute he was late.

Activity 2.2

1 Based on the example of breach of warranty above, calculate the amount Nicklas was fined by the club.
2 Working in pairs, use the internet to find other cases of breach of contract, e.g. in business, professional sports and entertainment. Prepare a mini-presentation for your classmates to explain the details of the case. You could use a poster, slideshow or infographic to display your findings.

DID YOU KNOW?

Giuseppe Reina, a player for a German football club, insisted on a clause in his contract that required the club to build him a house each year of his three-year contract. The clause didn't make clear what type or size of house should be built, so the club made him a Lego house for each year of his contract.

Remedies for Breach of Contract

If a party breaks a condition of a contract, the other party can take the case to court. A judge listens to the evidence of the breach and makes a decision on how the issue should be resolved.

For example, let's assume that Jill signed a contract with McHugh Motors and paid €26,000 for a blue Hyundai i10 car. On collection, Jill discovered that a different Hyundai model had been delivered and McHugh Motors refused to refund Jill her payment or re-order the correct model. Jill decided to take McHugh Motors to court for breach of contract.

The remedies for breach of contract are:

1 Compensation
2 Rescind the contract
3 Specific performance.

Remedy	Explanation	Example
1 Compensation	→ The judge can order the party that caused the breach to pay compensation for any losses suffered by the innocent party due to the breach.	→ The judge orders McHugh Motors to pay €26,000 compensation to Jill for refusing to re-order the correct model car.
2 Rescind the Contract	→ The judge cancels the contract. This returns both parties to the position they were in before the breach occurred.	→ The judge cancels the contract between Jill and McHugh Motors and orders: • McHugh Motors to return the €26,000 paid by Jill • Jill to return the incorrect Hyundai model to McHugh Motors.
3 Specific Performance	→ A judge can order the party that breached the contract to complete their side of the deal.	→ The judge orders McHugh Motors to complete their side of the contract by re-ordering and delivering the blue Hyundai i10 for Jill.

CASE STUDY

Singer Prince Ordered to pay €2m for Breach of Contract

MCD Promotions arranged for the singer Prince to perform a concert in Dublin. The company advertised the concert and sold tickets in advance of the performance. About two weeks before the concert, Prince cancelled the show without any explanation. MCD Promotions was forced to call off the concert and reimburse all ticket purchases. The company sued Prince for breach of contract in the Irish High Court. The High Court judge awarded MCD Promotions over €2m in compensation for the breach of contract.

Activity 2.3

Choose a word from the word cloud below, which relates to the law of contract. Define it for your partner without using the word chosen and they have to guess the word that you're explaining.

consent
offer
specific performance
rescind
condition
agreement
intention
consideration
compensation
contract
warranty remedies
breach acceptance

PART 2: CONSUMER CONFLICT

Consumers should use the principle of **caveat emptor** when purchasing goods and services. This Latin phrase means **'Let the buyer beware'** and implies that consumers should use common sense when they make a purchase. Consumers should do some basic research before buying goods and services to ensure they get good quality at a reasonable price.

Even if consumers have used the principle of caveat emptor, there may be times when conflict occurs between a consumer and a business, e.g. poor-quality goods or services, or misleading advertising.

It is very important that consumers are aware that there are a number of non-legislative and legislative ways of resolving conflict with businesses.

A Non-legislative Methods for Resolving Consumer Conflict

Consumers may try to resolve conflict with a business in a non-legislative manner. This means that they try to solve the conflict by themselves or with the help of others, without using any laws or legal agencies. The options for solving consumer conflict in a non-legislative way include:

1 Negotiation
2 Writing a letter of complaint
3 Assistance from a third party.

1 Negotiation

If a consumer is unhappy with a good or service that they purchased, they should:

1 Return to the retailer with their proof of purchase, e.g. a receipt or bank statement

2 Ask to speak to a manager and state clearly the problem with their purchase

3 Tell the retailer how they would like the problem to be resolved.

The retailer can respond to the consumer's complaint by accepting or rejecting it or suggesting an alternative solution.

2 Writing a Letter of Complaint

If a consumer is unable to speak to or visit a retailer, for example because they live too far away, it would be advisable to send a formal letter of complaint. Many people now send a letter of complaint as an email.

As in the negotiation process, the consumer should:

1 Outline the problem with the good or service
2 Explain how they would like this issue to be resolved
3 Include copies of any proof of purchase.

The retailer could: accept the complaint and deal with the issue as requested by the consumer; reject the complaint; or offer an alternative solution.

3 Assistance from a Third Party

If negotiation is not successful, the consumer can seek assistance from a third party to help resolve their problem with the retailer. Organisations that help consumers include:

- Consumers' Association of Ireland (CAI)
- European Consumer Centre Ireland (ECC Ireland).

Consumers' Association of Ireland

The CAI is an interest group that works on behalf of consumers. The CAI aims to ensure that consumers are aware of their consumer rights and receive high-quality goods and services at a reasonable price.

The CAI:

- Operates a website to inform consumers of their consumer rights (www.thecai.ie)
- Identifies areas where consumer legislation is weak and lobbies the government to improve this legislation.

DID YOU KNOW?

The CAI publishes a magazine called Consumer Choice. *It contains articles about consumer rights and independently compares goods and services in terms of value, performance and reliability.*

European Consumer Centre Ireland

ECC Ireland is part of an EU-wide network of consumer centres. ECC Ireland:

- Gives advice to Irish consumers on their rights when buying goods and services in other EU member states
- Helps to settle disputes between consumers in Ireland and traders in different EU countries.

CASE STUDY

European Consumer Centre Ireland

An Irish consumer rented a car while on holiday in Greece. The car was in a bad state of repair and after being driven for 20 km it caught fire. The consumer escaped from the car unharmed, but all his belongings, including clothing, documentation, mobile phone and cash, were destroyed. The consumer contacted ECC Ireland requesting assistance in obtaining €12,500 compensation from the car rental firm for items lost and damages. With the help of ECC Ireland, the Irish consumer and the Greek car company agreed on a settlement of €11,000.

B Legislative Methods for Solving Consumer Conflict

Sometimes a consumer will be unable to resolve an issue with a retailer using non-legislative methods. A consumer may need to use consumer laws in Ireland or use legal organisations to resolve the conflict with the retailer.

Legislative methods of resolving consumer conflict include:

1 Sale of Goods and Supply of Services Act 1980
2 Consumer Protection Act 2007
3 Competition and Consumer Protection Commission (CCPC)
4 Ombudsman
5 Small Claims Procedure.

Exam Tip!
Learn the full titles of the two consumer laws and the year they were introduced: the Sale of Goods and Supply of Services Act 1980 and the Consumer Protection Act 2007.

1 Sale of Goods and Supply of Services Act 1980

This Act applies to consumers when they buy goods and services for their own use from a registered business.

Under the Sale of Goods and Supply of Services Act 1980, consumers have a number of legal rights. These include:

A Rights of consumers when purchasing a good

B Rights of consumers when purchasing a service

C Remedies for breach of the Act

D Retailer's responsibility

E Guarantees

F Second-hand goods

G Inertia selling/unsolicited goods.

A Rights of Consumers when Purchasing a Good

Consumers have a number of rights under the Act when purchasing goods. These include:

Right	Description	Example
Goods must be of *merchantable quality*	→ Goods should be of an acceptable standard, taking into account their price and durability.	→ A new motorbike should not break down after travelling 10 km. → A new pair of football boots should not rip after being worn for one match.
Goods must be *fit for the purpose intended*	→ Goods should do what a consumer reasonably expects them to do.	→ A dishwasher should wash dishes. → A freezer should freeze food.
Goods must be *as described*	→ The description of the goods must match the packaging, the brochure or description given by the salesperson.	→ A laptop described as a silver colour in a brochure should actually be a silver colour. → A speaker described on the packaging as being voice-activated should be able to be activated by the consumer's voice.
Goods should *match the sample* **shown**	→ The sample shown to consumers by a seller should match the product purchased by the consumer.	→ A carpet sample shown to a consumer should match the complete order received.

B Rights of Consumers when Purchasing a Service

When a consumer buys a service, they have the right to expect that:

- The supplier of the service is qualified and has the skills needed to provide the service
- The supplier will provide the service with proper care and diligence
- The materials used by the supplier are sound and fit for the purpose intended
- Goods provided as part of the service must be of merchantable quality.

C Remedies for Breaches of the Act

In some circumstances, a consumer may feel that the good or service they purchased does not meet the legal standards.

Under the Sale of Goods and Supply of Services Act 1980, there are three solutions for breaches of the Act. These are commonly known as the **three Rs**.

Remedy	Explanation
Refund	→ If the fault is a major one, e.g. a washing machine that does not wash clothes, the consumer is entitled to a full refund of the price paid.
Repair	→ If the consumer used the item for some time and then discovered a fault in it, they are entitled to have the item repaired free of charge. The repair should permanently fix the problem.
Replacement	→ If the seller is unable to repair the item, they may replace it for the same item or an item of similar quality and price.

Note!

Consumers do not have the right to a refund, repair or replacement if they:
- *Are responsible for any fault*
- *Change their mind and want to return the good*
- *Delayed contacting the retailer once they had discovered the fault.*

D Retailer's Responsibility

Under the Sale of Goods and Supply of Services Act 1980, the consumer has a contract with the retailer when they buy goods and services. Therefore, if there is a problem with the good or service purchased, the seller must resolve the issue.

The retailer is not allowed to put up signs in their business that give consumers the impression that they have reduced consumer rights or that their rights are limited. Illegal signs include:

No Refunds

Credit Notes only

Goods not exchanged

Credit Note
A credit note acts like a voucher and allows the consumer to purchase items in the retailer's shop up to the amount stated on the credit note.

E Guarantees

Some manufacturers may give a written guarantee to consumers, which states that they will repair or replace a faulty item within a certain time period after it has been purchased, e.g. one year.

A guarantee is legally binding and is enforceable through the courts. The guarantee must show:
- What goods are covered
- The time frame involved
- The procedure required for making a claim.

F Second-hand Goods

Second-hand goods must be fit for the purpose intended, but consumers should not expect second-hand goods to be of the same quality as new goods. Consumers should carefully examine second-hand goods before purchasing as such goods are sold 'as seen'.

G Inertia Selling/Unsolicited Goods

This refers to goods that are sent to someone with a demand for payment, even though the person did not order the goods. It is illegal for an individual or a business to demand payment for unsolicited goods.

Example
In the past, some charities would send unsolicited goods, e.g. cards and pens, to people's homes and demand payment for these items.

The person who received the unsolicited goods can keep them without payment in the following circumstances:

- At the end of six months, as long as the consumer has not prevented the seller from collecting them
- After 30 days, if the consumer contacts the seller in writing and provides the address at which the goods can be collected and the seller does not collect them.

Evaluation of the Sale of Goods and Supply of Services Act 1980

The Sale of Goods and Supply of Services Act 1980 helps to protect consumers because:

- It ensures that consumers get a refund, repair or replacement if a good is faulty, or a service provided does not meet the required legal standard.
- It ensures that consumers are not misled by retailers using signs that reduce their responsibility to solve consumer complaints, e.g. 'credit notes only', 'no refunds'.

Activity 2.4

In pairs, prepare a consumer complaint roleplay. One of you plays the role of the consumer with a good or service that you feel breaches the Sale of Goods and Supply of Services Act 1980. The other plays the role of the retailer, who tries to resolve the complaint. Classmates must identify which part of the Act has been broken, e.g. goods were not as described.

2 Consumer Protection Act 2007

The Consumer Protection Act 2007 helps to protect consumers from unfair business-to-consumer commercial practices. The areas covered by the Act include:

A Misleading Descriptions

Sellers should not advertise goods and services in a way that deceives consumers, i.e. that is deliberately misleading, or by withholding information from consumers. This includes false or inaccurate claims about:

- The quantity, weight or volume of the good
- The country in which the good or service is made
- The ingredients and materials used in the good.

Example
- Stating that a bag of sugar weighs 1kg when it actually contains 800g of sugar.
- Stating that a jumper was made in Ireland when it was actually manufactured in China.

B Aggressive Practices

Traders cannot harass or coerce (force) consumers into buying a good or service. They are not allowed to use threatening or abusive language to force consumers to purchase a good or service that they would not buy under normal circumstances.

Example
- A car salesman threatens to hurt a consumer unless they sign a contract to purchase a car.
- Placing consumers under pressure to buy a product by falsely giving them the impression that the price of the good or service will increase tomorrow.

C Prohibited Practices

Certain practices are prohibited under the Act. These include:

- False claims that a product can cure an illness
- Running promotions or competitions when it costs money to claim the prizes
- Claiming that a business is closing down when this not the case.

Example
- A pharmaceutical company claims that a tablet manufactured by the firm will cure people suffering from asthma, even though there is no scientific proof of this claim.
- A consumer is asked to pay €50 to claim a prize they won in a competition.

D Price Display Regulations

The Act gives the Minister for Jobs, Enterprise and Innovation the power to require that the price of certain products must be displayed in a particular manner.

Example
- The full price of goods shown must be inclusive of all relevant taxes, e.g. value-added tax (VAT).
- The price shown on goods must be placed on the item or on a label on the edge of the shelf.
- Goods sold by weight must show the price per kg / g.

E Price Controls

The Act allows for price controls to be introduced in emergency situations. The decision to introduce price controls must be approved by the government.

Evaluation of the Consumer Protection Act 2007

The Act is good for consumers because they receive honest information from retailers about the good or service they want to purchase. This ensures that consumers know what they are buying and the price of the item.

Activity 2.5

Divide into two groups. Your teacher will assign your group either the Sale of Goods and Supply of Services Act 1980 or the Consumer Protection Act 2007. You have to work together to create a revision video using Powtoon, ShowMe or another appropriate software tool.

3 Competition and Consumer Protection Commission

The CCPC is an independent body that enforces competition and consumer protection law in Ireland.

The CCPC performs a number of functions, including the following.

A Informs Consumers of their Rights
B Investigates Breaches of Consumer Laws
C Advises the Government
D Personal Finance Information and Education
E Enforces Product Safety Regulations

Coimisiún um Iomaíocht agus Cosaint Tomhaltóirí | Competition and Consumer Protection Commission

A Informs Consumers of their Rights

The CCPC operates a website (www.ccpc.ie) and telephone helpline which gives consumers information about their consumer rights. It also gives consumers information to help them manage their money and runs campaigns to raise awareness of consumer rights, e.g. in newspapers and social media.

B Investigates Breaches of Consumer Laws

The CCPC investigates breaches of consumer legislation, e.g. product safety and misleading advertising. The CCPC has the power to:
- Issue on-the-spot fines for breaching price display legislation
- Prosecute traders who break consumer laws.

Example
Following an investigation by the CCPC, a Dublin-based car salesman was prosecuted for providing false information on a car's odometer (a display on a vehicle's dashboard that measures distance travelled). The car salesman was fined €500 and ordered to pay compensation of €7,000 to the consumer he had misled.

C Advises the Government

The CCPC conducts research to identify areas where consumers need greater protection. It informs the government about the impact any new laws or changes to existing consumer laws that would have on consumers.

D Personal Finance Information and Education

The CCPC provides financial information and education to consumers. The office runs public awareness campaigns and financial education programmes in workplaces and in schools.

E Enforces Product Safety Regulations

The CCPC ensures that producers and retailers obey relevant product safety regulations. The organisation shares information about dangerous products across the EU.

CASE STUDY — *CCPC*

The Irish toy market experienced a short-lived demand for fidget spinners. The CCPC, in collaboration with Revenue and Customs, seized approximately 200,000 fidget spinners as many did not comply with product safety legislation (they contained small parts that detached easily) and many did not have CE marking. Fidget spinners that were found not to comply with consumer laws were destroyed or returned to the manufacturer.

Definition: CE marking

This is a certification mark used on many products traded in the European Union. It shows that the product has met very high health, safety and environmental protection requirements.

---

4 Ombudsman

If a consumer cannot resolve a complaint with an organisation such as a government department or a bank, they can make a complaint to the relevant ombudsman. The services provided by the ombudsman are free of charge.

Consumers must have used the complaints process in the relevant organisation before they can bring a case to the ombudsman.

There are a number of ombudsmen in Ireland, including:

- The Financial Services and Pensions Ombudsman (FSPO)
- The Office of the Ombudsman.

DID YOU KNOW? Ombudsman *is a Swedish word meaning 'representative of the people'. An ombudsman investigates complaints from the public who feel that they have been treated unfairly by organisations. The king of Sweden appointed the first ombudsman in 1809 and there are now approximately 120 ombudsman offices around the world.*

Financial Services and Pensions Ombudsman

The FSPO deals with complaints made by individuals against financial institutions and pension providers, e.g. banks and employers that operate pension schemes.

- The FSPO aims to solve complaints through mediation and to find a mutually acceptable solution to the problem.

- If an agreement cannot be reached, the FSPO makes a decision on the case, which is legally binding.
- The FSPO can also award compensation if the complaint made is upheld.

> **!**
> **Definition: Mediation**
> This is when an independent third party helps to get two or more parties in dispute to reach a solution that is acceptable to both sides.

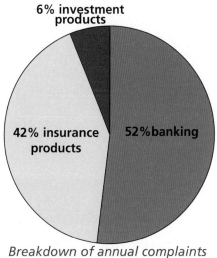

6% investment products

42% insurance products

52% banking

Breakdown of annual complaints to the FSPO

CASE STUDY · Financial Services and Pensions Ombudsman

A woman informed her insurance company that her car had been damaged in an attempted car theft. The insurance company removed the car from her home and told her that it would cost €2,200 to repair. Without consulting the owner, the insurance company crushed the car.

The car owner brought a complaint to the FSPO stating that the car had been crushed without her knowledge and sought €5,800 compensation from the insurance company. The insurance company was willing to pay €2,500 compensation.

The FSPO upheld the car owner's complaint and decided that the insurance company should pay her €3,000 compensation.

The Office of the Ombudsman

The Office of the Ombudsman investigates complaints from members of the public who believe they have been unfairly treated by a public body, including:

- The HSE (Health Service Executive)
- Local authorities, e.g. Limerick City and County Council
- Government departments, e.g. Department of Social Protection.

The Ombudsman may request files from the public body or demand to meet with employees of the government body involved in the case.

The Ombudsman then issues a recommendation on how they think the matter should be resolved, e.g. suggesting that the public body should issue an apology, an explanation or, in exceptional cases, financial compensation.

The public body generally carries out the recommendation of the Ombudsman.

DID YOU KNOW?

The Office of the Ombudsman receives approximately 3,000 complaints each year, the majority relating to government departments and local authorities.

Activity 2.6

There has been only one case in the 34-year history of the Office of the Ombudsman where the public body did not carry out the recommendation of the Ombudsman.

This took place in 2009, but the recommendation was recently implemented. Visit www.ombudsman.ie to find out more about this case and write it up as a newspaper article.

CASE STUDY *The Office of the Ombudsman*

A woman received a letter from her local office of the Department of Social Protection outlining that an overpayment of €19,900 had been paid to her. She contacted the Department requesting an explanation of the overpayment but received no reply.

The Ombudsman contacted the Department's local office and requested that they re-examine the woman's case. The local office discovered that her social welfare application had been processed incorrectly and that errors calculating her social welfare payments had been made. The Department found that not only had there never been an overpayment to the woman but she was entitled to an additional €700.

5 Small Claims Procedure

If a consumer cannot resolve a complaint with a business, they can take their case to the Small Claims Procedure at the District Court. Claims up to the value of €2,000 can be made for:

- Faulty goods
- Poor-quality production
- Damage to property.

It is a relatively easy, cheap and fast way for consumers to solve their dispute without the need to employ a solicitor.

There are a number of steps a consumer must follow to have their case heard in the Small Claims Procedure.

	Small Claims Procedure	
1	**Application**	→ The consumer submits an application form outlining the complaint and the amount they are claiming for. This application, together with a small fee, is sent to the local District Court.
2	**Small Claims Registrar**	→ The Smalls Claims Registrar organises a meeting with the consumer and business to resolve the dispute. If the claim cannot be resolved, the Small Claims Registrar refers the case to the District Court.
3	**Referral to the District Court**	→ The District Court judge listens to all witnesses and makes a decision on the case, which can include: • Awarding the amount claimed to the consumer • Ordering the goods to be repaired or the tradesperson to complete the work within a specific time period • Awarding financial compensation to the consumer.
4	**Appealing a Decision**	→ If a consumer or business is not happy with the judgment, an appeal can be made to the Circuit Court within 14 days of receiving the judgment.

Evaluation of the Small Claims Procedure

The Small Claims Procedure is effective for consumers because:

- It is a cheap, fast method of resolving conflict between the consumer and the business
- It is housed in the local District Court (there are 23 in Ireland), which means that consumers do not have to travel to Dublin to have their cases heard in court.

CASE STUDY · *Small Claims Procedure*

An Irish travel company was ordered by the Small Claims Procedure to pay compensation of €2,000 to a family after a week's holiday in Gran Canaria. The family endured late-night parties, an intruder on their fourth-floor accommodation and late-night building work on the hotel swimming pool.

KEY TERMS

Now you have completed this chapter, you should understand and be able to explain the following terms. In your copybook, write a definition of each term to build up your own glossary of terms.

- contract
- offer
- acceptance
- invitation to treat
- intention to contract
- capacity to contract
- consent to contract
- consideration
- legality of purpose
- legality of form
- contract termination
- performance
- agreement
- frustration
- breach of contract

- condition
- warranty
- compensation
- rescind the contract
- specific performance
- caveat emptor
- negotiation
- letter of complaint
- Consumers' Association of Ireland (CAI)
- European Consumer Centre Ireland (ECC Ireland)
- Sale of Goods and Supply of Services Act 1980

- inertia selling/unsolicited goods
- Consumer Protection Act 2007
- Competition and Consumer Protection Commission (CCPC)
- Financial Services and Pensions Ombudsman (FSPO)
- Office of the Ombudsman
- Small Claims Procedure

PowerPoint Summary

EXAM-STYLE QUESTIONS

Ordinary Level

Section 1 – Short Questions (10 marks each)

1 List **five** elements of a valid contract.
2 In contract law, distinguish between capacity to contract and intention to contract.
3 What is meant by the term *consideration* in relation to the law of contract?
4 Explain **two** remedies for breach of contract.
5 Outline **one** non-legislative method of resolving consumer conflict.
6 List **two** provisions of the Sale of Goods and Supply of Services Act 1980.
7 List **two** provisions of the Consumer Protection Act 2007.
8 Indicate by means of a tick (✔) which of these signs are legal.

Signs		
A	No cash refunds	
B	Credit notes only for faulty goods	
C	Faulty goods repaired only	
D	No refund on sale items	
E	Complaints should be made to the manufacturer	

Section 2 – Long Questions

1 Outline **four** elements of a valid contract. **(20 marks)**
2 Describe what is meant by the terms *(i) agreement* and *(ii) frustration* in relation to terminating a contract. **(15 marks)**
3 Discuss the remedies available for breach of contract. **(15 marks)**
4 'There are a number of non-legislative methods of resolving consumer disputes with retailers.' Describe **two** of these methods in detail. **(15 marks)**
5 Describe how the Consumers' Association of Ireland helps consumers. **(15 marks)**
6 Outline the main provisions of the Sale of Goods and Supply of Services Act 1980 in relation to the sale of goods. **(20 marks)**
7 Explain the responsibilities of suppliers of a service under the Sale of Goods and Supply of Services Act 1980. **(15 marks)**
8 Outline **three** provisions of the Consumer Protection Act 2007. **(20 marks)**
9 Outline how a consumer can take a case to the Small Claims Procedure. **(20 marks)**
10

> Christine purchased a mobile phone in a local phone shop. On arriving home, she discovered that she could not make calls or receive text messages. She returned to the shop, but they told her that she would have to contact the manufacturer to resolve the issue. Christine decided to contact the Competition and Consumer Protection commission to ask their advice.

(i) Name the law that protects Christine in this situation. **(10 marks)**
(ii) Describe **two** of Christine's rights under this law. **(10 marks)**

Higher Level

Section 1 – Short Questions (10 marks each)

1 Explain the term *invitation to treat*.

2 Write the correct answer in the following statements.

  (i) A contract can be terminated by **agreement / acceptance**.

  (ii) The exchange of money or goods in a contract is known as **capacity to contract / consideration**.

  (iii) All social agreements are **legally binding / are not legally binding**.

  (iv) The legal ability to enter into a contract is known as **capacity to contract / capability to contract**.

  (v) A remedy for breach of contract is called **specific performance / specific production**.

3 Explain the term *capacity to contract*. Give **two** examples of a time when a person does not have the capacity to contract.

4 Distinguish between legality of purpose and legality of form.

5 Using examples, explain the difference between a warranty and a condition in a contract.

6 Explain what is meant by the term *unsolicited goods*.

7 Identify the correct organisation described in the following sentences:

  (i) This person is responsible for resolving issues between consumers and public sector organisations.

  (ii) This state agency is responsible for informing consumers of their rights and ensuring that businesses comply with consumer legislation.

  (iii) This is a non-commercial organisation established to promote consumer rights in Ireland and that publishes a magazine called *Consumer Choice*.

  (iv) This is a court that deals with consumer complaints in a fast and cheap manner without the need for a solicitor.

8 Name the law that protects consumers from misleading practices and prices. List **two** other provisions of this piece of legislation.

Section 2 – Applied Business Question (80 marks)

Law of Contract – Rapid Sports Ltd

Judy Murphy is 25 years old and has recently set up her own business called Rapid Sports Ltd. She spotted a gap in the market to sell sports clothing online to customers throughout Europe.

Judy understood that for her business to be a success she would need to engage the services of a reliable courier company. She arranged a meeting with David Cody, the owner of Swift Couriers Ltd. In their meeting David offered a one-year courier service at a cost of €15,000 with delivery to be made to consumers within 48 hours. Judy accepted the terms offered by David – she will pay David €15,000 and he will provide a delivery service for one year. Both parties entered into the contract voluntarily and signed a written contract to deliver sports clothing across Europe.

To keep up with the demand from consumers, Judy employed ten staff and has found new suppliers to add to her website to increase the range of stock that she carries.

Unfortunately there have been some problems with Swift Couriers Ltd as there have been complaints from consumers who have not received their orders for 72 hours. Judy has tried to contact the owner of Swift Couriers Ltd, but he has not replied to her emails or voicemails.

Judy called a management meeting and sought suggestions from staff as to how to solve the problems with the courier firm. Joanne, the marketing manager, suggested that they should take Swift Couriers Ltd to court for breach of contract. Tommy, the finance manager, thinks they should complete the contract and then source a new courier. Diarmuid, the distribution manager, thinks that Judy should get David to agree to end the contract.

Judy doesn't know what to do. She doesn't want to get a bad reputation among her consumers by not keeping her promise of delivery within 48 hours, but she is also concerned about the legal costs of dealing with a breach of contract.

A Identify the main stakeholders in Rapid Sports Ltd. Refer to the text in your answer. **(30 marks)**

B Identify and describe the main elements of a contract that exist between Rapid Sports Ltd and Swift Couriers Ltd. **(30 marks)**

C Outline the ways in which Rapid Sports Ltd could terminate its contract with Swift Couriers Ltd. **(20 marks)**

Section 2 – Applied Business Question (80 marks)

Consumer Conflict – TV City

Alex decided to purchase a new silver model TXX television, which was manufactured in Ireland, for €2,500 from TV City. Even though it was a very expensive purchase, Alex was happy with the detailed technical information he received from the salesperson and the fact that he was supporting jobs in Ireland with his purchase.

Alex paid for the TV and was surprised to find that the TV actually cost €3,025, as the price tag had shown the price excluding VAT.

A week later the television arrived and Alex was disappointed to find that he had received the correct television but in the wrong colour. He had ordered the silver model, but TV City had delivered the grey model. He also saw a label on the box stating that the television was manufactured in Taiwan, even though in the store the sign above the television stated that it had been made in Ireland.

A few weeks later Alex began to notice some problems with the television. He could not view any of the TV channels and the sound had stopped working.

Alex returned to TV City and asked to speak to the manager. While he was waiting, Alex noticed that the TV he had purchased was still priced at €2,500. Alex had been told that this was a special offer price for one day only and he was annoyed that three weeks later, the special offer was still running in store.

Alex outlined the problems he had experienced with the television and showed the manager his receipt. The manager said that she couldn't help, as the manufacturer is responsible for fixing any problems experienced by consumers. She also told Alex that if he couldn't get in contact with the manufacturer, the store would offer Alex store credit to the value of €2,500. Alex asked for the name and address of the branch manager so he could write a letter of complaint, as he was not happy with the options presented by the store manager.

While Alex was in the store he noticed a poster for an instore competition to win a new television. The poster stated that the winner would have to pay €20 to receive the top prize. He pointed this out to a salesperson, who simply said, 'It's a large television and we can't be expected to deliver it to the winner for free!'

Alex is concerned about the consumer practices at the TV City store and intends to refer to the CAI website and contact the CCPC for advice regarding the faulty TV.

A Outline Alex's rights as set out in the Sale of Goods and Supply of Services Act 1980. **(30 marks)**
B Describe the legal responsibilities of TV City under the Consumer Protection Act 2007. **(20 marks)**
C Recommend **three** non-legislative methods that Alex could use to solve this problem
  with TV City. **(30 marks)**

Section 3 – Long Questions

1 Outline **four** ways in which a contract can be terminated. **(20 marks)**
2 Evaluate the remedies available for breach of contract. **(20 marks)**
3 Evaluate the non-legislative methods which can be used to solve conflict between the
  consumer and the business. **(15 marks)**
4 Outline the forms of redress available to consumers under the Sale of Goods and
  Supply of Services Act 1980. **(15 marks)**
5 Illustrate the main provisions of the Consumer Protection Act 2007. **(20 marks)**
6 Evaluate the role of the CCPC in protecting consumers in Ireland. **(20 marks)**
7 Outline the role of the European Consumer Centre (ECC) in resolving consumer complaints. **(15 marks)**
8 Discuss the role of the Small Claims Procedure in resolving consumer conflict with traders. **(20 marks)**

PREVIOUS LEAVING CERTIFICATE EXAM QUESTIONS

Ordinary Level

Section A – Short Questions (10 marks each)

1 Column 1 is a list of business terms relating to contract law. Column 2 is a list of possible explanations for these terms. One explanation has no match.

Business Terms		Explanations
1 Capacity	A	An unforeseen event makes it impossible for a contract to be fulfilled
2 Contract	B	A person must be legally able to enter into a contract
3 Consideration	C	The parties entering the contract must do so of their own free will
4 Consent	D	The legally binding agreement made between two or more parties
5 Frustration	E	Some contracts must be drawn up in a certain way if they are to be legal contracts
	F	Something of value exchanged between the parties to the contract

Match the two lists in your copybook by writing your answers in the form *number = letter* (e.g. 1 = A).

[LC OL 2016]

2 Explain the term *breach of contract*. **[LC OL 2014]**

3 Complete the following table, which refers to the Sale of Goods and Supply of Services Act 1980, by placing a tick (✔) in the correct box for each statement. **[LC OL 2014]**

Consumer Issue	Not of Merchantable Quality	Not Fit for the Purpose	Not as Described	Does Not Match the Sample
Waterproof coat that allows water in				
Curtains have a different pattern to that seen in the shop				
A black phone inside a box labelled silver phone				
The water dispenser of a fridge is leaking				

Section B

1

> Consumers in Ireland are also protected in relation to the sale of goods, hire purchase agreements and contracts for the supply of services. www.consumerhelp.ie

Name a consumer law other than the Consumer Protection Act 2007, that protects consumers in Ireland. **(10 marks) [LC OL 2017]**

2 If a consumer purchases a faulty product, who is responsible – the retailer **or** the producer? Explain your answer and name the law that protects the consumer in this case. **(15 marks) [LC OL 2018]**

Section B *continued*

3

Funky Fotos

Jenny spotted an offer from Funky Fotos on a daily deals website of 100 photos printed for just €5.99. Jenny signed up for the deal and went to Funky Fotos. She uploaded her 5" x 7" photos for printing and was told to come back the next day to collect them as they were extremely busy.

Jenny returned the following day to collect the photos. She was told the price was €10.99. She referred to the 'deal' that she signed up for but the shop assistant told her that the deal was for 4" x 6" photos only. Jenny contacted the Competition and Consumer Protection Commission which had already received many similar complaints about the Funky Fotos offer.

TODAY'S DEAL
Funky Fotos
Photos printed immediately
Special Offer
100 Photos
Only €5.99

Explain how Funky Fotos has broken the terms of the Consumer Protection Act 2007. (Refer to the text in your answer.) **(15 marks) [LC OL 2014]**

4 The Small Claims Court procedure can be used to resolve consumer complaints.

Outline **two** advantages for a consumer of taking a case to the Small Claims Court. **(15 marks) [LC OL 2018]**

Higher Level

Section A – Short Questions (10 marks each)

1 Fill in the appropriate words to complete each of the following statements.

(i) R_____, replacements and repairs are forms of redress available to a consumer under the Sale of Goods and Supply of Services Act 1980.

(ii) The _____ provides a solution to consumer conflicts and can award compensation up to €2,000.

(iii) The term merchantable quality in consumer law implies that consumer products are of a reasonable quality having regard to their _____.

(iv) The _____ is responsible for investigating, enforcing and encouraging compliance with consumer law.

(v) The Sale of Goods and Supply of Services Act 1980 states that all providers of services will supply a service with _____. **[LC HL 2018]**

Section B

1

The band Stand and Deliver officially cancelled their upcoming tour due to the death of their singer Richard Stears.

(i) Explain the method of terminating the legal contract referred to in the text above.

(ii) Outline **three** other methods for terminating a legal contract, providing an example in each case. **(25 marks) [LC HL 2018]**

2 Outline a consumer's legal rights under the terms of the Sale of Goods and Supply of Services Act 1980, with reference to any **three** of the following:

(i) Merchantable Quality

(ii) Guarantees

(iii) Signs limiting consumer rights

(iv) Unsolicited Goods **(20 marks) [LC HL 2014]**

3

The National Consumer Agency (NCA) now known as the Competition and Consumer Protection Commission (CCPC) launched an investigation into the motor vehicle emissions scandal at the car manufacturer Volkswagen.

Evaluate the functions of the NCA (CCPC) with regard to protecting the interests of consumers. **(20 marks) [LC HL 2016]**

 Solutions

CHAPTER 3

RESOLVING CONFLICT IN THE WORKPLACE

Learning Outcomes

When you have completed this chapter, you will be able to:

1. Explain the term *industrial relations*

2. Understand the importance of positive industrial relations in the workplace

3. Identify and explain areas of conflict in business

4. Identify and describe the different types of industrial action

5. Outline the impact of industrial action on business stakeholders

6. Describe non-legislative methods of resolving industrial relations conflict

7. Identify and explain legislative methods of resolving industrial relations conflict.

Literacy Link

Industrial relations, trade unions, bargaining, negotiation, conciliation, arbitration, discrimination, equality

Numeracy Link

Division, multiplication, percentages, addition

Cross-curricular Link

Home Economics – employment, equal pay
Religious Education – discrimination, equality

CASE STUDY — Industrial Relations at the ESB Group

The ESB Group is a state-owned electricity company with approximately 7,800 employees. The company strives to have **positive industrial relations** between management and staff through ongoing communication.

The company understands the importance of complying with all relevant **employee legislation** such as the **Employment Equality Acts 1998–2015** and the **Unfair Dismissals Act 1977–2015**.

A number of different **trade unions** represent employees across the organisation. They aim to **provide support and advice** to their members and seek **improved pay and working conditions**.

The ESB and its unions have not always experienced positive industrial relations. In 1991 ESB electricians went on **official strike** for five days, causing power cuts across Ireland. The dispute related to **pay and productivity claims**. Electricity supplies were 30% lower than needed and some farmers complained that they had to dump milk as there was no electricity to keep supplies fresh.

In recent years, the ESB Group wanted to close some peat-fuelled

ESB — Energy for generations

power generation plants. When staff at the Rhodes plant in Co. Offaly rejected a closure package, there were concerns that **unofficial wildcat action** would take place. However, management and unions worked together to resolve the issue.

Some years ago the unions served **notice of strike action** on the company in a dispute over the company's pension scheme. However, following **negotiations** between the parties, agreement was reached between the unions and company at the **Workplace Relations Commission (WRC)**.

Given the sheer size of the company and the range of employees in the firm, ESB management and trade unions must continue to work together to ensure positive industrial relations continue in the business.

INDUSTRIAL RELATIONS

Industrial relations refers to the relationship between the employer and employees in an organisation. The aim is to have a positive industrial relations environment.

Benefits of Positive Industrial Relations

Benefit	Reason
Recruitment and Retention	→ It is easier to recruit and retain staff when there are positive industrial relations in the business. Current employees want to stay and the business is an attractive workplace for potential staff.
Employee Motivation	→ Happy employees tend to be more motivated and are more willing to work hard for the benefit of the business.
Intrapreneurship	→ Employees are willing to suggest ideas for new products and processes, which may increase business profits or reduce business costs.
Change	→ Employees are more accepting of change in the workplace when the employer is open and honest about the reasons why changes are needed.
Industrial Action	→ Employees are more likely to speak to management about problems before they develop into serious issues. This helps to reduce the likelihood of industrial action.

Causes of Industrial Relations Conflict

There are a number of reasons why industrial relations conflict can develop between management and employees in a business. These can include disputes over:

Potential for Conflict and Example	
Pay	→ Disputes with the employer over rates of pay, overtime payments and pension contributions.
Working Conditions	→ Disagreement with the employer in relation to hours of work, health and safety in the workplace and holiday time.
Technology	→ Resistance to the introduction of new technology if there is the belief that: • The employer has not provided adequate training • The use of new technology will increase workloads or lead to staff redundancies.
Redundancy	→ Unhappiness at the way staff were chosen for redundancy or with the redundancy terms offered by the employer.
Unfair Dismissal	→ Belief that that co-workers were unfairly dismissed based on factors such as disability or race. Employees may fear for their own job security in the future.

CASE STUDY _Vita Cortex Industries_

Thirty-two employees at Vita Cortex Industries in Cork staged a sit-in at the factory after the company closed without any redundancy payments to staff. The employees received messages of support from many people, including former president of Ireland Mary Robinson and former Manchester United manager Sir Alex Ferguson. The dispute ended after 161 days when the company agreed to make redundancy payments to staff.

PAY CLAIMS

The most common forms of pay claims include the following:

1 Cost of Living Claim

This occurs when employees want their pay to keep up with the rate of inflation. For example, if the rate of inflation is 3%, employees want at least a 3% pay increase.

> **Definition: Pay Claim**
> A demand made by employees to their employer for an increase in pay.

> **Definition: Inflation**
> The increase in the cost of goods and services from one year to the next.

Activity 3.1

An employee of a manufacturing company earns €67,250 per year and wants her pay to remain in line with inflation levels in Ireland. If inflation increases by 2% and the employee seeks and receives a 2% pay increase, how much will she now earn per year?

2 Comparability Claim

Employees want a pay increase because people doing similar work have received a pay increase. For example, SuperValu cashiers get a pay increase and Dunnes Stores cashiers demand the same increase from their employer.

3 Productivity Claim

Employees seek a pay rise because their workload has increased or they have adapted to changes introduced by management, e.g. the introduction of new machinery.

4 Relativity Claim

This occurs when the pay of one group of workers is linked to the pay of another group, even though they are performing different jobs. If one group receives a pay increase, the other group will also want an increase of the same percentage to maintain a pay gap. For example, if the waiting staff in a restaurant receive a 10% pay increase, the chefs demand a 10% pay increase to maintain a 10% difference in pay.

Activity 3.2

Use a website such as www.postermywall.com to create a Wanted poster to explain one type of pay claim that you have learned about.

TRADE UNIONS

A trade union is an organisation that aims to protect and improve the pay and working conditions of its members. An employee can join a trade union by paying a yearly subscription.

Trade unions can represent employees in one sector, e.g. ASTI (the Association of Secondary Teachers, Ireland); or employees in many sectors, e.g. SIPTU – Services, Industrial, Professional and Technical Union.

> **DID YOU KNOW?**
> *Around 29% of the working population in Ireland are members of a trade union. SIPTU is the largest trade union with over 180,000 members.*

Activity 3.3

Working in pairs, research trade unions in Ireland. Choose one trade union and examine its website (e.g. www.asti.ie). Create a presentation about the trade union to include the following information:
- Name of the trade union
- Number of members
- Types of workers it represents
- Campaigns it supports/has supported.

Shop Steward

The shop steward is elected by trade union members in a workplace and acts as the union's representative in that workplace.

The duties of a shop steward include:

- Providing feedback to the union on the views of union members
- Giving advice and support to members on workplace issues, e.g. sick leave
- Helping to resolve disputes between employees and management, e.g. the introduction of new working hours.

Benefits of Trade Union Membership for Employees

There are a number of benefits for employees when they become members of a trade union, including:

Benefit	Reason
Protects Employment Rights	→ It makes employees aware of their rights in the workplace, e.g. working conditions, and protects members if the business breaches any of these rights.
Information and Support	→ Provides information and support to members on issues such as pay and leave entitlements.
Better Pay and Working Conditions	→ The trade union negotiates with management on behalf of the staff to gain better pay and working conditions, e.g. an increase in basic pay.
National Level	→ The union can increase awareness of employees' concerns by providing information to the media, e.g. on problems with health and safety in the workplace.

 DID YOU KNOW? *In 1945 the Irish Women Workers' Union organised a three-month strike to improve working conditions. They successfully obtained the right to two weeks' annual leave for all workers in Ireland.*

Benefits of Trade Union Membership for Employers

While many people believe that trade unions benefit only employees, this is not the case. For many employers there are a range of benefits of trade union membership.

Benefit	Reason
Faster Negotiations	→ It is faster for employers to negotiate with the shop steward, rather than with individuals or groups of employees. This saves the business time and money.
Introducing Change	→ It can be easier for the employer to introduce change, e.g. new technology. The shop steward can explain to the employees why the changes are needed.
Improved Health and Safety	→ Employees inform the shop steward of health and safety issues in the workplace. This information can be passed to management and can help to improve health and safety at the firm.

ICTU (Irish Congress of Trade Unions)

ICTU is the umbrella body that represents and campaigns on behalf of trade union members in Ireland.

ICTU aims to:

- Provide training and information to trade unions and their members
- Help resolve disputes between unions and employers
- Negotiate on behalf of unions in national pay agreements with the government and social partners.

STRONGER TOGETHER
CONGRESS
Irish Congress of Trade Unions

 DID YOU KNOW? *Forty-four trade unions are members of ICTU in the Republic of Ireland and Northern Ireland. They represent over 800,000 workers across the island of Ireland.*

BARGAINING

In most organisations, managers and employees meet to discuss a wide range of issues including pay and working conditions. This process is known as *bargaining*. It can be conducted in the following ways:

1 Individual bargaining
2 Collective bargaining
3 National collective bargaining.

1 Individual Bargaining
Individual employees meet with the employer to negotiate the best pay and working conditions for themselves. This often occurs in businesses where there is little or no trade union membership.

2 Collective Bargaining
The employer negotiates pay and conditions of employment with groups of employees, often represented by the trade union shop steward.

3 National Collective Bargaining/Social Partnership
This involves the social partners negotiating pay and working conditions at a national level. The aim of this type of bargaining is to achieve moderate wage increases in return for positive industrial relations in the economy and reductions in income tax for employees. Past social partnership agreements have included: Programme for Prosperity and Fairness; and Sustaining Progress.

> **! *Definition*: Social partners**
> Social partners are groups that work together with government to achieve an agreed goal, which benefits all the groups involved e.g. moderate pay increases in return for improvements in public services. Social partners include: Ibec, ICTU, IFA and CIF (Construction Industry Federation).

TYPES OF INDUSTRIAL ACTION

Despite managers and employees engaging in bargaining, sometimes conflict between the parties cannot be resolved. This may lead to employees taking industrial action. There are different types of industrial action, including:

A Legal Types of Industrial Action

1 Official strike
2 All-out strike
3 Work to rule
4 Token stoppage
5 Overtime ban

B Illegal Types of Industrial Action

1 Unofficial strike
2 Wildcat/lightning strike
3 Political strike

A Legal Types of Industrial Action

1 Official Strike
Employees refuse to enter the workplace and perform their normal duties. An official strike requires that:
- A secret ballot is held
- At least one week's notice of industrial action is given to the employer
- The strike action is approved by the trade union.

Trade union members may receive strike pay from their trade union during an official strike.

2 All-out Strike

All employees in the business go on strike, even employees who are not directly involved in the dispute.

The decision to strike must be made by a secret ballot and seven days' notice must be given to the employer. ICTU approval is needed for this type of industrial action.

3 Work to Rule

Employees carry out their workplace duties as stated in their contract of employment or job description. They do not carry out any other duties, e.g. nurses would not perform any cleaning or administrative duties.

4 Token Stoppage

Employees refuse to work for a short period of time (e.g. one day). This gives the employer a warning that more serious industrial action may be taken in the future if agreement is not reached.

> **Example**
> Nurses at Sligo General Hospital staged a one-day work stoppage to protest against job cuts and the non-renewal of temporary nursing contracts.

5 Overtime Ban

Employees refuse to work overtime for the employer. This may put the employer under pressure to resolve the issue quickly so the dispute does not have a negative impact on the business, e.g. missing deadlines.

> **Example**
> Train drivers in a firm are in dispute with management and go on strike. Ticket inspectors and maintenance workers not involved in the dispute also go on strike.

> **Definition: Overtime**
> Overtime is when employees work more hours than their standard working week.

B Illegal Types of Industrial Action

1 Unofficial Strike

Employees take strike action but do not meet all or some of the requirements of an official strike, e.g. they do not conduct a secret ballot. Trade union members do not receive strike pay.

2 Wildcat/Lightning Strike

Employees take strike action without giving any warning to the employer. These disputes are often resolved quickly.

> **CASE STUDY** — *Wildcat Strike in the Prison Service*
>
> A change in court sittings meant that prison escort drivers' work rosters had to change. The drivers were unhappy with these changes and 33 drivers were accused of engaging in wildcat strike action. They arrived for duty but 'forgot' their driving licences, so they were unable to perform their driving duties for that day. The Irish Prison Service and the trade union representing the drivers, the Irish Prison Officers' Association, reached agreement within a week of the wildcat action.

3 Political Strike

Employees leave the workplace to protest against the government's actions, e.g. the introduction of new laws. This is an illegal form of strike action, as employees should not punish their employer for a dispute they have with the government.

> **Note!**
> *Illegal types of industrial action are not approved by the trade union and striking employees do not receive strike pay.*

In pairs, work together to create a cloze test on the legal and illegal types of industrial action that can be taken by employees. Swap cloze tests around the classroom and complete a test prepared by another pair of students to test your knowledge.

THE IMPACT OF INDUSTRIAL ACTION ON STAKEHOLDERS

Industrial action taken by employees can have a negative impact on the organisation's stakeholders.

Stakeholder	Negative impact
Employer	→ Industrial action disrupts business activity and may result in missed deadlines, e.g. failure to fulfil a customer's order. This can damage the firm's reputation.
Investors	→ Profits can fall during industrial action, leading to lower dividends for investors.
Employees	→ The longer the industrial action continues, the greater the threat to employees' job security.
Suppliers	→ Suppliers may not be paid by a business experiencing industrial action. They may be unable to pay their own bills and could go out of business.
Government	→ Industrial action can reduce government tax revenue, e.g. income tax from employees. This results in less government income to spend on public services, e.g. health and education.
Consumers	→ Consumers may be unable to buy goods and services due to industrial action and decide to purchase from competitors. They may continue to purchase from competitors in the future.

Activity 3.5

Industrial action can have a negative impact on business stakeholders. Which stakeholder do you think could be most affected by industrial action? Discuss this in groups and give reasons for your choice of stakeholder.

RESOLVING INDUSTRIAL RELATIONS CONFLICT

Industrial relations conflict can be resolved by using:

- Non-legislative methods
- Legislative methods.

Non-legislative Methods

The employer and employees involved in industrial relations conflict should first try to resolve the dispute in a non-legislative manner through, in order of formality:

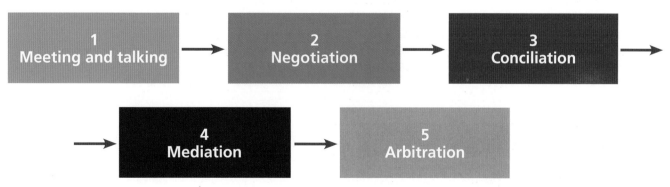

1 Meeting and Talking

A meeting is arranged between the employer and employees. The human resources (HR) manager might represent the employer and the shop steward might represent the employees. They discuss the issue and try to resolve the problem.

2 Negotiation

Both parties meet and bargain with each other. They make offers and counter-offers until a compromise is reached that is acceptable to both sides.

3 Conciliation

The dispute is referred to an independent conciliator who listens to both sides of the dispute. The conciliator tries to get both sides to come to an agreed solution.

Definition: Conciliator
A person who brings disputing parties together to try to resolve the dispute.

4 Mediation

An independent mediator hears both sides of the dispute and outlines how they think the problem should be resolved.
Mediation encourages the employer and employees to solve the dispute together.

Definition: Mediator
An independent person who aims to get two parties in a dispute to reach an agreement by acting as a go-between.

5 Arbitration

An independent arbitrator listens to both parties in the dispute and makes a decision on how the problem should be resolved. This recommendation is not legally binding and can be rejected by one or both of the parties.

Definition: Arbitrator
An independent person who examines an issue and makes a recommendation on how it should be solved.

Definition: Binding arbitration
In some cases the employer and employees may agree in advance to accept the decision made by the arbitrator. This is known as binding arbitration.

Legislative Methods

Sometimes a dispute between management and staff cannot be resolved using non-legislative methods. There are a number of legislative methods of resolving industrial relations conflict, which we will examine in detail. These include:

1 Industrial Relations Act 1990

2 Workplace Relations Commission (WRC)

3 Labour Court

4 Unfair Dismissals Acts 1977–2015

5 Employment Equality Acts 1998–2015

1 Industrial Relations Act 1990

The Industrial Relations Act was introduced to improve industrial relations in Ireland and to help to resolve industrial relations disputes. The main features of the Act include the following.

A Trade Disputes

This relates to any dispute between employers and employees, which is connected with:

- The employment or non-employment of a person, or
- The terms or conditions of employment of any person.

The Act outlines the difference between legal and illegal disputes.

Legal Trade Disputes	Illegal Trade Disputes
1 Pay and working conditions	1 Disagreement about how the business is run
2 Discrimination against an employee	2 Discontent about how the government is running the country
3 Dismissal of an employee	3 Closed-shop agreements, e.g. insisting that employees join a particular trade union such as SIPTU

B Secret Ballot

For official industrial action to be taken, trade union members must vote in a secret ballot. This is a confidential vote in which employees decide whether to take industrial action. If the majority of votes cast are in favour of industrial action, the trade union decides on the most effective form of action to be taken, e.g. an official strike.

C Minimum Notice

The employees must give the employer a minimum of seven days' notice before taking industrial action.

D Picketing

Primary picketing takes place at the employees' workplace. It involves employees walking outside the workplace carrying placards indicating that they are taking strike action. Placards often contain information on the name of the trade union and the reason for the industrial action.

Secondary picketing takes place outside the workplace of another employer. It is legal to do this if the employees believe that this employer is helping their employer to break their strike action.

> **Example – Secondary Picketing**
>
> Employees of DJ Sports are on strike. The owner of Super Sport sends employees to open DJ Sports stores and operate the tills. As Super Sport is helping to break the strike at DJ Sports, secondary picketing is allowed to take place. Employees from DJ Sports can now picket outside Super Sport shops too.

E Immunity

The employer cannot sue the trade union or its members for losses incurred by the business due to official strike action. The employees must have conducted a secret ballot and given the employer a minimum of seven days' notice to be protected by immunity under the Act.

Activity 3.6

Examine the image and answer the following questions.

1 What is the name of the trade union involved in the industrial action?
2 What type of industrial action are employees taking? Explain this form of industrial action.
3 Name the law that protects employees when they picket.
4 Do these employees have immunity while they picket? Give a reason for your answer.

2 Workplace Relations Commission (WRC)

The WRC is an independent body that provides a range of industrial relations services to employers and employees.

DID YOU KNOW? *The WRC was set up under the Workplace Relations Act 2015.*

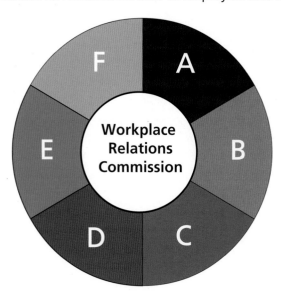

A Information

B An advisory service

C Conciliation

D Mediation

E An adjudication service

F Codes of practice

A Information

The WRC provides information on employment law and industrial relations to employers and employees through its website (www.workplacerelations.ie) and phone service.

B Advisory Service

The advisory service works with businesses to build and maintain positive industrial relations in the workplace. The advisory service can visit the firm and provide workshops and training, e.g. on issues in the workplace.

C Conciliation

An independent conciliator hears the dispute and helps both parties to reach a mutually acceptable agreement. The conciliator may offer a solution if they believe it will be accepted by both parties.

D Mediation

The mediation officer tries to get both parties to reach a mutually acceptable solution to their dispute. If mediation is successful, the mediation officer records the agreement in writing and it becomes legally binding. Unsuccessful mediation is referred to an adjudication officer.

E Adjudication Service

Adjudication officers investigate cases when mediation has been unsuccessful. They hear both sides of the dispute and make a decision on how the case should be solved. Decisions made by adjudication officers can be appealed to the Labour Court.

F Codes of Practice

The WRC formulates codes of practice, which are written rules that define how people or organisations must act in particular situations. Examples include bullying in the workplace, and disciplinary procedures.

Activity 3.7

Working in pairs, complete a fishbone graphic organiser summarising the services provided by the Workplace Relations Commission (WRC). Swap your completed graphic organiser with a pair of students close to you. Check that the information contained in the diagram is correct and fill in any missing details.

3 Labour Court

The Labour Court is the **court of last resort** for industrial relations disputes. It is not a court of law but an industrial relations tribunal. The aim of the Labour Court is to resolve and adjudicate on industrial disputes quickly, fairly and informally.

The functions of the Labour Court include:

THE LABOUR COURT
An Chúirt Oibreachais

A Investigates Disputes
The Labour Court investigates trade disputes between employers and employees and issues a decision on the case. If either party is unhappy with the decision, it can be appealed to the High Court.

B Hears Appeals
Decisions made by an adjudication officer at the WRC can be appealed to the Labour Court. The Labour Court issues a binding judgment on the case.

C Establishes Joint Labour Committees (JLCs)
The Labour Court sets up a JLC for employees in certain sectors, e.g. security or hairdressing. A JLC improves pay and working conditions for staff in these sectors.

D Registers Employment Regulation Orders
An Employment Regulation Order (ERO) is drawn up by a JLC and fixes minimum rates of pay and working conditions for people working in specific industries, e.g. contract cleaning. The ERO is adopted by the Labour Court and becomes legally binding.

E Interpretation of Codes of Practice
The Labour Court gives its opinion on the interpretation of the codes of practice formulated by the WRC, e.g. grievance and disciplinary procedures. It also investigates complaints about breaches of codes.

Definition: Joint Labour Committee (JLC)
A JLC is used in sectors with low trade union membership. It is made up of an equal number of employer and employee representatives appointed by the Labour Court, and a chairperson. It sets minimum pay and working conditions for these workers.

Example
An ERO was registered in 2017 for security operatives in the security industry. This increased hourly rates and sick pay entitlements for employees across the entire industry.

CASE STUDY — Luas Drivers at the Labour Court

Luas drivers represented by the trade union SIPTU demanded a pay increase from their employer Transdev. The employer refused this increase and the drivers took four months of industrial action, including a work to rule and 12 days of all-out strike. In response to the industrial action, Transdev docked pay from the drivers who participated in the industrial action.

The dispute was referred to the Labour Court and in May 2016 it ruled that the drivers were entitled to a wage increase of between 15.6% and 18.3% over four years and that they should receive an immediate payment of €750. The court also ruled that the employer must restore pay docked during the dispute.

The Labour Court recommended that Transdev should drop their demand to increase the employees' shift length from nine to nine and a half hours. In return the drivers agreed to co-operate with the extension of Luas services and that the starting salary for new recruits would be 10% lower than colleagues' pay.

Activity 3.8

Create a mind map summarising the services provided by the Workplace Relations Commission and the Labour Court. You could use websites such as https://coggle.it or www.canva.com to create your mind map. Both text and images help to create a memorable mind map.

4 Unfair Dismissals Acts 1977–2015
Dismissal is when an employer removes an employee from their job. The Unfair Dismissals Acts were introduced to prevent employees being dismissed from their roles for unfair reasons. The Acts apply to employees with one year's continuous employment with the employer.

Under the Acts, all dismissals are deemed to be unfair and the burden of proof lies with the employer, i.e. they must prove that the dismissal was fair.

Fair Dismissal

There are a number of grounds under which dismissal is deemed to be fair:

Ground for dismissal	Explanation
Redundancy	→ The employer can dismiss an employee if a genuine redundancy situation exists, e.g. falling sales. Employees must be chosen fairly for redundancy, e.g. dismissing the least qualified employees.
Incompetence	→ The employee can be dismissed if they do not perform their role to an appropriate standard, e.g. poor performance or failure to reach agreed targets.
Qualifications	→ If the employee does not have the relevant qualifications for performing their role, e.g. failing to pass professional accounting exams that would enable them to work as a qualified accountant.
Employee Misconduct	→ It can relate to a number of minor incidents that when viewed together warrant dismissal, e.g. persistent lateness or absenteeism. **Definition: Misconduct** Unacceptable behaviour of an employee in the workplace. → Gross misconduct is more serious and can result in instant dismissal, e.g. stealing from the business.
Legal Reasons	→ An employee can be dismissed if continuing their employment would break the law, e.g. a non-EU employee who does not possess a valid work visa to work in Ireland.

Procedure for Fair Dismissal

The business should develop a dismissal policy to ensure that dismissals are carried out fairly. An employee cannot be dismissed on a whim of the employer, e.g. because of a personality clash.

During the procedure for fair dismissal the employee can:

- Bring a colleague or trade union representative to the meetings
- Respond to the complaint at all stages of the procedure.

1 Counsel employee

2 Verbal warning

3 First written warning

4 Final written warning

5 Suspension

6 Dismissal

The steps in the procedure for fair dismissal may include the following:

1 **Counsel employee:** The employer notices that an employee is underperforming and arranges an informal meeting. The employer outlines the improvements that need to be made and offers assistance, e.g. extra training.

2 **Verbal warning:** The employee's performance has not improved and a formal meeting with management is organised. The employer outlines the improvements that need to be made and a timeline to achieve them.

3 **First written warning:** This is issued to the employee if their performance shows no improvement. Additional training may be offered by the employer to improve performance.

4 **Final written warning:** This is given to the employee if there has not been any significant improvement in performance. If employee performance does not improve within a specified time frame, they may be suspended or dismissed.

5 **Suspension:** The employee may be suspended with or without pay while the employer conducts a further investigation into the employee's underperformance.

6 **Dismissal:** The employer removes the employee from their job as their performance has not improved to the required standard, despite additional training and support from the business.

CASE STUDY _Fair Dismissal_

A former security guard took a case of **unfair dismissal** to the **Adjudication Officer** at the **WRC**. He had worked for his employer for nine years and had been dismissed for using his mobile phone during working hours.

On one occasion he had missed a serious security breach at the premises of a client as he was using his mobile phone instead of monitoring the CCTV cameras. The employer gave him a **written warning** and informed him that his job was at risk if he continued to use his mobile phone while working.

Six months later, a site manager noticed that the security guard had his phone beside him during working hours. The company conducted

an **investigation** and two months later the security guard was dismissed.

The security guard believed that he had been **unfairly dismissed** and that instead of dismissing him, his employer could have disciplined him in some other way. He explained that he had an addiction to his mobile phone but had worked hard to get it under control and wanted to return to work.

The adjudication officer found that the security guard's behaviour had breached the company's mobile phone policy and, coupled with previous breaches, the **dismissal** was deemed to be **fair**.

Unfair Dismissal

There are a number of ways in which the dismissal of an employee can be deemed to be unfair. These include dismissal based on the employee's:

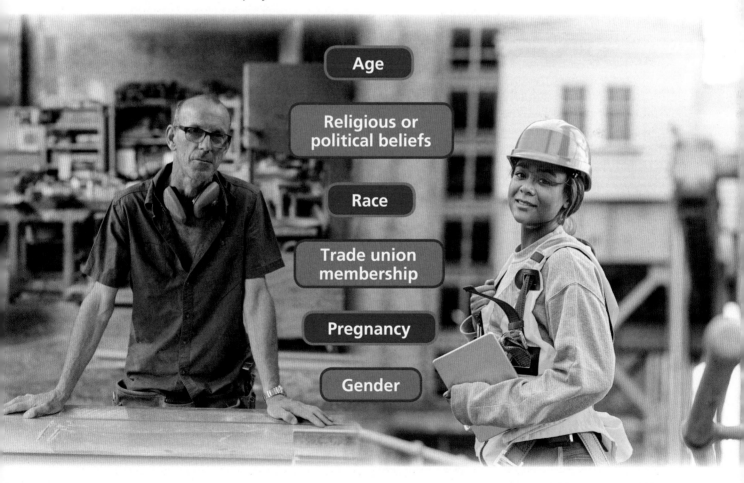

Age

Religious or political beliefs

Race

Trade union membership

Pregnancy

Gender

Activity 3.9

Working in groups, create a roleplay showing a scene where an employee is dismissed. The other students need to identify whether the dismissal was fair or unfair based on the roleplay.

Redress for Unfair Dismissal

If an employee has been found to have been unfairly dismissed, the options for redress are as follows.

1 Reinstatement

The employee:

- Gets their old job back
- Is entitled to back pay from the date of dismissal
- Is entitled to any improvements in conditions of employment while they were dismissed.

2 Re-engagement

The employee:

- May get their old job back or go to an alternative job approved by the WRC
- Is not entitled to any back pay from the date of dismissal.

3 Compensation

The employee gets:

- Up to two years' salary if they have suffered from financial loss due to the dismissal.
- Up to four weeks' salary if they have not suffered a financial loss.

Activity 3.10

An employee of a financial services company earns €77,000 per annum. At the WRC he is awarded compensation for unfair dismissal. The compensation payment is for 1.5 years of his salary. How much compensation will the employee receive?

CASE STUDY — *Unfair Dismissal*

An IKEA employee took a case of unfair dismissal against the company after he was dismissed for drinking a milkshake from the company café without paying for it.

The employee had worked for the company for five years and was a member of the bistro staff. IKEA employees are allowed to drink tea, coffee and soft drinks free of charge. However, a manager noted that the employee drank a milkshake without purchasing a company token as payment.

Management viewed the consumption of the milkshake as theft and the employee was suspended. An investigation and disciplinary meeting was arranged, but he did not attend. The employee said that he had not been notified of the meeting as he had taken a pre-planned holiday in France with his family. On his return he was informed that he had been dismissed.

It was judged that drinking the milkshake did not warrant dismissal and he was awarded €30,000 for unfair dismissal.

Activity 3.11

Lots of cases of unfair dismissal are reported in local and national newspapers. Can you find any interesting cases where employees received compensation or were reinstated to their roles? Post the article(s) on your class collaboration wall, such as Lino (www.linoit.com) or Wakelet (https://wakelet.com) for your classmates to read.

Constructive Dismissal

This occurs when an employee resigns from their job due to their employer's conduct towards them. The employee feels that the employer has made their working life so difficult that is impossible to remain in their job.

In cases of constructive dismissal, the burden of proof lies with the employee to show that the resignation was justified.

Before resigning, the employee should have tried every other possibility to solve the issue with the employer.

CASE STUDY: Constructive Dismissal

Philip Smith, the former CEO of Royal Sun Alliance (RSA) Ireland, was awarded €1.25m in compensation for constructive dismissal. This was the largest compensation ever awarded under the Unfair Dismissals Act.

Senior management at the company had blamed him for financial irregularities and announced his suspension on national television. Mr Smith claimed that his treatment by the company gave him no other option but to resign his position.

The claim for constructive dismissal was upheld for the following reasons:

1 Suspending Mr Smith on national television damaged his professional reputation around the world.

2 The financial irregularities were known to at least 24 other employees at RSA for a long period of time. Therefore, the company could not blame Mr Smith solely for these problems.

5 Employment Equality Acts 1998–2015

The Employment Equality Acts 1998–2015 prohibits discrimination in the workplace.

The Act applies to temporary, full- and part-time employees in both the public and private sectors. It also applies to many areas of employment, including:

- Equal pay
- Training
- Promotion.

Discrimination is illegal under the following nine grounds:

> **Definition: Discrimination**
> **Discrimination** occurs when one person is treated less favourably than another is, has been or would be treated in a comparable situation.

> **Exam Tip!**
> Make sure that you can **define** discrimination. You must be able to give a **precise meaning** of the term.

Ground for discrimination	Type of Discrimination
Age	→ Age-related discrimination, e.g. against an older or a younger person
Gender	→ Male, female and transgender
Disability	→ Physical disability, learning disability or chronic illness
Sexual Orientation	→ Heterosexual, bisexual or homosexual
Membership of the Traveller Community	→ People from the Traveller community
Family Status	→ Parent or acting as a parent for a child under the age of 18 years, or over the age of 18 years and with a disability requiring care on a continuous basis
Civil Status	→ Single, married, separated, divorced, widowed or in a civil partnership
Race	→ Race, colour, nationality or ethnic origin
Religious Beliefs	→ People who have a religion/faith and those who do not follow a religion

Activity 3.12

Working in groups, create a revision video on the Unfair Dismissals Act 1977–2015. You could use Powtoon, Explain Everything or other suitable software.

Resolving Complaints of Discrimination in the Workplace

Employees who believe that they have been discriminated against may use non-legislative or legislative means to resolve the issue.

Non-legislative

Meet with management:

- A meeting is arranged between management and the employee to discuss the employee's complaint about workplace discrimination.
- The employee may bring their shop steward or another union member for support to this meeting.
- The employee outlines their complaint to management and both parties try to solve the problem internally.

Legislative

1 Mediation:

- If an employee cannot resolve the issue of discrimination with the employer, they can take their case to the Workplace Relations Commission and request mediation.
- The aim of mediation is to try to get both parties to reach a mutually acceptable solution. The solution is recorded in writing, signed by both parties and becomes legally binding.

2 Adjudication:

- Unsuccessful mediation is referred to an adjudication officer.
- The adjudication officer hears the case and makes a legally binding decision on the dispute.
- If discrimination is proved, the adjudication officer can order the employer to:
  - Pay compensation to the employee
  - Provide equal pay and/or equal treatment
  - Take a specific course of action to prevent discrimination occurring again.

CASE STUDY

Employment Equality Acts 1998–2015

A highly qualified and widely published lecturer at an Irish university took a case of gender discrimination after she was unsuccessful at her fourth attempt at gaining promotion to senior lecturer position.

It was found that she had been discriminated against based on her gender. An investigation uncovered the following:

- No training had been given to the interviewers.
- A male candidate who was not eligible to apply for promotion was offered the position of senior lecturer.
- Male lecturers had a one in two chance of being promoted to senior lecturer; female lecturers had less than a one in three chance.

The female lecturer was awarded the full salary difference she had lost and a tax-free lump sum of €70,000 in compensation. The university was ordered to appoint her to the post of senior lecturer and to review its policies and procedures relating to promotion.

KEY TERMS

Now you have completed this chapter, you should understand and be able to explain the following terms. In your copybook, write a definition of each term to build up your own glossary of terms.

- industrial relations
- pay claims
- trade unions
- shop steward
- Irish Congress of Trade Unions (ICTU)
- bargaining
- official strike
- all-out strike
- work to rule
- token stoppage

- overtime ban
- unofficial strike
- wildcat/lightning strike
- political strike
- negotiation
- conciliation
- mediation
- arbitration
- Industrial Relations Act 1990
- trade dispute

- Workplace Relations Commission (WRC)
- Labour Court
- Joint Labour Committee (JLC)
- Unfair Dismissal Acts 1977–2015
- discrimination
- Employment Equality Acts 1998–2015

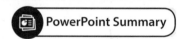
PowerPoint Summary

EXAM-STYLE QUESTIONS

Ordinary Level

Section 1 – Short Questions (10 marks each)

1 Outline **two** areas of conflict that can arise between an employer and an employee.

2 Distinguish between a cost of living pay claim and a productivity pay claim.

3 Name **three** non-legislative methods of solving industrial relations conflict.

4 Indicate in your copybook which of the following disputes are legal or illegal.

Reason for Dispute	
A	Discrimination against employees
B	The way the government runs the country
C	Employee unfairly chosen for redundancy
D	The way the business is run by the owners
E	Trade union recognition

5 Describe **two** benefits for employees of joining a trade union.

6 Explain the difference between primary and secondary picketing.

7 Distinguish between a work to rule and a token stoppage as forms of industrial action.

8 What do the letters (i) ICTU and (ii) WRC stand for?

9 List **two** services provided by the Workplace Relations Commission.

10 Outline **two** reasons for fair dismissal under the Unfair Dismissals Act 1977–2015.

Section 2 – Long Questions

1 Benefits of positive industrial relations include:
   (i)   Improved employee motivation
   (ii) Less industrial action and
   (iii) Improved employee recruitment and retention.
   Describe **two** of these benefits in greater detail. **(15 marks)**

2 Employers and employees will not always agree on workplace related issues.
   Outline **three** legitimate trade disputes between an employer and employee. **(15 marks)**

3 Twenty-nine per cent of the Irish workforce are members of a trade union.
   (i) What is a trade union?
   (ii) Describe the role of the trade union shop steward in the workplace. **(15 marks)**

4 During industrial relations disputes, employees can take legal types of industrial action.
   Describe **three** legal types of industrial action which can be taken by employees. **(20 marks)**

5 Outline the non-legislative methods that can be used to resolve industrial relations disputes. **(20 marks)**

6 Describe the services provided by the Workplace Relations Commission. **(20 marks)**

7 The Labour Court <u>investigates disputes</u>, <u>hears appeals</u> and <u>sets up JLCs</u>. Describe **two** of the underlined terms. **(15 marks)**

8 Describe the steps that should be taken in order to dismiss an employee fairly. **(20 marks)**

9 Outline the forms of redress available to employees who have been unfairly dismissed. **(15 marks)**

10 Explain **three** grounds on which discrimination is unlawful under the Employment Equality Acts 1998–2015. **(15 marks)**

Higher Level

Section 1 – Short Questions (10 marks each)

1 Outline the benefits of positive industrial relations for an employer.

2 Distinguish between a relativity pay claim and a comparability pay claim.

3 Discuss the role played by the shop steward in a business.

4 Distinguish between arbitration and conciliation.

5 What is the ICTU? What services does it provide to its members?

6 Identify the correct type of industrial action described in the following sentences.
   (i)   The employees carry out their duties in accordance with their employment contract but refuse to perform any additional duties.
   (ii) Employees refuse to work more than their normal working week.
   (iii) Employees refuse to work for a short period of time, which leads to disruption of work.
   (iv) Employees hold a secret ballot and give the employer seven days' notice of strike action. Employees do not enter the workplace and do not perform their normal duties.
   (v)   Employees go on strike without giving their employer any advance notice. This is an illegal form of industrial action.

7 Name **four** services provided by the Labour Court.

8 What is meant by the term *discrimination*?

9 Distinguish between constructive dismissal and unfair dismissal.

10 Indicate whether each of these statements is true or false.

Statements		True or False
A	The Workplace Relations Commission interprets codes of practice.	
B	The Labour Court is known as the court of last resort.	
C	Adjudication officers provide a service at the Labour Court.	
D	There are seven grounds for discrimination under the Employment Equality Acts 1998–2015.	
E	Compensation, reinstatement and re-engagement are remedies available for employees who have been unfairly dismissed.	

Section 2 – Applied Business Question (80 marks)

McGovern Enterprises

Cara McGovern is the owner and managing director of McGovern Enterprises, a manufacturing company based in Kilkenny. She employs 40 staff and most employees have worked at the company for more than five years. They are motivated to provide high-quality goods and customer service to the firm's customers.

Cara and her human resources manager have worked hard with the trade union shop stewards over the years to create a positive relationship between management and staff. The current shop steward, Michael O'Keeffe, works with the trade union to improve pay and working conditions for the union members. He ensures that the business complies with all relevant employment legislation. Michael also provides advice to employees on their rights in the workplace.

Cara regularly meets with the trade union shop steward to ensure that employee complaints do not escalate into industrial action.

Cara believes that she has open communication with her staff and is always eager to listen to any ideas for improvements in products and processes from her employees. Last year a suggestion by a machine operative saved the company €25,000 per year.

Demand for the firm's products has increased and Cara wants to introduce new machinery to increase output. She also wants to implement a new IT system to improve communication with customers and suppliers. Cara has arranged a meeting with the shop steward to discuss these changes as she feels that this would be more efficient than speaking to staff members individually.

A week later, Michael requested another meeting and outlined that staff are very unhappy about the proposed changes. There are suggestions among the staff that they will vote to take industrial action. Some are suggesting that they should not give Cara any notice of their strike action. Cara is shocked that her staff would react in this way to the planned changes. She tells Michael that she will not tolerate the staff picketing outside the workplace and that if unofficial strike action is taken, she will take legal action for loss of earnings and sales.

Cara hopes that Michael and the employees can negotiate a resolution to their current industrial relations issues, as she does not want her employees to go on strike.

A (i)   What is meant by the term *industrial relations*?
    (ii) Evaluate the advantages of positive industrial relations for McGovern Enterprises.   **(30 marks)**
B (i)   What is a shop steward?
    (ii) Outline the merits of trade union membership for the employer and employees of
        McGovern Enterprises.   **(30 marks)**
C Describe how the provisions of the Industrial Relations Act 1990 impact on trade unions.   **(20 marks)**

Section 3 – Long Questions

1 Negative industrial relations has wide-ranging consequences.
  Discuss this statement in relation to the impact on business stakeholders.   **(20 marks)**
2 Outline the different forms of bargaining that can be used by employers when
  negotiating with employees.   **(15 marks)**
3 Do you think employees should join a trade union? Discuss the advantages and
  disadvantages of trade union membership for employees.   **(20 marks)**
4 Name **four** stakeholders that can be affected when industrial action is taken by employees in a
  business. Describe the impact the industrial action has on **three** of these stakeholders.   **(20 marks)**
5 Evaluate the non-legislative methods of resolving industrial relations conflict.   **(15 marks)**
6 The provisions of the Industrial Relations Act 1990 include:
  (i) Trade dispute
  (ii) Secret ballot
  (iii) Picketing
  (iv) Immunity.
  Discuss **three** of the four provisions listed.   **(20 marks)**

Section 3 – Long Questions continued

7 Evaluate the role of the Workplace Relations Commission in settling disputes between employers and employees. **(25 marks)**

8 The Labour Court is the court of last resort for industrial relations disputes.

The role of the Labour Court includes:

(i) Hearing appeals

(ii) Establishing JLCs

(iii) Interpreting codes of practice

(iv) Registering employment regulation orders.

Explain **three** of the roles mentioned above. **(20 marks)**

9 Under the terms of the Unfair Dismissals Acts 1977–2015, outline the grounds for dismissal that are deemed to be unfair. **(20 marks)**

10 Outline the steps management should take to fairly dismiss an employee. **(20 marks)**

PREVIOUS LEAVING CERTIFICATE EXAM QUESTIONS

Ordinary Level

Section A – Short Questions (10 marks each)

1 Outline **two** functions of a trade union. **[LC OL 2011]**

2 Outline **two** reasons for fair dismissal and **two** reasons for unfair dismissal under the Unfair Dismissals Acts 1977–2015. **[LC OL 2012]**

3 List **three** grounds on which discrimination is outlawed under the Employment Equality Acts 1998–2015. **[LC OL 2017]**

Section B

1

Junior Doctors Industrial Action

In October 2013, junior doctors held a one-day strike action against the Health Service Executive (HSE) in relation to working hours and conditions. They were represented by their <u>trade union</u>, the Irish Medical Organisation (IMO), and they engaged in <u>picketing</u> outside public hospitals. Following the industrial action, the IMO and the HSE returned to the Workplace Relations Commission (WRC).

(i) List **three** reasons, other than working conditions, which may cause industrial relations disputes. **(15 marks)**

(ii) Explain the underlined terms above. **(15 marks)**

(iii) Explain **two** functions of the Workplace Relations Commission. **(15 marks) [LC OL 2014] (Adapted)**

2

Train drivers at Irish Rail were involved in an industrial relations dispute with their employer. The train drivers were represented by their Trade Unions, the NBRU (National Bus and Rail Workers Union) and SIPTU (Services, Industrial, Professional and Technical Union).

Outline **two** types of official industrial action a trade union can take as part of an industrial relations dispute. **(20 marks) [LC OL 2016]**

(i) Outline **two** benefits to an employee of being a member of a Trade Union. **(20 marks)**

(ii) State **one** example of a Trade Union in Ireland. **(20 marks) [LC OL 2015]**

Higher Level

Section A – Short Questions (10 marks each)

1 (i) Define the term *trade dispute*.

  (ii) Outline **two** types of official industrial action available to employees involved in an industrial dispute with employers. **[LC HL 2016]**

2 Distinguish between primary picketing and secondary picketing as types of industrial action available to employees. **[LC HL 2015]**

3 Outline **two** types of industrial action that employees could take in an attempt to get employers to meet their demands. **[LC HL 2011]**

4 Explain the term *constructive dismissal*. **[LC HL 2013]**

Section B

1

> 'The purpose of the Industrial Relations Act 1990 is to put in place an improved framework for the conduct of industrial relations and the resolution of disputes.'

  (i) Outline **three** factors that can lead to industrial disputes in business.

  (ii) Discuss **two** types of official industrial action available to employees in an industrial dispute with employers. **(25 marks) [LC HL 2014]**

2 Under the terms of the Unfair Dismissals Acts 1977 to 2015, explain the grounds for dismissal that deemed to be **fair**. **(20 marks) [LC HL 2018]**

3 Outline the procedures an employer should follow under the Unfair Dismissals Acts of 1977–2015, before dismissing an employee. **(20 marks) [LC HL 2012]**

4 (i) Outline **two** reasons for fair dismissal as set out under the Unfair Dismissal Acts 1977–2015.

  (ii) Explain the term *constructive dismissal*, providing an example to support your answer.

  (20 marks) [LC HL 2016]

 Solutions

ENTERPRISE

🎯 Learning Outcomes

When you have completed this chapter, you will be able to:

1. Define *enterprise*
2. Identify and describe enterprise in daily life
3. Name and outline the characteristics of entrepreneurs and enterprising people
4. List and explain the skills of entrepreneurs and enterprising people
5. Apply enterprise skills to areas such as the home, school, business start-ups, the local community and government departments
6. Define *intrapreneurship* and outline the ways in which it can be encouraged
7. Analyse the importance of enterprise in business and the community.

Literacy Link
Enterprise, risk-taking, human relations, charisma, decision-making, intrapreneurship

Numeracy Link
Division, multiplication, percentages

Cross-curricular Link
Economics – factors of production

CASE STUDY — *Freshly Chopped – The Healthy Food Company*

Brian Lee is a serial **entrepreneur**. Aged eleven, he borrowed money from his father to purchase a lawnmower. He printed business cards and made a profit by mowing neighbours' lawns. Throughout his teenage years, Brian, who is highly **self-motivated**, set up other businesses, including selling mobile phone covers at school and running market stalls around Dublin.

Brian has always had a strong interest in sports, particularly mixed martial arts. He believed there was a gap in the market for a studio-style gym. While many gyms closed during the recession, Brian took a **risk** and decided to set up Fit Studios. He believed that his hard work and **determined** attitude would make it successful.

Brian realised that the health and exercise sector was growing but there were very few options for healthy and nutritious fast food. He established Chopped – The Healthy Food Company with the aim of serving 'delicious, healthy food fast – natural and full of flavour. Food we would be happy to give our children.'

Many people doubted his business idea and some even said 'people won't queue for salad', but Brian had the **self-confidence** to believe that his business would be successful. When he opened a store in Dublin city centre, there were queues along the street from the first day of opening.

Creativity and **being proactive** are the key for business growth and Brian plans to introduce healthy lunch boxes for children and adapt menus based on location.

Chopped employs over 600 people in more than 40 stores across Ireland, the UK and Cyprus.

Brian's advice to teenagers is 'Stay in school. Get your Leaving Cert. If you're entrepreneurial then start young. You won't have anything to lose. You can make mistakes and bounce back.'

ENTERPRISE

Enterprise is when an individual or group of people take a risk and decide to start something new. For example, a person is enterprising when they start a new hobby such as learning to play the guitar.

An **entrepreneur** is a person who spots a gap in the market and comes up with an idea that they can turn into a business in order to fill the gap. An entrepreneur takes financial and personal risks when setting up a business. They hope to earn a profit from their successful business idea.

Example
Irish entrepreneur Marissa Carter used her creativity to develop a range of high-quality self-tanning products and established the business Cocoa Brown.

Unit 2

Almost 21,000 new businesses are established in Ireland every year. Counties Cork, Donegal and Wexford have the most entrepreneurial activity.

Activities 4.1

1 If there are on average 21,000 new businesses established in Ireland per year, how many are established per month and per week?
2 In pairs, make a list of entrepreneurs you know of and the goods or services they provide. How many Irish entrepreneurs can you name?

WHY DO PEOPLE BECOME ENTREPRENEURS?

People become entrepreneurs for a number of reasons, including:

1 **Being your own boss:** Many entrepreneurs do not want to take orders from other people and want to be their own boss. They get to make all the decisions on behalf of the business, e.g. location and opening hours.
2 **Varied work day:** They like the different types of work associated with being an entrepreneur. Days are varied as the entrepreneur might have to, for example, meet with customers and prepare a marketing campaign.
3 **Unemployment:** Someone who can't find work might become an entrepreneur out of necessity.
4 **More money:** Many entrepreneurs believe that they can earn more money by owning their own business rather than working for others.

Eight in every 100 people in Ireland is involved in entrepreneurship – either planning to launch a new business or running an existing business.

Activity 4.2

Name the entrepreneurs in the images below and the businesses they founded. Search online to find out how much each of these people is worth in monetary terms.

Activity 4.3

Examine the infographic below and answer the questions that follow.

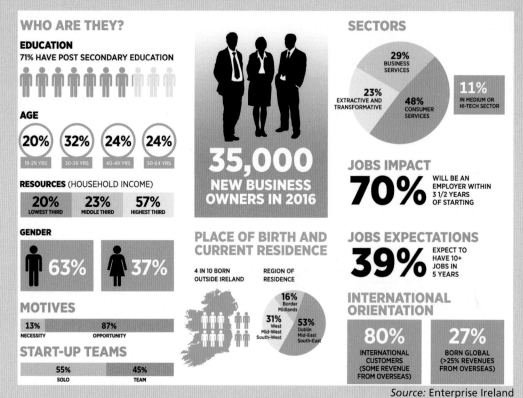

Source: Enterprise Ireland

1   How many people became new business owners in 2016?
2   What age group produced the highest percentage of new business owners?
3   Which sector had the highest percentage of new business owners?
4   What percentage of people became entrepreneurs out of necessity?
5   Why, do you think, are only 37% of the new business owners female?

ENTERPRISE IN DAILY LIFE

Many people assume that enterprise is only found in businesses. However, it can also be found in other areas of life, including the home, school, a new business, a government department and the local community.

Examples of Enterprise in Daily Life

1 Enterprise in the home

- A parent enrols on a course, e.g. to learn German.
- A teenager offers piano lessons to local students for a fee.

2 Enterprise in school

- A group of students organise a charity event, e.g. a table quiz.
- TY students set up a business as part of the Student Enterprise Awards programme.

3 Enterprise in a new business

- An entrepreneur spots a gap in the market for homemade ice cream and sets up an ice cream shop in a busy shopping centre.
- An entrepreneur opens a suit shop in a business district to provide office wear to professionals.

4 Enterprise in a government department

- The Department of Health launched the Healthy Ireland programme to improve the health and wellbeing of people in Ireland.
- Local Enterprise Offices (LEOs) have been set up to support and encourage entrepreneurship and employment in local areas.

You will learn more about LEOs in Chapter 26.

5 Enterprise in the local community

- A group of local people set up a Tidy Towns committee to improve the appearance of the local area and make it a better place to work, visit and live.
- A group of local people establish a meals-on-wheels service for elderly people in their area.

Social Enterprise

A social enterprise/not-for-profit enterprise has a social or environmental aim, e.g. to reduce poverty or to protect the environment. It is run like a business and profits are used to benefit the cause rather than the owners.

CASE STUDY

The Big Issue

Gordon Roddick and A. John Bird established a **social enterprise** – the *Big Issue* street magazine in 1991 – in response to the increasing number of rough sleepers in London. The magazine is written by professional journalists and sold by homeless people or those at risk of homelessness.

Vendors (sellers) of the *Big Issue* buy the magazine with their own money for half of the cover price and sell it to their customers at a profit. This means that the vendors are given the opportunity to earn their own income. The aim of the company is to give homeless people 'a hand up rather than a hand out'.

The *Big Issue* operates in a number of countries, including Australia, Ireland and the USA. In the UK alone, over 200 million copies of the *Big Issue* have been sold since 1991.

Activity 4.4

Can you think of other social entrepreneurs in Ireland or elsewhere? Research some social entrepreneurs in Ireland and abroad.

Prepare a mini-presentation to the class outlining the causes that these enterprises have championed. You could make a poster, slide show or use a website such as www.canva.com to create an infographic.

CHARACTERISTICS OF AN ENTREPRENEUR

Characteristic	Explanation	Example
Decision-making	→ An entrepreneur makes quick and clear decisions. They weigh up the pros and cons of a situation and choose the best option for the business. The entrepreneur takes full responsibility for all their decisions.	*Camile Thai* → Brody Sweeney **decided** to introduce a new type of takeaway to the Irish market. He created Camile Thai, a takeaway restaurant that delivers healthy, restaurant-style food direct to people's homes.

Characteristic	Explanation	Example
Risk-taking	→ Entrepreneurs take financial and personal risk and view failure as a learning experience. They ensure they take a calculated risk, i.e. a risk where there is a reasonable chance of success.	*Paddy Wagon Tours* → Cathal O'Connell took the **risk** of investing his last €550 into his business, Paddy Wagon Tours. The firm provides escorted tours around Ireland and owns six hostels. He now employs over 100 staff and has sales of €7 million per year.
Determination	→ Entrepreneurs are determined to find a way of solving problems. They do not give up easily when they are faced with obstacles or failures.	*Dyson* → James Dyson was **determined** to make a bagless vacuum cleaner. He made 5,127 prototypes over a five-year period before he created a successful product.
Self-motivation	→ Entrepreneurs are motivated from within to succeed. They have the personal drive and ambition to achieve their goals.	*Honda* → Soichiro Honda was an unsuccessful job applicant at Toyota. He was unemployed but **self-motivated** and began to make scooters at home. He established Honda, which is now the world's largest motorcycle manufacturer.
Self-confidence	→ Entrepreneurs believe in themselves and their idea. They are not put off by other people's opinions.	*Innocent* → The three founders of Innocent Drinks had the **self-confidence** to quit their jobs and develop a range of fresh drinks and smoothies, despite people telling them that the business would not be a success.
Creativity	→ Entrepreneurs think outside the box and come up with new ideas and new ways of doing things.	*VOYA Seaweed Products* → Mark Walton used his **creativity** to create products from seaweed harvested in County Sligo. The company's products are now sold in 37 countries worldwide.

Activity 4.5

A mnemonic uses the first letter of each word to create a catchy word or sentence to help you to remember information. In pairs, create a mnemonic to help you to remember the characteristics of an entrepreneur. Share your mnemonic with your classmates.

SKILLS OF AN ENTREPRENEUR

Entrepreneurs possess a range of skills that help them to make their idea a success. They should be able to identify their entrepreneurial skills and exploit them to gain the largest benefit for themselves and their business.

Definition: Skill
A **skill** is an ability to perform a particular task well. Skills can be learned and improved.

Entrepreneurial skills include:

1 Decision-making

2 Being proactive

3 Networking

4 Risk management

5 Human relations

6 Realism

We will now examine the skills of an entrepreneur in the following five scenarios.

- **Home:** Parents rent a room in the home to earn additional income.
- **School:** Students show enterprise by organising a bake sale to raise money to fund a school trip.
- **New business:** An entrepreneur spots a gap in the market and decides to set up a juice and smoothie shop in a local shopping centre.
- **Government:** Local Enterprise Offices (LEOs) have been established by the government to encourage entrepreneurship in local areas.
- **Local community:** A group of local people show enterprise by setting up a committee to create a tourist attraction in their area.

Exam Tip!
You should be able to apply the enterprise skills to a range of scenarios, including in the home and in the local community.

1 Decision-making

Enterprising people make quick, clear decisions. They weigh up the pros and cons of a situation and make decisions that bring the greatest benefit. They take full responsibility for all decisions made and do not blame others for their own poor decision-making.

Home	→ Parents decide to renovate a spare bedroom and rent it out to earn extra income.
School	→ A group of students decide to organise a school bake sale to raise money to fund a school trip.
New Business	→ An entrepreneur decides to open a juice and smoothie shop in a busy city centre location.
Government Organisation	→ The LEO decides to offer a range of programmes for entrepreneurs who want to set up their own business.
Local Community	→ A group of local people decide to renovate an old building and turn it into a museum.

2 Being Proactive

Enterprising people take action and make changes before they need to be made rather than waiting for a situation or problems to arise.	
Home	→ The parents get the room listed with local colleges and place advertisements on house rental websites such as www.daft.ie.
School	→ The students create a number of social media accounts, e.g. on Facebook and Snapchat, to promote the bake sale.
New Business	→ The entrepreneur attends a marketing course to learn how to promote the juice and smoothie shop to increase consumer awareness of the new business.
Government Organisation	→ The LEO conducts market research to identify the types of workshops and training courses needed by entrepreneurs in the local area.
Local Community	→ The committee applies for grants from government agencies to fund the renovations of the building.

3 Networking

This skill involves meeting new people and exchanging information. The people you meet may be useful to you in your professional or social life.	
Home	→ Friends of the parents inform them that there is a high demand for student accommodation in the local area and the local college is seeking rooms for rent in people's homes to accommodate students.
School	→ A relative of a student owns a bakery and provides ingredients for the cakes free of charge.
New Business	→ A contact in the industry gives the business some second-hand equipment for the juice and smoothie shop, thus saving the business the cost of purchasing new items.
Government Organisation	→ The LEO has built a network of successful business owners and industry experts who can give guest talks and lectures at the workshops organised for new entrepreneurs.
Local Community	→ The committee contacts heritage groups in other areas to seek their advice about the renovation and development of the local museum.

4 Risk Management

Entrepreneurs can be exposed to commercial, physical and financial risks. They must identify these risks and find ways to reduce the likelihood of the risk occurring. For example, the entrepreneur can reduce: • **Physical risks by installing fire alarms** • **Commercial risks by increasing advertising to increase their market share** • **Financial risks by taking out employee embezzlement insurance in case of employee theft.**	
Home	→ The parents request a deposit of one month's rent from the new tenant. This ensures that if the tenant causes any damage, the deposit will cover the cost of repair.
School	→ The students take out public liability insurance to cover claims made by members of the public for illness or injury that may happen on the school premises during the bake sale.
New Business	→ The entrepreneur provides health and safety training to all staff to ensure drinks are prepared in compliance with food safety standards.
Government Organisation	→ The LEO has a detailed review process to ensure that grants are awarded to businesses with the greatest chance of success.
Local Community	→ The committee provides high-visibility jackets and hard hats for volunteers working on the renovation.

5 Human Relations

This skill is used to build relationships with people and to bring out the best in them. Enterprising people use their human relations skills to persuade people to help them.

Home	→ The parents persuade family members to help them with renovations. This helps to reduce the renovation costs for the parents.
School	→ The bake sale committee persuades local businesses to donate cakes for the event.
New Business	→ The entrepreneur builds relationships with producers and suppliers. This helps the entrepreneur to negotiate discounts on products for the juice and smoothie shop.
Government Organisation	→ The LEO persuades officials in government departments to increase funding to support new and existing businesses.
Local Community	→ The committee persuades local people to volunteer in the renovation project, e.g. painting walls and bricklaying.

6 Realism

It is very important that entrepreneurs recognise when things are going wrong and take action to make positive changes.

Home	→ The parents realise that they have set the rental price too high and reduce the price to attract more applicants.
School	→ The students realise that there are not enough volunteers for their bake sale. The students make an announcement at a school assembly to encourage more people to help at the event.
New Business	→ The entrepreneur realises that they do not have enough money to buy stock for the business and applies to the bank for a bank overdraft to pay for the stock.
Government Organisation	→ The LEO notes that registrations for its programmes are very low. It launches a social media campaign to encourage further applications from entrepreneurs.
Local Community	→ The committee realises that the renovations are taking longer than expected and they decide to postpone the opening for three months.

Activity 4.6

Search online for the mini-documentary about Fenu Health. Using the grid given to you by your teacher, identify the characteristics and skills shown by Annie and Kate Madden in creating and running their business.

Definition: Employee embezzlement insurance
The business owner receives financial compensation if it is found that an employee has stolen from the business or has damaged property.

INTRAPRENEURSHIP

This means that the employees of a business act like entrepreneurs within that business. The employees come up with new ideas, new ways of solving business problems or create a new production process, which help to increase business profits or reduce costs.

DID YOU KNOW?

Google uses a scheme called Innovation Time Off to encourage their engineers to spend 20% of their working week on projects that interest them. During this time, the engineers came up with Gmail and Google News.

DID YOU KNOW?

A Sony employee spent hours improving his daughter's Nintendo console to make it more powerful and user-friendly. His work helped to develop the Sony PlayStation.

CASE STUDY — *Intrapreneurship at ESB*

Energy for generations

ESB Group has a strong history of encouraging **intrapreneurship** among its 7,800 employees. The firm runs the 'Little Big Things' campaign to encourage employees to use their **creativity** and **innovation** to add value to the firm. Some of the intrapreneurial ideas include:

- ESB eCars developed an electric carpooling scheme for employees travelling on business. This saved the company €57,000 on taxi and mileage expenses. It also reduced CO_2 emissions by 4,000 tonnes per year.

- A team of workers from across the organisation created an app called PowerCheck to provide information to consumers on planned and unplanned power supply disruptions and reconnection times. To date the app has received over one million hits.

- The Powering Kindness charity initiative encouraged members of the public to do an act of kindness and bank it in favour of three charities selected by ESB to share a prize fund of €190,000.

Methods of Encouraging Intrapreneurship

1 Training Programmes
Employees can receive training on how to come up with and develop new ideas that benefit the business.

2 Rewards
Employees can be offered financial rewards for ideas used by the business to reduce costs or increase profits, e.g. a bonus payment.

3 Workplace Culture
The business creates a workplace culture where employees know that it is okay to make mistakes. This can encourage employees to develop new ideas for the business without fear of punishment if the ideas are not successful.

4 Teamwork
The business should give employees the opportunity to work in teams. This can encourage employees to brainstorm and develop better ideas as a group.

> *Definition:* **Brainstorming**
> When people meet together to come up with as many ideas as possible.

5 Resource Provider
The business can give employees access to the resources needed to help them to come up with new ideas to benefit the business. These resources can include raw materials, time and finance.

REWARDS AND RISKS OF BECOMING AN ENTREPRENEUR

There are a number of risks and rewards of becoming an entrepreneur, including:

Rewards		Risks	
Control	→ Entrepreneurs have control of the business and make all the decisions, e.g. product range, opening hours.	Income	→ Entrepreneurs may be unable to take an income from the business for a number of years. Money earned may need to be reinvested in new stock and to pay bills.
Income	→ Entrepreneurs believe that if their business idea is successful, they could earn more money than they would earn if they worked as employees for other businesses.	Decision-making	→ Entrepreneurs cannot be experts in all areas of the business. They may make mistakes when making decisions, which could damage the firm's reputation.
Challenge	→ Entrepreneurs enjoy the challenge of setting up a business and working hard to make it successful.	Long Working Hours	→ Entrepreneurs often work very long hours. This can have a negative impact on their personal life and lead to high levels of stress.

Activity 4.7

Can you think of any other risks or rewards of becoming an entrepreneur? Would you like to work for yourself? What type of business would you create? Discuss these questions with other students in your class.

THE IMPORTANCE OF ENTERPRISE IN BUSINESS

1 **Encourages intrapreneurship:** Enterprise encourages intrapreneurship in the business. Employees identify new ideas for products or processes which can increase business profits or reduce costs.
2 **Greater efficiency:** Enterprise encourages businesses to use their resources more creatively. This can lead to cost savings and greater efficiency in the business.
3 **Spin-off businesses:** Enterprise in business can identify spin-off businesses that can be developed by the firm. This can help to generate additional sales and profits for the business.
4 **Business culture:** A business culture where enterprise is encouraged can help employees to come up with ideas without the fear of punishment for unsuccessful results.

THE IMPORTANCE OF ENTERPRISE IN THE COMMUNITY

1 **Encourages enterprise:** Successful entrepreneurs encourage others to take the risk, set up their own businesses and become entrepreneurs.
2 **Wealth creation:** Local people spend their wages/salaries in local shops and restaurants. This helps these businesses to be successful and generates more wealth in the local economy.
3 **Creates employment:** Enterprise creates direct and indirect employment. The wages earned give people a higher standard of living than they would have if they remained on social welfare.
4 **Community engagement:** Entrepreneurs can get involved in the community by sponsoring local teams and events, e.g. sporting teams and festivals. They can also offer work experience to local people who want to increase their skills and experience.

Activity 4.8

Working in groups, create a revision video on the topics covered in this chapter. You could use tools such as Explain Everything, Adobe Spark or another suitable program.

KEY TERMS

Now you have completed this chapter, you should understand and be able to explain the following terms. In your copybook, write a definition of each term to build up your own glossary of terms.

- enterprise
- entrepreneurship
- social enterprise
- enterprise characteristics
- decision-making
- risk-taking
- determination

- self-motivation
- self-confidence
- creativity
- enterprise skills
- being proactive
- networking
- risk management

- human relations
- realism
- workplace culture
- intrapreneurship
- spin-off businesses

PowerPoint Summary

EXAM-STYLE QUESTIONS

Ordinary Level

Section 1 – Short Questions (10 marks each)

1 What is meant by the term *enterprise*?

2 Name **two** Irish and **two** international entrepreneurs.

3 What is meant by the term *social enterprise*? Name **two** social enterprises.

4 List **four** characteristics of an entrepreneur.

5 Explain the enterprise skill of networking and outline how it would be used by a new business.

6 Column 1 is a list of business terms. Column 2 is a list of possible explanations for these terms. Match the two lists in your copybook by writing your answers in the form *number = letter* (e.g. 1 = A).

Terms		Explanations	
1	Risk-taking	A	An entrepreneur is driven from within to make the business a success
2	Risk Management	B	An entrepreneur believes their idea will be successful
3	Determination	C	An entrepreneur identifies risks and finds ways to reduce them
4	Self-motivation	D	An entrepreneur is not afraid to take a chance to try something new
5	Self-confidence	E	An entrepreneur does not quit when faced with obstacles

7 Distinguish between an entrepreneur and an intrapreneur.

8 Outline two reasons why enterprise is important to the Irish economy.

Section 2 – Long Questions

1 Outline **three** reasons why people become entrepreneurs. **(15 marks)**

2 Risk-taking, decision-making and creativity are important entrepreneurial characteristics. Explain each of the underlined characteristics. **(15 marks)**

3 Illustrate the enterprise skills of realism, human relations and risk management in a government organisation. **(20 marks)**

4

> Lauren Power runs her own IT business creating apps for businesses with large numbers of staff. She took out a bank loan and got a friend to invest in her business to set up an office in the city centre. She now wants to employ two staff members to help her with app design and marketing to gain more clients.

Describe **two** skills and **two** characteristics that Lauren possesses as an entrepreneur. **(20 marks)**

Section 2 – Long Questions *continued*

5 What is the difference between enterprise and being an entrepreneur? Describe **two** risks an entrepreneur takes when setting up a business. **(20 marks)**

6 Intrapreneurship is very important for a business. Describe **three** ways in which intrapreneurship can be encouraged in a business. **(15 marks)**

7 Outline **three** rewards of becoming an entrepreneur. **(15 marks)**

8 Explain **three** advantages of enterprise in the local community. **(15 marks)**

Higher Level

Section 1 – Short Questions (10 marks each)

1 Distinguish between the enterprise characteristics self-motivation and self-confidence.

2 Fill in the blanks in the following sentences.
   (i) An entrepreneur spots a _____ in the market.
   (ii) An entrepreneur takes _____ risks and _____ risks when setting up a business.
   (iii) Most entrepreneurs hope their business will be successful and earn a _____.

3 Illustrate your understanding of the term *realism* as an entrepreneurial skill.

4 Distinguish between the enterprise skills of (i) decision-making and (ii) risk management.

5 Describe examples of enterprise in (i) a government department and (ii) a school.

6 Complete the sentence: Intrapreneurship involves …

7 Outline the ways in which a business can encourage intrapreneurship.

8 Explain the importance of enterprise in business.

Section 2 – Applied Business Question (80 marks)

Finn's Fine Foods

Shane Finn has always wanted to own his own restaurant. Every year during his school holidays he worked in cafés and restaurants and decided that he wanted to train as a chef. After completing his studies, Shane spotted a gap in the market and decided to set up a restaurant specialising in traditional Irish foods. He believed that he had the talent to make the business a success.

He approached his local bank and borrowed €70,000 to set up Finn's Fine Foods. He knew that it was important to get the restaurant up and running for the summer tourist season, so he drew up a plan of all the items he needed to purchase to establish the restaurant. He rented premises in the city centre and installed all the necessary fire prevention equipment such as smoke alarms and fire extinguishers. He then recruited ten staff to make sure the restaurant would run efficiently.

Shane enjoyed meeting and greeting customers and liked to tell them about the local producers who supplied the restaurant. Some customers have told Shane that he is an inspiration to young people in the local community.

Shane was determined to make the restaurant a success and was delighted to find that the tourist season had been very profitable.

During the winter months, Shane read some online customer reviews that criticised his menu, saying that it had become boring. Shane is determined to make some changes and decided to involve all staff in revamping the menu. He organised the staff into teams, set aside time during the work day and encouraged them to come up with as many ideas as possible. He gave all staff access to ingredients and time in the kitchen to develop new dishes. He also told the staff that he was open to hearing all their suggestions and even offered a monetary reward for the best ideas.

Shane is confident that collaborating with his employees will help him to solve the problems in the restaurant and will help to make the restaurant a lasting success.

A Identify the enterprise characteristics and skills used by Shane. Refer to the text in your answer. **(30 marks)**

B (i) Illustrate your understanding of the term *intrapreneurship*.
   (ii) Describe the methods Shane could use to encourage intrapreneurship in his restaurant. **(30 marks)**

C Discuss the importance of enterprise in the local community. **(20 marks)**

Section 3 – Long Questions

1 Entrepreneurs tend to have similar characteristics. Describe the characteristics displayed by entrepreneurs. **(20 marks)**

2 Identify two skills of an entrepreneur and outline how they can be used in the local community. **(15 marks)**

3

> 'Water and juice-based drinks containing more than five grams of sugar per 100ml are now liable for the Sugar Sweetened Drinks Tax.' (RTÉ News, May 2018)

Discuss how enterprise skills have been used in the Department of Health to introduce this tax. **(20 marks)**

4 Using examples, analyse the importance of the enterprise skills risk management, time management and realism. **(20 marks)**

5 Outline the importance of enterprise in business. **(15 marks)**

6 Describe the importance of enterprise in the community. **(15 marks)**

PREVIOUS LEAVING CERTIFICATE EXAM QUESTIONS

Ordinary Level

Section A – Short Questions (10 marks each)

1 Indicate whether each of the following is an example of intrapreneurship or entrepreneurship by writing **INTRAPRENEUR** or **ENTREPRENEUR** after each of the following statements.

PlayStation	An employee at Sony coming up with the idea for the Sony PlayStation.	
Snapchat	Two Stanford University graduates setting up a photo-sharing app business known as Snapchat.	
Like	An employee at Facebook coming up with the idea of the like button as a method of communicating that you like a post or photograph.	
Gmail	An employee at Google coming up with the idea for an email service, which became known as Gmail.	
Poco	Irish fashion and beauty blogger Pippa O'Connor launching her own range of jeans.	

[LC OL 2018]

2 Explain the following entrepreneurial characteristics:
   (i) Innovative
   (ii) Risk taker. **[LC OL 2015]**

Section B

1

> **Superfoods by SuperDudes**
>
> Michelle, a gym goer, found it very difficult to source healthy 'food on the go' in Ireland. She gave up her job and invested her savings in Superfoods by SuperDudes, a pop-up restaurant serving healthy fast food in Dublin city centre, near many local gyms. The business employs seven staff. Their customers include athletes, fitness enthusiasts, office workers, families, students, etc. She holds weekly meetings with her staff and recently announced plans to offer a delivery service to customers who sign up for a weekly meal plan. The business will order more stock every week from suppliers to fulfil orders for its delivery service.

Outline **three** entrepreneurial characteristics/skills displayed by Michelle. (Refer to the text in your answer.) **(15 marks) [LC OL 2018]**

2

> **Fitness Fanatics**
>
> Seán spotted a gap in the market for a personal training business in his home town. He used his personal savings to open a fitness studio. Within one year he had over 150 clients in training. Seán hired five full-time personal trainers to help him with the workload. He regularly consults with his staff and values their opinions.

(i)   Outline **three** characteristics/skills of an entrepreneur. **(15 marks)**

(ii) Explain **two** risks for Seán of setting up his own business. **(15 marks) [LC OL 2016]**

Higher Level

Section A – Short Questions (10 marks each)

1 Outline **two** methods of promoting intrapreneurship. **[LC HL 2018]**

Section B

1 Outline **two** reasons why a person might become an entrepreneur. **(10 marks) [LC HL 2018]**

2

> Stripe, the fast-growing online payments business, was established by Limerick brothers Patrick and John Collison when they were aged just 22 and 19. Stripe enables websites to accept credit and debit card payments. It employs over 600 people globally and is worth more than $9bn.
>
> *Source: adapted from www.siliconrepublic.com and the* Irish Times

Outline the characteristics/skills that you would associate with entrepreneurs. **(20 marks) [LC HL 2017]**

3

> **The Mayfair Hotel**
>
> The Mayfair Hotel is a five-star city centre hotel which is celebrating 100 years in business. To celebrate this centenary, the management of the hotel is planning various events. The General Manager, Ann Johnson has suggested organising staff into various project teams, with a project leader to plan for this centenary celebration.

Discuss how the hotel staff could apply entrepreneurial characteristics/skills to develop the various centenary events. **(20 marks) [LC HL 2016]**

4

> EducaPrint Ltd is a business publishing schoolbooks in Ireland. John O'Leary, the Production Manager, suggested introducing some of its traditional print books in eBook format. He wanted to tap into the improvements in broadband speed and the major developments in mobile devices. The eBooks were launched onto the market in 2013 to great success.

(i)   Explain the term *intrapreneurship*.

(ii) Outline methods of promoting intrapreneurship in EducaPrint Ltd. **(20 marks) [LC HL 2013]**

Solutions

CHAPTER 5 | INTRODUCTION TO MANAGEMENT

Learning Outcomes

When you have completed this chapter, you will be able to:

1. Define *management*
2. Provide a summary of management skills and activities
3. Describe and apply management skills and activities to daily life
4. List and describe the characteristics of a manager
5. Distinguish between enterprise and management.

Literacy Link

Management, management skills, leading, motivating, communicating, management activities, planning, organising, controlling, management characteristics

Numeracy Link

Multiplication, division, subtraction

Cross-curricular Link

English – communicating and planning
Geography – planning a geographical investigation
History – political leadership
Home Economics – managing resources
Languages – communicating orally, visually and in writing
Religion – women and leadership

CASE STUDY

A Day in the Life of a Store Manager

Kate Fitzgerald is a manager at Smart Tech, a shop specialising in smartphones, tablets and laptops. The store employs ten staff in a range of roles including customer service and repairs. **Leading** is an area of management that Kate has had to develop over the years. She now uses a **democratic leadership** style and delegates tasks such as stock ordering and supplier payments to employees. Kate trusts her staff and **delegation** gives her time to focus on managerial issues such as recruiting and training new employees.

Kate has a busy role and spends every Friday morning **planning** the staff rota for the following week to ensure that there are enough staff in the store to deal with customer sales and product repairs.

Communicating regularly with staff is also very important to Kate. She holds a staff meeting every Monday morning at which employees have the opportunity to give feedback and raise any concerns. She likes to use the time to **motivate** staff by reading out positive reviews written by customers on the store's website and congratulating them on work well done.

At today's meeting, an employee suggested that the store should hold an event for the launch of a new smartphone model. Kate thinks that this is a great idea and **organises** the employees into teams to brainstorm ideas for the launch.

Kate has realised that she must introduce better **control** procedures in the store. Today three customers visited the store to purchase the new Icon 24 tablet but Kate had to inform them that the item was out of stock. The consumers were disappointed and told Kate that they would purchase the tablets from another store instead. Kate realises that she needs to introduce a better **stock control** system to ensure that this loss of sales does not happen again.

While Kate loves her role as manager of Smart Tech, she realises that she still needs to develop her **management skills** of **leading, motivating** and **communicating** to ensure that she gets the best out of her staff. She also knows that to ensure the success of the store, she must improve the common **management activities** of **planning, organising** and **controlling**.

WHAT IS MANAGEMENT?

For a business to be successful, it must have effective and efficient management in place.
Management involves getting people to work together for a common organisational goal using the skills of leading, motivating and communicating. Good managers use the management activities of planning, organising and controlling to co-ordinate resources such as employees, materials and capital to ensure business success.

The most senior management position in the business is the CEO (chief executive officer). The managing director (MD) is responsible for the day-to-day running of the business and is responsible for the overall actions of the firm. A business may also employ managers who are responsible for running different departments in the firm, e.g. marketing manager.

One out of every three managers in the EU is a woman. Female managers earn on average almost 25% less than their male counterparts, despite doing the same job. Latvia is the only EU member state where there are more female managers than male, with a rate of 53% of the workforce.

Activity 5.1

The average pay gap between male and female managers in the EU is 23%. If a male manager earns €65,000 per annum, what would the female manager earn if there is a 23% pay gap between them?

MANAGEMENT SKILLS AND ACTIVITIES

MANAGEMENT SKILLS

Leading

Motivating

Communicating

MANAGEMENT ACTIVITIES

Planning

Organising

Controlling

Management Skills Summary

1 Leading
Managers have a clear vision for the future which they share openly with employees. They encourage employees to work together for a common organisational goal. Managers choose the most appropriate leadership style, e.g. autocratic, democratic or laissez-faire, for business success.

Example
General Electric Company (GE) is an American technology and financial services company. When Jack Welch became CEO he used strong leadership to grow the company from sales of €1.3 billion to sales of €12.7 billion.

2 Motivating

Managers must find out what motivates their employees in the workplace. They can offer financial rewards, e.g. bonus payments, and non-financial rewards, e.g. additional holidays, as incentives to encourage employees to work harder. Motivational theories such as Maslow's Hierarchy of Needs and McGregor's Theory X and Theory Y are useful in finding the best ways to motivate staff.

> *Leadership styles and motivational theories will be described in greater detail in Chapters 6 and 7.*

Example

Vodafone employees are motivated in the workplace through a range of benefits, including: access to a 24-hour gym and wellness centre; discounts on Vodafone products; flexible working; and days off work to volunteer for charities.

3 Communicating

A good manager must be able to exchange information effectively with stakeholders such as employees and consumers. Effective communication is the ability to use oral, written and visual communication through a range of methods, e.g. email, meetings and charts. Good communicators know that their message must be clear and concise so that employees understand the tasks assigned and the quality standards expected.

Example

Toyota US recalled 2.3 million vehicles due to faulty brakes. Consumers began to sue the company and the brand name was damaged. The Toyota CEO went on a live online conversation session with consumers. More than 1,000 questions were submitted and no questions were filtered. The CEO was open and honest about the quality issues and reassured consumers that the quality of Toyota vehicles would be improved.

Activity 5.2

In pairs, draw the outline of a person on a large sheet of paper. Find images to show the skills needed by this person to manage others (i.e. leading, motivating and communicating). You could draw these skills or use images from magazines or online sources. Present your image of a manager to your classmates.

Management Activities Summary

1 Planning

Managers must identify the overall business goals and break them down into more manageable tasks. The manager should develop plans to achieve these goals using the business resources available, e.g. employees and capital. Managers make short-, medium- and long-term plans to ensure business success. For example, a manager should have a contingency plan in place to deal with an unforeseen event

Example

The CEO of Yahoo! announced plans to reduce the workforce by 15% and to close five foreign offices in order to ensure the survival of the company.

> *You will learn more about types of planning in Chapter 10.*

> *You will learn more about organising in Chapter 11.*

2 Organising

Managers identify the roles and tasks that need to be performed by staff. They then put an organisational structure in place to enable these tasks to be completed. Management can choose from a range of organisational structures including functional, geographic and product.

Example

Procter & Gamble (P&G) changed from a traditional functional organisation structure, in which employees are divided into departments, to a product organisation structure. This helped to focus staff on specific product ranges in the business and increase innovation and efficiency in the firm.

3 Controlling

Management should build control mechanisms into the business, such as stock control, financial control and quality control. The manager can identify when targets have not been met and take necessary action to ensure the business achieves its goals.

Example

Birds Eye has a strong quality control policy for its frozen peas. Once the peas arrive at the factory, a sample is taken. A 'tenderometer' is used to check the firmness of the peas. Only the best peas are frozen, packaged and distributed to retailers.

Activity 5.3

In pairs, create a crossword using the vocabulary from management skills and activities. Try to make your clues as imaginative as possible. You could use websites such as www.discoveryeducation.com/free-puzzlemaker to create your crossword.

> ### Exam Tip!
> *It is very important that you know the difference between management skills and activities. Management skills include **leading**, **motivating** and **communicating**. Management activities are **planning**, **organising** and **controlling**.*

MANAGEMENT SKILLS AND ACTIVITIES IN DAILY LIFE

While many people associate management with business, management skills and activities are also important in other areas of life. We will examine these areas below.

Home
Example: managing a healthy lifestyle.

Skill/Activity	Adults ...
Leading	→ Lead by example by taking part in sports, showing children the importance of physical activity.
Motivating	→ Motivate children to get involved in sport by praising participation.
Communicating	→ Give clear communication so that children know why fitness is important for a healthy life.
Planning	→ Plan family outings to include physical activity, e.g. walks in the countryside.
Organising	→ Organise meals to ensure that there is healthy food available in the home.
Controlling	→ Control the family budget to ensure there is money available to pay for sporting activities.

School

Example: managing a school.

Skill/Activity	The principal ...
Leading	→ Leads a school by creating a positive learning environment for students.
Motivating	→ Motivates staff and students by praising work well done.
Communicating	→ Holds regular meetings with staff to communicate important information.
Planning	→ Plans for the school year by creating timetables for staff and students.
Organising	→ Organises which staff will teach specific subjects.
Controlling	→ Is responsible for controlling the school budget to avoid overspending.

Local Community

Example: managing a food festival.

Skill/Activity	The local community committee ...
Leading	→ Shows leadership by deciding to run a food festival.
Motivating	→ Motivates people to volunteer by highlighting the economic and social benefits that such an event would bring to the local area.
Communicating	→ Communicates with the public by creating a website and social media campaign.
Planning	→ Plans the events that will be held during the festival.
Organising	→ Organises volunteers and assigns roles for the volunteers during the event, e.g. car park attendants.
Controlling	→ Controls the project by having regular financial review meetings to ensure that it does not overspend.

CASE STUDY

Management at the West Waterford Festival of Food

In 2008, a group of local people in west Waterford showed **leadership** when they created a food festival based in the town of Dungarvan. A committee was formed, consisting of people from the local community, business representatives and sponsors. The committee **planned** a series of events for the festival, including food workshops, demonstrations and food tours.

Members of the local community were **motivated** to get involved in the festival because it would bring visitors to the area, which would increase sales and profits for local businesses.

Active **communication** was key to increasing the public's awareness of the festival. The committee set up a dedicated food festival website as well as social media accounts on Facebook, Instagram and Twitter to interact with the public.

The committee **organised** volunteers into groups and allocated roles such as stewards, administration and catering, to ensure that the festival would run smoothly.

At the end of the festival, the committee met to review the success of the events held during the festival. This is a **control** mechanism to ensure that the festival continues to grow and to attract attendees.

The festival has become an annual event and last year attracted over 25,000 people to the local area.

Business

Example: managing employees.

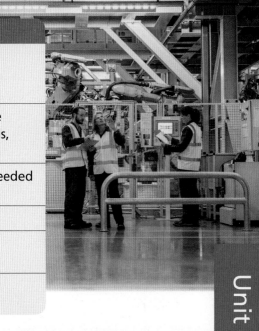

Skill/Activity	The manager ...
Leading	→ Shows leadership by deciding to introduce new machinery into the factory to improve production quality.
Motivating	→ Motivates employees to learn how to operate the new machinery by offering them financial rewards, e.g. a bonus.
Communicating	→ Communicates the reason why new machinery is needed in the firm.
Planning	→ Plans the type of employee training required.
Organising	→ Organises employees into teams to take part in training.
Controlling	→ Controls the process by conducting quality checks on the finished products.

Government

Example: managing exam marking.

Skill/Activity	The State Examination Commission ...
Leading	→ Shows leadership by encouraging teachers to apply to correct state exam papers such as the Leaving Certificate.
Motivating	→ Motivates teachers to correct exam papers by offering them insights into how to improve their standard of teaching.
Communicating	→ Regularly communicates with the correctors to ensure that they meet the deadlines for correcting the exam papers.
Planning	→ Plans the timetable for state examinations such as the Leaving Certificate and Leaving Certificate Applied.
Organising	→ Organises groups of teachers to correct the exam papers.
Controlling	→ Arranges for supervisors to monitor samples of corrected exam papers to ensure quality control in the correcting process.

Activity 5.4

Working in pairs, create a quiz with ten questions and answers related to management skills and activities in daily life. Swap the questions with another pair of students in the class and receive a set of ten questions for you and your classmate to answer. Return the answers to the pair who created the quiz and find out your score out of ten.

Unit 3

CHARACTERISTICS OF A MANAGER

1 Problem-solving 2 Flexibility 3 Charisma

4 Hard-working

5 Initiative

Managers often have a range of common traits that help them to be successful. These characteristics include:

1 Problem-solving ability: A good manager should be able to identify problems in the business and find solutions to deal with them quickly and effectively.

2 Flexibility: Managers need to be flexible when dealing with unexpected situations in the business. Good managers understand that they must adapt their management techniques to achieve the best results.

3 Charisma: Charismatic managers have the ability to inspire others. They encourage employees to use their knowledge and creativity for the benefit of the business.

4 Hard-working: Managers must set a good example for employees by working hard in the firm. They do not quit until tasks are completed.

5 Initiative: Managers do not wait for others to tell them what to do. They start something new and take the lead before others.

THE DIFFERENCES BETWEEN ENTERPRISE AND MANAGEMENT

A successful entrepreneur may not always be a good manager. Entrepreneurs need to be able to recognise when they need help to run the business and employ a manager.

Entrepreneurs and managers need to work together to make the business a success. However, there are a number of differences between enterprise and management.

Unit 3

1 Idea Generation

Entrepreneur	Manager
This is the ideas person in the organisation – they have noticed a gap in the market and have developed an idea to fill the gap.	The manager is responsible for implementing the entrepreneur's ideas to ensure business success.

2 Risk-taking

Entrepreneur	Manager
Entrepreneurs take a personal and financial risk when they set up a business. If the business is unsuccessful, they may lose all the money they have invested.	Managers take fewer risks – if the business fails, they can leave the firm and apply for a job in another business.

3 Running the Business

Entrepreneur	Manager
The entrepreneur should spend less time on day-to-day activities in the firm and instead focus on important tasks such as raising finance and recruiting employees.	The manager is responsible for the daily running of the business. Managers delegate tasks to employees to ensure that deadlines are met.

4 Control

Entrepreneur	Manager
The entrepreneur has full control over the business and makes all decisions. They do not need to consult with others if they do not wish to do so.	Managers must get approval from the entrepreneur before they make certain business decisions. Managers may need to report to the entrepreneur on a regular basis.

Activity 5.5

Working in pairs, create a gif to represent each difference between the entrepreneur and the manager. You could use websites such as https://giphy.com/create/gifmaker. Share your gifs with your classmates.

KEY TERMS

Now you have completed this chapter, you should understand and be able to explain the following terms. In your copybook, write a definition of each term to build up your own glossary of terms.

- management
- management skills
- leading
- motivating
- communicating
- management activities

- planning
- organising
- controlling
- problem-solving
- flexibility
- charisma

- hard-working
- initiative
- idea generation
- risk-taking

PowerPoint Summary

Unit 3

EXAM-STYLE QUESTIONS

Ordinary Level

Section 1 – Short Questions (10 marks each)

1 Explain the term *management*.
2 Complete the **two** missing management skills.

	Motivating	

3 List **four** characteristics of a manager and describe **one** of them.
4 Explain what the following letters stand for: (i) CEO, (ii) MD.
5 List **three** management skills and **two** management activities.
6 Identify the management activities in the following list: leading, planning, communicating, organising, controlling, motivating.

Section 2 – Long Questions

1 Managers must be able to <u>plan</u>, <u>organise</u> and <u>control</u> in their working lives. Outline the underlined terms. **(15 marks)**
2 Distinguish between the management skill of communicating and the management activity of controlling. **(15 marks)**
3 Describe the management skills of leading and motivating. **(15 marks)**
4 Explain how management can be seen in the following areas:
  (i) In the local community
  (ii) At school. **(15 marks)**
5 Outline **four** management characteristics. **(20 marks)**

Higher Level

Section 1 – Short Questions (10 marks each)

1 Indicate whether each of the following statements is true or false.

Statements		True or False
A	The most senior manager in an organisation is known as the CEO.	
B	Flexibility is the ability to put time and effort into tasks and not quit until a goal has been achieved.	
C	A manager takes a personal and a financial risk when running a business.	
D	Motivating refers to telling employees the task they need to complete.	
E	The management activities are planning, controlling and organising.	

2 Distinguish between the management skills of motivating and communicating.
3 Describe the management characteristics (i) problem-solving and (ii) hard-working.
4 Outline **two** management activities.
5 Explain how idea generation differs between entrepreneurs and management.

Section 2 – Applied Business Question (80 marks)

Medica Engineering Ltd
Entrepreneur Shola Mooge spotted a gap in the market for medical equipment used in eye surgery and took the risk of setting up a business manufacturing this equipment in Dublin.
Over the last five years the business has become very successful and Shola has decided to recruit a new general manager to oversee the day-to-day operation of the company. This will give Shola time to focus on planning and raising finance to fund the expansion of the production facility.

Section 2 – Applied Business Question (80 marks) *continued*

Erica Ryan was recruited as the new general manager and Shola decided to spend a day shadowing Erica to see what her typical day consists of at Medica Engineering Ltd.

Erica is responsible for running the manufacturing plant and managing its 12 staff. She uses a democratic leadership style and likes to involve staff in the decision-making process in the business. She has organised the employees into teams of four and at the beginning of each week meets with them to discuss their plans for the week ahead. Erica has introduced a reward system for intrapreneurial ideas from the employees. Her enthusiasm for her work has inspired staff to come up with some excellent ideas, which have saved the business a large amount of money.

Erica is disappointed to learn from the production team that a planned delivery of mechanical components has not arrived from a supplier. She rings a local supplier and convinces them to supply the components within an hour. Shola is delighted by Erica's ability to solve production line problems and is relieved that late deliveries and unhappy customers will not damage the company's reputation. Shola meets with Erica to discuss the events of the day. Erica gives a detailed report on the company's performance. She tells Shola that she has noticed some quality control issues on some of the medical components and will be conducting spot checks on the items for the foreseeable future.

Shola is delighted that her recruitment process identified such a capable and hard-working individual for the role of general manager.

A   Identify the main management characteristics shown by Erica in the extract.   **(20 marks)**
B   Compare the roles of the entrepreneur and manager at Medica Engineering Ltd.   **(30 marks)**
C   Evaluate the management activities and skills displayed at Medica Engineering Ltd.   **(30 marks)**

Section 3 – Long Questions

1 Evaluate the management activities of planning, controlling and organising.   **(15 marks)**
2 Describe, using examples, management in action in (i) the home and (ii) a business. **(20 marks)**
3 Differentiate between the roles of an entrepreneur and a manager in a business.   **(15 marks)**
4 Managers must inspire followers to achieve organisational goals. Describe the management
  characteristics that you think inspire workers to achieve business goals.   **(15 marks)**

PREVIOUS LEAVING CERTIFICATE EXAM QUESTIONS

Ordinary Level

Section A – Short Questions (10 marks each)

1 List **three** qualities of managers.   [LC OL 2003]
2 Name the **three** management activities.   [LC OL 2016]

Section B

1 List **three** management skills and explain **one** of them.   **(25 marks)** [LC OL 1999]

Higher Level

Section A – Short Questions (10 marks each)

1 Define *management*.   [LC HL 2006]
2 Illustrate the difference between enterprise and management.   [LC HL 2009]

 Solutions

6 | MANAGEMENT SKILLS 1: LEADING

CHAPTER

 Learning Outcomes

When you have completed this chapter, you will be able to:

1 Define *leading* as a management skill

2 Outline the features of autocratic, democratic and laissez-faire leadership styles

3 Describe the advantages and disadvantages of autocratic, democratic and laissez-faire leadership styles

4 Describe delegation and the advantages it brings to an organisation.

 Literacy Link

Leading, leadership styles, autocratic, democratic, laissez-faire, delegation

 Numeracy Link

Multiplication, exchange rates

 Cross-curricular Link

History – political leadership
Religion – women and leadership

CASE STUDY | *Leadership at Apple Inc.*

Steve Jobs co-founded Apple Inc. in 1976 with Steve Wozniak and Ronald Wayne. The business was initially very successful and floated on the stock exchange in 1981. Jobs was a visionary **leader** and was responsible for a team of employees who developed the Macintosh computer. When it was launched, the Macintosh received positive consumer reviews, but sales were low and this put the company under financial pressure.

Jobs made some **poor decisions** while leading this team. The team worked in isolation from other business units and team members complained that Jobs was too demanding as a **manager**. Some members of the board of directors referred to him as 'uncontrollable' and in 1985 he was voted out of the company he had established.

Jobs went on to create two more highly successful companies, NeXT and Pixar Animation Studios. At the same time, Apple was almost bankrupt, with annual losses of over $1 billion. In 1997 the board of directors asked Jobs to return to Apple Inc.

When he returned to the company, Jobs had changed his **leadership style**. He **communicated** his vision clearly and effectively to employees – he wanted the company's products to be sleek, functional and covetable. He **motivated** his employees to work hard for the benefit of the business, and over the years launched products such as the iPod, iTunes and the iPhone. He encouraged employees to make mistakes: 'Embrace every failure. Own it, learn from it, and take full responsibility for making sure that next time, things will turn out differently.'

The return of Steve Jobs to the helm of Apple Inc. heralded a change in fortune for the business. Apple became the world's first company to be valued at $1 trillion.

LEADING

We met the management skills of leading, motivating and communicating in Chapter 5. Now we shall examine the skill of leading in more detail. **Leading is a management skill that encourages people to work towards a specific goal.**

A strong leader must be able to:

- Clearly communicate business goals to all staff
- Find ways to motivate employees to achieve these goals
- Set an example to employees so they know what is expected of them
- Delegate tasks to staff.

> *We shall examine the other management skills of motivating and communicating in Chapters 7 and 8.*

Activity 6.1

Work in groups to create a collage of some inspirational management quotes to hang on the classroom walls. You could use a mixture of words and images to make your collage more attractive. Don't forget to do some research on the people behind the quotes so that you can tell your classmates about them.

Activity 6.2

Examine the images below. In pairs, discuss the following questions:
1 What, do you think, is the message conveyed by these images?
2 Can you name any famous leaders in the world of business, entertainment or sports? What approach to leadership do you think they take?

LEADERSHIP STYLES

There are a number of leadership styles that managers can use to achieve organisational goals. The most common styles are:

1 Autocratic
2 Democratic
3 Laissez-faire.

> *Exam Tip!*
> *You may be asked to **compare** the different leadership styles. This means that you should show the **similarities** and **differences** between them.*

Managers tend not to stick to one single leadership style at all times. Different scenarios and situations may require a manager to move between leadership styles to achieve their goals.

  Elon Musk, founder and CEO of SpaceX and Tesla Inc., said 'Leaders are expected to work harder than those who report to them and always make sure that their needs are taken care of before yours, thus leading by example.'

Activity 6.3

José Mourinho was one of the highest-paid football managers in the world. At one point he was earning £388,000 per week. How much was he earning per year?
Look up the current pound sterling/euro exchange rate and work out how much he was earning per week in euros.

1 Autocratic Leadership

Autocratic leadership is a management style where the manager makes all business decisions without input from employees. The manager does not trust the employees and uses the threat of punishment to motivate staff.

In autocratic leadership there is one leader who makes all the decisions and who orders subordinates to follow instructions. This leadership style is often associated with the military, McDonald's Ray Kroc and Sam Walton of Walmart.

> **Definition: Subordinate**
> A person in a lower rank or position in the organisation.

Features of Autocratic Leadership

A Authority: Autocratic leaders have complete power and control in the organisation. They give orders to subordinates and expect them to be carried out without question.

B Decision-making: Autocratic leaders do not consult with employees when making decisions. They believe that they have the knowledge and expertise to make the best decisions for the business.

C Trust: They do not trust employees and may believe that they are lazy and try to avoid work. Therefore, autocratic managers closely supervise the work of subordinates.

D Motivation: Autocratic leaders use threats and punishment to motivate their employees to work harder. Employees are afraid to make mistakes, as they may feel that they could lose their job.

AUTOCRATIC LEADERSHIP

✓ Advantages	✗ Disadvantages
1 Quick Decision-making Decisions can be made quickly as the autocratic leader does not consult with others. Therefore, the business does not miss out on opportunities in the market.	**1 Management Stress** The autocratic leader makes all business decisions and does not delegate tasks. This can lead to management stress and burnout.
2 Quick Task Completion The autocratic leader gives orders to staff to ensure that tasks are completed quickly and deadlines are not missed.	**2 Staff Motivation** Motivation levels are low as staff follow orders and jobs are not delegated to them. This can lead to higher absenteeism and staff turnover.
3 Improved Productivity Employees work hard as they know that they are being supervised by management. This can improve productivity in the workplace.	**3 Industrial Action** Employees may feel undervalued, which damages the relationship between management and employees. This may lead to increased industrial action, e.g. work to rule and official strikes.

CASE STUDY: *Autocratic Leadership*

Edward Mike Davis was CEO of Houston-based Tiger Oil Co. in the 1970s. He was an autocratic leader and regularly sent his staff memos outlining the behaviour and standards he expected in the business.
Some examples of his memos are given below.

MEMORANDUM

TO: All Employees

DATE: January 11, 1978

FROM: Edward Mike Davis

SUBJECT: Idle Conversation

Idle conversation and gossip in this office among employees will result in immediate termination.

Don't talk about other people and other things in this office.

DO YOUR JOB AND KEEP YOUR MOUTH SHUT!

EDWARD MIKE DAVIS

MEMORANDUM

TO: Secretaries

DATE: January 3, 1978

FROM: Edward Mike Davis

This is a business office. All correspondence and other things pertaining to this office will be typewritten.

Handwriting takes much longer than a typewriter — you're wasting your time, but more importantly, you're wasting my time. If you don't know how to type, you'd better learn.

EDWARD MIKE DAVIS

MEMORANDUM

TO: All Employees   DATE: February 8, 1978

SUBJECT: Celebrations of Any Kind

Per Edward Mike Davis' orders, there will be no more birthday celebrations, birthday cakes, levity, or celebrations of any kind within the office. This is a business office.

If you have to celebrate, do it after office hours on your own time.

Activity 6.4

Discuss in groups:
1 Would Edward Davis's behaviour towards staff be acceptable in the workplace today?
2 How would you have felt as an employee of Tiger Oil on receiving memos like these?
3 What, do you think, were the positive and negative consequences of this leadership style?

2 Democratic Leadership

Democratic leadership is also known as participative leadership. It encourages employees to participate in decision-making in the business. The democratic leader has ultimate authority and responsibility but values employees' ideas and suggestions.

Democratic leadership is a common management style used in many organisations today, e.g. marketing and accounting firms.

Unit 3

Features of Democratic Leadership

A Authority: Democratic managers delegate tasks to employees. They believe that their staff have the skills to complete tasks effectively. However, ultimate responsibility for all tasks lies with the manager.

B Decision-making: Democratic leaders include employees when they make business decisions. Employees have a wide range of skills and experience, which can help management to make better decisions.

C Trust: Democratic leaders trust their employees and empower them to make decisions on behalf of the business. This can help the business to develop fast solutions to problems when they arise.

D Motivation: Employees are motivated as they feel valued when they are delegated tasks and are involved in decision-making in the business. As a result, they work harder for the business.

Definition: Empowerment

Empowerment occurs when managers allow employees to make certain decisions on behalf of the business, without needing to consult with management.

DEMOCRATIC LEADERSHIP

✓ Advantages	✗ Disadvantages
1 Increased Intrapreneurship Democratic leadership encourages intrapreneurship. Employees are willing to come up with ideas that can help the business to increase sales or decrease business costs, e.g. a new product.	**1 Slow Decision-making** Decision-making is slow as managers consult with their employees before making major business decisions.
2 Future Promotion Delegation and empowerment help employees to develop new skills and knowledge. When promotions arise in the business they can apply for these roles.	**2 Frustrated Employees** Employees may feel frustrated if their ideas are not incorporated into business decisions. They may decide not to contribute their ideas in the future.
3 Employee Motivation Employees have high levels of motivation, as they feel valued. This can lead to higher productivity levels among staff.	**3 Management Resentment** Some managers may resent empowering employees, as it reduces their control in the business. Managers may ignore employees' suggestions, believing their own ideas are better.

CASE STUDY *Democratic Leadership*

Herb Kelleher and Rollin King founded Southwest Airlines in 1971. It is the world's largest low-cost airline carrier, employing over 47,000 people, and it has enjoyed 40 consecutive years of profitability.

The company has a strong **democratic leadership** style which focuses on ensuring that employees are happy in the organisation. Management believes that in order of importance employees rank first, ahead of consumers and shareholders. They believe that if employees are happy, they will treat customers well. This results in increased sales and profits, which means that shareholders are happy with their investment.

Managers clearly communicate the overall company objective and employees understand the important role they play in the business.

Employees are **empowered** to make decisions that benefit the business. Former CEO James Parker recalled an occasion when an elderly lady arrived at the airport and her son was unable to collect her. A Southwest Airlines employee drove her to the nearest airport to ensure she made an alternative flight. 'He didn't call headquarters and ask what to do,'

Parker said. 'He just went to the employee parking lot, got his car, and drove her to Tucson about 100 miles away.'

The company's democratic style is envied by many of its competitors, who try to copy its successful approach in their own airlines. Co-founder Herb Kelleher has said, 'They can buy all the physical things. The things you can't buy are dedication, devotion, loyalty – the feeling that you are participating in a crusade.'

Activity 6.5

Using a Venn diagram, compare and contrast autocratic and democratic leadership styles. Compare your Venn diagram with those drawn by other students in your class.

3 Laissez-faire Leadership

In laissez-faire leadership, management outlines the business goals and trusts the employees to decide on the best way to achieve these goals. Laissez-faire leaders take a hands-off approach to employees and allow them to make decisions that they believe are in the best interests of the business.

Laissez-faire leadership is most common in organisations where employees can work independently from management, e.g. research and development departments in pharmaceutical firms.

Features of Laissez-faire Leadership

A Authority: Laissez-faire managers set goals for employees and allow staff to decide how best to achieve those goals. While power is given to employees, overall responsibility rests with the manager.

B Decision-making: Laissez-faire managers empower employees to make decisions on behalf of the business. Management becomes involved only when very important decisions need to be made.

C Trust: Management outlines the business objectives and trusts employees to work independently without close management supervision.

D Motivation: Employees are highly motivated under this style of leadership, as they feel empowered to achieve the firm's goals. They work hard for the benefit of the business and want the firm to be successful.

LAISSEZ-FAIRE LEADERSHIP

✓ Advantages	✗ Disadvantages
1 Employee Motivation Employee motivation is high among empowered employees, as they feel trusted by management. They work hard for the benefit of the business and to achieve the firm's goals.	**1 Reduced Productivity** Some employees may take advantage of the lack of regular management supervision. This can create tension among team members and reduce business productivity.
2 Improved Skills and Knowledge Delegated work helps employees to improve their skills and knowledge. This prepares them for future promotions in the business.	**2 Poor Decisions** Some employees can make poor decisions that damage the firm's reputation or result in a business missing an opportunity in the market.
3 Intrapreneurship Employees use their intrapreneurial skills to develop new products or identify new processes. This can help to reduce business costs and improve sales.	**3 Poor Industrial Relations** Management may blame employees for mistakes made or for not achieving targets. This can lead to poor industrial relations between management and staff.

Activity 6.6

Working in pairs, complete a cross-classification chart to compare autocratic, democratic and laissez-faire leadership styles. When you have completed your chart, compare your results with another pair of students. Did you all record the same information? What changes would you make to the charts?

CASE STUDY

Laissez-faire Leadership

Warren Buffet is the **CEO** of Berkshire Hathaway, an American holding company that owns a wide range of firms, including Fruit of the Loom, Duracell and Helzberg Diamonds. The organisation also owns a large percentage of shares in companies such as Coca-Cola (9%), Kraft Heinz (27%) and American Express (16%).

How does Warren Buffet manage such a diverse range of companies with almost 377,000 employees? He uses a **laissez-faire leadership style**, buying and investing in businesses that are run by experienced managers. He takes a 'hands-off' approach and allows these managers to run the firm as they see fit.

In a Berkshire Hathaway annual report, Buffet said, 'We tend to let our many subsidiaries operate on their own, without our supervising and monitoring them to any degree. Most managers use the independence we grant them magnificently, by maintaining an owner-oriented attitude.' Put simply, Buffet trusts his managers to do their best for the business. However, that is not to say that he does not make difficult decisions in relation to managers. A biographer once noted, 'When a leader violates corporate values or generates reputational damage, the axe falls swiftly.'

Buffet publishes an annual letter to **shareholders** and often singles out employees and managers for specific praise. He does not **communicate** often with his managers, but when he does his words have a powerful effect.

When Warren Buffet first purchased shares in Berkshire Hathaway, he paid $7.50 per share. Today they trade at $300,000 per share.

Activity 6.7

Reflect on autocratic, democratic and laissez-faire leadership styles. Write a sentence that you think each type of leader might say.

Each student reads out their sentences and their classmates use mini-whiteboards to write down the type of leadership they think has been referenced.

DELEGATION

Delegation involves assigning tasks to another person, e.g. a manager delegates tasks to a subordinate. It is very important that the manager clearly communicates the assigned tasks to subordinates to prevent any confusion. When delegating, managers should choose subordinates with the appropriate skills and provide the necessary resources to complete the assigned task.

Requirements for Delegation

In order for delegation to be successful in an organisation, management must ensure that there is:

Open communication

Employee skills and experience

Managerial control

1 Open communication: Delegated tasks and the required standards should be clearly communicated to employees. This ensures that the tasks are completed to an appropriate standard.

2 Employee skills and experience: Management must choose employees with adequate skills and experience to complete the assigned task. The manager should trust in the employees' ability to complete the task successfully.

3 Managerial control: Ultimate responsibility for task completion lies with management. Therefore, managers must implement a control system to ensure that errors are identified and corrected quickly.

CASE STUDY *Delegation at the Marriott International*

Roy Jones worked for the Marriott International for €11 per hour and was delegated the task of managing the firm's Twitter account. He 'liked' a tweet from a Tibetan separatist group that had complimented the hotel on recognising Tibet as a separate country from China.

The Chinese government was outraged, because it views Tibet as part of China. Despite an apology from the Marriott, the Chinese government shut down the company's booking system in China for one week.

Roy Jones was fired, but he insisted that he had not received any training on dealing with political issues relating to China.

Who was really responsible for the error? The man earning €11 per hour who received the delegated task, or the manager who had assigned the task?

A wide range of business benefits arise from delegation in the workplace, including:

✓ Advantages	✗ Disadvantages
1 Management Workload Delegation reduces managerial workload and allows managers to focus their time on more important managerial tasks and decisions.	**1 Employee Stress** Some employees may not want the additional responsibility of delegated tasks and may become stressed and want to leave the firm.
2 Increased Employee Motivation Delegating tasks to employees shows that management trusts them. Increased motivation can help to boost productivity in the workplace.	**2 Poor Decision-Making** Employees lacking experience and suitable guidance may make poor decisions when they receive delegated tasks. This could damage the firm's reputation.
3 Management Training Delegation gives employees the opportunity to develop their skills and knowledge and helps them to train as managers. The business can promote from within when vacancies arise.	**3 Employee Resentment** Employees may resent management if they feel that the delegated tasks are simply tasks that the manager does not like to do. This can reduce employee motivation levels and lead to lower employee productivity.

BENEFITS OF LEADERSHIP

Good managers view leadership as a very important management skill. The benefits of strong leadership include:

1 Achieving organisational goals: Management clearly communicates the organisational goals to staff. This ensures that all employees are working towards achieving these business goals.

2 Management time: Delegation allows management to spend time on other managerial tasks. This reduces managerial stress and reduces the likelihood of management burnout.

3 Increased employee motivation: Good leaders involve employees in decision-making, which makes employees feel that they have an important role in the business. This helps to increase employee motivation levels.

4 Supporting change: Managers lead by example when changes are introduced in the business, e.g. new technology. Employees follow their lead and are more willing to accept the changes.

5 Staff recruitment and retention: Good leadership helps the business to recruit and retain high-quality staff. If employees are happy in the workplace they tend to have lower absenteeism levels and stay in their roles longer.

KEY TERMS

Now you have completed this chapter, you should understand and be able to explain the following terms. In your copybook, write a definition of each term to build up your own glossary of terms.

- leading
- leadership styles
- autocratic leadership
- democratic leadership
- empowerment
- laissez-faire leadership
- delegation

PowerPoint Summary

EXAM-STYLE QUESTIONS

Ordinary Level

Section 1 – Short Questions (10 marks each)

1 What is meant by the term *leadership*?

2 List **three** common leadership styles.

3 The following table shows five statements made by leaders. Tick (✔) the leadership style that is most likely to match the statement.

Terms		Autocratic	Democratic	Laissez-faire
A	The manager outlines a task to be achieved and tells staff that she will talk to them in six weeks.			
B	The manager organises regular staff meetings and encourages staff to voice their opinions.			
C	The manager holds staff meetings but does not want to hear suggestions from staff.			
D	The manager makes decisions in collaboration with staff.			
E	The manager allows employees to decide how best to achieve organisational goals.			

4 Explain the term *autocratic leadership*.

5 Why is slow decision-making a feature of democratic leadership?

6 Describe **two** features of laissez-faire leadership.

7 Identify a work situation that would be suitable for each type of leadership.

   (i)   Autocratic: _____

   (ii) Democratic: _____

   (iii) Laissez-faire: _____

8 In your copybook write the correct word(s) in the following statements.

   (i)   Democratic leaders **delegate/do not delegate** tasks to their employees.

   (ii) Autocratic leaders **involve/don't involve** employees in decision-making.

   (iii) Ultimate responsibility for delegated tasks lies with the **manager/employee**.

   (iv) Laissez-faire leaders **closely monitor/loosely monitor** employees.

   (v)   Managerial workload **increases/decreases** with delegation.

Section 2 – Long Questions

1 Explain the difference between a democratic leader and a laissez-faire leader. **(20 marks)**

2 Tim is the production manager at TOB Textiles. He thinks his employees are lazy and do not want to work. What style of leadership does Tim use? Outline **two** other features of this leadership approach. **(15 marks)**

3 Outline **two** advantages of using a laissez-faire leadership style. **(15 marks)**

4 Outline **two** disadvantages of a democratic leadership style. **(15 marks)**

5 Describe **three** requirements needed for delegation to be successful in a business. **(20 marks)**

6 Leadership requires managers to <u>manage their time</u> effectively, <u>improve staff motivation</u> and help to <u>achieve organisational goals</u>. Explain how **two** of the underlined terms are a benefit of leadership. **(15 marks)**

Unit 3

Higher Level

Section 1 – Short Questions (10 marks each)

1 List **four** features of democratic leadership.

2 Distinguish between autocratic and democratic leadership.

3 Complete the following sentence: Democratic leadership helps business because …

4 Outline the features of laissez-faire leadership.

5 Describe the difference between trust levels in democratic and laissez-faire leadership styles.

6 Outline why open communication is necessary for delegation to be successful in a business.

7 Indicate whether each of these statements is true or false.

Statements		True or False
A	A laissez-faire leader delegates and empowers employees.	
B	A democratic leader gives employees instructions and expects them to be obeyed without question.	
C	An autocratic leader motivates employees to work harder using fear and threats.	
D	An autocratic leader encourages employees to offer suggestions and opinions.	
E	A democratic leader encourages employees to become involved in business decisions.	

8 Illustrate your understanding of the term *delegation*.

Section 2 – Applied Business Question (80 marks)

Masood Consulting Ltd

Roman Masood is a management consultant with over twenty years' experience helping businesses to improve their leadership skills. He has received reports from two companies that are experiencing difficulties regarding their leadership styles and that require his assistance.

He knows how difficult it can be to introduce change in leadership style but firmly believes that it is necessary for business survival. However, management must be ready to make the changes needed to ensure that all employees are working towards the same goals.

Company 1

Cosmetico Ltd manufactures a range of cosmetic products and employs 50 factory floor staff. The manager believes that as the employees are unskilled, they are constantly trying to avoid work and can be lazy. The manager finds it stressful to have to make all decisions in the firm. The manager gives orders to the employees at the beginning of each work shift and never delegates tasks to staff because he does not trust them. Employees are closely supervised, and management have threatened staff with a pay reduction unless they maintain quality levels.

A group of employees have approached management with suggestions on how to increase efficiency on the production line but management has ignored their suggestions. Employees have now started to become uncooperative, staff turnover has increased and industrial relations have reached an all-time low.

Company 2

WhitWorld Ltd is a software engineering company providing a wide range of services to clients all over the world. Roman has learned that many employees working in the firm are very happy, highly motivated and enjoy working independently, developing their skills and experience. Others feel that management does not clearly communicate organisational goals. They give brief instructions and employees are left wondering in which direction they should work. Some employees are taking advantage of the lack of supervision by spending days out of the office, leaving their co-workers to fill their roles.

There have been increased incidences of poor decision-making and the company recently lost a large client to a competitor. Management blames the employees for the loss of such an important client, but the employees disagree.

Roman thinks that both companies require immediate help and sets to work to design a plan to improve leadership in the businesses.

Section 2 – Applied Business Question (80 marks) *continued*

A   Identify the leadership style used in Cosmetico Ltd. Outline the common features of this style of management.   **(20 marks)**

B   Identify the leadership style used in WhitWorld Ltd. Outline the disadvantages of using this management style.   **(20 marks)**

C   Strong leadership and delegation are important elements of a successful business.

   (i)   Outline what is meant by the term *delegation*.   **(10 marks)**

   (ii) Evaluate the importance of strong leadership. Illustrate with reference to the text.   **(30 marks)**

Section 3 – Long Questions

1   Outline the benefits and drawbacks to a firm using a democratic leadership style.   **(15 marks)**

2   Clodagh likes to leave tasks for her employees and get them to decide how they will complete them. What type of leadership style does Clodagh use? Describe the benefits and draw backs of this approach to leadership.   **(20 marks)**

3   Distinguish between a democratic leader and an autocratic leader under the headings trust, decision-making and employee motivation.   **(15 marks)**

4   Describe the environment needed for successful delegation to take place.   **(15 marks)**

5   Outline the advantages of a business delegating tasks to its employees.   **(15 marks)**

6   Describe the difficulties a business may face when implementing delegation in the workplace.   **(15 marks)**

7   Leading is the most important management skill. Discuss this statement.   **(20 marks)**

PREVIOUS LEAVING CERTIFICATE EXAM QUESTIONS

Ordinary Level

Section B

1

BestoPesto

Maria Conlon is the manager of BestoPesto, a manufacturer of cooking sauces. BestoPesto produces sauces in five different flavours. Recently there has been an increase in consumer complaints about the products. Maria realises that her business needs to improve its quality control measures. Maria sent a memo to the staff informing them of a staff meeting to be held on Friday 27 June 2014 at 9.00 a.m. in the conference room to discuss quality control issues.

Explain **two** types of leadership styles.   **(15 marks) [LC OL 2014]**

2

Fitness Fanatics

Sean spotted a gap in the market for a personal training business in his home town. Sean used his personal savings to open a fitness studio. Within one year he had over 150 clients in training. Sean hired five full-time personal trainers to help him with the workload. He regularly consults with his staff and values their opinions.

Explain **two** features of a democratic leadership style.   **(15 marks) [LC OL 2016]**

Section B *continued*

3

Ashfield Tidy Towns

The people of Ashfield village have decided to enter the National Tidy Towns competition, after it was suggested by local entrepreneur Alice Fitzgerald. Due to her democratic leadership style, Alice was appointed Chairperson of the Tidy Towns Committee and she will lead all volunteer teams in achieving the committee's objectives. The next monthly meeting of the committee will be held on Friday 26 June 2015 at 7.30 p.m., in Ashfield Community Centre, to discuss sources of finance for improvements to the local park.

Explain the difference between a democratic and an autocratic leader. **(15 marks) [LC OL 2015]**

Higher Level

Section A – Short Questions (10 marks each)

1 Define the term *delegation*. Outline **two** benefits of delegation within a business. **[LC HL 2012]**

Section B

1

How you communicate is as important as what you communicate.

Outline **two** styles of leadership and illustrate how each of these styles may be appropriate in different business situations. **(20 marks) [LC HL 2012]**

2 Outline **one** appropriate leadership style, which a manager in a retail outlet could adopt, giving reasons for your choice. **(20 marks) [LC HL 2018]**

3

The rules of good management remain the same in times of growth or slowdown.

Explain the term *delegation*. Describe the benefits of delegation for a manager. **(20 marks) [LC HL 2009]**

 Solutions

CHAPTER 7 | MANAGEMENT SKILLS 2: MOTIVATING

 Literacy Link

Motivating, motivational needs, Maslow's Hierarchy of Needs, esteem, self-actualisation, McGregor's Theory X and Theory Y

 Numeracy Link

Percentages

 Cross-curricular Link

Accounting – wages and salaries

Music – music interpretation

CASE STUDY | *Motivating Employees*

Virgin Media, with Richard Branson as a figurehead, provides television, phone and broadband services in the UK and Ireland. The philosophy at Virgin Media is that **motivated employees** are loyal to the business. Happy employees provide high levels of customer care and can help increase the business's sales and profits.

The company motivates employees using **McGregor's Theory Y**. This is a **motivational theory** that believes that employees who enjoy work are willing to work harder for the business. Employees feel trusted and engaged in the workplace. A recent internal survey has found that 82% of staff feel that they are engaged in work.

Virgin Media uses features of **Maslow's Hierarchy of Needs** to motivate its employees. The company satisfies employees' needs in the following ways:

• **Physiological needs** – good pay levels

• **Safety needs** – healthy and safe work environment

• **Social needs** – employees work in teams and management organises social events for staff

• **Esteem needs** – job titles, e.g. software developer, customer service representative

• **Self-actualisation needs** – promotions; one day per year is dedicated to raising money for charity.

Although **financial rewards** are a key factor in **motivating** employees, Virgin Media recognises that individual employees are motivated by a range of factors. As well as offering competitive salaries and bonus schemes, the firm also provides **non-financial rewards** including private health care, a company pension and staff saving schemes.

Virgin Media believes that all employees should be given **opportunities for development** within the company. For example, a programme called 'Your Story Framework' is used to help technicians develop a career plan.

Virgin Media has created a culture of 'doing the right thing'; it has created a workplace where people feel happy; and this makes for better business.

MOTIVATION

We learned about the management skill of leading in Chapter 6. We shall now examine the skill of motivation in greater detail. **Motivation is a willingness to do something, e.g. work or exercise**. It is what drives people, and it encourages them to work to achieve their goals.

DID YOU KNOW? *According to a global study, 64% of Irish workers are not engaged in their jobs.*

Activity 7.1

Individually, write down on sticky notes the types of things that motivate you in areas of your life, e.g. in school or hobbies. Place the sticky notes on the classroom wall and compare your notes with another student. Working together, classify both of your lists into categories, e.g. financial reasons or health reasons. As a class, compile a list of items that motivate all students. Use a website such as www.canva.com to create an infographic of the things that motivate the students in your class.

CLASSIC THEORIES OF MOTIVATION

There are two main theories of motivation:

1 Maslow's Hierarchy of Needs
2 McGregor's Theory X and Theory Y.

1 Maslow's Hierarchy of Needs

Abraham Maslow's theory of motivation is based on the idea that humans want to satisfy different needs as they grow and develop. Maslow believed that once one need is satisfied, the need immediately above it becomes the dominant motivator.

According to Maslow, in the workplace, employees must have their lower-level needs fully met by the business before being motivated by the next level.

Maslow identified five needs.

Exam Tip!
You must be able to draw and label Maslow's Hierarchy of Needs.

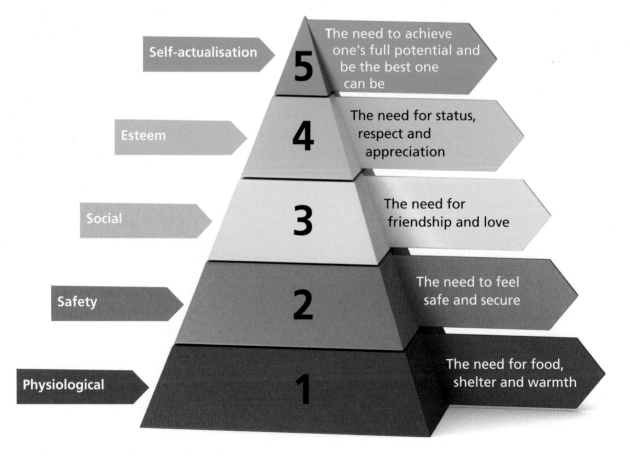

Self-actualisation — **5** The need to achieve one's full potential and be the best one can be

Esteem — **4** The need for status, respect and appreciation

Social — **3** The need for friendship and love

Safety — **2** The need to feel safe and secure

Physiological — **1** The need for food, shelter and warmth

Applying Maslow's Hierarchy of Needs in the Workplace
Management can use Maslow's theory to motivate staff at all levels.

1 Physiological Needs
- Paying a fair day's wage for a fair day's work
- Bonus payments for meeting targets
- Profit-sharing schemes

2 Safety Needs
- Offering employees long-term employment contracts
- Providing health insurance cover
- Providing a safe working environment, e.g. safety goggles and high-visibility jackets on construction sites

3 Social Needs
- Offering flexitime arrangements, which enables employees to spend more time with family
- Enabling employees to work in teams
- Organising social events, e.g. parties, sporting events

4 Esteem Needs
- Praise for work well done
- Providing job titles
- Offering employees an office of their own

5 Self-actualisation Needs
- Providing workers with a career plan, e.g. promotion to positions of responsibility
- Providing training and development opportunities for employees
- Employee empowerment (see Chapter 14)

Unit 3

Activity 7.2

In groups, create a poster of Maslow's Hierarchy of Needs. Draw the pyramid on A3 paper and use images to represent how each need is satisfied in the workplace. Use images from magazines/ newspapers or online sources. Display the posters on the classroom walls.

Advantages and Limitations of Maslow's Hierarchy of Needs
Maslow's theory of motivation is widely used by many different organisations to motivate people. However, as with all theories, there are advantages and limitations of Maslow's Hierarchy of Needs.

✓ Advantages	✗ Limitations
1 Rewards It recognises that people are motivated by more than money. They can be motivated by job titles, working in teams, praise and training and career development opportunities.	**1 Individual Needs** It assumes that all people are motivated by the same things at the same stage of their careers. It does not consider that people have different motivations at different life stages.
2 Changing Employee Needs It understands that people's needs change over time. Different rewards can be used to motivate individuals at different stages of their career.	**2 Self-actualisation** The concept of self-actualisation varies from person to person. A business may find it difficult to find ways to motivate employees at this level of the hierarchy.
3 Management Positions By providing training and development opportunities it prepares employees for future management positions.	**3 Value of Needs** Not all needs may be of equal value for employees, e.g. one employee may value esteem needs above safety needs.

Activity 7.3

Search on YouTube for a clip of Maslow's Hierarchy of Needs and, after watching it, answer the questions.
1 In what year did Maslow propose his theory of the Hierarchy of Needs?
2 Name **one** person Maslow considered to have reached their full or near to full potential.
3 Outline **two** ways in which a person could meet their esteem needs.
4 Identify **two** things that a person does when they reach the self-actualisation stage.

2 McGregor's Theory X and Theory Y

Douglas McGregor put forward two theories on employee motivation. He called these Theory X and Theory Y. These theories are two extremes of how management views employees' attitude to work.

Theory X is extremely negative; Theory Y is extremely positive. The optimal management approach would be somewhere between the two extremes, i.e. a manager could use motivational elements from both Theory X and Theory Y.

Theory X

Theory X managers believe that employees:
* Dislike work
* Avoid taking responsibility
* Lack ambition
* Are motivated by money.

The Theory X manager uses an autocratic style of leadership. Employees are not trusted and are closely supervised. Managers use threats and punishment to get staff to work hard.

The implications of a Theory X style of management include:

Demotivated workforce	→ An autocratic approach combined with a lack of trust and delegation leads to low morale among employees. Employees are less likely to use their own initiative.
Poor time management	→ As a Theory X manager does not delegate tasks to employees, management can become overworked and stressed.
High labour turnover	→ Unhappy workers leave their jobs. This increases costs for the business, e.g. recruitment and training costs.
Low-quality goods and services	→ Employees do not feel valued as they are not involved in decision-making in the firm. This reduces productivity and can result in lower-quality goods and services for consumers.

Theory Y

Theory Y managers believe that employees:
* Like work and are willing to work hard
* Want to take on additional duties and responsibility
* Are ambitious
* Are motivated by financial and non-financial rewards (you will learn more about these in Chapter 13).

Theory Y managers use a democratic or laissez-faire leadership style. They trust employees to do their work well. They also delegate tasks to staff and involve them in business decision-making.

Implications of a Theory Y management style include:

Motivated workforce	→ Because employees are trusted and given responsibilities, they are motivated and willing to work hard for the business.
Management time	→ As a Theory Y manager delegates tasks to employees, they have more time to focus on other managerial duties. This can reduce workplace stress.
Low labour turnover	→ Workers remain in the business longer, thus reducing recruitment and training costs.
High-quality goods and services	→ Employees take pride in their work and act as intrapreneurs by suggesting ways to improve products or processes. This results in higher-quality goods and services for consumers.

Advantages and Limitations of McGregor's Theory X and Theory Y

McGregor's Theory X and Theory Y is used by many different organisations to motivate people. The advantages and limitations include the following.

✓ Advantages	✗ Limitations
1 Employee Motivation Theory Y recognises that employees work better when trusted with responsibility. This increases motivation levels among staff.	**1 Unrealistic** It would be unusual for a manager to take a purely Theory X or Theory Y approach to management. Managers use aspects of both theories.
2 Recruitment and Selection Theory Y helps to create a positive work environment. This can help the business to attract high-quality employees and reduce labour turnover.	**2 High Staff Turnover** Employees tend to be unhappy when managers use a Theory X style of motivation. This can increase staff turnover, leading to higher recruitment costs for the business.
3 Improved Industrial Relations Regular communication between management and staff, as in Theory Y, helps to improve industrial relations in the business.	**3 Less Intrapreneurship** Employees are less likely to share ideas with managers that use a Theory X style of motivation e.g. suggesting product improvements. This can lead to lower-quality products for consumers.

Activity 7.4

Music and songs have always been known to motivate people. Listen to the following songs:
- 'Eye of the Tiger' (Survivor)
- 'Lose Yourself' (Eminem)
- 'We are the Champions' (Queen)

In pairs, write down **five** songs that help motivate you.

Compile a list of 10–15 songs from the whole class and create a motivational playlist for your class to use.

THE IMPORTANCE OF MOTIVATION

1 **Improved productivity:** Employees are more productive when they are motivated. As a result they produce better-quality products.

2 **Less staff turnover:** Employees remain in the business longer, so there is less staff turnover. This saves the business money on employee recruitment, selection and training.

DID YOU KNOW?

According to international recruitment agency Next Generation, 57% of employees say that a firm's reputation as a great place to work is the most important consideration when they are looking for a new job.

3 **Less absenteeism:** Motivated employees are absent from work less often. This reduces business disruption.

4 **Better business reputation:** High motivation among staff improves the business's reputation. This helps to attract high-quality employees to the firm.

5 **Less industrial relations conflict:** Employees have regular contact with management and are less likely to take industrial action.

Activity 7.5

In pairs, create a mind map summarising all aspects of motivation covered in this chapter. You could use an online tool such as Coggle or Canva.

KEY TERMS

Now you have completed this chapter, you should understand and be able to explain the following terms. In your copybook, write a definition of each term to build up your own glossary of terms.

- motivation
- Maslow's Hierarchy of Needs
- physiological needs
- safety needs

- social needs
- esteem needs
- self-actualisation needs
- McGregor's Theory X and Theory Y

PowerPoint Summary

EXAM-STYLE QUESTIONS

Ordinary Level

Section 1 – Short Questions (10 marks each)

1 Explain what is meant by the term *motivation*.
2 List the **five** levels of needs as identified by Maslow in his Hierarchy of Needs.
3 Copy the grid for McGregor's Theory X and Theory Y into your copybook and complete it.

Theory X	Theory Y
Theory X managers believe that:	Theory Y managers believe that:
(i) Most workers dislike work	(i)
(ii)	(ii)

4 Indicate whether each of these statements is true or false.

	Statements	True or False
A	The motivational Theory X and Theory Y was developed by Douglas McGregor.	
B	A safe, secure job is one of an employee's physiological needs.	
C	When staff are highly motivated they work harder in the business.	
D	According to Maslow's Hierarchy of Needs, self-actualisation is the first item that motivates each of us.	
E	Maslow's Hierarchy of Needs was based on the belief that when one set of needs is satisfied the next level of needs becomes the primary motivator.	

Section 2 – Long Questions

1 Describe Maslow's Hierarchy of Needs theory of motivation. **(15 marks)**
2 Explain McGregor's Theory X of motivation. **(15 marks)**
3 Describe **three** advantages of a manager using McGregor's Theory X and Theory Y to motivate employees. **(15 marks)**

Higher Level

Section 1 – Short Questions (10 marks each)

1 Define the term *motivation*.

2 Chart and label Maslow's Hierarchy of Needs.

3 (i) Complete the following sentence: 'Physiological needs' means _____.

   (ii) Name **two** other human needs Maslow identified in his Hierarchy of Needs.

4 Explain, with an example, what is meant by 'esteem needs' in Maslow's Hierarchy of Needs.

5 Outline the assumptions made about employees under McGregor's Theory Y theory of motivation.

6 Column 1 is a list of business terms about motivation. Column 2 is a list of possible explanations for these terms. Match the two lists in your copybook by writing your answers in the form *number = letter* (e.g. 1 = A).

Terms		Explanations	
1	Theory X and Theory Y	A	All employees' needs are arranged in a pyramid in order of their importance.
2	Motivation	B	A person's need to achieve their full potential and be the best at what they do.
3	Maslow's Hierarchy of Needs	C	The willingness of people to work hard to do a task and work to the best of their ability.
4	Self-actualisation	D	A theory that outlines the different attitudes managers can have towards staff.

Section 2 – Applied Business Question (80 marks)

O'Connell Dining

Patricia O'Connell is the owner of O'Connell Dining, a large restaurant in Galway city.

Patricia is responsible for the recruitment and selection of staff as well as their training and development. When staff members are trained as chefs, she offers them the opportunity to manage their own section in the kitchen such as starters or desserts. The chefs are given titles such as Executive Chef and Sous Chef. They are encouraged to develop new menus to increase the choice of meals for the growing number of customers. Several chefs have won quality awards in recent times. This played an important part in Patricia's ability to hire a head chef from a top Michelin-starred restaurant to join her team in Galway.

Patricia places emphasis on staff loyalty and rewards employees with regular bonuses and long-term contracts of employment. All the staff have remained in the business since they were first employed by the restaurant. Staff are paid per hour and all earn above the minimum wage. The business rarely experiences any industrial relations problems as staff can always talk to Patricia about any concerns that they have. She also has low absenteeism levels as employees are happy to come to work each day. This workplace culture is something that Patricia is very proud to have created.

Employees are treated well; they receive ongoing training and the firm has a rewards programme for innovative new ideas that help to increase business sales or reduce costs. Patricia knows that when her staff are highly motivated, she can concentrate on other areas of the business such as meeting with suppliers and producers.

Patricia understands the importance of creating a sense of community at the company. She organises events for staff to share and develop new dishes for each other. These events are fun and enjoyable. Staff have the opportunity to learn together while at the same time feeling part of one big happy family rather than just employees.

Patricia is now considering expanding her business further by establishing a chain of restaurants and even hotels. She has promoted one of her key personnel to the role of project manager and is searching for a suitable premises for their first restaurant outside Galway.

A Outline the advantages of motivating staff in a business such as O'Connell Dining. **(25 marks)**

B Does Patricia use McGregor's Theory X or Theory Y approach to motivate her staff? Outline the implications this has for the restaurant. Refer to the text in your answer. **(25 marks)**

C Illustrate how Patricia uses Maslow's Hierarchy of Needs to motivate her staff. **(30 marks)**

Section 3 – Long Questions

1 Analyse the implications for a business of a manager adopting a Theory X approach to managing. **(20 marks)**

2 Evaluate the motivational theories of Maslow and McGregor. **(25 marks)**

3 Contrast how a Theory X manager would motivate staff with a manager who uses the Theory Y approach to managing a business. **(20 marks)**

PREVIOUS LEAVING CERTIFICATE EXAM QUESTIONS

Ordinary Level

Section A – Short Questions (10 marks each)

1 Explain **two** benefits to a business of having highly motivated employees. **[LC OL 2014]**

2 Name levels 3, 4, 5 in Maslow's Hierarchy of Needs. **[LC OL 2013]**

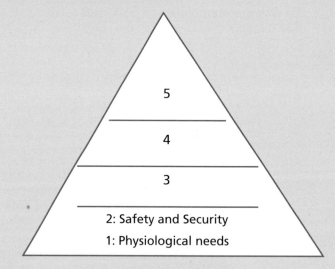

5

4

3

2: Safety and Security

1: Physiological needs

3 Explain the following needs in Maslow's Hierarchy of Needs.
   (i)   Basic needs
   (ii) Safety/Security needs

   [LC OL 2010]

Section B

1 (i) Identify the needs numbered 1 to 5 from the following list:
Social needs; Basic/Physical needs; Self-Actualisation needs; Esteem needs; Security/Safety needs.
Write your answers as follows:

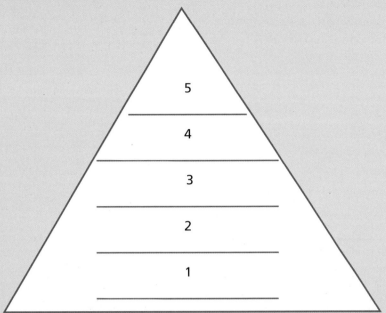

(ii) Outline using examples how a manager can satisfy the social needs of his/her employees.

(20 marks) [LC OL 2018]

2

> The Shareholders and Managing Director fulfil important roles in a company. Leadership and motivation are two management skills. Technology and modern developments in technology have changed the role of management.

Describe **one** of the following theories of motivation:

(i) Maslow's Hierarchy of Needs *or*

(ii) McGregor's Theory X and Theory Y.

(15 marks) [LC OL 2007]

Higher Level

Section A – Short Questions (10 marks each)

1 Maslow identified, in his hierarchical model, 'Self-actualisation' as a human need.
   (i) Self-actualisation means …
   (ii) Name **two** other human needs he also identified. **[LC HL 2007]**
2 Outline **two** possible implications for a business if a manager adopts McGregor's Theory X approach to managing. **[LC HL 2013]**

Section B

1 (i) Explain the 'Hierarchy of Needs' developed by Maslow in his theory of motivation.
   (ii) Discuss possible limitations to this theory. **(25 marks) [LC HL 2018]**
2 (i) Explain Maslow's theory of motivation.
   (ii) Illustrate how a manager could motivate workers by applying Maslow's theory in the workplace. **(20 marks) [LC HL 2011]**
3 Read the information supplied and answer the question which follows.

> 3 Dimension Ltd offers competitive salaries to its employees and a benefits programme that includes healthcare insurance. It is committed to providing a safe and healthy work environment. It holds weekly team meetings, enhancing workers' sense of belonging. It recognises and rewards staff achievement and provides opportunities for staff to develop new skills and experience new challenges.

Outline the different stages in Maslow's Hierarchy of Needs **and** illustrate how 3 Dimension Ltd applies this theory to motivate its employees. **(20 marks) [LC HL 2014]**
4 Analyse the implications for a business of a manager adopting a Theory X approach to managing. **(20 marks) [LC HL 2009]**

 Solutions

8 MANAGEMENT SKILLS 3: COMMUNICATING

Learning Outcomes

When you have completed this chapter, you will be able to:

1 Explain the role of communication in business and management
2 Describe the principles of effective communication
3 Distinguish between verbal, written and visual communication
4 Describe the different methods of communication
5 Draft a notice, agenda and minutes of a meeting
6 Describe the duties and characteristics of a chairperson and secretary at meetings
7 Present business data in the form of a memo, letter and report
8 Draft a visual presentation from given data
9 Identify and explain the main barriers to effective communication
10 Discuss the importance of communication skills.

Literacy Link

Communication, verbal, written, visual, meeting, notice, agenda, minutes, chairperson, secretary, quorum, memo, report

Numeracy Link

Percentages, statistics, charts

Cross-curricular Link

Accounting – preparing data, creating reports
Geography – sketch maps
Languages – verbal, written and visual communication
Maths – representing data in the form of graphs and charts

CASE STUDY

Communication at Tesla Inc.

Elon Musk is the founder and CEO of Tesla Inc., an American company that manufactures electric vehicles. He is a charismatic leader and uses his excellent **communication skills** to interact with stakeholders.

Musk uses **internal communication** to convey messages to employees. He regularly sends **emails** to all staff emphasising what the employees need to do to make the firm a success. He also insists that communication should travel along the shortest path, i.e. employees do not have to follow the **chain of command**. He has warned that managers who try to enforce a chain of command unnecessarily will be fired.

He has also written open **letters** to staff regarding **meetings** at the firm.

He has told staff to:

- Stop organising large meetings and frequent meetings unless they are useful to the employees
- Walk out of meetings if they don't add value to their work.

Tesla Inc. also uses **external communication** to communicate with **stakeholders** such as **consumers** and **investors**. Elon publish a quarterly **report** on the firm's website, www.tesla.com. These reports describe the cash flow, demand for products and future projections.

The company **chairperson** and **secretary** are responsible for sending out the **notice** and **agenda** to shareholders informing them of the Tesla Inc. **annual general meeting (AGM)**. During his AGM presentation, Musk uses a combination of **verbal**, **written** and **visual communication** to interact with shareholders. He uses detailed **graphs** and **charts** to highlight key information relating to sales and profits as well as future plans for the firm.

Elon Musk understands the importance of good communication and the power it has to positively impact Tesla Inc.

COMMUNICATION

In Chapters 6 and 7 we examined the management skills of leading and motivating. In this chapter we will examine in detail the management skill of communication.

Definition: Communication

The exchange of information between two or more parties. The sender of the information takes an idea and uses a combination of words, images and/or sound to turn it into a message. The message is then transmitted to the receiver using a medium such as email or telephone. The receiver processes the message and then takes action.

DID YOU KNOW? *Managers spend up to 75% of their time in the workplace communicating.*

Communication can be formal or informal. **Formal communication** is planned and is carried out through formal channels of communication, e.g. a job advertisement placed on a staff noticeboard by the human resources manager.

In **informal communication**, information is passed through an informal network within the organisation. This is often referred to as the grapevine.

Definition: Grapevine

Informal conversations which take place between people in an organisation, e.g. during breaks or at social events.

Internal and External Communication

Two types of communication can take place in an organisation:

1 Internal communication
2 External communication.

1 Internal Communication

This occurs between two or more people within an organisation, e.g. between management and employees. Examples of methods of internal communication include:

- Email
- Intercom
- Memos
- Staff notice board
- Meetings
- Intranet

Internal communication can take place in the following ways:

- **Upward communication:** Employees report up the chain of command, e.g. the marketing assistant reports to the marketing manager. Upward communication can include requesting information or offering suggestions.

- **Downward communication:** Information is sent down the chain of command, e.g. from the finance manager to an accountant. Management may give instructions or provide or request information.

Definition: Chain of command
The path of authority along which instructions are passed – from top management down to subordinates.

- **Horizontal (lateral) communication:** Communication between people at the same level in the organisation, e.g. between the sales manager and production manager.

2 External Communication

This communication takes place between the business and external stakeholders such as investors, consumers and suppliers. External methods of communication include:

- Email
- Video conferencing
- Telephone
- Letter
- Report
- Website
- Presentations

PRINCIPLES OF EFFECTIVE COMMUNICATION

To ensure that a message is effectively communicated to the receiver, communication should meet the following principles:

1. **Accuracy:** All the facts in the message should be accurate and the sender should have up-to-date knowledge on the topic.

2. **Appropriate language:** The language used should not be too technical or too difficult for the receiver to understand. The sender should avoid using unnecessary jargon and use short clear sentences.

Definition: Jargon
Words or phrases used by a profession or group of people that can be difficult for others to understand, e.g. many medical or legal terms would not be understood by the general public.

3. **Preparation:** Before communication takes place, the sender needs to research the audience to judge the tone and content of the message to be sent, e.g. education levels, experience.

4. **Confidentiality:** The method chosen should reflect the confidentiality of the content of the message. Sensitive information such as sales data should be communicated face to face, e.g. in a meeting.

5. **Feedback:** A feedback mechanism should be a feature in all methods of communication. It gives the receiver the opportunity to seek clarification and reduces the likelihood of misunderstandings.

Methods of Communication

The forms of communication used by organisations include:

- Verbal
- Written
- Visual.

The methods or media of these types of communication include the following:

Verbal Communication	Written Communication	Visual Communication
→ Telephone calls	→ Email	→ Bar chart
→ Meetings	→ Memo	→ Pie chart
→ Video conferencing	→ Letter	→ Line graph
→ Intercom	→ Report	→ Pictogram
→ Face-to-face conversations	→ Social media, e.g. Twitter	→ Break-even chart
→ Presentations	→ Business website	→ Business website

Activity 8.1

Individually, write down the different ways you have communicated today. In each case, what scenario were you in and why did you choose that method of communication? Compare your list with another student in your class. Which method of communication was most common?

THE ROLE OF COMMUNICATION IN BUSINESS AND MANAGEMENT

It is important that there is open and honest communication between the business and its stakeholders. This prevents misunderstandings and confusion and helps the business to run more efficiently.

Internal Communication

Managers	→ Managers should be able to communicate clearly with each other. This ensures that they have all the information needed to make decisions, which leads to better decision-making in the business.
Employees	→ Effective communication between management and staff ensures that staff understand their roles and responsibilities. This reduces confusion about tasks and staff are aware of the quality standards expected.

External Communication

Consumers	→ It is important that the business communicates clearly to consumers about new product launches or improvements to existing products. This can help to increase consumer loyalty and boost the firm's sales and profits.
Investors	→ The business should provide investors with honest information about the firm's financial performance. This increases trust between the business and investors and may encourage investors to provide additional finance if needed in the future.
Government	→ The business communicates with government agencies when it applies for grants or attends workshops and seminars run by bodies such as the Local Enterprise Office or Enterprise Ireland.
Local Community	→ The business communicates with the local community when it sponsors local events or clubs. It may also involve the local community in decisions regarding expansion, e.g. to limit the negative impact business expansion will have on the local area.
Suppliers	→ The business communicates regularly with suppliers to ensure that it has the correct quantity of raw materials needed at the appropriate time. This reduces the possibility of disruption to production schedules.

VERBAL COMMUNICATION

Verbal communication is part of our everyday lives; we regularly meet with others and speak face to face or speak on the phone.

Definition: Verbal communication
The exchange of information and ideas in speech, e.g. asking and responding to questions and giving instructions.

Verbal communication has a number of advantages and disadvantages, including:

✓ Advantages	✗ Disadvantages
1 Fast Communication It is the fastest form of communication as feedback can be instant.	**1 No Record** There is no record or proof that the communication took place.
2 Repeat the Message The receiver can ask the sender to repeat the message. This prevents misunderstanding or tasks being completed incorrectly.	**2 Not Listening** The receiver may not listen to the message, e.g. due to background noise or lack of concentration. They may miss important parts of the message.
3 Personal Connection It is a more personal form of communication as both tone of voice and facial expressions can be observed. It can help to create a connection with the listener.	**3 Lack of Preparation** If the sender of the message has not prepared in advance, the message may cause offence or confusion to the receiver.
4 Powerful Impact It is often a more powerful way of conveying a message, as tone and pitch can be used to emphasise important points.	**4 Message Length** It is not suitable for long messages, as the receiver may forget important information contained in the message.

Activity 8.2

Working in pairs, students sit back-to-back. One student chooses an image and describes it in words, while the other student attempts to draw this image based on the description given. Once the image has been described, the students compare the actual image with the drawing.
Did you experience any difficulties when completing this task? What would you do differently next time?

WRITTEN COMMUNICATION

Written communication involves using the written word to transfer information between people. Common types of written communication used in business include:

- Emails
- Memos
- Letters
- Reports
- Brochures
- Leaflets
- Social media
- Business documents, e.g. invoices, orders, quotations.

Unit 3

Written communication has a number of advantages and disadvantages, which include:

✓ Advantages	✗ Disadvantages
1 Record It is a permanent record that the communication took place. This could be useful if the information ever needs to be verified.	**1 Slow Feedback** Feedback is slower than with verbal communication, e.g. letters can take days or weeks to reach the receiver.
2 Reference Written material can be used as a reference. Information can be re-read if the reader needs to recall information.	**2 Security** There is a lack of confidentiality, as once something is written down, anyone can potentially read it, e.g. email hacking.
3 Speed Advances in IT have increased the speed of written communication, e.g. text message and email.	**3 Cost** The cost of paper, ink and printing equipment increases business costs.
4 Accurate People often have to take more time when preparing written communication. As a result, the message may be more accurate.	**4 Delayed Decision-making** As it is a slower method of communication, it can delay decision-making in the business until a response is received.

DID YOU KNOW? *The first written communication was used over 9,000 years ago.*

CASE STUDY — *Written Communication at Tesco*

A number of years ago, horse DNA was found in food products labelled as beef and pork in meat products in Ireland and thirteen other European countries. Consumers were concerned about food safety and traceability. Tesco had been selling beefburgers that actually contained 29% horsemeat. The company experienced a communication failure when the pre-scheduled tweet shown below was circulated as the media reported on the scandal:

> Tesco Customer Care @UKTesco
> It's sleepy time so we're off to hit the hay! See you at 8am for more #TescoTweets
>
> Tweet

The company deleted the tweet and apologised for the offence caused to consumers.

VISUAL COMMUNICATION

Visual communication involves using images, graphs, photos, maps and symbols to communicate messages. Visual methods are often used together with verbal or written communication to increase the impact of the message.

The advantages and disadvantages of visual communication include the following:

✓ Advantages	✗ Disadvantages
1 Easy to Understand It can help make large or complex pieces of information easier to understand, e.g. images can be used to replace text.	**1 Cost** Preparing information in visual format can be expensive and time-consuming, e.g. graphs and posters.
2 Easy to Recall It is often easier to remember information in the form of an image or chart.	**2 Cannot be Used Alone** Visual communication must be used in conjunction with written or verbal communication to ensure that the message is understood.
3 Presentation It can increase the impact of verbal or written communication, e.g. a bar chart can be used to show numerical information more clearly.	**3 Over-use** Over-use of visual communication can be distracting for the receiver of a message. They may miss out on key information contained in verbal or written communication.

We will examine the methods of visual communication in greater detail later in the chapter.

Ancient Egyptians used symbols called hieroglyphs over 5,200 years ago.

Activity 8.3

In pairs, write down ten scenarios where a business would have to communicate with stakeholders, e.g. the manager informing staff that there will be pay cuts to reduce business costs. Swap the ten scenarios with another pair of students, who must then identify the most appropriate method of communication to be used and explain their reasons for choosing this method.

MEETINGS

Meetings are used by organisations to exchange information. They can be informal or formal. An **informal** meeting is unplanned, often with no set agenda. At a **formal** meeting, the venue, time and agenda are known in advance.

> **Definition: Meeting**
> A gathering of at least two people to discuss a topic or topics with the purpose of making a decision on matters discussed.

Reasons for Holding a Meeting

- **Sharing information:** For example, sales targets are shared between management and staff.
- **Decision-making:** People with different skills and experience come together to make decisions to benefit the business.
- **Problem-solving:** People meet to brainstorm solutions to problems experienced by the organisation, e.g. declining market share.

Notice and Agenda

Before a meeting at a business or a club takes place, the secretary of the meeting sends out a notice and agenda.

> **Definition: Notice**
> An invitation for people to attend the meeting. It informs them of the date, time and venue.

> **Definition: Agenda**
> A list of items to be discussed at the meeting. Topics are listed in the order in which they will be discussed.

Unit 3

Notice and Agenda for a Company

Notice and Agenda for Fox Ltd

The Annual General Meeting of Fox Ltd will take place in the Wheel House Hotel, Bridgetown, Co. Leitrim at 3.30 p.m. on 6 March 2022. ← **Notice**

The agenda is as follows: ← **Agenda**

1 Minutes of the 2021 AGM

2 Matters arising from those minutes

3 Chairperson's report

4 Auditor's report

5 Dividend proposals for 2022

6 Election of new directors to the board of directors

7 AOB

Signed: *Richard Farrell*
  Richard Farrell
  Secretary

> **!**
> *Definition*: **Matters arising**
> The opportunity to discuss items arising from the previous meeting.

> **!**
> *Definition*: **AOB**
> AOB means 'any other business'. It gives people at a meeting the opportunity to bring up a topic they want to discuss that is not on the agenda.

Notice and Agenda for a Club

Notice and Agenda for Baldwinstown Hockey Club

The Annual General Meeting of the Baldwinstown Hockey Club will take place in the Clubhouse, Longridge Road, Co. Sligo at 8.30 p.m. on 3 January 2022. ← **Notice**

The agenda is as follows: ← **Agenda**

1 Minutes of the 2021 AGM

2 Matters arising from the minutes

3 Club chairperson's report

4 Club treasurer's report

5 Club subscriptions for 2022

6 AOB

Signed *Amy Kelly*
  Amy Kelly
  Secretary

Minutes

During the meeting the company or club secretary takes the minutes of the meeting.

> **!**
> *Definition*: **Minutes**
> A record of the meeting. They are taken by the secretary of the meeting and provide a summary of what was discussed, the people present and what decisions were made.

Minutes for the AGM of Fox Ltd

Minutes of the Annual General Meeting of Fox Ltd on 6 March 2022 were as follows:

1 The minutes of the 2021 AGM were read and approved.

2 There were no matters arising from the minutes.

3 The chairperson addressed the meeting and stated that there had been a 10% increase in sales this year. This was due to the firm expanding to new European markets.

4 The company's auditors, Parle & Wall, stated that the accounts give a true and fair view of the financial position of the firm.

5 The dividend for 2022 would be €0.15 per share.

6 Ann Delaney and John Keville were elected to the board of directors unopposed.

7 As there was no other business the chairperson closed the meeting at 5.30 p.m.

Signed: *Richard Farrell*
Richard Farrell, Secretary

Minutes for the AGM of Baldwinstown Hockey Club

Minutes of the Annual General Meeting of Baldwinstown Hockey Club on 3 January 2022 were as follows:

1 The minutes of the 2021 meeting were read and approved.

2 There were no matters arising from the minutes.

3 The chairperson addressed the meeting and stated that the year had been very successful for the club. Membership had increased by 5% and the U-16s had won the league competition.

4 The treasurer reported on the financial affairs of the club. The club has fully repaid the loan used to build the new club changing rooms.

5 The meeting voted by 10 votes to 4 to increase the club subscription for 2022 to €380 per year.

6 Since there was no other business, the chairperson closed the meeting at 10.30 p.m.

Signed *Amy Kelly*
Amy Kelly, Secretary

Note!

AGMs are formal meetings. The minutes of the AGM of a business or club would be more detailed than those described in these examples.

Key People Involved in Meetings

There are two key people involved in organising and running a meeting. These are the chairperson and the secretary.

1 Chairperson

A chairperson is responsible for opening, running and closing a meeting. The chairperson is elected by the attendees of a meeting, e.g. shareholders at a business AGM.

Role of the Chairperson

Notice and Agenda	→ The chairperson works with the secretary to draw up the notice and agenda for a meeting.
Opens the Meeting	→ The chairperson welcomes all present and begins the meeting by counting the quorum. If the quorum is present, the meeting continues.
Runs the Meeting	→ The chairperson ensures that the agenda is followed and that the standing orders are obeyed. The time given to each person to speak is monitored to ensure that a small number of individuals do not dominate the meeting.
Calls for Votes	→ The chairperson calls for votes on motions (topics that are discussed during the meeting). The chairperson has the casting (deciding) vote in the event of a tied vote.
Closes the Meeting	→ At the end of discussions, the chairperson closes the meeting.

Unit 3

> **Definitions:**
>
> **Quorum** – the minimum number of people who need to be present for the meeting to begin. If the quorum is not reached, the meeting is postponed. Having a quorum prevents a small number of people making decisions that affect the entire business or club.
>
> **Standing orders** – the rules for running a meeting, e.g. each person has no more than five minutes to speak.
>
> **Point of order** – when an attendee draws attention to the fact that a standing order has been broken.
>
> **Proxy** – a person who attends the meeting as a representative of a shareholder or club member who cannot attend. The proxy votes in accordance with the instructions given by the person who cannot attend.

A good chairperson should possess the following characteristics:

- **Unbiased:** They should be impartial and objective and not allow their own opinion to influence discussions at the meeting.
- **Knowledgeable:** They should know the standing orders. They should be able to refer to the rules of the meeting if any issues arise during the meeting.
- **Good time management:** They should be good at managing time. This ensures that people are given adequate time to discuss matters but individuals are not allowed to dominate the discussion.
- **Good communicator:** They should speak clearly to ensure that all attendees can hear and understand what they say during the meeting. This helps to prevent misunderstandings at the meeting.

2 Secretary

The secretary is responsible for organising the meeting, i.e. the administrative aspects of the meeting.

Role of the Secretary

Arranges the Venue	→ Organises the venue and facilities, e.g. books the room, organises refreshments and stationery.
Notice and Agenda	→ Sends the notice and agenda to attendees entitled to attend the meeting, e.g. shareholders for an AGM. The notice and agenda should be sent in adequate time to ensure that people can attend.
Minutes	→ Reads out the minutes from the previous meeting. Records the minutes during the current meeting.
Correspondence	→ Deals with the paperwork arising from the meeting, e.g. letters and emails from stakeholders.
Assists the Chairperson	→ If the chairperson needs help during the meeting, the secretary provides assistance, e.g. counting votes.

A good secretary should have the following characteristics:

- **Organised:** The secretary will need to be organised to ensure the notice and agenda are sent to people in advance of the meeting. The venue and facilities must also be booked in advance.
- **Discreet:** The secretary does not disclose sensitive information discussed at the meeting to members of the public.
- **Good at summarising:** The secretary will be able to take accurate notes at the meeting and summarise key points discussed.

Types of Meeting for a Private Limited Company

1 Annual General Meeting (AGM)

This is a meeting held once a year and is attended by the directors and shareholders of a limited company. At the AGM, the shareholders elect the board of directors and appoint the auditors. Shareholders are given the opportunity to ask the board of directors about the firm's policies.

> ### Note!
>
> *A company limited by shares (Ltd) is not required to hold an AGM, as long as it provides specific information to shareholders in written form. Shareholders return a signed document stating that they have received and approved the information.*

You will learn more about private limited companies in Chapter 24.

2 Extraordinary General Meeting (EGM)

This is a meeting of the board of directors and shareholders to discuss an urgent issue, such as a takeover bid, that cannot wait until the next AGM. This urgent matter is the only item discussed at this meeting.

3 Board Meeting

Board meetings are attended by the firm's board of directors and are usually held at regular intervals, e.g. once a month. They discuss the performance of the business and outline future plans for the firm.

4 Statutory Meeting

This meeting must be held once in the life of the company. It is the first meeting of the company and shareholders are informed about the business affairs of the firm.

5 Ad Hoc Meeting

This meeting takes place at short notice to discuss a matter that has arisen unexpectedly but needs to be resolved quickly.

6 General Meeting

These are meetings held on a regular basis between management and employees. Topics discussed can include: planning, sales forecasts and updates on the operation of the business.

CASE STUDY — Meetings at Amazon

Amazon founder Jeff Bezos has three simple rules for company meetings:

1 **Two pizzas** – the number of attendees can be no more than can be fed by two pizzas.

2 **No PowerPoint presentations** – attendees must prepare a detailed memo to be given to attendees at the meeting.

3 **Silence** – meetings begin with 30 minutes of silence as attendees read the memo. The attendees then discuss the matters outlined in the memo.

WRITTEN COMMUNICATION

Organisations use many forms of written communication, which can include:

1 Memos 2 Business letters 3 Reports.

1 Memos

A memo is used for internal communication in a business. It can be sent between employees at all levels of the organisation.

A typical memo would follow the layout below.

> **Definition: Memo**
> A short written message used by a business for internal communication. 'Memo' is an abbreviation of the word memorandum and is used primarily to remind people of items and events.

MEMO

To: All staff   **Date:**   18 October 2021
From: Managing Director   **Re:**   Password Security

Due to a suspected Internet security breach this morning, all staff must change their password to access the business network. This matter requires your urgent attention and co-operation.

Signed   Julie Duggan
              Managing Director

---

2 Business Letters

A business letter is a formal method of communication. It can be sent internally, e.g. from a manager to a subordinate. It can also be sent by the business to external stakeholders such as investors and suppliers. In modern businesses, many letters are sent by email.

Business letters are often used when:

- The content is important, e.g. the date of an appointment
- A written record is required, e.g. business negotiations
- Complex instructions need to be given.

Exam Tip!
In the exam, marks are awarded for the layout of a business letter.

The letter should be typed on official business stationery.

Reference numbers are used for filing purposes. They are used by both the sender and receiver.

The subject – what the letter is about.

The body of the letter usually contains at least three paragraphs:

1 Opening paragraph – what the letter is about
2 Middle paragraph(s) – detailed information
3 Closing paragraph – stating what should happen next.

The date the letter was sent.

The addressee – the person to whom the letter is sent.

Opening salutation to the person to whom the letter is addressed. If the person's name is unknown, 'Dear Sir/Madam' should be used.

Closing salutation. Formal ending to the letter : Yours sincerely if the salutation is the name of the person; Yours faithfully if the salutation is not a name.

Signature and title of person sending the letter on behalf of the business.

Power Ltd
23 High Street
Mooncoin
Co. Kilkenny
Tel: 053 3876453   Email: info@powerltd.ie

Your Ref: PLM
Our Ref: MOD TF/RH
Date: 16 August 2021

Ms Caroline Cullen
General Manager
The Castle Business Centre
Castle Street
Mooncoin
Co. Kilkenny

Conference Booking Confirmation

Dear Ms Cullen

Following our meeting on Friday 13 August, I would like to book a conference room for Monday 20–Wednesday 22 September 2021 inclusive.

Our business requires the room for a training programme on the General Data Protection Regulation (GDPR). We will also require refreshments and a light lunch to be provided. I have enclosed a schedule for the training days.

I would appreciate if you could confirm in writing that the booking has been accepted.

Yours sincerely

Michael O'Dwyer
Michael O'Dwyer
Managing Director
Power Ltd

Encl: Training schedule

Encl: any documents that are enclosed with the letter.

3 Reports

A report is a detailed document about a specific topic and is used for both internal and external communication.

A report can be written for a number of different reasons, including:

> **Definition: Report**
>
> A formal written document used to present data and information to the people who requested it to be written, e.g. a market analysis report for the sales manager.

1 **Information:** To provide information on a particular topic, e.g. a report on the financial performance of a business.
2 **Investigation:** To investigate the reason why an incident or accident occurred, e.g. a report on the cause of a fire in a warehouse owned by the business.
3 **Solution:** To find the best way to overcome an issue, e.g. a report on how a business can improve Internet security.
4 **Impact of a decision:** To assess the impact that a decision may have on the business, e.g. a report on the impact on company profits if the government increases corporation tax rates.
5 **Convince readers:** To convince readers of the report to act in a particular way, e.g. a report on the environmental damage caused by plastic might convince a restaurant to use paper straws instead of plastic ones.

Haworth Enterprises Ltd is considering opening a new canteen to offer hot meals to staff. The board of directors has hired a business consultant to investigate whether this would be a viable option.

Unit 3

The reason for compiling the report. It details who commissioned the report and who wrote the report.

A brief outline of the main findings and conclusion of the report.

This is the main body of the report. It sets out the results of any investigations.

Appendices contain the sources of information used to compile the report. The bibliography lists the works referred to by the author while compiling the report, e.g. books and articles.

REPORT

Title: Feasibility of introducing a hot meal canteen for Haworth Enterprises Ltd

To: Board of Directors, Hawarth Enterprises Ltd, New Street, Midleton, Co. Cork

From: AB Consultants, Rathangan, Co. Kildare

Date: 25 April 2021

Table of Contents

Executive Summary

The business should proceed with the introduction of a hot meal canteen for staff.

Predicted profits are €600 per day.

Terms of Reference

The purpose of this report is to investigate the viability of the introduction of a hot meal canteen in your business.

Findings

We surveyed 600 employees and our main findings are:

1 400 employees would be willing to purchase a hot meal at least three days per week.

2 On average 300 employees would purchase a meal every day.

3 The preferred meal choices are:

    (a) chicken with salad or jacket potato (360 staff)

    (b) chicken or beef curry with rice (150 staff)

    (c) a vegetarian dish (90 staff)

The business would make a daily profit of €600 based on 300 employees buying a hot meal every day.

Conclusion and Recommendations

We conclude that the business should proceed with this venture.

We recommend that the canteen be opened by January 2022.

Appendix and Bibliography

This lists the main sections of the report and relevant page numbers.

Sets out the purpose of the report. The terms of reference give the report writer the authority to prepare the report and set guidelines to be followed, e.g. the problem to be addressed and recommendations to be made.

A statement by the author of the report on the course of action that should be taken.

VISUAL COMMUNICATION

Earlier in this chapter, we briefly examined methods of visual communication. We also learned about the advantages and disadvantages of using visual communication in an organisation. We will now examine methods of visual communication in more detail.

Look at the findings in the report on the previous page. We could present the numerical information relating to the market research using visual communication to enhance the report. This can make it easier for the reader to understand and analyse the data.

Charts must be clearly labelled, with a heading, axis labels and a legend explaining colours and so on.

Bar Chart

Used to compare different categories of items, e.g. the different meal types.

No. of employees

400
350 — 360
300
250
200
150 — 150
100
50 — 90
0

| Chicken with salad or jacket potato | Chicken or beef curry with rice | Vegetarian dish |

Meal types

Pie Chart

This chart can also be used to compare different categories.

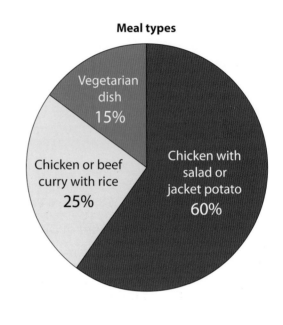

Meal types

- Chicken with salad or jacket potato 60%
- Chicken or beef curry with rice 25%
- Vegetarian dish 15%

Pictogram

Pictures are used to represent the different categories. For example, one picture represents 30 meals.

No. of meals preferred

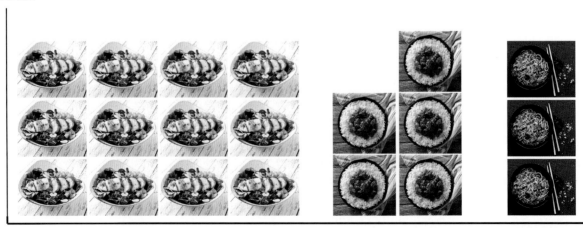

| Chicken with salad or jacket potato | Chicken or beef curry with rice | Vegetarian dish |

Meal types

Line Graph (Time Trend Graph)

This is used to show changes or patterns over a period of time, e.g. temperatures over the months or monthly sales.

Let's assume the following data was available for meals bought Monday–Friday.

Hot meals bought per day				
Monday	Tuesday	Wednesday	Thursday	Friday
280	350	90	250	530

This data could be shown on a line/trend graph as follows:

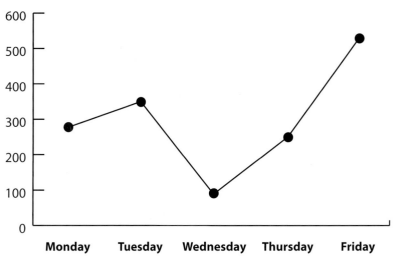

Hot meals bought per day

Gantt Chart

These are often used in project management, as they are useful for showing individual tasks and their completion against time.

New Canteen Construction

Tasks: Task F, Task E, Task D, Task C, Task B, Task A

28/04/22   14/11/22   01/06/23   18/12/23   05/07/24

■ Days Completed □ Break ■ Days Remaining

Maps

These are used to illustrate the physical location of a business premises. They are often used on an organisation's website to enable suppliers and consumers to find its location easily. The maps can be interactive and include information on transport links and other amenities in the area.

Organisation Charts
You will learn more about these charts in Chapter 11.

Break-even Charts
We shall study these charts in more detail in Chapter 19.

Unit 3

CHOOSING A METHOD OF COMMUNICATION

A manager must consider several factors when selecting the most effective method of communication to be used in the business. These include:

1 **Cost:** The manager must choose a communication method that brings the most value to the firm at the lowest price. Communicating by email is relatively cheap whereas face-to-face meetings that require the managers to travel to a venue can be more expensive.

2 **Message content:** The content of the message needs to be taken into consideration. If the content is detailed or technical, the message should be in writing with visual aids, e.g. a financial report with graphs and charts.

3 **Urgency:** A message that needs to be communicated urgently should be sent using the fastest means, e.g. an email or telephone call rather than a letter.

4 **Confidentiality:** Sensitive business information such as customer details should be kept confidential. This type of information may need to be communicated by email using encryption software to prevent the data being hacked or stolen.

5 **Record:** It is important to keep a record of certain communications, e.g. business negotiations. A written record should be kept as it may be used at a later date to prove that the communication took place.

BARRIERS TO EFFECTIVE COMMUNICATION

Effective communication is essential for running any type of organisation. If communications break down it can have serious consequences for the organisation.

Even if a manager has good communication skills, there are factors that can lead to a breakdown in the communication process. A manager must be able to identify the barriers to communication and find ways to overcome them to ensure that messages are delivered and understood.

> **Definition: Barrier to communication**
> Something or someone that stops a message reaching the intended audience.

	Barrier to Communication	Methods to Overcome Barrier
Timing	→ The sender may not give the receiver sufficient time to process and respond to the message.	→ The sender should not expect immediate feedback. The receiver should be given enough time to reply to the message.
Language	→ The sender may use jargon which is not understood by the receiver. The receiver may take incorrect action, e.g. not completing a task and missing a deadline.	→ Use simple language that can be understood by the receiver.
Information Overload	→ If there is too much information in the message, the receiver can become overwhelmed and the main points can be lost.	→ Keep the information concise and relevant.
Not Listening	→ People may not listen to the sender of the message, e.g. due to background noise or being preoccupied with other thoughts.	→ Summarise and repeat the message to ensure that it has been understood.
Lack of Trust	→ There may be a lack of trust between the sender and receiver of the message. The receiver may not believe some or all of the message.	→ Team-building training may be needed to strengthen relationships and build trust between employees.

ADVANTAGES OF EFFECTIVE COMMUNICATION

Effective communication between all stakeholders is essential in all organisations. Advantages of effective communication include:

1 **Productivity:** Employees know exactly what they have to do, which enables them to work faster. This increases productivity at the firm and reduces errors made.

2 **Industrial relations:** Effective communication ensures that there is no confusion over work standards between management and staff. Issues can be resolved quickly before they escalate into industrial relations problems.

3 **Customers:** Customers will have a more positive experience when doing business with the organisation. They are likely to share their positive experience with others, which will increase business sales.

4 **Improved decision-making:** Effective communication ensures that managers receive accurate information in clear language. This helps to improve decision-making in the organisation.

5 **Employee morale:** Effective communication means that employees receive clear instructions and are listened to by management. This increases staff morale and reduces stress levels.

KEY TERMS

Now you have completed this chapter, you should understand and be able to explain the following terms. In your copybook, write a definition of each term to build up your own glossary of terms.

- communication
- formal communication
- informal communication
- grapevine
- internal communication
- external communication
- upward communication
- downward communication
- horizontal communication
- principles of effective communication
- verbal communication
- written communication
- visual communication

- meetings
- notice
- agenda
- minutes
- chairperson
- secretary
- quorum
- standing orders
- point of order
- proxy
- AGM (annual general meeting)
- EGM (extraordinary general meeting)
- board meeting

- statutory meeting
- ad hoc meeting
- memo
- business letter
- report
- terms of reference
- bar chart
- pie chart
- pictogram
- line graph
- Gantt chart
- map
- barrier to communication

 **PowerPoint Summary**

121

EXAM-STYLE QUESTIONS

Ordinary Level

Section 1 – Short Questions (10 marks each)

1 Explain the term *communication*. List the methods of communication used by a business.
2 List **three** types of (i) verbal communication and (ii) written communication used in an organisation.
3 Name the key people involved in running a meeting. Outline **one** duty of each person.
4 What is meant by the term *Notice and Agenda* of a meeting?
5 Explain what is meant by the term *quorum*.
6 Outline **two** characteristics of a chairperson involved in running a meeting.
7 What do the following initials stand for? (i) AGM (ii) EGM.
8 Draft a memorandum (memo), using an appropriate format, from Catherine Higgins, managing director, reminding all staff that a meeting will take place on Tuesday 8 April at 10.30 a.m. in meeting room 102.
9 Draw a bar chart to illustrate the following information. Dimensions Ltd has recently reported its sales for the month for its top-selling clothes.

Small:	50	units
Medium:	120	units
Large:	80	units
XL:	25	units
XXL:	15	units

10 Draw a line graph to represent the following information. McConnell Motors published its car sales for the first six months of the year:

January	120	cars
February	90	cars
March	100	cars
April	75	cars
May	50	cars
June	2	cars

Section 2 – Long Questions

1 Describe **three** principles of effective communication. **(15 marks)**
2 List **three** methods of verbal communication in a business. Describe **two** advantages of verbal communication. **(20 marks)**
3 The Clonmore Dramatic Society are to hold their AGM next month.
  (i) Draft a suitable notice and agenda for this meeting. The agenda should have at least **five** items. Make relevant assumptions in your answer. **(15 marks)**
  (ii) Draft the minutes of the meeting of the Clonmore Dramatic Society. Make relevant assumptions in your answer. **(15 marks)**
4 Explain the terms (i) *quorum*, (ii) *ad hoc meeting* and (iii) *AOB* in relation to a business meeting. **(15 marks)**
5 Outline the role of (i) the chairperson and (ii) the secretary when organising and running a business meeting. **(20 marks)**
6 The managing director of Murphy Couriers wants to purchase a new delivery van from Hill Autos Ltd. Write a letter from Eamon Murphy, MD of Murphy Couriers, to Ray Doyle, sales director of Hill Autos Ltd, enquiring about the cost and delivery options for a new van. Write the letter using today's date and fictional addresses. **(25 marks)**
7 Describe the reasons why a report would be prepared. **(20 marks)**
8 Outline **four** barriers to effective communication. **(20 marks)**

Higher Level

Section 1 – Short Questions (10 marks each)

1 What is meant by the term *external communication*?

2 Describe **two** principles of effective communication.

3 Distinguish between upward, downward and horizontal communication.

4 Describe **one** advantage and **one** disadvantage of using visual communication.

5 Using an appropriate format, draft a memorandum (memo) from the CEO to all the managers informing them of an upcoming communications training day.

6 Explain the terms (i) *standing order* and (ii) *point of order* in relation to meetings.

7 Draft a bar chart from the following data:

Car Sales for 2022:

Audi	2,000	cars
BMW	1,500	cars
Citroën	500	cars
Mini	750	cars
Nissan	2,250	cars
Volkswagen	3,500	cars

8 List **five** barriers to effective communication.

Section 2 – Applied Business Question (80 marks)

Brideswell Industries Ltd

It is a very busy time of year for Temi Uduchukwu, owner of Brideswell Industries Ltd, with a product launch to plan and an AGM to organise. The firm has spent the last two years developing a new product for the engineering industry. Due to the top-secret nature of the product, Temi has organised a number of face-to-face meetings with potential investors. He knows that this is the fastest way to communicate all the information about his new invention.

Today Temi has organised a trial run of the presentation to investors with his sales team. He examines the promotional brochures for the product and is impressed with the bar charts and line graphs that make the technical and numerical information easy to understand. He knows that the investors will use these as reference after watching the investment pitches.

Temi is aware that a well-practised presentation helps to create a connection with the audience. He also wants to ensure that the team can answer every type of question posed by the potential investors. After listening to the presentation, Temi is unhappy with the fact that the sales team continues to use very technical information when describing the product. The team has already been informed that the investors come from different educational backgrounds and many will not understand the technical aspects of the product. Sometimes Temi wonders if his sales team listens to his instructions at all, as he has to repeatedly give the same instructions. He also thinks the team should include more images and charts to help the investors to recall important information.

Temi is relieved to see that the notice and agenda have been sent out for the firm's AGM, which will be held on 18 October at a local conference centre. Hopefully this will mean that a quorum will attend and the meeting will take place as planned. Last year's AGM wasn't successful as certain attendees spoke for longer than the agreed five minutes. Rules must be obeyed at this AGM and Temi is hopeful that the chairperson will strongly enforce them. There are lots of important matters to vote on, such as electing the new board of directors.

While these are busy times for Temi, he is delighted that his hard work and strong team have helped to build a successful business.

A Outline the principles of effective communication which guide communication at Brideswell Industries Ltd. **(20 marks)**

B Discuss the advantages of verbal, visual and written communication used by Brideswell Industries for its sales pitch to investors. **(30 marks)**

C Draft a report describing the duties of a chairperson and a secretary at the annual general meeting (AGM) of Brideswell Industries Ltd. **(30 marks)**

Section 3 – Long Questions

1 Managers spend most of their time communicating. Illustrate the factors that a manager should consider to ensure that they communicate effectively. **(25 marks)**

2 Evaluate the benefits of using written communication in business. **(20 marks)**

3 (i) Draft a bar chart or a line graph from the following information.

180 people were surveyed about their use of mobile phones. The results are shown below:

Phone calls	18
Text messaging	54
Internet	36
Social media	72

(ii) 'Visual communication helps to improve the communication of data.' Discuss this statement. **(20 marks)**

4 As the outgoing chairperson of your local football club, draft a letter to the incoming chairperson outlining their role as chairperson during the AGM. **(20 marks)**

5 Describe the duties and characteristics of a secretary at a meeting. **(25 marks)**

6 Discuss the reasons for formulating a report. **(20 marks)**

7 Draft a report to the chief executive officer (CEO) of a public limited company outlining the factors to be considered when choosing an appropriate method of communication. **(20 marks)**

8 Draft a letter to the managing director of a limited company explaining **four** main barriers to communications in a business. **(20 marks)**

PREVIOUS LEAVING CERTIFICATE EXAM QUESTIONS

Ordinary Level

Section A – Short Questions (10 marks each)

1 List **three** types of written communication that a business might use. **[LC OL 2016]**

2 The chart illustrates the projected sales of new cars for Maher Motors Ltd for the six-month period January to June 2017.

Projected Car Sales for Maher Motors Ltd from January to June 2017

(a) Name the method of visual communication presented above.

(b) (i) Identify the month with the highest projected sales.

(ii) Identify the projected number of cars that will be sold that month.

(c) Name **one** other method of visual communication. **[LC OL 2016]**

3 State whether the following are functions of the CHAIRPERSON or SECRETARY at an AGM. **[LC OL 2014]**

	Functions	Chairperson or Secretary
A	Opens and closes the AGM.	
B	Reads the minutes from the last AGM.	
C	Ensures the agenda is followed.	
D	Takes notes during the meeting and writes up the minutes after the meeting.	
E	Has the casting vote if a vote is tied.	

Section B

1

> Sport Trips Ireland Ltd intends to hold an Annual General Meeting (AGM) in the G Hotel, Co. Galway. The meeting will begin at 2 p.m. on the 30th September 2017. The company secretary Emma Butler is responsible for preparing the notice, the agenda and the minutes of this meeting.

(a) Explain the following terms:
   (i) the agenda of a meeting
   (ii) the minutes of a meeting.   **(15 marks)**

(b) Draft the Notice **and** Agenda for the AGM of Sport Trips Ireland Ltd. The Agenda must contain at least **five** items.   **(20 marks) [LC OL 2017]**

2

> Employment levels in the **hospitality sector** in Ireland:
>
> **2005:** 135,000   **2007:** 133,000   **2009:** 130,000   **2011:** 115,000   **2013:** 130,000
>
> The 2014 Budget retained the reduced 9% Value Added Tax (VAT) rate in the hospitality/tourism sector.

Construct a Line Graph to represent the above employment levels in the hospitality sector in Ireland.
                                                                    (15 marks) [LC OL 2014]

Higher Level

Section A – Short Questions (10 marks each)

1 The following sales information is taken from the books of the Grand Hotel.
   May 2004: Rooms €45,000 Bar €35,000 Restaurant €25,000 Functions €15,000
   May 2005: Rooms €60,000 Bar €40,000 Restaurant €30,000 Functions €95,000
   Illustrate this information in bar chart format.   **[LC HL 2005]**

2 (a) Distinguish between **two** types of meetings which are common in a business.
   (b) Outline **two** benefits of meetings as a method of communication.   **[LC HL 2011]**

3 Using today's date, draft a memorandum (memo) from Peter Murphy, Marketing Manager, to Mary O'Brien, Managing Director of a retail business outlining **two** different sales promotional incentives to encourage sales.   **[LC HL 2009]**

4 Draft a typical agenda for at the AGM of a Private Limited Company.   **[LC HL 2008]**

Section B

1

> Paul O'Brien is the Sales Manager with Water Solutions Ltd, a business which has recently developed a new water conservation product. Paul is due to make a presentation to the board of directors on the potential of this product. He will present the following projected sales data for the product for the next six months.
>
> | Month | July | August | September | October | November | December |
> |---|---|---|---|---|---|---|
> | Sales € | 50,000 | 60,000 | 40,000 | 30,000 | 20,000 | 10,000 |

(i) Illustrate the above data by means of a bar chart or a line graph.

(ii) Outline the principles Paul should consider to ensure he communicates his message effectively to the board of directors.   **(25 marks) [LC HL 2015]**

2 Distinguish between the duties of a chairperson and a secretary in the organising and running of an Annual General Meeting.   **(20 marks) [LC HL 2012]**

 Solutions

CHAPTER 9
INFORMATION AND COMMUNICATIONS TECHNOLOGY AND DATA PROTECTION

Learning Outcomes

When you have completed this chapter, you will be able to:

1. Identify the types of information and communications technology (ICT) used by organisations

2. Describe the advantages and disadvantages of the types of ICT used by organisations

3. Explain the benefits and risks associated with ICT

4. Explain the rights of data subjects under the General Data Protection Regulation (GDPR)

5. Explain the responsibilities of data controllers under the GDPR

6. Outline the functions of the Data Protection Commission.

Literacy Link

ICT, the Internet, email, cloud computing, video conferencing, spreadsheet, data protection, data subject, data controller, GDPR

Numeracy Link

Subtraction, multiplication, percentages

Cross-curricular Link

Computer Science – the Internet
Technology – ICT tools, using computers for research, using applications software

CASE STUDY

ICT and Data Protection at Amazon

Amazon was founded by Jeff Bezos in 1995. The firm initially sold books over the **Internet** but has since grown to become the largest online retailer in the world, now selling a variety of goods. Customers simply create an online account, search for products and place their order; they receive an order confirmation **email** and the products are shipped directly to their door.

While the firm is best known for Internet shopping, Amazon also owns a number of other businesses, including AWS and Amazon Chime. AWS provides **cloud computing** services to firms all over the world and is the market leader with over 30% of the market share.

Amazon Chime is a **video conferencing** service, which enables firms to hold HD-quality virtual meetings. The video conferencing technology can be controlled by Alexa. Users can use their voices to start meetings and control equipment.

With all these businesses, Amazon holds large volumes of data such as consumer names and addresses, as well as credit card details. The firm adheres strictly to the **General Data Protection Regulation (GDPR)**, a European Union regulation which was introduced across EU countries in May 2018. Amazon guards data by using firewalls, encryption software and passwords.

In 2017 Amazon acquired the supermarket chain Whole Food Markets for over €11 billion. The firm reported a security breach when **hackers** attempted to steal customer credit card details at the POS (points of sale) instore.

Amazon understands the importance of **social media** platforms as a means of connecting with customers. The firm has over 28 million followers on Facebook and 1.5 million followers on Instagram. It has recently entered into a deal with Snapchat whereby users can take a photo of a product on Snapchat and information from the

Amazon website appears, showing the user the price, the customer rating for the item and giving the option to purchase.

Constant innovation using **information and communications technology (ICT)** has made Jeff Bezos the richest person in the world with a wealth of over €95 billion.

PART 1: ICT AND BUSINESS

ICT is widely used in all types of businesses today. It is used in supermarkets with self-service scanning, and at airports where travellers print and scan their own boarding cards. Organisations are operating in a world where ICT is changing the way in which they do business.

The speed and amount of information that can be stored, transferred, accessed and manipulated is important in how organisations operate in the digital age.

> **Definition: Information and communications technology (ICT)**
> The use of computers and other electronic technology to **S**tore, **T**ransfer, **A**ccess and **M**anipulate (STAM) information.

> **Exam Tip!**
> *ICT is developing all the time, so keep up to date with technological advances by reading the technology sections in newspapers or online, e.g. www.bbc.com, www.independent.ie.*

Activity 9.1

In groups, brainstorm the types of ICT that are used in the home, school and local businesses. Swap your lists with other groups and see how many items you have in common.

Many forms of ICT are used in business. We will examine:

1 The Internet
2 Email
3 Electronic data interchange
4 Cloud computing
5 Video conferencing
6 Social media
7 Computer software applications.

1 The Internet

The Internet is a global network of computers that enables people to share and transfer data, text, pictures and videos instantly anywhere in the world. It is often referred to as the Net or the World Wide Web (www).

✓ Advantages	✗ Disadvantages
1 Fast Communication Access to information is instant and feedback can be given or received immediately. This enables businesses to make faster decisions and avoid missing out on business opportunities.	**1 Hacking** Cyber threats such as hacking occur when hackers find ways to access the firm's data illegally. The hackers may delete or steal confidential business information.
2 Reduce Costs The business can sell its products online through its own website. It does not need to set up shops around the world and employ staff. This reduces business costs.	**2 Fake News** It can be difficult to verify the accuracy of information. The business may make business decisions based on false information.

✓ Advantages *continued*	✗ Disadvantages *continued*
3 Improves Decision-making Managers can use search engines such as Google to access information, e.g. competitors, market share and suppliers. This enables work to be completed in different time zones without delay, improving business productivity.	**3 Cost** It is expensive to install the equipment needed to access the Internet, e.g. laptops and tablets. The business will also have to pay for maintenance and upgrades. Websites can be expensive to design and staff are needed to update and maintain them.
4 Advertising The business can promote its products to a worldwide audience, thus increasing consumer awareness of the brand. This can help to increase sales.	**4 Online Customer Reviews** Customers can leave negative reviews about the firm on online forums or websites. The comments might not even be true, but they can damage the firm's reputation.

CASE STUDY: PlayStation Hacked

The personal details of 77 million customers were stolen during a security breach of Sony's PlayStation Network. Hackers stole names and addresses as well as credit card numbers. Sony was forced to close the network for 20 days while they dealt with the problem, at a cost of approximately €145 million. The firm issued an apology to customers on its website and asked them to monitor their credit cards for fraudulent activity.

2 Email

Email is an abbreviation for electronic mail, which enables messages to be sent electronically around the world. A person must have an email account, e.g. Gmail, and an Internet connection to send an email. Emails can contain text, audio, pictures and video files.

✓ Advantages	✗ Disadvantages
1 Fast Decision-making Feedback from mail can be received instantly. This can help the business to get information and make faster decisions.	**1 Viruses** These are spread via email attachments and can damage the firm's computer system by deleting or damaging data.
2 Lower Cost The same message can be sent to many people located in different parts of the world. There are no stationery or postage costs, which reduces business costs.	**2 Incorrect Address** Emails can be sent to the incorrect address. Confidential information might be sent to the wrong organisation, which could be commercially damaging for the firm.
3 Accessibility Emails can be sent and received at any time of day, even when offices are closed. This can increase business productivity.	**3 Phishing** This is when a fake email, claiming to be from a legitimate business, is sent to a person with the purpose of scamming them for information, e.g. a bank account number. A business may lose money if it is a victim of phishing.
4 Record Emails can be stored to keep a record of information that was sent or received. This can be used as proof that the communication took place.	**4 Spam** Many emails may be unsolicited, i.e. junk mail. This can waste employees' time as they must filter the irrelevant emails.

Definition: Phishing
An attempt to illegally gain accesses to passwords and usernames for credit cards and bank accounts with the intention of stealing money.

Example
Computer virus I Love You was spread through email attachments in May 2000. Within ten days it had infected 10% of the world's networked computers. Businesses and governments were forced to close their email networks to protect their data. It caused over €6 billion-worth of damage worldwide.

Example
Italian football club S.S. Lazio received a fraudulent email from hackers. The email requested that the remaining instalment of a €2 million transfer fee be paid to an alternative bank account. S.S. Lazio complied with the request and later discovered that the money had been transferred to a false Dutch bank account.

DID YOU KNOW?
- Number of email accounts worldwide: 4.6 billion.
- 45% of email traffic is spam.
- 91% of us check our email daily.

3 Electronic Data Interchange (EDI)

EDI is computer-to-computer communication. It enables businesses to communicate information such as orders, invoices and payments electronically rather than using paper methods. The documents can be transferred without the need for human intervention.

For example, let's say that a supermarket has a minimum stock level of 1,000 units for tinned beans. When stock levels fall to 1,000 units, the EDI system automatically sends an order to the supplier to reorder the stock. All associated documents, such as invoices, payments and receipts, are sent through the EDI system and the tins of beans are automatically delivered to the supermarket.

✓ Advantages	✗ Disadvantages
1 Savings It is a cost-effective method of processing transactions. The cost of labour, office expenses and time are all reduced, as the EDI system does the work, with little or no intervention from employees.	**1 Cost** It is expensive to set up an EDI system due to the high cost of the hardware and software required. The system is also costly to maintain, e.g. requiring regular software updates.
2 Fewer Errors The scope for human error is reduced as the transactions are automated.	**2 Suitability** It is only cost-effective to install an EDI system for businesses that buy and sell in large volumes.
3 Speed The transactions are processed quickly, e.g. invoices are sent promptly once goods are delivered.	**3 Compatibility** Not all businesses use EDI, so the business will need to have alternative systems in place to deal with these suppliers, e.g. paper invoices.
4 Stock Control The business does not carry too much stock, thus reducing stock-holding costs, such as insurance and storage.	**4 Industrial Relations** Staff may be unhappy with the introduction of EDI, as it may replace employees. This can cause industrial relations problems in the firm.

4 Cloud Computing

This is the use of remote servers, hosted on the Internet, to store, manage and process data.

Cloud computing enables data to be accessed anywhere in the world at any time, as long as the user has the necessary passwords. The cloud can be accessed from devices such as laptops and smartphones. Examples include iCloud (Apple), Dropbox and Google Drive.

✓ Advantages	✗ Disadvantages
1 Inexpensive The operating and maintenance costs are lower than if the business installed its own server.	**1 Outages** As cloud computing is dependent on an Internet connection, outages may happen from time to time. This can reduce business productivity.
2 Global Access It is convenient for the business to be able to access data from anywhere at any time.	**2 Security** The information can be hacked. This could mean that confidential business information could be leaked to the public and to competitors.
3 Software Updates Software updates are carried out by the server, so the business does not have to employ staff to maintain the system.	**3 Cost** Although costs are reduced in terms of staff and hardware, there are ongoing costs, such as storage costs and service fees.
4 Data Security Cloud computing ensures that business data is backed up in the event of natural disasters or power failures. This reduces the likelihood of the firm losing important business information which can reduce business productivity.	**4 Lock-in** It may be difficult to change service providers, as cloud computing firms operate on different platforms.

5 Video Conferencing

This technology enables people in different locations to participate in a virtual face-to-face meetings. The equipment required includes a device such as a laptop or tablet together with a webcam, Internet connection and appropriate software. It allows attendees at a meeting to see and hear each other during the meeting. Examples of video conferencing products include Skype and Facetime.

✓ Advantages	✗ Disadvantages
1 Cost Savings The participants in a meeting do not have to travel to attend the meeting. This saves travel and accommodation costs as well as time.	**1 Cost** Installing and maintaining the equipment is expensive. Employees may also require training, which increases costs.
2 Speed Meetings can be organised quickly without requiring attendees to travel. This enables the business to make decisions more quickly.	**2 Technical Problems** A poor Internet connection can make it difficult to hear or see the other attendees. This can slow down decision-making at the meeting.
3 Regular Meetings Due to the cost savings, more regular meetings can be held, which improves communication at the firm.	**3 Time Zones** It does not overcome the problem of different time zones around the world. This can make scheduling meetings difficult.
4 Real Time Meetings can be conducted in real time even if the participants are in different locations.	**4 Personal Interaction** It is not a very personal form of face-to-face communication and it may take longer for meeting attendees to build up trust and a rapport.

6 Social Media

Social media consists of computer programs and websites that enable people to create and share content such as messages, images and videos around the world. Well-known social media platforms include Facebook, Instagram and Snapchat. These platforms can be accessed using computers and mobile devices such as smartphones and tablets.

✓ Advantages	✗ Disadvantages
1 Large Audience The business can promote its products to millions of potential customers around the world, e.g. Twitter has 328 million active users and Instagram has almost one billion active users each month.	**1 Brand Awareness** It is difficult to measure the effectiveness and monetary value of social media accounts. It may be more useful for the brand to spend money on traditional forms of advertising.
2 Low Cost It is a low-cost means of advertising, as many of the large social media accounts do not charge a sign-up fee.	**2 Negative Feedback** Users can post negative reviews about the business, even if they are untrue. This can damage the firm's reputation.
3 Customer Information It can be used to gather customer information, allowing for better business decisions, e.g. you can learn what consumers want from products based on the number of comments or likes on Facebook.	**3 Hacking** Social media platforms can be hacked and it can take a business a long time to build up followers again.
4 Consumer Loyalty It enables the business to create a personal relationship with consumers as they can interact with them in comment sections of social media. This can increase consumer loyalty.	**4 Time-intensive** It takes a lot of time and effort to maintain an interactive social media platform – monitoring the platform, responding to questions and feedback and posting updates.

Unit 3

Activity 9.2

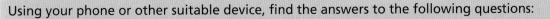

Using your phone or other suitable device, find the answers to the following questions:

1 Find the current number of users of (i) Facebook, (ii) Instagram and (iii) Snapchat.
2 How many tweets are sent on Twitter every day?
3 What is the average amount of time a person spends on social media each week?

CASE STUDY *Cadbury and Snapchat*

Cadbury wanted to raise awareness of Crunchie bars among the 16–24-year-old age range. It invested a significant amount of its marketing budget on Snapchat Lenses. Users who selected the Lens could see their face turned into a golden disco ball or with giant gold lips. The brand received 10 million views in the 16–24 target market for the Lens.

7 Computer Software Applications

Application	Explanation
Word Processing	→ Programs that produce typed documents such as business letters and reports using editing equipment, e.g. a laptop. Examples include MS Word and Apple Pages.
Spreadsheet	→ Programs that allow users to enter, calculate and store data in rows and columns. It can be used to prepare budgets and financial accounts. Examples of spreadsheet programs include MS Excel and Apple Numbers.
Database	→ An electronic filing system for organisations that enables them to store large volumes of information. This information can be easily accessed or updated. A database is often used together with EDI, e.g. preparing monthly statements for customers. Examples include MS Access.
Presentation Package	→ Programs that enable users to present information using text, sound, images and videos using a laptop and a digital projector. Examples include Apple Keynote and MS PowerPoint.
Desktop Publishing (DTP)	→ Programs that combine elements of word processing with graphics packages to enable the business to produce leaflets, brochures and newsletters. Examples include MS Publisher and Adobe InDesign.

Benefits and Challenges of ICT for Business

✓ Benefits	✗ Challenges
1 Faster Communication Information can be communicated more quickly, e.g. through email. This helps the business to make quick decisions.	**1 Security Issues** It can be difficult to keep electronic data safe, e.g. from hacking and computer viruses. Businesses should encrypt sensitive data and back up the data regularly.
2 Better Teamwork ICT such as video conferencing enables employees to work together on team projects. Combining expertise can result in better results for the firm.	**2 System Breakdown** Computers can break down and this can lead to a loss of productivity or loss of sales, e.g. when a website crashes.
3 Cost Savings ICT helps the business to reduce its costs, e.g. selling directly to customers online reduces the cost of renting shop space and employing staff.	**3 Cost** ICT systems are expensive to install and maintain. There are also training costs for employees.

✓ **Benefits** *continued*	✗ **Challenges** *continued*
4 Staff Morale ICT can make workplace tasks easier for employees. This improves staff morale and can increase productivity.	**4 Industrial Relations** Employees may fear for their job security when new technology such as EDI is introduced. This can result in industrial relations problems at the firm.
5 Improved Quality Computers are capable of producing consistently high-quality products. This improves the firm's reputation and reduces consumer complaints.	**5 Personal Touch** Some of the personal touch that customers like can be removed with the introduction of ICT, e.g. automated checkouts at supermarkets. Some people may prefer to shop where they can interact with humans rather than computers.

PART 2: DATA PROTECTION

General Data Protection Regulation (GDPR) 2018

Many organisations hold data on individuals, such as schools, doctors, banks and businesses. GDPR was introduced in May 2018. It is an EU-wide regulation that strengthens the rights of individuals and places more obligations in terms of data protection on organisations that hold data.

Unit 3

Activity 9.3

In pairs, make a list of the organisations that store data about you. What do these organisations do with your data? Where is the information stored? Share your lists with other students in the class.

Terms in the GDPR

Term	Explanation
Data Subject	→ The individual who the data is about.
Personal Data	→ Any information that relates to a data subject, e.g. name and address. The data can be stored in manual or computer files and can also include CCTV footage.
Data Controller	→ The person in a business who decides what data is collected and how it is processed.
Data Processor	→ Either the organisation or the person who processes data on behalf of the data controller.
Data Protection Commission (DPC)	→ The supervisory authority responsible for monitoring the application of the GDPR.

Rights of Data Subjects

All data subjects have rights under the GDPR, including:

 DID YOU KNOW? *Eighteen per cent of adults have had their personal information stolen.*

1 **Right of access:** The right to obtain details on why and how their data is being processed by an organisation.
2 **Copy of data:** The right to have a copy of the data held on them. This must be provided in electronic format within one month of the written request.
3 **Correction of data:** To have incorrect or incomplete data corrected.
4 **Erasure of data:** To have their data erased if the organisation has no legitimate reason to keep it.
5 **Complain to the Data Protection Commission:** Individuals who believe there has been a breach of the GDPR in the processing of their personal data can lodge a complaint with the DPC.

Responsibilities of Data Controllers

1 **Data collection:** Collect only data that is needed for their purposes.
2 **Provide copies:** Provide a copy of the requested data free of charge and within one month of a request from the data subject.
3 **Keep data secure:** Use encryption, back-up data and regularly review security measures.
4 **Report data breaches:** Notify the DPC of data breaches within 72 hours of a breach if the information could risk the rights and freedoms of data subjects.
5 **Appoint data protection officers (DPOs):** A DPO should be appointed in organisations that hold large volumes of personal data, e.g. hospitals and banks.

Functions of the DPC

1 **Monitors and enforces GDPR:** Order data controllers to provide information to the data subject when requested. It can also force a data controller to delete incorrect information held on the data subject.

> **Useful link:**
>
> *www.dataprotection.ie*

2 **Promotes public awareness of GDPR:** Informs the public about their rights under the GDPR through its website and publishes materials such as guidelines and infographics.
3 **Prohibits data transfer:** Stop the transfer of data outside Ireland in certain circumstances.
4 **Impose fines:** Impose fines of up to €20 million or 4% of annual turnover, whichever is larger, for very serious breaches of the GDPR.
5 **Data audits:** Investigates the processes used by data processors and controllers. It can enter a firm's premises, speak to relevant staff and inspect and copy information.

CASE STUDY

Crypto-ransomware at Primary School

The Data Protection Commission was informed that a primary school had been the victim of a crypto-ransomware attack. A hacker had encrypted one-third of the school's data and the school was unable to access it. The data contained personal details such as names, dates of birth and Personal Public Service Numbers (PPSNs). The hackers demanded a payment be made to release the data.

Data breaches must be reported to the Data Protection Commission and it found that the school was seriously deficient in terms of protecting their pupils' data. It did not fine the school but issued recommendations for the school to follow, including improving staff training about the risks associated with the use of personal USB keys and email.

KEY TERMS

Now you have completed this chapter, you should understand and be able to explain the following terms. In your copybook, write a definition of each term to build up your own glossary of terms.

- ICT
- Internet
- World Wide Web (www)
- hacking
- email
- computer virus
- phishing
- electronic data interchange (EDI)

- cloud computing
- video conferencing
- social media
- word processing
- spreadsheet
- database
- presentation package
- desktop publishing (DTP)

- GDPR (2018)
- data subject
- data controller
- data processor
- data protection officer (DPO)
- Data Protection Commission (DPC)

 PowerPoint Summary

EXAM-STYLE QUESTIONS

Ordinary Level

Section 1 – Short Questions (10 marks each)

1 What do the following letters stand for? (i) ICT (ii) EDI (iii) DTP.
2 Define the term *email*. List **two** advantages of using email as a method of communication.
3 What is video conferencing?
4 Draft a memorandum (memo) using an appropriate format to all staff outlining **two** advantages of using social media as a form of communication. Use today's date.
5 What is a spreadsheet?
6 List **three** ways in which ICT can benefit a business when communicating with its various stakeholders.
7 What does GDPR stand for?
8 Outline the difference between a data subject and a data controller.

Section 2 – Long Questions

1 Discuss the drawbacks to a business using the Internet. **(15 marks)**
2 State **two** advantages of video conferencing as a method of communication. **(15 marks)**
3 Explain the term *cloud computing*. **(15 marks)**
4 Organisations use <u>databases</u>, <u>presentation packages</u> and <u>desktop publishing</u> as part of their ICT strategy. Describe the **three** underlined terms. **(15 marks)**
5 Outline **two** benefits and **two** challenges of ICT to business. **(20 marks)**
6 Data controllers must have in-depth knowledge of the following terms: <u>data subject</u>, <u>data processer</u> and <u>Data Protection Commission</u>. Describe the **three** underlined terms. **(20 marks)**
7 Draft a letter to your doctor requesting a copy of all the data they hold about you. In your letter refer to your rights under the General Data Protection Regulation (2018). **(20 marks)**
8 Outline the main responsibilities of a data controller. **(20 marks)**

Higher Level

Section 1 – Short Questions (10 marks each)

1 Define the term *ICT*. List **three** methods of ICT used in business.
2 Distinguish between a computer virus and spam.
3 Outline **one** advantage and **one** disadvantage that using cloud computing brings to a business.
4 What is EDI? How does it work?
5 Distinguish between word processing and spreadsheets.
6 Outline **two** rights of data subjects.
7 Explain **two** responsibilities of data controllers.
8 Explain **two** functions of the Data Protection Commission.

Unit 3

Section 2 – Applied Business Question (80 marks)

Party2Go

Richard Cleary owns Party2Go, an online store for consumers to buy all they need for parties, such as costumes, balloons and decorations.

A number of years ago, Richard considered opening physical stores in Dublin and London, but the high cost of rent and recruiting employees made him reconsider this option. Now he is pleased to see that consumers all over the world order his products.

Richard has just received a call from his IT department detailing a security breach on the firm's website. The IT department suspect that a hacking attempt was made, with the hackers attempting to steal customer names and bank details. Richard is relieved that the firm invested heavily in firewalls and encryption software to protect consumer data.

While viewing the company website, Richard is disappointed to see that there have been a number of negative reviews about the quality of some party costumes. He intends typing a letter to the supplier to arrange a meeting to resolve the issue. Richard also spends some time researching new suppliers, as he always wants his online store to have the most up-to-date products.

Richard then spends time preparing for an important investor presentation next week. He emails the finance manager requesting an updated spreadsheet of the firm's sales and profits, so that he can include it in his presentation. He also needs to prepare a company newsletter for staff to update them on the progress of the firm.

While checking though his daily post, Richard opens a letter from a supplier requesting a copy of the data held by Party2Go on their firm. Richard logs on to the supplier's account and is worried when he sees that Party2Go has kept the supplier's credit card details even though they have not purchased from this supplier in over two years. Richard knows that under the GDPR, the Data Protection Commission has strong powers and he wonders if his own company policy is up to date. He plans to use the services of a GDPR expert to ensure that the firm is compliant with all the legislation.

A Outline the advantages and disadvantages of the Internet for a business such as Party2Go. **(25 marks)**

B Describe how the manager of Party2Go could use computer software packages as part of the day-to-day business operations. **(25 marks)**

C Describe how (i) the rights of the data subject and (ii) the responsibilities of the data controller, under the General Data Protection Regulation (GDPR), have impacted Party2Go. **(30 marks)**

Section 3 – Long Questions

1 Firms use <u>email</u>, <u>video conferencing</u> and <u>cloud computing</u> in the operation of their business. Outline the advantages of **two** of the underlined terms. **(20 marks)**

2 Describe the drawbacks of a business using social media as part of its ICT strategy. **(20 marks)**

3 Explain the benefits of ICT to modern business. Use examples to support your answer. **(20 marks)**

4 There is often a legal requirement under the GDPR for members of the public to hand over their personal information to public bodies. Discuss this statement in relation to the rights of data subjects and the responsibilities of data controllers under the GDPR (2018). **(20 marks)**

5 Evaluate the powers of the Data Protection Commission. **(20 marks)**

PREVIOUS LEAVING CERTIFICATE EXAM QUESTIONS

Ordinary Level

Section A – Short Questions (10 marks each)

1 Draft, using today's date, a Memorandum (Memo) from Mary Moore, IT manager, to all department managers reminding them to inform all staff of the importance of protecting sensitive data from cyber security threats. **[LC OL 2018]**

2 Explain **one** use of **each** of the following computer software programs for a business.

   (i) Microsoft Word   (ii) Microsoft Excel

   [LC OL 2017]

3 List **three** benefits to a business of investing in new technology. **[LC OL 2013]**

4 Which of the following acts governs how information is stored about people?
   (i) Consumer Protection Act 2007
   (ii) General Data Protection Regulation **[LC OL 2015]**

Section B

1
> ACE Toys Ltd is a successful Irish toy manufacturer. It uses a 'Batch Production' process. Each year it develops new products for the Christmas period, selling to the Irish and international markets. This year ACE Toys Ltd has produced 'SPRAOI', an interactive games console which uses basic Irish language, aimed at children aged 7–11. ACE Toys Ltd have set up a website called www.acetoys.com.

   Outline **two** benefits for ACE Toys Ltd of having its own website. **(10 marks) [LC OL 2013]**

2 Outline **three** advantages of Information Communications Technology to a business, giving examples. **(15 marks) [LC OL 2010]**

3 Under the General Data Protection Regulation people whose personal information is kept on a computer have several rights. Describe **two** of these rights. **(20 marks) [LC OL 2004]**

4 Apart from online selling, outline two ways in which developments in ICT (Information and Communications Technology) impact on a business. **(10 marks) [LC OL 2017]**

Higher Level

Section A – Short Questions (10 marks each)

1 Outline **three** problems with email in business. **[LC HL 2005]**

2 Outline **two** rights of a Data Subject under the terms of the General Data Protection Regulation. **[LC HL 2014]**

3 Outline **two** implications for management when a company develops its own website. **[LC HL 2013]**

Section B

1 Outline how developments in technology have benefited business communications. **(20 marks) [LC HL 2014]**

2 The General Data Protection Regulation (2018) sets out the following:
   (i)   The rights of Data Subjects
   (ii) The obligations of Data Controllers
   (iii) The functions of the Data Protection Commission
   Explain any **two** of the above. **(25 marks) [LC HL 2007]**

Unit 3

10 | MANAGEMENT ACTIVITIES 1: PLANNING

 Learning Outcomes

When you have completed this chapter, you will be able to:

1 Define the term *planning* as a management activity

2 Identify and explain the steps for effective planning

3 Describe the types of planning used in business

4 Outline the stakeholders who are affected by business planning

5 Describe the benefits that planning can bring to a business.

 Cross-curricular Link

Accounting – budgetary planning
Economics – economic planning
Geography – planning geographic investigations
History – planning a research study
Home Economics – meal planning, planning family routines and work schedules

 Literacy Link

Management activities, planning, SWOT analysis, mission statement, strategic plan, tactical plan, operational plan, contingency plan

 Numeracy Link

Currency conversion

CASE STUDY | *Planning at Adidas*

In order to be successful in the sportswear and sports equipment market, Adidas needs to undertake careful planning. The **mission statement** of the firm is very simple: 'To be the best sports company in the world.'

A **mission statement** cannot be achieved overnight, so Adidas must break down this overall goal into **strategic plans**.

As part of its strategic plan, Adidas wants to make its products more desirable to consumers. To achieve this, in 2015 the company signed Kanye West to create the Yeezy range of trainers, clothing and accessories. This approach helps to increase company sales and market share.

In order to achieve its strategic plans, Adidas formulates a number of **tactical plans**. These are short-term plans which break down the strategic plan into smaller steps.

The marketing department uses **tactical plans** to increase consumer awareness of the Yeezy range by creating inventive Snapchat and Instagram marketing campaigns.

Adidas uses **operational plans** for the day-to-day running of the company. Examples include recruiting staff for Adidas stores in key  cities such as London and New York, and ensuring that the stores have enough stock to meet consumer demand.

In 2018 US President Donald Trump announced the introduction of tariffs on imports from China, thus making Chinese imports more expensive than American-made goods. Adidas needed to develop **contingency plans** to deal with the price increases, as over 100 factories in China manufacture Adidas products.

While planning for a company as large as Adidas can be complex and time-consuming, it enables the entire firm to focus on the **mission statement**. With almost 57,000 employees worldwide and profits of €1.3 billion, Adidas must continue to invest in planning to ensure the future growth and success of the firm.

INTRODUCTION TO PLANNING

We met the management activities of planning, organising and controlling in Chapter 5. These are the three main tasks that are generally performed by managers in all industries, e.g. retail, construction and finance.

We all plan in our everyday lives – holidays, study schedules and leisure activities. For example, you might have a **plan** to go on holiday with your friends after you complete your Leaving Certificate exams. The **strategies** you might use to achieve this plan could include saving money received as gifts and getting a part-time job in order to pay for the holiday.

In a business, managers spend time planning in all areas of the firm, e.g. marketing plans and finance plans. It is the responsibility of managers to plan for the future to ensure the success of the firm.

> **Definition: Planning**
> Planning occurs when management looks to the future and sets specific goals for the business. The manager must put strategies in place in order to achieve these goals. Planning gives a business purpose and direction and reduces risk and uncertainty.

Activity 10.1

In pairs, read the planning quotes below and answer the following questions.

A goal without a plan is just a wish.
(Antoine de Saint-Exupery)

If you don't know where you're going, how will you get there?

Planning brings the future into the present so that you can do something about it now.

A plan is only as good as those who can see it through.

1 What is the key message of the quotes about planning?
2 Can you think of a time when you had to plan something, e.g. a party for a friend or a trip? How did you plan the event? Were your plans successful? Did you have to make any changes to your plan?

SMART PLANS

All plans need to be SMART plans. This means they must be:

		Explanation	Example for Adidas
S	Specific	The plan must clearly state its goal. Everybody should understand what the plan will achieve.	Adidas wants to increase sales in the US market.
M	Measurable	There should be evidence that the goal has been achieved, e.g. measured in units, sales or percentages.	Sales will increase by 50% in the US market to over €5 billion.
A	Achievable	The goal must be realistic. It should challenge the business to achieve it, but it should be possible to achieve.	With more people pursuing a lifestyle that promotes health and fitness, Adidas should be able to increase the sales of its products.
R	Relevant	The goal must be relevant to the overall business goals.	An increase in sales in the US market will increase overall company profits.
T	Timed	This is the target date when the goal should be achieved.	This goal will be achieved within three years.

Activity 10.2

Your class is organising an event in school to fundraise for a local charity. Working in groups, create a SMART plan for this event. Present your plan to your class using PowerPoint, Keynote or other presentation package.

STEPS IN THE PLANNING PROCESS

To make planning as effective as possible, the steps below should be followed:

1 Assess the current situation

2 Set a goal

3 Create a plan

4 Implement the plan

5 Review the plan

1 Assess the Current Situation

To assess the current situation in the business, managers conduct a SWOT analysis. This is an assessment tool used by management to identify the firm's Strengths, Weaknesses, Opportunities and Threats. The aim is to maximise strengths and opportunities and minimise the impact of weaknesses and threats.

Exam Tip!
Prepare a sample business on which to conduct a SWOT analysis. This will save you time during the exam.

SWOT Analysis for Samsung Electronics			
	Internal/ External	**Explanation**	**Examples**
Strengths	Internal	→ Strengths give the business a competitive advantage over competitors. → A firm should exploit its strengths.	1 Wide product range 2 Strong brand name 3 Loyal customers
Weaknesses	Internal	→ Weaknesses make it difficult for the business to achieve its objectives. They can put the business at a competitive disadvantage. → A firm should try to fix weaknesses as quickly as possible.	1 High selling price 2 Does not have its own operating system (e.g. Apple has iOS) 3 Damaged reputation due to the recall of Samsung Galaxy Note 7 smartphone
Opportunities	External	→ Opportunities enable the business to grow and increase profits. → A firm should take advantage of these opportunities.	1 Increased demand for smartphones in developing countries, e.g. Thailand 2 New product features, e.g. foldable screens 3 Sufficient cash to acquire other companies
Threats	External	→ Threats are obstacles that can reduce business profits or market share. → A firm should put plans in place to overcome these obstacles.	1 Saturated market in developed countries, e.g. Ireland 2 Strong market competition, e.g. Apple and HTC 3 Difficult to keep up with rapid changes in technology

Activity 10.3

As a class, choose another business on which to conduct a SWOT analysis. Working in smaller groups, prepare a SWOT analysis on this firm. Compare the results of the groups' SWOT analyses on the classroom whiteboard.

2 Set a Goal

The business analyses the results of the SWOT analysis. This helps the firm to decide which goals it wants to achieve. Some goals are long-term (more than five years), e.g. launching a new product or entering into a new market. Other goals are short-term (less than one year), e.g. to increase the marketing budget of the firm or to source a new supplier.

A business's most important goal is outlined in its **mission statement**. This is a **short written statement that sets out the firm's overall goal for the lifetime of the business**, i.e. the direction in which the business is going. It can be written by the entrepreneur who created the business or by the board of directors.

Example
Samsung's mission statement is: 'To inspire the world with innovative technologies, products and designs that enrich people's lives and contribute to a socially responsible, sustainable future.'

3 Create a Plan

To help the business to achieve its mission statement, it uses different types of planning, which include the following.

Name of Plan	Length	Written By	Explanation	Samsung Example
Strategic Plan	1–5 years	Senior management	→ Breaks down the mission statement into long-term business plans.	→ Samsung aims to grow annual sales to €345 billion and to ensure that the Samsung brand is ranked in the top five globally.
Tactical Plan	1–2 years	Middle management	→ Breaks down strategic plans into short-term plans. → Helps the business to achieve the strategic plan.	→ Samsung will launch new smartphone features such as artificial intelligence and foldable screens.
Operational Plan	0–1 year	All management levels	→ Plans for the day-to-day running of a business, e.g. annual marketing plans.	→ Samsung creates a worldwide marketing campaign when it launches a new product.
Contingency Plan	0–1 year	All management levels	→ Back-up plans used to deal with unforeseen events or emergencies, e.g. electrical failure or delayed delivery of raw materials.	→ If certain suppliers cannot supply raw materials, Samsung has contingency plans in place to source those materials from other suppliers in its network.
Human Resource (Manpower) Plan	0–1 year	Human resource manager	→ Ensures that the business has the correct number of employees, with the correct skills and qualifications to fill all roles in the firm.	→ Samsung fills job vacancies worldwide through its global website.
Financial Plan	0–1 year	Finance manager	→ Businesses prepare cash flow forecasts to predict the amount of income they will receive and spend in a particular period of time, e.g. six months.	→ Samsung uses cash flow forecasts to let shareholders know if it will be able to pay an annual dividend.

You will learn more about human resource manpower planning in Chapter 13. You will learn more about cash flow forecasts in Chapter 17.

DID YOU KNOW?

In 2019 only 20% of businesses in Ireland have a contingency plan in place to deal with issues that may arise due to the UK leaving the EU (Brexit).

Activity 10.4

The strategic plan of Toner Ltd is to increase sales in the UK market to £800 million. If the exchange rate is €1 = £0.83, what will the value of the sales be in euro?

CASE STUDY

Contingency Plans at Irish Ferries

Irish Ferries ordered a new ship for its fleet from a German shipyard at a cost of €144 million. A public competition was held to name the vessel and the name *W.B. Yeats* was chosen.

The company took 2,000 bookings for the ship, which was scheduled to travel from Dublin to Cherbourg in July 2018. In April, the German shipbuilder informed the company that the ship would not be completed for the July deadline.

Irish Ferries used **contingency planning** to try to rent another ship of similar size. Unfortunately no alternative ship could be found. Irish Ferries was forced to cancel all bookings for the ship for two weeks in July. Using further contingency planning, Irish Ferries was able to book the passengers on alternative sailings. This reduced the negative impact on consumers' travel plans.

Activity 10.5

Working in pairs, write out the key words relating to the types of planning on slips of paper. Fold the paper and place all the slips in a container/empty pencil case. Take turns to draw a slip and work together to write an explanation for the key term. Continue until all key terms have been explained.

4 Implement the Plan

Management chooses the plans to be implemented and communicates this information clearly to employees. Management also assigns tasks to employees to ensure that all staff are working towards the same goal.

5 Review the Plan

Regular review meetings should take place to ensure that the plans are progressing. If a plan has deviated, corrective action can be taken by management to ensure that the goal is achieved.

STAKEHOLDERS AND PLANNING

Business stakeholders can be affected by the different types of planning carried out by the firm. These include investors, employees and suppliers.

Investors

Financial planning can show investors that the business is able to repay loans borrowed. It also shows projected sales and profits, which may lead to increased dividends for shareholders.

Employees

Human resource planning can indicate to employees if there will be future promotion opportunities in the business. This can motivate employees to work harder to gain skills and experience to apply for these vacancies as they arise.

Suppliers

Strategic and tactical plans can indicate to suppliers that the business intends to expand. This can give the supplier the opportunity to sell more raw materials to the business. They can prepare these stocks in advance if they are aware of the firm's plans.

BENEFITS OF PLANNING

1 Anticipates Problems

Planning helps firms to anticipate future problems. It can then put plans in place to overcome these problems before they arise.

Example
Human resource planning identifies that the firm will have a shortage of staff. The business can recruit and select new employees to fill vacancies.

2 Identifies Strengths, Weaknesses, Opportunities and Threats

A SWOT analysis helps a business to identify and exploit its strengths and opportunities. It also helps the business to take action to minimise or remove weaknesses and threats.

Example
A SWOT analysis may identify that a business is using outdated machinery. The firm can purchase more efficient machines to increase production.

3 Benchmarking

The business monitors its progress by comparing its planned targets with actual results. This can help it identify what changes need to be made to achieve its targets.

Example
The business plans to increase sales by 5% but realises that sales have increased by only 2%. It may decide to increase promotion, e.g. introduce special offers to boost sales.

4 Improves Motivation

Planning ensures that all employees know the future goals of the business. This makes them feel that they have an important role in the business and increases motivation levels.

Example
The business may have a strategic plan to launch a new product. Employees will be motivated to work hard to make the product launch a success.

5 Finance

Financial planning helps the business to obtain finance, e.g. loans. It shows banks and investors that the firm will be able to repay its loans.

Example
The business prepares a cash flow forecast to show the bank manager that it will have enough cash to repay any loans.

Activity 10.6

Create a picture collage to summarise the benefits of planning. You could draw your images or use websites such as https://spark.adobe.com/ or www.canva.com.

KEY TERMS

Now you have completed this chapter, you should understand and be able to explain the following terms. In your copybook, write a definition of each term to build up your own glossary of terms.

- planning
- SMART plans
- SWOT analysis
- mission statement
- strategic plan
- tactical plan
- operational plan
- contingency plan
- human resource (manpower) planning
- financial planning
- benchmarking

PowerPoint Summary

EXAM-STYLE QUESTIONS

Ordinary Level

Section 1 – Short Questions (10 marks each)

1 Explain what is meant by the term *planning*.

2 List the **five** steps involved in planning.

3 Name **three** types of planning used in a business.

4 What do the following letters stand for? (i) SMART and (ii) SWOT.

5 In relation to SWOT analysis, give **two** examples each of a firm's (i) strengths and (ii) opportunities.

6 Circle the correct answer in the following sentences:

  (i)   A contingency plan is used for **long-term planning/unexpected events**.

  (ii) Human resource planning is also known as **manpower planning/human purpose planning**.

  (iii) A mission statement is formulated by **middle management/senior management**.

  (iv) A cash flow forecast is an example of a **strategic plan/financial plan**.

Section 2 – Long Questions

1 Conduct a SWOT analysis for a business of your choice. Include **one** point under each heading. **(25 marks)**

2 Distinguish between a mission statement and a strategic plan. Give **one** example of each. **(25 marks)**

3
> Ricky Lavelle owns a business creating custom-designed invitations for parties. He needs to take out a loan in order to purchase new printing equipment. To enable him to keep up with the demand for his products, he will need to employ some full-time and part-time staff.

Outline **two** types of plan that you think Ricky will need to help him to expand his business. **(15 marks)**

4 Explain how business planning can have an impact on **two** business stakeholders. **(15 marks)**

5
> Naomi Flynn plans to set up a beauty salon in her local town. She wants to get the business up and running as quickly as possible but has been advised to spend some time planning her business before she opens to the public.

Outline the benefits of planning for a business such as Naomi's. **(15 marks)**

Higher Level

Section 1 – Short Questions (10 marks each)

1 List **four** types of planning used in business and explain **one** of them.

2 Distinguish between a tactical plan and an operational plan.

3 Using the numbers 1–5 (with 1 being the first step), put the steps in planning in the correct order.

Implement a plan	
Create a plan	
Review a plan	
Assess the situation	
Set the goal	

4 Explain the concept of SMART planning.

5 Illustrate by an example why a business would prepare a contingency plan.

6 Describe how planning can be used by a business to anticipate future problems.

Section 2 – Applied Business Question (80 marks)

Beth's Boutique

Beth Jennings has owned Beth's Boutique in Kilkenny city for the past 15 years. She is passionate about fashion and her long-term business goal is to be the number-one destination for designer clothing in Ireland. She knows that her shop has a strong reputation in Ireland for providing high-quality designer clothes for special occasions.

Beth is now planning for future business growth and has carried out a SWOT analysis. The SWOT analysis has identified a number of interesting possibilities, such as opening a new store or launching a business website. It has also identified a number of areas that Beth will need to consider, such as the opening of two other high-end clothes shops in Kilkenny city and the high cost of rent for commercial premises.

Based on the information from the SWOT analysis, Beth has decided to open a second store in Limerick city by March 2021. There is a lot to plan before she can open her new store. She needs to find a suitable premises and recruit three new employees. She thought that she had found the ideal building but there were no customer car parking facilities nearby.

Beth knows that she does not have sufficient capital to fund the expansion of a new store. She will need to prepare a cash flow forecast and profit projections to include in her financial plans to apply for a bank loan.

Staff in her Kilkenny store are excited at the future plans for the business and Beth has included them in decision-making regarding the store location and shop fit-out. From past experience, Beth knows that planning can be used to compare planned with actual results and help to keep plans moving in the desired direction.

Exciting times lie ahead for Beth's Boutique and the planned expansion.

A (i) Explain what is meant by the term *planning*.
   (ii) Conduct a SWOT analysis for Beth's Boutique, using references to the text. **(25 marks)**
B Evaluate how different types of planning contribute to business success. Relate your answer to Beth's Boutique, making any appropriate assumptions. **(30 marks)**
C Discuss the benefits that planning can bring to Beth's Boutique. **(25 marks)**

Section 3 – Long Questions

1 (i) What do the letters SMART mean in relation to planning?
   (ii) Illustrate a SMART plan for a business of your choice. **(25 marks)**
2 There are high levels of competition in the Irish supermarket industry. Conduct a SWOT analysis on a supermarket of your choice. Include **two** examples under each heading. **(20 marks)**
3

> A good business plan always begins with a mission statement and involves many other forms of planning.

   (i) Outline what is meant by the term *mission statement*.
   (ii) Describe other forms of planning which can be used by businesses to improve the likelihood of success. **(20 marks)**
4 Describe the impact of planning on different business stakeholders. Illustrate your answer with reference to specific plans formulated in business. **(15 marks)**
5 Evaluate the benefits of planning for a business owner. **(25 marks)**

PREVIOUS LEAVING CERTIFICATE EXAM QUESTIONS

Ordinary Level

Section A – Short Questions (10 marks each)

1 Name the **three** management activities. [LC OL 2016]

2 Fill in the missing elements of a SWOT analysis in the spaces 2, 3 and 4 below:

  1 *Strengths*   2 _____   3 _____   4 _____ [LC OL 2018]

3 Column 1 is a list of business terms. Column 2 is a list of possible explanations for these terms. **(One explanation has no match.)** [LC OL 2014]

Business Terms		Explanations
1 Strategic Plan	**A**	A plan setting out expected cash inflows and cash outflows.
2 Mission Statement	**B**	A plan to ensure the business has the right number of employees with the right skills at the right time.
3 Contingency Plan	**C**	A specific plan to be achieved in a relatively short term.
4 Tactical Plan	**D**	The overall business aim to be achieved over the life of the business.
5 Manpower Plan	**E**	A back-up plan to cover unexpected events.
	F	A long-term plan providing a focus for the whole business.

Match the two lists in your copybook by writing your answers in the form *number = letter* (e.g. 1 = A).

Section B

1

West Coast Surf

In 2013, Jordan Casey was made redundant from his job at a factory in Sligo town. He received a redundancy package and decided he would like to set up his own business in the seaside town of Castlemore. Jordan has enjoyed surfing as a hobby since he was in school. He realised that surfing was becoming a very popular sport and spotted a gap in the market to provide surfing lessons at his local beach. He carried out a SWOT analysis of the potential business idea. Jordan was aware of his limitations. He approached the Local Enterprise Office, which provided a mentoring service to him.

Explain why Jordan should carry out a SWOT analysis. **(15 marks) [LC OL 2014]**

Higher Level

Section A – Short Questions (10 marks each)

1 What do the letters SWOT stand for? Explain its use in business. [LC HL 2007]

2 Distinguish between strategic planning and tactical planning. Give **one** example in each case. [LC HL 2008]

Section B

1 (i) What is meant by the term SWOT analysis?

  (ii) Conduct a SWOT analysis on a business of your choice. (Include **two** points under each heading.) **(20 marks) [LC HL 2010]**

2

Ryanair CEO Michael O'Leary has apologised for the cancellation of flights. The airline admits it 'messed up the planning of pilots' holidays'.

Source: Adapted from The Irish Times, 2017

  (i) Illustrate your understanding of the term *contingency plan*.

  (ii) Outline the importance of planning for an airline such as Ryanair. Refer to strategic, tactical and manpower planning in your answer. **(25 marks) [LC HL 2018]**

Solutions

CHAPTER 11 | MANAGEMENT ACTIVITIES 2: ORGANISING

Literacy Link

Organising, organisation chart, specialisation, span of control, chain of command, board of directors, CEO, middle management, delayering

Numeracy Link

Addition, subtraction, multiplication, percentages

Cross-curricular Link

Geography – geographical investigation
Home Economics – managing resources

CASE STUDY

Organising in Business

Bobby Riordan runs a toy manufacturing business in Ireland. He wants to expand the business by selling into Europe and by beginning to manufacture children's clothing.

Currently he employs forty staff in a range of roles, including marketing, finance, production and human resources. Bobby realises that with the prospect of expansion, he must put a **formal organisation structure** in place. Many employees do not know the **chain of command** and managers are unsure of the **span of control**.

Bobby asked his human resources manager to investigate the most suitable organisation structure for the business. The HR manager compiled a report, which outlined four different organisation structures: **functional**, **geographic**, **product** and **matrix**.

Bobby is interested in the **team-based aspects** of a **matrix** structure, as he believes that his employees would benefit from working in teams. However, a **functional** structure would allow for **greater specialisation of skills and knowledge**, as employees would be based in separate departments. Bobby also sees the merits of a **geographic** structure, as he plans to set up a European office in Berlin to help to increase sales in Europe. However, the decision to manufacture children's clothing makes Bobby consider the concept of using a **product** structure.

Bobby has a lot to think about and he must examine the advantages and disadvantages of each organisation structure and choose the one most appropriate for his business.

ORGANISING

In Chapter 10 we examined the management activity of planning. We will now look at the management activity of organising.

> **Definition: Organising**
> Organising occurs when the manager co-ordinates all business resources, e.g. employees, capital (money and machinery) and raw materials, into the most effective formation to achieve organisational goals.

Senior management may decide to create a **formal organisation structure** in a business in the form of an **organisation chart**. The organisation chart shows the:

- **Activities** undertaken in the business
- **Hierarchy** of employee and management positions
- **Roles** with responsibility for decision-making.

> **Note!**
> The organisation structure of a business can change over time, for example a business might change from a functional to a matrix structure. Some firms may even use elements from different organisation structures, rather than using one specific structure.

While many businesses have a formal organisation chart in place, such as a functional organisation chart, over time **informal structures** may develop. These structures develop in a business as a result of teamwork and workplace friendships. Employees may bypass the person assigned on the organisation chart to deal with an issue and instead direct their query to another employee.

An informal organisation structure can result in faster response times and can mean that tasks are completed more efficiently.

TYPES OF ORGANISATION STRUCTURE

There are different organisation structures used in business, including:

1 Functional

4 Matrix/team-based

2 Geographic

3 Product

> **Exam Tip!**
> Practise drafting the layout of an organisation chart for functional, geographic, product and matrix structures.

1 Functional Organisation Structure

This is the most common organisation structure used in business. The firm is divided into departments based on the functions they perform, e.g. finance, marketing and production. Each department has a manager who is responsible for achieving the department goal, e.g. the finance director in the finance department.

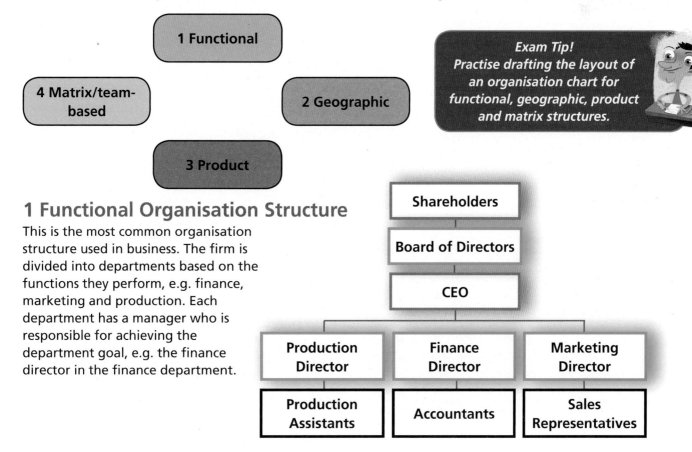

✓ Advantages	✗ Disadvantages
1 Employee Motivation Employees see that there is a promotional path in the firm. This encourages them to gain experience and skills, which can be used when future promotion opportunities arise.	**1 Focus on Department Goals** Employees may work towards departmental objectives rather than the overall business goals. This can slow down business growth.
2 Expert Knowledge It allows employees to become experts in a department, e.g. marketing. This improves productivity as employees can complete their duties faster and more efficiently.	**2 Slow Communication** Communication can be slow between departments. This can mean the business is slow to react to change, e.g. increased competition in the market.
3 Responsibility Employees know who is responsible for what jobs in the firm and to whom their queries and concerns should be directed.	**3 Lack of Teamwork** There may be a lack of trust between employees working in cross-departmental teams. This reduces productivity in the firm.

Example
Elon Musk, the CEO of Tesla Inc., understands the importance of employees working towards business goals. He said, 'We are all in the same boat. Always view yourself as working for the good of the company and never your department.'

Activity 11.1

Working in pairs, create a crossword using eight to ten words relating to a functional organisation structure. Swap crosswords among your classmates so that you complete a crossword that has been created by another pair of students.

2 Geographic Organisation Structure

In this type of organisation structure, the business is divided into geographical areas, e.g. based on region, country or continent.

Example
International IT firms such as Microsoft use a geographic organisation structure with sections of the business located in Africa, Europe, North and South America, Asia and the Middle East.

✓ Advantages	✗ Disadvantages
1 Local Managers Local managers provide local consumers with products that satisfy their needs. This helps to increase consumer loyalty.	**1 Duplication of Work** There may be duplicate departments working in different geographic areas, with employees doing the same job. This increases business costs.
2 Friendly Competition There is often friendly competition between the geographic units. Each unit tries to outdo the others in terms of increasing sales and reducing costs. This helps to increase profits for the entire business.	**2 Conflict between Management** Decisions made by senior management for the entire business can have a negative effect on local areas, e.g. redundancies. This can result in conflict between managers.
3 Promotion Managers in geographic units make decisions on behalf of the business in their region. This helps them to prepare for future promotion opportunities.	**3 Communication** There may be poor communication between geographic units. The development of new products or processes may not be shared, which can result in organisational inefficiency.

Example: Local Managers
Kellogg's has a local management team based in Dublin to meet the needs of Irish consumers. The firm views Ireland as an important market as on average Irish people eat 10kg of cereal per year, compared with 2–3kg consumption per person in France and Germany.

Example: Communication
Lack of communication at the Kraft Heinz Company meant that the invention of resealable packaging in the European unit was not shared with other geographic units. Management in the Latin America unit discovered that they had not known about the invention, despite it being very useful for their range of products.

Activity 11.2

Draw a geographic structure for a business that operates in the EU, the Americas, Africa and Asia. Include **two** countries for each geographic zone. Don't forget to label your organisation chart.

3 Product Organisation Structure

The business is divided into units based on the type of products it provides to consumers. Many large companies with a range of products use a product organisation structure, e.g. Toyota and Samsung.

Example
Samsung operates three product divisions and produces a range of consumer goods, including TVs, smartphones, medical devices and semiconductors. The Samsung Electronics unit earned the highest revenue for the company, with profits of €10.8 billion.

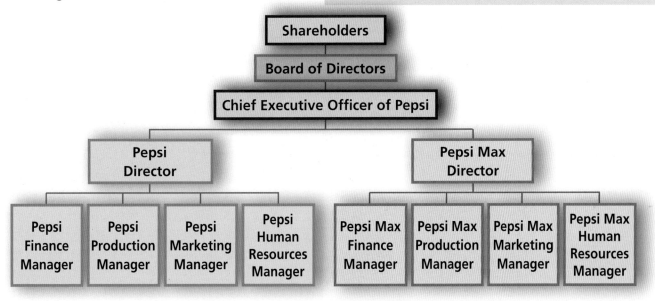

✓ Advantages	✗ Disadvantages
1 Consumer Demand As it is focused on specific products, this structure can meet consumer needs more effectively. The producer can react faster to changes in consumer demand.	**1 Duplication** There may be a duplication of units with multiple people doing the same job, e.g. marketing. This increases business costs.
2 Monitor Product Performance The business can monitor the performance and profits of each product unit. It may decide to discontinue underperforming products or increase promotion of products that are performing well.	**2 Product Competition** There may be rivalry between units as some of their products may be in direct competition with each other, e.g. car models such as the Toyota Yaris and Toyota Aygo.
3 Expert Knowledge Employees working in product divisions can develop expert knowledge. This means they can give a higher level of customer service to consumers.	**3 Poor Communication** Poor communication between the product units may result in the business missing opportunities in markets.

Example: Expert Knowledge

Kellogg's has a finance team based at the company's European Cereal headquarters in Dublin that manages the finances for Kellogg's Europe. This reduces the need for similar departments in other European countries.

Example: Product competition

The Coca-Cola Company produces a range of products competing against each other, such as Coca-Cola, Sprite, Smart Water and Innocent Drinks.

Activity 11.3

Draw a product organisation structure for a business with a wide range of products, such as Apple, Mercedes-Benz or Sony. Before you begin, visit your chosen firm's website to research some of the products it produces.

4 Matrix (Team) Organisation Structure

This structure combines elements of a functional organisation structure with a team-based structure. Employees work in various departments, such as finance and marketing, and then come together to work in cross-functional teams to complete business projects. The employees report to two managers: their department manager and the project manager.

For example, a business establishes a project team to develop a new product. The team includes employees from different departments, such as finance, marketing and production. The business believes that a cross-functional team will achieve better results as members have a greater range of skills and knowledge.

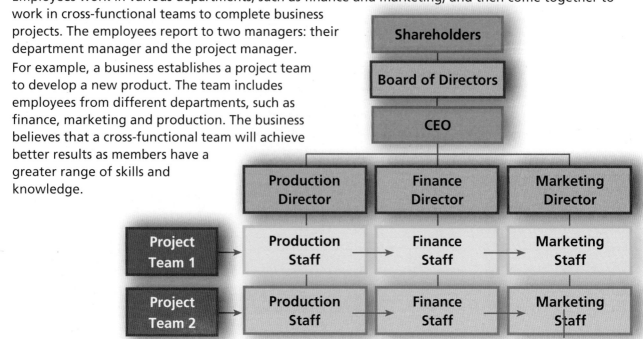

✓ Advantages	✗ Disadvantages
1 Increased Motivation Employees feel valued when they are part of a project team. This motivates employees and increases productivity.	**1 Multiple Managers** The employees may receive conflicting instructions from their department and project managers. They may struggle to decide which orders to prioritise.
2 Improved Communication Working with employees on a cross-business project improves communication. It helps employees from various departments to work towards common organisational goals.	**2 Training Costs** Employees working in teams need training in areas such as teamwork and communication to help the team work effectively. These training programmes increase business costs.
3 Improved Decision-making Project team members have a wide range of skills and experience. This can lead to better-quality decisions being made by the team.	**3 Lack of Trust** It may take the team longer to become productive, due to the lack of trust between employees from different parts of the firm.

Activity 11.4

Create a draft wiki page about a matrix organisation structure. The page should include some deliberate mistakes, e.g. false information about the structure. Swap your wiki page with another student. Identify and correct their errors and return the page to the author.

Unit 3

CASE STUDY — *Organisation Structure at Starbucks*

Starbucks operates over 24,000 stores in 70 countries. The growth of the company has led to changes in the organisation structure. Currently the company uses a mixture of organisation structures, including **functional** and **geographic**.

The company headquarters in Seattle operates a range of **functional departments** including finance, human resources and marketing for the entire company.

The company also operates in three **geographic divisions**: (a) the Americas; (b) Europe, Middle East, Africa and Russia; and (c) China and Asia Pacific. By operating in these separate geographic units, Starbucks can react quickly to local changes in consumer demand.

In the past, the Starbucks website featured a section called My Starbucks Idea. It allowed consumers in different regions to pitch ideas and product suggestions to the company. Consumers made more than 150,000 suggestions and 277 ideas were brought to market, including:

- New flavours such as Pumpkin Spice Latte
- Free Wi-Fi in stores
- A free birthday treat for customers.

Question
As an Irish consumer, what suggestions would you pitch to Starbucks to introduce to the Irish market?

Activity 11.5

Working in groups, create a mind map showing all four types of organisation structure, including the advantages and disadvantages of each. You could create your mind map on a large piece of paper or online using a website such as Coggle or Canva.

CHOOSING AN ORGANISATION STRUCTURE

Each business must identify which organisation structure is most appropriate for the firm. The business should consider the following factors:

Consumer Demand	→ A business may choose a product or geographic structure so that it can satisfy consumer needs more effectively. It allows the business to react quickly to changes in consumer taste, which helps to increase business sales and consumer loyalty.
Specialisation	→ If the business wants its employees to become experts in a particular business area, e.g. marketing, it may choose a functional organisation structure. This can improve customer service and productivity in the business.
Intrapreneurship	→ The business may choose a matrix organisation structure to encourage intrapreneurship and develop new products and processes for the firm. This can help to increase sales and reduce business costs.

CHAIN OF COMMAND

A chain of command shows the line of authority and communication in a business. It runs from the top of the organisation to people in positions at the bottom of the chain.

Span of Control

This relates to the number of employees who report directly to a manager. A business can have a wide or narrow span of control.

Wide Span of Control

A manager has a wide span of control when they have a **large number of employees** reporting directly to them. It is often used when employees do not require a high degree of supervision, e.g. employees completing repetitive tasks, such as factory workers or office cleaners.

Narrow Span of Control

A narrow span of control applies when a **smaller number of employees** report directly to the manager. It is used when employees require greater supervision, e.g. employees performing difficult or dangerous work, such as trainee doctors and miners.

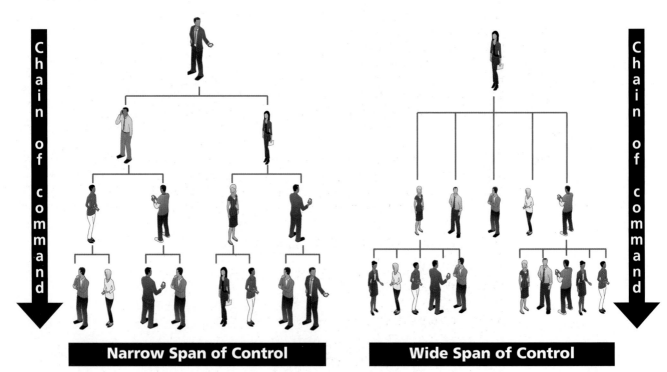

Narrow Span of Control   **Wide Span of Control**

Unit 3

Factors Affecting Span of Control

Trust	→ Management who trust staff tend to have a wide span of control. They do not closely monitor employees. A lack of trust between management and staff may result in a narrow span of control.
Employee Skills	→ Employees with fewer skills and less experience require greater management supervision; therefore a narrow span of control is needed. Skilled employees require less managerial supervision and the business can use a wide span of control.
Tasks	→ Employees performing repetitive tasks require less supervision; therefore management can use a wide span of control. Employees involved in complex tasks or performing dangerous work require greater supervision and the business should use a narrow span of control.
Managerial Workload	→ Managers perform a number of duties, including supervising staff and communicating with stakeholders. The manager may need to have a narrow span of control to ensure that they are not overwhelmed by their workload.

DID YOU KNOW?
Researchers have found that three or four reporting levels are optimal in most businesses. It is recommended that the span of control is between 15 and 20 employees for the best results.

Activity 11.6

In pairs, create a cloze test using the information you have learned on chain of command and span of control. Swap your exercises with other students in the class as a means of revision.

LEVELS IN AN ORGANISATION STRUCTURE

While businesses operate in different industries and sectors, many of them have similar organisational levels in their firms.

Shareholders

- These are individuals or organisations that have purchased shares in the firm.
- They are entitled to a share of the business profits, known as a dividend.

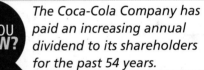

DID YOU KNOW?
The Coca-Cola Company has paid an increasing annual dividend to its shareholders for the past 54 years.

Board of Directors

- The board of directors are appointed by the shareholders of the business.
- They are responsible for creating the firm's mission statement and appointing a CEO to achieve it.

Example: Patagonia mission statement

Patagonia is an American outdoor clothing company that manufactures its products in a sustainable manner. The company's mission statement is to 'Build the best product. Cause no unnecessary harm. Use business to inspire and implement solutions to the environmental crisis.'

Senior Management

- The Chief Executive Officer (CEO) holds the most senior management position in the firm.
- The CEO sets the overall strategic plan for the firm and reports to the board of directors.

Middle Management

- Middle managers tend to be heads of specific departments, e.g. production manager.
- They are responsible for implementing the plans and policies set by senior management.

Supervisor

- Supervisors assign tasks to front-line staff and monitor employee progress.
- They are responsible for recruiting staff for their department and for providing training.

Front-line Staff

- These are the employees who carry out the day-to-day duties and tasks within a department, e.g. a marketing assistant in the marketing department.
- They are assigned roles by their supervisor.

Activity 11.7

In groups, prepare a roleplay which incorporates the various employee levels in an organisation, e.g. CEO. Each person in the group must play a role. Perform your roleplay for your classmates, who have to guess which student is playing what position in the firm.

DELAYERING

Delayering involves removing one or more management layers in an organisation structure. Businesses often remove middle management levels, which increases the span of control of senior managers.

For example, many retail outlets no longer have an area manager for the district or supervisors for each store. Instead the business appoints a regional manager to oversee the operation of a number of stores.

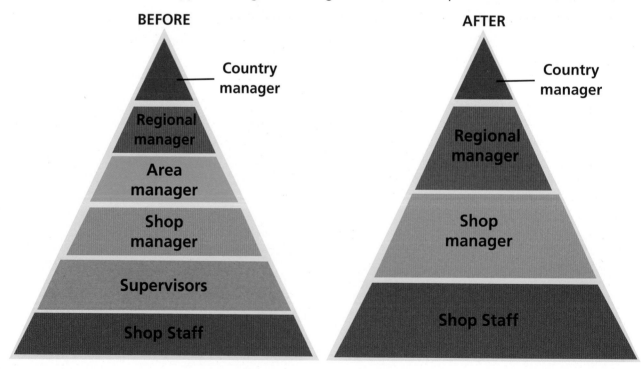

Before and after delayering

✓ Advantages	✗ Disadvantages
1 Improved Communication Faster communication throughout the organisation, as the messages pass through fewer levels.	**1 Decreased Motivation** Employees may fear for their own job security. This can decrease motivation and reduce productivity among staff.
2 Reduced Costs Delayering often involves removing managerial staff. This reduces wage costs for the business.	**2 Managerial Span of Control** Delayering can result in a wider span of control for managers. This increased workload may lead to stress and burnout.

CASE STUDY

Delayering at Tesco

In 2017, Tesco in the UK replaced 1,700 deputy managers in its Express convenience stores with 3,300 lower-paid 'shift leaders'. Twenty-two per cent of the managers affected chose to take voluntary redundancy, while 55% agreed to move to other roles with a lower rate of pay. The remainder moved to different roles at the same rate of pay.

Tesco claimed that the introduction of 'shift leaders' would ensure that there would be a greater number of employees on the shop floor of its stores. The company believes that this approach improves the quality of customer service across all its Express convenience stores.

Unit 3

Activity 11.8

Answer the following questions, referring to the Tesco Case Study above.
1   What percentage of deputy managers have remained on the same rate of pay performing different roles in Tesco?
2   How many deputy managers transferred to other roles within Tesco at a lower rate of pay?

Activity 11.9

Delayering at ABC Ltd
ABC Ltd has reviewed its organisation structure and is considering removing Layer 3 from its current structure. The HR department of ABC Ltd provides you with the following information:
- There are five layers in the organisation.
- The CEO is in Layer 1, i.e. the top layer, and is the only person in this layer.
- Each manager, including the CEO, has five people reporting directly to them.

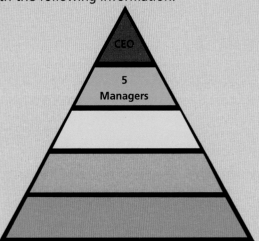

1   Draw the triangle in your copybook and complete the layers for the organisation structure as it currently stands.
2   Calculate the total number of people currently working in ABC Ltd.
3   If ABC Ltd delayered and removed Layer 3, how many staff members would it remove?

ADVANTAGES OF ORGANISING AS A MANAGEMENT ACTIVITY

The management activity organising has a number of benefits for an organisation, including:

1 **Clear chain of command:** It ensures that everybody in the business knows who reports to whom. Consumers and employees know to whom they should address their questions or problems. This ensures that issues are solved as quickly as possible.

2 **Improved communication:** It encourages better communication in the workplace. Management can send instructions down the organisation structure to staff. The staff can provide ideas to management by using upward communication.

3 **Management workload:** It is clear to see how many people report to a manager, so workload can be distributed more evenly to prevent managerial stress and work overload.

4 **Employee motivation:** It shows employees that there is a clear promotional path in the organisation. This motivates them to work to the best of their ability to prepare for these promotional opportunities in the future.

KEY TERMS

Now you have completed this chapter, you should understand and be able to explain the following terms. In your copybook, write a definition of each term to build up your own glossary of terms.

- organising
- formal organisation structure
- organisation chart
- informal organisation structure
- functional organisation structure
- specialisation

- geographic organisation structure
- product organisation structure
- matrix organisation structure
- chain of command
- span of control
- delayering

 PowerPoint Summary

EXAM-STYLE QUESTIONS

Ordinary Level

Section 1 – Short Questions (10 marks each)

1 What is meant by the term *organising*?

2 List **three** types of organisation structure.

3 Outline **two** disadvantages of a functional organisation structure.

4 What is a geographic organisation structure? Illustrate a geographic organisation structure with **three** geographic units.

5 Outline **two** advantages of a matrix organisation structure.

6 Column 1 is a list of business terms relating the management activity of organising. Column 2 is a list of possible explanations for these terms. Match the two lists in your copybook by writing your answers in the form *number = letter* (e.g. 1 = A).

Business Terms		Explanations
1 Supervisor	**A**	Carry out duties assigned by their supervisor
2 CEO	**B**	Receive a share of the profits, known as a dividend
3 Front-line staff	**C**	Elected by the shareholders of the business
4 Board of directors	**D**	Gives instructions to front-line staff and monitors their progress
5 Shareholders	**E**	Most senior management position in the firm

Section 1 – Short Questions (10 marks each) *continued*

7 Distinguish between the role of middle management and supervisors in a business.

8 Choose the appropriate words to complete the sentence below. (One word does not apply.)

Employee	Management	Removing

Delayering involves _____ one or more _____ layers in an organisation structure.

Section 2 – Long Questions

1 Name **one** type of organisation structure that can be used to divide employees into departments in a business. Outline **one** advantage and **two** disadvantages of this type of organisation structure. **(20 marks)**

2 Outline **two** advantages and **two** disadvantages of using a geographic organisation structure. **(20 marks)**

3 Draft a product organisation structure for a business of your choice. Describe **two** advantages of this type of structure. **(20 marks)**

4 Using a diagram, describe what is meant by the phrase 'a narrow span of control'. **(20 marks)**

5

> Emma Barry runs a mineral mining company with over 30 employees. She needs to decide on an appropriate span of control for her managers to ensure the safety of her staff.

Outline **two** factors that would affect the span of control in her business. **(15 marks)**

6 Shareholders, board of directors and the chief executive officer are featured in an organisation chart. Explain the role of **two** of the underlined terms. **(15 marks)**

7 Describe **two** benefits of a business delayering its organisation structure. **(15 marks)**

8

> Organising is one of the most difficult management activities, which managers must work hard to develop.

Describe **two** advantages of the management activity of organising for a business. **(20 marks)**

Higher Level

Section 1 – Short Questions (10 marks each)

1 Draft and label a functional organisation chart for a clothing manufacturer.

2 Describe the benefits for an organisation of using a matrix organisation structure.

3 Explain what is meant by the term *chain of command*.

4 Illustrate by using examples the difference between a narrow span of control and a wide span of control.

5 Outline the factors that affect the span of control of a business.

6 Explain what is meant by the term *delayering*. Use a diagram to support your answer.

7 Indicate whether each statement is true or false.

Statements		True or False
A	A matrix organisation structure organises people based on their location.	
B	Duplication of roles is a disadvantage of a functional organisation structure.	
C	A wide span of control is needed when employees perform dangerous or complicated tasks.	
D	Delayering involves adding a layer of employees to the business.	

8 Distinguish between senior management and middle management in an organisation.

Section 2 – Applied Business Question (80 marks)

Madra Rua Chocolates Ltd

Lauren Fox is the <u>CEO</u> of an Irish chocolate manufacturing company called Madra Rua Chocolates Ltd.

To ensure that her business would run as efficiently as possible, Lauren put a formal organisation structure in place when she started the business. She chose a functional organisation structure as she believed that it would benefit the business to have employees working in distinct departments, so that they could focus on specific tasks associated with their department.

Lauren has four <u>shareholders</u> in the business who have invested over €2 million into her firm. They require regular updates from <u>senior management</u> including the Chief Financial Officer and herself, the Chief Executive Officer. She also has four <u>middle managers</u> – a Finance Director, Production Director, Marketing Director and a Human Resources Director. At times Lauren thinks that the company has too many managers, which has led to increased wage costs.

Recently there have been a number of problems in the business. Lauren has received complaints from the employees that there are high levels of hostility and a lack of trust between the directors in each of the departments. Errors fulfilling customer orders have arisen in the past six months as employees received conflicting orders from the various department managers. Lauren is disappointed to find that departments are more concerned with achieving their own departmental objectives than the overall company goal.

Lauren has conducted some online research and wants to make some changes to the organisation's structure. She believes that a team-based structure is the most appropriate approach for her growing business. By assigning employees to teams, she feels that communication between employees will improve, thus reducing the current culture of hostility and distrust. Lauren believes that employees will be more motivated to work as part of a team and this will help to improve decision-making and innovation in the business.

A (i) Outline what is meant by the term *organisation structure*.

    (ii) Describe the disadvantages of Madra Rua Chocolates Ltd using a functional organisation structure. Refer to the text in your answer. **(25 marks)**

B (i) Illustrate, by means of a diagram, a matrix organisation structure which Lauren could use in her business.

    (ii) Outline the advantages to Lauren's business of organising staff in a matrix organisation structure. **(30 marks)**

C (i) Explain **two** of the underlined terms in the text above.

    (ii) What is meant by the term *delayering*? What are the advantages of delayering to Lauren's business? **(25 marks)**

Section 3 – Long Questions

1 Distinguish between a formal and an informal organisation structure that could exist in a business. **(15 marks)**

2 Draft and illustrate a functional organisation structure. Outline the advantages of this type of structure. **(20 marks)**

3 A business should always choose a geographic organisation structure for its business. Discuss this statement. **(15 marks)**

4 Choosing an appropriate organisation structure is a difficult decision for management. What type of organisation structure do you think is most effective? Explain your choice. **(15 marks)**

5 Discuss the factors that affect span of control in a business. **(15 marks)**

6 Outline the levels of management in an organisation structure. **(20 marks)**

7 Delayering is a complex process for a business to undertake. Discuss this statement with reference to the disadvantages a business may experience while delayering. **(15 marks)**

8 Describe the benefits to a business of organising as a management activity. **(15 marks)**

PREVIOUS LEAVING CERTIFICATE EXAM QUESTIONS

Ordinary Level

Section A – Short Questions (10 marks each)

1 Complete the functional organisational structure of a Private Limited Company with four departments.   **[LC OL 2015]**

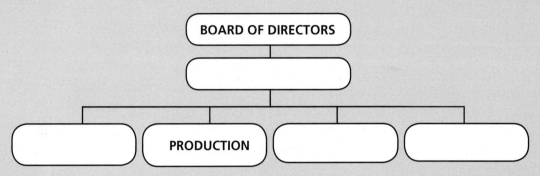

2 Copy and complete the functional organisation structure of a business with four departments.   **[LC OL 2013]**

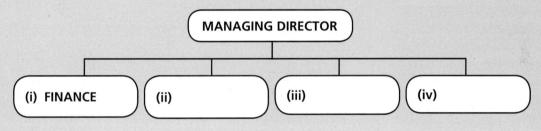

Higher Level

Section A – Short Questions (10 marks each)

1 Draft and label a matrix structure for a manufacturing organisation.   **[LC HL 2007]**

2 Explain the term *span of control* and outline a situation where a narrow span of control may be appropriate.   **[LC HL 2015]**

Section B

1 Outline the benefits to a business of a functional organisation structure.   **(15 marks) [LC HL 2015]**

2 Discuss the benefits and challenges for a business of developing a matrix organisation structure (team structure) to complete specific projects in a business.   **(20 marks) [LC HL 2016]**

 Solutions

12 | MANAGEMENT ACTIVITIES 3: CONTROLLING

Learning Outcomes

When you have completed this chapter, you will be able to:

1 Define *controlling* as a management activity

2 Describe the four main types of control: stock, quality, credit and financial

3 Outline the importance of control in an organisation.

Literacy Link

Stock control, JIT, quality control, quality circle, Q Mark, ISO, credit control, creditworthiness, bad debts, financial control

Numeracy Link

Multiplication, division, percentages

Cross-curricular Link

Accounting – stock control, credit control and financial control
Home Economics – food preparation and processing

CASE STUDY

Samsung Forms a New Quality Control Team

Within weeks of Samsung launching the Galaxy Note 7 in August 2016, the firm was inundated with reports of exploding phones and devices catching fire. The firm was forced to recall 4.3 million phones worldwide at a cost of over €4.5 billion.

As Samsung understands the importance of **quality control**, the firm launched an investigation into the cause of the problem. The firm tested over 200,000 devices and 30,000 batteries at a facility built specifically to identify what had caused the technology to fail. The investigation discovered that a problem with two battery suppliers had caused the fault in the smartphones.

After the Galaxy Note 7 fiasco the company was determined to prevent a similar issue occurring. The firm apologised to consumers and put together a new **quality control team**, which

reports directly to the company's president. The firm has also improved its quality processes, by introducing battery **inspections** and working with independent experts.

WHAT IS CONTROLLING?

Controlling is one of the three management activities. We have already learned about the activities of planning and organising in Chapters 10 and 11.

> **Definition: Controlling**
> A management activity that measures how well an organisation achieves the goals and objectives that it has set. It involves setting standards, measuring the actual performance against these standards and taking corrective action where necessary.

Steps in the Management Activity of Control

Step 1 – Set the standard

Step 2 – Measure performance

Step 3 – Compare performance with standard

Step 4 – Take corrective action (if necessary)

Step	Explanation	Business Example
1 Set the standard	→ The organisation sets the standard to be achieved, e.g. for a product or a process.	→ A firm's finance department sets the standard that all debts must be paid within 30 days of issuing an invoice to customers.
2 Measure performance	→ Actual performance is measured.	→ The firm records the number of days it takes customers to pay their bills.
3 Compare performance with standard	→ Management compares actual performance with the standards set. If there are differences, management analyses the situation to find out the cause.	→ The firm identifies that 80% of customers paid their bill within 30 days of receiving the invoice.
4 Take corrective action	→ Take action to avoid the same issues happening again. → Corrective action must be well planned and carried out quickly to prevent the problem worsening.	→ Send a reminder to customers, e.g. an email/text message to remind them of the payment date.

Activity 12.1

A business has 56 customers who have bought goods on credit. If the firm has bad debts of 20%, calculate how many businesses pay their bills in full and on time.

TYPES OF MANAGEMENT CONTROL

We will now look at the **four** main areas of a business which require control procedures to be in place:

1 Stock Control

2 Quality Control

3 Credit Control

4 Financial Control

> **Exam Tip!**
> You may be asked to evaluate the different types of control in a business. This means that you must **examine the information** presented and provide **your own conclusion**.

1 STOCK CONTROL

Types of Stock

A business holds **four** main types of stock:

1 **Raw materials:** For a manufacturing business these are the raw materials used to make the products, e.g. timber used for making tables.

2 **Work in progress:** Stock of goods that are partially completed, e.g. timber that has been cut to make into tables.

3 **Finished goods:** Goods that have been completed in the manufacturing process but have not yet been sold to customers, e.g. the finished tables ready for sale.

4 **Merchandise:** Goods bought by the firm to be sold on to consumers, e.g. bottled water.

> **Definition: Stock control**
> A management activity that aims to keep optimum stock levels so that the organisation doesn't have too much stock or too little stock.

Key Terms in Stock Control

Key Term	Explanation
Optimum stock level	→ This is the ideal level of stock that a business should have of a particular item, e.g. ice cream. The optimum stock level varies from time to time, e.g. a shop will carry more stocks of ice cream in summer than in winter.
Maximum stock level	→ The largest amount of stock that should be held. This can be limited by the space available in the businesses premises.
Minimum stock level	→ The lowest amount of stock that should be held.
Re-order level	→ The level of stock at which a new order for stock should be placed. This takes into account lead time.
Lead time	→ The time from when an order is placed to the stock arriving at the firm's stockroom.

Methods of Managing Stock Levels

Stock control needs to be in place for all items held by the business, i.e. from raw materials to finished goods. To aid this process, manual stock takes, EDI (electronic data interchange) and JIT (just in time) are used to control large volumes of stock.

1 Manual Stock Take

Employees physically count and record all stock in the business. The stock counted is compared to the quantities recorded on the firm's computer system to identify any differences, e.g. due to theft.

Activity 12.2

Do a stock take of all the items in your food cupboard at home. Repeat the task a week later. Identify any slow-moving items. Is there too much stock or too little stock of any items?

2 EDI (Electronic Data Interchange)

We learned about EDI in Chapter 9 – ICT and Data Protection. We know that EDI enables firms to communicate information such as orders, invoices and payments electronically rather than on paper. The documents can be transferred without the need for human intervention.

Using EDI has a number of benefits for stock control:

- **Quicker re-ordering process:** There are fewer instances of stock shortages.
- **Lower costs:** When the minimum stock level is reached, an order is immediately placed with the supplier. This reduces wage costs, as fewer staff are needed.
- **Lead times:** It is easier to track stock in real time.
- **Shorter processing times:** By reducing delivery times, businesses can reduce the amount of stock they need to carry.

3 Just in Time (JIT)

This method of stock control originates from Japan. The main features of this method of stock control include the following:

- The business holds the minimum amount of raw materials and receives regular deliveries from suppliers, thus ensuring that it never runs out of stock.
- The firm buys from reliable suppliers that provide the exact quantity and quality of stock when needed by the business.
- All finished goods are completed just in time for delivery to consumers.
- The system must be carefully planned, as any disruptions can lead to problems such as a shortage of raw materials for production.
- JIT helps to reduce business costs such as storage, insurance and security.

CASE STUDY
Just in Time at Toyota

In the 1970s, Toyota introduced a JIT stock control system as part of its business model. Toyota orders parts only after it has received a customer order for a vehicle. In order for JIT to be successful, the company must have:

- High-quality raw materials
- Reliable suppliers
- No machine breakdowns at the plant
- Fast methods to assemble vehicles.

Despite its success, Toyota's JIT concept almost came to a crashing halt. A fire at a supplier's factory meant that it was unable to produce brake parts for Toyota. The company was the sole supplier of the part and Toyota ran out of brake parts after just one day. Production lines shut down for two days until another supplier was able to start manufacturing parts. Other suppliers for Toyota also had to shut down

because the car manufacturer did not need their parts on the assembly line until the brake parts were manufactured. The fire cost Toyota nearly €13 billion in revenue and the manufacture of 70,000 cars was delayed due to its two-day shutdown.

Effective Stock Control

Effective stock control is an essential management activity in a business. It means that the business has optimum stock levels. Having optimum stock levels ensures that the business will have the right stock in the right place at the right time to meet:

- Production requirements
- Consumer demand.

There can be problems if a business carries either too much or too little stock.

If a business is carrying **too much stock**, it can lead to:

Lower profits	→ The business may have lower profits due to the high cost of storage, e.g. rent of warehouse space and insurance.
Obsolete stock	→ There is an increased risk of stock becoming outdated. For example, Cisco Systems had to write off almost €2 billion in outdated stock, including communication chips and optical lasers.
Theft	→ If large volumes of products are stored in the facility, management may not notice if stock is stolen.
Inefficient use of cash	→ There may be too much money tied up in stock. The firm could make better use of the money, e.g. placing it into a short-term investment.

If the business carries **too little stock**, this can lead to:

Loss of sales	→ Consumers shop elsewhere to buy the goods they need, thus reducing the firm's sales.
Loss of economies of scale	→ As the firm buys stock in smaller volumes, it may not receive discounts from suppliers for bulk purchasing.
Storage costs	→ The business may have to pay for warehouse and insurance costs, even if it runs out of stock.
Production delays	→ The business may be unable to meet production deadlines if it does not have sufficient stocks of raw materials.

For these reasons, management must operate an efficient stock control system. Managers need to make decisions about what the optimum stock levels are for all the products the business carries, i.e. raw materials, and finished goods and merchandise.

Definition: Economies of Scale
A firm benefits from buying items such as raw materials in bulk, i.e. the larger the amount of items purchased, the larger the discount received.

Benefits of Stock Control

Having a good stock control system benefits a business in the following ways:

1 **Increased efficiency:** Modern stock control systems are computerised and are often more accurate than humans. This increases efficiency and reduces the number of mistakes made.

2 **Feedback:** There is instant feedback on all stock levels for each item, enabling easy identification of slow- and fast-moving items.

3 **Reduced costs:** The costs associated with having too much stock, such as obsolescence and storage, and with having too little stock, e.g. stock-outs, are reduced.

4 **Theft:** It is easier to identify theft, as stock is accurately monitored.

2 QUALITY CONTROL

Definition: Quality control
A set of procedures used to check work completed to ensure it meets the standards set.

Quality control aims to ensure that goods and services provided by a business are of the highest standard at all times. They should meet legal requirements as outlined in consumer legislation such as the Sale of Goods and Supply of Services Act 1980, and meet or exceed the expectation of consumers.

The Purpose of Quality Control

Purpose	Explanation	Business Example
Detect	→ Identify whether there are any quality issues in the business.	→ The production manager has received complaints from consumers regarding the quality of the firm's products.
Prevent	→ Set up procedures that will prevent quality issues arising in the future.	→ The production manager sets up a new quality control team.
Correct	→ Take corrective action to prevent problems in the future.	→ The team recommends the replacement of faulty or outdated equipment that is causing faulty products.
Improve	→ The business should constantly strive for improvements in quality.	→ The team frequently reviews quality at the firm and strives for continuous improvement.

A business that fails to meet its customers' expectations will inevitably lose customers and will gain a reputation for poor-quality or unreliable products, which can be difficult to remove.

Achieving Quality Control

In order for quality control to be effective it must constantly be reviewed – quality can always be improved. A business can achieve quality control in a number of ways, for example:

A Inspections

B Quality circles

C Quality awards

D Total quality management (TQM).

A Inspections

Inspection uses trained inspectors to carry out tests on the finished goods. This can be done by either:

- Inspecting every single product produced; or
- Inspecting a limited number of products chosen at random, i.e. sampling.

Most firms use a random method of sampling. This involves selecting a number of products from the batch of products made, e.g. ten packets of biscuits for every 500 made. If the sample passes the inspection, the entire batch is passed. If the sample fails, the whole batch fails and is destroyed.

B Quality Circles

A group of factory floor employees volunteer to become part of a quality circle. The group meets regularly to identify and discuss quality issues at the firm. The quality circle recommends solutions to resolve quality concerns. Management can decide to accept, reject or amend these recommendations. Recommendations are then implemented by the quality circle.

The benefits of a quality circle include:

- **Employee motivation:** Employees feel valued when they work as part of a quality circle and when their recommendations are implemented. This increases employee motivation.
- **Reduced costs:** Higher-quality products reduce costs. There is less wastage of raw materials and fewer repairs of faulty goods and consumer refunds.
- **Improved quality:** Better-quality products encourage consumer loyalty, thus increasing a firm's sales.

C Quality Awards

These are awards given by independent organisations when a business achieves an agreed quality standard. The awards encourage firms to aim for very high-quality standards across all areas of their business. There are a number of quality awards, including:

- **Q Mark:** An Irish quality mark awarded by EIQA (Excellence Ireland Quality Association) to businesses that strive to continuously improve quality in their firms. Businesses awarded the Q Mark may be audited to ensure that they are maintaining high standards.
- **Bord Bia Quality Mark:** Awarded to firms that produce and process food in Ireland that meet the Bord Bia standards. These firms are allowed to use the Bord Bia Quality Assured label on their product packaging.
- **ISO 9000 series:** An international quality award system; firms must meet very high standards of quality control and are subject to regular spot checks. Irish firms that have achieved ISO awards include Bord Gáis Networks and ESB International.

 CASE STUDY ── *ISO Quality Award*

The ISO is an international standard for quality. The International Organisation for Standardisation (ISO) develops and maintains the ISO standards, but it does not itself carry out certification. Certification schemes are in operation in a number of countries, in which management systems or products are assessed for conformance to ISO standards by third parties (certification bodies). If organisations apply for an ISO award and the certification body are satisfied with every quality aspect, it delivers the ISO certificate.

The ISO members (see www.iso.org) provide up to date information about the certification bodies operating in their countries. There is only one member allowed per country. The Irish ISO member is the National Standards Authority of Ireland (NSAI) (see www.nsai.ie).

Unit 3

Activity 12.3

Watch the clip called 'What ISO Standards Do for You' and answer the following questions.
1 Name **two** effects that ISO has on the world.
2 List **two** advantages of ISO.
3 Name **two** global challenges that ISO can have an impact on.
4 How many ISO standards have been created?

Benefits of Quality Awards

The benefits to a business of achieving a quality award include:

- **Consumer trust:** Quality awards increase consumer trust in the firm. Consumers admire companies that invest in quality and this can increase consumer loyalty.
- **Marketing:** Quality awards can be used in a firm's marketing campaigns. This can give the business a competitive advantage over competitors in the market, leading to an increased market share.
- **Exports:** Certain quality symbols, such as the ISO 9000 series, are recognised internationally. This can open up markets for the business and increase the firm's sales.
- **Pricing:** Customers often associate quality symbols with high-quality goods and services. Firms can charge a higher price to consumers, leading to greater profits for the firm.

CASE STUDY

Quality Control at Bluebird Care

Bluebird Care provides high-quality care in the home and community for people of all ages and abilities. The firm employs over 145 staff and cares for over 600 people around Ireland.

It has been awarded a Q Mark for Best Homecare Provider and has also achieved the ISO 9001 international standard.

Activity 12.4

Using the Internet, find firms in your local area that have achieved quality awards such as the Q Mark or ISO. As a class, make an online collage of these firms and their products.

D Total Quality Management (TQM)

TQM is a system of quality management where the whole business seeks to improve quality in all areas of the firm. It involves ongoing improvements at every stage of the production process through to customer service. We will examine this management technique in Chapter 14.

Benefits of Quality Control

Any business that engages in effective quality management will achieve many benefits, including:

- **Customer satisfaction:** Consumers are satisfied with the high-quality products provided by the firm. This increases consumer loyalty and can help to increase the firm's sales and market share.
- **Quality awards:** These awards can be used as part of the firm's marketing campaigns and increase consumer trust in the business. The achievement of international awards such as ISO can be used by the firm to market its products abroad.
- **Reduced costs:** Effective quality control reduces business costs, as the firm does not spend money repairing and replacing poor-quality products for consumers.

3 CREDIT CONTROL

Many firms sell goods on credit, i.e. their customers (debtors) can buy now and pay later. Usually, the firm expects that the debtor will pay for the goods within 30 days. Every time a business sells goods or services on credit it runs the risk of incurring bad debts, i.e. not being paid in full.

Credit control ensures that customers who use credit facilities pay their bills in full and on time. It helps to improve cash flow for a business as it gives more certainty about when cash will be received from credit customers.

Definition: Debtor
A customer of a business who owes the business for goods or services previously sold on credit.

Definition: Bad debt
When a debtor fails to pay the amount owed for goods or services, for example because they are in financial difficulty.

Setting up a Credit Control System

There are a number of steps involved in establishing an effective credit control system.

1 Set Credit Limits

This is the maximum amount of credit that a business should provide to a customer. The credit controller sets limits for:

- **The entire business:** The total credit the business gives to all customers, e.g. €500,000.

- **Individual customers:** The maximum credit for each individual customer, e.g. €20,000.

Definition: Credit controller
The person in an organisation who decides the amount of credit given to a customer (debtor) and who is responsible for debt collection procedures.

Setting credit limits helps to reduce the firm's exposure to bad debts.

2 Check Customers' Creditworthiness

The firm assesses the potential customers' ability to repay the amount owed for goods sold to them on credit.
Creditworthiness can be checked by:

- Consulting *StubbsGazette*
- Asking the customer for a bank reference or trade reference.

DID YOU KNOW?

StubbsGazette *provides a range of services to businesses and consumers through its website and magazine. It enables customers to check on the credit rating of firms. It lists businesses and individuals who have gone into liquidation or bankruptcy.*

Definition: Liquidation
When an organisation is wound up because it is unable to pay its bills as they fall due.

Definition: Bankruptcy
When an organisation is declared by law that it is unable to pay its debts.

3 Efficient Administration

Once credit has been given, the firm must ensure that documents such as invoices and statements are accurate and are sent to customers on time.

4 Debt Collection Procedure

The firm needs to have an effective debt collection procedure to collect money owed to the business. This involves sending reminders, offering discounts to customers for early payments, and charging interest on any late payments.

Benefits of Credit Control

An organisation with an efficient credit control system will see many benefits, including:

- **Lower risk of bankruptcy:** A business that collects and pays its debts on time should avoid cash flow problems that can lead to bankruptcy.
- **Reduces bad debts:** The business gives only the most reliable customers credit terms. This reduces the incidence of bad debts.
- **Increased sales and profits:** By selecting the best and most reliable customers for credit purposes, businesses can build, maintain and increase sales.

4 FINANCIAL CONTROL

In business, financial control aims to ensure that the business is profitable and liquid (liquidity is the ability to pay bills as they fall due).

Any business that fails to keep proper financial control will run the risk of losses. These can eventually become unsustainable and could lead to the closure of the business.

There are a number of management tools that a manager can use in financial control.

Methods of Financial Control

Management Tool	Explanation
Cash Flow Forecast (You will learn more about this topic in Chapter 17)	→ A cash flow forecast is a financial plan that sets out planned future income and expenditure. An accurate cash flow forecast can help a business to ensure that it can pay its bills as they fall due.
Ratio Analysis (You will learn more about this topic in Chapter 18)	→ Ratio analysis can be used to obtain a quick indication of an organisation's financial performance and state of affairs.
Budget Allocation	→ The business sets a budget for each department, e.g. production, marketing, for a set period of time, such as a year. This helps the firm to control spending in the different areas of the firm.

THE IMPORTANCE OF CONTROL

The management activity of controlling is important to a business for the following reasons:

- **Business goals:** Control is used to compare actual performance with the standards set. Any deviations can be noted and corrective action taken immediately. This helps the firm to achieve its aims and objectives.
- **Maximises resources:** Efficient control procedures help a business to eliminate waste, e.g. fewer mistakes will be made, so fewer faulty products are manufactured.
- **Employee motivation:** Employees who are involved in improving quality at the firm tend to have higher motivation. This increases the firm's productivity levels.
- **Increases sales and profits:** Customers are loyal to firms that produce high-quality products. This can increase the sales and profits of a business.

Activity 12.5

In pairs, create a collage to summarise the different types of control used in business. You could use images from magazines or online tools such as Adobe Spark or Pic-Collage.

KEY TERMS

Now you have completed this chapter, you should understand and be able to explain the following terms. In your copybook, write a definition of each term to build up your own glossary of terms.

- controlling
- stock
- stock control
- electronic data interchange (EDI)
- just in time (JIT)
- quality control
- inspection
- quality circle

- quality awards
- Q Mark
- ISO
- total quality management (TQM)
- credit control
- debtor
- bad debt
- credit limit

- creditworthiness
- liquidation
- bankruptcy
- financial control
- cash flow forecast
- ratio analysis
- budget
- credit controller

PowerPoint Summary

EXAM-STYLE QUESTIONS

Ordinary Level

Section 1 – Short Questions (10 marks each)

1 List **four** types of control used in a business.
2 Outline **two** reasons why stock control is important to an organisation.
3 List **three** ways in which a manager could check the quality of goods produced.
4 What do the following abbreviations stand for?
   (i) JIT   (ii) TQM   (iii) ISO
5 Name **two** awards that a business could achieve for producing high-quality products.
6 What is a bad debt?
7 List **three** ways in which a manager can reduce the risk of a bad debt.
8 Indicate whether the following sentences are true or false.

	Statements	True or False
A	EDI stands for electronic data interchange.	
B	It is mandatory for factory floor staff to become members of a quality circle.	
C	Bad debts refers to customers who pay their bill in full and on time.	
D	Lead time refers to the length of time it takes to produce a good.	
E	Liquidation of a business occurs when a judge closes the firm as it cannot pay its bills.	

Section 2 – Long Questions

1 Describe the difference between the following types of stock: (i) raw materials; (ii) work in progress; and (iii) finished goods. **(15 marks)**

2
> Management in a business must introduce a <u>stock control</u> system. This ensures that the firm always has <u>optimum stock levels</u>. When re-ordering stock, the manager must consider the <u>lead time</u> involved.

Explain the underlined terms. **(15 marks)**

3 Outline the disadvantages of a business carrying too much stock. **(15 marks)**

4 Explain the term *quality control*. Describe how inspections can be used to improve quality at a firm. **(15 marks)**

5 A business can gain awards for producing top-quality goods. Name **three** of these awards and explain any **two** of them. **(20 marks)**

6 Name **three** ways in which management can assess the creditworthiness of a new customer to the business. Explain any **one** of these methods. **(15 marks)**

Section 2 – Long Questions *continued*

7 As part of financial control, describe how (i) cash flow forecasts and (ii) department budgets can help a business to remain profitable and liquid. **(15 marks)**

8 Outline **three** benefits that the management activity of controlling can bring to a business. **(20 marks)**

Higher Level

Section 1 – Short Questions (10 marks each)

1 Define the term *controlling* as a management activity. List **four** areas of a business where control is essential.

2 Outline what is meant by the term *stock control*. Outline **one** benefit that stock control brings to a business.

3 Describe **two** disadvantages of a firm carrying too little stock.

4 What is meant by the term *JIT*? Outline **two** advantages of this system.

5 Discuss **two** advantages of using quality circles in quality control.

6 Describe **two** benefits that a credit control system would give to a business.

7 Illustrate your understanding of the term *financial control*.

8 Describe **two** measures a business could undertake to reduce the likelihood of bad debts.

Section 2 – Applied Business Question (80 marks)

Beauty Cart

Louise Howard owns Beauty Cart, an online business selling beauty products on credit to beauty salons around Ireland. The beauty salons are given a credit limit of €5,000 and are expected to pay their bills within 30 days.

Beauty Cart sells over 45 different brands but Louise finds it very difficult to manage stock levels, which has a direct impact on the firm's profits. Last year she mistakenly ordered too much stock for Christmas. The Christmas packaging meant that consumers did not want to buy the items after Christmas. A report by her warehouse manager identified that after a manual stock check it was apparent that staff had stolen significant quantities of stock. Louise knows that she needs to work with the warehouse manager to order optimum stock levels this Christmas.

For a long time, Louise has wanted to supply high-end beauty salons across the UK. Many of these salons want the suppliers to have independent quality awards. The firm's quality control department wants Louise to apply for external quality awards, such as the Q Mark. Consumers trust brands that have achieved quality standards and are often willing to pay more for these products. The marketing manager agrees with this proposal and suggests to Louise that the awards could be displayed on the firm's website.

A meeting with the firm's finance manager has made Louise worried about the future of the firm. The annual report has indicated that Louise is not using money efficiently, due to the overstocking of products. The report also notes that despite rising sales figures, some of the beauty salons to which she has sold goods on credit have become bad debts. This is despite the finance department sending regular reminders of invoice payments. The finance manager thinks that Louise needs to introduce creditworthiness checks to reduce the incidences of bad debts.

Louise needs to spend some time considering all the issues at her firm. She knows that she must implement more robust control mechanisms to guarantee the future success of Beauty Cart.

A Define the term *stock control*. Describe the disadvantages for Beauty Cart of carrying too much stock. **(25 marks)**

B Evaluate the benefits to Beauty Cart of achieving independent quality awards. **(25 marks)**

C (i) What is meant by the term *optimum stock levels*?

(ii) Discuss the drawbacks to Beauty Cart of carrying too much stock. **(30 marks)**

Section 3 – Long Questions

1 Describe how a business introduces a control mechanism. Illustrate your answer with reference to a business of your choice. **(20 marks)**

2 Controlling is an important management activity. Name the **four** types of management control. Evaluate **one** of these methods of control in relation to running a successful modern business. **(20 marks)**

3 Having too little or too much stock can cause serious problems for a business. Outline the importance of having an efficient system of stock control. **(20 marks)**

4 Evaluate **two** methods of quality control, giving at least **one** advantage and **one** disadvantage of each method. **(20 marks)**

5 Describe the process a business needs to introduce to achieve an ISO award. **(20 marks)**

6 The credit controller in a firm must be aware of the dangers of bad debts, liquidation and bankruptcy when operating a credit control system in a business. Explain the underlined terms. **(20 marks)**

7 Credit control is a key management activity. Explain why managers need to engage in credit control. **(20 marks)**

8 In your opinion, which management control activity is the most important? Explain your answer. **(15 marks)**

PREVIOUS LEAVING CERTIFICATE EXAM QUESTIONS

Ordinary Level

Section A – Short Questions (10 marks each)

1 Outline **two** benefits of **quality control** for a business. [LC OL 2017]
2 Explain the term *stock control*. [LC OL 2010]
3 Outline **two** benefits of a good stock control system for a business. [LC OL 2012]

Section B

1 Explain each of the following terms: (i) *credit control* and (ii) *quality control*. **(20 marks)** [LC OL 2005]

2

> John and Martin Quinn are organic farmers in Co. Wicklow. They supply organic vegetables and meat to local shops, restaurants and butchers. Their business is expanding and they believe that with the correct channels of distribution and a suitable pricing policy they can become very successful.
>
> The brothers are concerned with their cash flow position and they know that credit control is a problem. They give their established customers 30 days' credit but some of their customers do not pay their bills on time.

Describe **two** methods to improve their credit control system. **(20 marks)** [LC OL 2009]

3 Explain the terms (i) *stock control* and (ii) *financial control*. **(15 marks)** [LC OL 2008]

Higher Level

Section A – Short Questions (10 marks each)

1 Name **three** types of control in business. [LC HL 2003]

Section B

1 Explain the methods a business could consider to minimise the risk of bad debts as part of its credit control system. **(20 marks)** [LC HL 2015]

2 Describe how stock control and financial control achieve efficiencies in business. **(20 marks)** [LC HL 2011]

3 Evaluate the contributions that stock control and credit control make to the successful management of a business. Use examples in your answer. **(20 marks)** [LC HL 2008]

CHAPTER 13 HUMAN RESOURCE MANAGEMENT

⊕ Learning Outcomes

When you have completed this chapter, you will be able to:

1 Define *human resource management*

2 Explain the functions of a human resource manager, including:

— human resource planning

— recruitment and selection

— training and development

— performance appraisal

— rewarding employees

— employer–employee relationships.

Literacy Link

Human resource management (HRM), recruitment and selection, training and development, performance appraisal, labour turnover, CV, rewards

Numeracy Link

Division, multiplication, percentages

Cross-curricular Link

English – oral and written communication
Home Economics – skills development

CASE STUDY — <u>Human Resource Management at Vodafone</u>

In 2015, Vodafone Ireland invested €60 million in developing a European sales centre in Dublin. **Human resource planning** identified that the firm needed to recruit and select 200 new staff to take up positions in the firm.

The company also employs workers through its graduate programme, with vacancies for twenty college graduates. During the **recruitment and selection** process, candidates complete an **application form** and then submit a **CV** to the firm. The HR manager **screens** the applications and makes a **shortlist** of candidates, who sit a series of **selection tests**. Candidates are then chosen to take part in a video **interview** with management. Successful applicants receive a **job offer** and then complete an eighteen-month graduate programme.

Employees at Vodafone receive a range of **financial rewards** such as a competitive **salary** and **bonus** payments based on performance. **Non-financial**

rewards are also used to motivate staff, including **employee share purchase plans** and health insurance cover.

Employees undergo an annual **performance appraisal** where management set targets to be achieved for the year. This also helps the HR manager to identify **training and development** needs among staff.

Vodafone offers a range of **on-the-job training** programmes such as **induction training** for new recruits as well as customer service training for existing staff.

There is a positive **employer–employee relationship** at Vodafone. A company survey indicated that 91% of staff believe that the firm treats them with respect and 87% of staff would recommend Vodafone as a place to work.

HUMAN RESOURCE MANAGEMENT (HRM)

Human resources (HR) are the employees who work for a firm. They possess skills and knowledge that help the business to run successfully.

Human resource management (HRM) is a system of recruiting employees to the business. They are then trained, developed and rewarded for their efforts. The responsibility for HRM lies with the firm's human resource manager.

> **Exam Tip!**
> Make sure that you can **list the functions of the human resource manager.**

Functions of an HR Manager

The functions/roles of the human resource manager include:

1 Human resource planning (HR planning)	2 Recruitment and selection	3 Training and development
6 Employer–employee relationships	**FUNCTIONS OF AN HR MANAGER**	4 Rewards
	5 Performance appraisal	

1 HUMAN RESOURCE PLANNING

The HR manager carries out human resource planning (HR planning). This ensures that the business has the correct number of staff with the necessary skills and qualifications to fill all vacancies in the business. HR planning involves the following steps.

Step 1: Review Current Staff

The HR manager reviews the current staff numbers and each staff member's qualifications, skills and experience.

Step 2: Forecast Human Resource Needs

The HR manager estimates (forecasts) the number of employees and the types of skill that will be needed to fill all future roles at the firm. Forecasting can be influenced by factors such as future business expansion or changes in consumer demand.

Step 3: Estimate Labour Turnover

The HR manager estimates the number of employees who will leave the business. This can be as a result of ill health, retirement or employees leaving to take jobs in other firms.

Example

Germany's state rail company Deutsche Bahn estimated that it would need to employ 19,000 new employees in 2018 due to retirements from the firm. It had recruited 60,000 new employees over the previous five years.

Labour turnover refers to the proportion of employees who leave the workforce. Some labour turnover is healthy in a business as new employees can bring new ideas and skills to the firm. However, high labour turnover may have a negative impact on the business, for example:

- High training costs as a result of the number of new recruits
- Low productivity while new recruits settle into their roles
- High recruitment costs, e.g. for advertising vacancies.

Businesses can reduce labour turnover by:

- Offering financial rewards, e.g. bonus payments, and non-financial rewards, e.g. flexitime or job sharing
- Improving the recruitment and selection process to reduce the likelihood of employing unsuitable candidates.

Step 4: Create an HR Plan

The HR manager formulates a plan to ensure that the firm has the correct number of employees with the required skills when needed.

If the firm:

- Needs more employees – it recruits extra staff
- Requires different skills – it recruits new staff or trains existing staff
- Needs fewer staff – the HR manager makes some employees redundant.

Step 5: Review the Plan

The HR plan should be reviewed regularly. If the plan does not meet the needs of the business, changes can be made, such as increasing recruitment, training additional staff or making staff redundant.

Activity 13.1

The formula to calculate labour turnover in a business is:

$$\frac{\text{Number of employees leaving}}{\text{Average number employed}} \times 100$$

During 2020 Irish Country Tours employed on average 95 employees. The business recruited 20 new employees to replace the 29 who retired or left the business. Calculate the annual labour turnover for Irish Country Tours.

Benefits of Human Resource Planning

- **Training needs:** The HR manager can identify training needs and provide training programmes for staff. This enables employees to carry out their jobs effectively.
- **Enough staff:** The business always has enough staff with the required skills to complete all tasks in the business. This enables the business to provide high-quality goods and services to customers.
- **Labour turnover:** HR planning identifies labour turnover in the firm. If the figure is high, the HR manager can take steps to reduce it, e.g. improve recruitment and selection. This helps to reduce recruitment and selection costs for the firm.

2 RECRUITMENT AND SELECTION

The HR manager is responsible for the recruitment and selection process in a business.

Definition: Recruitment
Recruitment involves attracting suitable candidates with the relevant skills, qualifications and experience to apply for job vacancies in the firm. It includes preparing a job description and person specification as well as creating and placing a job advertisement.

Definition: Selection
The process of deciding which applicant is the most suitable for the advertised job vacancy. It involves screening applicants, conducting selection tests and interviews, making job offers, formulating employment contracts and notifying unsuccessful candidates.

The Recruitment and Selection Process

The recruitment and selection process involves some or all of these steps:

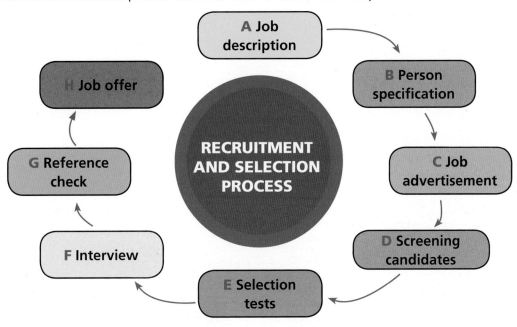

RECRUITMENT AND SELECTION PROCESS

- A Job description
- B Person specification
- C Job advertisement
- D Screening candidates
- E Selection tests
- F Interview
- G Reference check
- H Job offer

A Job Description

Once the HR manager has identified a vacancy in the business, they prepare a job description. This is a written outline of the job title, duties and responsibilities associated with the role. It may include details of pay and the person to whom the employee will report.

Job Description for a Marketing Assistant at Bennett Ltd	
Job Title:	Marketing Assistant
Reporting to:	Marketing Director
Duties:	Organising company events
	Managing the firm's social media platforms
Salary:	€25,000

B Person Specification

This sets out the ideal candidate for the job vacancy. It outlines the qualifications, skills, characteristics and experience needed by the person to fill the role. A person specification helps the HR manager draft an accurate job description in order to attract the most suitable candidates.

Person Specification for a Marketing Assistant at Bennett Ltd	
Essential:	Bachelor's degree in business or marketing
	Excellent communication and interpersonal skills
Desirable:	One year's experience in a similar role
	Proficiency using Microsoft Office

C Job Advertisement

The HR manager creates a job advertisement based on the job description and person specification. The vacancy should be advertised in a location that will be seen by the largest number of potential candidates, such as on the firm's website, in newspapers or on recruitment websites, e.g. www.irishjobs.ie.

The advertisement usually contains the following information:

- Main duties of the advertised role
- Qualifications and skills required
- Pay and benefits, e.g. annual salary and private health insurance
- Location of the job
- Method by which candidates should apply, e.g. CV and cover letter and the address it should be sent to.

Job Advertisement

Bennett Ltd has an immediate vacancy for a Marketing Assistant to join their busy Marketing Department in their offices in Limerick city.

Duties and responsibilities include:

- Organising company events
- Managing the firm's social media platforms.

The ideal candidate will have:

- A bachelor's degree in business or marketing
- Excellent communication and interpersonal skills
- One year's experience in a similar role
- Proficiency using Microsoft Office.

Salary: €25,000 per annum

To apply for this role, please send your CV and cover letter to Michelle Clancy at hr@bennett.ie by 5 p.m. on Friday 18 November.

Bennett Ltd is an equal opportunities employer.

Definition: Equal opportunities employer
This employer respects the Employment Equality Acts 1998–2015 when recruiting, selecting, promoting and training employees. It does not discriminate against employees based on grounds such as gender, age and race.

You learned about the Employment Equality Acts 1998–2015 in Chapter 3.

D Screening Candidates

The HR manager matches the job applications received against the job description and person specification. A shortlist is made of suitable candidates. Applications that do not meet the criteria are rejected.

Methods Used When Applying for Jobs

CV
A curriculum vitae is a written document that outlines a person's qualifications, skills and experience. It contains details such as education, work experience, interests and hobbies.

Cover Letter
This is a letter written by the candidate giving details about why they want the job and the benefits they would bring to the business if selected.

Application Form
This contains a number of questions, which the employer asks all candidates to complete. It can include information on qualifications and experience. It can make it easier for the employer to compare all job applicants as they all answer the same questions.

E Selection Tests

The HR manager may conduct a range of selection tests to further shortlist the candidates. These tests could include:

- **Intelligence tests** – measure numerical and language reasoning
- **Personality tests** – identify whether the candidate's personality is suitable for the job advertised
- **Work sample tests** – candidates perform sample jobs to identify whether they have the necessary skills for the role, e.g. drafting a report or memo.

DID YOU KNOW? *Selection tests are used by companies such as Microsoft, KPMG and Ford Motors.*

Note!
Not all businesses use selection tests as part of their recruitment and selection process.

F Interview

Candidates who perform successfully at the selection test stage are called for interview. At the interview, the candidate is asked job-related questions to assess their suitability for the job.

Definition: Interview
A formal meeting between the applicant and representative(s) of the company, e.g. the HR manager.

- **One-to-one interviews** take place between the candidate and a representative of the business, e.g. department manager.
- **Panel interviews** involve the candidate and a number of interviewers, e.g. the HR manager and the manager of the relevant department. This helps to reduce interviewer bias and ensure that the most suitable candidate is chosen.

G Reference Check

The HR manager conducts a reference check on the candidates who performed best at interview. The reference is usually provided by someone who can confirm the education and work experience details given by the candidate. Referees might include a former employer or school principal.

DID YOU KNOW?

According to recruitment company Monster.ie, almost 60% of managers decide not to offer a job to a candidate due to a poor reference.

H Job Offer

The HR manager makes a job offer to the successful candidate, usually by phone. A formal job offer is then sent to the candidate in writing and it includes details such as the job title, salary and length of probationary period. The HR manager also contacts the other candidates to inform them that they have not been successful in obtaining the role.

Definition: Probationary period
A trial period during which the employer and the new employee can decide whether they are a suitable fit for each other. If the employer is unhappy with the performance of the new recruit, they can end their contract; likewise, if the employee decides they are not comfortable in the role they can leave the post.

Activity 13.2

Working in pairs, find **five** job advertisements for jobs that require candidates who speak a foreign language. You could use recruitment websites such as www.irishjobs.ie or local and national newspapers. Compare the jobs you have found with those your classmates found. Do all the job advertisements contain the same type of information? Which are the highest-paid and lowest-paid jobs you found?

Internal Recruitment

Internal recruitment means that the business fills job vacancies with existing employees in the workforce. Internal recruitment can be achieved by:

DID YOU KNOW?

At Vodafone, the majority of job vacancies are filled using internal recruitment.

- Promotion – an employee moves to a higher-ranking role in the firm
- Redeployment – an employee moves from one section of the business to another.

External Recruitment

Employers use the external labour market to find new employees to fill job vacancies. External recruitment might be conducted by:

- Placing job advertisements on the firm's website, recruitment websites or in newspapers and on social media
- Using a recruitment agency, which shortlists candidates for the employer
- Headhunting – a specialised agency identifies and approaches people employed in firms to fill job vacancies in other businesses.

Unit 4

179

EXTERNAL RECRUITMENT

✓ Advantages	✗ Disadvantages
1 Best Candidate The employer can appoint the best candidate for the job from a wider pool of applicants than from internal recruitment.	**1 Lower Employee Motivation** Employees may have lower motivation as they can feel that it is pointless to work hard if promotions are awarded to external candidates.
2 New Ideas External candidates can bring new ideas to the business. These ideas can increase business productivity.	**2 Cost** It can be expensive for the business to place job advertisements in newspapers or on recruitment websites.
3 Introduce Change It may be easier for the new employee to introduce change to the business, as they do not have an existing relationship with staff.	**3 Slower Integration Time** It can take the external candidate a while to integrate into the business. This reduces workplace productivity.
4 More Skills Current employees may learn or improve their skills by working with a new employee who has different skills and experience from them.	**4 Unsuitable Employee** While the external candidate may have performed well at interview, they may not be suitable for the role. They may leave the role and the business will have to begin the recruitment and selection process again.

Benefits of Recruitment and Selection

- **Increased productivity:** Recruitment and selection help the business to find and choose the best candidates for job vacancies. This can increase productivity in the business.

- **New ideas:** New staff can bring new ideas into the business, e.g. production methods or sales techniques. These can help the firm reduce costs or increase sales.

- **Employee retention:** By selecting the most suitable candidate for the job vacancy, the HR manager reduces the likelihood of the new recruit leaving the firm. This improves employee retention and reduces recruitment and selection costs.

3 TRAINING AND DEVELOPMENT

Training

Training is a process that ensures that employees have the skills, knowledge and attitudes needed to carry out their jobs effectively.

When a new employee starts their job, they complete **induction training**. Induction training helps new employees to become familiar with the business, employees, culture and procedures. It ensures that employees have the work skills to make them fully productive as quickly as possible. The training can include:

- A general introduction to the business
- Information on the layout of the building
- Health and safety rules
- Business goals.

Example
New employees at Marks & Spencer receive 1–2 weeks of induction training, which includes an overview of the business as well as job-specific training.

Unit 4

New employees may receive an induction pack, which includes detailed information on health and safety rules and the business's code of conduct.

Businesses want their staff to possess a wide range of skills. This makes employees more adaptable to changes in the workplace. Firms offer two types of training: on-the-job training and off-the-job training.

A On-the-job Training

This type of training takes place in the workplace. It can include:

- **Work shadowing:** Observing a more experienced staff member, e.g. new staff watch an existing member of staff use the firm's computer system.
- **Demonstration:** Showing a new employee how to carry out their role, e.g. a sales assistant shows a new employee how to operate the till.
- **Job rotation:** The new employee moves around the firm doing different jobs, e.g. spending three months working in the HR department and the next three months in the marketing department.

ON-THE-JOB TRAINING

✓ Advantages	✗ Disadvantages
1 Cheaper This type of training is cheaper than formal training, as the business does not have to pay an external organisation to run a course.	**1 Quality of Training** The quality of the training depends on the ability of the trainer and the time given to train the new employee.
2 Faster Integration As the new employee learns on the job, they become familiar with how the business is run. This helps them to integrate into the organisation more quickly.	**2 Staff Resentment** Some staff may resent having to train new employees. They may become uncooperative, as they believe that training is not part of their job description.
3 Increased Productivity Training takes place in the workplace. This reduces time spent away from the workplace and increases productivity.	**3 Bad Habits** Bad habits of the trainer may be passed on to the new employee, e.g. filing paperwork incorrectly. This may reduce productivity in the workplace.

B Off-the-job Training

This type of training takes place in a venue outside the workplace and can include:

- Workshops
- Lectures
- Demonstrations
- Courses.

Examples

- Employees in the marketing department attend a social media marketing workshop in a local training centre.
- A trainee accountant attends lectures to become a qualified accountant.

DID YOU KNOW?
A Eurostat survey has shown that 23% of Irish employees took part in training courses related to their area of work compared to 61% of employees in the Netherlands.

Unit 4

OFF-THE-JOB TRAINING

✓ Advantages	✗ Disadvantages
1 High Quality Specialists in specific areas, e.g. communication, provide the training. This often means that the training is of higher quality than on-the-job training.	**1 Expensive** It is more expensive than on-the-job training. Costs can include travel expenses, training course fees and possibly overtime payments if the course takes place during the employee's free time.
2 Exchanging Ideas Employees can meet staff from other organisations and exchange ideas. These ideas can be used in the business to reduce costs or increase sales.	**2 Lack of Relevancy** Off-the-job training may include skills and knowledge that are not relevant to the employee. This can be a waste of time and money for the business.
3 Lower Workplace Absenteeism Some training may take place during the employee's free time, e.g. courses and seminars. This reduces the time the employee is absent from the workplace.	**3 Reduced Productivity** Employees may need to attend off-the-job training during working hours. This reduces productivity in the workplace.

Development

Development can include employees taking educational courses or developing career plans. It increases employees' self-esteem and prepares them for promotion.

While a development programme for employees can be costly for a business, it is beneficial because employees can become more productive and motivated.

> **Definition: Development**
> Development is a long-term approach used for existing employees. It encourages them to take on new challenges and focus on career development. It ensures that employees have a higher level of skills, which improves their professional development.

Example
Virgin Atlantic organised a personal development workshop for their managers. The workshop included individual coaching sessions where managers set personal development goals. This led to increased motivation and retention of managers and increased internal recruitment for management roles by 10%.

Advantages of Training and Development

- **Increased productivity:** Employees have the correct skills and knowledge to complete their duties effectively. This increases workplace productivity.
- **Industrial relations:** Training and development ensures that employees understand the quality standards expected by management. This reduces the likelihood of industrial relations problems between management and staff.
- **Future managers:** Training and development prepares staff for management roles in the firm. Employees are motivated to work harder as there will be opportunities for promotion in the future.

Activity 13.3

Using a Scrabble board (given to you by your teacher), work in pairs to note as many terms as possible associated with training and development. Now add up the total score for each word you recorded. Which word earned the highest score?

4 REWARDS

The HR manager is responsible for creating a rewards package to motivate employees. This package can include financial and non-financial rewards. Motivated employees work harder and there are lower levels of absenteeism and labour turnover.

Financial Rewards

These are monetary payments received by employees for their workplace effort. They can include:

Reward	Explanation	Advantages	Disadvantages
Time Rate	→ Employees receive a fixed amount of pay per hour and work an agreed number of hours per week, e.g. €12 per hour for 35 hours.	→ Easy for the employer to calculate.	→ Employees may complete their work slowly to obtain more overtime hours at higher pay.
Piece Rate	→ The employee is paid per item produced or job completed, e.g. per table assembled.	→ Motivates employees to work faster, because the quicker they work, the more pay they receive.	→ It can lead to poor-quality products, as employees hurry to complete work.
Salary	→ Employees are paid a fixed sum regardless of the number of hours worked.	→ The employer can accurately plan future expenditure, as it knows how much the firm's wage bill will cost.	→ No incentive for the employees to work harder, as they know they will receive the same payment regardless of effort.
Commission	→ Employees earn a percentage of the total sales they have achieved. Sales staff are likely to earn commission.	→ Motivates employees to work harder to sell goods or services to consumers.	→ Employees may be too pushy in order to gain a sale. Consumers may decide to buy elsewhere.
Bonus	→ This is an extra payment received by the employee for reaching a target or at specific times of the year, e.g. Christmas.	→ Motivates employees to work harder to reach a target.	→ Expensive for the firm to pay out to staff, especially if business profits have fallen.
Employee Profit-sharing	→ A percentage of the firm's annual profits is shared among employees.	→ Motivates staff to work as a team to achieve business goals. They know that if the business is profitable, they will earn a share of the profits.	→ Hard-working employees may resent the fact that less productive staff earn the same share of the profit. This can cause dissatisfaction and demotivate staff.
Employee Share Purchase Plan (ESPP)	→ Employees can buy shares in the business, often at a discounted price.	→ Makes employees feel that they are an important part of the business and motivates them to work harder to make the business a success.	→ It can be expensive for a business to manage an employee share purchase plan, e.g. legal and administrative costs.

Example: Bonus
American energy company Hilcorp achieved its goal of increasing the value of the company eight months ahead of schedule. As a reward for this achievement, the company gave each of its employees a bonus of $100,000 (€85,000).

Example: Employee Share Purchase Plan
ESB Electric Ireland operates an ESPP. Current and former employees collectively own a 5% stake in the company.

Activity 13.4

Amelia works in a clothes shop and earns €10.50 per hour for a 40-hour week. If she works over 40 hours she earns a rate of time and a half. If Amelia worked 48 hours this week, calculate her gross pay.

Non-financial Rewards

Non-financial rewards are the rewards received by an employee that are not in the form of money. They can include:

Reward	Explanation	Advantages	Disadvantages
Benefit-in-Kind (BIK) (also known as perks or fringe benefits)	→ Employees receive products, services or discounts instead of money as part of their income, e.g. a company car or meal vouchers.	→ It can help to attract new employees and retain current staff.	→ It can be difficult for the employer to find a BIK that motivates all staff.
Job Enlargement	→ Employees are given additional duties on top of their normal role in the firm.	→ It helps to reduce employee boredom and can make the role more satisfying for the employee.	→ Employees may be unhappy with the changes imposed by management and could become uncooperative.
Job Enrichment	→ Employees are given more responsibilities and are able to make decisions on behalf of the business.	→ It prepares employees for future promotions in the business.	→ Employees could make poor decisions, which could damage the firm's reputation.
Job Sharing	→ Employees share a position in the firm, e.g. office assistant. Job sharing can be done in a number of ways: —working one week on, one week off —working alternate days.	→ It improves work–life balance and can help to retain staff.	→ Poor communication between the employees who are job sharing can result in slow task completion.

Note!

A benefit-in-kind can be viewed as a financial reward if the item is taxable, e.g. a company car. If it is not taxable (e.g. canteen lunch or vouchers worth less than €200) it is not viewed as a financial reward.

Reward	Explanation	Advantages	Disadvantages
Extra Holidays	→ Employees are given more annual leave, e.g. an extra five days' holidays per year.	→ It can help to retain staff in the business who value personal time over work time.	→ It can be difficult for management to schedule holidays and ensure that there are sufficient numbers of staff available at all times to run the business effectively.
Flexitime	→ Employees choose their own working hours within an agreed time frame, e.g. staff must be in the workplace between 10 a.m. and 4 p.m.	→ It helps to retain staff as it can reduce their commute time and improve work–life balance.	→ It can be difficult to schedule meetings as employees may want to start and end their work day at different times.

Example

Europe's largest telecommunications company, Deutsche Telekom, gives employees fourteen additional days' holiday to increase retention rates among staff.

CASE STUDY

Financial and Non-financial Rewards at Pret A Manger

Pret A Manger is a worldwide chain of sandwich stores. It provides the following financial and non-financial rewards for store managers:

- Commuter Club – support with public transport costs
- Bonus – generous quarterly bonus scheme
- Free food from the store – when the manager is working
- Discount of 50% off the store's food – when the manager is not working
- Family support – life assurance and childcare vouchers
- Private healthcare – private health insurance.

Benefits of Rewards

- **Employee motivation:** Rewards help to motivate staff to work harder to provide higher-quality products to consumers. This can lead to increased sales and profits for the firm.
- **Employee recruitment and retention:** Good financial and non-financial rewards can help the firm recruit and retain high-quality staff.
- **Increased job satisfaction:** Rewarding employees for high-quality work increases their job satisfaction. This, in turn, increases their loyalty to the business.

DID YOU KNOW? *According to research carried out by Glassdoor, 67% of job applicants viewed pay as the most important factor when applying for jobs.*

Activity 13.5

Working in pairs, one of you draws an image to represent a financial or non-financial reward. Your partner must guess the reward and outline an advantage or disadvantage of each reward, gaining a point for each correct answer given. Swap roles to see which of you can earn the most points.

5 PERFORMANCE APPRAISAL

Performance appraisal is a review of an employee's performance and is usually carried out by the employee's direct manager or the HR manager. The manager meets with the employee and agrees goals to be achieved within a period of time, e.g. a year. At the end of the period they meet again to evaluate the employee's performance.

There are a number of steps in the performance appraisal process:

Step 1 – Set performance targets

Step 2 – Measure employee performance

Step 3 – Performance appraisal meeting

- **Step 1 – Set performance targets:** The employee and HR manager meet to set the targets to be achieved by the employee within a particular time frame, e.g. one year.
- **Step 2 – Measure employee performance:** The HR manager meets with the employee on a regular basis to measure and track progress. The employee may be given additional help from management to achieve the target, e.g. training or resources.
- **Step 3 – Performance appraisal meeting:** The HR manager and employee meet for the formal performance appraisal. The HR manager compares the target set against the actual performance achieved by the employee. The employee may receive a pay increase if targets have been met. Additional training may be given to employees who do not meet their targets.

Benefits of Performance Appraisal

Many benefits arise from a business conducting performance appraisal, including:

- **Training needs:** It can help identify training needs for employees and these can be organised by the HR manager, e.g. workshops or work shadowing.
- **Promotion:** It can help the HR manager to identify candidates for future promotion. These employees have achieved the targets set and may want more responsibility in the firm.
- **Performance-related pay:** It can be used to decide on financial and non-financial rewards for employees. For example, an employee who performs well may receive an increase in pay or a benefit-in-kind such as the use of a company car.
- **Employee motivation:** As employees know that their work is monitored, they may be more motivated to work harder. This can improve business productivity.
- **Industrial relations:** Employees can highlight problems in the business during a performance appraisal. This can help management to deal with issues quickly and improve industrial relations in the workplace.

CASE STUDY — *Performance Appraisal at IBM*

Technology company IBM decided to adapt their annual performance appraisal to improve the effectiveness of the process.

The company introduced an app called Checkpoint, which enables staff to give feedback on all staff members regardless of title or rank. Supervisors and employees meet 3–4 times per year to discuss and receive feedback. The new performance appraisal process has improved communication and connections between management and staff.

Activity 13.6

Working in pairs, complete a ladder graphic organiser to summarise the steps in performance appraisal and the benefits the process brings to the business.

6 EMPLOYER–EMPLOYEE RELATIONSHIPS

The HR manager works hard to ensure that there is a positive employer–employee relationship in the firm. Positive relationships can result in increased staff productivity, less industrial action and improved recruitment and retention of staff.

A positive employer–employee relationship can be achieved in the following ways:

1 **Honest communication:** Regular face-to-face meetings enable the business to communicate with staff openly and honestly. At these meetings management can inform staff of the issues facing the business and receive employee feedback.

2 **Training:** Training can improve employees' skills and knowledge so that they can perform their duties to a high standard. This reduces conflict with management over quality standards.

3 **Social activities:** HR managers organise social activities, e.g. sports events, to meet Maslow's social needs (see Chapter 7). This helps management and staff build informal relationships.

4 **Health and safety:** The HR manager ensures that the work environment is healthy and safe for all staff. Health and safety training should be given to new and existing staff, e.g. manual handling training and fire safety.

5 **Grievance procedure:** The HR manager is responsible for formulating a grievance procedure to deal with staff complaints, e.g. disagreements with superiors, pay disputes. Staff use this procedure to make an official complaint to management and resolve the issue.

> *Definition*: **Grievance procedure**
> A formal method of resolving workplace problems and complaints.

> *Definition*: **Manual handling**
> The physical lifting of items in the workplace, e.g. boxes. Staff should be trained on how to handle bulky or heavy items to reduce the risk of injury.

Benefits of Good Employer–Employee Relationships

Good employer–employee relationships produce a pleasant working atmosphere, which benefits everyone. Specifically, it helps with:

- **Employee motivation:** High-quality training and organised social activities can help to make employees feel valued in the workplace, which increases their motivation.

- **Lowers absenteeism:** Health and safety training can reduce the likelihood of accidents in the workplace. This lowers absenteeism levels among employees and reduces business disruption.

- **Employee recruitment and retention:** Positive industrial relations between management and staff helps to recruit and retain staff in the business. This reduces recruitment and training costs for the firm.

Activity 13.7

Create a collage of images to represent the ways in which an HR manager can encourage positive employer–employee relationships and the benefits that it brings to the business. Present your collage to other students for them to identify what each image represents.

KEY TERMS

Now you have completed this chapter, you should understand and be able to explain the following terms. In your copybook, write a definition of each term to build up your own glossary of terms.

- human resource management (HRM)
- human resource manager
- human resource planning
- labour turnover
- recruitment
- selection
- job description
- person specification
- selection tests
- interview
- reference check
- CV
- cover letter

- application form
- equal opportunities employer
- internal recruitment
- external recruitment
- training
- development
- on-the-job training
- off-the-job training
- induction training
- financial rewards
- time rate
- piece rate
- salary

- commission
- bonus
- employee profit-sharing
- employee share purchase plan (ESPP)
- non-financial rewards
- benefit-in-kind (BIK)
- job enlargement
- job enrichment
- job sharing
- flexitime
- performance appraisal
- employer–employee relationships

PowerPoint Summary

EXAM-STYLE QUESTIONS

Ordinary Level

Section 1 – Short Questions (10 marks each)

1 List **three** duties performed by an HR manager.

2 Write the steps in HR planning in the correct order in your copybook. Label the first step number 1 and the final step as number 5.

Steps in HR Planning	
A	Human resource forecasting
B	Create a HR plan
C	Review current staff
D	Review the HR plan
E	Estimate labour turnover

3 List **two** pieces of information that would be included in (i) a job description and (ii) a person specification.

4 Outline **two** advantages of internal recruitment for a business.

5 State **two** ways, other than advertising on the firm's website, in which a business can recruit new staff.

6 Explain the term *induction training*.

7 What do the following letters stand for? (i) HRM, (ii) CV and (iii) BIK.

8 Indicate whether the following statements are true or false.

Statements		True or False
A	A job description includes details of the duties and responsibilities of the vacant role in the business.	
B	Induction training is given to new employees in the firm.	
C	Off-the-job training can include work shadowing and attending a course.	
D	Time rate is paid based on the number of hours worked.	
E	A grievance procedure is used to solve problems between the business and the public.	

Unit 4

Section 2 – Long Questions

1 What is meant by the term *HR planning*? Describe the steps taken by the HR manager during the HR planning process. **(25 marks)**

2
> Labour turnover can indicate that employees are unhappy in the workplace.

Outline **three** ways in which a business can reduce labour turnover. **(15 marks)**

3 Employees can apply for job vacancies using a <u>CV</u> and <u>cover letter</u> or an <u>application form</u>. Explain the **three** underlined terms. **(20 marks)**

4
> HR managers may carry out an interview as part of the selection process for new employees.

(i) What is an interview?
(ii) Describe the difference between a one-to-one interview and a panel interview. **(15 marks)**

5 Outline **two** advantages and **one** disadvantage of off-the-job training. **(15 marks)**

6 What is performance appraisal? Describe **two** benefits of performance appraisal for the employer. **(15 marks)**

7
> Olivia Jacob is the HR manager at Cullinan Ltd, a cosmetics manufacturer. She is currently designing the firm's reward package and will include financial and non-financial rewards, such as: <u>commission</u>, <u>bonus</u> and <u>flexitime</u>.

(i) Distinguish between financial and non-financial rewards.
(ii) Explain **two** of the underlined terms. **(20 marks)**

8 Describe **two** ways in which the HR manager can improve the employer–employee relationship in a business. **(15 marks)**

Higher Level

Section 1 – Short Questions (10 marks each)

1 Describe **two** benefits of human resource planning for a business.
2 List **four** pieces of information contained in a job advertisement.
3 State **five** functions of an HR manager in a business.
4 Column 1 is a list of business terms. Column 2 is a list of possible explanations for these terms. Match the two lists in your copybook by writing your answers in the form *number = letter* (e.g. 1 = A).

Business Terms		Explanations	
1	Training	**A**	Improving an employee's skills and knowledge to prepare them to take on new challenges in the business.
2	Recruitment	**B**	A review of the employee's workplace performance.
3	Development	**C**	Deciding which job applicant is most suitable for a job vacancy.
4	Selection	**D**	A process that ensures that employees have the necessary skills, knowledge and attitude to carry out their role.
5	Performance Appraisal	**E**	Attracting suitably qualified and experienced candidates to apply for job vacancies.

5 Distinguish between (i) screening candidates and (ii) selection tests, as part of the recruitment and selection process.
6 What is meant by the term *development* in relation to HRM?
7 Distinguish between job enlargement and job sharing.
8 Outline the benefits of an HR manager conducting a performance appraisal with an employee.

Section 2 – Applied Business Question (80 marks)

Rowley's Department Store

Niall Rowley is the HR manager at Rowley's department store in Dublin. He is responsible for 100 staff, including product buyers, sales assistants, warehouse employees and administrative staff. It is September, and while Christmas shopping may seem far away, Niall must begin the process of human resource planning. He has examined the current staff numbers and realises that ten staff members will be leaving the firm – some are retiring and others have decided to leave and work for other businesses.

Niall knows that some employees are demotivated as they find the work repetitive and boring. To increase motivation he is considering sharing some of the business's profits with employees who have five or more years' service in the business.

Based on this analysis Niall realises that he needs to come up with a plan to make sure all vacancies are filled. He will need to recruit 35 additional staff members from October to January, as this is always the store's busiest period. Last year he didn't recruit enough staff, so Niall knows that he must plan more carefully this year.

Niall needs to recruit and select 20 sales assistants and 15 warehouse employees. He placed a <u>job advertisement</u> on the firm's website and outlined the <u>job description</u> and a description of the ideal candidate. Employees will be paid per hour and employees in some positions will be able to choose their own working hours.

Niall has received many <u>CVs</u> – some even stretch to five pages. He has read through many <u>cover letters</u> and has found it difficult to identify potential candidates. He is considering using an <u>application form</u> to simplify the process.

Niall has a busy time ahead to make sure he has all the staff he needs recruited and trained for the busy Christmas season.

A Explain the **five** underlined terms relating to the recruitment and selection process at Rowley's department store. **(20 marks)**

B Human resource planning is important at Rowley's department store. What is meant by the term *human resource planning*? Describe the steps that must be undertaken when conducting human resource planning. **(30 marks)**

C (i) Describe **two** types of financial and non-financial rewards used by Rowley's department store.

(ii) Outline the benefits of a rewards system for staff and management at Rowley's department store. **(30 marks)**

Section 3 – Long Questions

1 Describe the work undertaken by the HR manager in the following steps of the HR planning process: (i) reviewing current staff; (ii) estimating labour turnover; and (iii) creating an HR plan. **(15 marks)**

2 List the steps involved in recruiting and selecting the most appropriate job applicants. Outline any **four** of these steps. **(20 marks)**

3

> HR managers must ensure that they prepare a detailed and accurate <u>job description</u>, <u>person specification</u> and <u>job advertisement</u>. This helps them to recruit the most suitable candidates for vacant positions in a business.

Explain the underlined terms above. **(15 marks)**

4

> Stephen O'Rourke is the HR Manager at SuperPet, a pet supplies manufacturer. He has received complaints from staff about the weak reward packages available in the firm. Some staff are threatening to leave and seek better pay and conditions elsewhere. Stephen knows that he must act quickly to create improved financial and non-financial rewards for staff.

Formulate a rewards package that includes financial and non-financial rewards for the staff at SuperPet. Outline the advantages and disadvantages of each reward chosen. **(30 marks)**

5

> 'Irish workers are far less likely to participate in on-the-job training.' *Irish Independent, March 2018*

(i) Define *on-the-job training*.

(ii) Describe the benefits of on-the-job training for a business. **(20 marks)**

Section 3 – Long Questions *continued*

6 Discuss the benefits to a business of staff training and development. **(15 marks)**

7

> 'Companies move to ditch the dreaded performance review.' *Irish Times, August 2015*

Do you think employers should stop conducting performance appraisals? Support your answer with detailed reasons. **(15 marks)**

8 Discuss the importance of maintaining positive employee–employer relationships in a business. **(15 marks)**

9 Evaluate the role of the human resource manager in a business. **(20 marks)**

PREVIOUS LEAVING CERTIFICATE EXAM QUESTIONS

Ordinary Level

Section A – Short Questions (10 marks each)

1 Outline **two** methods for rewarding employees. [LC OL 2013]

Section B

1

> Maire de Paor had an idea for an app which would help students set study goals, track their study progress and enable reminders for weekly study targets, etc. Maire's business proved very successful. The app is the market leader amongst second-level students in Ireland and Maire needs to hire staff to cope with the increasing demand. Maire needs to prepare a Job Description for the new position of Sales Manager. Maire will offer an attractive financial rewards scheme to motivate her staff.

(i) Explain the term *Job Description*.

(ii) Draft the Job Description Maire prepared for the new position of Sales Manager.

(20 marks) [LC OL 2017]

2 Read the information supplied in the following advertisement and answer the question that follows.

> **IRISH NATURAL JUICES LTD**
> FINANCE MANAGER REQUIRED
>
> **The ideal candidate:** Will have a Business Degree, excellent leadership, communication and analytical skills. Two years' experience in a similar role is essential.
>
> **The position:** Involves managing the Finance Department.
>
> **Responsibilities include:** Preparation of monthly and annual accounts.
>
> Apply by 1st August 2013 with a letter of application, including a CV, to:
> Marion Pender, HR Manager,
> Irish Natural Juices Ltd, Newtown Industrial Park, Newtown, Co. Tipperary.
> *Irish Natural Juices Ltd is an Equal Opportunities Employer*

Deirdre Keegan, 37 Oaklands, Athlone, Co. Westmeath applied for the position advertised.
Using today's date, draft Deirdre's letter of application. **(20 marks) [LC OL 2013]**

3

> Lucia noticed a job advertisement for a Team Leader at Aztec Insurance. The advertisement includes details such as <u>salary</u>, <u>benefit-in-kind</u>, <u>person specification</u> and details about the <u>training</u> the successful candidate will receive.

Explain any **three** of the terms underlined above. **(15 marks) [LC OL 2018]**

Higher Level

Section A – Short Questions (10 marks each)

1 Distinguish between induction training and staff development. **[LC HL 2018]**

2 Illustrate your understanding of the term *performance appraisal*. **[LC HL 2002]**

Section B

1

> The Area Manager Programme is a critical part of our business. What sets us apart from our competitors is the calibre of people in our stores.
>
> *Source: www.aldirecruitment.ie*

Discuss the role of the following in the effective recruitment and selection of an Area Manager for a large supermarket chain:

Person Specification   Job Description   Panel Interview   **(20 marks) [LC HL 2018]**

2

> ### SuperSave
>
> SuperSave, a supermarket chain located in the south west, is considering updating its IT system to link all its stores and to modernise all its operations. It intends to implement a new Quality Assurance programme throughout all its stores. It is also considering a major recruitment campaign.

Discuss the benefits of both internal **and** external recruitment for management positions for a business such as SuperSave.   **(20 marks) [LC HL 2016]**

3

> Performance appraisals are a valuable way to communicate with employees and may boost business productivity in difficult times.

(i)   Explain what is meant by the term *performance appraisal*.

(ii)   Outline the benefits of performance appraisal for a business.   **(20 marks) [LC HL 2010]**

4 Outline the financial rewards used for motivating employees.   **(15 marks) [LC HL 2017]**

5 Outline the stages in a 'recruitment and selection' process using the following headings:

(i)   Internal and External Recruitment

(ii)   Job Description and Person Specification

(iii) Job Interview   **(25 marks) [LC HL 2014]**

Solutions

Unit 4

14 MANAGING CHANGE

Learning Outcomes

When you have completed this chapter, you will be able to:

1 Describe the reasons for change in business

2 Outline the reasons why employees resist change and the strategies used to overcome this resistance

3 Describe the changing role of a manager from controller to facilitator

4 Understand the importance of employee participation

5 Outline the steps in team formation

6 Describe the benefits that teamwork brings to an organisation

7 Describe the impact of technology on the role of management, business costs, business personnel and business opportunities

8 Discuss the importance of total quality management.

Literacy Link

Change management, employee empowerment, employee participation, employee works council, worker director, teamwork, total quality management (TQM)

Numeracy Link

Addition, subtraction, multiplication

Cross-curricular Link

English – communicating
Geography – changes in the levels of economic development
History – political, population and climatic changes
Home Economics – the impact of societal and technological changes on family, industry and the economy; teamwork

---

CASE STUDY *Change Management at An Post*

The **state-owned company** An Post has experienced many changes over the past thirty years. **Changes in consumer habits**, including the greater use of **email**, have led to a decrease in the number of letters it handles. Competition has also increased in the postal market with the arrival of **competitors** such as DPD and Parcel Motel.

Management at An Post has informed staff that large-scale changes will need to take place to guarantee the future success of the business. Over 800 post offices have closed over the past 25 years and many staff members are **resistant to further changes**. Employees **fear for their job security**, as management has announced that

2,000 jobs will need to be cut.

To encourage open and honest communication between management and staff, five An Post staff have

been elected as **worker directors**. They sit on the board of directors and represent the views of staff during board meetings.

In order to compete with competitors in the market, An Post has focused on **continuously improving quality**. It has been awarded two **quality awards** from the **ISO**: for improving the quality of customer service and for IT security.

Technology has brought positive changes to the business. The company has an interactive website which contains up-to-date information about the services available at An Post branches, e.g. Passport Express and savings accounts. **Changes in technology** have also enabled An Post to **develop new products** such as Address Pal, which enables consumers to use a US or UK postal address for deliveries from online UK or US retailers.

An increase in online orders from companies such as Zara and Amazon has led to an increase in parcel deliveries. An Post is Amazon's preferred delivery partner in Ireland and in 2017 Christmas parcel deliveries increased by 30% on the previous year.

While uncertain times may lie ahead for An Post, the company is putting measures in place to deal with changes and ensure the long-term success of the business.

REASONS FOR CHANGE IN A BUSINESS

Today's business environment is dynamic and ever-changing. Businesses that do not adapt to change may go out of business.

In order for businesses to survive and grow, they must be able to react to changes in:

Definition: Change management
The processes used to identify and adapt to changes in the business environment.

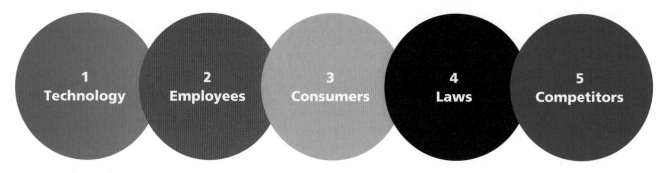

| 1 Technology | 2 Employees | 3 Consumers | 4 Laws | 5 Competitors |

1 Technology

- The introduction of technology such as CAD, CAM and CIM (see later in this chapter) has increased the speed and quality of production.
- E-commerce and social media enable firms to promote and sell their goods and services online to consumers worldwide.
- Using technologies such as email and video conferencing has increased the speed of communication between businesses and their stakeholders while at the same time reducing costs.

2 Employees

Changes in the education and skill level of employees has created a need for:

- Greater flexibility in the workplace, e.g. flexitime and teleworking
- More varied financial and non-financial rewards, e.g. profit-sharing and job enrichment
- Interesting and challenging work.

3 Consumers

Consumers today have more complex demands than consumers in the past. Businesses must be able to react to:

- Changes in consumer tastes
- Demand for a greater choice of goods and services
- A growth in demand for environmentally friendly and ethical products.

Example
There has been a change in consumer demand for vegan products. European vegan sales of meat substitutes have increased by 451% over the past four years. Irish food businesses have reacted to this demand by increasing their range of vegan products, e.g. Strong Roots and Dee's.

4 Laws

New national and EU laws can change the way businesses operate, e.g. environmental laws and consumer protection regulations.

5 Competitors

Businesses must monitor changes introduced by competitors, including the:

- Launch of new and improved goods and services
- Methods used by competitors to reduce costs, e.g. automated customer service helplines
- Growth of competitors through mergers and acquisitions.

Example

The EU has introduced food labelling laws, which require businesses to include features such as nutritional information and country of origin on food packaging.

Activity 14.1

Using an online voting website such as www.mentimeter.com, hold a class vote on which reason you believe is the main cause of change in a business. As a class, discuss the results of the vote.

RESISTANCE TO CHANGE

Business managers possess in-depth knowledge of the internal and external business environment and they understand the reasons why changes need to be introduced. They must be prepared to expect some resistance to these changes from staff. There are a number of reasons why employees may resist change, including:

1 **Fear of failure:** Employees may be afraid that they will not be able to cope with the changes in the workplace, e.g. the introduction of new production processes.
2 **Redundancy:** Employees may feel the changes introduced will lead to redundancy, e.g. new machinery replacing workers.
3 **Loss of control:** Changes to a regular routine can make an employee feel that they are losing control of their work life. This can make some employees uncooperative when changes are introduced.
4 **Lack of rewards:** Employees may feel that they should be rewarded for accepting changes in the business, e.g. a bonus payment. This may cause industrial relations conflict with management.
5 **Laziness:** Some employees will resist change as it will require them to make more of an effort to learn new processes or systems in the workplace.

Overcoming Resistance to Change

To reduce or remove the resistance to change, managers can use the following strategies.

1 **Open communication:** Management must communicate honestly about the reasons for change in the business. They should outline the consequences of not making these changes, e.g. loss of market share or redundancies.
2 **Employee involvement:** Employees should be encouraged to express their opinion about the changes happening at the firm. This gives them a sense of ownership in the change process.
3 **Leading by example:** Management shows employees that they believe in the benefits of change. Staff will follow the example set by management and be more accepting of the changes introduced.
4 **Rewards:** Management may give rewards to employees for co-operating with the introduction of changes in the business, e.g. a bonus payment.
5 **Training:** If a business introduces changes such as new processes or technology, staff should be given adequate training. This provides them with the skills needed and reduces their resistance to change.

Unit 4

Activity 14.2

Working in pairs, take turns to choose a term from the word cloud. Explain how the term relates to:

(a) The reasons for resistance to change; or

(b) The strategies that can be used to overcome resistance to change.

Word cloud: Fear, Control, Laziness, Training, Leading, Reward, Redundancy, Consultation, Communication

CASE STUDY · Resistance to Change at Eastman Kodak

The Eastman Kodak company was established in the USA in 1880. It became one of the world's most well-known global brands for cameras and camera film. At one point, it sold 90% of all camera film and 85% of all cameras in the USA.

However, management at the company was slow to react to changes in technology. In 1975, an employee invented the first digital camera but was surprised that the reaction from senior management was 'That's cute, but don't tell anyone about it.' Market research at the firm estimated that it would take ten years before mainstream customers would use digital cameras. Over the next ten years, management at Eastman Kodak did little to prepare for changes in consumer demand. They focused instead on creating cameras that incorporated film, so that customers would need to develop and print their photos.

Consumers had changed: they now wanted to take photos instantly and share these images online. Competitors also began manufacturing digital cameras and in time mobile phones with inbuilt cameras reduced the demand for traditional cameras.

Senior management continued to resist changes that were taking place in the camera market.

Finances at the firm fell rapidly as sales of cameras and camera film declined. Eastman Kodak sold shares in many of the companies it owned; it even demolished buildings on its campus to reduce the cost of property tax.

A company that once employed almost 145,000 staff with profits of over €2.1 billion had seen its share price fall by over 90%.

Management at the company finally recognised the need to change in order to survive. The firm now focuses on printer technology and in 2018 announced the launch of a cryptocurrency, a virtual (digital) currency. A cryptocurrency is not legal tender, i.e. not backed by a government, and exists only online. Examples include Bitcoin and litecoin. Kodak employs 6,600 staff with annual profits of over €80 million.

CHANGE FROM A CONTROLLER TO A FACILITATOR MANAGEMENT STYLE

In the past, many managers used a traditional controller managerial style. This is associated with autocratic leadership and the motivational approach of McGregor's Theory X.

In order to accept and embrace changes in the business environment, managers use a facilitator management style. This is associated with democratic leadership and the motivational approach of McGregor's Theory Y.

> You learned about leadership styles in Chapter 6 and motivational theories in Chapter 7.

	Controller Manager	Facilitator Manager
Authority	→ The manager gives orders and expects employees to obey without question.	→ Authority is shared between management and employees. Staff are delegated responsibility for certain tasks.
Motivation	→ Staff are viewed as lazy and unmotivated. Management uses money to motivate employees to work harder.	→ Employees are offered a range of financial and non-financial rewards to motivate them in the workplace, e.g. salary and additional holidays.
Training and Development	→ Employees are trained only to perform their duties. Managers believe that employees do not want more responsibility so do not invest in further training and development.	→ Management invests in training and development to improve the skills and experience of employees. This prepares employees for future managerial vacancies in the firm.
Management Supervision	→ Managers closely supervise employees to ensure that they are constantly working.	→ Managers delegate tasks to employees. Employees are trusted to perform their duties without constant management supervision.
Decision-making	→ Managers make all decisions and do not consult with staff.	→ Employees are empowered to make decisions on behalf of the business without the need to consult with management.

EMPLOYEE EMPOWERMENT

There are a number of methods managers can use to encourage empowerment in the workplace, including:

- **Investment in training:** Ensure that employees have the skills to make decisions on behalf of the business.
- **Rewards:** Offer financial and non-financial rewards to encourage employees to take on more responsibility.
- **Trusting employees:** Create a culture of trust where management believes in the abilities and skills of staff.
- **Control mechanism:** Management must be able to monitor empowered staff to ensure that mistakes are identified and corrected quickly.

Definition: Employee empowerment
Management gives employees a certain amount of independence and responsibility for decision-making in the business. This enables employees to make decisions on behalf of the business without needing to get permission from management.

Exam Tip!
*Make sure that you can **describe** the features of employee empowerment. **Describe** means **giving an account** of the topic and providing **advantages**, **disadvantages** and **examples**.*

CASE STUDY *Employee Empowerment at the Ritz-Carlton*

Employees at the global hotel chain Ritz-Carlton are empowered to make decisions on behalf of the hotel to resolve guest complaints or to improve the guest's stay. Empowered employees can spend up to €1,700 to ensure that the customer has a positive experience at the hotel.

Employees receive training and guidelines regarding empowerment and know that management respects their decisions. If mistakes are made, managers deal with the situation sensitively so as not to damage the trust that has been built between management and staff.

EMPOWERMENT

✓ Benefits	✗ Risks

✓ Benefits

1 Decision-making
Employees have the skills and knowledge needed to make decisions on behalf of the business. This can lead to faster and better decision-making.

2 Employee Motivation
Empowered employees are motivated because they feel that they have an important role in the business. This can lead to increased productivity.

3 Management Time
Empowered employees require less supervision as they are trusted to make decisions. This allows managers to focus their time on other areas of the business such as strategic planning.

4 Better Customer Service
Employees are encouraged to solve consumer issues quickly and effectively. This can lead to improved customer service and increase consumer loyalty.

Example
A customer on a Southwest Airlines flight tweeted to complain that the Wi-Fi that she had paid for on board her flight was not working and she was unable to view a basketball game. Rather than refer the complaint to management, the employee operating the Twitter account decided to live tweet the game to the customer. Media outlets around the world used the story in their news feed and this increased consumer awareness of the brand.

✗ Risks

1 Employee Training
If empowerment is introduced without adequate training, employees may make mistakes that could damage the firm's reputation and increase business costs.

2 Managerial Control
Some managers may be unhappy with giving power and responsibility to employees. This could lead to industrial relations conflict between management and staff.

3 Lower Motivation
Some employees may not want the extra responsibility associated with empowerment. It can increase employee stress and lead to lower motivation.

4 Less Managerial Supervision
Less supervision from management may encourage some empowered employees to take unnecessary business risks. This can lead to poor decision-making and cost the business money.

Example
An employee at Mizuko Securities intended to sell one company share for ¥610,000 (approx. €4,200) but instead sold 610,000 shares at ¥1 each. The mistake cost the company €194 million.

Activity 14.3

In pairs, create a cloze test to revise employee empowerment. Swap the cloze test with another pair of students to see if they can fill in all the blanks correctly.

EMPLOYEE PARTICIPATION

Employee participation relates to management encouraging staff to actively take part in running and improving the business. Management can encourage employee participation in the following ways.

1 Employee Works Councils

As part of an EU directive, employees in businesses with at least 1,000 staff across Europe have the right to set up a works council. Employees elect representatives for the works council and this gives staff a direct line of communication with senior management in the business.

A works council ensures that:

You will learn more about EU directives in Chapter 30.

- Employees across all EU countries receive information from management about business plans at the same time
- Representatives share the information with their colleagues and formulate a common response to these plans.

Before implementing the plans, senior management must take into account the views of the works council.

Example
Sodexo, a multinational food services company, has a European works council that meets four times per year. There is currently one Irish representative on the works council and representatives have helped the business to improve health and safety standards across all its European sites.

2 Worker Directors

These are employees who have been elected by colleagues to sit on the board of directors of a business. They participate in decision-making at a senior level in the firm. There are worker directors in many Irish state-owned firms, including the ESB and An Post.

3 Employee Share Purchase Plan (ESPP)

Employees can buy shares at a reduced price or may receive shares as part of their reward package. Employees become owners in the business and can vote at the AGM.

Example
Food delivery service Deliveroo has given all permanent employees shares in the firm at a cost of over €11 million to the business.

Importance of Employee Participation

- **Increased motivation:** Employees feel that they are valued and respected by management. This increases motivation levels and boosts productivity.
- **Improved industrial relations:** Employee representatives speak to management about issues such as pay and working conditions. These issues can be resolved quickly and lead to improved industrial relations between management and staff.
- **Improved decision-making:** Management can make better decisions when they include suggestions from employees. Staff possess skills and experience that can aid decision-making in the firm.

TEAMWORK

In the past, controller managers closely monitored employees while at work. These managers did not trust employees to work as a team. Nowadays, facilitator managers understand the importance of teamwork and the benefits that it can bring to a firm.

In many businesses a matrix organisation structure is used to promote teamwork. (You have already learned about this in Chapter 11.) Employees from different departments work together on a project for the business.

Definition: Team
A group of people who work together to achieve a common goal or complete a task. The team members possess skills, knowledge and experience that help the team to achieve the goal.

Stages in the Formation of a Team

Teams go through the following four stages:

Stage 4 – Performing

Stage 3 – Norming

Stage 2 – Storming

Stage 1 – Forming

Stage 1: Forming
The team members come together for the first time. There may be a lack of trust between the members. The team leader tries to build relationships and outlines the overall goal of the team, e.g. to complete a project.

Stage 2: Storming
Conflict can arise at this stage, as the members have different opinions. There may be personality clashes within the group. The team leader must work hard to manage conflict between the team members.

Stage 3: Norming
There is greater trust between the team members and they develop ground rules, i.e. rules regarding behaviour and work standards. These ground rules enable the team to function effectively.

Stage 4: Performing
The team focus on achieving the team goal. They trust each other and work hard to make decisions and solve problems quickly and effectively.

CASE STUDY — *Teamwork at Google*

The Google Doodle team consists of a group of artists, designers and engineers who adapt the Google logo to celebrate cultural, historic and artistic events. The team holds regular brainstorming sessions to decide which event they will commemorate. They develop images, games and puzzles to interact with Google users.

Some famous doodles that the team created were celebrations of:
- 30 years of the arcade game Pac-Man – the public spent 48 million hours playing the doodle game
- The birth of Shakespeare
- St Patrick's Day.

Benefits of Teamwork

- **Greater employee motivation:** Employees are often more motivated when they work as part of a team. This can help a business recruit and retain high-quality staff.
- **Improved communication skills:** Teamwork can improve employees' communication and interpersonal skills, as they deal with the different personalities of team members.
- **Better decision-making:** Team members have knowledge and experience which can help the team to make better business decisions.
- **Faster task completion:** Team members are assigned specific roles in the team, often based on their own skills and experience. This can result in faster task completion.

Activity 14.4

Examine the image.
1 What is the key message?
2 What are the benefits of teamwork that you can see in the image?

TOTAL QUALITY MANAGEMENT

To adapt to a changing business environment, many firms focus on developing total quality management (TQM). To be successful, TQM requires the business to provide goods and services that meet the needs and quality standards of its customers.

The principles of TQM include:

1 **Focus on consumers:** The business conducts market research to identify consumer needs. It can then provide the goods and services that consumers want to buy.

2 **Continuous improvement:** Every person in the firm aims to constantly improve the quality of the goods and services provided by the firm. They aspire to provide defect-free goods and services.

3 **Employee empowerment:** Employees make decisions on behalf of the business to ensure that customers always get the best-quality goods and services.

4 **Quality assurance:** The business focuses on incorporating quality in all stages of the design process. Businesses may be awarded an ISO to recognise quality assurance.

5 **Teamwork:** Employees work in teams to find ways to improve quality in the firm, e.g. quality circles. The business also works with suppliers as a team. These suppliers must provide the highest-quality raw materials for the firm.

Definition: Total quality management (TQM)
A commitment by management and employees to continuously promote and encourage quality in all aspects of a firm's operations. All employees work together to create high-quality goods and services for consumers.

Definition: Quality assurance
A system, put in place by senior management at a firm, that guarantees quality at every stage of the production process from design to customer sales.

> You learned about quality circles and ISO in Chapter 12.

Unit 4

TOTAL QUALITY MANAGEMENT

✓ Benefits	✗ Risks
1 Improved Quality Everyone in the business is focused on quality. This leads to high-quality goods and services for customers.	**1 Slow Process** It can take a business a long time to develop the processes for TQM. It can then take a number of years before the business sees any benefits from introducing it.
2 Lower Costs High-quality products have fewer defects. This reduces the cost of wasted materials and refunds to unhappy customers.	**2 Pressure on Staff** There can be constant pressure on staff and management to continuously improve quality standards in the business. This can lead to stress among staff.
3 Employee Motivation Employees are motivated to work hard and improve quality standards. This can boost employee productivity.	**3 High Costs** Total quality management is expensive to introduce, as there are costs for training staff, equipment and maintenance.
4 Increased Sales The business develops a reputation for providing high-quality goods and services. This can attract new customers to the business and increase sales.	**4 Staff Resistance** Some staff may resist the introduction of TQM, due to the effort that is required to implement it properly into the firm. This can make it difficult for the firm to make it a success.

Activity 14.5

Working in pairs, create a fishbone diagram to summarise the principles of TQM and the associated benefits and drawbacks to a firm of using TQM.

TECHNOLOGY IN BUSINESS

Technology is constantly changing the way businesses operate. In Chapter 9, we looked at some examples of this technology, such as EDI, video conferencing and cloud computing.

There are other types of technology that can impact on the production, marketing and distribution of a firm's goods and services. These include:

- **CAD (computer-aided design):** Software that can be used by businesses to create 2D and 3D models of new products, e.g. cars.
- **CAM (computer-aided manufacturing):** Software used to control and monitor manufacturing machinery, e.g. on a car assembly line.
- **CIM (computer-integrated manufacturing):** The use of computers to control the entire production process of a product from design to production, e.g. tinned products such as beans and peas.

- **Voice recognition software:** Software that recognises the human voice and can command a device to perform a particular task. It can also be used to convert words to text, e.g. a person speaks into a computer or tablet and the words appear on the screen, for example in a word processing program.

Impact of Technology on Management

1 **Wider span of control:** Technology can help to increase the manager's span of control, as they can monitor a larger number of employees more efficiently, e.g. by using video conferencing.

2 **Speed of communication:** Technology enables faster communication between management and stakeholders such as employees and suppliers, e.g. by using email and social media.

3 **Management stress:** Managers may suffer from stress and burnout as they are accessible 24 hours a day via tablets and laptops.

4 **Improved decision-making:** Managers have access to large amounts of data online and this can help them to make better business decisions.

5 **Production:** Production technology such as CAM and CAD have helped to improve production efficiency. Products can be made faster and with fewer faults.

IMPACT OF TECHNOLOGY ON BUSINESS COSTS

Increased Business Costs	Reduced Business Costs
1 Large Capital Costs Technology such as CAD and CAM is a very large capital cost for a business. Associated costs include installation, updating and maintenance.	**1 Improved Quality** Technology such as CAD and CAM can improve the quality of goods produced. This reduces the cost of repairing faulty goods and issuing refunds to dissatisfied customers.
2 Employee Training Employees must receive training to learn how to use new technology. The business may need to hire external trainers, which increases business costs.	**2 Staff Redundancies** Technology can increase business productivity and efficiency, thus requiring fewer employees. Staff redundancies can reduce wage costs for the firm.

Activity 14.6

ACE Pottery employs 80 staff who produce 50 plates per day. The employees are paid €16 per hour and work eight hours per day.

The owner of the company is considering purchasing new machinery which will produce 400 plates per day. The running cost for the machinery is €7,500 per day.

Calculate the amount of money that will be saved by ACE Pottery if they purchase the new machinery to replace the staff.

Impact of Technology on Business Personnel

1 **Teleworking:** This can help a business recruit and retain high-quality staff who may be unable or unwilling to spend time commuting to and from work.

> **Definition: Teleworking/e-working**
> This enables employees to work from home via the firm's computer system.

2 **Staff training:** Technology has changed the way in which employees do their jobs, e.g. most office work is now computer-based. Employees need to receive training to ensure that they can perform their work duties.

3 **Staff qualifications and skills:** Technology has replaced many low-skilled jobs, e.g. sewing machinists in clothes factories. Employees now need to have higher educational qualifications and skills than employees in the past in order to find work.

4 **Efficiency:** Technology helps employees to perform their duties more efficiently, e.g. the use of spreadsheets to calculate financial information. Employees can then spend time on more complex aspects of their jobs.

Unit 4

Impact of Technology on Business Opportunities

1 **New products/services:** Advances in technology have led to the development of new products for businesses, e.g. voice recognition software in Amazon Alexa. This can open up a new market for the business and increase business sales and profits.

> **Example**
> Novel Effect is a voice-activated app that adds sound effects to children's story books as they are read aloud. The company appeared on the US version of *Dragon's Den* and received a €420,000 investment for a 15% share in the company.

2 **Faster production:** Improved technology can increase production speed. The business can produce and deliver goods to customers more quickly.

3 **E-commerce:** The business uses technology such as the firm's website and social media, e.g. Facebook, to promote their products around the world. Consumers can order products online and have them delivered direct to their home.

> **Definition: E-commerce**
> Buying and selling goods and services over the Internet. These transactions can be: business to consumer (B2C); business to business (B2B); or consumer to consumer (C2C).

4 **Improved decision-making:** Technology such as the Internet gives the business access to larger amounts of information. This can help to improve decision-making in the business.

Activity 14.7

Working in groups, create a revision quiz for this topic using an online tool such as Kahoot!, Socrative or Quizizz.

KEY TERMS

Now you have completed this chapter, you should understand and be able to explain the following terms. In your copybook, write a definition of each term to build up your own glossary of terms.

- change management
- controller manager
- facilitator manager
- employee empowerment
- employee participation
- employee works council
- employee share purchase plan (ESPP)
- worker directors

- teamwork
- total quality management (TQM)
- quality assurance
- computer-aided design (CAD)
- computer-aided manufacturing (CAM)
- computer-integrated manufacturing (CIM)
- teleworking
- e-commerce

 **PowerPoint Summary**

EXAM-STYLE QUESTIONS

Ordinary Level

Section 1 – Short Questions (10 marks each)

1 Outline what is meant by the term *change management*.

2 List **four** factors that might cause a business to change.

3 Outline **two** reasons why employees may be resistant to changes introduced in the business by management.

4 Describe a strategy that can be used by managers to help employees overcome their resistance to change.

5 Describe **two** characteristics of a facilitator manager.

6 Describe **one** advantage and **one** disadvantage of the use of total quality management in a business.

7 What do the letters CAD and TQM stand for?

8 Copy the table below into your copybook and fill in the missing elements of team formation in the spaces 2, 3 and 4.

1	Forming
2	
3	
4	

Section 2 – Long Questions

1 Describe how changes in consumer and employee demands have caused businesses to change. **(15 marks)**

2
> Management must help employees to adjust to changes in the business.

Describe the methods used by managers to reduce employee resistance to change. **(20 marks)**

3 Describe the characteristics of a controller manager. **(15 marks)**

4 What is meant by the term *employee empowerment*? Describe **two** ways in which a manager can encourage empowerment in the workplace. **(20 marks)**

5
> Harry Carter is the managing director of Carter Construction. He is overwhelmed by all the decisions he makes in the business every day and wants to empower employees to take more responsibility in the workplace.

Outline the benefits that empowerment would bring to Carter Construction. **(15 marks)**

6
> It is important that employees feel engaged and participate in the workplace.

Outline how employee works councils and worker directors can increase employee participation. **(15 marks)**

7 Describe the stages in the formation of a team. **(20 marks)**

8 Discuss how the introduction of technology can reduce business costs. Illustrate your answers with relevant examples. **(15 marks)**

Unit 4

Higher Level

Section 1 – Short Questions (10 marks each)

1 Describe why management may need to introduce change in a business due to the impact of (i) consumers and (ii) competitors.

2 State whether each of the following statements is true or false.

Statements		True or False
A	A controller manager invests in the training and development of employees.	
B	TQM stands for Total Quantity Management.	
C	Employee works councils can be established in businesses in the EU with at least 1,000 employees.	
D	The stages in team formation are: storming, forming, norming and performing.	
E	CAD is used to control the entire production process from design to manufacture.	

3 Complete the following sentence. Empowerment benefits a business by _____

4 Describe the role of a worker director in a business.

5 Outline the stages norming and performing in the formation of a team.

6 Explain the term *quality assurance*.

7 Outline **two** risks for a business using total quality management.

8 Describe **two** ways in which changes in technology have impacted on business costs.

Section 2 – Applied Business Question (80 marks)

Divine Desserts Ltd

Olga Adamczyk is the CEO and owner of Divine Desserts Ltd, a desserts manufacturer. The dessert industry is highly competitive and Olga faces competition from both national and international competitors. To promote the firm's products, the marketing department is active on the firm's Facebook and Instagram accounts.

Olga has heard rumours in the media that the government intends to extend the sugar tax to apply to dessert products. In reaction to this rumour she has decided to create a range of desserts with a lower sugar content. This will appeal to the growing number of health-conscious customers. Olga will need to introduce a CAM system to enable the factory to increase the efficiency of production.

Today at a management meeting the HR manager informed Olga that some staff are unhappy. They feel that they could improve decision-making in the company but their opinions are ignored. Other staff would also like to have the option of more flexible working arrangements such as working from home.

Olga is disappointed to hear that her staff are unhappy and wants to find ways to motivate and engage them in the workplace. The HR manager suggests implementing a system of employee empowerment, which can help the firm to improve employee motivation and customer service. The marketing manager believes that only managers should be making decisions in the business as they have the highest level of skills and experience. Olga feels that they should introduce empowerment and delegates the task of creating a training programme to the HR manager.

Olga decides to organise a meeting with all staff to explain the reason for the introduction of a CAM system in the firm. She knows that some machine operatives are afraid that they will be replaced by the new technology. Olga reassures the staff that their jobs are secure and extensive training will be provided so that they will learn the skills to use the new machinery.

A What are the main reasons Olga must introduce changes in her business Divine Desserts Ltd? **(20 marks)**

B What is meant by the term *employee empowerment*? What potential benefits and drawbacks could empowering employees bring to Divine Desserts Ltd? **(30 marks)**

C Explain what is meant by the term *CAM*. Outline the impact that technology has had on (i) personnel and (ii) business opportunities at Divine Desserts Ltd. **(30 marks)**

Section 3 – Long Questions

1
> 'The workplace is changing.' *Irish Independent, June 2017*

   Describe the factors that can cause changes in the workplace. **(20 marks)**

2
> Empowering workers may not always lead to positive results for a business.

   Discuss this statement. **(15 marks)**

3 Evaluate the use of employee works councils and employee share ownership as methods of increasing employee participation in the workplace. **(15 marks)**

4
> Teamwork brings enormous benefits to all types of businesses.

   Evaluate this statement. **(20 marks)**

5 In order to be successful, TQM must have (i) a focus on consumers, (ii) continuous improvement and (iii) quality assurance. Describe the **three** principles in detail. **(20 marks)**

6 Explain the term *TQM* and outline the benefits of it to a business and its employees. **(20 marks)**

7 Illustrate the impact that technology has had on the role of management. **(15 marks)**

8 Discuss how technology can have an impact on personnel. Illustrate your answer with relevant examples. **(15 marks)**

PREVIOUS LEAVING CERTIFICATE EXAM QUESTIONS

Ordinary Level

Section A – Short Questions (10 marks each)

1 Choose the appropriate words to complete the sentence below. (One word does not apply.)

POWER   DECISIONS   TARGETS

Employee empowerment provides staff with more _____ to make their own _____ about how to do their jobs. **[LC OL 2016]**

2 List **three** benefits to a business of investing in new technology. **[LC OL 2013]**

Section B

1 Explain what Employee Empowerment means and outline **two** benefits of empowerment. **(20 marks) [LC OL 2003]**

2 Outline **two** benefits of teamwork in a business. **(15 marks) [LC OL 2018]**

3 Using examples, describe **three** ways in which technology has changed the role of management. **(15 marks) [LC OL 2007]**

Higher Level

Section A – Short Questions (10 marks each)

1 Outline **two** strategies management could use to help employees adapt to change. **[LC HL 2011]**

2 Forming, storming, norming and performing are stages in team development.
   Outline your understanding of storming and norming. **[LC HL 2015]**

Section B

1 People are at the heart of every successful business. Describe **two** strategies that a business organisation can use to manage change. Use examples to support your answer. **(20 marks) [LC HL 2008]**

2 Discuss the benefits and risks of empowering employees within a business. **(20 marks) [LC HL 2012]**

3 Discuss the benefits of TQM to a manufacturing business. **(20 marks) [LC HL 2009]**

4 Analyse the impact of new technology on business costs and on business opportunities. Provide examples to support your answer. **(20 marks) [LC HL 2016]**

Solutions

15 MANAGING A BUSINESS AND A HOUSEHOLD: INSURANCE

⊕ Learning Outcomes

When you have completed this chapter, you will be able to:

1 Describe how a household and business manage risk
2 Outline the principles of insurance
3 Calculate a basic insurance premium for a household and a business
4 Describe the different types of insurance for a household and a business
5 Explain the similarities and differences between insurance for a household and a business
6 Outline the importance of insurance for a household and a business.

Literacy Link

Risk management, insurance, insurable interest, utmost good faith, indemnity, contribution, subrogation, average clause, material facts, premium

Numeracy Link

Addition, subtraction, multiplication, division percentages, calculation of formulae, Venn diagrams

Cross-curricular Link

Accounting – accruals and prepayments
Home Economics – types of insurance, fire safety

CASE STUDY

Insurance at SuperValu

SuperValu operates more than 200 stores across Ireland and employs over 55,000 people. The firm, like many in Ireland, has experienced increasing **insurance premiums** in recent years. Research by Ibec has shown that the cost of **employer** and **public liability insurance** for retailers has increased by between 5% and 10% over the past five years. To reduce the incidence of **insurance claims**, which would increase their premiums in the future, SuperValu has invested time and resources in **risk management**. Following health and safety laws, the firm has clearly marked fire exits in its stores, as well as fire alarms and sprinkler systems. Each store has a health and safety officer and a fire warden. Staff also undertake training in manual handling and first aid.

CCTV is in operation in the stores to protect against stock theft. Many stores also employ on-site security personnel. SuperValu pays **PRSI** on all staff employed at the firm.

SuperValu operates a fleet of trucks that deliver to every SuperValu store around the country. By law, the vehicles must be covered by at least **third party motor insurance**.

SuperValu has also entered the insurance market and partnered with **insurer** AIG to provide **motor**, **house** and **travel insurance** to customers online. Customers can view **insurance proposal** forms and their **insurance policy** online. **Insurance claims** can also be made through the SuperValu insurance website.

RISK MANAGEMENT

Risk management involves identifying all the risks that a business or household *might* incur. Once the business/household has identified possible risks and found ways to minimise these risks, it should take out insurance cover.

> **Definition: Risk management**
> A planned approach used by businesses and households to deal with risks that can affect them. It involves identifying all possible risks (e.g. fire, personal injury) and calculating the cost of protecting themselves against these risks.

Activity 15.1

Working in pairs, identify the risks you can see in the image. Outline how you would overcome each risk you identify.

Ways to Minimise Risks

The business and household can minimise risks in the following ways:

1 **Install security systems:** Security risks can be reduced by installing alarms, CCTV cameras and motion-sensor lights.

2 **Training:** Everyone should be aware of health and safety procedures, e.g. what to do in the event of a fire, CPR training for a medical emergency. In the workplace the employer may provide protective clothing and equipment to reduce the risk of injury or illness.

3 **Appoint a health and safety officer:** Appointed in the workplace to report safety issues and conduct regular safety inspections. Management may replace or upgrade equipment based on recommendations made by the health and safety officer.

4 **Health and safety:** Ensure that employees are aware of health and safety rules, e.g. wearing a hard hat on a construction site. Warning signs should use images, which will be clearly understood by all staff.

5 **Insurance:** Take out insurance cover to transfer the risk to an insurance firm in return for paying a premium. The insurance firm will pay for any loss incurred.

INSURANCE

Individuals and businesses are exposed to risks every day, e.g. a person's car could be stolen or a fire could damage a business premises. After undertaking a risk assessment, an individual and business can decide to take out insurance cover to protect against possible losses. In return for the premium (fee) paid by the insured to an insurance company, they receive compensation for any loss suffered.

DID YOU KNOW? *Starbucks pays more for its employees' health insurance than it does for its coffee beans.*

> **Definition: Insurance**
> Financial protection against possible loss.

Before we examine insurance in more detail, let's look at some important insurance terms.

Insurance Terms

	Term	Explanation
1 The Forms	Proposal form	→ The form you fill in when applying for insurance.
	Claim form	→ The form you fill in when making a claim, e.g. when a fire has damaged a building.
2 The Documents	Insurance policy	→ The document you receive when you buy insurance. It is a legally binding contract and it must be in writing. It sets out the terms and conditions of the policy, i.e. what risks are covered.
	Renewal notice	→ This document is sent out before the policy is due for renewal. It reminds the insured that their policy is due for renewal and the premium for renewing the policy.
	Cover note	→ A document that proves that insurance is in place. It is used until the full policy document is sent to the insured.
3 Other Terms	The insured	→ The household or business that takes out the insurance policy.
	The insurer	→ The insurance firm with which the insured has taken out their insurance policy, e.g. Axa, Allianz.
	Insurance premium	→ The fee paid for insurance. It consists of a basic premium plus any loadings or discounts that may apply.
	Policy excess	→ When a claim is made by the insured, the first portion of the claim is paid by the insured, e.g. if the claim is €1,000, the insured pays the policy excess of €200 and the insurance firm pays €800 compensation.
	Loading	→ An additional charge on top of the basic premium because of an extra risk that may apply in certain circumstances, e.g. a driver with a provisional licence.
	No claims bonus	→ A reduction in the premium charged if no claim has been made on the policy since the last renewal date.
	Days of grace	→ A short period of time given to the insured to pay the insurance premium. (This does not apply to motor insurance.)
	Average clause	→ This applies in cases of under-insurance. (You will learn more about this later in the chapter.)

DID YOU KNOW? Approximately 15,000 people are employed in the insurance industry in Ireland.

DID YOU KNOW? In Japan, keen golfers buy insurance because if they get a hole in one, they are expected to buy gifts and drinks for their friends. The policy covers them for a party worth up to €2,500, for the premium of €56 per year.

Unit 4

People in Insurance

The insurance industry employs a large number of people in some of the following roles:

Job title	Role
Actuary	→ Calculates the premium to be paid by the insured.
Assessor	→ Calculates the amount of compensation to be paid.
Loss adjuster	→ When a loss occurs, the amount of compensation to be paid is decided by the insurance firm. If the insured is unhappy with this amount, an independent person known as a loss adjuster is appointed to assess the situation. The loss adjuster may adjust the amount of compensation.
Insurance agent	→ A person or business who sells insurance on behalf of one insurance business, e.g. an agent for Axa.
Insurance broker	→ A person or business who sells insurance on behalf of a number of different insurance companies. They are paid a commission by the insurance company with which the final policy is taken out, e.g. Chill Insurance.

Activity 15.2

Working in pairs, create a crossword using terms associated with insurance. Swap your crossword with that of another pair of students and complete each other's grids.

The Principles of Insurance

These are the basic rules of insurance. If any of these rules is broken, the insurance policy will be void and no compensation will be paid. There are five such principles.

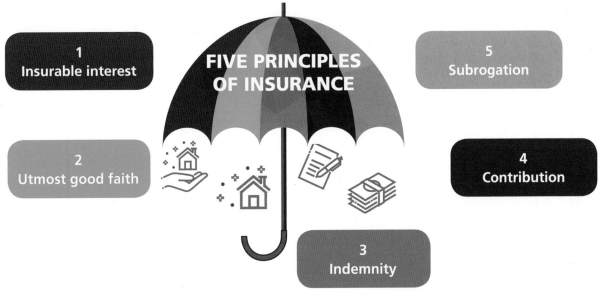

FIVE PRINCIPLES OF INSURANCE

1 Insurable interest
2 Utmost good faith
3 Indemnity
4 Contribution
5 Subrogation

Principle 1: Insurable Interest

This means that the insured person must own the item to be insured. They must benefit from its existence and suffer **financially** from its loss.

It is important to remember that the insured must suffer financially from the loss of the item, e.g. we cannot insure the Spire in Dublin against damage just because we would feel sad if anything were to happen to it. We would not lose money as a result of its damage, therefore we cannot insure it.

Example

A household or a business may insure its own valuables, e.g. buildings and vehicles. You can insure your own car but not your neighbour's car as you wouldn't suffer financially from its loss.

Principle 2: Utmost Good Faith

Utmost good faith (or *uberrimae fidei*) means that when you are completing the proposal and claim forms, you must be completely truthful. When taking out insurance you must give full and truthful facts. This includes material facts which may not be asked for on the forms but may affect the premium or compensation to be paid.

Definition: Material facts

Information that may not be asked on the insurance proposal form but could affect the premium or compensation paid for insurance. For example, a household fails to mention that their house is located near a river that is prone to flooding; if a flood occurs and damages the house, it is unlikely the home owner will receive compensation as they did not reveal all material facts.

Principle 3: Indemnity

This means that you cannot make a profit from insurance. You cannot be better off after a loss has occurred than you were before the loss happened.

The insurer will pay compensation only to the value of the loss suffered. This must be measurable in financial terms.

It is the responsibility of the insured to ensure that they have adequate insurance cover. If you under-insure an item to make a saving on your insurance premium, then if a loss occurs the insurance company will apply the rule of **average clause**.

Definition: Average clause

Used by insurance firms to calculate compensation when an item is insured for less than its actual value. If the item is fully destroyed and it is underinsured, the insurance firm will pay the amount for which it was insured.

Example

If you insure your property for €260,000 and its rebuild cost is only €250,000, the compensation payable is €250,000, i.e. you cannot make a profit from insurance.

However, if there is partial loss, the following formula for average clause is applied when calculating the amount of compensation to be paid:

$$\text{Amount of compensation payable} = \frac{\text{Amount item insured for} \times \text{Claim}}{\text{Real value of the item}}$$

Exam Tip!
*Don't forget to **write the formula** when calculating average clause.*

Note!
Any excess will be deducted after the claim has been reduced by the average formula.

Example

Rowe Ltd had insured its premises for €250,000. The rebuild cost of the premises was €320,000. A fire destroyed the kitchen, causing €40,000 worth of damage. How much compensation is the owner entitled to and why?

$$\frac{\text{Amount item insured for} \times \text{Claim}}{\text{Real value of the item}} \qquad \frac{250{,}000 \times 40{,}000}{320{,}000} = €31{,}250$$

Compensation paid: €31,250.

Reason: Rowe Ltd receives €31,250 as the premises was under-insured at the time the fire occurred. As a result of the principle of indemnity the average clause rule applies and only a proportion of the claim is paid in compensation to reflect the proportion under-insured.

There is also no point in over-insuring an item, i.e. insuring it for more than it is actually worth, as you will be compensated only for the actual value of the item. Over-insurance also means that you will pay a higher premium.

Example

Tom, Richard and Harriet each purchased a house in a new housing estate at Lakelands. The rebuild cost of each house was €320,000.

- Tom insured his house for €240,000 – under-insured
- Richard insured his house for €320,000 – adequately insured
- Harriet insured her house for €350,000 – over-insured

On 18 October a fire caused €15,000 damage to each house.

(i) How much compensation is each person entitled to and why?

(ii) If the fire had completely destroyed the houses, how much compensation would each person receive?

		Tom	Richard	Harriet
(i) Partial damage	Compensation	$\frac{240,000 \times 15,000}{320,000}$ = €11,250	€15,000	€15,000
	Reason	• Under-insured • Average clause applies to partial loss due to the principle of indemnity	• Adequately insured • Fully compensated	• Over-insured • €15,000, as the principle of indemnity applies, i.e. you cannot profit from insurance
(ii) Completely destroyed	Compensation	€240,000	€320,000	€320,000
	Reason	• Under-insured • Average clause applies due to the principle of indemnity	• Adequately insured	• Over-insured • You cannot profit from insurance due to the principle of indemnity

Principle 4: Contribution

This principle is linked to indemnity. It is used when a household or business insures an item with two or more insurance firms. This might occur if an individual or business tries to make a profit from an insurance claim by claiming from each insurance firm. Any compensation payable will be divided between them in proportion to the value insured with each. The claim is made to one insurance company, which then recovers a proportion of the claim from the other insurance company or companies.

This ensures that the insured cannot make a profit by insuring an item with more than one insurance company with the hope of making a full claim under each policy.

If a loss occurs, the following formula is used by the insurance company to calculate the amount of compensation to be paid by each company the claimant is insured with for the particular insurable interest:

$$\frac{\text{Amount insured with insurance company} \times \text{Claim}}{\text{Total amount insured (all insurance companies)}}$$

Example 1

Eamon Hayes insured his delivery van for €25,000 with two insurance firms. The van was completely destroyed in an accident.

How much compensation will he receive from each insurance firm? Why?

In this case the van was insured for €25,000 with both insurance firms. Therefore, each insurance firm pays compensation equally. He will receive €12,500 from each insurance firm.

This is because of the principles of contribution and indemnity. Since he lost an item valued at €25,000 the maximum compensation is €25,000 – you cannot make a profit from insurance.

Example 2

Eamon's van is worth €25,000. He has insured it with Company A for €18,000 and with Company B for €12,000. How much compensation will he receive from each insurance company?

The item is not insured equally. Therefore the amount of compensation payable will be divided in proportion to the amount insured with each insurance company.

	Company A	Company B
	$\dfrac{18,000 \times 25,000}{30,000}$	$\dfrac{12,000 \times 25,000}{30,000}$
Compensation payable:	€15,000	€10,000

Reason: The total amount of compensation payable is €25,000. This will be divided in the ratio (direct proportion) between the two insurance firms under the principle of contribution.

Principle 5: Subrogation

This principle is also linked to the principle of indemnity. It states that once you have received compensation, you give up your right to make any further claims. The insurance firm can pursue the business or individual that caused the damage for compensation.

Let us look at two examples to explain this principle further.

Example 1

Jenny crashed her car and it is completely written off. The car was worth and insured for €20,000. The insurance company pays her compensation of €20,000.

Under the principle of subrogation she gives up all her rights to the car. The car now becomes the property of the insurance company, and they can sell it.

If Jenny had kept her car after she received her compensation and sold it for scrap she would have made a profit. This is not permitted under the principle of indemnity.

Example 2

Nadine had her premises insured for fire. A fire occurred, caused by the negligence of an electrical contractor she had employed to work on the premises. The insurance company paid compensation in full for the damage suffered.

Nadine cannot then sue the electrical contractor. She has given up this right once she received compensation from the insurance company. To do so she would make a profit and this is not allowed under indemnity.

The insurance company has the right to sue the electrical contractor as it can sue a third party who caused the loss to occur.

Insurance Premium Calculations

Insurance is a large cost for both households and businesses. The premium to be paid is calculated by an actuary and is based on a number of factors, including:

1 **Risk:** The more likely the risk is to occur, the higher the premium. The actuary uses statistics when calculating the risks, e.g. the number of claims in the past, the different risks involved.

2 **Claims:** The amount paid out by insurance firms in the past will affect the level of the premium. The higher the amount paid out, the higher the premium will be.

Activity 15.3

In pairs, discuss the reasons why motor insurance is so expensive for younger drivers when they start driving. Have you or your siblings tried to get car insurance? Do you think the high cost is fair? Share your thoughts with others in the class.

3 **Value:** The higher the value of the item, the higher the premium. The basic premium is a percentage of the value, e.g. a car valued at €40,000 will cost more to insure than a car that cost €15,000.

4 **Loadings:** These increase the cost of insurance premiums as they add extra risk to the policy, e.g. smokers pay more for life assurance than non-smokers; people living in certain areas pay more for property insurance as the risk of theft is greater.

Activity 15.4

In pairs, think of other possible loadings that would result in higher insurance costs. Compile a list of loadings with others in your class and design an infographic to display in the classroom.

5 **Discounts:** The person seeking insurance can reduce the premium by taking steps to reduce the risk, e.g. installing a smoke alarm. Insurance firms can also reward insurers for not making claims, e.g. a no claims bonus.

Let us now take a look at some examples of how insurance premiums are calculated.

Example 1

As new homeowners, Jack and Gretta, who live in Dublin, want to take out insurance on their home and its contents. Their home's rebuild value is €400,000 and contents are valued at 30% of this figure. They have a monitored alarm and CCTV. They have no previous claims.

They have received the following quotation from Lewis Insurance Ltd, based on the fact that they are new customers:

Buildings:	€1.20 per €1,000 valuation
Contents:	€3.40 per €1,000 valuation
Loadings:	Dublin address 15%, Previous claims 12%
Discounts:	No previous claims 4%, Alarm systems 8%, New customer 2%

Calculate the premium they will have to pay if they decide to take out their policy with Lewis Insurance Ltd.

Exam Tip!
When calculating an insurance premium, any loadings or discounts are calculated as a percentage of the basic premium.

Solution to Example 1

			€	€
Basic Premium				
	Buildings	(400 × €1.20)		480.00
	Contents	(120 × €3.40)		408.00
	Basic Premium			888.00
Add Loadings	Dublin Address	(€888 × 15%)	133.20	133.20
				1,021.20
Less Discounts	No claims	(€888 × 4%)	35.52	
	Alarm system	(€888 × 8%)	71.04	
	New business	(€888 × 2%)	17.76	(124.32)
Premium Due				**€896.88**

Example 2

Cullen Enterprises has buildings with a rebuild value of €700,000, contents valued at €250,000 and stock to the value of €40,000. Its average cash held in the office is €1,500. It has 15 employees and owns three vans, each valued at €25,000. The general manager, Brian Cullen, has received the following quotation, as a first-time client, from Mullins Insurance Ltd:

Buildings:	€9 per €1,000 value	Cash on hand:	€16 per €500 value
Contents:	€14 per €1,000 value	Vans:	€1,800 per van
Stock:	€16 per €1,000 value	New client discount: 5%	

Calculate the premium Cullen Enterprises would have to pay if Brian, the general manager, takes out insurance with Mullins Insurance Ltd.

Solution to Example 2

		€
Basic Premium		
Buildings	(700 × €9)	6,300.00
Contents	(250 × €14)	3,500.00
Stock	(40 × €16)	640.00
Cash	(3 × €16)	48.00
Vans	(3 × €1,800)	5,400.00
Basic Premium Total		15,888.00
Less Discount – new client (5%) (€15,888 × 5%)		(794.40)
Premium Due		**€15,093.60**

Exam Tip!
Remember: when calculating a premium always work it out in this order:
Premium = Basic Premium + Loadings – Discounts

Think!
Why, do you think, there is a higher rate for insuring cash?

Insurance summary

Step 1 – Contact an insurance agent or broker

Step 2 – Complete an insurance proposal form

Step 3 – Premium, calculated by the actuary

Step 4 – Insurance policy issued to consumer

Step 5 – Insurance claim if loss occurs

Step 6 – Receive compensation

TYPES OF INSURANCE

Both households and businesses need insurance to cover various risks that might arise. Some of these risks are similar. However, a business tends to have more varied and more complex risks than a household. Common types of household and business insurance include:

Household Insurance

Health
Mortgage protection
Income protection
Personal accident
Travel
Identity theft
Life assurance

Property/premises
Contents
Motor
PRSI

Business Insurance

Product liability
Public liability
Employer's liability
Key personnel
Fidelity guarantee
Consequential loss
Cash in transit
Plate glass

DID YOU KNOW? *Alien abduction insurance has been available in the USA since 1987.*

SIMILARITIES AND DIFFERENCES BETWEEN BUSINESS AND HOUSEHOLD INSURANCE

Similarities

1 Property/Premises Insurance
- **Household:** Protects the home from damage or loss including fire, storm and burst pipes.
- **Business:** Covers the business premises for events such as storm damage and fire.

2 Contents Insurance
- **Household:** Household contents such as furniture and electrical goods need to be insured against risks such as theft. Items of higher value such as laptops and expensive jewellery may need to be listed individually on policies.
- **Business:** A business should also insure its contents, including trading stock and fixtures and fittings, against damage or theft.

> **Note!**
> *When taking out an insurance policy on property the premium will be based on its replacement cost, i.e. the cost to rebuild it, not on the price paid for the property or its current market valuation.*

3 Motor Insurance

- **Households:** Anybody who owns a motor vehicle is required by law to have at least a third-party policy.
- **Businesses:** Businesses that have their own vehicles, e.g. delivery vans and company cars, must hold valid insurance policies (at least third party) for all vehicles and all drivers.

 DID YOU KNOW? *Motor insurance is compulsory in Ireland – the minimum requirement is third-party insurance.*

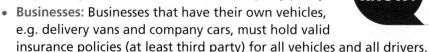
Motor Insurance

Three is a magic number – there are three parties to a motor insurance policy and three main types of policy available.

The three parties:

- **The insured:** The person or business who owns the vehicle(s).
- **The insurance firm:** The insurance company covering the risk.
- **The third party:** The injured party in an accident, e.g. the driver or passenger of the other vehicle.

The three policies:

- **Third party:** The insurance company pays compensation for damage caused by the insured to the third party and property.
- **Third party, fire and theft:** The insurance company pays compensation for damage caused by the insured to the third party and property. It also covers the insured person's own car from damage due to fire or theft.
- **Comprehensive:** This policy includes all losses covered in third party, fire and theft. It also covers the insured for accidental damage to their vehicle.

Activity 15.5

1 In small groups, discuss the reasons why you think that motor insurance is compulsory but home insurance is not. Share your thoughts with other groups in the class.

2 In groups, select a model of car. Use www.carzone.ie to find the value of the car of your choice. Using the Internet, research how much it would cost you to insure this car for 12 months. Each group should use different criteria, e.g. full licence vs. provisional, male vs. female, value, alarms. Compare your results with other groups. Which are the most expensive policies? Which are the least expensive?

4 PRSI (Pay Related Social Insurance)

This insurance is compulsory and must be paid by both the employee and the employer.

- **Household:** Employees pay PRSI from their gross pay and it is used by government to pay for items including Jobseeker's Allowance and state pensions.
- **Business:** Employers pay PRSI on behalf of each of their employees. This is known as employer's PRSI.

Differences

Insurance Policies for Households

1 **Health insurance:** Protects individuals and families against the cost of hospital fees and day-to-day medical expenses. Health insurers include VHI and Laya Healthcare.

2 **Mortgage protection:** Covers the cost of mortgage repayments if the household cannot meet their payments, e.g. due to illness or redundancy. This is often a compulsory part of a mortgage contract.

3 **Income protection:** Covers the financial loss to a household if the main earner is unable to continue to work either for a short period of time or permanently, e.g. due to illness. Most policies provide for 75% of salary earned.

4 **Personal accident insurance:** Covers loss if the insured person has a serious accident. People who need their body, or parts of their body, to earn income often take out this type

 DID YOU KNOW? *'Lord of the Dance' Michael Flatley insured his legs for €34.5 million. Coffee taster Gennaro Pelliccia has had his taste buds insured for €8.6 million by his employer, Costa Coffee.*

of insurance, e.g. the actor Daniel Craig insured his body for €6.6 million when he was filming the movie *Casino Royale*.

5 **Travel:** Covers risks such as loss of baggage and delayed flights. It also covers cancellation costs if a travel plan has to be cancelled due to a family emergency.

6 **Identity theft:** Covers losses against your identity being stolen, e.g. all the money is cleared out of your bank account. Identity theft insurance covers expenses such as phone bills and lost wages or salary.

7 **Life assurance:** Pays compensation to a named person (e.g. husband or wife) when the person who took out the policy dies. Life assurance firms in Ireland include Irish Life Assurance and Zurich Life.

Life Assurance

There are three main types of life assurance policy.

A **Whole life policy:** A person pays a premium until they die. When the person dies, the insurance policy pays out to a named person, e.g. a family member. These policies are often used to help with funeral expenses and other financial needs of immediate family members. The policy pays out only after the person dies.

B **Term life policy:** A person takes out this policy for a certain length of time, e.g. 25 years. The policy only pays out if the person dies within the timeframe of the policy, i.e. during the 25 years. If the person lives past this period, no payout is made.

C **Endowment policy:** This policy will pay out when (a) the policy reaches maturity, e.g. on the insured person's sixty-fifth birthday, or (b) the person dies, whichever happens first.

Insurance Policies for Businesses

1 **Product liability:** Covers a business against claims made by customers who were injured or became ill while using the firm's products, e.g. by food poisoning.

2 **Public liability:** Covers a business against claims made by members of the public who are injured while on the business's premises, e.g. a fall on a shop floor.

3 **Employer's liability:** Covers against claims made by an employee for accident, illness or injury in the workplace.

4 **Key personnel:** Covers the loss a business may suffer when a key employee leaves the business, e.g. when a manager with specialised skills leaves to join a rival firm. The cost of finding a suitable replacement is covered by this policy. Key personnel are highly specialised and trained employees.

5 **Fidelity guarantee:** Covers a business against any loss suffered due to fraudulent activities by employees, e.g. theft by employees or an employee giving away product ideas to rival businesses.

6 **Consequential loss:** Covers a business against a loss that can arise as result of another risk happening. For example, if a restaurant is damaged in a fire and has to close for a week for repairs, the lost revenue and profits as a result of this closure can be insured against, i.e. the loss of income is a direct consequence of the fire.

7 **Cash in transit:** Covers a business against theft of cash while it's off the premises, e.g. when in transit from the business premises to the bank. This is essential for businesses with a lot of cash sales, e.g. a restaurant, or when a sales representative collects cash from customers.

8 **Plate glass:** Covers a business against large shop windows being broken or damaged.

DID YOU **KNOW?**

The 9/11 terrorist attack in the USA resulted in insurance payouts totalling over €37 billion. Compensation was paid for claims made across a range of insurance policies, including: property, aviation, business interruption, employees and life assurance.

Unit 4

Unit 4

Activity 15.6

In small groups, create a leaflet or poster describing the main types of insurance taken out by households or businesses.

SIMILARITIES AND DIFFERENCES BETWEEN HOUSEHOLD AND BUSINESS INSURANCE

Similarities	Differences
1 Policies Both households and businesses take out common types of insurance, e.g. motor, contents, pay related social insurance and property.	**1 Risks** Businesses are exposed to a greater number of risks than households. A business usually has to take out more insurance policies than a household, e.g. plate glass and employer's liability.
2 Forms Both truthfully complete insurance proposal and claim forms.	**2 Premiums** Businesses tend to pay higher premiums than households.
3 Risk Management Both identify risks and take steps to manage risk, e.g. installing smoke alarms and CCTV cameras to deter burglars.	**3 PRSI** Households pay PRSI on their own earned income as employees. A business must pay PRSI for all its employees.
4 Review Policies Both regularly review their policies to ensure that the value of items insured is accurate.	**4 Business Expenses** The cost of insurance is a business expense and can be used to reduce the firm's tax liability.

The Importance of Insurance

Insurance is important to households and businesses for the following reasons:

Cost saving	→ The cost of the premium is usually less than the cost incurred if the risk happens, e.g. a premium of €150 for motor insurance is a lot lower than the cost of repairs, which could run into thousands of euros. A claim for negligence or injury could run into hundreds of thousands of euros.
Legal requirements	→ Some types of insurance, e.g. motor insurance, are required by law. Failure to pay such policies can result in fines.
Risk management	→ Insurance helps households and businesses to reduce their risk as they must carry out a risk assessment before taking out insurance, e.g. installing a smoke alarm. This helps to reduce the likelihood of a risk occurring, e.g. a fire.

KEY TERMS

Now you have completed this chapter, you should understand and be able to explain the following terms. In your copybook, write a definition of each term to build up your own glossary of terms.

- risk management
- insurance
- proposal form
- claim form
- insured
- insurer
- premium
- loading
- actuary
- assessor
- loss adjuster
- insurance agent
- insurance broker
- principles of insurance
- insurable interest

- utmost good faith
- average clause
- contribution
- subrogation
- material facts
- indemnity
- property insurance
- contents insurance
- motor insurance
- PRSI
- health insurance
- mortgage protection insurance
- income protection insurance

- personal accident insurance
- travel insurance
- life assurance
- product liability insurance
- public liability insurance
- employer's liability insurance
- key personnel insurance
- fidelity guarantee insurance
- consequential loss insurance
- cash in transit insurance
- plate glass insurance

Unit 4

EXAM-STYLE QUESTIONS

Ordinary Level

Section 1 – Short Questions (10 marks each)

1 List **three** ways in which the manager of a restaurant could reduce risks in their business.

2 Distinguish between an insurance proposal form and a claims form.

3 Explain what is meant by the term *premium*. Who calculates it?

4 Indicate whether the following statements are true or false.

Statements		True or False
A	A loading is a reduction in the basic premium.	
B	Indemnity means you cannot profit from insurance.	
C	An assessor calculates the premium.	
D	Motor insurance is compulsory in Ireland.	
E	Utmost good faith means you must tell the truth when completing a compensation form.	

5 List the main principles of insurance.

6 List **three** insurance policies a typical household might have.

7 Distinguish between product liability insurance and employer's liability insurance.

8 Outline **two** similarities between household and business insurance.

Section 2 – Long Questions

1 What is the difference between (i) an insurance agent and an insurance broker and
   (ii) an actuary and an assessor? **(20 marks)**

2 State any **four** principles of insurance. Explain **two** of these principles. **(15 marks)**

3 List **four** factors to be considered when calculating an insurance premium. Describe **two**
   of these factors in more detail. **(15 marks)**

4 A house rebuild is valued at €600,000 and insured for €500,000. Calculate the compensation
   payable in the event that a fire partially damages the house causing damage to the
   value of €35,000. **(15 marks)**

5

> Carol Power runs her own fruit and veg business, Spuds and Plums, in a busy town in Kilkenny.
> She employs three full-time staff. She operates from her own premises, which has a rebuild value
> of €350,000 but is insured for €300,000. A flood causes damage to the premises to the value of
> €120,000. Carol submits a claim to her insurance company for €120,000.

   (i)   Name the form that Carol will complete to make this claim.
   (ii) Calculate the amount of compensation that Carol will receive from the insurance company.
   (iii) Name the principle of insurance which applies in this case.
   (iv) Name the person who will calculate this compensation for the insurance company. **(20 marks)**

6 Name and explain **three** documents regularly used in insurance. **(15 marks)**

7

> John Tyrell insured his van with Sinnott Insurance Ltd for €24,000. The van was worth €30,000.
> Vandals caused €9,000 worth of damage to the van.

   (i)   Calculate the compensation to be paid to John.
   (ii) Which principle of insurance applies in this case?
   (iii) List **two** ways in which John can reduce the risk happening again. **(30 marks)**

8 Outline **two** similarities and **two** differences between insurance for business and
   insurance for households. **(20 marks)**

Higher Level

Section 1 – Short Questions (10 marks each)

1 Explain the following terms: (i) *premium*, (ii) *loading*, (iii) *no claims bonus*.

2 Distinguish between the insurance principles of (i) *indemnity* and (ii) *insurable interest*.

3 Differentiate between the principles of (i) *subrogation* and (ii) *contribution*.

4 Lily has her apartment insured for €140,000. The cost of rebuilding the apartment is currently €180,000.
   A fire caused €30,000 worth of damage. How much compensation will Lily receive? Explain your answer.

5 Aodhnait insured her café with three different insurance companies as follows:

One Insurance Ltd	Whole Insurance Ltd	Maxi Insurance Ltd
€200,000	€300,000	€400,000

   A flood has recently caused €50,000 worth of damage. How much compensation will Aodhnait receive
   from each insurance company? She was adequately insured. Explain your answer.

6 Column 1 is a list of key business terms associated with Insurance. Column 2 is a list of possible
   explanations for these terms. Match the two lists in your copybook by writing your answers in the
   form *number = letter* (e.g. 1 = A).

Terms		Explanations	
1	Loading	A	A person or business who sells insurance on behalf of one insurance company.
2	Insurable interest	B	This document is sent out before the policy is due for renewal.
3	Premium	C	An extra charge on top of the basic premium because of an extra risk that may apply in certain circumstances.
4	Insurance agent	D	The fee charged or the price paid for insurance.
5	Renewal notice	E	This means that the insured person must own the item and benefit by its existence and suffer financially from its loss.

Unit 4

Section 1 – Short Questions (10 marks each) *continued*

7 Distinguish between the following types of insurance: (i) fidelity guarantee; and (ii) consequential loss.

8 Choose the correct answer from the words in bold in each sentence.

   (i) An insurance broker sells insurance on behalf of **one/more than one** insurance company.

   (ii) A loading on an insurance policy **increases/decreases** the cost of insurance.

   (iii) An **actuary/assessor** calculates the risk involved and the price charged for insurance.

   (iv) The **premium/policy** is the price charged for insurance.

   (v) When a customer is injured on a business premises he or she is protected by **product/public** liability insurance.

Section 2 – Applied Business Question (80 marks)

A Cut Above the Rest

A Cut Above the Rest is a hair salon in Carrick-on-Suir owned by Geraldine Casey. The premises has large window frontage on the main street, which helps to attract customers into the salon. Geraldine employs six full-time staff and has recently introduced a mobile hairdressing unit. Two stylists travel in the firm's car to clients and Geraldine has seen a large increase in demand for this service.

Local newspaper articles have highlighted that there has been an increase in burglaries in the area. This is a concern to Geraldine as she brings the takings from the salon to the bank at the end of each day. She is considering installing a 24-hour monitored CCTV system to deter burglars and provide some protection to the staff. A number of local properties have been set on fire due to anti-social behaviour in the area and Geraldine is worried about the damage a fire could cause to her premises.

After a client slipped and broke her leg on a wet floor at the salon, Geraldine realised that she had to take a more formal approach to <u>risk management</u>. She appointed Sheila as the salon's health and safety officer. Sheila organised a first aid training session for all staff and has placed safety signs around the salon, e.g. reminders that equipment such as hair straighteners can be very hot and burn the skin.

Geraldine recently received a <u>renewal notice</u> from her insurance company. She is surprised to discover that her <u>insurance premium</u> for the business premises has increased by 25%. Geraldine contacted her <u>insurance agent</u>, Sinead O'Donnell, who explained that a number of items on the premises such as hairdryers and straighteners have added a <u>loading</u> to her premium. A recently submitted <u>claim form</u> to pay for the hospital bill of the client injured at the salon has also increased the premium.

A Insurance is considered to be part of a risk management strategy for reducing the costs of running a business.

   (i) Describe what is meant by the term *risk management*.

   (ii) Outline ways in which Geraldine could take steps to reduce risks for her business. **(25 marks)**

B Outline your understanding of the underlined insurance terms with reference to A Cut Above the Rest. **(25 marks)**

C Describe the types of insurance appropriate to Geraldine's business. **(30 marks)**

Section 3 – Long Questions

1 Insurance is part of the risk management strategy of a business. What is meant by the term *risk management*? Outline the ways in which a business can manage its exposure to risk. **(20 marks)**

2 Insurance is based on five main principles. Select and describe **three** of these principles in detail. **(15 marks)**

3 The fee charged by insurance companies is called the premium. Describe the factors that determine this premium. **(15 marks)**

4 Meaghan wants to take out insurance on her home and contents. The house is located in Limerick city and is valued at €250,000. Contents are valued at 20% of the value of the house. Meaghan has an alarm system installed. She has made no previous claims. She has received the following quotation from Allied Insurance Ltd:

    Buildings: €1.30 per €1,000

    Contents: €3.20 per €1,000

    Loadings: City address 15%

    Discounts: No previous claims 2%, Alarm system 4%.

Calculate the premium that Meaghan will pay to Allied Insurance Ltd. **(15 marks)**

5

> Brady Ltd is a building contractor that employs 15 staff. The employees travel to work in vans owned by the business. Cash earned from jobs is deposited by the staff in a night safe at a local bank each evening.

Outline the types of insurance that you would recommend the management at Brady Ltd should take out. **(20 marks)**

6 Describe the different life assurance policies that a household can take out from an insurance provider. **(15 marks)**

7 Insurance is essential for households and businesses. Discuss **two** similarities and **two** differences between insurance for a household and for a business. **(20 marks)**

8 Describe the benefits that insurance cover can have for a household and a business. **(15 marks)**

PREVIOUS LEAVING CERTIFICATE EXAM QUESTIONS

Ordinary Level

Section A – Short Questions (10 marks each)

1 Outline the purpose of the following insurance forms (i) Proposal Form (ii) Claim Form. **[LC OL 2015]**

2 Write TRUE or FALSE for each of the following statements: **[LC OL 2014]**

	Statements	True or False
A	Indemnity states that you must gain from the item's existence and suffer financially from its loss.	
B	Loading is an extra charge on the basic premium due to increased risk.	
C	An insurance policy is a contract.	
D	Utmost good faith states that the insured must be truthful about all the material facts when applying for insurance.	
E	An assessor calculates the premium the insurer must pay.	

3 Distinguish between employer's liability insurance and public liability insurance. **[LC OL 2007]**

Section B

1

> **Kevin's Garage**
>
> Kevin owns a garage and has a recovery truck. He employs seven people. Kevin received his annual insurance bill for the garage. He was disappointed to discover that his insurance premium had increased by 50%. He decided to shop around, getting online quotes for insurance from several companies.

Outline **three** types of insurance you would expect the business to have.   **(20 marks) [LC OL 2016]**

2

> InsuranceDepot.com is an insurance broker based in Cork City. It employs 8 sales staff in the Cork office. Due to increased online demand they are currently recruiting 3 more sales staff.

(A) Explain **two** types of insurance that InsuranceDepot.com might sell to its customers.   **(15 marks)**

(B) Explain **two** of the following principles of insurance and give **one** example in **each** case:
   (i)   Indemnity
   (ii) Insurable Interest
   (iii) Utmost Good Faith   **(20 marks) [LC OL 2015]**

3

> It is important that a business identifies, assesses and tries to reduce risks before taking out insurance.

(A) Outline **four** different types of insurance policies you would expect a factory to have.   **(20 marks)**

(B) Outline **three** ways in which a manager can reduce risks in a factory.   **(20 marks)**

(C) Name and explain the functions of **two** documents commonly used in insurance.   **(15 marks) [LC OL 2008]**

Higher Level

Section A – Short Questions (10 marks each)

1 Illustrate the difference between the insurance principles Insurable Interest and Indemnity.   **[LC HL 2010]**

2 Distinguish between public liability and fidelity guarantee as types of insurance.   **[LC HL 2009]**

3 John O'Neill owned a house worth €350,000 and insured it for €300,000 when a fire caused a partial loss of €63,000. Calculate the amount of compensation the insurance company will have to pay. Name the principle of insurance that applies in this case.   **[LC HL 2008]**

Section B

1

> PRIVATE MOTOR INSURANCE PROPOSAL FORM DECLARATION
>
> I/we declare to the best of my/our knowledge and belief that the information given on this form is true and complete in every respect.

(i)   Outline the function of an insurance proposal form.

(ii) Explain the principle of insurance referred to in the contract from the above private motor insurance proposal form.

(iii) Outline **two** other principles of insurance that apply to insurance contracts.   **(20 marks) [LC HL 2015]**

2 Explain what it means to be underinsured and outline **one** possible effect of being underinsured on a business.   **(15 marks) [LC HL 2014]**

Solutions

16 MANAGING A BUSINESS AND A HOUSEHOLD: TAXATION

⊕ Learning Outcomes

When you have completed this chapter, you will be able to:

1 Outline the reasons for taxation

2 Describe the taxes paid by households and businesses

3 Explain how the PAYE system operates

4 Calculate the tax liability of an employee

5 Explain the implications of taxation for households and businesses

6 Outline the similarities and differences between household and business taxes.

📖 Literacy Link

Taxation, direct tax, indirect tax, Revenue Commissioners, VAT, PAYE, PRSI, capital gains tax, tax credit

Numeracy Link

Addition, subtraction, percentages, manipulation of formulae, income tax calculation, corporation tax calculation

Cross-curricular Link

Accounting – PAYE, PRSI and VAT, procedures for the treatment of taxation

Economics – government income

Home Economics – household income, household expenditure, PRSI

CASE STUDY · Dalata Hotel Group

Dalata Hotel Group plc is one of the largest hotel operators in Ireland with a portfolio of thirty-nine hotels, which include the brands Maldron and Clayton. Like many businesses across Ireland, Dalata is responsible for paying a number of taxes to the **Revenue Commissioners**.

Through the **Pay As You Earn (PAYE)** system Dalata collects **income tax** and **PRSI** payments on income earned by its 4,300 employees and sends them to the Revenue Commissioners. Dalata also pays **employer's PRSI** on each member of staff it employs. The total annual employer's PRSI paid by Dalata amounts to €8.5 million. The firm also pays **corporation tax** on its profits of over €9 million.

Some of the hotels operated by Dalata offer a shuttle bus service to the local airport, so the firm ensures that it pays the correct rate of **motor tax** on its vehicles.

Guests at the hotels pay **VAT** on room rates and products purchased at the hotel such as meals. The hotel bars and restaurants stock a range of alcoholic drinks on which **excise duties** are paid. Imports of alcohol from countries outside the European Union are also subject to **customs duties**.

The firm values environmental sustainability and has reduced its **carbon tax** liability by using 100% renewable energy, which is supplied by Bord Gáis Energy.

Dalata hotels pay **commercial rates** to their local authority. This enables the council to maintain and improve roads in the area, as well as providing street cleaners and water supplies.

WHAT IS TAXATION?

Taxation is a levy imposed by government on individuals and businesses. It is paid on income, the purchase of goods and services, and on property. The Revenue Commissioners, often referred to as Revenue, is the government agency responsible for collecting taxes on behalf of the Irish government.

> **Note!**
> The Department of Finance, through the Minister for Finance, is responsible for setting the rates of taxation to be levied on households and businesses.

 DID YOU KNOW? *In recent years the Revenue Commissioners has collected on average €50 billion in taxes from individuals and businesses.*

REASONS FOR TAXATION

A country needs taxation for a number of reasons, including:

Government Revenue	→ For a country to function the government needs to raise income through taxation. The government collects taxes to fund the daily running of the country, i.e. to provide essential services such as healthcare and education.
Redistribution of Wealth	→ Taxation takes money from higher earners through the PAYE system and redistributes it among the less well off in society using the social welfare system. This lessens the gap between the rich and the poor with the aim of making a country a fairer place to live in.
Discouraging Consumption	→ The government places higher taxes on products that are unhealthy. This makes them more expensive to purchase and discourages citizens from buying these items, e.g. excise duty on tobacco products and alcohol.

 DID YOU KNOW? *In 2018 a sugar tax was introduced on juices and soft drinks with more than 5g of sugar per 100ml.*

Activity 16.1

In pairs, discuss the effects of the sugar tax and its consequences for households and for businesses operating in the soft drinks industry.

 DID YOU KNOW? *In 1696 the King of England introduced a tax on homes with more than six windows. As a result, houses were built with no more than six windows and home owners began to fill in windows with bricks. The phrase 'daylight robbery' comes from this period and refers to homes where bricked-up windows prevented rooms from receiving any sunlight. People began to suffer health problems from lack of sunlight, and the tax was repealed in 1851.*

DIRECT AND INDIRECT TAXATION

Taxation can be classified into two types: direct and indirect.

Direct Taxation	**Indirect Taxation**
These are taxes levied on the income earned by a household or businesses and paid directly to the government. Examples include PAYE income tax and corporation tax.	These are taxes levied on what people spend, rather than earnings. Examples include VAT and import duties.

Unit 4

TAXES PAID BY HOUSEHOLDS AND BUSINESSES

	Type of Tax	Households	Businesses
1	Value added tax (VAT)	✓	✓
2	Motor tax	✓	✓
3	Capital gains tax (CGT)	✓	✓
4	Customs duty	✓	✓
5	Excise duty	✓	✓
6	Carbon tax	✓	✓
7	Pay related social insurance (PRSI)	✓	✓
8	Pay As You Earn (PAYE) income tax	✓	✗
9	Self-assessment income tax	✓	✗
10	Universal social charge (USC)	✓	✗
11	Deposit interest retention tax (DIRT)	✓	✗
12	Local property tax (LPT)	✓	✗
13	Capital acquisitions tax (CAT)	✓	✗
14	Corporation tax	✗	✓
15	Commercial rates	✗	✓

Taxes Paid by Both Households and Businesses

The following taxes are paid by both households and businesses in Ireland.

1 Value Added Tax (VAT)

VAT is a tax on goods and services paid by both households and businesses. Some goods and services are exempt from VAT, and not all goods and services have the same rate applied. The standard rate of VAT is 23%.

- **Households:** VAT is paid by households when they buy goods and services. This tax is included in the selling price of products.
- **Businesses:** Businesses have a dual role in the VAT system. They pay VAT and also collect VAT on behalf of the Revenue Commissioners, if they are registered for VAT with Revenue. The system operates as follows:

  — A business pays VAT on the goods and services it purchases.

  — A business collects VAT on the goods and services it sells.

  — The business can claim the VAT paid on purchases against the VAT collected on sales.

  — If a business pays more VAT than it collected from sales in a particular period it will be entitled to a VAT refund from the Revenue Commissioners; if it collects more VAT than it pays, it transfers the balance to the Revenue Commissioners.

Activity 16.2

Research the current rates of VAT on the following items in Ireland.

Rate	Items subject to rate
___%	Basic food items, children's clothes and medicines
___%	Hospitality/tourism activities including hotel rooms and cinema tickets
___%	Services and home buildings/heating, e.g. electricity and home heating
___%	Chocolates, sweets, computers

Compare your answers with other students' answers to ensure that all students have identified the correct rates.

2 Motor Tax

Motor tax is paid on all motor vehicles that use public roads. The rates are set by the government and the tax is collected through local authorities, e.g. Offaly County Council.

- **Households:** Households pay motor tax on the vehicles they own. The amount of motor tax paid depends on CO_2 emissions or engine size.
- **Businesses:** Businesses also pay tax on all their vehicles, e.g. trucks, vans and cars. These vehicles are subject to a business rate of motor tax.

3 Capital Gains Tax (CGT)

This is a tax on the gain made when a household or business sells an asset, e.g. land or company shares. The capital gain is the difference between the selling price and the original price paid for the asset. The current rate of CGT on most assets is 33%.

Activity 16.3

Eve bought shares in a company for €12,000. The shares later rose in value on the stock market. She sold the shares for €18,000. Calculate the capital gains tax Eve paid, using the rate of 33%.

4 Customs Duty

This tax is levied on goods imported to Ireland from countries outside the European Union. This makes the imported goods more expensive and encourages citizens to purchase more goods grown or manufactured in the EU.

5 Excise Duty

This tax is paid on certain goods such as alcohol and tobacco products and is used by the government to discourage consumption of these items. Different rates of excise are applied to different goods.

6 Carbon Tax

A tax levied on products that emit carbon into the atmosphere, e.g. heating oil, diesel and petrol. The objectives of a carbon tax include:

- To discourage our use of such products as they damage the environment
- To help pay for climate change programmes.

7 Pay Related Social Insurance (PRSI)

PRSI is a statutory deduction made by employers on behalf of the Revenue Commissioners. It is a tax charged on both employers and employees and is used to fund social welfare benefits, e.g. pensions and medical cards.

- **Households:** For employees, the amount of PRSI to be paid is deducted from their wages, with different rates payable depending on the amount they earn.
- **Businesses:** Businesses that employ staff pay employer's PRSI. The PRSI payment by the employer is based on the amount earned by the employee.

> *Employers make deductions from employees' pay on a statutory or non-statutory (voluntary) basis.*
> - **Statutory deductions:** *Employers are required by law to make these deductions, e.g. PAYE and PRSI.*
> - **Non-statutory deductions:** *Employees request that their employer makes certain deductions from their pay, e.g. trade union subscriptions and private health insurance.*

Taxes Paid by Households Only

The following are some of the main taxes paid by households:

1 Pay as You Earn (PAYE) Income Tax

This is a direct tax on employees' wages and salaries and is collected through the PAYE system. It is a statutory deduction which is deducted at source by the employer and paid directly to the Revenue Commissioners. There are two rates of tax:

- The standard rate, which is currently 20%
- The higher rate (marginal rate), which is currently 40%.

> **Note!**
> *Many people refer to PAYE as a tax, or use the term when referring to income tax. However, the term PAYE relates to the **system** used to collect income tax from employees.*

2 Self-Assessment Income Tax

This is a tax paid by self-employed people on their business profits and other income earned. By 31 October each year, an estimate of tax due (known as preliminary tax) for the current year must be paid, in addition to any amounts outstanding from the previous year.

3 Universal Social Charge (USC)

USC is paid by all employees and self-employed people who earn more than €12,000 per annum.

4 Deposit Interest Retention Tax (DIRT)

DIRT is a tax on interest earned on savings in deposit accounts in banks, post offices and credit unions. The financial institution is responsible for deducting this tax at source. The DIRT rate for 2019 is 35%.

5 Local Property Tax (LPT)

This tax is based on the value of residential property, e.g. a main home, holiday home or property rented to other people. It is paid by the household or landlord each year to their local authority.

6 Capital Acquisitions Tax (CAT)

This is a tax on gifts and inheritances. The amount of tax paid is based on the relationship between the person giving and receiving the gift or inheritance. The closer the relationship to the person giving the gift or inheritance, the lower the amount of tax that will be paid by the recipient, e.g. there is no CAT between spouses or civil partners. CAT is charged at 33%.

Activity 16.4

In pairs, look up houses for sale in your local area on www.daft.ie or www.myhome.ie and calculate the LPT on the property. Use the 'Calculate your Local Property Tax' link on the Revenue website, www.revenue.ie.

Taxes Paid by Businesses Only

The following are the main taxes paid by businesses only.

1 Corporation Tax

This is a tax on a firm's profits. The standard rate of corporation tax in Ireland is 12.5%. This low rate of corporation tax relative to other European Union countries has been a major factor in attracting foreign direct investment (FDI) to Ireland, e.g. firms such as Google and Facebook.

> **You will learn more about FDI in Chapter 28.**

Activity 16.5

Working in pairs, research the different rates of corporation tax rates around the world. Create a table in Microsoft Excel or a similar application listing the countries and their corporation tax rates.

Activity 16.6

Empire Ltd recorded a profit of €150,000. How much corporation tax would it be liable for if it was based in (i) Ireland, (ii) the USA and (iii) France?

---

2 Commercial Rates

Commercial rates are levied by the local authority on a firm's property and are used to finance local government services, e.g. street cleaning and lighting. The amount paid is based on the value of the property as well as the size and nature of the business, e.g. a large supermarket in a prime location will pay a higher commercial rate than a small shop on the outskirts of a town.

> **DID YOU KNOW?** *Brown Thomas on Dublin's Grafton Street pays annual commercial rates of over €1 million to Dublin City Council.*

Activity 16.7

In pairs, draw a Venn diagram in your copybook. Fill in the diagram to show the similarities and differences between the taxes paid by households and businesses.

Note!
Some taxes are progressive; others are regressive.

Definition: Progressive tax
Taxes that impose higher rates for those on higher incomes, e.g. PRSI and PAYE income tax.

Definition: Regressive tax
The amount of tax is levied uniformly. As a result, a regressive tax takes a larger percentage of income from low income earners than high income earners, e.g. VAT.

THE PAYE SYSTEM

Every person employed in Ireland is subject to tax on their income. The collection system in Ireland is known as PAYE – Pay As You Earn. As we have already learned, there are two rates of PAYE income tax, 20% and 40%. The standard rate of tax (20%) applies to income up to a certain level, known as the standard rate cut-off point (SRCOP). Any income earned above this level is subject to the higher rate of tax (40%).

The amount of PAYE payable by individuals varies and depends on their own personal circumstances, e.g. whether they are single, married or widowed. The amount of tax payable can be reduced by claiming tax credits.

Definition: Tax rate/band
This specifies the range of income for an individual that is subject to the standard rate of income tax (20%) and any balance that is subject to the higher rate of tax (40%).

Definition: Tax credits
A tax credit reduces the amount of PAYE income tax paid by an employee. There are a number of different tax credits available, including:
- Single person tax credit
- Employee tax credit
- Home carer tax credit.

 DID YOU KNOW? *Approximately €800 million in tax credits goes unclaimed each year in Ireland.*

PAYE Modernisation

In the past, employers in Ireland dealt with many taxation forms relating to the employment and end of employment of staff. This created annual paperwork of almost 5 million forms for employers throughout Ireland.

There has been a growth in the number of employers and employees in Ireland, and over 200,000 people are in more than one employment, e.g. a person working part-time for three different employers. In order to reflect these changes in the employment market, reduce taxation paperwork and increase efficiency, the Revenue Commissioners have introduced PAYE modernisation.

From 2019 the PAYE system operates as follows.

1 Commencing Employment

An individual registers with the Revenue Commissioners using their PPSN (Personal Public Service Number), creates an online account and enters details about their employer. The Revenue Commissioners then assigns this individual the correct **tax bands** and **tax credits**, which is known as the **RPN (Revenue Payroll Notification)**.

The information contained in the RPN is used by the employer to ensure that the employee pays the correct rates of tax and receives the correct tax credits.

Definition: PPSN
A PPSN (Personal Public Service Number) is a unique reference number assigned to each person in Ireland; it enables people to access social welfare benefits and public services and identifies them for employment and tax purposes.

Unit 4

> **Emergency Tax**
>
> If an employer does not have an employee's PPSN or RPN, it must impose emergency tax on the employee's income. If after four weeks the employer still does not have the required information, all income is taxed at the higher rate of PAYE income tax, i.e. 40%.

2 During Employment

An employee can log on to their account with the Revenue Commissioners and obtain up-to-date information on the amount of taxes that they have paid. They can also check to ensure that the correct tax rates and tax credits have been applied to their income.

An end-of-year statement will be available for employees via their online account with the Revenue Commissioners. It will include details of all their pay and tax deductions from all employments for that tax year.

3 Ending Employment

When an employee ceases employment with an employer, the employer communicates the end date with the Revenue system. This information is available to the individual's:

- New employer – so that they can register the tax band and tax credits of the new employee
- Local social welfare office – so that he/she can access the relevant social welfare payments, e.g. Jobseeker's Benefit.

Benefits of PAYE Modernisation

	Employer	Employee
S	**Seamless** → The employer's payroll systems can integrate with Revenue's system. This means that information on employees can be exchanged automatically, which saves time.	**Simplified** → Employees can access information on their tax credits and tax bands through their online account on the Revenue website.
M	**Minimise costs** → There are lower costs for the employer, as less staff time is taken up with preparing and processing forms, e.g. P60 and P45.	**Maximise the use of tax credits** → The employee can monitor their allocation of tax credits during the year to ensure that they don't overpay taxes.
A	**Abolition of forms** → It has led to the abolition of forms such as the P45 (when an employee ended their employment).	**Automatic review** → The system undertakes an automatic end-of-year review of tax paid. Employees receive a tax refund if they are found to have overpaid taxes during the year.
R	**Right tax** → It ensures that employees and employers pay the correct amount of taxes. It also reduces the number of employees who pay emergency tax.	**Real-time reporting** → Employees can log on to their Revenue account to see what taxes they have paid to date.
T	**Time savings** → It saves the employer time as forms such as P45s and P60s will not have to be created by the employer, which was time-consuming.	**Transparency** → Employees can see that tax deducted by their employer has been paid to Revenue.

> **Example**
>
> Boxform Ltd, a building contractor, pleaded guilty to five Revenue offences, which included the failure to transfer PAYE and PRSI deducted from employees to the Revenue Commissioners. The fraud was initially discovered when former employees attempted to claim social welfare benefits and found no appropriate records in respect of themselves. In total, the company owed over €2.5m to the Revenue Commissioners. Now, under PAYE modernisation, an employee can check that taxes collected by their employer have actually been paid over to the Revenue Commissioners.

TAX NON-COMPLIANCE

Nobody likes paying taxes. However, taxes are essential in a fair society and for a country to function. Some individuals and businesses will try to **evade** paying their taxes (illegal) or find ways to **avoid** paying their taxes (legal).

> **Definition: Tax evasion**
> Households and businesses avoid paying the correct amount of tax by under-declaring income or over-claiming tax deductions. This is **illegal**, and heavy penalties are applied by the Revenue Commissioners for tax evasion.

> **Example**
> The former director of an Irish firm was sentenced to three years in prison for tax evasion. The director was found guilty of unpaid taxes, including VAT, PRSI and PAYE, amounting to €2.1 million.

DID YOU KNOW?
It is estimated that in a ten-year period, tax evasion in Ireland amounted to €1 billion.

> **Definition: Tax avoidance**
> This reduces the tax liability for households and businesses. Unlike tax evasion, tax avoidance can be done **legally** by using the tax laws (sometimes referred to as loopholes) to reduce tax liability, e.g. by maximising tax deductions and tax credits while minimising taxable income.

To reduce the incidence of tax evasion, the Revenue Commissioners conduct random revenue audits. During these audits, officers compare the tax returns of households and businesses with their tax records to see if they have underpaid tax.

TAX CALCULATIONS

The employer is responsible for calculating and collecting taxes paid by employees. It is very important that employees understand how to calculate their own pay to check that the correct tax band and tax credits are applied. The amount of tax owed by an employee is based on:

- Gross pay: basic pay plus overtime and bonuses
- The financial value of any benefits-in-kind.

Once gross income has been calculated, the **gross PAYE tax** is calculated using the standard rate and higher rate of tax (if applicable). Tax credits available to the employee are then deducted from the gross PAYE tax in computing the **net PAYE tax**.

> **Pay as You Earn (PAYE) Income Tax Calculation Summary**
>
> - **Gross pay = basic pay + overtime + bonuses**
> - **Gross income = gross pay + financial value of benefits in kind**
> - **Gross PAYE tax = gross income × appropriate tax rates**
> - **Net PAYE tax = gross PAYE tax – tax credits**

PRSI and USC charges are then calculated and subtracted from gross income to arrive at **net pay**:

Net pay (also known as take-home pay) = gross income – PAYE – PRSI – USC.

Unit 4

Tax Calculations: Sample Questions

The tax rates below are used in the following three sample calculations.

Standard rate of tax	20%
Higher rate of tax	40%
Standard rate cut-off point	€33,800
Employee's PRSI	4%
USC (first €12,012)	0.5%
USC (next €7,360)	2%
USC (next €50,672)	4.75%
USC remainder at	8%

Exam Tip!
Taxation rates will be supplied in taxation questions in the Leaving Certificate exam. You are not required to know the current rates for calculation purposes.

Example 1

Ashley works as a part-time mechanic with FM Motors Ltd. His salary is €23,500 per annum. Ashley has been allocated a personal tax credit of €2,200 per annum. Calculate Ashley's net annual pay (take-home pay).

Solution

	€	€	€
Gross Pay			23,500.00
Step 1: Calculate Gross PAYE Tax			
Standard rate: €23,500 × 20%	4,700.00		
Higher rate: (nil, since salary is below the standard rate cut-off point)	0		
Gross PAYE Tax		4,700.00	
Less Tax Credits		(2,200.00)	
(A) Net PAYE Tax		2,500.00	
Step 2: Calculate PRSI (levied on gross pay)			
(B) €23,500 × 4%		940.00	
Step 3: Calculate USC			
First €12,012 × 0.5%	60.06		
Next €7,360 × 2%	147.20		
Remainder (€23,500 − €19,372) × 4.75%	196.08		
(C) Total USC Payable		403.34	
Total Deductions (A + B + C)		3,843.34	
Step 4: Subtract Total Deductions from Gross Pay			(3,843.34)
Net Pay (Take-home Pay)			19,656.66

Example 2

Tom Wall is an employee at Parle Distributions Ltd and earns an annual salary of €92,000. His personal tax credits consist of a single person tax credit of €1,760 and an employee tax credit of €1,760. Calculate his net annual pay (take-home pay).

Solution

	€	€	€
Annual Salary			92,000.00
Gross PAYE Tax			
Standard rate: €33,800 × 20%	6,760.00		
Higher rate: €58,200 × 40%	23,280.00		
Gross PAYE Tax		30,040.00	
Less Tax Credits			
Single person	1,760.00		
Employee	1,760.00	(3,520.00)	
(A) Net PAYE Tax		**26,520.00**	
(B) PRSI			
92,000 × 4%		**3,680.00**	
USC			
First €12,012 × 0.5%	60.06		
Next €7,360 × 2%	147.20		
Next €50,672 × 4.75%	2,406.92		
Remainder (92,000 – 70,044) × 8%	1,756.48		
(C) Total USC Payable		**4,370.66**	
Total Deductions (A + B + C)			(34,570.66)
Net Pay (Take-home Pay)			**57,429.34**

Example 3

Shauna Butler is an employee at Meadowlands Resources plc. She earns an annual salary of €76,000. She also has the use of a company car during the year with an estimated value to her of €6,000. This is treated as a benefit-in-kind for taxation purposes and is taxed accordingly. Shauna has the following tax credits: employee €1,760; single person €1,760; dependent relative €900.

Calculate Shauna's net annual pay (take-home pay).

Unit 4

Solution

	€	€	€
Income			
Gross Salary		76,000.00	
Add Benefit-in-Kind (Company Car)		6,000.00	
Gross Income			82.000.00
Gross PAYE Tax			
Standard rate: €33,800 × 20%	6,760.00		
Higher rate: €48,200 × 40%	19,280.00		
Gross PAYE Tax		26,040.00	
Less Tax Credits			
Employee	1,760.00		
Single person	1,760.00		
Dependent relative	900.00	(4,420.00)	
(A) Net PAYE Tax		21,620.00	
(B) PRSI			
€82,000 × 4%		3,280.00	
USC			
First €12,012 × 0.5%	60.06		
Next €7,360 × 2%	147.20		
Next €50,672 × 4.75%	2,406.92		
Remainder (82,000 − 70,044) × 8%	956.48		
(C) Total USC Payable		3,570.66	
Total Deductions (A + B + C)			(28,470.66)
Net Pay (Take-Home Pay)			53,529.34

THE IMPLICATIONS OF TAX FOR HOUSEHOLDS AND BUSINESSES

POSITIVE IMPLICATIONS

Households	Businesses
1 Redistribution of Wealth Taxation helps to redistribute wealth in society. Employee PRSI is used to provide social welfare payments such as Jobseeker's Benefit.	**1 Tax Incentives** Tax incentives can be used to encourage businesses to expand or establish in disadvantaged areas. This reduces the cost of setting up or expanding a business.
2 Improved Public Services The government uses tax revenue to provide public services, e.g. education. This improves the standard of living for all citizens.	**2 Lower Rates of Corporation Tax** Low corporation tax rates in Ireland increases the amount of profits that a business can keep.

NEGATIVE IMPLICATIONS

Households	Businesses
1 Reduces Disposable Income PAYE, PRSI and USC reduce employees' take-home pay. This means that households have less disposable income, i.e. the amount they have available to spend.	**1 Overtime** High rates of income tax may discourage employees from working overtime, which can make it difficult for firms to fulfil orders at busy times of the year.
2 Higher Prices VAT, customs duty and excise duty increase the price of goods and services. Consumers may buy fewer of these products and/or purchase from businesses outside Ireland to reduce costs.	**2 Employer's PRSI** Employers must pay employer's Pay Related Social Insurance (PRSI) for each employee, which increases business costs.
3 Regressive Taxes Regressive taxes such as VAT result in those on lower incomes paying a larger portion of their income in tax than wealthier people.	**3 Discourages Enterprise** High rates of taxation such as employer's PRSI and commercial rates discourage enterprise. People do not take the risk of setting up their own businesses.

Activity 16.8

As a class, debate the following motion. 'Taxation is simply a burden on society and only serves to increase prices.'

Definition: Depreciation of assets
Depreciation is the loss in value of a fixed asset over its useful economic life due to wear and tear and passage of time.

SUMMARY: HOUSEHOLD AND BUSINESS TAXES

Both households and businesses are liable for many taxes. There are similarities and differences between them in relation to taxation.

HOUSEHOLD AND BUSINESS TAXES

✓ Similarities	✗ Differences
1 Registration Both households and businesses register for tax with the Revenue Commissioners.	**1 Reduced Tax Liability** Businesses can reduce their tax liability in more ways than a household. For example, legitimate business expenses can be written off for tax purposes, e.g. depreciation of assets.
2 Tax Compliance They both pay the correct amount of tax.	**2 Reclaim VAT** A VAT-registered business can claim back VAT paid on its purchases of goods and services.
3 Tax Avoidance Households and businesses use only legal methods to reduce their tax liability, i.e. tax avoidance strategies.	**3 Greater Range of Taxes** More taxes apply to businesses, e.g. corporation tax and commercial rates.
4 Record Keeping Both households and businesses must keep a record of the amount of taxes owed and taxes paid to the Revenue Comissioners.	**4 Tax Collection** Businesses act as collectors of taxes on behalf of the Revenue Commissioners.

KEY TERMS

Now you have completed this chapter, you should understand and be able to explain the following terms. In your copybook, write a definition of each term to build up your own glossary of terms.

- taxation
- direct tax
- indirect tax
- value added tax (VAT)
- motor tax
- capital gains tax (CGT)
- customs duty
- excise duty
- carbon tax
- Pay Related Social Insurance (PRSI)

- Pay As You Earn (PAYE) income tax
- self-assessment income tax
- Universal Social Charge (USC)
- deposit interest retention tax (DIRT)
- local property tax (LPT)
- capital acquisitions tax (CAT)

- corporation tax
- commercial rates
- progressive tax
- regressive tax
- tax credits
- tax band
- PAYE modernisation
- tax evasion
- tax avoidance
- revenue audit
- net take-home pay

PowerPoint Summary

EXAM-STYLE QUESTIONS

Ordinary Level

Section 1 – Short Questions (10 marks each)

1 Name **three** taxes paid by a household.

2 Name **three** taxes paid by a business.

3 What do the following letters stand for? (i) VAT, (ii) PRSI and (iii) DIRT.

4 What do the following initials stand for? (i) CGT, (ii) PAYE and (iii) CAT.

5 What is meant by the term *emergency tax*?

6 Tony Mowbray's annual salary is €26,000. PAYE is paid at 20% on the first €32,000 and 40% on the remainder. PRSI is charged at 3%. Calculate Tony's annual take-home pay if he has an employee tax credit of €3,200 per annum. Show your workings.

7 Brian Finnegan has an annual salary of €68,000. PAYE is paid at 20% on the first €34,000 and at 40% on the remainder. PRSI is charged at 4%. Calculate Brian's annual take-home pay if he has a single person's tax credit of €3,900 per annum. Show your workings.

8 Indicate whether the following statements are true or false.

Statements		True or False
A	VAT stands for value appreciated tax.	
B	Deposit interest retention tax is a tax paid on the interest earned on savings in a bank or post office.	
C	Tax avoidance is a legal way of reducing your tax liability.	
D	PAYE is an example of an indirect tax.	
E	Corporation tax is a tax on a company's profits.	

Unit 4

Section 2 – Long Questions

1
> John Murphy works at Ross Printers. He earns €34,000 annual salary and from this saves €100 per month with his local post office in a post office savings account. He has a car and owns his own house.

   Outline **four** taxes that John would be likely to pay. **(20 marks)**

2 Broderick plc has a taxable profit of €96,000. Corporation tax is charged at 12.5%. Calculate the amount of tax to be paid by Broderick plc. **(15 marks)**

3 Calculate Susan Griffin's annual net take-home pay from the following information: Annual salary €54,000, Tax credits €2,900, Standard PAYE rate 20%, Higher rate 40%, Standard cut-off point €34,000, PRSI is charged at 4%, USC is charged at 1% up to €12,000, 3% between €12,000 and €22,000 and 7% on the remainder. **(20 marks)**

4 Calculate Michael Acheson's annual net take-home pay from the following information: Annual salary €85,600, Employee tax credit €1,600, Married person tax credit €1,600, Standard PAYE rate 20%, Higher rate 42%, Standard cut-off point €34,000, PRSI is charged at 5%, USC is charged at 2% up to €14,000, 4% between €14,000 and €25,000 and 8% on the remainder. **(20 marks)**

5 Irish households are overburdened with taxation. Describe the taxes paid by households in Ireland. **(25 marks)**

6 Outline the implications of taxation for a household. **(15 marks)**

7 Outline **two** similarities and **two** differences in relation to taxation for a household and a business. **(20 marks)**

Higher Level

Section 1 – Short Questions (10 marks each)

1 Outline the reasons for taxation.

2 Distinguish between a direct tax and an indirect tax. Illustrate your answer with relevant examples.

3 List **five** taxes that both households and businesses pay.

4 Distinguish between corporation tax and commercial rates.

5 Explain what is meant by the term *tax credit*.

6 Distinguish between tax evasion and tax avoidance. Illustrate your answers with relevant examples.

7 Column 1 is a list of taxation terms. Column 2 is a list of possible explanations for these terms. Match the two lists in your copybook by writing your answers in the form *number = letter* (e.g. 1 = A).

Terms			Explanations
1	VAT	A	A tax on the gain made when an individual or business sells an asset, e.g. land and buildings or company shares.
2	Progressive Tax	B	Levied by the local authorities on business property. The purpose is to help finance local government services, e.g. street cleaning and lighting.
3	PPSN	C	A tax on goods and services paid by both consumers and businesses.
4	Capital Gains Tax	D	A number unique to an individual that is used for employment purposes and to access social welfare benefits and public services in Ireland.
5	Commercial Rates	E	Taxes that impose higher rates for those on higher incomes.

8 Choose the correct option in each of the following sentences.

  (i) Tax **evasion/avoidance** is an illegal process whereby individuals and business do not pay the correct amount of tax.

  (ii) VAT is levied on **goods and services/income**.

  (iii) The tax payable on alcohol and tobacco products is called an **import/excise** duty.

  (iv) **Local property tax/local premises tax** is based on the value of residential property.

  (v) When a business or individual inherits an item, e.g. a property, it is subject to **capital gains tax/ capital acquisitions tax**.

Section 2 – Applied Business Question (80 marks)

Kian's Kitchen

Kian Finnegan set up his restaurant Kian's Kitchen five years ago. He chose a village in Carlow to locate his business, as the government offered tax incentives and reduced corporation tax for firms that set up in the area. Kian knows of other chefs who have chosen not to set up their own business due to the high cost of commercial rates, especially in city locations.

Kian uses high-quality international produce in his restaurant. He imports manuka honey from New Zealand and wine from a small importer in the UK. Kian has purchased a van and one member of staff travels to Dublin each week to collect the produce from Dublin port.

Kian has recently employed a new chef as he found it difficult to get his existing staff to work overtime each week. He knows that the new chef is an additional cost to the business, especially in terms of taxation, but business is busy and he does not want the quality standards in the restaurant to suffer.

The new chef has an annual salary of €54,000 together with health insurance premiums paid at a cost of €2,000. Kian reminds the new chef to log on to www.revenue.ie to check that he is registered on the Revenue system and that he has received the correct <u>tax credits</u>. In the past some staff have had <u>emergency tax</u> applied and Kian does not want this to happen to the new recruits.

A   Describe the taxes that Kian Finnegan would have to pay as owner of Kian's Kitchen. **(30 marks)**

B   (i)   Explain the underlined tax terms.

   (ii)   Calculate the chef's take-home pay using the following information.
   PAYE: the standard rate is 20%, higher rate is 41%. The standard cut-off point is €32,000.
   PRSI is levied at 3% on gross income.
   USC is charged at 3% on the first €13,000, 4% on the next €7,000 and 7% on the remainder.
   Employee Tax Credit of €2,100. **(30 marks)**

C   The taxation policy of a government can have positive and negative implications for business. Describe how these policies can affect businesses such as Kian's Kitchen. **(20 marks)**

Section 3 – Long Questions

1 Discuss the reasons why the government imposes taxes on society. **(15 marks)**

2
> Laura is single and works as a scientist at a large pharmaceutical company. She owns her own home and has recently received a large monetary inheritance.

   Describe the taxes that Laura would be liable to pay. **(20 marks)**

3 Employees pay a number of statutory deductions. Describe **three** statutory deductions paid by employees in Ireland. **(15 marks)**

4 Describe the changes that have occurred with the introduction of PAYE modernisation. **(20 marks)**

5 Managing a business and running a household are similar when it comes to the area of taxation. Evaluate this statement. **(20 marks)**

6 Contrast the different taxes associated with running a household and managing a business. **(20 marks)**

Section 3 – Long Questions *continued*

For questions 7 and 8 use the information supplied below:

PAYE		PRSI	
Standard rate	21%	First €52,000	4%
Higher rate	42%	Remainder	6%
Standard cut-off point	€33,200		
USC		Tax credits	
First €14,000	2%	Single person	€1,500
Next €8,000	4%	Married person	€3,000
Remainder	8%	Employee	€1,600
		Dependent child	€900

7 Catherine McDonald is single and recently began work for the first time. Catherine's net salary will be €28,000 a year.
   (i) What is meant by the term *emergency tax*?
   (ii) Calculate Catherine's annual take-home pay. **(30 marks)**

8 Anthony Kelly is married with two dependent children. He has worked as a project manager for a number of years and has an annual salary of €102,000.
   (i) Outline the purpose of a tax credit.
   (ii) Calculate Anthony's annual take-home pay. **(25 marks)**

PREVIOUS LEAVING CERTIFICATE EXAM QUESTIONS

Ordinary Level

Section A – Short Questions (10 marks each)

1 Calculate Joanne Heffernan's net annual take-home pay from the following details. Show your workings:

Name: Joanne Hefferman		€	€
Gross Pay			**70,000**
Deductions			
PAYE (20% of €34,550) (40% of €35,450)	6,910 <u>14,180</u> 21,090		
Less tax credits	4,200		
Net PAYE		16,890	
PRSI (4% of €70,000)		(i)	
USC (3% of €70,000)		(ii)	
Total Deductions			(iii)
Net Annual Take Home Pay			(iv)

[LC OL 2018]

2 What do the following initials stand for? (i) PAYE and (ii) USC. [LC OL 2013]

3 A limited company has a taxable profit of €68,400. Tax is charged at a rate of 12.5%.
   (i) Calculate the amount of tax to be paid. (Show your workings.)
   (ii) What is the missing word in the following sentence? The tax paid on profits of a limited company is called _____ tax. [LC OL 2006]

Section B

1 List **two** taxes other than motor tax that a business might pay. **(15 marks) [LC OL 2016]**

2

> Elaine McGrath works as an Assessor for Insure2Bsure Ltd. Her job includes processing claims from customers and deciding on compensation. She earns Gross Pay of €32,000 per annum. She pays PAYE at the standard rate of 20%. Assume PRSI is 4% and the Universal Social Charge (USC) is 3%, both calculated on her gross pay. Her annual tax credit is €3,600.

(i) Explain the **three** underlined terms. **(15 marks)**

(ii) Calculate Elaine's Net Annual take-home pay. **(20 marks) [LC OL 2012]**

Higher Level

Section A – Short Questions (10 marks each)

1 Distinguish between VAT and corporation tax. **[LC HL 2016]**

2 What do the letters PAYE stand for? Outline **two** main features of the PAYE tax system. **[LC HL 2015]**

3 Explain the difference between tax rates and tax credits. **[LC HL 2012]**

Section B

1

> Audrey Stapleton is an employee at BAT Resources Ltd and earns a gross annual salary of €78,000. Her employer provides her with a holiday voucher worth €2,000. This is treated as a benefit-in-kind for tax purposes and taxed accordingly.
>
> The standard rate band for a single taxpayer is €32,800. (This means that the first €32,800 is taxed at the 20% standard rate and the remainder is taxed at the higher rate of 41%.)
>
> Audrey has the following tax credits: Single Person Tax Credit €1,650, Employee Tax Credit €1,650 and Rent Tax Credit €320.
>
> The Universal Social Charge (USC) rates on Audrey's gross income are 2% on the first €10,036, 4% on the next €5,980 and 7% on the balance of her gross income. Audrey pays PRSI at 4% of her gross income.

Calculate Audrey Stapleton's net monthly take-home pay. **(20 marks) [LC HL 2013]**

2 Pay As You Earn (PAYE), Value Added Tax (VAT) and Corporation Tax are examples of taxes relevant to businesses.

(i) Explain **each** tax underlined above.

(ii) Evaluate the implications of **each** tax for a business. **(25 marks) [LC HL 2011]**

3 From the following information calculate the net annual take-home pay of Ms Joan McCormack.

> Joan McCormack is an employee of Lynch Printers Ltd and earns a gross annual salary of €84,000. She is allowed the following tax credits: Single person credit of €1,760 and employee credit of €1,760. The income tax rates are: 20% on the first €34,000 (standard cut-off point) and 41% on the balance. The employee PRSI Rate is 6% on the first €48,800 and 2% on the balance.

(20 marks) [LC HL 2007]

 Solutions

17 MANAGING A BUSINESS AND A HOUSEHOLD: FINANCE

⊕ Learning Outcomes

When you have completed this chapter, you will be able to:

1 Outline the methods used by businesses and households to plan and monitor cash flow

2 Analyse a cash flow forecast for a business and a household budget

3 Identify and describe the main sources of finance available to businesses and households

4 Explain the factors to be considered when choosing a source of finance

5 Describe the criteria used by financial institutions to provide loans to businesses and households

6 Identify and outline the features of a current account

7 Describe the current account services provided by financial institutions

8 Compare managing business and household finance.

 Literacy Link

Cash flow, budget, finance, financial institution, accrued expenses, factoring, hire purchase, leasing, loan, debenture

 Numeracy Link

Percentages, addition, subtraction

 Cross-curricular Link

Accounting – bank accounts, bank reconciliation statements, debentures, loans
Economics – interest rates
Home economics – household budgets, credit facilities, home finance

---

CASE STUDY

Irish Continental Group (ICG)

Irish Continental Group provides direct ferry links from Ireland to the UK and Europe under the brand name Irish Ferries. Each year over 1.6 million passengers use its ferry services to connect to ports such as Holyhead and Cherbourg.

ICG requires a range of **sources of finance** to enable it to deliver services to its customers, as well as to pay its bills as they fall due. Sources of finance can be short-, medium- or long-term. Some of the sources of finance used by ICG include:

Short-term

AIB (Allied Irish Banks) provides a €16 million **bank overdraft** facility to ICG. The company uses this throughout the year as required.

The firm also uses **trade credit**, whereby it buys items on credit and pays for them at a later date. The average period of trade credit that ICG obtains from suppliers is 69 days.

Medium-term

The company uses **leasing** to acquire plant and equipment. Leases are at least three years in duration, and carry an **interest** cost of 5.5%.

Long-term

To enable the firm to pay for the construction of a new ship, ICG obtained a **debenture** of €80 million from the European Investment Bank (EIB). The debenture is repayable over 12 years with a **fixed interest rate** of 1.6% per year. To obtain the loan, ICG prepared **cash flow forecasts** to show the EIB that it had the ability

to repay the loan. ICG paid the German ship builder 20% of the contract price in **instalments** during the construction phase, with the 80% balance paid on delivery.

The company has a policy to invest any **surplus cash balances** on a short-term basis in **deposit accounts**. The management of the company monitors cash flow forecasts to ensure that the **liquidity** of the company is adequate.

ICG currently employs over 300 staff and has generated **retained earnings** of over €200 million.

CASH FLOW FORECAST

Financial planning for a business involves preparing a **cash flow forecast.** This is a financial plan that shows the business how much money it expects to receive (receipts) and spend (payments) over a specific period of time.

A cash flow forecast can have three possible outcomes:

1 A cash **surplus** – more cash coming into the business than going out.

2 A cash **deficit** – more cash going out of the business than coming in.

3 A **balanced** cash flow – the same amount of cash coming in and going out.

> *You will learn more about liquidity in Chapter 18.*

If a business has continuous cash flow deficits, it may experience liquidity issues, i.e. it will have difficulty paying its debts as they fall due. Poor liquidity is one of the main reasons for business failure. We will now examine a cash flow forecast for a business.

> **Definition: Liquidity**
> The ability of a business to pay its debts as they fall due.

Examples of receipts: sales, investment income, sale of assets, receipt of grants

Examples of payments: purchases, wages and salaries, overheads (day-to-day running expenses), e.g. light and heat, postage, stationery

Cash Flow Forecast for Reilly Musical Enterprises Ltd				
	July	August	September	Total July– September
Receipts				
Sales	17,600	10,400	23,000	51,000
(A) Total Receipts	**17,600**	**10,400**	**23,000**	**51,000**
Payments				
Purchases	8,000	6,800	8,900	23,700
Wages	4,000	4,000	4,000	12,000
Overheads	2,100	2,900	2,900	7,900
(B) Total Payments	14,100	13,700	15,800	43,600
(A-B) Net Cash Flow (1)	3,500	(3,300)	7,200	7,400
Opening Cash (2)	3,000	6,500	3,200	3,000
Closing Cash (1+2)	**6,500**	**3,200**	**10,400**	**10,400**

There is a positive cash flow for the month of July, i.e. receipts are greater than payments

This is the opening cash available to the business at the start of July

There is a negative cash flow for the month of August, i.e. payments are greater than receipts

This is the closing cash balance at the end of September

Unit 4

Activity 17.1

In pairs, create a fishbone graphic organiser to show the main cash inflows and outflows you think a business would have. Using your graphic organiser, create a poster/infographic of the main inflows and outflows of cash for a business to display on the classroom wall.

Purpose of a Cash Flow Forecast

It is important for a business to prepare a cash flow forecast for a number of reasons. These include:

- **Identifying periods of cash surpluses:** The business can identify periods of time in the future when it should have a cash surplus. It can then plan to use these surplus funds, e.g. place them in a high interest earning deposit account or purchase equipment for expansion.
- **Identifying periods of cash deficits:** The business can identify when it is likely to have a cash deficit. It can take corrective action to deal with the deficit, e.g. arrange a bank overdraft.
- **Applying for finance:** The cash flow forecast is part of the business plan given to investors such as banks when applying for a loan. It shows that the business will be able to make loan repayments.
- **Financial control:** A cash flow forecast can be compared with the actual cash inflows and outflows, i.e. it is a financial control mechanism. Managers can identify whether actual cash flow is on target with the budgeted figures. If not, corrective action can be taken, e.g. reduce payments.

When preparing a cash flow forecast, it is important to consider:

- **Delays:** There may be a delay in payments from credit customers (debtors).
- **Seasonal fluctuations:** Some seasonal businesses will have periods of high and low cash flow, e.g. ice cream manufacturers.
- **Bad debts:** When someone who purchased goods on credit does not pay the amount owed.

 DID YOU KNOW? *In Ireland the average yearly bad debt for small and medium enterprises is €14,000.*

Failure to take these into account may lead to a less effective cash flow forecast.

How to Deal with a Cash Flow Forecast Deficit

When a business encounters a cash flow deficit it can overcome it in a number of ways:

1 **Increase selling price:** It may be able to charge more for its goods or services without reducing sales levels.
2 **Reduce selling price:** It could reduce the selling price to increase business sales.
3 **Discounts:** It could offer cash incentives for early payment from debtors, e.g. 10% discount if the amount owed is paid within 14 days.
4 **Finance:** It could obtain finance to cover the deficit, e.g. a bank overdraft. However, there may be high interest rates charged on repayment.
5 **Adjust payments:** It could decrease its cash payments by, for example, sourcing cheaper suppliers or asking employees to take a pay cut.

HOUSEHOLD BUDGETS

Individuals and households prepare a household budget. This ensures that they live within their means, i.e. they can pay their household expenses as they fall due.

Now let us look at an example of a household budget.

Definition: Household budget
A financial plan of future income and expenditure.

Household Budget for the Walters Family					
	January	February	March	April	Total
Income					
Wages	3,400	3,400	3,400	3,600	13,800
Child Benefit	200	200	200	200	800
Lotto win			1,500		1,500
(A) Total Income	**3,600**	**3,600**	**5,100**	**3,800**	**16,100**
Expenditure					
Fixed					
Mortgage	800	800	800	800	3,200
Car Loan	200	200	200	200	800
Subtotal (1)	**1,000**	**1,000**	**1,000**	**1,000**	**4,000**
Irregular					
Petrol	50	70	40	120	280
Groceries	300	340	380	190	1,210
Gas	60	70	40	30	200
Subtotal (2)	**410**	**480**	**460**	**340**	**1,690**
Discretionary					
Entertainment	300	500	400	400	1,600
Holiday	—	500	—	2,500	3,000
Subtotal (3)	**300**	**1,000**	**400**	**2,900**	**4,600**
(B) Total Expenditure (1+2+3)	1,710	2,480	1,860	4,240	10,290
(A-B) Net Cash (X)	1,890	1,120	3,240	(440)	5,810
Opening Cash (Y)	2,000	3,890	5,010	8,250	2,000
Closing Cash (X+Y)	3,890	5,010	8,250	7,810	7,810

Examples of income: wages, salaries, unemployment benefit, interest on savings, child benefit, sale of items, e.g. old furniture

Examples of expenditure: mortgage, electricity, car running costs, clothing, food, entertainment

There is a positive cash flow for the month of January

There is a negative cash flow for the month of April

The total amount that the household will save over the budget period

The amount of cash the household will have at the end of the budget period

Exam Tip!
Make sure that you know how to calculate net cash, opening cash and closing cash.

Household expenditure is classified as fixed, irregular or discretionary.

Expenditure	Explanation	Examples
Fixed	→ Expenditure where the amount remains the same regardless of usage.	→ Mortgage → Car tax
Irregular	→ The amount paid varies based on usage.	→ Electricity → Groceries
Discretionary	→ Expenditure on non-essential items.	→ Entertainment → Presents

Activity 17.2

Individually write down on sticky notes as many items of income and expenditure relating to households as you can think of. Place the sticky notes on the wall and work in pairs to categorise the items into fixed, irregular or discretionary expenditure.

Reasons for Preparing a Household Budget

- **Identify cash surplus:** The budget shows when the household will have a cash surplus. This surplus could be invested into a bank deposit account to earn interest.
- **Identify cash deficit:** The budget shows when the household will have a cash deficit. The household can arrange finance to deal with the deficit, e.g. a bank overdraft.
- **Apply for loans:** A household can use a household budget to support a loan application. Bank managers will be able to see that the household can make the loan repayments.

DEALING WITH A BUDGET SURPLUS AND DEFICIT	
Surplus	**Deficit**
What a household can do with a cash surplus: • Make payments to reduce mortgage owed • Invest it to earn more money, e.g. in a deposit account • Save it in order to reduce future borrowing	How a household can deal with a cash deficit: • Spread payments over a longer period, e.g. pay car tax quarterly rather than annually • Postpone expenditure, e.g. holiday • Shop around for cheaper suppliers, e.g. electricity, using a website such as www.bonkers.ie

SOURCES OF FINANCE

Many businesses and households will not have enough of their own money to operate on a day-to-day basis. They will need to obtain this money from other sources, e.g. bank overdraft or grants.

Businesses need finance to:
- Set up the business, e.g. purchase premises
- Operate the business, e.g. pay wages
- Expand the firm, e.g. move to bigger premises.

Households need finance to:
- Buy a home
- Pay for day-to-day living costs, e.g. groceries
- Improve their standard of living, e.g. holidays.

Sources of finance can be:

1 **Short-term** – repaid within one year
2 **Medium-term** – repaid between one and five years
3 **Long-term** – repaid after more than five years.

Sources of finance can also be internal or external.

- **Internal sources:** Finance obtained inside the business or household, e.g. retained profits (business) or savings (household).
- **External sources:** Finance obtained outside the business or household, e.g. borrowing from a bank.

1 Short-term Sources of Finance

This is finance to cover short-term business and household expenditure and is paid back within one year.

	Short-term Sources of Finance	Business	Example of Use	Household	Example of Use
A	→ Bank overdraft	✓	→ Wages and salaries	✓	→ Holidays
B	→ Credit card	✓	→ Insurance premium	✓	→ Kitchen appliances
C	→ Accrued expenses	✓	→ Light and heat	✓	→ Electricity
D	→ Factoring	✓	→ Paying bills, e.g. rent of premises	✗	—
E	→ Trade credit	✓	→ Purchasing stock	✗	—

Unit 4

A Bank Overdraft (Business and Household)

This is a facility where a bank allows its customers who have a current account to withdraw more money from their account than they have in it, up to an agreed limit. It is used by businesses to pay for e.g. wages and salaries. Households might use a bank overdraft to pay for holidays and/or for day-to-day items too, such as buying food and fuel.

> **Definition: Security/collateral**
> Assets used to secure certain types of finance. They can be seized by the finance provider if the household or business fails to make repayments as they fall due.

✓ Advantages	✗ Disadvantages
1 Interest Interest is paid only on the amount used, rather than the maximum overdraft limit approved by the bank.	**1 High Interest Rate** The interest rates charged on the amount used is high, e.g. 8–14%.
2 No Security No security is needed for a customer to obtain a bank overdraft.	**2 Penalties** If a household or business exceeds the agreed limit or fails to pay it back on time, penalties are applied.
3 Application Process Fast application and approval process.	**3 Damage to Credit Rating** Failure to make repayments can negatively affect the borrower's credit rating.

B Credit Card (Business and Household)

A customer pays for goods and services using their credit card at the point of sale. The credit card firm pays the store or supplier and the customer repays the credit card company within an agreed time frame. Examples of credit cards used in Ireland are Mastercard and Visa.

✓ Advantages	✗ Disadvantages
1 No Interest Charge No interest charge applies if the balance on the card is repaid within an agreed period of time.	**1 High Interest Rate** Interest charged on outstanding balances can be very high, e.g. 14–20%.
2 Safety Safe method of payment for goods and services. Credit cards are often used as a secure method for making online payments.	**2 Overspending** There is a temptation to overspend and buy items that are not needed.
3 Worldwide Widely accepted as a form of payment all over the world.	**3 Government Tax** Annual government tax is €30 per card payable on 1 April each year.

C Accrued Expenses (Business and Household)

This is when a supplier of services allows the business or household to use their service and pay later, e.g. electricity and gas. The supplier invoices the household or business at the end of the period and sets the date when the payment should be made. As payment is in arrears this enables the business or household to allocate money for other more urgent uses before the payment is due.

Unit 4

✓ Advantages	✗ Disadvantages
1 Free Finance It is a free source of finance.	**1 Loss of Services** Services will be cut off if bills remain unpaid.
2 No Security No security is needed to use this short-term source of finance.	**2 Limited Availability** Limited availability, i.e. it is only offered by certain service providers such as electricity and gas.
3 Improves Cash Flow Because the service provider is paid in arrears, cash is available for other uses, e.g. paying wages.	**3 Loss of Discounts** Discounts may be lost if bills are not paid on time.

D Factoring (Business Only)

This is when a business sells its sales invoices (debtors) to a factoring firm (debt-collection business) at a discounted price. The factoring firm then collects the amounts owed directly from debtors and makes a profit.

Example
Daly Ltd sold goods on credit to Fleming Ltd to the value of €120,000. Daly Ltd sold this debtor balance to Griffin Finance for €100,000. Management of Daly Ltd will receive the €100,000 immediately and Griffin Finance will in turn collect the full €120,000 from the debtor.

Definition: Debtor
A debtor receives goods or services on credit from a business and agrees to pay by a set date in the future.

There are two types of factoring:

1 Factoring **without recourse**: Daly Ltd will not have to pay back the factoring firm if Fleming Ltd fails to pay amounts owed.
2 Factoring **with recourse**: If Fleming Ltd fails to pay the amount owed, Daly Ltd will have to reimburse Griffin Finance.

✓ Advantages	✗ Disadvantages
1 No Security No security is needed to obtain this source of finance.	**1 High Fees** Factoring companies charge high fees.
2 Immediate Finance is received immediately.	**2 Risk of Bad Debts** If the debts are factored with recourse, the business is still exposed to the risk of bad debts.
3 No Loss of Control There is no impact on ownership, i.e. the owner does not lose any control of the business.	**3 Business Relationship** The relationship between the business and its customers may be damaged. Customers may prefer to deal directly with the business rather than the factoring company.

Unit 4

249

E Trade Credit (Business Only)

This is when a business receives goods or services from its suppliers and pays by an agreed date in the future. The amount of credit available is dependent on the creditworthiness of the buyer.

Using trade credit is also referred to as 'leaning on the trade'.

Definition: **Creditworthiness**
The ability to borrow money or pay later for goods and services. A lender or supplier will consider the creditworthiness of an individual or business when deciding whether they are eligible for credit.

✓ Advantages	✗ Disadvantages
1 Free Finance It is a free source of finance – no interest is charged if bills are paid on time.	**1 Loss of Discounts** Cash discounts may be lost if goods are not paid for up front in cash.
2 No Security No security is needed to use this short-term source of finance.	**2 Damage to Credit Rating** A business could damage its credit rating if it fails to pay on time. It may have difficulty buying goods on credit in the future.
3 Immediate Use The business gets immediate use of the goods.	**3 Credit Businesses Only** Credit terms are not offered by all suppliers.

Implications of Using Short-term Sources of Finance

Source of Short-term Finance		Security Required	Loss of Control	Cost Incurred
Bank Overdraft	Business/Household	No	No	Yes
Credit Card	Business/Household	No	No	Free if paid in full
Accrued Expenses	Business/Household	No	No	No
Factoring	Business	No	No	Yes
Trade Credit	Business	No	No	Free if paid in full

2 Medium-term Sources of Finance

This is finance to cover medium-term business and household expenditure and is paid back over one to five years.

	Medium-term Sources of Finance	Business	Example of Use	Household	Example of Use
A	→ Hire purchase	✓	→ Delivery van	✓	→ Car
B	→ Medium-term loan	✓	→ Machinery	✓	→ New kitchen
C	→ Leasing (renting)	✓	→ Company car	✓	→ Apartment

A Hire Purchase (Business and Household)

A business or household (buyer) may be unable to afford to pay the full purchase price of an item upfront. For some purchases, e.g. a car, household appliance or production equipment, the purchaser can enter into a hire purchase agreement to enable them to buy the item and pay for it in instalments.

How Does Hire Purchase Work?

1 The buyer, the hire purchase firm and the retailer enter into a hire purchase agreement.
2 The hire purchase firm pays the retailer for the cost of the item requested by the buyer.
3 The buyer pays a deposit to the hire purchase firm, e.g. 10% of the cost of the item.

4 The retailer gives the item to the buyer.

5 The buyer pays the remaining balance owed plus interest to the hire purchase firm in an equal number of instalments, e.g. €340 per month for 36 months.

6 When the last instalment has been paid, the buyer legally owns the item.

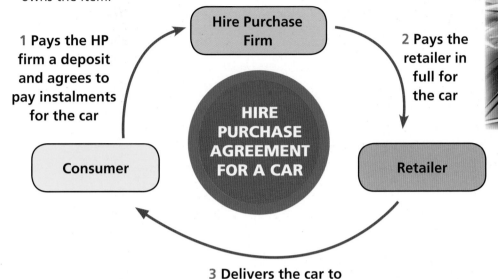

1 Pays the HP firm a deposit and agrees to pay instalments for the car

Hire Purchase Firm

2 Pays the retailer in full for the car

HIRE PURCHASE AGREEMENT FOR A CAR

Consumer

Retailer

3 Delivers the car to the consumer

Activity 17.3

If an item costs €5,600 and the consumer pays an initial deposit of 12.5%, how much would they have to pay the hire purchase company as a deposit?

✓ Advantages	✗ Disadvantages
1 Immediate Use The buyer gets immediate use of the item once a deposit is paid to the hire purchase firm.	**1 Delayed Ownership** The buyer does not own the item until the final instalment is paid.
2 No Security No security is needed to use this medium-term source of finance.	**2 High Rate of Interest** It can be an expensive source of finance as the hire purchase firm charges a high rate of interest.
3 Fast A hire purchase agreement is relatively quick and easy to arrange.	**3 Risk of Repossession** The hire purchase firm can repossess the item if the buyer does not pay the instalments as agreed.

Activity 17.4

A personal contract plan (PCP) is an alternative form of finance that can be used to purchase cars. Working in pairs, research how PCP differs from hire purchase when buying cars.

B Medium-term Loan/Personal Loan (Business and Household)

The borrower takes out a loan from a financial institution (e.g. a bank or credit union) and repays it, with interest, at regular intervals over a period of between one and five years. The interest rates may be fixed or variable. The terms and conditions of the loan, e.g. duration and monthly repayments, can be tailored to meet the needs of the business or household.

> **Note!**
> A medium-term loan for a household is referred to as a personal loan.

Unit 4

Business Application for a Medium-term Loan

Outlined below is the type of information sought by financial institutions from businesses applying for a medium-term loan.

Information required	Explanation
Business Details	→ Nature of the business, e.g. construction
Loan Details	→ Purpose of the loan, e.g. purchase of vans → Amount required
Business Reputation/ Creditworthiness	→ Length of time the business has been established → Reputation of the owners/directors of the business → Business credit rating
Business Plan (Ability to Repay)	→ Cash flow forecast → Trading, profit and loss account → Balance sheet (statement of financial position)

Household Application for a Medium-term Loan (Personal Loan)

This is a sample of the information sought by financial institutions from households applying for a personal loan.

Information required	Explanation
Personal Details	→ Name → Date of birth
Loan Details	→ Purpose of loan → Amount required
Employment Details	→ Occupation → Employer's name and address
Financial Details	→ Present savings and borrowings → Regular monthly income → Assets
Bank Details	→ Name and address of the borrower's bank
Creditworthiness	→ Credit rating

✓ Advantages	✗ Disadvantages
1 Interest Rate Lower interest rates than hire purchase.	**1 Interest Charged** Interest is charged on the sum borrowed.
2 No Security For smaller amounts no security is generally required by the lender.	**2 Risk of Repossession** Security is required for larger loans. Failure to meet the repayments may lead to repossession of the item used as security.
3 No Loss of Control For businesses, there is no impact on ownership.	**3 Repayments May Increase** A rise in interest rates will cause the repayments to increase, when variable rates apply.

C Leasing/Renting (Business and Household)

A business or household (lessee) enters into a lease agreement with the owner of the asset (lessor). The lessee makes regular payments to the lessor for an agreed period of time while they are using the asset, e.g. two to five years. Leasing is commonly used by businesses and households to rent items such as a car. At the end of the agreement the asset is returned to the lessor.

✓ Advantages	✗ Disadvantages
1 Immediate Use The lessee gets immediate use of the item.	**1 Ownership** The lessee will never own the asset.
2 No Security No security is needed to use this medium-term source of finance.	**2 Cost** Leasing can be more expensive than buying the item if it is leased for a long period of time.
3 Access to Up-to-Date Items The business or household can have access to the most up-to-date items, e.g. computers.	**3 Risk of Repossession** Items can be repossessed if the business or household cannot make repayments.

Implications of Using Medium-term Sources of Finance

Source of Finance	Business or Household	Security Required	Loss of Control	Cost Incurred
Hire Purchase	Business/Household	No	No	Yes
Medium-term Loan	Business/Household	If there are large amounts borrowed	No	Yes
Leasing/Renting	Business/Household	No	No	Yes

Activity 17.5

Working in pairs, create a chatter box (your teacher will provide you with a template) with eight questions relating to short- and medium-term sources of finance. Swap the chatter boxes around the room so that you answer the questions from other students.

3 Long-term Sources of Finance
This is finance to cover long-term business and household expenditure and is paid back over a term greater than five years.

	Long-term Sources of Finance	Business	Example of Use	Household	Example of Use
A	→ Mortgage	✗	—	✓	→ House purchase
B	→ Savings	✗	—	✓	→ House extension
C	→ Retained Earnings	✓	→ Pay off existing loans	✗	—
D	→ Equity Capital	✓	→ Purchase a new business	✗	—
E	→ Grants	✓	→ Business start-up	✗	—
F	→ Debenture	✓	→ New premises	✗	—
G	→ Sale and Leaseback	✓	→ Purchase machinery	✗	—
H	→ Venture Capital	✓	→ Business expansion	✗	—

A Mortgage (Household Only)
A mortgage is a long-term loan used to purchase property. It can be obtained from a bank or building society for between 20 and 35 years at a fixed or variable rate of interest.

The buyer obtains the mortgage by using the property as security. A mortgage is repaid in monthly instalments.

Unit 4

Definition: Tracker mortgage
This is a variable rate mortgage where the interest rate charged follows (tracks) the interest rates charged by the European Central Bank (ECB). A borrower on a tracker mortgage will benefit when the rate is low but will have to pay more when rates rise.

✓ Advantages	✗ Disadvantages
1 Amount A large amount of money can be borrowed.	**1 Risk of Repossession** If the borrower fails to meet the repayments their property can be repossessed.
2 Long Repayment Period The payments can be spread over a long period, which makes instalments smaller and more affordable.	**2 High Overall Cost** The overall cost of the property can be almost double the cost price.
3 Low Rate of Interest The rate of interest charged on a mortgage is low relative to other forms of finance.	**3 Repayments May Increase** If the variable rate increases, the cost of repayments also increases.

B Savings (Household Only)

Savings refers to cash that a household has not spent but saved for a future purpose. It is usually saved in a deposit account in a financial institution, e.g. a bank or credit union. Savings are often used to pay for expensive items such as a car or home improvements.

Definition: Deposit account
A type of account used for savings. Money is lodged by the saver and interest is earned.

✓ Advantages	✗ Disadvantages
1 No Security There is no security needed to use this long-term source of finance.	**1 Low rate of interest** There are low rates of interest available on deposit accounts. The interest earned is subject to DIRT.
2 No Financial Cost No financial cost, as there is no money borrowed.	**2 Savings Period** It takes a long time to build up savings and the household may be unable to wait to buy the item.
3 No Application Process No application process to obtain the funds.	**3 Regular Saving** The household must be disciplined to save the money on a regular basis.

C Retained Earnings (Business Only)

These are profits that a business has saved over time. The firm can reinvest this money back into the business, e.g. to expand activities, upgrade equipment or pay off existing loans.

✓ Advantages	✗ Disadvantages
1 Large Amount of Finance A large amount of finance can be available if the business is profitable.	**1 Savings Period** It can take a long time to build up retained earnings to use in the business.
2 No Financial Cost There is no cost involved as the business is using its own money.	**2 One-off Payment** It is only available once – when the money is spent it is no longer available.
3 No Security No security is required as there is no borrowing involved.	**3 Impact on Dividends** It reduces profits available for paying dividends.

D Equity Capital (Business Only)

The business owners sell shares in the business to investors. The investors become shareholders and have a say in the running of the business. Investors can vote at the firm's AGM and are entitled to a share of the profits, known as dividend.

> **Definition: Dividends**
> The portion of profits paid to shareholders. The dividend policy of the business is decided by the board of directors.

✓ Advantages	✗ Disadvantages
1 No Security No security is needed – owners invest money at their own risk.	**1 Loss of Control** Dilutes the existing owner's control as each share sold equals one vote at the business's AGM.
2 No Financial Cost No interest payments as no money is borrowed. This enables the business to keep more of the firm's profits, which can be used to fund expansion.	**2 Shareholders May Sell Shares** If the business does not pay sufficient dividends, the shareholders may become dissatisfied and sell their shares. For public companies, this can result in a fall in the share price and/or a potential takeover.
3 Repayment Money raised does not have to be repaid until the firm ceases trading.	**3 Shareholder Disputes** Shareholder disputes can arise, which can damage the reputation of the business.

E Grants (Business Only)

A grant is a sum of money given to a business by a government agency, e.g. LEO or Enterprise Ireland, and can be used to fund expansion. It does not have to be repaid as long as the business adheres to certain conditions and the grant is used for the purpose intended.

✓ Advantages	✗ Disadvantages
1 Amounts Available Large sums of money can be made available to support the business, e.g. to purchase machinery.	**1 Criteria for Grant** Grants must be used for the specific reasons for which the money was received.
2 No Financial Cost Grants do not have to be repaid as long as certain terms and conditions are met.	**2 Application Process** The application process for grants can be slow.
3 No Security No security is needed.	**3 Partial Funding** The grant may fund only a portion of the money required, and therefore the business will have to source the shortfall elsewhere.

Unit 4

F Debenture (Business Only)

This is long-term debt finance similar to a loan. It is obtained using the firm's assets as security, e.g. deeds to property. The business makes interest-only payments on the debenture and repays the amount borrowed in one lump sum at a future date.

Example

A business takes out a 9% €200,000 debenture 2029.
This means that the borrower will pay 9% interest on the loan each year. They will repay the €200,000 as one lump sum in 2029.

Activity 17.6

Calculate the annual interest on a 9% debenture loan of €200,0000 repayable in 2029.

✓ Advantages	✗ Disadvantages
1 Fixed Interest Rate As the interest rate is fixed, the business knows how much interest is to be repaid each month.	**1 Costs** There is a cost to this source of finance as interest must be paid.
2 No Loss of Control Control of the business is not affected. Debenture holders do not have a say in the running of a business.	**2 Risk of Losing Asset** The asset used as security can be taken by the debenture holder if payments are not met.
3 Amounts Available Debentures give firms access to large amounts of finance. This money can be used to fund expansion, e.g. purchase machinary and land.	**3 Risk of Business Failure** Debentures increase the business's gearing and risk of business failure. (You will learn more about gearing in Chapter 18.)

G Sale and Leaseback (Business Only)

This is when a business sells an asset, e.g. premises, and then leases it back from the buyer. This allows the business to continue to use the asset while at the same time gaining extra finance. In some cases, when profits allow, the business may be able to buy back the premises.

✓ Advantages	✗ Disadvantages
1 Amounts Available A large amount of money can be raised quite quickly if a buyer can be found.	**1 One-off Source** The business no longer owns the asset. This makes it a one-off source of finance and the business has to pay rent each year on the item sold.
2 Operation The business can continue operating as normal while it is gaining extra finance.	**2 Assets Reduced** The value of the firm's assets is reduced on the balance sheet. This limits the amount of security available for future loans or debentures.
3 No Loss of Control There is no impact on ownership of the business.	**3 Time** It may take time to find a buyer for the asset.

H Venture Capital (Business Only)

Venture capital firms invest money (capital) into new businesses where there is potential for a high return on their investment. These firms often provide finance when other finance providers won't take on the higher risk. They invest a sum of money for a share in the business. Once the business has become successful, the venture capital firm sells its shares at a profit.

✓ Advantages	✗ Disadvantages
1 Expertise A venture capital firm can bring expertise to the business, e.g. in marketing and distribution.	**1 Loss of Control** A share of the business is given to the venture capital firm, which has a say in the running of the business.
2 No Interest As the business does not borrow money, no interest payments are paid on this form of finance.	**2 Profit Share** Profits are shared with the venture capital firm.
3 Amounts Available Venture capital firms may have access to large amounts of finance, which the firm can use to purchase equipment or expand.	**3 Time** Funding by the venture capital firm may be paid over a period of time rather than upfront.

CASE STUDY

Dragons' Den

Dragons' Den is a reality television programme featuring entrepreneurs pitching their business ideas in order to secure investment finance from a panel of **venture capitalists**.
Simon Stenson established the Cherry Blossom Bakery and creates additive- and preservative-free breads and cakes for a growing healthy food market. Simon received the largest ever *Dragons' Den* Ireland **investment** of €200,000 in return for a 40% stake in the business. The firm used the investment to purchase new and larger equipment and has agreed a deal with Musgrave to supply SuperValu and Centra stores throughout Ireland.

Unit 4

Implications of Using Long-term Sources of Finance

Source of Finance	Business or Household	Security Required	Loss of Control	Cost Incurred
Mortgage	Household	✓	✗	✓
Savings	Household	✗	✗	✗
Retained Earnings	Business	✗	✗	✗
Equity Capital	Business	✗	✓	✗
Grants	Business	✗	✗	✗
Debentures	Business	✓	✗	✓
Sale and Leaseback	Business	✗	✗	✓
Venture Capital	Business	✗	✓	✗

Activity 17.7

In pairs, create a cross-classification graphic organiser to illustrate the different sources of finance available to households and businesses.

FACTORS WHEN CHOOSING A SOURCE OF FINANCE

A number of factors should be taken into account when choosing a source of finance.

1 **Purpose of finance (matching principle):** This means that the source of finance chosen should match the time frame of the item being purchased. For example, a short-term source of finance should be used to finance a short-term want or need, e.g. a household could use a bank overdraft to pay for a holiday.

2 **Security (collateral) required:** The household or business may need to provide an asset as security in order to obtain finance, e.g. deeds of property to obtain a mortgage. In the event that repayments are not met as agreed, the lender takes ownership of the asset.

3 **Tax implications:** Only certain sources of finance may be tax-deductible for the business or household. This means that the tax paid to the Revenue Commissioners is reduced. For example, interest charged on a medium-term loan is tax-deductible, whereas dividends paid to shareholders are not.

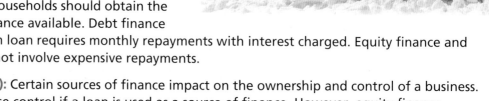

4 **Cost:** Businesses and households should obtain the cheapest source of finance available. Debt finance such as a medium-term loan requires monthly repayments with interest charged. Equity finance and retained earnings do not involve expensive repayments.

5 **Control (business only):** Certain sources of finance impact on the ownership and control of a business. A business does not lose control if a loan is used as a source of finance. However, equity finance dilutes control as shareholders have a say in the running of the business.

LOAN CRITERIA

When a household or business applies for a loan or debenture, financial institutions such as banks and credit unions consider the following factors when deciding on granting finance. These are the four Cs – Collateral, Character, Capacity and Creditworthiness.

Criterion	Explanation
Collateral	→ The borrower pledges an asset as collateral (security) against the loan. This reduces the risk for the lender in the event of non-payment by the borrower, as the asset can be seized.
Character	→ The lender wants to ensure that the borrower has good character and reputation. Some business types and occupations are viewed as less risky for lenders, e.g. providing mortgages to people in permanent jobs rather than temporary jobs.
Capacity	→ The household or business must provide evidence of their ability to repay the loan. For example, a household would provide evidence of income and a business would provide a business plan showing projected sales.
Creditworthiness	→ The lender checks the borrower's credit history, e.g. by obtaining a bank or trade reference, checking with the Irish Credit Bureau or *StubbsGazette*.

BANKING

Bank Accounts

There are two main types of bank account:

1 **Current account** – for day-to-day banking, including paying bills
2 **Deposit account** – for savings.

A current account is a type of bank account used for managing cash inflows and cash outflows. This account offers the account holder a range of services, including the facility to lodge and withdraw cash. A list of services offered with a current account include:

Type of Service	Service	Explanation
Money Transmission	Standing order (SO)	→ An instruction to the bank by the account holder to pay a **fixed** amount on a regular basis to a named individual or organisation, e.g. a mortgage payment.
	Direct debit (DD)	→ An instruction to the bank by the account holder to pay a **variable** amount on a regular basis to a named individual or organisation, e.g. paying a gas bill.
	Credit transfer (CT)	→ Money can be transferred between accounts belonging to different people or businesses, either online or by completing a form in the bank.
	Cheque	→ A written instruction to a bank to pay a stated sum of money to a named person (the payee).
	Bank overdraft	→ See page 248.
	Paypath	→ Wages are paid electronically from the employer's bank account into the employee's bank account via the payroll system.
Plastic Cards	Debit card	→ It can be used to pay for goods and services instead of cash. The amount is transferred automatically from the user's bank account to the retailer's bank account. → It can be used at an ATM to withdraw cash and check the balance on the account, e.g. Visa Debit.
	Credit card	→ See page 248.
Other Payments	Phone payments	→ Payments can be made from a credit or debit card using a smartphone app, e.g. Apple Pay.

Banking Abbreviations

ATM   automated teller machine

PIN   personal identification number

PAC   personal access code (similar to a PIN, but used for online banking access with some banks)

IBAN   international bank account number (this uniquely identifies the account of a customer at a financial institution and makes it easier and faster to process cross-border bank payments)

BIC   bank identifier code (This uniquely identifies the name and country, and sometimes the branch, of the bank.)

Bank Statements

- A bank statement is a document sent by a bank to its customers (business and households) on a regular basis.
- It shows all transactions that took place during a specific time period, e.g. one month.
- It shows the balance on the account at the beginning and end of the period.
- Customers can view their bank statement on their online banking account.

Bank of Ireland
Main Street, Clonmel
Co. Tipperary

Tel: 053 984 0104
Branch Sort Code: 90-67-12
Branch ID: BIK6178EH

STATEMENT OF ACCOUNT

Ms Claire Finnegan
23 St Joseph's Lodge
Clonmel
Co. Tipperary

Account name:	Claire Finnegan
Account number:	98704912
IBAN	IE234BOI906712987049
Date	30 April 2020
Statement Number	607

Money going out of the account

Money going into the account

The balance in the account after each transaction

Date	Transaction Details	Dr	Cr	Balance
01.4.2020	Balance			506.00
02.4.2020	Paypath		2,340.00	2,846.00
03.4.2020	SO – Mortgage	1,200.00		1,646.00
06.4.2020	DD – Bord Gais	235.00		1,411.00
06.4.2020	J. Donohoe Motors	1,500.00		89.00 DR
07.4.2020	Cheque no. 28950	456.00		545.00 DR
09.4.2020	PayPath		2,340.00	1,795.00
13.4.2020	Bank charges	32.40		1,762.60
15.4.2020	Interest	24.60		1,738.00
18.4.2020	INET – Visa	780.00		958.00
21.4.2020	ATM	120.00		838.00
23.4.2020	Lodgement CT 560		1,000.00	1,838.00

The opening balance at the beginning of the period covered by the statement

The closing balance at the end of the period covered by the statement

---

Activity: Discussion 17.8

As a class, discuss and explain Claire Finnegan's bank statement using the following questions:
1 What type of account is this? Give **two** reasons for your answer.
2 What is Paypath?
3 Explain the transactions on (i) 3 April – SO; (ii) 6 April – DD; (iii)18 April – INET – Visa; and (iv) 23 April – CT.
4 What are bank charges?
5 Why is DR written after the transactions of 6 and 7 April?
6 Why is interest charged on the account on 15 April?

COMPARISON BETWEEN MANAGING BUSINESS AND HOUSEHOLD FINANCE

There are similarities and differences associated with managing business and household finance.

Similarities

1 **Financial planning:** Cash flow forecasts and household budgets help businesses and households plan future income and expenditure. They highlight future cash surpluses and deficits so that appropriate steps can be taken to deal with a financial situation, e.g. invest cash if there is a surplus or arrange a bank overdraft if a deficit arises.

2 **Record-keeping:** Up-to-date and accurate financial records must be maintained to monitor finances and keep tax affairs in order.

3 **Sources of finance:** Businesses and households use common short-, medium- and long-term sources of finance, e.g. bank overdraft and hire purchase.

4 **Bank accounts:** Businesses and households use services offered by financial institutions on current accounts, e.g. debit cards and electronic transfer of money.

Differences

1 **Financial planning:** Financial projections are more detailed for a business than for a household. For example, a business prepares a detailed business plan to obtain finance from a financial institution.

2 **Amount borrowed:** Businesses tend to borrow larger amounts of money than households and are therefore exposed to higher risks.

3 **Taxes:** Businesses can claim the costs of finance against their profit, thus reducing their tax bill. They also have more dealings with the Revenue Commissioners, e.g. they submit VAT returns.

4 **Sources of finance:** There are more sources of finance available to businesses than to households, e.g. factoring, debentures, equity capital.

Unit 4

KEY TERMS

Now you have completed this chapter, you should understand and be able to explain the following terms. In your copybook, write a definition of each term to build up your own glossary of terms.

- cash flow forecast
- household budget
- deficit
- surplus
- short-term sources of finance
- bank overdraft
- credit card
- accrued expenses
- factoring
- trade credit
- creditworthiness
- medium-term sources of finance
- hire purchase
- medium-term loan
- personal loan
- leasing/renting
- long-term sources of finance
- mortgage
- savings
- retained earnings
- equity capital
- grants
- debenture
- sale and leaseback
- venture capital
- collateral/security
- current account
- deposit account
- standing order
- direct debit
- bank statement
- cheque

 PowerPoint Summary

EXAM-STYLE QUESTIONS

Ordinary Level

Section 1 – Short Questions (10 marks each)

1 Explain **two** reasons why a business prepares a cash flow forecast.
2 List **three** items that could be included in the receipts section of a cash flow forecast.
3 List **three** short-term sources of finance for a household.
4 Explain the term *hire purchase*.
5 List **three** sources of long-term finance available to a business.
6 Outline **one** advantage and **one** disadvantage of using savings as a source of finance for a household.
7 Indicate whether each of these statements is true or false.

Statements		True or False
A	A bad debt is when someone who purchased goods on credit fails to pay the amount owed on time.	
B	Medium-term finance is borrowing for between three and eight years.	
C	Factoring is when a business sells its loans to debtors.	
D	With hire purchase, ownership of the goods does not pass until the final instalment is paid.	
E	Equity capital is the ordinary share capital of a business.	

8 Name **four** factors a business or a household should consider when deciding on a source of finance.
9 What do the following letters stand for? (i) PIN, (ii) PAC, (iii) ATM.
10 State a suitable source of finance for a business for the following: (i) a new computer system costing €40,000; and (ii) an extension to premises costing €250,000.

Section 2 – Long Questions

1 Baxter Ltd has prepared the following cash flow forecast:

	January €	February €	March €	April €	May €	Total €
Total Income	3,000	1,800	2,300	3,000	2,400	12,500
Total Expenditure	2,700	3,800	1,200	1,700	3,000	12,400
Net Monthly Cash						

  (i) Copy the above cash flow into your copybook and complete the net cash for each month.
  (ii) In which month(s) will Baxter Ltd experience a deficit? In which month(s) will it have a surplus?
  (iii) Explain how Baxter Ltd might deal with the financial problem identified in this cash flow forecast. **(30 marks)**
2 Describe the differences between a credit card and trade credit as sources of finance for a business. **(15 marks)**
3 The Keelan household is considering buying a new car. Describe **two** sources of finance that the Keelan household could use to purchase a new car. **(20 marks)**
4 What is meant by the term *mortgage?* What are the disadvantages of a mortgage as a source of finance for a household? **(15 marks)**
5 Name **two** sources of long-term finance available to a household. Describe **one** of these sources of finance in detail. **(15 marks)**
6 Explain the differences between short-, medium- and long-term sources of finance and list **two** examples of each. **(25 marks)**
7 The cost of money is a factor when deciding on a source of finance. Explain why cost is a factor to consider and name **three** other factors that should be considered. **(20 marks)**
8 Outline **two** similarities between managing a household and managing a business in relation to finance. **(15 marks)**

Higher Level

Section 1 – Short Questions (10 marks each)

1 Outline the reasons why a household would prepare a budget.
2 Explain what is meant by the term *accrued expenses*.
3 Explain what is meant by the term *factoring*.
4 Distinguish between a medium-term loan and leasing as sources of finance for a business and household.
5 Outline the advantages of equity capital as a source of finance for a business.
6 List the factors that a lending institution will consider when it receives a loan application before deciding whether to grant a loan.
7 Distinguish between a standing order and a direct debit.
8 Outline the function of a bank statement. Illustrate your answer with relevant examples.
9 List **two** similarities and **two** differences between managing the finances of a business and of a household.
10 Fill in the appropriate words to complete each of the following statements.
  (i) In a cashflow forecast there is a cash s_____ when there is more cash coming in than going out.
  (ii) A household b_____ is a financial plan of future income and expenditure.
  (iii) M_____card and V_____ are examples of companies that provide credit cards.
  (iv) P_____ a_____ c_____ is used to access online banking information.
  (v) A s_____ o_____ is an instruction to the bank by the account holder to pay a fixed amount on a regular basis to a particular person or organisation.

Section 2 – Applied Business Question (80 marks)

CandyCakes Ltd

For many years Karl Sheridan worked as a confectioner specialising in cupcakes in a local cake shop in Arklow, Co. Wicklow. The shop owner decided to retire and Karl was about to be made redundant from his job. Karl did not know what he was going to do – he had a mortgage and a car loan on PCP to pay.

Karl discussed his options with friends and family and he decided to buy the cake shop with his sister. They would use Karl's redundancy money and their joint savings to buy the business from its current owner, Catherine McDonald.

They met with an accountant who advised them to prepare a detailed business plan and include a cash flow forecast. This would show the likely income and likely outgoings for the first six months of trading.

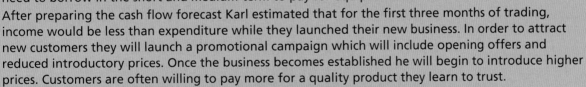

Karl and his sister Molly set up the business as a private limited company with the aim of producing and selling top-quality cupcakes and other confectionery in their store. They called the new business CandyCakes Ltd. The start-up costs were high and despite having savings of €40,000 they would need to borrow €160,000 to buy premises. The accountant, Laura O'Connor, advised them that the best source of finance for this was to take out a large loan. They would also need to borrow in the short and medium-term to pay for equipment and stock.

After preparing the cash flow forecast Karl estimated that for the first three months of trading, income would be less than expenditure while they launched their new business. In order to attract new customers they will launch a promotional campaign which will include opening offers and reduced introductory prices. Once the business becomes established he will begin to introduce higher prices. Customers are often willing to pay more for a quality product they learn to trust.

The overheads of running the business would also need to be further analysed. He made arrangements with his bank to set up an overdraft facility to cover the cost of wages and opening stock. He also looked at other ways to spread the costs over a period of time, for example by taxing the delivery van for three months at a time. CandyCakes Ltd has bought a delivery van to deliver cakes and sandwiches to business clients, a service that is currently unavailable in the area.

A Outline the main sources of finance that Karl could use to finance the setting up of the new business. **(30 marks)**

B Business start-ups are known to experience cash flow deficits. Identify, with reference to the text, ways in which a business can overcome such cash flow problems. **(25 marks)**

C Outline the factors that a lender would consider before granting finance to Karl. **(25 marks)**

Unit 4

Section 3 – Long Questions

1 The business cash flow forecast of Casey Security Ltd is set out below.

	March €	April €	May €	June €	Total €
Receipts	45,000	43,000	38,000	41,000	167,000
Payments	50,000	41,000	34,000	34,000	159,000
Net cash	(5,000)	2,000	4,000	7,000	8,000
Opening cash	1,000	(4,000)	(2,000)	2,000	1,000
Closing cash	(4,000)	(2,000)	2,000	9,000	9,000

(i) Outline **two** reasons why Casey Security Ltd would prepare a cash flow forecast.

(ii) Analyse the cash flow forecast of Casey Security Ltd. Explain any problems you think the business might have and provide a solution to any problems you have identified. **(20 marks)**

2 The Hayes family want to go to Spain on holiday. Recommend, with reasons, **two** sources of finance to fund their holiday. **(20 marks)**

3 Describe **three** medium-term sources of finance for a business. Evaluate **one** of these sources. **(30 marks)**

4 Mannion Ltd wants to expand its manufacturing plant and needs to fund a new extension. Evaluate debentures and equity capital as possible sources of long-term finance to fund this extension. **(20 marks)**

5 Evaluate venture capital as a source of finance. **(20 marks)**

6 Outline the criteria used by banks when considering loan applications. **(20 marks)**

7 Describe the factors a household and a business should consider when choosing an appropriate source of finance. **(15 marks)**

8 Managing a business and a household is similar when it comes to finance. Discuss this statement. **(25 marks)**

PREVIOUS LEAVING CERTIFICATE EXAM QUESTIONS

Ordinary Level

Section A – Short Questions (10 marks each)

1 Outline **two** advantages of leasing as a medium-term source of finance. **[LC OL 2013]**

2 Outline **two** advantages for a business of preparing a cash flow forecast. **[LC OL 2012]**

3 Indicate by means of a tick (✔) the appropriate source of finance for the following:

	Short-Term	Medium-Term	Long-Term
Delivery van			
Purchase of stock			
Extension to a factory			
Payment of an electricity bill			

[LC OL 2011]

Section B

1 (i) Explain the term *bank overdraft*. **(10 marks)**

(ii) Explain **three** factors that a bank would consider before giving a loan to a business.

(20 marks) [LC OL 2016]

2

> ### Sanders Household
>
> Linda and Paul Sanders live in their own home with their two children. Linda works as an Office Manager in a large printing company. Paul is a Sales Representative for a furniture store. Linda prepares a household budget every year and must include the purchase of a second car in the expenditure this year. The Sanders family are considering taking out a medium-term bank loan to purchase the car. They currently have an overdraft facility on their current account.

(i) Outline **two** reasons why the Sanders household would prepare a Household Budget. **(15 marks)**

(ii) Outline **two** factors the Sanders household must consider before taking out a medium-term bank loan. **(15 marks)**

(iii) Outline **three** features of a current account. **(15 marks)**

(iv) Outline **one** similarity and **one** difference for Linda between managing her office and managing her home. **(15 marks) [LC OL 2014]**

Higher Level

Section A – Short Questions (10 marks each)

1 Explain the term *short-term finance*. Illustrate a business situation where short-term finance would be appropriate. **[LC HL 2011]**

2 Identify a suitable source of finance for the purchase of a delivery van in a new business enterprise. Give **two** reasons for your choice. **[LC HL 2008]**

Section B

1 The cash flow forecast for Amrod Ltd for the final quarter of 2015 is set out below:

Cash Flow Forecast for Amrod Ltd for the 4th Quarter of 2015				
2015	**October €**	**November €**	**December €**	**Total €**
Total Receipts	70,000	180,000	90,000	340,000
Total Payments	100,000	165,000	120,000	385,000
Net Cash	(30,000)	15,000	B	(45,000)
Opening Cash	20,000	A	5,000	C
Closing Cash	(10,000)	5,000	(25,000)	(25,000)

(i) Explain the reasons Amrod Ltd would prepare a cash flow forecast.

(ii) Calculate the figures represented by the letters A, B and C on the cash flow forecast. (Show your workings.)

(iii) Explain how Amrod Ltd might deal with the financial problem identified in this cash flow forecast. **(25 marks) [LC HL 2015]**

2

> Marie Nolan is the owner of 'Marie's Pizzas', a successful pizza restaurant with a home-delivery service. Demand for take-aways has increased, as more people are eating at home due to the economic downturn. Marie is planning to expand her business through franchising and her accountant recommends that a business plan should be prepared before going ahead.

(i) Discuss the factors that should be considered when choosing between different sources of finance.

(ii) Analyse **two** appropriate sources of finance for acquiring an additional delivery van at 'Marie's Pizzas'. **(30 marks) [LC HL 2010]**

 Solutions

Unit 4

18 MONITORING THE BUSINESS

Profit   Loss

⊕ Learning Outcomes

When you have completed this chapter, you will be able to:

1 Use, interpret and understand financial business data

2 Analyse the final accounts of a business, namely the profit and loss account and balance sheet

3 Calculate and interpret the main ratios using formulae for liquidity, profitability and gearing

4 Outline the limitations of using ratio analysis.

Literacy Link

Profit and loss account, balance sheet, liquidity, profitability, gearing, debt, equity

Numeracy Link

Calculation of formulae, use of percentages

Cross-curricular Link

Accounting – interpretation of accounts
English – communication, report writing
Mathematics – percentages, formulae, addition, multiplication and division of numbers

CASE STUDY _Applegreen_

Applegreen plc opened its first service station in Ballyfermot, Dublin in 1992 and now operates over 360 sites in Ireland, the UK and the USA.

At a recent **AGM**, the company presented its financial accounts for the year to its **shareholders** for approval. These included the **profit and loss account** and the **balance sheet**.

The financial accounts showed that the firm used **retained earnings** and **debt** to finance growth. Debt finance was obtained from Ulster Bank Ireland and AIB through **debentures**. The firm also raised **equity finance** through an **IPO**.

Applegreen plc is listed on the Irish Stock Exchange with the ticker symbol APGN. The company conducts regular **ratio analysis** to

monitor the operation and financial health of the firm. The company has the following data on its ratios.

Gross profit margin	11.74%
Return on investment	15.8%
Current ratio	0.64:1
Gearing ratio	0.37:1

The firm uses these ratios to help plan for future growth, including acquiring new companies and developing new service area sites.

FINANCIAL INFORMATION

Every organisation, both commercial (e.g. a business or sole trader) and non-commercial (e.g. a charity or school) must prepare a set of financial statements. These statements, which include financial accounts, record all money coming into and going out of the organisation. This is required because:

- The organisation needs to see if it is profitable and therefore sustainable.
- The organisation needs to know if it is liquid (can pay its bills as they fall due for payment).
- By law the organisation needs to ensure that appropriate amounts of tax are paid.
- If the organisation applies for loans from financial institutions it will need to show that it can meet the repayments, and if it applies for grants from government agencies it will need to show that it can meet the terms of the award.

THE ACCOUNTS

The financial accounts prepared at the end of the financial year are the:

- Profit and loss account (P&L account)
- Balance sheet
- Cash flow forecast (you learned about this in Chapter 17).

Information in these financial accounts includes:

- **Sales** (also known as turnover, revenue or income): The total income from products sold that the firm normally trades in, e.g. groceries or building materials.
- **Cost of sales:** The cost of making or purchasing goods or of supplying services.
- **Gross profit:** Sales less cost of sales, i.e. the profit from trading before deducting overhead expenses.
- **Expenses:** Day-to-day running costs (overheads) of the business, e.g. insurance, rent.
- **Net profit:** The overall profit after all costs have been deducted.

Unit 4

The Profit and Loss Account

The profit and loss account records the sales less all the expenses the organisation incurred throughout the financial year.

A simple profit and loss account looks as follows:

Income from the sale of goods and supply of services a business normally trades in

Profit and Loss Account	
	€
Sales (turnover)	1,340,000
Less Cost of Sales	(840,000)
Gross Profit	500,000
Less Expenses	(100,000)
Net Profit	**400,000**

The cost of the goods sold or services provided.
Calculated by
Opening Stock + Purchases – Closing Stock

The profit earned from buying and selling the goods or services, i.e. trading, before deducting overhead expenses

The profit after all costs and overhead expenses have been deducted

Overheads – the day-to-day running costs of the business, e.g. insurance, advertising, telephone, staff wages and electricity

A more detailed profit and loss account will look as follows:

Profit and Loss Account of Butler Ltd for the year 2021	
	€
Sales	2,400,000
Less Cost of Sales	(1,300,000)
Gross Profit	1,100,000
Less Expenses (Overheads)	(600,000)
Net Profit	500,000
Less Dividend Paid	(262,500)
Retained earnings for the year	237,500
Retained earnings at start of year (1/1/2021)	40,000
Retained earnings at end of year (31/12/2021)	277,500

The portion of net profit paid to shareholders of the business

The portion of net profit retained in the business at the end of 2021 for future needs, e.g. to fund expansion

Activity 18.1

If Keeny Ltd has profits of €700,000 and pays corporation tax of 12.5%, how much corporation tax will it have to pay to the Revenue Commissioners?

What Can We Learn from the Profit and Loss Account?
As financial results are presented in numbers, it is relatively easy to compare performance from one financial period to the next, or between one business and another.

Gross Profit: What Can it Tell Us?
Gross profit is the profit made from buying and selling goods or services that the firm normally trades in. It can be compared from year to year or with other businesses.

If gross profit is **low or falling**, the business is either:

- Not charging enough for its goods/services, or
- Paying too much for raw materials or to turn them into finished goods.

The business will have to either:

- Increase its selling price, or
- Shop around for a cheaper supplier.

Net Profit: What Can it Tell Us?
Net profit is the profit made by the business after all costs have been paid, i.e. the overall profit the firm made for the financial year. The net profit figure also gives management information on the amount of dividends it can afford to pay to shareholders.

If net profit is **low or falling**, the business is either:

- Spending too much money on day-to-day running costs, e.g. electricity or wages, or
- Making less efficient use of its resources, e.g. too many delivery vans in use given the sales volume.

The business will have to either:

- Reduce its running costs, e.g. wage cuts, or
- Shop around for cheaper alternatives, e.g. switch energy providers.

Unit 4

The Balance Sheet

A balance sheet is a snapshot of the financial health of a business at a point in time. **It shows how much wealth a business has generated by providing a statement of its assets and liabilities as well as its sources of finance.** The balance sheet is also referred to as a statement of financial position.

A simple balance sheet would look as follows:

Items a business **OWNS** for more than one year. Examples include:
(i)   Tangible fixed assets – physical items, e.g. premises, vehicles
(ii) Intangible fixed assets – non-physical items, e.g. patents, brands

Items a business OWNS for less than one year, with their value changing regularly, e.g. the amount owed by debtors changes daily

Short-term liabilities that the business OWES which are due to be paid within one year, e.g. money owed to suppliers, a bank overdraft

The money available to pay day-to-day expenses. Adequate working capital is essential for a business to pay its debts as they fall due. Negative working capital may result in business closure

The long-term sources of finance for the business, i.e. debt and equity capital

Money invested in the business by its owners, i.e. ordinary shareholders

These are amounts the business OWES which will be paid after 12 months and include long-term liabilities such as debentures

Balance Sheet of Butler Ltd as at 31/12/2021

	€	€
Fixed Assets		
Premises		850,000
Vehicles		135,000
Office Equipment		85,000
		1,070,000 Y
Current Assets		
Closing Stock	23,500	
Debtors	30,000	
Cash	4,000	
	57,500 A	
Less Current Liabilities		
Creditors	22,000	
Bank overdraft	18,000	
	40,000 B	
Working Capital (A–B)		17,500 Z
Total Net Assets		**1,087,500** Y+ Z
Financed by		
Long-term Liabilities		
10% Debenture 2023		200,000
Equity Capital		
Ordinary Share Capital (Equity)	610,000	
Retained Earnings	277,500	887,500
Capital Employed		**1,087,500**

The total amount of money invested in the business by all parties, i.e. debt and equity capital

> **Definition: Debtors**
> Individuals or businesses (i.e. customers) that owe the business money after buying goods or services on credit.

> **Definition: Creditors**
> Individuals or businesses that the business owes money to, e.g. suppliers. It has bought goods on credit and will pay for these at an agreed future date.

What Can We Learn from the Balance Sheet?

A **balance sheet** tells us a lot about the financial position of the business, such as:

- The current value of the business, i.e. as at the date of the balance sheet.
- Whether the business has enough money to pay its short-term debts as they fall due (from the working capital figure). This is referred to as **liquidity**.
- The level of debt and equity in the business (from the 'Financed by' section). This is referred to as **gearing**.

> ### Activity 18.2
>
> Working in pairs, create a Blockbusters game grid using the terms associated with the profit and loss account and the balance sheet.

INTERPRETING ACCOUNTS: THE USE OF RATIO ANALYSIS

Ratio analysis is a technique used to compare the financial performance of a business relative to previous years and to its competitors. It highlights the key underlying trends affecting the business. Businesses are assessed using ratios under three main headings:

1 Profitability	2 Liquidity	3 Gearing

We shall now examine the financial accounts of Butler Ltd, using the information from pages 268 and 269. We shall calculate the profitability, liquidity and gearing ratios.

1 Profitability Ratios

Ratio	Formula	Application to Butler Ltd
(A) Gross Profit Margin *(Gross Margin)*	$\dfrac{\text{Gross Profit} \times 100}{\text{Sales}} = \%$	$\dfrac{1{,}100{,}000 \times 100}{2{,}400{,}000} = 45.83\%$
(B) Net Profit Margin *(Net Margin)*	$\dfrac{\text{Net Profit} \times 100}{\text{Sales}} = \%$	$\dfrac{500{,}000 \times 100}{2{,}400{,}000} = 20.83\%$
(C) Return on Investment (ROI) *(Also known as Return on Capital Employed (ROCE))*	$\dfrac{\text{Net Profit} \times 100}{\text{Capital Employed}} = \%$	$\dfrac{500{,}000 \times 100}{1{,}087{,}500} = 45.98\%$

Note!

Capital employed is calculated as follows: Ordinary share capital + retained earnings + long-term loans + preference shares

Definition: Preference shares

These shares entitle the holder to a fixed dividend that will be paid in priority over dividend payments to ordinary shareholders.

What do Profitability Ratios Tell Us?

- **Gross profit margin** shows the percentage profit on all items sold. This is the profit percentage on trading (buying and selling). The higher the percentage the better, as the business will have more money to cover its overhead expenses. For example, if the gross profit margin is 30%, this means that for every €100 of sales, the business generates €30 of gross profit, which it uses to cover its overhead expenses.

- **Net profit margin** shows the overall percentage profit for the business after covering all costs, including expenses. As the business aims to make a profit, the higher the net profit margin the better. For example, if the net profit margin is 10%, this means that for every €100 of sales, the business makes €10.

- **Return on investment (ROI)** measures the level of profit the business can generate from the money invested by shareholders and banks. It is often compared with the interest rate offered on deposit accounts.

2 Liquidity Ratios

Ratio	Formula	Application to Butler Ltd
Current Ratio *(Working Capital Ratio)*	Current Assets : Current Liabilities	57,500 : 40,000 **1.44:1**
Acid Test Ratio *(Quick Ratio)*	Current Assets – Closing Stock : Current Liabilities	57,500 – 23,500 : 40,000 34,000 : 40,000 **0.85:1**

Unit 4

What do Liquidity Ratios Tell Us?

Current ratio:

- It shows the ability of a business to pay its current liabilities as they fall due.
- The calculation includes closing stock as an asset.
- The ideal ratio is 2:1.This means that for every €1 owed by the business it has €2 available to pay its bills.

> ### Note!
> *If the current ratio rises to, e.g., 5:1 or more it could indicate that the business is making inefficient use of its resources. It may be holding too much closing stock or have large amounts of cash that it should consider returning to its shareholders.*

> *Closing stock is excluded from the acid test ratio as it may not be possible for the business to sell its stock quickly to pay its bills.*

Acid test ratio:

- This is similar to the current ratio, except it excludes closing stock when calculating assets.
- The ideal ratio is 1:1. This means that for every €1 owed by the business it has €1 available to pay its bills.

How can a Business Overcome a Liquidity Problem?

- **Credit control:** Limit the amount of credit given to customers, both in terms of the amount and the period of time. Encourage early payment of debts by offering discounts.

- **Stock control:** Keep stock levels to a minimum, e.g. JIT – just in time (see Chapter 12).

- **Raise finance:** Look at ways of increasing cash in the business to repay debts sooner, e.g. raising equity finance by selling shares.

- **Financial planning:** Prepare cash flow forecasts to identify times of surplus and shortfalls of cash. Periods with shortfalls in cash can be avoided by putting in place credit facilities, e.g. a bank overdraft.

Definitions:

Liquidity
The ability of a business to pay its **short-term** liabilities as they fall due.

Solvency
The ability of a business to pay **all** its debts (short- and long-term liabilities) as they fall due.

Unit 4

3 Gearing Ratios

Ratio	Formula	Application to Butler Ltd
Debt/Equity Ratio	Debt Capital : Equity Capital	200,000 : 887,500 **0.23:1**

Definitions:

Debt capital = bank loans + debentures + preference shares
Equity capital = ordinary share capital + retained earnings

What Does the Gearing Ratio Tell Us?

- It shows the level of debt and equity capital invested in the business.
- The level of debt compared to the level of equity is known as gearing.
- A high level of gearing can indicate a risk of business collapse.

- **Low gearing** – *debt capital is less than equity capital.*

- **High gearing** – *debt capital is greater than equity capital.*

- **Neutral gearing** – *debt capital is equal to equity capital.*

Problems Facing a Highly Geared Business

- **Dividends:** More of the firm's profits are used to pay interest payments, so there is less money to pay dividends on ordinary shares. Shareholders in a plc (public limited company – you will learn more about plcs in Chapter 24) may become dissatisfied and decide to sell their shares.
- **Extra debt finance:** The business will have difficulty obtaining further loans. Lenders may view the firm as a higher risk and charge a higher interest rate or seek additional security. New loans would also further disimprove (worsen) the debt/equity ratio.
- **Extra equity finance:** The business may have difficulty raising additional equity finance as the ordinary shareholders would view the business as having a higher risk of bankruptcy. Also, where more ordinary shares are issued, this reduces the amount of dividend that can be issued per share.
- **Management stress:** Management of a highly geared business may suffer from additional stress. They would be under significant pressure to increase profits to meet interest payments and provide an adequate dividend to shareholders.

Activity 18.3

In pairs, use a graphic organiser of your choice to create a revision chart showing the formulae for the ratios to calculate profitability, liquidity and gearing.

Sample Set of Financial Accounts and Analysis

Using two ratios in each case, analyse the profitability, liquidity and gearing of Dowling Autos Ltd from the following extracts of the financial accounts.

Dowling Autos Ltd		
	Year 1 €	**Year 2 €**
Retained Earnings	204,000	263,500
Closing Stock	37,400	44,200
Net Profit	81,600	59,500
Sales	1,326,000	1,088,000
Current Assets	115,600	122,400
Gross Profit	204,000	136,000
Equity Share Capital	1,190,000	1,190,000
Current Liabilities	71,400	108,800
Long-term Loan	300,000	200,000

> **Exam Tip!**
> Include the correct unit of measurement in your answer, e.g. € or %. Round your answer to two decimal places.

Before we analyse the profitability, liquidity and gearing we must first calculate the relevant ratios for each year so as to understand the underlying trends.

Profitability

		Year 1	Year 2
(i) Gross Profit Margin			
	$\dfrac{\text{Gross Profit} \times 100}{\text{Sales}}$	$\dfrac{204,000 \times 100}{1,326,000}$	$\dfrac{136,000 \times 100}{1,088,000}$
Answer		15.38%	12.5%
(ii) Net Profit Margin			
	$\dfrac{\text{Net Profit} \times 100}{\text{Sales}}$	$\dfrac{81,600 \times 100}{1,326,000}$	$\dfrac{59,500 \times 100}{1,088,000}$
Answer		6.15%	5.47%
(iii) Return on Investment			
	$\dfrac{\text{Net Profit} \times 100}{\text{Capital Employed}}$	$\dfrac{81,600 \times 100}{1,694,000}$	$\dfrac{59,500 \times 100}{1,653,500}$
Answer		4.82%	3.6%

Capital employed Year 1 = 1,190,000 + 204,000 + 300,000 = 1,694,000

Capital employed Year 2 = 1,190,000 + 263,500 + 200,000 = 1,653,500

Analysis

Gross Profit Margin

What changed?	→ The gross profit margin has **decreased** from 15.38% in year 1 to 12.5% in year 2.
Cause?	→ The selling price decreased or the cost of producing the item increased.
Solution?	→ The business should increase the selling price or try to reduce cost of sales, e.g. by shopping around for cheaper raw materials.

Net Profit Margin

What changed?	→ The net profit margin has **decreased** from 6.15% in year 1 to 5.47% in year 2.
Cause?	→ An increase in business expenses, e.g. insurance.
Solution?	→ The business should try to reduce its day-to-day running expenses, e.g. shop around for cheaper insurance providers.

Return on Investment

What changed?	→ The ROI has **decreased** from 4.82% in year 1 to 3.6% in year 2.
Cause?	→ The business is making a lower return from the capital invested in it in year 2. The managers are not using the firm's assets as efficiently compared to year 1.
Solution?	→ The business should consider retraining or replacing the managers.
Alternative Investment	→ It is worth noting that the ROI is still greater than the return currently being offered on risk-free investments. For example, the current interest rate return from banks or state savings is typically less than 1%.

Liquidity

	Year 1	Year 2
(i) Current Ratio		
Current Assets : Current Liabilities	115,600 : 71,400	122,400 : 108,800
Answer	**1.62 : 1**	**1.13 : 1**
(ii) Acid Test Ratio		
Current Assets – Closing Stock : Current Liabilities	115,600 – 37,400 : 71,400	122,400 – 44,200 : 108,800
Answer	**1.09 : 1**	**0.72 : 1**

Analysis

The Current Ratio

What changed?	→ The current ratio has **disimproved** from 1.62:1 in year 1 to 1.13:1 in year 2. This indicates that the business has less cash to pay its bills as they fall due.
Cause?	→ The business may be using more of its bank overdraft and failing to collect on amounts owed from debtors, i.e. an increase in bad debts.
Comparison to ideal ratio	→ The current ratio is less than the ideal ratio of 2:1.
Solution	→ The business should try to raise equity finance or sell non-core fixed assets, including investments (if any).

The Acid Test Ratio (Quick Ratio)

What changed?	→ The acid ratio has **disimproved** from 1.09:1 in year 1 to 0.72:1 in year 2. This indicates that the business has less cash to pay its debts as they fall due.
Cause?	→ The firm is tying up funds because it is buying more stock.
Comparison to ideal ratio	→ The acid ratio is less than the ideal ratio of 1:1.
Solution	→ The business should improve stock control and sell off excess stock at a discount. In addition, it should consider raising equity finance or selling non-core fixed assets including investments.

Gearing

	Year 1	Year 2
Debt/Equity Ratio		
Debt Capital : Equity Capital	300,000 : 1,394,000	200,000 : 1,453,500

Equity capital Year 1 = 1,190,000 + 204,000
Equity capital Year 2 = 1,190,000 + 263,500

	Year 1	Year 2
Answer	0.21 : 1	0.14 : 1

Analysis

Debt/Equity Ratio	
What changed?	→ The debt/equity ratio **decreased** from 0.21:1 in year 1 to 0.14:1 in year 2.
Cause?	→ This is because the firm has reduced its long-term debts by repaying part of the amount borrowed.
Solution?	→ The business should continue to reduce borrowings through regular repayments.

How a Business Can Deal with Trends in Profitability, Liquidity and Gearing

Ratio		Improving Ratio	Disimproving Ratio
Gross Profit Margin	Reason	→ Cost of sales has fallen → Selling price has risen	→ Cost of sales has risen → Selling price has fallen
	Solution	→ Continue as is	→ Find a cheaper supplier → Charge a higher selling price
Net Profit Margin	Reason	→ Business expenses have decreased → Gross profit % has improved	→ Expenses have risen → Gross profit % has disimproved
	Solution	→ Continue as is	→ Reduce expenses → Charge a higher selling price
Return on Investment	Reason	→ Increasing net profit generated from capital investment	→ Lower net profit generated from capital invested
	Solution	→ Continue as is	→ Put business resources to more efficient uses
Current Ratio or Acid Test Ratio	Reason	→ Business is better at managing cash flow, stock control and payment of debts	→ Increased overdrafts → Increased use of creditors as a form of finance
	Solution	→ Continue as is	→ Sell non-core fixed assets (e.g. investments) to generate cash

Ratio		Improving Ratio	Disimproving Ratio
Gearing	Reason	→ Loans have been repaid or new funds raised from shareholders	→ New loans have been taken out
	Solution	→ Continue to pay off loans and use more equity capital	→ Raise new equity capital → Sell non-core fixed assets (e.g. investments) to repay loans

Limitations of Ratio Analysis

1 **Industrial relations:** Ratios do not show if there are poor industrial relations in a firm.

2 **Accounting policies:** When comparing one business with another, different accounting policies may be used, which distorts comparisons, e.g. how a business values stock.

3 **Ethical behaviour:** Ratios show how well a business is performing financially. However, they don't show if the business is acting sustainably or ethically.

4 **Non-financial information:** This can be excluded from the financial analysis, e.g. staff morale, staff retention and economic climate.

5 **Past performance:** Ratios show how a business performed in the past. However, they give no indication of what the future holds.

WHO USES FINANCIAL INFORMATION?

Many different people and organisations have an interest in the financial affairs of a business, for a range of different reasons.

Users (Stakeholders)	Stakeholders' Interests	Relevant Ratios Include
Investors (Banks)	→ **Liquidity:** The ability of the business to pay interest on loans. → **Gearing:** The effect that any new loans would have on the debt/equity ratio. Too much debt could lead to business failure and loans not being repaid.	→ **Liquidity:** Acid Test Ratio → **Gearing:** Debt/Equity Ratio
Management	→ **Profitability:** To compare the profit trend year on year and understand how this compares to the industry average. → **Liquidity:** To ensure the business can pay its debts as they fall due. → **Gearing:** This is monitored so that the level of debt in the business is appropriate.	→ **Profitability:** Net Profit Margin → **Liquidity:** Current Ratio, Acid Test Ratio → **Gearing:** Debt/Equity Ratio
Investors (Shareholders)	→ **Profitability:** To assess how the business is performing compared to last year and the industry average. → **Liquidity:** The ability of the business to pay its debts as they fall due, in order to determine the security of their investment.	→ **Profitability:** Net Profit Margin, Return on Investment → **Liquidity:** Current Ratio, Acid Test Ratio
Suppliers (Creditors)	→ **Liquidity:** The firm's ability to pay for the goods supplied on credit. A supplier will not want to sell goods where the risk of non-payment is high or the business is at risk of going into liquidation.	→ **Liquidity:** Current Ratio, Acid Test Ratio

Users (Stakeholders)	Stakeholders' Interests	Relevant Ratios Include
Employees	→ **Profitability:** To see the level of business profits and the likelihood of receiving a pay rise. → **Liquidity:** The employees will be concerned about their job security. This is shown by the firm's ability to pay its bills as they fall due and therefore to continue to trade.	→ **Profitability:** Net Profit Margin → **Liquidity:** Current Ratio
Competitors	→ **Profitability:** To understand how profitable the business is, compared to their own firm's performance. → **Gearing:** To examine the level of debt in the firm, when considering a possible takeover.	→ **Profitability:** Net Profit Margin → **Gearing:** Debt/Equity Ratio
Government (including the Revenue Commissioners)	→ **Profitability:** To ensure that the correct amount of tax on profits is paid. → **Liquidity:** State agencies such as Enterprise Ireland will examine the financial affairs of the business before allocating government or EU grants.	→ **Profitability:** Net Profit Margin → **Liquidity:** Current Ratio, Acid Test Ratio

Definition: Liquidation

When a business is unable to pay its debts as they fall due, suppliers can have a liquidator appointed to the business. The liquidator will try to raise enough cash to pay the suppliers, e.g. by selling assets or stock (liquidation sale).

Activity 18.4

Working in groups, create a mind map showing the main users of financial information and the ratios each user is interested in. You could create your mind map on a large piece of paper/card or online using a website such as www.coggle.it or www.popplet.com.

Definition: Receivership

If a business fails to repay the interest on a debenture, the lender can take legal action against the firm by appointing a receiver. The receiver takes ownership of the asset used to secure the loan, e.g. the deeds of premises.

KEY TERMS

Now you have completed this chapter, you should understand and be able to explain the following terms. In your copybook, write a definition of each term to build up your own glossary of terms.

- profit and loss account
- gross profit
- net profit
- retained earnings
- balance sheet
- fixed assets
- current assets
- debtors
- current liabilities
- creditors

- working capital
- capital employed
- ratio analysis
- profitability ratios
- net profit margin
- gross profit margin
- return on investment (ROI)
- liquidity ratio
- current (working capital) ratio

- acid (quick) ratio
- liquidity
- solvency
- gearing
- debt capital
- debt/equity ratio
- liquidation
- receivership

 **PowerPoint Summary**

EXAM-STYLE QUESTIONS

Ordinary Level

Section 1 – Short Questions (10 marks each)

1 Name the financial accounts prepared by a business organisation.

2 Explain what is meant by the term *gross profit*.

3 List **two** current assets and **one** fixed asset that you would find in a business's balance sheet.

4 Distinguish between current liabilities and long-term liabilities.

5 The following information was taken from the books of Mullins Ltd:

    Sales €600,000   Gross Profit €360,000   Net Profit €240,000

    Calculate (i) gross profit margin and (ii) net profit margin.

6 The following information was taken from the books of Howlin Ltd:

    Current Assets €108,000   Current Liabilities €75,600

    Calculate (i) the figure for working capital and (ii) the current (working capital) ratio.

7 The following information was taken from the books of Kehoe Ltd:

    Current Assets €1,520,000   Current Liabilities €912,000   Closing Stock €608,000

    Calculate (i) the current (working capital) ratio and (ii) the acid (quick) test ratio.

8 The following information was taken from the books of Sinnott Ltd:

    Equity Capital €1,050,000   Debt Capital €700,000   Retained Earnings €350,000

    Calculate the debt/equity ratio.

9 Rewrite the following sentence in your copybook using the appropriate words to complete the sentence. (One word does not apply.)

    Assets   **Liabilities**   **Working Capital**   **Balance Sheet**

  A _____ is a snapshot of a business at a particular point in time. It provides a statement of _____ and _____ and the sources of finance for the business.

10 Indicate whether each of these statements is true or false.

	Statements	True or False
A	Gross profit is calculated by Sales – Cost of Sales.	
B	Dividends is the portion of profits paid to a supplier for goods purchased on credit.	
C	Capital is the amount of money invested by an owner(s) into a business.	
D	ROI stands for Republic of Ireland for business accounts purposes.	
E	Working capital is the money available to pay day-to-day expenses of a business.	

Section 2 – Long Questions

1 Explain the purpose of a balance sheet. Name **one** current asset and **one** current liability found on the balance sheet.   **(15 marks)**

2 Outline the information a business owner can learn from analysing the gross profit of a company.   **(15 marks)**

3 The following figures have been taken from the books of Griffin Ltd:

	Year 1 €	Year 2 €
Sales	230,000	276,000
Gross Profit	138,000	151,800
Net Profit	92,000	73,600

  (i) Calculate the gross margin for both years and comment on the trend.

  (ii) Calculate the net margin for both years and comment on the trend.   **(20 marks)**

4 The following figures have been extracted from the books of Foynes Plc:

	Year 1 €	Year 2 €
Sales	4,400,000	5,225,000
Net Profit	1,100,000	825,000
Capital Employed	2,200,000	3,300,000

  (i) Calculate the net margin for both years and comment on the trend.

  (ii) Calculate the return on investment (ROI) for both years and comment.   **(20 marks)**

Section 2 – Long Questions *continued*

5 The following figures have been extracted from the books of Hand CLG:

	Year 1 €	Year 2 €
Current Assets	540,000	810,000
Current Liabilities	270,000	486,000
Closing Stock	170,000	432,000

(i) Calculate the current (working capital) ratio for both years and comment on the trend.

(ii) Calculate the acid (quick) ratio for both years and comment on the trend. **(20 marks)**

6 The following figures have been extracted from the books of Munroe DAC:

	Year 1 €	Year 2 €
Equity Capital	108,000	162,000
Debt Capital	54,000	113,400
Retained Earnings	27,000	32,400

Calculate the debt/equity ratio for both years and comment on the trend. **(20 marks)**

7 Name **three** stakeholders in a business that would be interested in the financial information of a business. Explain the reasons why **one** of these stakeholders would be interested in the final accounts of the business. **(20 marks)**

8 Describe **three** limitations of a firm using ratio analysis. **(15 marks)**

Higher Level

Section 1 – Short Questions (10 marks each)

1 Distinguish between debtors and creditors.

2 Describe the information a person can obtain from analysing a firm's balance sheet.

3 The gross profit percentage has fallen from 32% to 24% over the past 12 months. Identify **two** possible causes for this decrease.

4 The net profit percentage has increased from 15% to 23% over the past 12 months. Identify **two** possible causes for this increase.

5 Identify how a firm could overcome a liquidity problem.

6 Distinguish between equity capital and debt capital.

7 The following figures have been extracted from the books of Gibbons Ltd:

	Year 1 €	Year 2 €
Current Assets	3,960,000	3,630,000
Current Liabilities	2,760,000	2,415,000
Closing Stock	879,000	1,242,000

Calculate (i) the current ratio and (ii) the acid test ratio for both years. Comment on the trend.

8 The following figures have been extracted from the books of Behan Ltd:

	Year 1 €	Year 2 €
Equity (ordinary) Share Capital	980,000	1,050,000
Debt Capital	350,000	210,000
Retained Earnings	70,000	105,000

Calculate the debt/equity ratio for both years and comment on the trend.

9 Column 1 is a list of terms associated with monitoring a business. Column 2 is a list of possible explanations for these terms. Match the two lists in your copybook by writing your answers in the form *number = letter* (e.g. 1 = A).

Terms		Explanations	
1	Current Assets	**A**	The ability of a business to pay its short-term debts as they fall due.
2	Liquidity	**B**	Items that a business owns for more than one year.
3	Capital Employed	**C**	Items that a business owns but their value changes regularly.
4	Fixed Assets	**D**	Long-term loans and preference shares.
5	Debt Capital	**E**	Ordinary share capital + Retained earnings + Long-term loans and preference shares.

Section 1 – Short Questions (10 marks each) *continued*

10 Choose the correct option in each of the following sentences.
   (i)   A current liability is an amount **owed to/owed by** a business and must repaid **within/after** one year.
   (ii) Solvency is the ability of a business to pay **short-term/long-term/all** debts as they fall due.
   (iii) The **net profit/gross profit** margin shows the overall percentage profit for the business after covering all expenses.
   (iv) When calculating the acid test ratio closing stock is **included/excluded.**
   (v)   When debt capital is less than equity capital a business is **lowly/highly** geared.

Section 2 – Applied Business Question (80 marks)

SF Shoes
Senan Fitzmaurice established SF Shoes ten years ago using his own savings as well as investment from his family and a loan from the bank. He employs ten staff at his factory in Donegal, which manufactures shoes for customers who want high-quality design and materials.

At times, Senan uses an autocratic management style and his staff are unhappy with this approach. He doesn't involve them in decisions about new designs and a number of staff have left the firm in the last two years.

While sales have increased, Senan has noticed a steady increase in expenses such as electricity and broadband services.

As expenses have increased, the cost of raw materials such as leather has decreased. He has received phone calls from suppliers as he has missed a number of payment deadlines. These suppliers are threatening to impose a credit limit on his orders.

Senan wants to purchase some new machinery to increase production. He has applied to his Local Enterprise Office for a grant and is hopeful that this will be approved.

Senan recently met with Adam Merriman, the firm's accountant, who presented the financial accounts of the business for the past two years.

	2022	2023
Sales	300,000	320,000
Cost of Sales	150,000	140,000
Expenses	90,000	120,000
Current Assets (incl. closing stock)	80,000	65,000
Closing Stock	40,000	45,000
Current Liabilities	20,000	30,000
Debentures and other loan capital	120,000	100,000
Equity Capital (incl. retained earnings)	200,000	200,000

The accountant explained that while sales have increased, there are some areas of concern. Senan is accumulating bad debts, as he is selling shoes to shops around Ireland but these stores are not paying for the items delivered. He is also building up too much stock and his accountant wants him to find ways to reduce his stock levels. He is also worried about the firm's ability to pay its debts as they fall due. If this continues, SF Shoes could go out of business. Senan has missed making a recent VAT payment to the Revenue Commissioners.

Senan organises a meeting with his staff and investors. Upon hearing the financial analysis, the employees begin to raise concerns about the future of their jobs.

After the meeting, Senan's parents mentioned that they had hoped that their investment would provide for their retirement. The number of missed payments to suppliers and the Revenue Commissioners is also a concern. Senan's father mentions that he has received accounts on a comparable company in Antrim, which has a net profit margin of 25%. Senan says that he will need to talk to his accountant as he thinks that there are different accounting policies in the UK. Senan feels under pressure to satisfy all his stakeholders.

A   Using your knowledge of ratio analysis, comment on the performance of SF Shoes over the two years. Identify the trends and comment appropriately.   **(40 marks)**

B   Which stakeholders would be interested in the financial statements of SF Shoes? Outline what type of information they would use with reference to relevant ratios.   **(20 marks)**

C   Describe the limitations of using ratio analysis.   **(20 marks)**

Unit 4

Section 3 – Long Questions

1 Explain the purpose of preparing (i) a Profit and Loss Account and (ii) a Balance Sheet. **(15 marks)**

2 Describe the information that can be learned from examining a firm's (i) gross profit and (ii) net profit. **(15 marks)**

3 The following figures have been extracted from the books of Collins Ltd:

	Year 1	Year 2
Current Assets	201,125	228,750
Current Liabilities	108,000	156,000
Closing Stock	100,250	122,500
Equity Capital	625,000	625,000
Debt Capital	150,000	632,500
Retained Earnings	45,000	50,000

(A) Calculate the (i) current ratio, (ii) acid ratio and (iii) debt/equity ratio for both years.

(B) Comment on the trends. Would you advise someone to invest in this business? Give reasons for your answer. **(30 marks)**

4 The following figures have been extracted from the books of Clancy Ltd:

	Year 1	Year 2
Current Assets	60,420	63,840
Current Liabilities	30,780	28,120
Closing Stock	34,580	47,120
Sales	644,100	598,500
Gross Profit	171,570	155,610
Net Profit	57,380	28,120
Equity Capital	380,000	399,000
Debt Capital	140,000	140,000
Retained Earnings	76,000	79,800

(A) In the case of profitability and liquidity, calculate **two** ratios each and identify the trend.

(B) Explain **one** reason why working capital is so important to a business. **(20 marks)**

5 The following figures have been extracted from the books of Rigney Ltd:

	Year 1	Year 2
Current Assets	31,050	35,535
Current Liabilities	21,630	18,860
Closing Stock	18,860	23,230
Sales	325,450	279,450
Gross Profit	133,975	97,888
Net Profit	31,250	30,480
Equity Capital	195,000	195,000
Debt Capital	110,000	110,000
Retained Earnings	16,300	37,800

(A) Analyse the profitability trends in the above business.

(B) Analyse the liquidity trends in the above business. **(25 marks)**

6 The following figures have been extracted from the books of Farrelly Ltd:

	Year 1	Year 2
Fixed Assets	500,000	650,000
Current Assets	134,500	156,000
Liabilities due within 1 year	97,800	104,500
Closing Stock	32,000	43,500
Sales	967,000	890,000
Gross Profit	123,400	115,500
Net Profit	78,000	68,000
Equity Capital	350,000	400,000
Debt Capital	200,000	190,000
Profit and Loss (Retained Earnings)	25,600	24,900

Section 3 – Long Questions *continued*

(A) Calculate for both years the:
  (i) Net Profit Margin
  (ii) Return on Capital Employed
  (iii) Working Capital Ratio and
  (iv) Quick Ratio.

(B) Analyse the above company's performance in relation to profitability, liquidity and level of gearing. Is the business (i) liquid and (ii) solvent? **(30 marks)**

7 Discuss the issues that may affect a highly geared business. **(15 marks)**

8 Evaluate the limitations of ratios as a method of interpreting financial information. **(15 marks)**

PREVIOUS LEAVING CERTIFICATE EXAM QUESTIONS

Ordinary Level

Section A – Short Questions (10 marks each)

1 The following information is available from the final accounts of Navona Ltd:
  Sales €420,000
  Gross Profit €84,000
  Net Profit €31,500

  (i) Calculate the Gross Profit Margin.
  (ii) Calculate the Net Profit Margin. [LC OL 2012]

2 The following information has been taken from the books of Dalton Ltd on 31/12/2010:
  Net Profit: €40,000   Capital Employed: €500,000

  Calculate the Return on Capital Employed. [LC OL 2011]

3 The following information is available from the final accounts of Daly Ltd on 31/12/2012:
  Current Liabilities €140,000
  Current Assets (includes closing stock €70,000) €280,000

  (i) Calculate the Working Capital Ratio.
  (ii) Calculate the Acid Ratio. [LC OL 2013]

Section B

1 The following information is available from the final accounts of Doherty Ltd.

	2007 €	2008 €
Sales	600,000	750,000
Gross Profit	200,000	300,000
Net Profit	120,000	210,000

  (i) Calculate the Gross Profit Margin for 2007 and 2008 **and** comment on the trend. **(20 marks)**
  (ii) Calculate the Net Profit Margin for 2007 and 2008 **and** comment on the trend. **(20 marks) [LC OL 2009]**

2 Use the information below and answer the questions which follow.

Balance Sheet – Brady's Hotel (Extract)		
	2010 €	2009 €
Current Assets	900,000	800,000
Current Liabilities	500,000	400,000

  (i) Calculate the Working Capital ratio for 2010 and 2009.
  (ii) Explain whether the ratio has improved or disimproved. **(20 marks) [LC OL 2011]**

Section B *continued*

3 The following information is extracted from the accounts of Sweeney Sports Ltd.

Balance Sheet (Extract) as on 31 December		
	2007 €	2006 €
Current Assets	300,000	290,000
Liabilities due within 1 year	200,000	145,000

(i) Identify **two** items that could be included under the current assets section of the Balance Sheet of Sweeney Sports Ltd. **(15 marks)**

(ii) Calculate the Working Capital Ratio for 2006 and 2007 and **comment** on the trend. **(25 marks) [LC OL 2008]**

Higher Level

Section A – Short Questions (10 marks each)

1 (i) Using the figures below calculate the Net Profit Percentage (Margin) of Auburn Publishing Ltd for 2014.

	€
Sales	50,000
Gross Profit	22,000
Expenses	12,000

(ii) If the Net Profit Percentage for 2013 was 25% outline how management could use this information in making decisions. **[LC HL 2015]**

2 (i) Explain the term *Return on Investment (ROI).*

(ii) Using the figures below calculate the Return on Investment for Natural Options Ltd.

	€
Net Profit	57,000
Ordinary Share Capital	140,000
Reserves	56,000
Long Term Loan	24,000

[LC HL 2011]

3 (i) Using the figures below calculate the Current Ratio for Sentry Ltd.

	€
Debtors	12,000
Bank Overdraft	20,000
Cash	15,000
Creditors	50,000
Closing Stock	8,000

(ii) Comment on the liquidity position of Sentry Ltd. **[LC HL 2013]**

4 (i) Using the figures below calculate the Debt/Equity ratio (Gearing) of Lalco Ltd for 2015.

	€
Reserves	130,000
Long Term Loan	700,000
Ordinary Share Capital	220,000

(ii) Outline whether Lalco Ltd is highly geared or lowly geared **and** the possible effect this result has on the business. **[LC HL 2016]**

Section B

1 The following figures have been taken from the final accounts of Flame Ltd for 2013.

	€
Authorised Share Capital	900,000
Issued Share Capital	450,000
Long Term Capital	200,000
Retained Earnings	150,000

(i) Explain the term *Debt/Equity Ratio*.

(ii) Calculate the Debt/Equity ratio for 2013. Show your workings.

(iii) Discuss the importance of the Debt/Equity Ratio when deciding on new sources of finance for Flame Ltd. **(20 marks) [LC HL 2014]**

2

> Bianua Ltd, a medium sized company operating in the agrifood sector, supplies quality prepared food to producers in Ireland and in the UK market.

The average performance of companies in the same industry as Bianua Ltd (Agrifood) for 2011 is detailed below.

Industry Average Results 2011	
ROI	11%
Current Ratio	2:1
Acid Test Ratio	1.2:1
Debt Equity Ratio	0.3:1

The following figures are taken from the final accounts of Bianua Ltd for 2011.

Bianua Ltd figures for 2011	€
Net Profit	50,000
Sales	975,000
Current Assets (Including closing stock)	155,000
Long-term Loan	300,000
Ordinary Share Capital	500,000
Current Liabilities	85,000
Retained Earnings	100,000
Closing Stock	80,000

(i) Calculate the following for 2011 for Bianua Ltd:
   (a) Return on Investment (ROI)   (b) Current Ratio
   (c) Acid Test Ratio   (d) Debt/Equity Ratio   **(20 marks)**

(ii) Analyse the profitability and liquidity of Bianua Ltd for 2011, with reference to the industry average results shown above **and** make recommendations for Bianua Ltd. **(20 marks) [LC HL 2012]**

Section B *continued*

3 (i) From the figures below for 2009 calculate the following for CES Ltd.

(a) Net Profit Margin   (b) Acid Test Ratio

(c) Current Ratio   (d) Debt/Equity Ratio   **(20 marks)**

Information for 2009	
Sales	€135,000
Net Profit	€33,750
Current Assets (including closing stock)	€84,500
Current Liabilities	€65,000
Closing Stock	€39,000
Ordinary Share Capital	€300,000
Long Term Debt	€192,000
Retained Earnings	€20,000

Results for 2008	
Net Profit Margin	32%
Current Ratio	2:1
Acid Test Ratio	1.1:1
Debt/Equity Ratio	0.4:1

(ii) Analyse the significance of the trends over the two years (2008/2009) for the following stakeholders:

(a) Investors/Shareholders

(b) Suppliers

(c) Employees   **(20 marks) [LC HL 2010]**

 Solutions

Learning Outcomes

When you have completed this chapter, you will be able to:

1. Identify and contrast the main sources of ideas for new and existing businesses
2. Explain the term *market research*
3. Outline the reasons for conducting market research
4. Identify and describe the different methods of obtaining information about a market
5. Explain the importance of carrying out market research
6. Outline the stages involved in the development process of a new product
7. Calculate the break-even point and margin of safety
8. Draft and label a break-even chart.

Literacy Link

Brainstorming, market research, consumer panel, product development, feasibility study, prototype development, break-even point, margin of safety

Numeracy Link

Percentages, statistics, calculation of formulae, plotting a graph

Cross-curricular Link

Accounting – break-even point, marginal costing, budgeting
Economics – consumer demand

CASE STUDY

Product Development at Dyson Ltd

Out of **frustration** at the poor performance of his vacuum cleaner, James Dyson decided to take the machine apart and examine the components. He set about trying to make a vacuum cleaner that was more efficient and quieter than models on the market. Five years later, after developing 5,127 **prototypes**, he successfully created the world's first bagless vacuum cleaner.

With the income generated from sales of this product, James established Dyson Ltd and set up a dedicated **research and development (R&D) department**. Over the years, the R&D department has used **brainstorming** to generate ideas for new products. The team has taken ideas and used the processes of **product screening** and **concept development** to create successful products such as the bladeless fan and hand dryer. The **product development process** can take a long time at the firm, with some products taking up to ten years

to get from **idea generation** to **product launch**.

Dyson products always have a **USP** that makes them stand out from competitors' products. The USP of the firm's new hairdryer is that it dries hair eight times faster than a standard hairdryer. The R&D department spent five years and almost €57 million developing 600 prototypes to create this product.

Dyson also monitors **customer feedback**, particularly the bad reviews, to find ways to improve its products or identify new product ideas.

The firm has recently announced its intention to enter the electric car market. Dyson has pledged to invest almost €3 billion in **product development**.

IDEAS FOR BUSINESS

Every new business begins with an idea. Entrepreneurs get ideas for new business ventures from many different sources.

Existing businesses also develop ideas, for example creating new products or modifying existing ones. Ideas for new and existing businesses come from both within the organisation (internal) and outside it (external).

Internal Sources of Business Ideas

Internal sources come from within the business.

Internal Sources of Business Ideas for Entrepreneurs

1 **Interests and hobbies:** The entrepreneur looks at what they enjoy doing. They might be able to turn their hobby into a successful business. For example, a person who collects model trains could set up their own model train store.

2 **Unexpected events:** The eureka moment – a thought or event provokes an idea for a good or service, for example trying to solve a problem leads to a completely different product or invention, e.g. Dr John Pemberton first developed Coca-Cola as a medicine.

3 **Frustration:** An entrepreneur may be frustrated about the lack of a product on the market. For example, entrepreneur Joy Mangano developed the Miracle Mop, a self-wringing cleaning mop, when she grew frustrated with wringing out mops with her hands. She has now sold over €8 million worth of mops.

4 **Skills and knowledge:** An entrepreneur may have particular skills or knowledge that can be turned into a business. For example, a person who has very good historical knowledge of a local area sets up a business providing history tours to tourists.

Internal Sources of Business Ideas for Existing Firms

1 **Brainstorming:** People from different areas of the business come together to think of as many ideas as possible. Some ideas will be rejected; others will be put forward and developed further. For example, three friends developed the Irish Fairy Door Company when they were brainstorming ideas around the kitchen table.

2 **Intrapreneurship:** Intrapreneurship means that ideas come from employees, through suggestion schemes or boxes. Since they work with the products they may be best placed to come up with ideas on how to improve them, e.g. by adding new features. Many businesses encourage intrapreneurship by offering employees incentives such as bonus payments.

3 **Research and development (R&D):** A specialised department in the business that develops new goods or services and new ideas for existing products, e.g. Apple and Samsung.

 Kerry Foods Group has an R&D department based in Naas, County Kildare. The firm spends €180 million on R&D each year.

Activity 19.1

Google's revenue was €96 billion. The company spent 12.5% of that on research and development. Calculate the amount Google spent on R&D.

 The Rubik's Cube was developed when Erno Rubik used a cube as a teaching tool to help students understand 3D objects. He had a eureka moment when he tried to put the cube back together and realised he had created a puzzle.

Activity 19.2

In groups, brainstorm ideas for improvements at your school. Select **one** idea from each group and present it to your student council representative.

 A Bacon and Cabbage Roll

A butcher in Wexford invented the bacon and cabbage roll to cater for consumers who want a traditional Irish dinner in a roll. Richie Doyle and Sons in Wexford created the roll using creamed potatoes, spring onion, Irish bacon, buttered cabbage, and a drizzle of Chef brown sauce.

They say it's possibly 'more Irish than a breakfast roll'. It's all the goodness of a bacon and cabbage dinner, stuffed into a roll.

External Sources of Business Ideas

These are ideas that come from outside the business, e.g. the marketplace.

For Entrepreneurs

1 **Family and friends:** Ideas for new products can come from family members, friends and colleagues. Complaints, frustrating experiences and casual stories may help the entrepreneur spot a gap in the market.

2 **Networking:** Meeting with people to build relationships and share business ideas and information, e.g. at corporate functions such as exhibitions, conferences or golf outings. For example, Dublin City LEO organises a range of networking events for female entrepreneurs and food start-ups.

For Entrepreneurs and Existing Businesses

1 **Media:** Ideas for products can come from the media, e.g. television, newspapers and social media. For example, the PopSocket was developed to be used as a grip to enable smartphone users to take selfies and videos with a steadier hand.

2 **Market trends:** A business keeps an eye on market trends to identify new goods and services to satisfy consumer needs. For example, many brands are using additional protein in their products to attract health-conscious consumers, e.g. Avonmore Protein Milk, Cadbury Boost + Protein bar.

3 **State agencies:** State agencies such as Enterprise Ireland provide information on worldwide markets and growth statistics. This can provide firms and entrepreneurs with ideas for new products or markets.

4 **Import substitution:** When an Irish business or entrepreneur makes a product that is currently imported, i.e. there is no Irish-made product available.

 DID YOU KNOW? *Enterprise Ireland runs a voucher scheme that provides innovation vouchers worth €5,000 to SMEs that engage with third-level institutions to work on new product/process development.*

For Existing Businesses

1 **Competitors:** A business might copy or adapt a competitor's goods or services. The business then creates its own product. For example, Ryanair was the first European airline to operate a no-frills service. Other airlines, including Aer Lingus, copied the idea to compete in the airline market.

2 **Customer feedback:** This gives the business insight into products that consumers would like to buy. The firm can develop new or improved products to meet consumer needs.

Unit 5

CASE STUDY

Customer Feedback for the Instant Pot

Robert Wang created the Instant Pot, a small kitchen appliance that cooks food quickly. The product has over 39,000 **reviews** on Amazon and Robert tries to read every review left by customers to look for **ideas to improve the** **product**. Based on **customer feedback**, the firm launches an updated version of the Instant Pot every 12–18 months. The product is so popular that 300,000 units were sold on Amazon Prime Day over the course of 30 hours.

MARKET RESEARCH FOR BUSINESS IDEAS

Market research is essential for a business to be successful. A business will only succeed if it not only **meets** but **exceeds** the needs, wants and expectations of its customers. To find out what these needs and wants are, the business must engage in market research.

Definition: Market research
The process of collecting and analysing information about the target market. It is used by the business to identify trends and make marketing decisions.

Reasons for Conducting Market Research

Businesses conduct market research for many reasons, including:

- **To find out the size of the market:** To find out the overall market size and identify the size of the target market, e.g. how many 14–18-year-old males live in the area.
- **To identify competitors:** To find out information about competitors in the market, e.g. the number of competitors and their market share.
- **To find out consumer needs and wants:** The business identifies what the consumer wants from the good or service. This also includes feedback on packaging, price and quality.
- **To identify trends:** The business may want to identify current and future market trends, e.g. growth in wearable technology such as fitness trackers or an increase in demand for adventure holidays.

Stages in Market Research

When a business decides to engage in market research it must decide:

What information will be researched?	For example, market size or competition in the marketplace.
How will the data be collected?	Using primary and/or secondary research.
Who will collect the information?	The firm's own marketing department or market research agencies.
How long will it take to complete?	For example, three days, three weeks or three months.
How much will it cost?	The budget available for market research.

Once a business has made these decisions, the next stage is to:

1 **Gather:** The information must be gathered and compiled.
2 **Analyse:** The information must be studied in detail to identify trends and statistics.
3 **Report:** A report is compiled and given to the appropriate decision-makers. They use the information to make decisions regarding the future of the business, e.g. to produce a new product or enter a new market.

Types of Market Research

There are two types of market research:

- **Primary** (field) research
- **Secondary** (desk) research.

WE WANT YOUR FEEDBACK

Primary (Field) Research

Primary research involves gathering first-hand information from the marketplace. Researchers go into the marketplace (field) and find out information by making direct contact with potential customers.

Common forms of primary (field) research include the following:

1 Observation

Market researchers watch consumer behaviour and learn from their reactions, e.g. observing consumers reacting to a product display in a shop. Businesses use this information to improve the layout of the shop to maximise sales.

- **Advantage:** Consumers are unaware that they are being observed, so the retailer can gain accurate information on consumer behaviour.
- **Disadvantage:** It shows **how** people behave, but because there is no direct interaction it does not explain **why** they behave as they do.

2 Consumer Panels (Focus Groups)

Groups of consumers or potential consumers meet to discuss a firm's products. This gives the firm information on consumer habits and opinions, which can be used to develop new products or improve existing products.

- **Advantage:** The business can gain detailed insight into the consumers' attitudes and opinions.
- **Disadvantage:** It can be time-consuming and expensive to run.

3 Surveys

Market researchers conduct an interview with consumers or potential consumers. These surveys can take place:

- Face-to-face, e.g. stopping people on the street or calling to people's homes
- By telephone
- Online, e.g. using a website such as SurveyMonkey or Google Forms.

Surveys provide the business with quantitative data (statistics and facts) and qualitative data (people's opinions). Businesses often provide an incentive for people to take part in the survey, such as discounts or vouchers.

- **Advantage:** The firm can obtain detailed information from respondents.
- **Disadvantage:** Non-response rate can be high, e.g. people can refuse to complete telephone or face-to-face surveys.

4 Mystery Shoppers

Anonymous shoppers evaluate customer service and store operations. Businesses can also use mystery shoppers to monitor competitors, e.g. buying a basket of goods in a competitor's store to compare prices.

- **Advantage:** It encourages employees to provide high-quality customer service at all times because they don't know which customers are mystery shoppers.
- **Disadvantage:** Information gathered by the mystery shopper is subjective and depends on his/her personal tastes and preferences.

CASE STUDY — Consumer Panel at Boots

Boots has a **consumer panel** of people who test their cosmetic products at home. The firm sends out approximately 30,000 products to members of the panel each year. Panellists are required to **test the items** on average five times over a two-week period. **Feedback** is given through **surveys** created by the firm on SurveyMonkey. Panellists are not paid for their feedback in order to maintain the independence of the testing.

Unit 5

Activity 19.3

In pairs, decide how the following survey questions devised for a local cinema can be improved.
1 What is your income to the nearest €20?
2 Are you an occasional or frequent user of the cinema?
3 Do you like this cinema? Yes or No.
4 How many times have you been to see a film you saw advertised on TV?
5 What were the most splendiferous and awe-inspiring attributes of the cinema and the movie?
Can you think of any other questions that could be included in the survey? Write them down and share them with the class.

Activity 19.4

In groups, create a survey about a topic of your choice, e.g. mobile phone usage, school canteen meals. Think carefully about what information you need to find out. Use a variety of questions. Create an online version of the survey using a website such as SurveyMonkey.

PRIMARY RESEARCH

✓ Advantages	✗ Disadvantages
1 Specific Information The business can obtain very specific market information relevant to its own products.	**1 Time-consuming** It can take a long time to plan, conduct and analyse primary research data.
2 Better Analysis The information collected can be examined and analysed by the business according to its own needs. It does not rely on other people's interpretation of the information.	**2 Cost** It is more expensive than secondary research because the business is involved in all stages of the process from design to analysis.
3 Timing The information collected is recent, which makes it more accurate.	**3 Inaccurate Feedback** Responses can be untrue or biased and can therefore provide the business with inaccurate information.
4 Confidentiality The information gathered is owned by the business and is not shared with other businesses. This gives the firm an advantage over its competitors.	**4 Business Resources** Many of the firm's resources are tied up in data collection and analysis, e.g. staff and computers. This can take business resources away from other important areas, e.g. raising finance.

Secondary (Desk) Research

This involves gathering and reviewing existing information that has already been collected by others.
It consists of looking through reports, files and the Internet, and is carried out sitting at a computer or desk.

Secondary (desk) research includes the following.

1 Business Reports

A business can use reports created by other organisations to increase their knowledge of competitors or markets, e.g. competitors' annual reports. This information can help the business improve decision-making.

- **Advantage:** Many of these reports are available free of charge.
- **Disadvantage:** It can be time-consuming to read through the report, and not all of the information will be relevant.

2 Government Publications

Government departments provide useful information to businesses about markets, both at home and abroad, e.g. the census from the Central Statistics Office (CSO) and Enterprise Ireland's reports on export markets.

The census gathers information on everybody in Ireland on census night. It provides details on the social and living conditions across Ireland. The first census was conducted in 1821 and the next census is expected to take place in 2021.

DID YOU KNOW?

- **Advantage:** They provide accurate information from a reliable source.
- **Disadvantage:** It can be difficult to find these reports as they are published on a wide variety of government websites.

3 Internet

Businesses can use the internet to carry out searches using search engines such as Google. They can also view websites, social media platforms and consumer forums to find out information about the market.

- **Advantage:** Most of the information is available free of charge.
- **Disadvantage:** There is an enormous amount of information on the Internet and it can be difficult to check the validity of sources.

4 Commercial Research Agencies

These businesses conduct market research on a range of topics and markets, e.g. Ipsos MRBI. They often use a blend of telephone and online surveys to gather data. The information is then sold to businesses.

- **Advantage:** They provide detailed information.
- **Disadvantage:** Agencies charge a fee for the information.

5 Media

Newspapers, magazines and TV can provide valuable insight into markets, e.g. a business may read an article on economics when planning its pricing policy for the market.

- **Advantage:** A wide range of information from a range of sources is available.
- **Disadvantage:** Information the business requires may not be available from the media at the time the business needs it.

Activities 19.5

1. On average there are 40,000 search queries per second on Google. Calculate how many searches take place (i) per minute (ii) per hour (iii) per day.
2. Examine the summary of Census 2016 and answer the following questions.

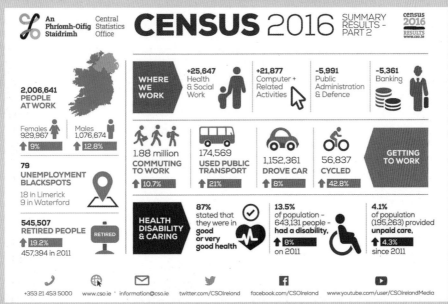

   (i) How many people were working in Ireland in 2016?
   (ii) What percentage of these workers were male?
   (iii) Which employment sector experienced the largest increase in workers?
   (iv) How could entrepreneurs and existing businesses use this information to help them develop a new product?

SECONDARY RESEARCH

✓ Advantages	✗ Disadvantages
1 Cheaper than Primary Research Large amounts of information can be accessed free of charge.	**1 Non-specific** A lot of information is available, but it may not be exactly what the user needs.
2 Faster than Primary Research The information already exists so it can be faster for the business to find and process the information.	**2 Outdated** Information that has not been collected recently may have become outdated and therefore be inaccurate.
3 Large Volume of Information The information available is extensive and covers a wide range of topics.	**3 Copyright** Some secondary sources may be subject to copyright; and reproducing data without permission can lead to costs and possible legal consequences.
4 Accurate Many sources are available online, which means that results can be cross-checked for accuracy.	**4 Information Overload** If there is too much information it needs to be filtered for the business's needs, which can take time.

Benefits of Market Research

Market research helps a business to:

1 **Identify the target market:** Market research reveals the target market – the people at whom the product is aimed, e.g. teenagers or adults. It shows why they are likely to buy the product.

2 **Reduce costs:** Information from consumers can help the business to provide products that satisfy consumer needs and wants. This saves the business time and money by avoiding making items that consumers won't purchase.

3 **Evaluate an advertising campaign:** It can be used to find out if the firm's advertising campaign was effective. For example: Did consumers remember the advertising? Did the advertising create interest in the product? If the answers are negative the business can make changes to future advertising campaigns.

4 **Forecast future trends:** Market research helps to identify future market trends, so the business can create products to meet future consumer needs.

5 **Identify problems:** It can identify problems that consumers are experiencing with the firm's products. It enables the business to take action before the issue damages the firm's reputation.

Activity 19.6

In pairs, use desk research to find out information about your nearest town, for example population and age/gender statistics. Create an infographic with at least **five** pieces of information to display your findings.

DEVELOPMENT PROCESS OF A NEW PRODUCT

To be successful, the development of new products needs to be well thought out and planned. This involves a number of key stages:

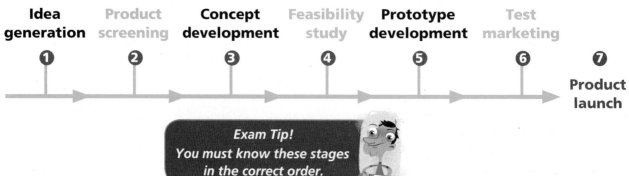

Idea generation	Product screening	**Concept development**	Feasibility study	**Prototype development**	Test marketing	
❶	❷	❸	❹	❺	❻	❼

Product launch

Exam Tip!
You must know these stages in the correct order.

Unit 5

Stage 1: Idea Generation

Ideas for new products can come from internal sources, such as a firm's R&D department or brainstorming sessions. External sources such as suggestions from friends and family or customer feedback can also provide ideas.

Example: The New Škoda Kodiaq

Employees working at the R&D department at Škoda brainstormed ideas for different car models that the firm could develop.

Stage 2: Product Screening

All ideas generated are vetted and those deemed to be impractical or unworkable are dropped. The ideas most likely to be successful are chosen for further development. This saves the business time and money developing a product that consumers will not buy.

Example

Škoda's R&D team considered making a new car model in segments of the market where the firm was already competing. However, the screening process identified a gap in the market for a large SUV (sports utility vehicle).

Stage 3: Concept Development

This is when the idea is turned into an actual product to meet the needs of consumers. The USP of the product is identified and this differentiates it from other products on the market.

Definition: USP

A **unique selling point** is the features that make a product stand out from its competitors. For example, the USP of Mercedes-Benz is high-quality luxury cars.

Example

Škoda decided to develop a large but affordable seven-seater SUV which would attract new customers to the brand. The SUV model would also include features such as a windscreen ice scraper under the fuel cap and umbrellas in the front doors.

Stage 4: Feasibility Study

A feasibility study is carried out to investigate whether the product is commercially viable.

The feasibility study has three main aims:

1 **Production feasibility:** Can the product physically be made? Will it meet government regulations, e.g. safety standards?

2 **Financial feasibility:** What will it cost to make the product?

3 **Marketability:** Is there a demand for the product?

Example

Škoda looked at the capacity of its production plants to manufacture the car. It also considered the size of the market segment to ensure that there would be sufficient sales.

Škoda carried out a detailed cost analysis. It ensured that production costs were kept in line with those of other models. This involved a break-even analysis (see next page).

The study found that the product was likely to be successful and profitable.

Stage 5: Prototype Development

At this stage a sample product or mock-up is produced to see:

- Can it be made?
- What materials are required to make it?
- Does it appeal to customers?

The prototype can be used to test the product to see if it meets standards and to determine whether any adjustments or improvements can be made. The business may create many prototypes to overcome initial flaws before deciding to go into full production.

Example

The Škoda team created 47 prototypes of the Kodiaq, each of which took one month to build. The prototypes tested different features such as the number of seats, boot space, dashboard features. Engineers and car testers covered 700,000 kilometres test driving the prototypes.

Unit 5

Stage 6: Test Marketing

The product is launched into a small section of the market, e.g. in the local area rather than nationwide. The business can evaluate how consumers react to the product and whether further changes are needed.

Example

It is difficult for a car firm to test market a new vehicle. However, the Kodiaq roadshow gave Irish customers a chance to see the new car at first hand. Car dealers in Ireland were able to get feedback from customers and relay it to Škoda Ireland.

Stage 7: Product Launch

The product is launched into the entire market and full-scale production begins. A strong marketing campaign is needed to raise consumer awareness of the product. Pricing and distribution channels are established, with the aim of making the product a success.

Example

The Škoda Kodiaq launched into the Irish market accompanied by an extensive advertising campaign on TV, in newspapers and online. Škoda Ireland received pre-orders for 50% of their projected sales.

Development Process of a New Product: Summary

Stage		Explanation
1	Idea generation	→ Ideas found through brainstorming, market research, staff, suggestions and customer feedback.
2	Product screening	→ Ideas are vetted. Impractical/unworkable ideas are dropped and the best ones are chosen.
3	Concept development	→ The idea is turned into an actual product.
4	Feasibility study	→ Identifies whether the product is technically and commercially viable.
5	Prototype development	→ The first working model is made and tested.
6	Test marketing	→ A small launch to get consumers' initial feedback.
7	Product launch	→ Product launched to the entire market and full-scale production begins.

BREAK-EVEN ANALYSIS

One of the seven stages of product development is a feasibility study. The aim is to find out whether the product is commercially viable, i.e. whether it can be produced and sold at a profit. The feasibility study involves conducting a **break-even analysis**.

In order to conduct a break-even analysis, a business must be able to identify and categorise fixed and variable costs. It must also be able to calculate the break-even point, as well as the margin of safety.

Fixed Costs

These are costs that do not change with the level of production. For example, a baker pays the same fixed rent on their bakery regardless of whether they bake 100 or 1,000 cakes. Other fixed costs include insurance and interest payments on loans.

Variable Costs

The amount changes directly with the level of production, i.e. these costs increase if more products are made and decrease if fewer products are made. Examples include raw materials and labour.

Break-Even Point

The break-even point for a business arises when income earned from selling a product is the same as the cost of making the product, i.e. the business is making neither a profit nor a loss.

The formula used to calculate the break-even point is:

$$\text{Break-Even Point (units)} = \frac{\text{Fixed Costs}}{\text{Contribution per Unit*}}$$

*Contribution per Unit = Selling Price per Unit – Variable Costs per Unit

Margin of Safety

This is the difference between a firm's forecast output (sales) and its break-even point. It is measured in units and shows how far sales can fall before the break-even point is reached. The formula used to calculate the margin of safety is:

Margin of Safety = Forecast Output (Sales) – Break-Even Point

Break-Even Chart Sample Question

Examining a sample question will help you to understand how to draft a break-even chart:

Jack is planning to set up a business manufacturing coffee machines. He wants to find out how many machines he needs to sell per week in order to break even. Jack prepares the following information:

Fixed costs	€200,000
Variable Cost per unit	€55
Selling Price per unit	€80
Forecast Output (Sales)	10,000 units

Jack needs to calculate:

1 Break-even point in units and euro   2 Profit at forecast output   3 Margin of safety at forecast output. What will Jack's calculations look like?

Solution

1 Break-Even Point in Units and Euro

Jack must calculate the break-even point to find out the number of coffee machines (units) he needs to sell in order to break even. He uses the following formula:

$$\text{Break-even Point} = \frac{\text{Fixed Costs}}{\text{Contribution per Unit}} = \frac{200,000}{25^*} = 8,000 \text{ units}$$

(Contribution per Unit = Selling Price per Unit – Variable Costs per Unit = €80 – €55 = €25)

Jack also wants to find out what his gross income will be at the break even point.

Break-Even Point in euro = Break-Even Point × Selling Price per Unit

8,000 units × €80 = €640,000

2 Profit at Forecast Output

Jack needs to calculate the amount of profit he can earn if he sells all manufactured coffee machines, i.e. the forecast output (sales).

He must first calculate the **Total Revenue**, i.e. the total amount of money he will receive if he sells all the coffee machines (forecast output).

He must then calculate the **Total Costs**, i.e. the fixed costs and variable costs associated with selling all the coffee machines (forecast output).

The difference between these two figures will show Jack his profit at forecast output.

Profit at forecast output is calculated as follows:

	€	€
Total Revenue		800,000
Total Costs		
Fixed costs	200,000	
Variable costs	+ 550,000	– 750,000
Profit at Forecast Output		50,000

Total Revenue = Forecast Output × Selling Price = 10,000 units × €80 = €800,000
Total Costs = Fixed Costs + Variable Costs (Forecast Output × Variable Costs Per Unit) = €200,000 + 550,000 (10,000 units × €55) = €750,000

Unit 5

3 Margin of Safety at Forecast Output

Jack then calculates the margin of safety to find out the difference between the forecast output (sales) and the break-even point.

Margin of Safety = Forecast Output (Sales) – Break-even Point

10,000 units – 8,000 units = 2,000 units

Steps in Drawing a Break-Even Chart

The break-even point can also be found by constructing a break-even chart. This visually aids the understanding of break-even analysis.

> *Exam Tip!*
> *Marks are awarded for labelling the break-even chart correctly. Make sure that you:*
> * *Give the chart a title, e.g. Break-Even Chart for Jack.*
> * *Label the x-axis Output in Units and the y-axis Value of Sales / Costs €.*
> * *Label the Fixed Costs, Total Revenue and Total Costs lines.*
> * *Clearly label the Break-even Point and the Margin of Safety.*

Step 1: Label the diagram

Begin by giving the chart a title. In this case, the break-even chart will be labelled **Break-Even Chart for Jack**.

Draw a horizontal axis (x) and title it **Output in Units**. This line will extend as far as the figure given for forecast output. In Jack's case, the horizontal axis will go as far as 10,000 units. You can decide which interval to use on the x-axis. In this case we will use intervals of 2,000 units.

Draw a vertical axis (y) and title it **Value of Sales/Costs €**. The highest point on this line records the figure calculated for total revenue. In this case, the y-axis will reach €800,000. We will use intervals of €100,000 to label the y-axis.

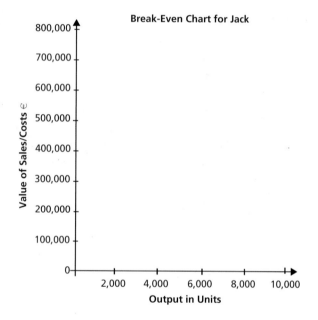

Step 2: Draw the Fixed Costs line (FC)

This is a horizontal line drawn parallel to the x-axis. Locate the fixed costs value on the y-axis, in this case €200,000, and draw a horizontal line straight across the chart. Label this line FC (Fixed Costs).

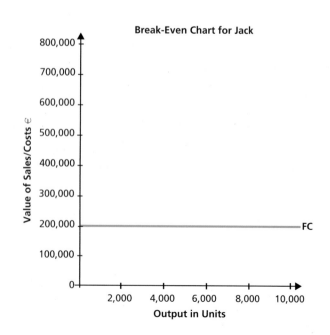

Step 3: Plot and Label the Total Revenue line (TR)

There are two points required in order to plot the Total Revenue line. Begin by plotting the Total Revenue line at zero, because if the business does not sell any coffee machines, the sales revenue will be zero. The second point is located at the intercept of €800,000 on the y-axis and 10,000 units on the x-axis, as shown in the diagram. This shows that the total revenue earned by Jack at forecast output (10,000 units). Draw a line between these two points to complete the Total Revenue line. Label this line TR (Total Revenue).

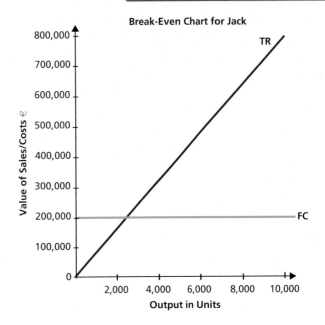

Step 4: Plot and Label the Total Costs line (TC)

Plot the Total Costs line by beginning at the same point on the y-axis where you started your Fixed Costs Line. In this case the line will begin at €200,000. The second point on the Total Costs line is located at the intercept between €750,000 on the y-axis and 10,000 units on the x-axis, as shown in the diagram. The second point shows that if Jack sells at forecast output (10,000 units), he will have costs of €750,000. Draw a line between these two points in order to complete the Total Costs line. Label this line TC (Total Costs).

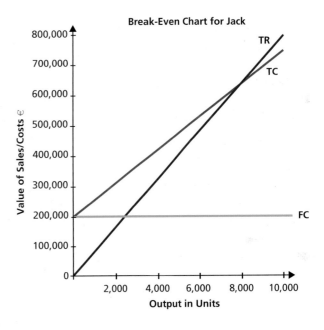

Step 5: Label the Break-even Point (BEP)

The point where the Total Revenue and Total Costs lines intersect is the break-even point. Label this point BEP. Draw a dashed line from this point straight down to the x-axis. The reading on the x-axis confirms the break-even point of 8,000 units. If you follow the break-even point horizontally across to the y-axis, it indicates that Jack's revenue at the break-even point is €640,000.

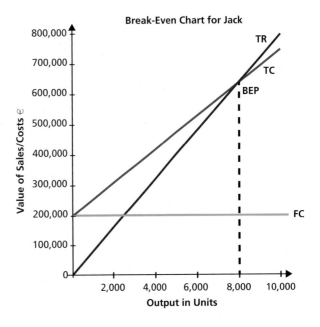

Unit 5

Step 6: Label the Profit at Forecast Output

Draw a double-headed arrow between the Total Revenue and Total Costs lines, as shown on the chart. Label the arrow Profit. This indicates the profit that will be made by Jack if he sells 10,000 units, i.e. €50,000.

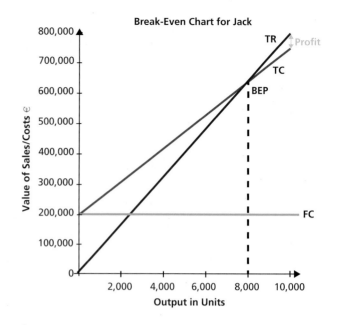

Break-Even Chart for Jack

Step 7: Label the Margin of Safety (MoS)

Draw a vertical line down from the highest point of the Total Revenue line (€800,000) to the forecast output on the x-axis. In this case the figure will be 10,000 units. The distance on the x-axis between the break-even point and forecast output should be indicated using a double-headed arrow and labelled MoS (Margin of Safety).

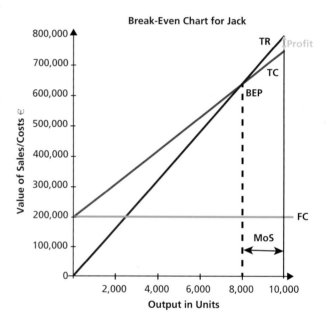

Break-Even Chart for Jack

Limitations of Break-Even Analysis

Break-even analysis is not, however, an accurate measure. It has limitations, which include:

- **Sales:** It assumes that all products manufactured will be sold. In times of low demand a firm may have difficulty selling all its products.
- **Selling price:** It assumes that selling price per unit remains the same for all items sold. It does not take into account times when the business may sell the items at a lower price, e.g. discounts for bulk buying or end-of year sales.
- **Faulty products:** It assumes that there is always 100% quality 100% of the time.
- **Classification of costs:** It assumes that the business knows all its costs and can categorise them into fixed and variable costs.
- **Changes in selling price:** It does not take into account the effect a change in price may have on sales – a price increase usually leads to a fall in demand for the product and vice versa.

Unit 5

KEY TERMS

Now you have completed this chapter, you should understand and be able to explain the following terms. In your copybook, write a definition of each term to build up your own glossary of terms.

- internal sources of business ideas
- brainstorming
- research and development (R&D)
- external sources of business ideas
- networking
- import substitution
- market research
- primary (field) research

- observation
- consumer panels
- survey
- mystery shopper
- secondary (desk) research
- commercial research agencies
- development process of a new product
- idea generation
- product screening

- concept development
- feasibility study
- prototype development
- test marketing
- product launch
- unique selling point (USP)
- break-even chart
- break-even point
- fixed costs
- variable costs
- margin of safety

PowerPoint Summary

EXAM-STYLE QUESTIONS

Ordinary Level

Section 1 – Short Questions (10 marks each)

1 Name **five** internal sources of ideas for businesses.
2 List **three** external sources of ideas for businesses. Describe **one** of these sources.
3 What is meant by the term *market research*? Outline **one** reason why a business might carry out market research.
4 Explain the **two** types of market research, giving an example of each.
5 List in the correct order the stages involved in the development of a new product.
6 What is a feasibility study?
7 Explain the terms (i) *break-even point* and (ii) *margin of safety*.
8 Sketch a labelled break-even chart showing clearly (i) the fixed cost line, (ii) the total cost line, (iii) the sales revenue line and (iv) the break-even point.
9 Circle the correct option in each of the following sentences.
  (i) An employee who comes up with suggestions for new business ideas is an **entrepreneur/ intrapreneur**.
  (ii) When a business conducts its own market research this is called **primary/secondary** research.
  (iii) Observation is an **internal/external** form of market research.
  (iv) A product's **USC/USP** is what will make the product stand out against its competitors.
  (v) The selling price of a product less variable costs is equal to **contribution/compensation** per unit.
10 Indicate whether the following statements refer to field or desk research.

	Statements	Field/Desk
A	A cinema conducts an online survey, e.g. using SurveyMonkey.	
B	The managing director of a company downloads a competitor's annual report.	
C	Supermarket customers are observed as they shop in the store.	
D	A business uses www.cso.ie to find out how many teenagers live in Ireland.	
E	A group of consumers are asked to test a product and give feedback on it.	

Section 2 – Long Questions

1 Brainstorming is one of the methods used to generate ideas for a business. Describe **three** other methods that can be used by entrepreneurs or existing firms to develop business ideas. **(15 marks)**

2 What is meant by the term *desk research*? Explain clearly **one** method a business could use to carry out desk research. **(15 marks)**

3 Describe the benefits of a firm carrying out market research. **(20 marks)**

4 Distinguish between (i) prototype development, (ii) test marketing and (iii) product launch, as part of the development process of a new product. **(20 marks)**

5 Outline the **five** stages in the development of a new product, using a product of your choice. **(30 marks)**

6 Distinguish between the terms *break-even point* and *margin of safety*. **(15 marks)**

7 Distinguish between (i) fixed costs and (ii) variable costs. Draw a graph to represent both of these costs. **(15 marks)**

8 Give **two** benefits to a business of carrying out a break-even analysis. At what stage of the development process will it take place? **(15 marks)**

Higher Level

Section 1 – Short Questions (10 marks each)

1 What is meant by the term *import substitution*? Name **one** product not currently made in Ireland which is imported.

2 Explain the terms (i) *desk research* and (ii) *field research*. Give **one** example of each.

3 Describe one advantage and disadvantage of a firm undertaking field research.

4 *Product screening* and *concept development* are important stages in the development of a new product. Explain these terms.

5 Column 1 is a list of terms relating to formulating business ideas. Column 2 is a list of possible explanations for these terms. Match the two lists in your copybook by writing your answers in the form *number = letter* (e.g. 1 = A).

Terms		Explanations	
1	Eureka moment	A	People meet formally or informally to build up relationships and to create business ideas and share information.
2	Brainstorming	B	Groups of people (consumers) meet to discuss a business or its products.
3	Networking	C	When a thought or event unexpectedly becomes an idea for a product or service.
4	Consumer panel	D	This is when the idea becomes an actual product or service.
5	Concept development	E	People from different areas of the business come together to creatively think of as many ideas as possible.

6 Calculate the break-even point for a business where the selling price per unit is expected to be €20, variable costs per unit are €12, and estimated fixed costs are €64,000. If the costs increased to €72,000 how many extra units would have to be sold to break even?

7 Indicate whether each of these statements is true or false.

Statements		True or False
A	R&D stands for research and deployment.	
B	The first stage in product development is product screening.	
C	A feasibility study is carried out to see if a product idea is commercially viable.	
D	Test market is when the new product/service is launched onto the entire market.	
E	At break-even point a business is not making a profit or a loss.	

Section 2 – Applied Business Question (80 marks)

Kilmore Crisps

Deborah Murphy is the managing director of Kilmore Crisps, a crisp manufacturer based in County Kilkenny. At a recent meeting, the marketing manager, Billy Jones, informed her that sales are in decline. Billy has already conducted some online research and discovered that their nearest competitor, Barron's Bites, has launched a range of vegan crisps. Deborah is worried about the impact this new launch will have on the firm's market share and asks Billy to prepare a report to outline ways that they can find out what products consumers want from the firm.

Billy organises for a group of customers to visit the firm and take part in a discussion about the brand and its products. One of the customers suggests that Kilmore Crisps needs to develop some new flavours. Billy asks the customers to log on to www.surveymonkey.com to complete a written questionnaire that he will prepare on future products for the firm.

Deborah holds a meeting with the R&D department to discuss possible new products. Billy presents the results of his research and the team work together to decide which ideas have the potential to be turned into actual products. The R&D team believes that a range of crisps based on traditional Irish food would give their range a USP. The R&D leader explains that they already have the equipment to produce the new flavours. Deborah likes the idea but is worried about the cost of such a venture.

She asks her finance manager to investigate the cost of developing the project. Deborah plans to sell the crisps in boxes of 30 bags and she wants to find out information such as the break-even point and margin of safety. The finance manager produces the following figures:

Forecast Output (Sales)	60,000 units
Selling Price per unit	€30
Fixed Costs	€400,000
Variable Costs per unit	€20

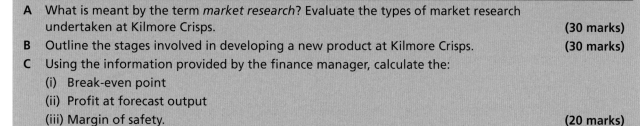

The R&D department made a number of sample flavours: Irish Stew, Dublin Coddle and the Full Irish. A panel of consumers tasted the range and the feedback indicated that Dublin Coddle was the least favourite as it was too salty. The R&D department made the necessary changes and the range of three flavours was launched in a small number of stores close to the factory. The range of crisps was launched nationwide and the firm used social media platforms such as Instagram and Snapchat to promote the products.

A What is meant by the term *market research*? Evaluate the types of market research undertaken at Kilmore Crisps. **(30 marks)**

B Outline the stages involved in developing a new product at Kilmore Crisps. **(30 marks)**

C Using the information provided by the finance manager, calculate the:
  (i) Break-even point
  (ii) Profit at forecast output
  (iii) Margin of safety. **(20 marks)**

Section 3 – Long Questions

1 Businesses can get ideas for new products from a range of sources. Describe **four** external sources of new product ideas. **(20 marks)**

2 Define *market research*. Explain **three** reasons why a business would undertake market research. **(20 marks)**

3 Analyse **two** market research techniques for a product or service of your choice. **(20 marks)**

4 Describe the steps involved in conducting market research. **(25 marks)**

5 Outline the stages in the development process of a new product. **(20 marks)**

6 Evaluate concept development and test marketing in the development process of a product of your choice. **(15 marks)**

Section 3 – Long Questions *continued*

7 Cassidy Ltd manufactures and sells a range of clothes. The business is considering the introduction of a new line of school uniforms. The following figures are available:

Fixed costs	€300,000
Cost per unit	€7.50
Selling price	€22.50
Forecast output	45,000 units

(i) Illustrate by means of a break-even chart the:
    (a) Break-even point
    (b) Profit at forecast capacity
    (c) Margin of safety.
(ii) Explain the term *margin of safety*.   **(30 marks)**

8 A break-even chart provides management with a range of financial information relating to <u>fixed costs</u>, <u>variable costs</u> and <u>break-even point</u>. Explain each of the underlined terms.   **(15 marks)**

PREVIOUS LEAVING CERTIFICATE EXAM QUESTIONS

Ordinary Level

Section A – Short Questions (10 marks each)

1 List **three** sources of new business ideas for an entrepreneur.   **[LC OL 2009]**

2 Explain the following stages in the development of a new product or service.
  (i) Feasibility Study and (ii) Prototype Development.   **[LC OL 2014]**

3 State whether the following market research techniques are desk or field research.
  (i) Questionnaire, (ii) Central Statistics Office statistics, (iii) Government Publications, (iv) Focus groups and (v) Observation.   **[LC OL 2013]**

Section B

1

Theo's Mexican

Theo had many years of experience working as a chef in Mexican food restaurants. He noticed how popular food trailers had become when attending various music festivals. Theo conducted market research and decided to open his own food trailer selling authentic Mexican food. He purchased a jeep and a food trailer. The brand name, Theo's Mexican Street Food, now has an excellent reputation for high-quality affordable food. Theo communicates his sales promotions through social media such as Facebook and Twitter.

(i) Explain **three** sources of new product/service ideas for a business.   **(15 marks)**
(ii) Outline **two** reasons why a business would carry out market research.   **(15 marks) [LC OL 2016]**

2 Outline **two** benefits of carrying out market research.   **(15 marks) [LC OL 2015]**

3

West Coast Surf

In 2013, Jordan Casey was made redundant from his job at a factory in Sligo town. He received a redundancy package and decided he would like to set up his own business in the seaside town of Castlemore. Jordan has enjoyed surfing as a hobby since he was in school. He realised that surfing was becoming a very popular sport and spotted a gap in the market to provide surfing lessons at his local beach. He carried out a SWOT analysis of the potential business idea. Jordan was aware of his limitations. He approached the Local Enterprise Office, who provided a mentoring service to him.

Jordan turned his hobby into a business opportunity. Outline **two** other sources of new business ideas.   **(15 marks) [LC OL 2014]**

Higher Level

Section A – Short Questions (10 marks each)

1 In break-even analysis a distinction is made between *fixed costs* and *variable costs*. Explain these terms, and give **one** example in each case. **[LC HL 2013]**

2 Column 1 is a list of business terms. Column 2 is a list of possible explanations for these business terms. (One explanation does not refer to any of the business terms.) Match the two lists by writing your answers in the form *number = letter* (e.g. 1 = A).

Business Terms		Explanations	
1	Idea Generation	**A**	It involves developing a sample or mock-up of a product.
2	Concept Development	**B**	Brainstorming is one of the methods used.
3	Product Launch	**C**	Is carried out to assess if a product has a profit potential.
4	Prototype Development	**D**	The product is made available to the market.
5	Feasibility Study	**E**	Unworkable ideas are dropped.
		F	A unique selling point (USP) is identified.

[LC HL 2014]

3 Distinguish between prototype development and test marketing as stages in the development process of a new product. **[LC HL 2010]**

Section B

1
> Google's '20 Percent Time' strategy gives engineers time and space to work on their own projects.

Outline the internal and external sources of new product ideas for technology companies like Google. **(20 marks) [LC HL 2013]**

2 Feasibility Study, Test Marketing, Product Screening and Prototype Development are stages in the New Product Development Process.
(i) List the **four** stages above in the **correct order**.
(ii) Outline your understanding of any **three** of these stages. **(20 marks) [LC HL 2015]**

3
> Medron plc manufactures medical devices and its R&D department is currently working on a prototype for a tube to be used in vascular surgery.

(A) Outline the reasons why businesses engage in prototype development. **(15 marks)**

(B) Read the information supplied and answer the questions which follow.
Medron plc has supplied the following financial information for the new medical device:

Forecast Output (Sales)	60,000 units
Selling Price per unit	€30
Fixed Costs	€400,000
Variable Costs per unit	€20

Illustrate the following by means of a break-even chart:
(i) Break-even point
(ii) Margin of safety at the forecast output
(iii) Profit at forecast output. **(25 marks)**

(C) Following a review of costs, Medron plc decreased its variable costs per unit to €10.
(i) Calculate the new break-even point and illustrate on your break-even chart the new total cost line (TC2) and the new break-even point (BE2).
(ii) Outline **one** limitation of a break-even analysis when making business decisions. **(20 marks) [LC HL 2016]**

 Solutions

Unit 5

CHAPTER 20 MARKETING

⊕ Learning Outcomes

When you have completed this chapter, you will be able to:

1. Explain the term *marketing*
2. Identify the main elements of a marketing strategy
3. Outline the methods and benefits of market segmentation
4. Explain the term *target market*
5. Describe niche marketing
6. Explain and evaluate the elements of the marketing mix – product, price, place and promotion.

Literacy Link

Marketing, marketing mix, market segmentation, target market, niche market, product positioning, trademark, patent, channel of distribution, merchandising

Numeracy Link

Multiplication, division, addition, percentages

Cross-curricular Link

Art – design
Economics – price
English – communication
Geography – locations
Home Economics – marketing, advertising

CASE STUDY

Marketing at Rolex

Hans Wilsdorf created a new brand of wristwatch in London in 1905. He chose the **brand name** Rolex, as he wanted a name that was easy for consumers to pronounce. The **brand logo** consists of a small crown and the **slogan** 'A crown for every achievement'.

As many wristwatches at this time did not keep time accurately, Wilsdorf invested heavily in **product design** to develop accurate and precise timepieces. This precision has remained the **unique selling point (USP)** of Rolex watches.

Rolex's **target market** appreciate the quality and craftsmanship of the watches. This has enabled the firm to use a **premium pricing strategy**. Today, the entry level price for Rolex watches is almost €4,500.

Rolex has always understood the importance of **promotion** as part of the **marketing mix**. Over the years it has used **newspaper advertising** to announce new product developments, such as the first waterproof watch. It uses **public relations** to **sponsor** prestige events including the Masters

Tournament in golf and the Australian Open in tennis.

Rolex uses celebrity **endorsements** to promote the brand. Elite athletes are paid to act as brand ambassadors and their photos are used in **advertisements** and **merchandising** displays. Brand partners include tennis champion Roger Federer and golfer Jordan Spieth.

To maintain the **product positioning** of exclusivity and luxury, Rolex watches can be purchased only from official Rolex retailers. The **channel of distribution** used by Rolex involves the firm selling directly to consumers in its own stores or through **retailers** around the world. **Direct selling** is used by staff who provide high-quality customer service and have the expertise and skills to help consumers choose a Rolex watch that meets their needs.

The strong marketing mix of **product, price, place** and **promotion** has helped the company to achieve estimated sales of over €3.8 billion.

INTRODUCTION TO MARKETING

In the past, businesses used a marketing and selling approach that focused on providing the largest possible quantity of products to consumers in order to maximise business profits. They did not consult consumers about what goods and services they would like to buy and instead chose a marketing and selling concept based on the principle 'If we make it they will buy'.

Today, with increased competition in the market and more demanding consumers, businesses must use a more consumer-focused marketing concept.

Marketing Concept

The business focuses on understanding the needs and wants of consumers in the market. This allows the firm to provide the goods and services demanded by consumers more effectively and efficiently than its competitors.

The marketing concept is achieved through the marketing process.

> **Definition: Marketing concept**
> The marketing concept ensures that the business always focuses on the needs of consumers first, before it develops a good or service.

Marketing

Marketing is the business processes that are used to understand, anticipate and satisfy consumer needs and wants both now and in the future. Marketing requires the business to:

1 Conduct market research
2 Develop a marketing strategy and marketing plan
3 Formulate the marketing mix.

> *You learned about market research in Chapter 19.*

MARKETING STRATEGY AND MARKETING PLAN

It is important that the business develops a marketing strategy and marketing plan to raise consumer awareness of its goods and services and persuade consumers to buy them.

Marketing Strategy

The marketing strategy examines the overall business objectives and develops marketing activities to help the business to achieve these goals. The marketing strategy can include: deciding the market within which the business should compete; and identifying the target market.

Once the business has developed a marketing strategy it should formulate a marketing plan. The strategy is '*what* needs to be done'; the plan is '*how* it will be done'.

Marketing Plan

The marketing plan is used to implement the firm's marketing strategy. For example, a firm's marketing strategy could include launching a product into a new market segment. The marketing plan would include the development of an advertising campaign to raise consumer awareness of the product.

To create an effective marketing plan, the business should undertake the following:

Conduct a SWOT Analysis	→ Identify its internal strengths and weaknesses and examine its external threats and opportunities. This gives the business a detailed overview of its current situation.
Market Segmentation	→ Decide on a market at which it will target its product.
Research the Target Market	→ Find out the needs and wants of consumers in this market.
Develop a Marketing Mix	→ Based on the analysis of the target market, the business can develop the marketing mix. This will ensure that it uses the most appropriate product, price, place and promotion to persuade consumers to buy the product.

Target market

Role of the Marketing Plan in a Business

1 Business Goals
The marketing plan helps the business to focus on achieving its goals. This can mean that the business achieves these goals more effectively and efficiently.

2 Finance
The marketing plan shows potential investors that the business has conducted an in-depth analysis of the market. This can persuade investors to provide finance for business start-up or expansion.

3 Benchmarking
The business can use the marketing plan to benchmark planned performance against actual results. If results are below those expected, e.g. sales in a new market are lower than expected, the firm can take corrective action, e.g. increase advertising or sales promotion.

> **Definition: Benchmarking**
> Setting a standard and comparing performance against this standard.

MARKET SEGMENTATION

It is unlikely that the same product will satisfy the needs of all consumers in a market. Therefore, a business may decide to aim the product at a specific group of consumers. In order to identify the target market, the business will need to first undertake market segmentation.

There are a number of ways to segment the market, including:

1 **Geographic:** The market is divided into different geographic zones or areas, e.g. region, country or county.

2 **Demographic:** The market is divided into segments based on certain common characteristics such as age, gender, income and occupation.

> **Definition: Market segmentation**
> The market is divided into different sections (segments). The most common forms of segmentation are **geographic**, **demographic** and **psychographic**. Market segmentation enables the firm to target its products and services more effectively at the relevant consumers.

> **Example**
> In Ireland there are many regional newspapers, which cater for the needs of people living in a particular area, e.g. *Longford Leader*, *Sligo Champion*.

> **Example**
> Cadbury Dairy Milk Buttons are aimed at children. The target market for Cadbury's Wispa bar is adults.

3 **Psychographic:** The market is divided into segments based on beliefs, attitudes, social status and lifestyles. For example, a consumer who is concerned about the environment might purchase only brands that use recyclable materials.

> **Example**
> The 'one for one' strategy used at TOMS shoes attracts consumers who want their purchase to make a difference to the lives of others. For every pair of shoes a consumer buys, TOMS donates a pair of shoes to people in developing countries.

Benefits of Market Segmentation

Increased Sales	→ It provides a product that meets the needs of the target market. This can increase consumer loyalty and boost a firm's sales and profits.
Market Share	→ Established brands can make it difficult for a new firm to enter the market. Market segmentation enables the firm to focus on a small section of the market and allows the business to grow over time.
Lower Costs	→ The business does not waste time and money trying to sell to different target markets. Instead it focuses its marketing message on a smaller market but can do so more frequently. This helps to reduce the firm's marketing costs.

Unit 5

CASE STUDY: Market Segmentation at L'Oréal

L'Oréal is an international cosmetics **brand** with a large **product portfolio** including brands such as Maybelline and Lancôme. The company sells its products in over 140 countries on all continents.

Senior marketing managers at the firm use **market segmentation** to divide up the skincare, haircare and cosmetics markets. The firm can then sell specific brands into each of these markets. For example:

- YSL and Giorgio Armani – targeted at consumers with higher disposable income who are attracted to luxury products
- Garnier and Maybelline – targeted at consumers who want functional products but are unable or unwilling to pay high prices
- Redken and Kerastase – targeted at professional hair salons
- Urban Decay – targeted at young, adventurous consumers.

Activity 20.1

As a class, choose a market, e.g. clothing, footwear or toiletries. Working in pairs, segment the market and compare your answers with other pairs of students. Did you all identify the same markets? Is it possible to segment the market even further?

TARGET MARKET

Definition: Target market

A target market is the specific group of consumers who have common needs and wants. The business aims its products and services at this market.

Once the business has segmented the market, it can identify the target market for its products. For example, the target market for:

- The Mini Cooper is young drivers
- Brown Thomas department store is high income earners
- The *Irish Farmers Journal* is farmers and people working in farming-related industries.

Activity 20.2

Working in pairs, identify the target market for the following:
- Dr Oetker frozen pizzas
- Penneys clothes
- Magnum ice cream
- Lexus cars
- Nike trainers
- Lego sets
- Coca-Cola Zero Sugar
- Nestlé Milkybar

Niche Market

The needs of most consumers in a market are met by the goods or services provided by businesses. A **niche market** is **a small group of consumers in a larger market who have different needs from the majority of consumers**. They are willing to pay a higher price for goods and services to meet their needs.

Example
- Consumers who purchase the Hermès Birkin bag are a niche market. The bag is made in limited quantities and has a starting price of over €6,000. These consumers are willing to pay very high prices for what they consider to be exclusivity, luxury and quality materials.
- Consumers who buy organic food are concerned about the impact of chemicals and pesticides on the environment and on their health. They are willing to pay a higher price for a product that they believe is healthier than non-organic products.

NICHE MARKET

✓ Advantages	X Disadvantages
1 Less Competition There is less competition in a niche market, as other businesses focus on the larger general target market. This can help the business to increase market share.	**1 Economies of Scale** The business might not benefit from economies of scale as it produces goods in smaller quantities. For example, it might not receive discounts from suppliers as it does not buy raw materials in large enough quantities.
2 Consumer Loyalty Consumers are loyal to the goods and services that satisfy their specific needs in a niche market. This can help to increase business sales and profits.	**2 Competition** Larger competitors enter the market and the smaller business may be unable to compete on price. It may lose market share to the larger firm.
3 New Products A business selling in a niche market may be able to launch new products into the market more easily. Consumers trust the brand and are willing to try new products from the firm.	**3 Growth** As niche markets tend to be small, the business may find it difficult to grow. Profit margins are also lower in smaller markets.

Activity 20.3

Identify a niche market in the following markets: (i) ice cream; (ii) cleaning products; and (iii) coffee.

PRODUCT POSITIONING

Once the business has segmented the market and identified the target market it must then consider product positioning.

Definition: Product positioning
Creating a positive image for the product that stays in consumers' minds. The image could emphasise the fact that the product saves the consumer money, makes their life easier or makes them more fashionable.

Example
- Products that **save consumers money**: Fairy washing-up liquid lasts 50% longer than other brands.
- Products that **make life easier**: the Dyson hairdryer dries hair eight times faster than other hairdryers on the market.
- Products that are **fashionable**: fashion brand Supreme is highly sought after as it limits the quantity of clothing it produces.

MARKETING MIX

The marketing mix is the toolkit used by the business to persuade consumers to buy its products.
The marketing mix is often referred to as the **4 Ps of marketing**. It consists of:

1 Product   2 Price
3 Place   4 Promotion

1 Marketing Mix – Product

This is a good or service provided by a business to satisfy consumer needs and wants. All products should have a USP: a unique selling point that makes the product stand out from its competitors.

Some businesses sell only one product to consumers, e.g. Michelin sells tyres; other businesses sell a range of products, known as a product portfolio, e.g. Coca-Cola sells water and fizzy drinks.

Definition: Product
A good or a service.

Definition: Product portfolio
The range of products sold by a business.

Activity 20.4

1 Identify the companies that own the brands featured in the images below.
2 For one company, carry out further research online and list three other products in its product portfolio.

The product element of the marketing mix contains a number of distinct areas, which include:

A Product design
B Brand name
C Packaging
D Product life cycle.

A Product Design

When designing a product, a business should carefully consider the:

1 **Function**
2 **Materials**
3 **Manufacturing**
4 **Appearance**
5 **Cost**

1 **Function:** The product should do what consumers expect it to do and comply with all relevant safety standards, e.g. Sale of Goods and Supply of Services Act 1980.

2 **Materials:** The business identifies what materials are needed and where they will be sourced. It should ensure that materials are ethically sourced and limit environmental damage.

3 **Manufacturing:** The business should find out if the product can be made and where it can be manufactured.

4 **Appearance:** The product should be attractive to consumers in terms of shape, colour and image.

5 **Cost:** The business should take into account the cost of manufacturing and distributing the product. It must be able to charge a price to cover these costs and make a profit.

Example
A consumer should be able to make phone calls and use the Internet on a smartphone.

Unit 5

Impact of Good Product Design

- **Increased sales:** Well-designed products are visually appealing and easy for consumers to use. Good design gives the product a competitive advantage over competitors and helps to increase sales.
- **Lower costs:** There is less wastage of raw materials when products are well designed. There are also fewer consumer complaints about faulty or underperforming products. The business saves money on product recalls and repairing products.

Activity 20.5

Working in pairs, identify **five** well-designed products. Give reasons for your choice and compare products with other students in your class.

Legal Protection for Product Design

If the product is a brand new invention, the business will want to prevent competitors from copying their idea. The business may register a patent.

 For 25 consecutive years, IBM has registered more patents than any other company in the world. Irish employees of IBM register approximately one patent per week.

Definition: Patent
This gives exclusive legal ownership rights to the inventor of a product or process. No other business or individual can use this invention without the agreement of the patent owner. In Ireland, most patents last for 20 years.

Activity 20.6

Working in groups, visit the US Patent and Trademark Office website at www.uspto.gov. Identify **five** inventions and the year in which they received a patent.

B Brand Name

In order to increase consumer recognition of a firm's name and its products, many businesses use branding.

To enhance the brand name, many firms also develop a **brand logo**: images, words or shapes used to identify a brand and its goods and services. Logos help a firm stand out from its competitors and increase consumer awareness of a firm's products.

Definition: Brand name
A distinctive name given to a business and the goods and services it develops. A brand name is usually registered (in Ireland with the Irish Patents Office) and cannot be used by others, e.g. Cadbury and Nestlé.

 The designer of the Nike logo took her inspiration from the wings of the Greek goddess Nike to develop the now famous Swoosh logo. She was paid $35 for her work.

Firms may also develop a **brand slogan**, a catchy, memorable phrase. Examples include:

- 'Have a break – have a KitKat' – Nestlé KitKat
- 'Eat fresh' – Subway
- 'Impossible is nothing' – Adidas.

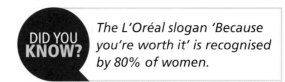

DID YOU KNOW? *The L'Oréal slogan 'Because you're worth it' is recognised by 80% of women.*

CASE STUDY — *Brand Slogan: KFC*

Fast food company KFC used the slogan 'Finger-lickin' good' for over 60 years. However, senior management decided to change the slogan because of a move by consumers to healthier food.

The company revealed the new slogan 'So good' and at the same time announced healthier options changes to their menu.

Businesses can spend a lot of time and resources developing a brand name, logo and slogan. To legally protect these, a business can register a trademark.

Trademark

A business can register words, logos, letters and numbers that distinguish its identity and products from those of its competitors.

Registering a trademark with the Irish Patents Office prevents other businesses or individuals using it without the firm's permission. Examples of trademarks include Tayto and Aer Lingus.

BRAND NAME

✓ Advantages for Business	✓ Advantages for Consumers
1 Recognition A brand name makes a product recognisable and consumers can distinguish the product from those of competitors, e.g. Volkswagen, Ford and so on.	**1 Consumer Image** Consumers may purchase certain brands to enhance their self-image, e.g. people who are perceived to be successful drive BMW cars.
2 New Products Consumers are more likely to try new products from a recognised brand. This can help a business build market share quickly, e.g. Cadbury.	**2 Benefits of the Product** Brands can communicate the benefits that the product will bring to the consumer when used, e.g. Wash and Go shampoo.
3 Higher Price Consumers associate brand names with higher quality. This enables firms to charge a higher price for branded products, e.g. Nespresso, Lindt, Puma and Chanel.	**3 Reduces Disappointment** Consumers buy familiar brands as they believe that they will not be disappointed with the product purchased. For example, people on holiday often purchase meals from well-known outlets such as Subway rather than unfamiliar local outlets.
4 Consumer Loyalty Consumers can become loyal to a particular brand. Even if the price increases, these consumers remain loyal to the brand, e.g. Kellogg's.	**4 High-quality Products** Consumers benefit from high-quality products, as branded businesses tend to invest heavily in R&D, e.g. Dyson.

Unit 5

Activity 20.7

Working in pairs, choose a well-known brand name. Create a mini-presentation about this brand, including images of the brand logo and product. Describe the advantages and disadvantages branding has had for this product. Present your findings to the class.

Own-Brand Products

These are products that are sold by retailers under the retailer's name and logo. They are often referred to as 'private labels'. Supermarkets such as Tesco and SuperValu have their own branded products, e.g. Tesco Value and Tesco Finest and SuperValu's Daily Basics and Signature Tastes ranges.

CASE STUDY *Killowen Farm*

Killowen Farm in Co. Wexford has created **own-brand** yoghurts for Aldi since 2011. The firm uses milk from its 120-strong herd of cows to create the Specially Selected range of yoghurts. The Specially Selected range has won a number of awards over the years at Blas na hÉireann and the Great Taste awards.

OWN-BRAND PRODUCTS

✓ Advantages for Retailers	✗ Disadvantages for Retailers
1 Product Specification The retailer can instruct the manufacturer to make the product to particular specifications, e.g. shape, colour and content.	**1 Increased Advertising** Consumers may perceive own-brand products to be of lower quality than branded items. The retailer may have to invest in advertising to change consumer perception of the brand.
2 Profits Retailers can sell own-brand products at lower prices than branded items. This can increase the retailers' sales and profits.	**2 Business Reputation** The retailer is dependent on the quality produced by the manufacturer. If it produces low-quality products, this can damage the retailer's reputation.
3 Consumer Loyalty The retailer can sell a wide range of products under the own-brand label. This can increase consumer awareness of the brand and lead to increased consumer loyalty.	**3 Cost** The retailer spends time and money developing the product, packaging and image for own-brand products. This can be expensive if the product is unsuccessful.
4 Different Target Markets Retailers can develop own-brand products to appeal to different target markets and charge different prices. For example, Tesco has created the Tesco Value, Standard and Finest ranges.	**4 Economic Conditions** A rise in employment levels can increase sales of branded goods and reduce the demand for own-brand products.

Activity 20.8

In pairs, use a graphic organiser of your choice to summarise the features of branded and own-brand products. Swap your summary with another pair of students and fill in any missing information in the graphic organiser that you have received.

C Packaging

Product packaging is often the consumer's first interaction with a product. It is important that it not only looks attractive but also performs the following functions:

- **Product protection:** The packaging should protect the product from damage when it is transported from the producer to the consumer. Materials used to protect the product include glass, plastic and cardboard.
- **Image:** The colour, shape and text used on the packaging can portray a particular image for a product. This can persuade consumers to buy the product.
- **Convenience:** Product packaging should be designed in a way that is convenient for consumers to use. For example, consumers can buy Maltesers mini bags for children, large pouches for sharing and gift boxes for occasions such as birthdays.
- **Information:** Packaging provides useful information, such as nutritional content and instructions for storage and use.
- **Recognition:** Attractive packaging that is well designed increases consumer recognition of the product. Even when a product is near competitor products, the consumer is able to identify and choose the product, which helps to increase sales.

Example
Consumers instantly recognise the triangular peaks of Toblerone chocolate or the distinctive orange foil packaging of a Terry's Chocolate Orange.

Activity 20.9

Using your smartphone or other device, take photos of innovative product packaging you see in shops. Share your photos with your classmates. As a class, discuss the features that make the product packaging distinctive. What advantages do you think attractive packaging has for consumers?

D Product Life Cycle

The product life cycle describes the stages that a product goes through from introduction to decline. It charts the five common stages: introduction, growth, maturity, saturation and decline.

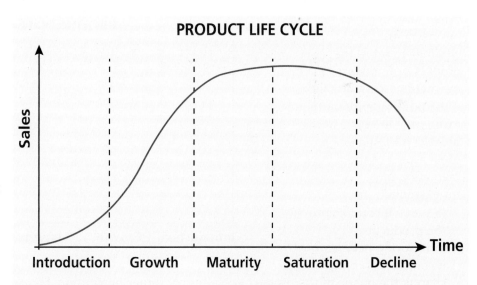

PRODUCT LIFE CYCLE

1 Introduction

Sales are low as the product is launched on the market. The firm invests in promotion to increase consumer awareness of the product. The business may have a negative cash flow and does not usually make a profit at this stage.

Example: driverless cars, robots in the home.

2 Growth

Sales increase and the business invests in production to keep up with consumer demand. Production costs begin to fall as the business begins to benefit from economies of scale. The business may not have enough cash to pay all its expenses.

Example: voice-command devices, e.g. Apple HomePod, augmented reality headsets.

Unit 5

3 Maturity

Sales and profits reach their peak and the business will have a positive cash flow. Competitors enter the market and the business may need to increase advertising or use special offers to attract consumers.

Example: activity trackers, smartphones.

4 Saturation

Sales and cash flow begin to slow down as consumers have purchased the product from the business or competitors. Costs increase as the business spends money on advertising and promotion to maintain market share. The firm may need to reduce the price of the product to encourage consumers to buy.

Example: breakfast cereals, chocolate bars.

5 Decline

Sales and profits decline and the business must decide whether it will continue to sell the product or retire it. The business has negative cash flow as expenditure is greater than sales revenue.

Example: iPods, CDs.

DID YOU KNOW? *Volkswagen has decided to retire its iconic Beetle car after nearly 80 years in production.*

Note!

Some products reach the decline stage of the product life cycle faster than others, e.g. fidget spinners had a short life cycle whereas the life cycle for Cadbury Dairy Milk has continued since 1905.

Note!

Ideally, a firm should have a product at each stage of the product life cycle, so that when one product is in decline, other products continue to generate revenue.

Extending the Product Life Cycle

When sales begin to fall, the business must decide whether to retire the product or find ways to maintain or increase sales.

If the business chooses to extend the life cycle of the product it must change some aspect of the marketing mix, for example:

1 **Product:** It could improve the product by introducing new features. It could also rebrand to change the image of the product and alter consumer perception. For example, TV station TV3 rebranded to Virgin Media Television.

PRODUCT LIFE CYCLE

PRODUCT EXTENSION

Sales — Time

Introduction | Growth | Maturity | Saturation | Decline

Definition: **Rebranding**
A marketing strategy to change the name, logo, image or products of a firm. It can occur as a result of changes in the target market or advances in technology.

---

2 **Price:** A change in pricing strategy can reach a new target market, e.g. the firm could reduce prices to attract new consumers.

3 **Place:** The business could change where the product is sold in order to reach a larger target market, e.g. in foreign markets or online through the firm's website.

4 **Promotion:** A new advertising campaign could be used, e.g. on Instagram and Facebook. The firm could also introduce new sales promotion techniques to increase consumer demand, e.g. vouchers or loyalty points.

Unit 5

CASE STUDY — *Extending the Product Life Cycle at Eir*

Senior management at telecommunications firm Eircom decided to rebrand the company and call it Eir. The rebranding involved:

- 1,500 new uniforms for technicians
- 1,500 vans being rebranded
- 116 stores receiving a refit
- 2,000 web pages being redesigned
- €5 million spent on advertising, with 6,500 TV and 4,500 radio advertisements

2 Marketing Mix – Price

Price relates to the amount of money consumers pay for the product offered by a business. The business must ensure that it charges a price that will earn the firm a profit.

Price Strategies

The business must be aware that the price charged can influence sales and consumer perception of the product. There are a number of pricing strategies that a business can use when setting the prices for its goods and services.

Low Price Strategies

1 **Penetration pricing:** The business sets a price lower than that of its competitors' products in order to gain a greater share of the market quickly. Over time the business may increase prices when it gains a stronger market position.

2 **Predatory pricing:** A business sets a price lower than that of its competitors' products to push them out of the market. Some firms may enter into a price war, in which each firm reacts to price cuts by reducing its own prices.

Example
When Sky broadband launched in Ireland, the firm offered introductory low prices to new consumers in order to gain market share.

Example
Airlines such as Ryanair and Aer Lingus engage in predatory pricing, with both businesses reducing prices on popular routes.

3 **Loss leader (below-cost selling):** The business sells a product below cost price, i.e. at a lower price than it paid to buy or manufacture the item. The firm hopes that when customers visit their shop, they will purchase more items, thus increasing the firm's sales.

Example
Supermarkets often use a loss leader pricing strategy to sell fruits and vegetables. Each week Aldi sells six fruit and vegetables below their cost price in the Super Six offer.

High Price Strategies

1 **Premium pricing:** The business charges a higher price than competitors in the market. This gives consumers the impression that the product is of a superior quality.

Example
Designer brands such as Chanel and Gucci use premium pricing for their clothing.

2 **Price skimming:** A high price is charged when the product is launched so that the business can recover R&D costs quickly before competitors enter the market. Price skimming can be used to attract 'early adopters' – consumers who are willing to pay more to buy the newest product on the market.

> **Example**
> Samsung used premium pricing to launch the Galaxy Note 9 at a price of over €1,000.

Other Price Strategies

1 **Psychological pricing:** This strategy is based on the theory that certain prices have a bigger psychological impact on consumers. It gets consumers to buy based on emotions rather than common sense.

> **Example**
> Consumers associate numbers ending in 99 with lower prices, e.g. €4.99 is associated with €4 rather than €5, even though there is only one cent in the difference between €4.99 and €5. This is sometimes called 'charm pricing'.

2 **Mark-up pricing:** The business adds a profit percentage to the cost price of the item, e.g. 10%.

> **Example**
> A restaurant calculates that it costs €3.50 to make a dessert. It adds a mark-up of 70% to the cost price and charges diners €5.95.

3 **Tiered pricing:** Consumers choose the price level that fits their budget. It allows a business to gain market share at different price points and is common in the motor industry.

> **Example**
> Car manufacturers often sell different variations of the same car model, e.g. the basic VW Tiguan Comfortline model and the more expensive Tiguan R-Line model.

4 **Price discrimination:** Different segments of the market are charged different prices for the same product.

> **Example**
> This is commonly used on Irish rail, where consumers pay different prices for the same journey, e.g. student, adult and child fares.

5 **Bundle pricing:** The business sells multiple items together for a lower price than they would cost separately. This can be used to sell slow-moving stock and gives consumers the impression that they are getting value for money.

> **Example**
> Consumers can buy TV, broadband and phone bundles from providers such as Sky and Virgin Media.

Activity 20.10

Working in pairs, write the name of as many pricing strategies as you can think of on sticky notes and place them on a desk or the wall. Categorise the strategies into low, high and other. Choose **five** of these strategies and write about them in your copybook.

Factors that Influence Price

1 **Cost:** The price charged to customers should cover the firm's costs, which include production, marketing and distribution, as well as a profit margin.

Activity 20.11

It costs a business €18.75 to manufacture a pair of shoes and the firm sells the shoes at a 94% mark-up. Calculate the price paid by the consumer.

2 **Competitors' prices:** Firms must consider the prices charged by competitors in the market. The business needs to decide whether it will charge a price that is lower, higher or the same as its competitors.

3 **Stage of the product life cycle:** The different stages of the product life cycle influence the price charged. For example, a price-skimming strategy might be used for the product launch stage.

4 **Product image:** The pricing strategy chosen should reflect the image of the product, e.g. premium pricing is used to give the impression of a luxury or superior quality product.

5 **Consumer demand:** Higher demand can enable the business to charge higher prices. For example, a hotel can charge higher prices during busy periods, e.g. summer holidays and local events such as matches and concerts.

3 Marketing Mix – Place

Place refers to where consumers can buy goods and services sold by the business. To reach the largest possible number of consumers, **the business must choose the most appropriate channel of distribution.** This is the way in which the product gets from the producer to the consumer.

Some channels of distribution feature an intermediary, who acts as a go-between between the producer and the consumer. Examples of intermediaries include wholesalers, agents and retailers.

> *Definition*: **Wholesaler**
> Wholesalers buy in large quantities from producers and sell these products in smaller quantities to retailers. Musgraves is an example of an Irish wholesaler.

> *Definition*: **Agents**
> Agents sell the producer's goods and services in a particular area, e.g. a country or region. The agent usually receives a commission based on sales made.

> *Definition*: **Retailer**
> A retailer buys products from either a wholesaler or a producer. Retailers can operate in physical stores or solely online (e-tailers). Examples of retailers include Dunnes Stores and ASOS.

The most common channels of distribution are illustrated below:

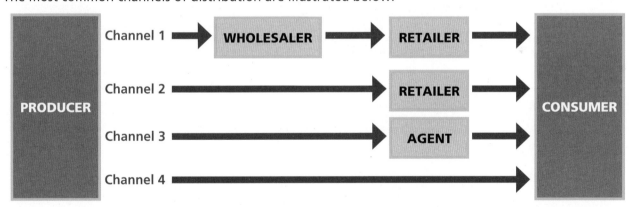

Some producers use a number of channels of distribution to sell products to consumers. A producer could sell its product to retailers but also sell directly to consumers on its own business website.

Channel 1 – Producer ➜ Wholesaler ➜ Retailer ➜ Consumer

The producer sells to the wholesaler in large quantities. The wholesaler then 'breaks bulk', i.e. they distribute smaller quantities to retailers. Consumers then purchase the items from these retailers.

> **Example**
> Products using this channel include grocery items such as tins of beans and packets of biscuits.

Unit 5

CHANNEL 1 – PRODUCER → WHOLESALER → RETAILER → CONSUMER

✓ Advantages	X Disadvantages
1 Target Market Potential to reach a large target market – the wholesaler can sell the products to many retailers.	**1 Cost** The product is more expensive for the consumer. A mark-up is added at each stage of the channel of distribution, which increases the price paid by the consumer.
2 Consumer Convenience It is more convenient for consumers as they can buy the product from a range of retailers instead of having to rely on one shop.	**2 Consumer Feedback** The producer may be unable to obtain direct feedback from consumers. This could lead to a delay in reacting to changes in consumer demand.
3 Simplified Distribution It simplifies the distribution process, as the wholesaler stores the products and sells in smaller quantities to retailers.	**3 Profits** The producer must give some of the profits earned to the wholesaler. This reduces the profits received by the producer.

Channel 2 – Producer → Retailer → Consumer

In this channel of distribution, the producer sells direct to the retailer, thus removing the need for a wholesaler. The retailer can obtain discounts from bulk buying and therefore offer lower prices to consumers.

The producer may also manufacture own-brand products for the retailers and these items are distributed using this channel of distribution, e.g. Tesco Finest range.

Example
- Producers such as Cadbury sell their products (e.g. Dairy Milk bars) direct to Dunnes Stores and SuperValu.
- Bakery firm Comerford Brothers in Co. Kildare produces a range of own-brand cakes for Lidl stores nationwide.

CHANNEL 2 – PRODUCER → RETAILER → CONSUMER

✓ Advantages	X Disadvantages
1 Target Market Large retailers buy direct from producers. This increases the size of the target market that the producer can reach.	**1 Discounts** Retailers may place pressure on the producer to sell them their products at a large discount. This can significantly reduce the profits of the producer.
2 Lower Prices Consumers benefit from lower prices, as there are fewer stages in the channel of distribution.	**2 Transport** The producer must transport the products to the retailer, e.g. to a distribution facility or individual stores. This can increase costs for the producer.
3 Promotion A large retailer may have a nationwide promotional campaign. This can increase consumer awareness of the product and help to increase sales.	**3 Copycat Products** The retailer may see the success of the product and make an own-brand copy. This can reduce the producer's sales.

Channel 3 – Producer → Agent → Consumer

The producer sells direct to an agent, who is responsible for selling the product in a particular market. This is often used when a business launches its product into a foreign market.

CHANNEL 3 – PRODUCER → AGENT → CONSUMER

✓ Advantages	✗ Disadvantages
1 Target Market The agent is familiar with the target market and may already have a network of potential buyers. This can help the firm to establish a market share quickly.	**1 Loss of Control** The producer may lose some control over the brand image and marketing, as this will be carried out by the agent.
2 Lower Costs The firm does not need to establish a physical outlet in the foreign market. This reduces recruitment, training and employee wage costs.	**2 Loyalty** Some agents will work for a number of different brands. It can be difficult to ensure that they are loyal to working on behalf of your brand.
3 React to Changes As the agent is based in the market, they can react quickly to changes in consumer demand and pass them on to the producer. This can help to increase the producer's sales and profits.	**3 Costs** The producer is responsible for marketing, transport and distribution of the product to consumers. This can be expensive for the producer.

Example
Avon is an American company that sells its own brand of cosmetics, homeware and fashion items. The firm recruits agents all over the world to sell its products to customers. Agents distribute catalogues to people's homes and receive a commission on items ordered. Last year the company sold €4 billion worth of goods to consumers worldwide.

Channel 4 – Producer → Consumer

The producer sells direct to the consumer, e.g. in stores, at markets or trade fairs, or online.

Example
Bespoke suits and dresses can be designed to customers' requirements and sold direct from the producer to the consumer in their own store or online.

CHANNEL 4 – PRODUCER → CONSUMER

✓ Advantages	✗ Disadvantages
1 Profits As there are fewer stages in the channel of distribution, the producer gets to keep more of the profit.	**1 Costs** The producer needs to take on all costs, e.g. transport, marketing. These can be expensive to set up and maintain.
2 Consumer Feedback Direct consumer feedback can help the producer develop new products to meet consumer needs.	**2 Expertise** The producer may not have all the expertise needed to sell direct to consumers, e.g. marketing, finance and transport.
3 Consumer Awareness A company website can promote the producer's products worldwide. This can increase consumer awareness of the product and increase sales.	**3 Time-consuming** Many small producers sell direct to consumers at weekly markets and events. It can be time-consuming travelling to these markets and customer numbers can vary.

Unit 5

CASE STUDY ## Channels of Distribution at Nicholas Mosse Pottery

Nicholas Mosse Pottery, based in Bennetsbridge, Co. Kilkenny, has produced handmade pottery for more than fifty-five years. The company uses different **channels of distribution** to sell its products.

- **Direct to consumers:** in its shop in Bennetsbridge and through the firm's website
- **Through retailers:** the firm sells to retailers around Ireland including Arnotts and House of Ireland.

Activity 20.12

These jeans are made in Mexico, assembled in the US and retail for $150, but the profit differs considerably depending on whether they're sold online or at a physical store.

OFFLINE

Cost of goods sold	$45
Store payroll	27.00
Freight to retail store	4.50
Rent*	22.50
Other retail operating costs	12.00
Marketing	15.00
Profit	**$24.00** 16%

ONLINE

Cost of goods sold	$45
Free standard shipping & returns	10.00
Warehouse/fulfilment	5.00
Operating costs (software maintenance)	30.00
Marketing	15.00
Profit	**$45.00** 30%

* Assuming an average of $120/square foot for premium retail
Source: Onestop Internet Inc.

Examine the image and answer the following questions.

1 Excluding the cost of goods sold, what is the largest expense for a business selling jeans (i) offline and (ii) online?

2 Outline **one** advantage and **one** disadvantage of a business selling its products online.

3 State **one** reason why this designer manufactured the jeans in Mexico rather than in the USA.

4 Name **one** business that sells their products exclusively online rather than in retail outlets.

Unit 5

Factors Affecting the Channel of Distribution

Factor	Reason
Cost	→ The producer should choose the cheapest but most effective channel of distribution. This increases the profits earned by the producer.
Nature of the Product	→ If the product is perishable or has a short shelf life, it is important to use a channel of distribution that gets the product to the consumer as quickly as possible, e.g. flowers can be sold direct to retailers and then to consumers.
Target Market	→ The business should choose a channel of distribution that reaches the largest possible target market. Producers may sell to wholesalers to reach a larger market, which can help increase sales.
Business Image	→ To maintain a brand image, a producer may need to choose a particular channel of distribution. The firm may sell direct to consumers online through the firm's website or to specific retailers that reflect the brand image. For example, Nespresso products can only be purchased direct from the firm's website and its stores, or through authorised retailers, e.g. Arnotts.
Market Size	→ In some cases, wholesalers may store the producer's products and transport them to retailers. This may be the most financially viable option for a producer to distribute their products to a wide range of consumers.

4 Marketing Mix – Promotion

Promotion is used to increase consumer awareness of the brand and the goods and services that it sells. It uses techniques to persuade consumers to buy the firm's products over those of competitors.

Promotional Mix

The **promotional mix** is the range of methods used by businesses to persuade consumers to buy their products.

The methods used can include:

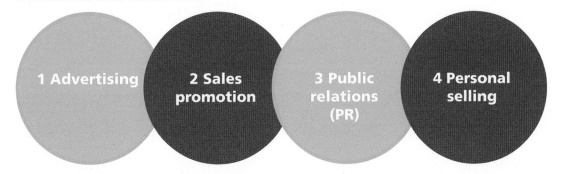

1 Advertising 2 Sales promotion 3 Public relations (PR) 4 Personal selling

1 Advertising

Advertising communicates information about a firm's goods and services to consumers. It aims to Remind, Inform and Persuade people about a brand and its products.

Types of advertising include:

1 **Informative advertising:** The advertisement gives consumers information about the product. It shows or explains what the product does and gives factual information about the item.

> **Example**
> - TV advertisements for cleaning products show consumers how the product will remove stains easily, e.g. Flash.
> - Magazine advertisements featuring new car models show images of the car and provide model specifications, e.g. *Car Buyers' Guide*.

2 **Reminder advertising:** This type of advertising reminds consumers about the brand and its products. It is often used when a product is in the decline stage of the product life cycle.

> **Example**
> Kellogg's Corn Flakes ran a TV advertising campaign called 'My Perfect Bowl', with different people discussing their favourite time to eat a bowl of Corn Flakes. The campaign resulted in a 20–30% increase in sales of the cereal.

3 **Persuasive advertising:** This type of advertising persuades consumers that they need the product. It can be used in the introduction stage of the product life cycle to generate interest in the product and persuade consumers to buy.

4 **Generic advertising:** Advertising a specific good or service from an industry rather than a particular brand or company. The advertising is often financed by a state-owned organisation or a number of businesses in the industry.

5 **Comparative advertising:** The brand or product is advertised as superior to those of other competitors based on quality, price or choice.

Example
Advertisements for supermarket retailers such as Aldi and Tesco often compare prices to convince consumers about savings that can be made.

Example
Advertisements for cosmetics often use models to persuade consumers that they will be more attractive if they use the products.

Example

Activity 20.13

Working in groups, find examples of each of the types of advertising listed above. Present your findings to your class.

Advertising Medium

The advertising medium is the way in which the business communicates its marketing message to consumers. The aim is to target as many consumers as possible and persuade them to buy the firm's goods or services. Advertising media include:

- Television
- Social media
- Radio
- Business website
- Newspapers

Advertising Medium	Advantages	Disadvantages
Television	1 Possible to reach a large target market. 2 Detailed information can be shown using images and sound.	1 It is an expensive medium. 2 Viewers can switch channels during the advertisements.
Radio	1 Cheaper than TV advertising. 2 More effective way to reach the target market, e.g. advertising on local radio stations.	1 Easy to forget as only sound is used in the advertisements. 2 Competition from similar products advertised.
Newspapers	1 Cheaper than TV and radio advertising. 2 Reach a local target market by advertising in local newspapers, e.g. the *Wicklow People*.	1 Fewer people buy newspapers than watch TV or listen to the radio. 2 Newspapers have a short shelf life and are generally not read the day after publication.
Social Media	1 Possible to reach a large target market. 2 Ability to interact directly with consumers.	1 Trolls can damage the brand by posting untrue negative comments. 2 Limited to the target market with social media accounts, e.g. Facebook, Instagram.

Unit 5

Advertising Medium	Advantages	Disadvantages
Business Website	1 The business can control all information contained on the website. 2 Relatively cheap method of advertising.	1 The website could be hacked and the business may have to invest money to increase security. 2 The technology must be upgraded regularly to ensure that the website is user-friendly.

Choosing an Advertising Medium

The business must take into account a number of factors when deciding on the most suitable advertising medium to use. These factors include:

1 **Cost:** Businesses should use their advertising budget wisely to have the greatest impact on consumers and ensure they get value for money, e.g. TV campaign.

2 **Type of product/service:** The method chosen should reflect the image of the product. For example, a designer brand of clothing such as Dior would not advertise on a local radio station; to reflect its brand image it might advertise in fashion magazines or on the firm's website.

3 **Target market:** The business should use a method that reaches the largest possible target market. Social media could be used to target a teenage audience; TV and newspaper advertisements are traditionally targeted at older customers.

> **Example**
> Kylie Jenner used Snapchat to build up a social media presence and interact with a largely teenage target market. At the age of 18 she launched Kylie Cosmetics. She owns 100% of the company, which is now worth approximately €700 million.

4 **Stage of the product life cycle:** Intense advertising may be needed in the launch stage of the product life cycle, e.g. TV and billboard advertisements. As the product moves into the maturity stage, online advertising can be used to maintain and increase consumer awareness of the product.

2 Sales Promotion

Examples of sales promotion include:

- **Loyalty cards:** The cardholder earns points for every euro they spend in the store and these points can be exchanged for goods and services, e.g. Boots Advantage Card and Tesco Clubcard.

> **Definition: Sales promotion**
> Short-term gimmicks used by businesses to attract consumers to buy products and services.

- **Special offers:** These are incentives offered to consumers to persuade them to buy the product, e.g. discounted prices, buy one get one free offers and free gifts. For example, pharmacy chain Boots uses '3 for 2' offers on Christmas gift sets.

- **Free samples:** Consumers receive a sample of a product to test. It gives them the opportunity to see if they like it enough to buy it. Money-off vouchers are often used in conjunction with free samples to convince consumers to buy the product at a reduced price.

- **Discount codes:** The firm offers consumers discount codes which reduce the price of their products. Many brands collaborate with social media influencers and offer discount codes through their social media platforms.

- **Merchandising:** This refers to the materials used in retail outlets to promote products, e.g. window displays, posters and specially designed display stands. Merchandising can often be placed at the point of sale (POS), i.e. where the consumer pays for the product.

Activity 20.14

Working in groups of three or four, create a poster showing the different sales promotion methods used by businesses.

Unit 5

3 Public Relations (PR)

Large firms may have their own PR department with a **public relations officer (PRO)** or they can employ the services of a PR company to protect and promote a positive image of the firm.

> **Definition: Public relations (PR)**
> A marketing technique used to create a positive public image for a business and the products or services it sells. It aims to generate positive publicity for the firm with stakeholders such as consumers and the local community.

PR Methods

- **Sponsorship:** The business pays money to an individual or group of people to display their brand name, e.g. Avonmore sponsors the Kilkenny hurling team.

  Sponsorship can also take place at events, where the firm's brand name is advertised on buildings or in stadiums, e.g. the Olympic Games.

Example

SoftCo, a finance software provider, paid approximately €20,000 to sponsor the Irish women's hockey team. The team was the first Irish team to reach a world cup final. This gave SoftCo increased media coverage and boosted consumer awareness of the brand.

- **Endorsements:** The business pays recognisable people, including actors, athletes and social media influencers, to promote the brand and its products. The business may pay these people to take part in advertising campaigns on TV, in print or online.

Example

Irish golfer Rory McIlroy signed endorsement deals with Taylor Made (a golf club manufacturer) for €92 million and Nike for almost €184 million.

- **Press communication:** The PR company may issue a press release or organise a press conference to communicate information via various media outlets, e.g. newspapers and TV. This can be used to launch new products or create positive publicity for the firm.

- **Charities:** Businesses can make direct monetary donations to charities and encourage staff to donate their time to charitable organisations.

Example

Vodafone Ireland has donated €8 million to charities such as the ISPCC and Concern Worldwide. Staff can take three days off per year to undertake charity work and are paid by Vodafone while volunteering.

DID YOU KNOW? *Last year 56 Irish businesses donated €32 million and over 227,000 volunteer hours to charities and community groups.*

4 Personal Selling

Sales staff meet consumers face to face, provide information on products and persuade the consumer to purchase them. In venues such as stores or trade fairs the sales staff promote the product through their appearance, knowledge of the product and their customer service approach.

Example

Personal selling is used in stores such as Harvey Norman and DID Electrical. Staff representatives provide information and advice to consumers about products such as TVs, computers and household appliances.

Unit 5

Promotion at Fulfil Nutrition

Irish brand Fulfil Nutrition produces a range of low-sugar, protein-enriched bars. The firm uses a range of promotion methods to increase consumer awareness of the products and persuade people to buy.

Advertising

It uses **social media** accounts such as Facebook, Instagram and Twitter to advertise its product range. Followers receive regular **reminder advertising** about existing flavours and **informative advertising** about the launch of new flavours.

Sales Promotion

Fulfil Nutrition uses eye-catching merchandising to display its products. It has also set up a **pop-up café** where the bars can be transformed into snacks such as smoothies or crêpes.

Personal Selling

Launch events for new flavours give consumers the opportunity to get **information from staff** about the brand, ingredients and product features.

Public Relations

Fulfil Nutrition signed a **sponsorship** deal to become an official snack sponsor of the FAI. The business has also used **endorsement** to engage a number of Irish brand ambassadors such as former Olympic athlete David Gillick.

PROTECTING CONSUMERS

Consumers need to be protected from businesses using unethical marketing methods. Businesses may deliberately mislead or omit information which can persuade consumers to buy when in ordinary circumstances they would not.

You learned in Chapter 2 that the Consumer Protection Act 2007 makes it illegal for firms to provide misleading descriptions about goods, services or the price of products.

Consumers can make a complaint about misleading advertising to the following bodies:

1 **Competition and Consumer Protection Commission (CCPC):** See Chapter 2.

2 **Advertising Standards Authority for Ireland (ASAI):** This is an organisation set up and financed by the advertising industry. It aims to ensure that advertising in Ireland is legal, decent, honest and truthful. Members of the public can make a complaint about advertisements, which are then investigated by the ASAI. While the ASAI cannot force businesses to remove advertisements, members of the ASAI agree to not breach the ASAI code of standards.

Social Influencers and the ASAI

The ASAI received a complaint from a member of the public that a social media influencer had used a filtered and photoshopped image to promote a beauty product on her Facebook and Instagram accounts. The influencer has over 190,000 Instagram followers and had received payment from a cosmetics company to promote the product. The company had also used the images on its social media accounts.

The complainant believed that the post was misleading as it would give people the impression that consumers would achieve the same results by using this product.

This was the first complaint made to the ASAI about social media influencers and the ASAI upheld the complaint. The company and social media influencer agreed to remove the photograph from all social media accounts.

EVALUATION OF THE MARKETING MIX

In an exam, you may be required to undertake an evaluation of the marketing mix for a specified product or one chosen yourself. We'll look at how to go about this by the example of Lindt chocolate bars in the panels on the right of the page.

Exam Tip!
You should be able to apply the marketing mix to a good and service of your choice. Choose a product and prepare an answer in advance of the exam. This will save you time in the exam.

Product

The product is the good or service sold by the business. The firm must ensure that the product meets consumer needs and quality expectation. A brand name should be developed to increase consumer awareness of the product. The firm should also ensure that product packaging is attractive and protects the good from damage during transport.

Example
The brand name Lindt was created by Rodolphe Lindt. The chocolate bars use high-quality ingredients sourced from around the world. The packaging of the bars is strong to protect the chocolate and uses bright colours to make it stand out from competitors' products.

Price

The business must ensure that the pricing strategy chosen for its product covers production costs. The firm can use a range of strategies including penetration pricing, premium pricing and tiered pricing.

Example
Lindt chocolate bars use a premium pricing strategy. They cost more than competitors' products, which indicates to consumers that they are of a superior quality.

Place

Place refers to the where the consumers can buy the product and the channel of distribution used to get the product from the manufacturer to the consumer. The firm may use a channel such as transferring the product from the wholesaler to the retailer and then to the consumer.

Example
Lindt chocolate bars are on sale in shops and supermarkets around Ireland. The firm primarily uses two channels of distribution: Channel 1 (Producer → Wholesaler → Retailer → Consumer); and Channel 2 (Producer → Retailer → Consumer). These channels of distribution enable the firm to reach the largest possible number of consumers.

Promotion

Promotion is used to increase consumer awareness of the brand and the products it sells. Promotion can include advertising, such as TV and radio advertisements. It can also include sales promotion techniques such as loyalty cards and free samples. Public relations can be used to improve the image of the brand through sponsorship and endorsements.

Example
Lindt uses advertising on TV and in magazines. It also uses sales promotion by offering free samples of its products in shops and special discounts, e.g. buy two bars for €2. Lindt uses endorsement and has appointed tennis player Roger Federer as a brand ambassador.

Example: Evaluation
In my opinion, Lindt has carefully examined the four elements product, price, promotion and place to create an effective marketing mix. This has helped to increase consumer awareness of the chocolate bars and enabled the firm to charge a higher price than competitors, using a premium pricing strategy.

KEY TERMS

Now you have completed this chapter, you should understand and be able to explain the following terms. In your copybook, write a definition of each term to build up your own glossary of terms.

- marketing
- marketing concept
- marketing strategy
- marketing plan
- market segmentation
- geographic segmentation
- demographic segmentation
- psychographic segmentation
- target market
- niche market
- product positioning
- marketing mix
- product
- product portfolio
- patent
- brand name
- brand logo

- brand slogan
- trademark
- own-brand products
- packaging
- product life cycle
- price
- pricing strategies
- penetration pricing
- predatory pricing
- loss leader
- premium pricing
- price skimming
- psychological pricing
- tiered pricing
- price discrimination
- bundle pricing
- place
- channel of distribution
- wholesaler

- retailer
- agent
- promotion
- promotional mix
- advertising
- informative advertising
- reminder advertising
- persuasive advertising
- generic advertising
- comparative advertising
- sales promotion
- merchandising
- public relations
- sponsorship
- endorsements
- personal selling
- Advertising Standards Authority for Ireland (ASAI)

PowerPoint Summary

EXAM-STYLE QUESTIONS

Ordinary Level

Section 1 – Short Questions (10 marks each)

1 List the 4 Ps of marketing.

2 Name **two** methods of segmenting a market.

3 Explain the term *brand name*. Give **two** examples of well-known Irish brand names.

4 What is an own-brand product? Outline **one** advantage to a business of own-brand products.

5 Choose the correct answer in each of the following sentences.

(i) A market that is segmented based on regions or areas is known as **geographic/demographic** segmentation.

(ii) A company's logo can be legally protected by registering a **patent/trademark**.

(iii) The second stage in the product life cycle is **maturity/growth**.

(iv) Launching a product into the market at a low price is known as **penetration pricing/price skimming**.

(v) PRO stands for public relations **official/officer**.

6 Distinguish between premium pricing and tiered pricing.

7 Name **two** channels of distribution and draw **one** of these channels for a product of your choice.

8 Distinguish between a wholesaler and a retailer.

9 List **three** sales promotion methods. Choose **one** method and explain it in detail.

10 What is meant by the term *PR*?

Section 2 – Long Questions

1 What is meant by the term *market segmentation*? Describe **two** ways in which a market can be segmented. **(15 marks)**

2

> Pippa Crawford has set up her first business making handmade candles. Pippa has developed a candle that has never been seen in the industry before and wants to protect her invention. She knows that she needs to develop a strong <u>brand name</u>, <u>brand logo</u> and <u>brand slogan</u>.

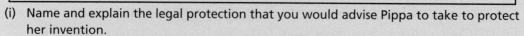

   (i)   Name and explain the legal protection that you would advise Pippa to take to protect her invention.
   (ii) Outline the underlined terms in the paragraph above. **(25 marks)**

3 Product packaging plays an important role in marketing a product. Describe **two** functions of product packaging. **(15 marks)**

4 Explain the term *product life cycle*. Draw a diagram illustrating the product life cycle and label each stage. **(20 marks)**

5 Outline **two** pricing strategies that a business could use to launch a new product. **(15 marks)**

6

> 'Snapchat loses three million users in three months.' *Irish Independent, August 2018*

Describe **two** advantages and **two** disadvantages of using social media as a method of advertising. **(20 marks)**

7 Advertising can be used to inform and remind consumers. Outline the meaning of the terms *informative advertising* and *reminder advertising*. **(15 marks)**

8 Describe the elements of the marketing mix, using a product/service of your choice to support your answer. **(25 marks)**

Higher Level

Section 1 – Short Questions (10 marks each)

1 Explain the term *marketing strategy*.
2 What is a niche market? Discuss the advantages and disadvantages of selling in a niche market.
3 Distinguish between brand name and rebranding.
4 Describe the term *product* in the marketing mix. Describe **two** factors that a business should consider when designing a product.
5 Outline how product packaging can be used to (i) protect the product and (ii) provide information.
6 Distinguish between the following pricing strategies: (i) penetration pricing and (ii) bundle pricing.
7 Distinguish between a trademark and a patent as legal protection for a business.
8 Illustrate a channel of distribution for a product of your choice. Name the product.
9 The following table gives examples of promotion. Using a tick (✔), identify the correct type of sales promotion described in each example in the following table.

Example	Advertising	Sales Promotion	Public Relations
Buy one, get one free			
Radio			
Loyalty cards			
Endorsements			
Newspapers			

10 Complete this sentence: Loyalty cards help a business _____

Section 2 – Applied Business Question (80 marks)

Sophie's Soups

As a vegan, Sophie Curran has been disappointed with the limited choice of vegan food available in Irish supermarkets. Many of the large food producers have ignored the growth in the number of vegan consumers. Sophie knows that vegan customers are loyal to vegan brands and are often willing to pay a little more for high-quality products.

Sophie decided to set up a company selling a small range of vegan soups. She wanted to convey a 'home-made' image and chose the name Sophie's Soups as her brand name. She is passionate about her products but knows the risks of new competitors entering the market and the high production costs that she will face.

Sophie has employed a marketing consultant to help her make product packaging and pricing decisions. The consultant has advised Sophie to package her soup range in strong plastic tubs rather than cartons, to enable consumers to heat the product and then eat from the tub. The consultant has also prepared a sample packaging design for Sophie to review. Sophie really likes the colour scheme chosen for the packaging and believes that it will make the range stand out on the shelves.

Sophie is impressed that the packaging features images of all the natural and fresh ingredients that go into her soups. She also likes the fact that the storage and use instructions are clear and easy for consumers to follow.

One of the most important decisions to be made relates to pricing. Sophie knows that she will need to charge a higher price than her competitors, as she does not benefit from economies of scale from her small production size. The marketing consultant believes that she should set a high price for her range of soups, to gain profits quickly before competitors enter the market. She has even suggested ending the price with .99c to persuade consumers to buy her range over her competitors'.

Sophie must also decide how she will distribute her products to consumers. She wants to reach as many consumers as possible and thinks that this can be achieved by selling direct to retailers. Supermarkets such as SuperValu use Irish brands in their TV advertising campaigns and Sophie admires the support they give to small producers.

Sophie has a lot of decisions to make before she launches her range of Sophie's Soups. She is excited about the future and is determined to make her new business a success.

A What is a niche market? Describe the advantages and disadvantages for Sophie of operating in a niche market. **(25 marks)**

B Outline the importance of product packaging for a business such as Sophie's Soups. **(25 marks)**

C (i) Describe the pricing strategies that you would recommend Sophie to use to launch her range of vegan soups. **(15 marks)**

 (ii) Illustrate a channel of distribution that you would recommend for Sophie's Soups based on the text. Outline **two** advantages of the channel of distribution that you have chosen. **(15 marks)**

Section 3 – Long Questions

1 Outline the steps in developing a marketing plan. **(15 marks)**

2 The image shows the geographic segmentation of the worldwide cosmetics market.

 (i) What is market segmentation?

 (ii) Describe **two** other methods of segmenting a market. **(15 marks)**

BREAKDOWN OF THE MARKET BY GEOGRAPHIC ZONE

36.9% ASIA, PACIFIC
24.7% NORTH AMERICA
19.3% WESTERN EUROPE
10.2% LATIN AMERICA
6% EASTERN EUROPE
2.9% AFRICA, MIDDLE EAST

3 Here is an example of the L'Oréal product portfolio, which includes many well-known international brands.

L'ORÉAL PARIS	MAYBELLINE™	NYX	ESSIE	IT COSMETICS
LANCOME PARIS	YVES SAINT LAURENT	GIORGIO ARMANI	URBAN DECAY	SHU UEMARA

 (i) What is a product portfolio?

 (ii) Outline the benefits of brand names for businesses such as L'Oréal and for consumers. **(20 marks)**

Section 3 – Long Questions *continued*

4 Many businesses have invested heavily in developing own-brand products. Discuss the advantages and disadvantages of creating own-brand products. **(20 marks)**

5 Outline the ways in which a business can extend the product life cycle. **(20 marks)**

6 Examine the channel of distribution below and outline the benefits that this channel can bring to a business. **(15 marks)**

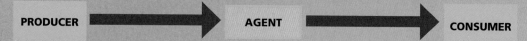

PRODUCER → AGENT → CONSUMER

7 Describe the factors that a business must consider when deciding on the most suitable channel of distribution for its products. **(15 marks)**

8 Evaluate the sales promotion methods used by businesses. Use an example to illustrate your answer. **(25 marks)**

PREVIOUS LEAVING CERTIFICATE EXAM QUESTIONS

Ordinary Level

Section A – Short Questions (10 marks each)

1 The diagram of the Product Life Cycle below is incomplete. The **Saturation** stage has been filled in and the names of the other stages are missing. Fill in the **missing** stages below. **[LC OL 2016]**

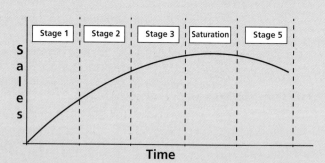

Stage 1 | Stage 2 | Stage 3 | Saturation | Stage 5

Sales

Time

Stage 1 _____

Stage 2 _____

Stage 3 _____

Stage 4 **Saturation**

Stage 5 _____

2 Complete the following table, which refers to examples of promotion techniques, by placing a tick (✔) in the correct box for each example.

	Promotion Techniques		
Examples	Advertising	Sales Promotion	Public Relations
Buy One Get One Free			
Billboards			
Press Conference			
Free Samples			

[LC OL 2015]

3 Give **three** examples of sales promotion. **[LC OL 2006]**

Section B

1

Sweetdreams Ltd

Sweetdreams Ltd, based in Dublin since 1997, is a large manufacturer of chocolate and confectionery. The company is continuously researching the market to ensure it maintains its market position for its brand.

(A) (i) Explain what is meant by the term *Channels of Distribution*.

(ii) Illustrate, using a diagram, a suitable channel of distribution for Sweetdreams Ltd. **(15 marks)**

(B) Describe **two** Sales Promotion methods that Sweetdreams Ltd may use to increase sales. **(10 marks)**

(C) Outline **three** factors Sweetdreams Ltd must consider when setting the price of its products. **(15 marks)**

(D) Outline **three** advantages of branding for Sweetdreams Ltd. **(15 marks) [LC OL 2012]**

2

SPRAOI

ACE Toys Ltd is a successful Irish toy manufacturer. It uses a 'Batch Production' process. Each year it develops new products for the Christmas period, selling to the Irish and international markets. This year ACE Toys Ltd has produced 'SPRAOI', an interactive games console which uses basic Irish language, aimed at children aged 7–11. ACE Toys Ltd have set up a website called www. acetoys.com.

(i) Draft and label the Product Life Cycle for 'SPRAOI'. **(15 marks)**

(ii) Choose a suitable advertising medium to bring 'SPRAOI' to the attention of consumers, and outline **two** reasons for your choice. **(20 marks) [LC OL 2013]**

Higher Level

Section A – Short Questions (10 marks each)

1 Explain the meaning of the term *Own-brand products*. Outline **two** reasons why retailers use own-brand products. **[LC HL 2011]**

2 Outline **two** methods of extending a product's life cycle and provide **one** example to illustrate your answer. **[LC HL 2016]**

Section B

1 Explain the factors a business should consider when designing a product. **(15 marks) [LC HL 2017]**

2 Many businesses spend large sums of money developing a brand name. Illustrate the benefits of branding for the business and the consumer. **(25 marks) [LC HL 2010]**

3 (i) Explain the term *Public Relations (PR)*.

(ii) Discuss methods a business could consider to generate good Public Relations. **(20 marks) [LC HL 2015]**

 Solutions

Unit 5

CHAPTER 21 GETTING STARTED IN BUSINESS

Learning Outcomes

When you have completed this chapter, you will be able to:

1. Describe the different business structures available to new businesses
2. Identify and explain the factors affecting the choice of business location
3. List the main sources of finance available for new businesses
4. Identify and describe methods of production, i.e. job, batch and mass production
5. Draft a business plan
6. Discuss the reasons for and importance of preparing a business plan.

 Literacy Link

Sole trader, partnership, private limited company, co-operative, job production, batch production, mass production, business plan

 Numeracy Link

Percentages

 Cross-curricular Link

Accounting – financial planning
Engineering – robotics, manufacturing
Geography – business location

 CASE STUDY ## Keogh's Crisps

Generations of the Keogh family have farmed land in north Co. Dublin for over 200 years. The family grows a range of crops including potatoes, tomatoes and broccoli.

In 2011 Tom Keogh, a third-generation farmer, decided to **diversify** and set up a business producing crisps, called Keogh's. The firm was established as a **private limited company**, which gives the owners **limited liability**.

With **access to a range of raw materials** grown on the farm, Keogh's produces 11 different flavours of crisps, including Shamrock and Sour Cream, and Chorizo and Cherry Tomato. The crisps are manufactured using **batch production** in kettle fryers purchased from Pennsylvania, USA.

Good transport links in Ireland allow the company to purchase ingredients from Irish suppliers, such as cheddar cheese and Atlantic sea salt from Co. Cork and shamrock from Co. Kerry.

High-quality labour is available in the local area and the firm currently employs 35 people.

With increased demand and need for expansion, Keogh's received a **grant** of €92,000 from the **LEADER** programme to purchase new equipment and machinery. The firm  now supplies supermarkets nationwide and exports to countries such as China, the USA and Germany. Keogh's has a **market share** of 30% of the luxury Irish crisp market and 8% of the overall crisp market in Ireland.

In 2018 the firm was awarded the contract as official snack provider for Emirates airline's first-class passengers. This creates a market for an additional one million bags of crisps per year and an additional ten jobs at the firm.

With **retained earnings** of over €1 million, the future looks bright for Keogh's.

When an entrepreneur decides to take the risk of setting up a new business, they have many important decisions to make, including:

1 Ownership structure of the business
2 Location
3 Sources of finance
4 Production method (if applicable).

Once these decisions have been made, the entrepreneur must prepare a detailed business plan.

DECISION 1: OWNERSHIP STRUCTURE OF THE BUSINESS

The entrepreneur must decide which ownership structure the business will use, for example:

- Sole trader
- Partnership
- Private limited company
- Co-operative.

> *Ownership structures are explained in more detail in Chapter 24.*

Sole Trader

A sole trader is a business owned and run by one person. The entrepreneur makes all business decisions. It is a very common form of business structure in Ireland as it is easy and quick to set up. A sole trader structure is suited to small businesses such as local shops, farmers and taxi drivers.

> *A sole trader using his or her own name can begin trading immediately, e.g. Philip Hayes. However, if the sole trader wants to use a different name, e.g. Speedy Hayes Couriers, this business name has to be registered with the Companies Registration Office (CRO).*

SOLE TRADER

✓ Advantages	✗ Disadvantages
1 Easy to Set Up There are few legal requirements unless a licence is needed to trade, e.g. a pharmacy. The sole trader must also register the business for tax purposes, e.g. VAT (if applicable) and self-assessment income tax.	**1 Unlimited Liability** The owner is personally responsible for all businesses debts and losses. The sole trader may have to sell personal assets, e.g. their private house or car, to pay these debts.
2 Keep all the Profits The owner gets to keep all the profits the business makes.	**2 No Continuity of Existence** When the owner dies or retires the business may close down if there is nobody else to take it over.
3 Decision-making The owner has complete control over all the decisions to be made, e.g. what to sell, business hours.	**3 Stress** The sole trader can experience high levels of stress due to long working hours, decision-making and raising finance. This can lead to burnout.
4 Confidentiality Sole traders are not required by law to publish their financial accounts, so their financial position remains confidential.	**4 Lack of Capital** The sole trader may have difficulty obtaining capital from financial institutions as sole traders are seen as having a high risk of business failure.

Companies Registration Office (CRO)

The CRO is the organisation where information on Irish companies and business names is stored and managed. The functions of the CRO include:

- The incorporation of companies, i.e. it is the authority for registering new companies in Ireland
- Receipt and registration of relevant documents required to set up a company in Ireland
- Making information available to the public, e.g. company name and registered office.

Partnership

A partnership is a business with between two and twenty partners. Common types of business that are set up as partnerships include accountants, solicitors and doctors. A partnership must register with the Revenue Commissioners and also register its name with the CRO. Each partner pays self-assessment income tax (i.e. is responsible for their own tax) on their share of the partnership's profits.

> *Definition*: **Business name**
> A trading name that differs from the names of the persons or the organisation who own the business.

> **Note!**
> *The number of partners can exceed twenty in certain circumstances, e.g. a practice of accountants or solicitors.*

PARTNERSHIP

✓ Advantages	✗ Disadvantages
1 Easy to Set Up A partnership is relatively easy to establish by drawing up a deed of partnership between the interested parties.	**1 Unlimited Liability** Partners have unlimited liability, i.e. they are responsible for all business debts. They may have to use personal assets, e.g. a private house, to repay business debts.
2 Decision-making Partners have a range of skills and experience, which can help to improve decision-making in the business.	**2 Profits** Profits are shared between the partners. The deed of partnership specifies how this is done, e.g. whether profits are shared equally or in line with the amount of capital each partner invested.
3 Increased Capital More people are available to invest in the business, so raising additional capital can be easier. New partners may be admitted if necessary to increase the capital.	**3 Decision-making** Can be slower as all partners have to be consulted. Differences of opinion may arise, which if not resolved may lead to the partnership being dissolved.
4 Confidentiality Partnerships are not required by law to publish their financial accounts, so their financial position remains confidential.	**4 Legal Entity** The partnership and the business are not separate legal entities, i.e. the partners – not the business – can be sued in law.

> *Definition*: **Deed of partnership/partnership agreement**
> A legal agreement signed by all partners that sets out the rules of the partnership on all matters, e.g. how to admit new partners, how profits will be shared and the procedure for partners to leave.

Activity 21.1

In pairs, draw a Venn diagram in your copybook. Fill in the diagram to show the similarities and differences between a sole trader and a partnership.

Private Limited Company

This is a common form of business structure and under the Companies Act 2014 there are a number of variations of a private limited company. For example, a private company limited by shares allows for between one and 149 people to become owners of the business. An owner of a share is referred to as a shareholder. In Ireland a private limited company must register with the CRO.

The shareholders elect a board of directors to run the business on their behalf. Shareholders have one vote per share and are entitled to attend and vote at the company's AGM.

DID YOU KNOW?

While one vote per share is the common voting structure for companies, some international technology firms such as Facebook and Google have established a structure that gives ten votes per share. This gives the founder (Mark Zuckerberg in the case of Facebook) full control of the company, even though its shares are traded on the stock exchange.

See Chapter 24 for more on setting up a company limited by shares and the documents required. Chapter 24 also looks at public limited companies.

PRIVATE LIMITED COMPANY

✓ Advantages

1 Limited Liability
The owners are not personally responsible for business debts. If the business fails, they lose only the amount they invested.

2 Continuity of Existence
The business continues to exist even after the death of one of the shareholders.

3 Separate Legal Entity
A private limited company is a separate legal entity from its owners. This means that the company can sue and be sued in its own name, and enter business contracts.

4 Taxation
The company pays corporation tax of 12.5% on its profits, which is a lower rate than self-assessment income tax paid by partnerships and sole traders. If the owners work in the company, they are employees of it and so pay the same rates of tax as all other employees.

✗ Disadvantages

1 Expensive to Set Up
A private limited company is more expensive to set up than a sole trader or partnership.

2 Profits are Shared
The profits of the business are shared between all the shareholders of the company, in contrast with a sole trader, who keeps all the profits.

3 Less Confidentiality
The accounts of the business must be submitted to the CRO. Summarised versions are made available to the public and other businesses.

4 Time
It takes longer to set up and start a private limited company as the business cannot begin trading until it receives a certificate of incorporation from the CRO.

Definition: Certificate of incorporation
When the CRO receives and processes all the relevant documents required to set up a company it issues a certificate of incorporation. This document enables the company to begin trading. It is sometimes referred to as the birth certificate of the company.

Activity 21.2

Working in pairs, create an infographic to summarise the features, advantages and disadvantages of a sole trader or private limited company. You could use websites such as www.canva.com or www.piktochart.com. Present your infographic to the class.

Unit 5

Co-operative

This type of business structure is set up, owned and controlled by members rather than shareholders. It operates for the benefit of its members and registers with the Registry of Friendly Societies. Each member has an equal say in how the business is run, i.e. one person, one vote. A co-operative must have at least seven members and there is no maximum number of members.

There are four main types of co-operative business:
- Producer co-operatives
- Worker co-operatives
- Community co-operatives
- Financial co-operatives.

DID YOU KNOW? *There are over 150,000 members of co-operatives in Ireland. Co-operatives employ 12,000 people in Ireland and have an annual turnover of €10 billion.*

Activity 21.3

If there are 2.4 million people in the labour force in Ireland, calculate the percentage who work in co-operatives.

CO-OPERATIVE

✓ Advantages	✗ Disadvantages
1 Limited Liability Members of a co-operative are protected by limited liability, i.e. they are not personally responsible for business debts. If the business fails, they lose only the amount they invested.	**1 Lack of Capital** As each member has only one vote there is a lack of incentive to invest more capital. This can delay expansion of the firm.
2 Taxation Co-operatives' profits are taxed under the corporation tax rate of 12.5%, in contrast with sole traders.	**2 Registration** This is more complex than for a sole trader. The co-operative must register with the Registry of Friendly Societies. Its name must include 'Society' and 'Limited'.
3 Continuity of Existence The co-operative continues to operate as a business even if a member dies or sells their shares.	**3 Profits** Profits have to be shared among the members, in contrast to a sole trader, who keeps all the profits.
4 Democratic Decision-making All members have an equal say in the running of the co-op as each member has one vote, regardless of the number of shares they own.	**4 Confidentiality** Co-ops must publish annual financial accounts, which reduces confidentiality.

DID YOU KNOW? *FC Barcelona is a fan-owned co-operative with over 143,000 members.*

See Chapter 24 for more on co-operatives.

Unit 5

Activity 21.4

Take photos of businesses in your local area. Share your images on a sharing website such as www.linoit.com. Work as a class to classify these businesses into sole traders, partnerships, private limited companies and co-operatives.

DECISION 2: LOCATION

The choice of location is an important decision when establishing and developing a successful business. Modern technology and the ability to source raw materials and customers across a wide geographic area means that many firms can locate almost anywhere in the world.

Businesses choose their business location based on the following factors:

Employees
- Access to a wide range of suitably qualified staff
- Education facilities, e.g. schools, colleges, training centres

Infrastructure
- Well-developed transport links for employees, raw materials and the distribution of goods
- Availability of high-speed broadband
- Good public utilities, e.g. waste disposal, energy and water supplies

Market
- Easy access to a wide range of customers
- Consumers with sufficient disposable income to spend on the firm's products or services
- Knowledge of competitors in the market

BUSINESS LOCATION

Land
- Affordable land and buildings available to rent or buy
- Opportunity to expand operations

Local Environment
- Clean, healthy, safe environment
- Positive support from the local community

Raw Materials
- Access to a stable supply of raw materials, e.g. close to a quarry

Government
- Politically stable government with low incidence of corruption or bribery
- Government programmes for encouraging business, e.g. grants

Definition: Footloose business

A business that can set up anywhere and is not tied to a specific location. It can move when the need arises. Many multinational businesses move to locations with more favourable trading conditions, e.g. Dell relocated from Limerick to Poland.

!

Advances in technology and the ability to trade globally mean that a business can be more flexible when it comes to deciding on a location.

CASE STUDY *Netwatch*

Netwatch is a security prevention firm based in Carlow that employs 150 staff. The business uses live audio warnings to alert potential intruders that they are being monitored. Carlow was chosen as the business location in part because of the availability of highly **educated staff** and the well-developed **transport links** with other major towns and cities across Ireland.

netwatch°

CASE STUDY *Stats*

Sports data company Stats provides sports teams and the media with statistical data relating to teams and events such as the World Cup. Stats chose Limerick as the location for its European headquarters because of the sports-related **education courses** at the University of Limerick. Graduates of the university's master's course in AI (artificial intelligence) and sports entrepreneurship have the right type of skills for the business.

DECISION 3: SOURCES OF FINANCE

An entrepreneur will rarely have enough money (capital) of their own to set up their business. They will need to make a decision on the best ways to finance their business.

As you learned in Chapter 17, sources of finance can be classified under three headings:

1 Short-term – repaid within one year

2 Medium-term – repaid between one and five years

3 Long-term – repaid after more than five years.

Note!

Retained earnings and sale and leaseback are not options for financing the setting up of a business.

See Chapter 17 for more details on sources of finance.

The Main Sources of Finance Available to a Business

Type	Examples	Uses
Short-term Less than 1 year)	→ Bank overdraft → Accrued expenses → Trade credit	→ Purchase of trading stock → Day-to-day running costs, e.g. wages, insurance
Medium-term (1–5 years)	→ Medium-term hire purchase → Term loan → Leasing	→ Purchase of fixed assets such as delivery vans and equipment
Long-term (More than 5 years)	→ Debentures → Equity capital → Grants	→ Purchase of land and buildings → Development of new products and ideas (research and development)

Activity 21.5

Working in pairs, create a crossword with appropriate clues based on the sources of finance available to set up a business. Swap crosswords around the room and complete a crossword created by another pair of students.

DECISION 4: PRODUCTION METHOD

If the business is involved in producing goods it also needs to decide which method of production to use. There are three main methods of production:

- Job production
- Batch production
- Mass (flow) production.

A business might use only one production method or a combination of methods to manufacture their products.

> **Exam Tip!**
> Make sure that you can **describe** the different production methods. This means giving an account of each, providing advantages and disadvantages and giving an example.

Job Production

Description	Labour	Machinery	Cost	Examples
→ Unique item made to customers' specifications → High-quality product	→ Highly skilled labour → Employees receive a high wage	→ Flexible, capable of producing a wide range of different products	→ Raw materials, labour and machinery are expensive → High price charged to customers	→ Tailor-made clothes → Private planes → One-off, specially designed house

Activity 21.6

Watch the online video 'Savile Row Tailoring: The Maurice Sedwell Experience' and answer the following questions.
1 Explain the word *bespoke*.
2 In how many countries has the business made suits for individuals?
3 How many hours does it take to create the perfect suit before the second fitting?
4 How does wearing a bespoke suit made by Maurice Sedwell make the customer feel?

Batch Production

Description	Labour	Machinery	Cost	Examples
→ Limited number of identical items are made in a production run → Goods are produced for stock	→ Less skilled than job production → Employees receive lower wages	→ Flexible, when one batch ends the machinery is used to make different products	→ Lower costs than with job production → Multiple items can be made at the same time → Increased efficiency and less waste	→ Bread → Clothes made in different sizes → Various flavours of soft drinks or crisps, e.g. Keogh's

> **Definition: Production run**
> The machinery in the factory is configured to make one product. When the production run of the product is completed, the machines are reset and reconfigured to enable a batch of another product to be manufactured.

Unit 5

Activity 21.7

Search the Internet for the video 'Made in Ireland: How Keogh's makes luxury crisps in north Dublin' and, after watching it, answer the following questions.
1 What is the first production process that happens to the boxes of potatoes?
2 Explain what happens in the crisp house.
3 How long are the crisps hand-cooked in the fryers?
4 How many different types of machinery did you observe during the crisp-making process? Explain the function of each piece of equipment.

Mass (Flow) Production

Description	Labour	Machinery	Cost	Examples
→ Identical items are made continuously → Goods are produced for stock in very large quantities	→ Unskilled assembly line workers → Repetitive work, so morale may be low → Low pay	→ Large capital investment → Automated machinery is specialised and can do only one job	→ High cost of machinery → Benefits from economies of scale, which reduces production costs	→ Pens → Batteries → Baked beans → Toilet rolls → Toothpaste

DID YOU KNOW?

One of the first businesses to use the technique of mass production was Ford. The method was introduced by Henry Ford when the company began to produce the car known as the Model T. He famously said that you could have any colour of Model T as long as it was black.

Activity 21.8

Search the Internet for the video 'Inside the World's Biggest Baked Beans Factory' and, after watching it, answer the following questions.
1 Where do the beans used in Heinz Beanz come from?
2 Why are the beans cooked inside the can?
3 How much steel is used to make the cans?
4 How many cans of baked beans are produced: (i) Each day? (ii) Each year?

Implications of Changing Production Methods

Changes in the business such as expansion or increased competition may result in a business deciding to change its production method, e.g. from batch production to mass production. The implications for this include:

- **Investment:** Batch and mass (flow) production methods are both heavily automated. This requires a large investment in machinery, equipment and premises.
- **Finance:** Additional long-term sources of finance may be needed to set up a new production process, e.g. mass production. If the firm does not have sufficient retained earnings, it may need to obtain a debenture or raise equity capital.
- **Ownership structure:** The business may have to change its structure in order to be able to raise the finance necessary for the investment, e.g. from a sole trader to a private limited company, which would allow it to sell shares and benefit from limited liability. This involves a loss of control of the business.

Unit 5

- **Changes to stock control:** If the business changes from job production to batch production, it will no longer be making goods to order for the customer. Both batch and mass production create goods for stock, so an efficient stock control system will need to be developed. This leads to increased business costs.
- **Marketing plan:** A revised marketing plan will need to be developed and implemented to cater for the increased level of goods being produced.

Activity 21.9

In pairs, create a cloze test on production methods. Swap your cloze test with another pair in your class. Complete the cloze test in pairs and return it to the authors to correct.

SUBCONTRACTING/OUTSOURCING

Subcontracting or outsourcing means that a business employs another firm to manufacture or produce part of a product or a whole product. For example, Nissan and Renault each manufacture cars, but they both outsource the manufacturing of the engines to another business.

Example

In order to reduce costs, many multinational companies (MNCs) outsource their technical and customer support helplines. Irish company Voxpro provides telephone support for firms such as Google, Airbnb and Stripe.

✓ Advantages	✗ Disadvantages
1 Cost Savings Less money is needed for the purchase of expensive machinery and equipment.	**1 Loss of Control** The business can lose control over aspects of production such as quality. Poor quality products could damage the firm's reputation.
2 Staff Savings Fewer staff are needed; the cost of labour is the responsibility of the business to which the jobs are outsourced.	**2 Industrial Relations** Staff may fear for their jobs, as fewer employees may be required if their work is now being done by employees in another business. This can lead to industrial relations issues in the firm.
3 Meet Demand If the demand for a businesses' product is greater than what the business can produce, it can be quicker and cheaper to outsource the extra products needed. The business does not lose any potential sales.	**3 Competition** The business to which the work is subcontracted may decide to manufacture the product themselves. They would then become a competitor in the market, manufacturing a similar product and selling it under their own brand name. The initial contract for outsourcing should include a clause that does not allow this.
4 Less Bureaucracy Regulations such as employment law are the responsibility of the manufacturing firm.	

Unit 5

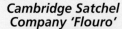

CASE STUDY — Outsourcing at the Cambridge Satchel Company

Cambridge Satchel Company 'Flouro'

11" – €98
13" – €102
14" – €105
15" – €108

Zatchels 'Metallic' Satchel

11.5" – €99
13" – €102
14.5" – €109
15" – €115

The Cambridge Satchel Company in the UK manufactures a range of fashionable satchel-style bags. A rapid increase in demand led to the company **outsourcing** production to another manufacturer. A year later a similar satchel appeared on the market under the name Zatchels.

It was discovered that the company to which the Cambridge Satchel Company had outsourced production had copied their design and materials and had begun to manufacture their own range of satchels.

The Cambridge Satchel Company took a case of **breach of contract** and won an out of court settlement for an undisclosed sum of money.

THE BUSINESS PLAN

It is important that the business has a clear idea of its aims and objectives and how to achieve them. This information can be incorporated into the firm's business plan.

> **Definition: Business plan**
> A detailed written document which includes information about the business. It outlines the firm's aims and objectives and the strategies, such as marketing and production, that will be used to achieve them.

Reasons for Preparing a Business Plan

A business plan is essential for the following reasons.

1 **To obtain finance:** Investors such as banks and government agencies will want to examine a business plan before they provide funding. A detailed business plan shows investors that the business has spent time planning and this increases the likelihood of business success.

2 **To measure performance:** The firm can use the business plan to set a standard against which it measures, for example, sales and production figures. If the standards are not achieved, action can be taken to remedy the situation, e.g. increase advertising to boost sales figures.

3 **To identify problems:** A business plan can help a firm to identify future problems, e.g. lack of finance. The business can then put plans in place to overcome these issues, e.g. obtain a bank overdraft.

4 **To formulate strategies:** A business plan sets out short- and long-term strategies, e.g. one year and five years. It sets out steps that a business will take to achieve its goals, e.g. earn a profit within five years of opening.

Elements of a Business Plan

There is no 'one size fits all' when it comes to preparing a business plan. Each business must prepare its own plan to suit its particular needs. However, some common headings included in a business plan are:

- **Business details:** Information about the firm's directors, shareholders and the legal structure, e.g. sole trader.

- **Objectives:** The overall aims and objectives of the business, including its mission statement.

- **Product details:** A brief description of the products or services that it will produce or sell. This section also refers to the product's unique selling point (USP).

- **Market details:** Analysis of market research, e.g. market size, competitors and target market. It outlines the marketing mix that will be used to maximise sales and market share.

- **Production details:** The production method the business will use, e.g. job or batch production. It includes the type of machinery required and production targets to be met.

- **Financial details:** How much money will be needed to set up the business and how the money will be sourced, e.g. equity finance and loans. This section may also contain a cash flow forecast and projected profits.

However, preparing a business plan does not guarantee business success. There are many risks and uncertainties when setting up and running a business, and even the best-laid plans cannot protect the business from, for example:

- **Unexpected events:** These can increase or decrease demand for a product or service, e.g. water pollution could see a huge increase in demand for bottled water.

- **Changes in tastes/fashions:** Changes in personal tastes and fashion can be difficult for a business to predict, e.g. people are buying fewer deep fat fryers due to health concerns over the use of oil when cooking food.

- **Competition:** New competitors can threaten market share. For example, there is intense competition between Apple and Samsung. Both firms compete to create the most innovative products for their consumers.

- **The economy:** Changes in the economy, e.g. a recession, can reduce consumers' disposable income. This can make trading difficult, despite the plans formulated by the business.

Stakeholders and the Business Plan

A business plan is important to many different stakeholders in a business, including the following.

Stakeholder	Interests
Employees	→ The business plan can reduce employees' concerns about the survival of the business and their job security. → Employees are also interested in the firm's plans to expand as there may be future promotional opportunities.
Investors (equity)	→ Investors are interested in projected sales figures and market research findings. This may persuade them to provide capital needed by the business.
Investors (financial institutions)	→ Financial institutions (e.g. banks) use a business plan to assess whether the business will be able to make repayments on money borrowed.
Manager	→ The business plan is used as a benchmark to measure actual performance against the goals set out in the plan.
Suppliers	→ Suppliers examine the business plan to ensure that the business can repay any credit facilities given to it.
Government Agencies	→ Government agencies such as the Local Enterprise Office (LEO) use the business plan to assess whether the business qualifies for financial assistance, e.g. a grant.

A Sample Business Plan

Business Plan for JB's Scoop Shop

Business Details

The directors of the company are James Byrne and Mary O'Brien. James holds a degree in management from UCD and Mary holds a master's degree in food science from UCC. Each shareholder has over 15 years' experience in the food industry.

JB's Scoop Shop has been established as a private limited company and is located at 45 Main Street, Carlow.

Objectives

The business produces handmade ice creams using milk from local suppliers. The mission statement of the firm is: To create the best ice cream in Ireland using natural, wholesome and local ingredients.

Marketing Mix

- Product – The business will produce a range of ice cream flavours free from additives and preservatives. Milk will be sourced from farms within a 50km radius of the store.
- Price – JB's Scoop Shop will charge a higher price than other competitors in the market, reflecting the cost of high-quality ingredients.
- Place – The ice creams will be sold directly to consumers at JB's Scoop Shop, 45 Main Street, Carlow.
- Promotion – The firm will advertise the shop on local radio stations and newspapers. JB's Scoop Shop has set up social media accounts on Facebook and Snapchat.

Production

JB's Scoop Shop will use batch production to manufacture the different ice cream flavours. The firm will use industrial mixers, freezers and fridges to make and store the product.

Finance

JB's Scoop Shop requires €160,000 in finance: €80,000 will be raised by equity finance from the owners, while the remainder will be raised through a bank loan.

Initial sales projections are based on market research on other frozen desserts throughout Ireland.

Initial Costs at Start-up	€	€
Annual rent of premises	31,000	
Purchase of equipment	84,000	
Purchase of delivery van	35,000	
Initial day-to-day running costs, i.e. working capital	10,000	160,000

Source of finance	€	€
James Byrne personal investment	40,000	
Mary O'Brien personal investment	40,000	
Bank overdraft (short-term loan facility)	10,000	
Long-term loan (bank)	70,000	160,000

Projected Profits	Year 1 €	Year 2 €	Year 3 €
Total revenue (sales)	55,000	65,000	75,000
Total expenditure	103,000	67,000	55,000
Net profit (loss)	(48,000)	(2,000)	20,000

It is expected to be loss-making for two years due to initial set-up costs. However, by the end of Year 3, the company will be profitable.

Unit 5

Activity 21.10

In groups, draft a sample business plan for a new business that you are setting up. Present the plan to the class using IT resources that are available to you.

CHALLENGES FOR BUSINESS START-UPS

A new business faces many challenges, including:

- **Ownership structure:** A business start-up must decide on its structure, e.g. sole trader. The different structures have different effects on the business in terms of risk, control and liability, e.g. limited or unlimited.

- **Finance:** A new business may have difficulty raising finance. If it uses debt finance, e.g. a long-term loan, it will need to make loan repayments regardless of profitability.

- **Production methods:** The business must choose an appropriate method of production that suits the type of product, e.g. job or batch production. Each method has different requirements in terms of machinery, staffing and storage.

- **Staff recruitment:** It can be difficult for new businesses to attract top employees. New firms may be unable to afford to pay wages as high as those paid by established businesses, and jobs may be less secure.

- **Competition:** It can be difficult for a new business to enter a market where there are well-established brands competing in that market, e.g. bringing a new cola into a market dominated by Coca-Cola and Pepsi.

DID YOU KNOW? *In Ireland the number of new start-ups has increased by 13% in recent years. The finance sector has seen the largest rise in the number of new firms, followed by construction.*

Why New Businesses Fail

When an entrepreneur starts a business, failure isn't something they want to think about. However, many start-ups don't succeed due to:

- **Poor management:** Lack of expertise in the day-to-day running of a business can lead to poor decision-making.

- **Insufficient capital:** Not enough capital was invested in the business. This means that it will not have enough resources to make it successful, e.g. spending on machinery or advertising.

- **Location:** The business was set up in an unsuitable location, e.g. the customer base was too small (low footfall).

- **Business plan:** The business plan was poorly prepared and was not used to anticipate future problems for the firm.

- **Expanding too fast:** The business grew too rapidly, which was unsustainable.

Usually no single reason will lead to a business start-up failing; it is usually caused by a combination of factors.

Unit 5

KEY TERMS

Now you have completed this chapter, you should understand and be able to explain the following terms. In your copybook, write a definition of each term to build up your own glossary of terms.

- sole trader
- Companies Registration Office (CRO)
- partnership
- business name
- deed of partnership/partnership agreement
- private limited company
- certificate of incorporation
- co-operative

- footloose business
- sources of finance
- job production
- batch production
- mass production
- production run
- subcontracting/outsourcing
- business plan

PowerPoint Summary

EXAM-STYLE QUESTIONS

Ordinary Level

Section 1 – Short Questions (10 marks each)

1 Name **three** different types of business ownership.
2 Describe **two** advantages of a partnership as a type of business organisation.
3 Outline **one** advantage and **one** disadvantage of a private limited company as a type of business organisation.
4 Explain the term *limited liability*.
5 Outline **three** factors to be considered when deciding where to locate a business.
6 List **three** types of production methods and explain any **one** of them.
7 List **four** headings used in a business plan. Outline the information contained under **one** of these headings.
8 Choose the correct answer in each of the following statements.
   (i)   When products are identical and made continuously the production process is called **batch/flow** production.
   (ii) A bank overdraft is an example of **short-/medium-**term finance.
   (iii) A **footloose/hands-free** business is one that can set up anywhere.
   (iv) A business name is a trading name that **differs from/is the same as** the names of the persons or the company who own the business.
   (v)   **Unlimited/limited liability** is when the owner is responsible for all business debts.

Section 2 – Long Questions

1 Describe **two** benefits and **two** risks of setting up in business as a sole trader. **(20 marks)**
2 What is a co-operative? Outline **two** advantages of co-operatives as a type of business organisation. Name **one** example of a co-operative operating in Ireland today. **(20 marks)**
3 Explain the term *subcontracting/outsourcing*. Outline the drawbacks of a business outsourcing production to another business. **(15 marks)**
4 Explain any **four** factors to be considered when deciding on the location of a business. **(20 marks)**
5 Describe **three** different methods of production. **(15 marks)**
6 Distinguish between batch production and mass production. **(15 marks)**
7 Describe **three** advantages of preparing a business plan. **(15 marks)**

Unit 5

Section 2 – Long Questions *continued*

8

Niamh Cullen opened her first cupcake shop in March 2018 after completing her degree in culinary arts. Her shop offers specially designed cakes and cupcakes for all occasions, both for general sale and made to order. She also sells to local supermarkets and has a kiosk in the local shopping centre. She now wants to expand the business into another retail outlet in a nearby town. This will cost €400,000, of which she can fund €150,000 from her personal savings. The remainder will need to be borrowed.

Draft a suitable business plan for Niamh that she can take to her bank when seeking the extra finance. Use the following headings: (i) Business Details; (ii) Market Details; (iii) Finance Details.

(30 marks)

Higher Level

Section 1 – Short Questions (10 marks each)

1 Define *sole trader* as a form of business. Give **two** advantages of this type of business structure.
2 What does CRO stand for? Describe **two** functions of the CRO.
3 Distinguish between a partnership and a co-operative as forms of business ownership.
4 Outline the importance of (i) employees and (ii) land when deciding on a location for a business.
5 List **three** types of long-term sources of finance that may be required when setting up a new business. Describe **one** of these sources in more detail.
6 What is meant by the term *outsourcing*?
7 List the main headings you would find in a business plan. Explain **two** reasons why it is essential to prepare a business plan.
8 Column 1 is a list of business terms relating to business start-ups. Column 2 is a list of possible explanations for these terms. (One explanation does not relate to any of these terms.) Match the two lists in your copybook by writing your answers in the form *number = letter* (e.g. 1 = A).

	Terms		Explanations
1	Batch Production	A	State agency that provides finance and advice to business start-ups.
2	Outsourcing	B	When a number of similar items are produced for a time and then the equipment is reset to make a number of different items.
3	Bank Overdraft	C	When a business produces an individually designed product to a customer's specifications.
4	Local Enterprise Office (LEO)	D	A business employs another business to manufacture or produce part of a product or a whole product for the original business.
5	Limited Liability	E	Short-term source of finance available to business start-ups for buying , e.g., stock.
		F	The owner(s) of a business will be liable for any business debts only up to the amount invested in the business.

Section 2 – Applied Business Question (80 marks)

Stewart Suits

Daniel Stewart is a sole trader who owns and runs Stewart Suits. The business produces bespoke suits for men and is based in Ranelagh, Dublin. During the recession, trade was slow and at one point Daniel thought that he would lose his home to pay the company's debts. Thankfully, the recession has ended and trade has increased so much that even with three highly skilled employees, Daniel cannot keep up with the demand from clients.

Most of the suit production, from measuring the client to cutting the fabric, is done by hand. Daniel has bought specialised sewing equipment manufactured in Italy to maintain quality standards. He charges customers over €1,000 for a suit and believes that this is good value, based on the amount of time it takes to produce each garment.

Section 2 – Applied Business Question (80 marks) *continued*

Daniel is considering making some radical changes to his business. He wants to register the business as a private limited company. He knows that there is lots of paperwork to complete and he must also wait for the certificate of incorporation to begin trading. While he waits for this documentation, he has viewed a unit in a small shopping centre in the IFSC (Irish Financial Services Centre) in Dublin city centre. It is near the Luas line and Connolly train station and the rent is very reasonable considering the location. Lots of business people and solicitors work in the IFSC and Daniel believes that this would be the ideal location to gain new clients.

While the firm's profits have risen to €80,000 this year, Daniel has had to pay high taxes on these earnings. He needs to obtain a loan from the bank and is hopeful that as a private limited company the loan will be easier to access.

A fashion college is located in the city centre and Daniel is hoping to employ some of the graduates to work in his store, as they understand pattern cutting and have excellent sewing skills.

Daniel rings his accountant to arrange a meeting about preparing and filing future financial accounts for the business. He also wants her to research whether he can apply for any grants from the Dublin City Local Enterprise Office.

A What type of production method is used at Stewart Suits? Describe the main features of this method of production. **(20 marks)**

B Describe the factors that Daniel should consider before moving business premises. **(30 marks)**

C Daniel is considering changing the organisation structure to a private limited company. Discuss the advantages that this form of business structure would bring to Daniel. **(30 marks)**

Section 3 – Long Questions

1 Distinguish between a sole trader and a private limited company as types of business organisation. **(20 marks)**

2 A friend is considering setting up a new business as a sole trader. Outline **two** benefits and **two** risks associated with this type of business structure. **(20 marks)**

3 Outline the main factors to be considered when deciding on the location of a new business. **(20 marks)**

4 Contrast the **three** different types of production process used by businesses. **(15 marks)**

5
> Warren and Margaret have recently moved to Ireland from the UK, having worked for many years with a large multinational business in Burnley. They have decided to move here because of Brexit and wish to set up their own business together in Roscommon manufacturing organic jams and preserves. Margaret has expertise in food science and preparation and Warren in finance, marketing and sales.

Draft a business plan for this proposed new business using **five** main headings and outlining the contents under each heading. **(30 marks)**

6 Evaluate the purpose of preparing a business plan when setting up a business. **(20 marks)**

7 Describe the reasons why different stakeholders would examine a firm's business plan. **(25 marks)**

8
> Alicia Gerdes was recently made redundant and has decided to establish her own business enterprise. Alicia's business will manufacture individually designed disposable glasses and party ware for private parties in homes, hotels and restaurants. Alicia understands that for her business to succeed, an idea alone will not be enough to ensure its success.

Outline the challenges that Alicia may experience while setting up her own business. **(15 marks)**

PREVIOUS LEAVING CERTIFICATE EXAM QUESTIONS

Ordinary Level

Section A – Short Questions (10 marks each)

1 Explain the term *batch production* and illustrate your answer with an example of a product produced using batch production. **[LC OL 2004]**

2 Indicate, by means of a tick (✔), the features that most likely apply to the different production processes.

	Job Production	Batch Production	Mass Production
Goods are produced in groups			
Continuous production of identical products			
Unique made-to-order products			

[LC OL 2009]

3 List **three** of the main headings in a business plan. (Example: Production) **[LC OL 2007]**

Section B

1
> **Dolly's Delicious Delights**
>
> Baking was always a hobby for Dolly O'Brien until she won the Great Irish Bake Off in 2015. She decided to operate as a sole trader. Dolly uses a batch production system to produce cakes and buns. She sells her products direct to her consumers at farmers' markets. Dolly decided to make customised wedding cakes as a new product. She introduced her wedding cakes to her target market at wedding fairs.

(i) Outline **two** factors of batch production.

(ii) List the other **two** types of production used in business. **(20 marks) [LC OL 2016]**

2
> Local Enterprise Offices (LEOs) across Ireland provide advice and assistance to potential start-up businesses. This includes help in setting up the business, drawing up a business plan, assessing finance, marketing and day-to-day running of the business. Mentors are provided for the new business owner, to offer independent advice in order to aid decision making.

(A) Explain **two** differences between a sole trader and a partnership as forms of business ownership. **(15 marks)**

(B) (i) List **two** headings included in a business plan.

(ii) Explain **two** benefits of preparing a business plan. **(20 marks)**

(C) Explain **two** features of Job Production. **(15 marks)**

(D) Outline **two** challenges for start-up businesses in Ireland. **(10 marks) [LC OL 2018]**

Higher Level

Section A – Short Questions (10 marks each)

1 Describe **two** features of job production. [LC HL 2016]

2 The following table shows three types of production and four qualities. For each quality, tick (✔) the type of production which is **most** likely to match that quality. [LC HL 2005]

	Job	Batch	Mass
Unique products			
Groups of products			
Highly skilled direct labour			
Expensive products			

Section B

1 Read the information supplied and answer the questions which follow.

> Sarah Fleming is a wedding dress designer and has worked for over 20 years in the bridal and clothing industry. She specialises in creating unique wedding dresses with an emphasis on personal service. Business is good and Sarah has applied for a bank loan of €10,000 to finance expansion.

   (i)   Name the type of production process used by Sarah.

   (ii) Outline **two** challenges for Sarah of this type of production process.

   (iii) Discuss **two** implications for Sarah of changing to another type of production process. **(25 marks) [LC HL 2014]**

2 Discuss **three** challenges facing business start-ups. **(15 marks) [LC HL 2014]**

3

> In 2015 a Slovakian company, AeroMobil, revealed its prototype of the AeroMobil 3-0 – a flying car. It is a road ready vehicle with foldable wings. It can navigate both traffic and airspace.
>
> *Source: Forbes* magazine, *March 2015*

   (i)   Outline the main sections contained in a business plan.

   (ii) Explain the importance of a business plan for **two** different stakeholders. **(20 marks) [LC HL 2017]**

 Solutions

Unit 5

CHAPTER 22 BUSINESS EXPANSION

Learning Outcomes

When you have completed this chapter, you will be able to:

1. Identify and explain the reasons for business expansion
2. Describe the methods of expansion available to businesses
3. Outline the main sources of finance for expansion
4. Compare and contrast debt and equity capital as sources of finance for expansion
5. Analyse the importance of Irish business expansion in domestic and foreign markets.

Literacy Link

Empire building, diversification, asset stripping, organic growth, licensing, franchising, inorganic growth, strategic alliance/joint venture, merger, takeover/acquisition, debt capital, equity capital

Numeracy Link

Percentages

Cross-curricular Link

Accounting – finance for expansion
Economics – job creation, consumer demand

CASE STUDY Costa Coffee

Italian brothers Bruno and Sergio Costa created their coffee blend in London in 1971. Initially they sold their coffee to local caterers and then in 1978 decided to **expand** the business and establish their first coffee shop, known as Costa Coffee. By 1995, they had 39 coffee shops and the brothers sold the chain to Whitbread plc. With **retained earnings** and access to **debt finance** such as **debentures** and **bank loans**, Whitbread, as the **holding company**, undertook large-scale expansion of the Costa Coffee brand. It **diversified** its product range further by introducing a new breakfast and lunch menu into the shops. It also expanded into **new markets**, including Ireland, and used a **franchise** model to open stores in Dublin and Cork.

Today Costa Coffee has almost 4,000 shops and 8,000 vending machines in 32 countries around the world. The business uses a range of expansion strategies to grow the brand,

including company-owned stores, franchised outlets and stores opened by **joint ventures**.

In 2018, Whitbread plc agreed to sell Costa Coffee to the Coca-Cola Company for over €4 billion. The Coca-Cola Company is using **inorganic growth** methods such as **acquisitions** to gain an immediate and significant position in the hot drinks market.

With a reduction in consumer demand for sugar-filled soft drinks and governments imposing sugar taxes, Coca-Cola needs to diversify its **product portfolio** and can use this acquisition to do so. There is lots of scope for Coca-Cola to earn large profits as the worldwide coffee market is estimated to be worth €86 billion.

REASONS FOR BUSINESS EXPANSION

A business may want to expand for a number of reasons, including:

1 Psychological
2 Defensive
3 Offensive.

> *Psychological needs for expansion are linked to Maslow's Hierarchy of Needs (see Chapter 7). Entrepreneurs' need for self-actualisation inspires them to expand and grow their business.*

1 Psychological Reasons for Expansion

Challenge

Some entrepreneurs love the challenge of setting up their own business. They know that starting and operating a business is difficult, but they enjoy the satisfaction when the business is a success.

Example
Brody Sweeney set up Camile Thai takeaways and Pat McDonagh set up Supermac's and SÓ Hotel Group.

Ambition

Some entrepreneurs want to have the biggest and best business in their particular industry. This is referred to as 'empire building'.

Example
Jeff Bezos has built an empire around online retailing (Amazon) and has expanded into other industries such as cloud computing.

Definition: Empire building
An attempt to increase the size of a firm's staff and assets. Empire builders want to dominate the market locally, nationally and/or globally.

2 Defensive Reasons for Expansion

A business may expand to protect itself from competition in the marketplace. Defensive reasons for expansion include reducing costs, diversifying, protecting supplies and protecting channels of distribution.

Reducing Costs

As the business becomes larger, it benefits from economies of scale. It will have greater buying power and it may receive larger discounts from suppliers, thus reducing business costs. It can then offer lower prices to consumers, resulting in higher sales and profits.

Example
Tunnock's uses 25 tonnes of coconut per week to make the Snowball. Comerford and Brothers bakery uses 15,000 eggs per week to make cakes for Lidl Ireland. Both businesses receive discounts from suppliers as they purchase in such large quantities.

Diversification

Larger businesses can produce a wide range of products and sell into different markets. This reduces the risk of failure as the business is not dependent on one product or market. If sales of one product or in one market decline, sales of other products or in other markets can offset the decline.

Definition: Diversification
When a business widens the range of goods and services it sells, or enters into new markets. For example, a food manufacturer decides to manufacture a clothing line, or enters into a new market, e.g. exports its food range to markets in Europe.

Example
Samsung has a diversified product range which includes smartphones, military hardware, apartments, ships and an amusement park.

Unit 5

Protecting Supplies

A business may protect its supplies by using backward vertical integration. This occurs when a business merges or takes over a supplier of its raw materials. This protects the quality and quantity of raw materials and helps to control their cost.

> **Definition**: **Backward and forward vertical integration**
> **Backward vertical integration** is when a business expands back into the supply chain, e.g. an ice cream manufacturer buys a dairy farm.
> **Forward vertical integration** is when a business expands forward into the market for its products, e.g. an ice cream manufacturer such as Ben & Jerry's opens a chain of ice cream shops.

Example
Starbucks purchased a coffee farm in Costa Rica. This will ensure that Starbucks has access to high-quality coffee beans at a reasonable price.

Protecting Channels of Distribution

A business might use forward vertical integration to control the channel of distribution used to get its products to the consumer. It might merge with or take over a business that sells its products.

Example
Netflix purchases, commissions and produces television series and films. The firm then sells these to consumers through its streaming website and app.

3 Offensive Reasons for Expansion

The business may expand in order to maximise profits and increase market share. Offensive reasons for business expansion include the following.

Increasing Profits

A business may want to grow in size in order to make more profits. These firms tend to have larger sales and lower costs as they benefit from economies of scale.

Example
Arnotts department store earns more profit than smaller independent retailers such as clothing and homeware shops.

Acquire New Products

A business may not have the time or money to develop new products for consumers. Instead it might buy other businesses that have developed or are in the process of developing newer products.

Example
To increase the range of products for customers, Facebook has acquired a number of other businesses, including Instagram and WhatsApp.

Asset Stripping

A business may buy a company purely to gain access to certain assets owned by that business. It intends to use those assets rather than continue to run the acquired business.

Example
Facebook has purchased a number of businesses in order to close them and bring innovative employees from those businesses into the Facebook organisation, e.g. Nextstop and Hot Potato.

Eliminating Competition

A business can expand by taking over competitors to maintain a dominant position in the market, thus increasing the firm's market share.

Example
Topaz acquired both Maxol and Esso service stations. A number of years later Topaz was taken over by the French-Canadian company Couche-Tard and now trades under the brand name Circle K. There are over 420 Circle K sites operating in Ireland.
Question: What is the English translation for *couche tard*?

Unit 5

Activity 22.1

Working in pairs, write **ten** key terms and definitions on the template provided by your teacher. Cut out the terms and definitions, mix them around and place them face down on the desk. Now try to match each term with the correct definition. The student to match the most terms wins the game. Move around the room to complete as many games as possible in the time allocated by your teacher.

CASE STUDY — *Business Expansion at Sheehy Motors*

The Sheehy Motor Group was established in Carlow in the 1970s. The business began as a retailer of Volkswagen passenger cars.

Since then the business has expanded for many reasons – psychological, defensive and offensive. The **entrepreneur** knew the **challenges** ahead when setting up the business, but also enjoys the success it has had over the years.

The business expanded using an **organic** method by increasing sales of passenger vehicles. It became the main dealer for Volkswagen and Mercedes-Benz, thereby increasing its **product portfolio**. It later added Volkswagen commercial vehicles to its business line up in Carlow.

As part of its **empire building**, Sheehy Motor Group opened its second dealership in Naas, Co. Kildare. It expanded by means of a **takeover** when it acquired the existing

dealership for Volkswagen and Audi in Naas. The Sheehy Motor Group is currently the main dealer for Audi, Škoda and Volkswagen passenger cars, and Volkswagen commercial vehicles, in Naas.

Sheehy Motor Group also expanded through **diversification**. It retails quality used cars and supplies a range of other services to the people of Carlow, Kildare and surrounding counties. The firm is the main dealer, sales and service **agent** for vehicles manufactured by the Volkswagen Group and Mercedes-Benz. Further diversification into sales of car accessories, such as roof boxes for people going on holiday, boot liners for family pets and bicycle holders, has attracted new customers to the firm. This expansion has led to increased sales and profits for the business.

Activity 22.2

1 Search for Sheehy Motors Co. Kildare or Co. Carlow on Google Earth. Using a distance calculator find our how far you would have to travel to get to one of their showrooms.

2 In groups, select a local business of your choice. Create a flowchart or decision tree to outline how you would expand the business. Share your thoughts and ideas with other students in your class to compare and contrast the various methods of business expansion.

METHODS OF BUSINESS EXPANSION

A business can grow using organic and inorganic methods of expansion.

1 **Organic** (internal) growth occurs when the business expands gradually over time using its own resources.

2 **Inorganic** (external) growth occurs when the business expands by using mergers, takeovers or forming strategic alliances with another business or businesses.

1 Organic (Internal) Growth

Organic growth can be achieved in the following ways:

A Growing sales

B Licensing

C Franchising.

A Growing Sales

A business can grow sales by increasing sales of an existing product or developing a new product.

Increasing Sales of an Existing Product

A business could grow sales of an existing product by increasing promotion of the product, e.g. advertising or sponsorship of local and/or national events. It could also decide to export the product into new markets in other countries, e.g. the UK and USA.

✓ Advantages	X Disadvantages
1 Lower Costs This method costs less than developing a new product, thus saving the business time and resources.	**1 Finance** The business may experience difficulty sourcing sufficient finance to invest in new markets or for increased advertising.
2 Product Knowledge The business can use its knowledge of previous product launches and promotions to successfully increase product sales.	**2 Slow Sales** It can be difficult to grow brand recognition in overseas markets, which can result in slow sales growth for the business.

Developing a New Product

The business could develop a completely new product by using internal and external sources of ideas, e.g. R&D or customer feedback. The firm uses the marketing mix to make consumers aware of the product and increase sales. It could sell this product on the domestic and international markets.

DID YOU KNOW? *According to international research, 67% of new products fail within the first three years of being launched onto the market.*

✓ Advantages	X Disadvantages
1 High Profits The business has the potential to earn high profits from selling into a new market or developing a successful new product.	**1 Cost** It can be expensive for a firm to develop a new product, e.g. R&D costs. It is also expensive to establish distribution channels and marketing to launch products into new markets.
2 Consumers Consumers are more willing to buy from brands they recognise. This can help the business to persuade consumers to buy their new product and boost sales.	**2 High Failure Rate** New products have a high failure rate for a variety of reasons, including a poor marketing mix and a lack of consumer awareness.

Activity 22.3

Choose a well-known brand and make a list of the products it sells and the markets into which it sells. You may need to use the Internet to find this information. Compare your list with other groups and compile a detailed list based on information from the entire class.

B Licensing

A business (licensor) agrees to allow another firm (licensee) to use its designs and products in return for a royalty payment (payment made for the ongoing right to use the design and products). The royalty paid may be based on product sales. Licensing is very popular for certain products, e.g. toys based on popular movies and television shows such as the Star Wars and Harry Potter films and the television series *PAW Patrol*.

DID YOU KNOW? *The Walt Disney Company is the world's most successful licensor with sales of almost €50 billion for merchandise (e.g. toys, clothes and books) including Mickey Mouse, Star Wars and Marvel's Avengers.*

<table>
<tr><td>

✓ Advantages

1 Low Cost
It is a fast method of expansion, as the licensor bears the cost of manufacturing, distribution and marketing.

2 Continuous Income
The licensor can earn a continuous income stream, while the licensee carries out the work.

</td><td>

✗ Disadvantages

1 Quality Control
The licensee may develop a poor-quality product that damages the licensor's reputation.

2 Loss of Control
The licensor will experience a loss of control, as the licensee makes decisions relating to production, distribution and marketing of the licensed products.

</td></tr>
</table>

C Franchising

A business (franchisor) agrees to let another business (franchisee) use its name, logo and business idea in return for a fee and a percentage of profits. The franchisee is trained how to operate the business and they must adhere to strict guidelines laid down by the franchisor.

FOR THE FRANCHISOR

<table>
<tr><td>

✓ Advantages

1 Low Capital Costs
This form of expansion requires a low capital investment by the franchisor, as the money used for expansion, e.g. to purchase equipment and premises, comes from the franchisees.

2 Rapid Expansion
Franchising allows for rapid expansion, as the capital from the franchisees can be used to set up a large number of outlets in a short period of time.

3 Franchise Cancellation
The franchisor can end the franchise contract if the franchisee does not adhere to the rules of the contract. This can prevent the franchisee damaging the firm's reputation, e.g. poor hygiene.

4 Economies of Scale
The franchisor can enter into deals with suppliers and obtain discounts from bulk buying. This can help to increase the franchisor's profit.

</td><td>

✗ Disadvantages

1 Control
The franchisor loses control of the day-to-day management of the franchised businesses. It can be difficult to monitor all the franchised outlets to ensure that they adhere to the rules set out in the franchise agreement.

2 Business Reputation
The reputation of the entire franchise could be damaged by the actions of one franchisee, e.g. poor quality standards.

3 Franchise Training
To increase the likelihood of success, the franchisor needs to invest in training for the franchisees. This can be expensive and time-consuming to establish.

4 Regular Monitoring
The franchisor needs to monitor franchisees regularly to ensure that quality standards are maintained. This can also help to identify problems, e.g. poor customer service, and solve them quickly.

</td></tr>
</table>

FOR THE FRANCHISEE

✓ Advantages	✗ Disadvantages
1 Franchise Support Support is provided to the franchisee in the form of training, e.g. in marketing, human resource management and finance.	**1 Cost** It can be very expensive to purchase a franchise. Many franchises cost hundreds of thousands of euro to buy, e.g. Subway, McDonald's.
2 Advertising The franchisee benefits from national or international promotion through advertising and sponsorship of events. This increases consumer awareness of the brand and can boost sales.	**2 Revenue** The franchisee must pay a percentage of their revenue to the franchisor each year.
3 Less Risk There is less risk of failure, as the franchise model has already proved successful.	**3 Rules** The franchisee must follow strict rules set out in the franchise agreement. There may be little scope for innovation or change unless it is introduced by the franchisor.

Activity 22.4

Working in groups, brainstorm as many well-known franchises as you can think of. Choose **one** of these franchises and research the following information: (i) the number of franchisees and their locations; (ii) the cost of purchasing the franchise; and (iii) the amount of profit to be paid to the franchisor. Present your findings using an infographic prepared on a website such as www.canva.com.

CASE STUDY — *Camile Thai*

Brody Sweeney spotted a gap in the market for restaurant-quality Thai food delivered direct to consumers' homes. He set up Camile Thai, which operates across Ireland and the UK. As the **franchisor**, Camile Thai helps **franchisees** find a suitable location, build, equip and stock the outlet. The location chosen must have a population of at least 20,000 people. The cost of a Camile Thai franchise involves an investment of between €250,000 and €400,000. The franchisee must then contribute 5% of net sales to a national advertising fund as well as a further 5% for a management fee.

Activity 22.5

1 If you opened a franchise of Camile Thai and had net sales of €80,000, calculate your contribution to the national advertising fund.
2 Working in groups, research how many towns in Ireland would be eligible for a Camile Thai franchise. Display your findings on a poster.

2 Inorganic (External) Growth

A Business may decide to expand inorganically through:

A Strategic alliance/joint venture

B Merger

C Takeover/acquisition.

A Strategic Alliance/Joint Venture

A strategic alliance arises when two or more businesses agree to work together on a common project that benefits both firms, e.g. developing a product. The businesses agree to co-operate and share resources for their mutual benefit. The businesses project is often temporary and the firms remain legally independent.

> **Example**
> - BMW and Toyota co-operate on research into hydrogen fuel cells and vehicle electrification.
> - Google, Kia and Hyundai have worked together to integrate Google Maps into new cars.
> - Apple and Mastercard have developed Apple Pay to enable customers to pay for items using their phone.

✓ Advantages	✗ Disadvantages
1 Success There is an increased likelihood of success as the businesses share knowledge, skills and resources. The businesses create a better product by working together.	**1 Slow Decision-making** Decision-making can be slow due to the number of different businesses involved in the strategic alliance.
2 New Markets The strategic alliance can open up new markets for both firms. This can help to increase sales and profits for each business.	**2 Disagreements** There may be disagreements between the businesses, e.g. regarding costs and leadership.

B Merger

A merger occurs when two or more businesses join together for their mutual benefit. Mergers can involve horizontal integration or conglomerate integration. The businesses join together and form a legal entity. When a merger takes place, the names of both or all the businesses are often used to create the new business, e.g. Irish Permanent Building Society merged with Trustee Savings Bank and became Permanent TSB.

> **Definition: Horizontal integration** !
> Two competing businesses join together, e.g. Disney and Pixar – both firms are involved in the entertainment industry.

> **Definition: Conglomerate integration** !
> A merger between businesses that are in unrelated industries, e.g. Amazon and Whole Foods supermarkets.

✓ Advantages	✗ Disadvantages
1 Economies of Scale The now combined larger business benefits from economies of scale and may receive discounts from suppliers. This reduces business costs.	**1 Redundancies** There may be duplication of jobs in both businesses. This can result in the merged firm making staff redundant.
2 New Products The merged business may be able to develop products faster using the combined resources of both firms. This can help to increase business sales.	**2 Conflict** Different business cultures can cause conflict between the staff of the merged firm. This can lead to industrial relations problems at the business.
3 Increased Profits The firm may benefit from increased profits due to the large customer base and lower costs.	**3 Decision-making** Making decisions can be a slow process if there is a lack of trust between the merged workforce. The business may then miss out on opportunities.

C Takeover/Acquisition

In a takeover/acquisition, one business purchases at least 51% of another business in either a hostile or a friendly manner. The business may take over a firm in the same or, in some cases, a different industry. The acquiring firm absorbs the other firm and it becomes part of the acquiring company. The business that owns the majority shareholding is called the **holding company**. The business that is acquired is known as a **subsidiary company**.

> **Definition**: **Hostile takeover**
> One firm acquires another business even though management oppose the acquisition. For example, AOL acquired Times Warner in a hostile takeover bid valued at almost €142 billion.

✓ Advantages	✗ Disadvantages
1 Spreads Risk By diversifying into new products or markets, it spreads risk for the acquiring business.	**1 Expensive** It can be expensive for the acquiring business as a large amount of capital may be required to finance the takeover.
2 Economies of Scale The larger business benefits from discounts from suppliers due to bulk buying. This reduces business costs.	**2 Staff Redundancies** There may be too many staff performing the same duties when one business is taken over by another. Staff redundancies will be needed to reduce business costs.
3 New Products The combined resources of the firms may result in faster development of new products. This can increase a firm's sales and profits.	**3 Industrial Relations** Some staff may be unhappy with the takeover and possible redundancies. This can increase the likelihood of industrial relations conflict at the firm.

Activity 22.6

Working in pairs, create a mind map to summarise the different methods of organic and inorganic growth. You can hand design the map or use a website such as www.canva.com.

CASE STUDY

Mergers

Many of the world's best-known brands have been created through mergers. Some have been successful, while others have failed.

Success: Disney and Pixar

Disney had a contract to release all Pixar's movies. When the contract was about to run out, the two businesses decided to merge. Following the merger, the company produced the highly successful *WALL-E*, *Up* and *Frozen*.

Frozen is the highest-grossing animated movie they've released.

Failure: Daimler-Benz and Chrysler

Daimler-Benz (a German firm) and Chrysler (a US firm) merged. However, there were cultural and communication difficulties between the two firms that the merger could not resolve. Daimler-Benz separated from Chrysler nine years after the merger.

HOW IS BUSINESS EXPANSION FINANCED?

You learned in Chapter 17 that businesses can obtain short-, medium- and long-term sources of finance. When choosing a source of finance it is important to make sure that the need is matched with the source, i.e. short-term finance is used for short-term needs. For example, a business could use a bank overdraft to purchase stock.

Unit 5

Expansion is part of a business's long-term strategy. Therefore, sources of finance required for expansion are long term. They include:

1 Equity capital
2 Retained earnings
3 Grant
4 Debt capital
5 Sale and leaseback
6 Venture capital.

> *The business should consider factors such as the impact on business control, risk and cost when deciding on the most appropriate source of finance for expansion. These factors are explained in greater detail in Chapter 17.*

1 Equity Capital

Equity capital is money raised when the business sells shares in the business or from direct investment of owner capital in a sole trader business.

This is done by:

- **Private limited companies:** Inviting existing shareholders or new shareholders to purchase shares in the business.
- **Public limited companies:** Selling more shares on the stock market, e.g. ISEQ (the Irish stock exchange).
- **Partnerships:** Inviting new partners into the business in return for a share of the business.
- **Sole trader:** The entrepreneur may invest more of his/her own money into the business.

The business owners sell shares in the company to investors. The investors become shareholders and have a say in the running of the business. Investors can vote at the firm's AGM and are entitled to a share of the profits, known as dividend.

2 Retained Earnings

The business uses profits that it has saved over time to finance expansion. There is no need to borrow, which reduces the cost of expansion. However, it can take a long time to build up enough profits to finance the expansion.

3 Grant

This is a sum of money given to the business by a government agency to support the expansion of the firm. Grants do not have to be repaid as long as the terms and conditions are met. The main sources are:

- **Local Enterprise Offices (LEOs):** Given to small local firms that wish to expand in the local area.
- **Enterprise Ireland:** Issued to domestic businesses that want to expand into foreign markets.
- **IDA Ireland:** Given to foreign business that operate in Ireland.
- **European Union:** Provides a range of grants, e.g. to highly innovative small and medium businesses.

 CASE STUDY ## Financial Supports Provided by Enterprise Ireland

Enterprise Ireland was an early investor in Brite:Bill, providing €400,000 in **equity capital** in the company. Brite:Bill provides ways for businesses to make bills easier for customers to understand. After a number of years of successful trading, Brite:Bill was **acquired** by an Israeli company called Amdocs for €75 million. As Enterprise Ireland held a 7% **equity** stake in Brite:Bill, the sale to Amdocs enabled it to make a profit on its original investment.

Note!

Under certain funding programmes, Enterprise Ireland provides equity capital in return for a maximum 10% stake in a business.

4 Debt Capital

The business takes out a long-term loan known as a debenture, using the firm's assets as security, e.g. deeds to property. The business makes interest-only payments on the debenture and repays the lump sum amount borrowed at a future date. If the business cannot repay the debenture, the lender can take ownership of the asset used to secure the loan.

Example

Irish security firm Netwatch raised €19.5 million to fund growth in the UK and US markets. Included in that funding was debt finance provided by Bank of Ireland, which amounted to €10.5 million.

Unit 5

5 Sale and Leaseback

The business sells an asset, e.g. premises, to a buyer, who then leases it back to the business. This gives the business a lump sum payment and allows it to continue to use the asset.

Example
Irish telecommunications company Digicel raised €77 million from a sale and leaseback of 451 of its telecom towers in Jamaica.

6 Venture Capital

A venture capitalist invests in a business in return for shares in the firm. The venture capitalist often gives the firm expertise, support and access to their own contacts. Once the business has become successful, the venture capital firm sells its shares at a profit.

Example
Dragons' Den Ireland gives entrepreneurs the opportunity to pitch their product ideas to a panel of investors. These venture capitalists invest in firms with the aim of making a profit on their investment. Kildare entrepreneur Noelle O'Connor received a €45,000 investment for a 45% stake in her business TanOrganic after an appearance on *Dragons' Den* Ireland. The brand is the only eco-certified self-tanning brand in the world and TanOrganic achieved sales of €1 million in the first three months of trading.

Activity 22.7

In groups, debate the benefits and drawbacks of the most common sources of finance used for business expansion. Which source of finance do you think brings the most benefits to the firm?

Using Debt or Equity Capital to Fund Expansion

For many businesses, expansion is a long-term strategy and requires the use of long-term sources of finance, particularly debt capital and equity capital. We will examine these forms of finance in greater detail under the headings Control, Interest Repayments /Dividends, Risk, Collateral and Tax.

Exam Tip!
*You should be able to **contrast** debt and equity capital. This means that you should be able to identify and explain the differences between the types of finance used by a business for expansion.*

	Debt Capital	**Equity Capital**
Control	→ Debt capital does not lead to a loss of control of the business.	→ Issuing shares dilutes the owner's control of the business as shareholders have a say in the running of the business.
Interest Repayments/ Dividends	→ Fixed interest repayments must be made on a debenture, regardless of business profitability.	→ The business does not have to pay a dividend to shareholders. However, if dividends are frequently small or not paid, the shareholders may sell their shares. This can result in a fall in share price.
Risk	→ If the business cannot make the fixed interest repayments, creditors may seek to have the business wound up and assets liquidated to pay debts.	→ A business that uses more equity than debt finance has low gearing. The business may be less likely to become bankrupt.
Collateral	→ The business must provide an asset as collateral to obtain debt finance, e.g. deeds of property.	→ No collateral is required to obtain equity capital.
Tax	→ Interest payments are a tax-deductible expense, i.e. they can be used to reduce a firm's tax liability.	→ Dividends paid to shareholders are not a tax-deductible expense.

Unit 5

IMPLICATIONS OF BUSINESS EXPANSION

Business expansion has short-term and long-term implications for the business and its stakeholders.

Implications for the Business

	Short-term Implications	Long-term Implications
Organisation Structure	→ The firm may introduce a formal structure such as a functional organisation structure. This outlines the chain of command and span of control in the firm.	→ The structure may need to change, e.g. the functional structure may be replaced with a geographic structure to support expansion into new geographic markets.
Product Mix	→ The firm's product range will increase to suit the wider range of market segments, e.g. Volkswagen acquired Škoda to give them a wider customer base.	→ Different marketing mixes will have to be put in place for the wider range of products in the firm's product portfolio.
Profitability	→ Profits will decrease due to increased expenditure on assets, e.g. machinery, buildings and IT.	→ Sales and profits will increase as the firm establishes itself in the market, and costs will be reduced by economies of scale, e.g. bulk buying.
Employment	→ Restructuring may lead to job losses as some roles are eliminated because of duplication, e.g. only one sales manager is needed instead of two.	→ As the business establishes itself in the market, the HR department will be able to recruit new employees as part of its staff planning.

Implications for Stakeholders

Consumers	→ As a business benefits from economies of scale, this may lead to lower prices for consumers. The business may also invest in R&D, thus giving consumers a wider choice of products.
Government	→ Growing firms employ more staff and may earn more profits. This increases the tax revenue received by the government, e.g. PAYE income tax, PRSI and corporation tax. This can be used by the government to pay for services such as education and health.
Local Community	→ Expanding firms provide jobs in the local community and they may invest in community initiatives, for example sponsoring local sports teams. Construction of manufacturing facilities may cause noise pollution and traffic congestion in the short term.
Employees	→ A larger business often requires more layers of management. This can increase promotional opportunities for employees.
Investors	→ A growing business may expand using equity finance. This decreases the control of existing shareholders.

THE IMPORTANCE OF BUSINESS EXPANSION

In the Domestic Economy

Expansion in the home market leads to:

- **Increased employment:** Increased demand may result in the business employing more staff. This increases employment and reduces the amount of government spending on social welfare payments.

- **Increased tax revenue:** Larger firms pay more taxes to the government, e.g. corporation tax. The government can use the tax revenue to develop infrastructure, e.g. new motorways.

- **Further expansion:** Larger businesses spend more money in the local economy purchasing raw materials and using services. This has a spin-off effect and leads to the expansion of other businesses. For example, as Lidl has grown in the Irish market, bakery Comerford Brothers has increased the size of its factory three times. It now supplies stores across Ireland with one million buns and 200,000 cakes per week.

- **Lower prices:** Large businesses benefit from economies of scale. They purchase items in bulk and obtain discounts from suppliers. This lowers the cost of production and can be passed on to consumers in the form of lower prices.

In Foreign Markets

Expansion in foreign markets leads to:

- **Increased employment:** As sales increase in foreign markets, more jobs are created in the Irish economy.

- **Increased exports:** This improves the balance of trade. A balance of trade surplus has a positive effect on a country as it means more employment and an increase in the standard of living.

- **Foreign currency:** Ireland needs to import goods such as oil, citrus fruits and cars. By increasing exports we bring in foreign currency to pay for the imports.

- **Spreading risk:** By selling products in other countries, a business is less dependent on the domestic market. If one market experiences low growth, sales in another market can compensate.

- **Improved international relations:** International trade encourages good relations between Ireland and the rest of the world.

HOW IS BUSINESS EXPANSION RESTRICTED?

Business expansion is restricted if either the Irish government or the EU believes that expansion is not in the best interests of consumers, e.g. if the larger business will have a dominant or monopoly position in the marketplace.

In Ireland, restrictions on business expansion are enforced by the Competition and Consumer Protection Commission (CCPC).

Business expansion is regulated by:

- **Irish law:** Mergers and takeovers above a certain financial value must be examined by the CCPC before they are allowed to proceed. If the CCPC believes that a proposed merger or takeover will have a negative impact on consumers, e.g. higher prices or less choice, the proposal will be denied.

- **EU law:** Under European competition law the EU Commission appoints a Commissioner for Competition to investigate all large mergers and takeovers above a certain financial value. Proposed mergers and acquisitions are prevented from taking place if they are not in the best interest of consumers, e.g. they create a monopoly in the market. For example, the EU Commission prevented a takeover of Aer Lingus by Ryanair as it would have created a dominant business in the airline market.

CASE STUDY *Apple's Takeover of Shazam*

After undertaking a detailed investigation, the **EU Commission** approved the **acquisition** by Apple of Shazam. The Commission believes that the **takeover** will not have a negative impact on competition across the EU. Shazam enables users to identify a song after hearing a fragment of the music. It has been downloaded over one billion times and is used to identify more than 20 million songs per day.

WHY DO SOME BUSINESSES REMAIN SMALL?

While many businesses want to expand in order to increase their sales and profits, some businesses may want to keep their firms relatively small in size.

✓ Advantages	✗ Disadvantages
1 Easier to Manage There are fewer products and fewer employees. These are easier to manage and control.	**1 Costs** Smaller businesses may have higher costs as they do not benefit from economies of scale, e.g. large firms receive better discounts from bulk buying.
2 Customer Loyalty Customers can receive a more personal service from staff, which can increase customer loyalty.	**2 Lack of Capital** A small business can find it difficult to raise finance, as investors may view the business as having a higher risk of failure.
3 Change Smaller businesses are flexible and may be able to adapt to changes in the market faster than larger firms. This can help to increase their sales and profits.	**3 Staffing** It can be difficult to attract and retain staff. Smaller firms may be unable to provide the better pay and working conditions offered by larger firms.
4 Faster Decision-making As there are fewer people and usually fewer management levels in a small business, decisions can be made faster.	**4 Profits** The firm's profits tend to be smaller than profits earned by larger businesses.

Activity 22.8

Divide the class into two teams. Your teacher will make a statement, e.g. 'It is better for business to remain small.' A student from one team makes a statement in favour of the topic and a student from the other team immediately makes a statement against the topic. This continues until one side of the room can no longer think of any relevant points to make on the topic.

KEY TERMS

Now you have completed this chapter, you should understand and be able to explain the following terms. In your copybook, write a definition of each term to build up your own glossary of terms.

- business expansion
- psychological reasons for expansion
- empire building
- defensive reasons for expansion
- diversification
- backward vertical integration
- offensive reasons for expansion

- forward vertical integration
- asset stripping
- organic growth
- licensing
- franchising
- inorganic growth
- strategic alliance/joint venture
- merger
- takeover/acquisition

- equity capital
- debt capital
- Competition and Consumer Protection Commission (CCPC)
- European Union Commissioner for Competition

PowerPoint Summary

EXAM-STYLE QUESTIONS

Ordinary Level

Section 1 – Short Questions (10 marks each)

1 List **three** reasons why a business might decide to expand.
2 Outline **one** defensive and **one** offensive reason for expansion.
3 Distinguish between organic growth and inorganic growth.
4 Describe **one** method of organic growth that a business might use for expansion.
5 Explain the term *strategic alliance*. Name **one** business formed by strategic alliance.
6 List **three** ways in which a business can finance its expansion.
7 Indicate whether each of the following statements is true or false.

Statements		True or False
A	Empire building is an attempt to increase the size of a business so that it can dominate the market.	
B	Forward integration is when a business expands by buying its own retail outlets.	
C	Organic growth is also known as external growth.	
D	All parties to a strategic alliance lose their independence.	
E	A hostile takeover is when a business takes over another in a friendly manner.	

8 Using the words below, fill in the gaps in the following sentence. (One word does not apply.)

franchisee   franchise   franchisor   fee

One business, known as the_____, agrees to let another business – the _____ – to use its name, logo and business idea in return for a _____ and a percentage of profits.

Section 2 – Long Questions

1 Outline defensive reasons why a business might decide to expand. **(15 marks)**
2 Explain the difference between organic growth and inorganic growth. **(15 marks)**
3 Explain the terms (i) *merger* (ii) *takeover* and (iii) *strategic alliance*. **(15 marks)**
4 Name **three** sources of finance that a business could use to fund its expansion. Explain **two** of these sources in detail. **(20 marks)**
5 Explain what is meant by the term *sale and leaseback*. What are the disadvantages of this source of finance? **(15 marks)**
6

> Cullen Ltd is a clothing manufacturer located in Swords Business Park. The company manufactures and distributes work uniforms to businesses across Ireland. It also has one retail shop based nearby in the retail park. Cullen Ltd hopes to expand more into the retail market and is considering a merger with the clothing store Uniforms4u Ltd, which has a chain of shops throughout Ireland, offering Cullen Ltd an opportunity to obtain access to a channel of distribution for their products.

   (i)   Explain what is meant by a merger and outline the benefits of a merger to Cullen Ltd. **(15 marks)**
   (ii) Name **two** sources of finance that Cullen Ltd may be able to use to finance this merger. Explain **one** of these sources of finance. **(15 marks)**
7 What are the short- and long-term implications of expansion on a firm's (i) product mix, (ii) profitability and (iii) organisation structure? **(30 marks)**
8 Describe the impact that business expansion has on the following business stakeholders: (i) employees and (ii) consumers. **(15 marks)**

Higher Level

Section 1 – Short Questions (10 marks each)

1 Describe **two** offensive reasons why a business makes the decision to expand its operations.

2 Distinguish between forward integration and backward integration in relation to the expansion of a business.

3 Outline the advantages and disadvantages of franchising as a method of expansion for the franchisee.

4 Distinguish between a merger and a joint venture.

5 Outline **two** advantages of using debt finance as a source of finance for expansion.

6 Fill in the appropriate words to complete each of the following statements.

   (i) A g_____ is a sum of money given to a business by a government agency to support the expansion of the firm.

   (ii) Licensing and franchising are forms of o_____ g_____

   (iii) C_____ integration is when two businesses with nothing in common join together.

   (iv) A s_____ a_____ is when two or more businesses agree to work together on a common project that benefits both firms.

   (v) E_____ b_____ is a reason for business expansion. It occurs when the business wants to be the largest and most successful firm in the market.

7 Choose the correct option in the following sentences.

   (i) When a business expands by taking over a supplier business this is called **backward/forward** integration.

   (ii) **Asset stripping/asset salvaging** occurs when a business purchases another simply to obtain items of value from the firm.

   (iii) A **takeover/merger** occurs when two businesses join together.

   (iv) **Equity/debt capital** is money raised through the issue of shares in the business.

   (v) The **CCPC/RSA** is responsible for enforcing restrictions on business expansion.

8 Describe the impact that business expansion has on (i) the local community and (ii) the government.

Section 2 – Applied Business Question (80 marks)

Toni's Italian Restaurants

Toni Kelly owns and runs two very successful Italian restaurants, both called Toni's, in Limerick city centre. The business is in a healthy financial position, as during the recession he bought the two buildings in which his restaurants are located at bargain prices. The firm has also built up considerable retained earnings.

He is considering opening more restaurants in other towns and cities across Munster. While other entrepreneurs want to stay small, Toni wants to own the largest chain of Italian restaurants in Ireland. Toni knows that he will require a large amount of finance to fund this planned expansion. He has spoken with his bank manager and she can offer him a loan of €300,000. She has also suggested that he could sell his premises and rent them back from the new owners, to reduce the amount of money he needs to borrow.

Toni enjoys the variety of tasks associated with setting up a business, from finding premises to developing marketing campaigns to attract customers. While travelling around Munster, Toni has viewed a number of restaurant buildings for sale with fully equipped kitchens. These are very attractive options as they would enable him to get the restaurants up and running quickly. He has also seen some small restaurants in prime retail locations and wonders if he should try to buy the owners out and set up his restaurants in these areas.

Today Toni received an interesting phone call from another restaurant owner in Tipperary, who wants to meet to discuss the possibility of joining their restaurants together. On his way home to Limerick, Toni hears an advertisement on the radio for the Limerick Local Enterprise Office and wonders if he could get some financial support for expansion.

Section 2 – Applied Business Question (80 marks) *continued*

Toni knows that owning and running a restaurant is hard work. His accountant has suggested that there are other options available for expansion. She asks him to consider selling his business idea to others in return for a fee. Toni is unsure if he wants to lose control of his firm and tells her that he needs time to consider his options.

A	Describe the reasons why Toni Kelly might decide to expand his business.	(30 marks)
B	Outline the methods that Toni could use to expand his Italian restaurant business.	(30 marks)
C	Evaluate the sources of finance that Toni could use if he decided to expand his business.	(20 marks)

Section 3 – Long Questions

1 Describe **three** reasons for business expansion other than to increase profits. (20 marks)

2 Distinguish clearly between the following terms: (i) *backward integration*; (ii) *forward integration*; (iii) *horizontal integration*; and (iv) *conglomerate integration*. Illustrate your answer with relevant examples. (20 marks)

3 Discuss the benefits and drawbacks of a firm using a merger as a form of expansion. (20 marks)

4 Evaluate franchising as a method of expansion for a restaurant. (20 marks)

5 Evaluate debt capital versus equity capital as sources of finance for business expansion. (20 marks)

6 Describe the ways in which business expansion can be restricted. (15 marks)

7

Jack and Greta Rose set up their own business in Dublin manufacturing wooden toys. They know that the Irish market is too small for them to increase profitability and want to expand into the EU market.

(i) Explain **two** methods of expansion you would advise them to consider. (20 marks)

(ii) Outline the implications for Ireland when Irish firms export to foreign markets. (15 marks)

8 Describe the advantages and disadvantages of a business remaining small. (20 marks)

PREVIOUS LEAVING CERTIFICATE EXAM QUESTIONS

Ordinary Level

Section A – Short Questions (10 marks each)

1 Choose the appropriate words to complete the sentence below. (Two words do not apply.)

MERGER; FRANCHISE; STRATEGIC ALLIANCE; TAKEOVER.

A _____ involves two businesses voluntarily joining together to form a single business, while a _____ involves two businesses working together on a specific project without any change of ownership. [LC OL 2018]

2 Describe what is meant by the term *franchise*. [LC OL 2002]

3 Indicate by means of a tick (✔) in the correct box, the method of expansion to which each statement below relates:

Statements	Merger	Takeover	Franchise	Strategic Alliance
Apple buys Beats by Dr Dre for $3bn.				
Avonmore Foods plc and Waterford Foods plc joined forces to form Glanbia plc				
Irish grocery retailer SuperValu has announced a new partnership with Bank of Ireland as part of its 'Real Rewards' loyalty programme.				
The Zip Yard have expanded by allowing other parties to use the business model and trademark in exchange for a fee and a percentage of profits.				

[LC OL 2017]

Section B

1

> David Mason operates a car dealership in Co. Kildare. He sells both new and used cars and also provides mechanic services. He is currently thinking of expanding the business. He will require long-term finance for the expansion. David has recently met with his local Bank Manager and presented his Business Plan.

(i) Outline **two** reasons why David Mason might wish to expand his business. **(15 marks)**

(ii) Explain **two** sources of long-term finance David Mason could use to expand his business.
(15 marks) [LC OL 2015]

2

> Pratai plc was set up fifty years ago and makes potato crisps for the domestic and export markets. It has expanded through organic growth and now is a major employer in the local area. The demand for its products is growing but the company has limited production capacity. Recent competition from other snack food companies has decreased Pratai's market share.

(i) Illustrate what is meant by organic growth. **(5 marks)**

(ii) Describe **four** reasons why Pratai plc would like to expand their business. **(20 marks)**

(iii) Describe **two** methods of expansion that Pratai plc could use. **(10 marks)**

(iv) Identify **three** sources of finance that Pratai plc could use for expansion. Explain any **one** of these sources. **(20 marks) [LC OL 2000]**

Higher Level

Section A – Short Questions (10 marks each)

1 Illustrate the difference between a strategic alliance and a takeover as methods of business expansion. **[LC HL 2014]**

2 Illustrate the difference between a merger and a strategic alliance. **[LC HL 2015]**

Section B

1

> SuperToys Ltd, a large retail chain with 45 shops throughout Ireland, had sales of €100 million in 2011. It has just commissioned a firm to design and manufacture a new range of soft toys for babies. These will be available for sale in its shops from Summer 2013. SuperToys Ltd plans to open its first shop in the UK in 2014.

Discuss the possible reasons for business expansion and growth at SuperToys Ltd.
(20 marks) [LC HL 2012]

2

> Kilronan Ltd produces a range of chilled food products. Made from natural ingredients, the firm's award-winning products have become household names. It is now one of the leading brands in Ireland and supplies all the major supermarket chains. Kilronan Ltd is considering either a 'merger' or a 'takeover' as a method of expansion within the Irish market. It is also considering how it will finance growth.

(A) (i) Illustrate the difference between a merger and a takeover as methods of business expansion.

(ii) Discuss the benefits and risks of a merger as a method of expansion for Kilronan Ltd.
(25 marks)

(B) Distinguish between debt capital and equity capital as sources of finance for the expansion of Kilronan Ltd. **(15 marks) [LC HL 2011]**

 Solutions

23 CATEGORIES OF INDUSTRY

When you have completed this chapter, you will be able to:

1. Identify and explain the factors of production and their associated rewards
2. Recognise and illustrate the categories of industry: primary, secondary and tertiary
3. Understand and explain the trends and challenges affecting the primary, secondary and tertiary sectors
4. Outline the benefits that the primary, secondary and tertiary sectors bring to the Irish economy.

Literacy Link

Primary sector, secondary sector, manufacturing, construction, agribusiness, tertiary (services) sector

Numeracy Link

Division, multiplication

Cross-curricular Link

Agricultural science – soil, crops, plants, trees
Economics – factors of production
Geography – primary, secondary and tertiary activities

CASE STUDY   *Combilift*

Combilift is an **indigenous** Irish **manufacturing** company operating in the Irish **secondary** sector. As a materials handling solutions provider, Combilift produces multi-directional forklifts, side loaders, articulated forklifts, pedestrian stackers and Straddle Carriers, enabling customers to improve loading and offloading times.

The firm, based in Co. Monaghan, is recognised as the world leader in the design and manufacturing of multi-directional forklifts, producing gas, LPG, electric and diesel products.

The business has sold more than 43,000 units in over 85 countries worldwide. Combilift invests 7% of its revenue into **R&D** and launches at least one new model per year. The company **exports** 98% of its products, with 25% of exports sold to the UK. Other fast-growing markets include the USA and Scandinavia.

The company has won many awards, and has been named Irish Exporter of the Year and Deloitte Best Managed Company. Managing Director, Martin McVicar, was named EY Entrepreneur of the Year in 2007.

Combilift is loyal to the local Monaghan area and has invested

COMBiLiFT
LiFTING INNOVATION

€50 million to develop a new global headquarters and manufacturing facility which will allow Combilift to double output. It was officially opened in 2018 by An Taoiseach Leo Varadkar TD. Combilift announced the creation of an additional 200 in the **tertiary sector**, providing jobs for skilled technicians and design engineers.

There are 650 people employed at Combilift in Monaghan and an additional 100 globally. A traineeship scheme was recently developed to ensure that the company has a supply of skilled workers. Trainees spend 50% of their time in college and 50% working and learning onsite in the Combilift factory.

Combilift also led the development of the Original Equipment Manufacturing **Apprenticeship** which is designed to meet the skills gap faced by Irish equipment manufacturing firms.

Combilift has a **turnover** of more than €240 million per annum and expects this figure to grow to €1 billion within the next ten years.

FACTORS OF PRODUCTION

Four essential elements, known as the **factors of production**, are needed to start a business: **land, labour, capital** and **enterprise**. The entrepreneur who spots a gap in the market for a business must combine land, labour, capital and enterprise to provide goods and services to consumers.

Factor of Production	Description		Economic Return/Reward
Land	→ All natural resources that are used to provide goods and services, e.g. rivers, land, air, coal, minerals and metals.		→ Rent
Labour	→ The human effort needed to provide goods and services. A business needs workers with a wide range of skills and expertise to run the firm effectively. Labour can include factory operatives, retail assistants and office staff.		→ Wages
Capital	→ Items used to produce goods and services, e.g. machinery, equipment, money and buildings.		→ Interest
Enterprise	→ This is the factor of production that combines the other three factors – land, labour and capital – and creates a business to provide goods and services.		→ Profit

Activity 23.1

Working in pairs, identify the goods and services needed to produce a Cadbury's Dairy Milk bar. When you've made your list, categorise the items into land, labour, capital or enterprise.

SECTORS IN THE ECONOMY

The sectors in an economy are divided into primary, secondary and tertiary (services).

1 Primary Sector

The **primary sector** refers to the **extraction of raw materials from the earth**. It includes industries such as farming, fishing, forestry and mining.

The primary sector provides:

- Fuel for businesses to operate, e.g. oil and gas
- Raw materials needed to produce goods, e.g. wood, metals and crops.

Example
Fish caught in Irish waters are used to make Donegal Catch frozen products.

Macroom Buffalo Cheese

Farmer Johnny Lynch was disappointed with the price paid by supermarkets for cows' milk. He wanted to find a way to increase his farm's income and decided to **diversify** into buffalo farming.

Johnny purchased 31 buffalo from Italy and established the first milking buffalo farm in Ireland. He knew that the market demand for products made from buffalo milk was increasing and decided to manufacture Irish mozzarella. At a cost of €500,000, Johnny built a cheese plant on his farmland and together with a local cheesemaker began to make Macroom Buffalo Cheese. Johnny now employs ten people and produces 70 tonnes of cheese from a herd of 200 buffalo on his 150-acre farm. The company supplies many of the supermarket chains around Ireland.

Johnny has plans to **expand** the herd **organically** by 40% over the next few years and to increase production. In May 2018 he signed a deal with Aldi, whereby Macroom Buffalo Cheese will supply €1 million of mozzarella cheese to the supermarket over a two-year period.

Activity 23.2

1 One hectare is the equivalent of 2.47 acres of land. Calculate how many hectares of land Johnny Lynch owns.

2 Search on the Internet for a video of the Aldi Ireland advertisement 'Italian Buffalo Mozzarella?' to see Johnny Lynch and his herd of buffalo.

Trends and Challenges in the Farming Industry in Ireland

Farming includes arable and dairy farming. There are almost 140,000 family farms in Ireland, with most agricultural land used to grow grass and cereals such as barley. The southern and eastern regions have almost 80% of all dairy farms in the country.

DID YOU KNOW? *A standard GAA pitch measures approximately three acres.*

Trends			Challenges		
Changes in Consumer Demand	→ Many farmers have begun to produce organic and GMO-free products to cater for changes in consumer demand. This can help to increase farm income and profits.		**Farm Loans**	→ Farmers typically pay more interest on bank loans than other businesses as they are viewed to have a higher risk of failure, e.g. due to bad weather affecting farm output. This has reduced farmers' ability to expand their farms and modernise their machinery.	
Job Vacancies	→ Job vacancies in the dairy sector may encourage people to begin careers in farming or encourage people to return to the dairy sector.		**Reduce Greenhouse Gases**	→ Farmers are under increasing pressure from the government to reduce their emissions of pollutants such as methane gas, which is a greenhouse gas. This can increase farming costs.	

Trends		Challenges	
Free Trade	→ A free trade agreement with the EU and Japan enables Irish farmers to export their products to Japan free from tariffs. This could lead to an increase in Irish exports and increase farm profits.	**Brexit**	→ Many farmers fear that Brexit will lead to the reintroduction of border tariffs between Ireland and the UK. This will increase the cost of Irish farming exports and may result in lower profits for farmers.
Modernisation	→ The EU offers grants to farmers to modernise their farming methods and machinery. This can help to increase the quality and quantity of their farm output.	**Farm Accidents**	→ To reduce the number of deaths on farms, the government must increase spending on farm safety awareness programmes.

There are more cattle than people in Ireland – 4.7 million people and 6.4 million cattle.

Definition: Brexit
The withdrawal of the UK from the European Union.

Definition: GMO
A genetically modified organism is a plant or animal whose genetic structure has been altered in a laboratory. This process is often used to make plants more resistant to weeds, diseases and pests. Common GMO products include corn, soy beans and cotton.

Activity 23.3

Working in pairs, write out the key words relating to the farming industry in Ireland on slips of paper. Fold the papers and put them in a container/empty pencil case. Take turns to draw a slip and work together to write an explanation for the key term. Continue until all key terms have been explained.

Trends and Challenges in the Fishing Industry in Ireland

The fishing industry employs more than 14,000 people across Ireland and contributes €1.15 billion to the Irish economy. The two main fishing ports in Ireland are Killybegs in Co. Donegal and Castletownbere in Co. Cork.

Trends		Challenges	
Growing Demand	→ There is a growth in demand for seafood products around the world, e.g. in Chile and China, where disposable incomes have increased.	**Increased Regulation**	→ Stricter EU regulations and quotas have been introduced to prevent overfishing. This has reduced fishing incomes and led to an increased number of fishing industry workers leaving their jobs.
Growth of New Business	→ There has been an increase in the number of new businesses in the nutritional supplements sector, e.g. fish oils. This has led to more job opportunities in the industry.	**Brexit**	→ Currently Irish fishing boats can fish between six and twelve nautical miles off the UK coast. After Brexit this may not be allowed, which will reduce fish catches and income for the Irish fishing fleet.

Trends			Challenges		
Movement of Species	→ Seafood species have begun to migrate from traditional fishing grounds due to climate change and other environmental factors. This has enabled fishing industry workers to catch new species and open up new markets for their produce.		**Price of Fuel**	→ The fishing industry is highly dependent on oil as a source of fuel. Higher oil prices will affect the industry, so it must work with experts to find alternative fuel sources to help reduce costs.	
Traceability	→ Consumers demand greater traceability of the seafood they consume. The fishing industry needs to spend more money on technology to increase traceability, which can increase consumer trust.		**Aquaculture**	→ The aquaculture sector can have a negative impact on the environment if not managed correctly, e.g. the transmission of diseases to wild fish. High standards should be maintained at all times to limit environmental damage.	

DID YOU KNOW?

Sixty-four per cent of mackerel and 39% of prawns caught by Irish vessels come from UK waters.

The World Bank estimates that by 2030, 60% of the world's fish for human consumption will come from the aquaculture industry.

Definition: **Aquaculture**
Breeding and harvesting plants and animals, e.g. shellfish, seaweed and farmed fish, in water environments.

Activity 23.4

One nautical mile is equal to 1.1508 statute miles (land miles). How many statute miles are in 12 nautical miles?

Trends and Challenges in the Forestry Industry in Ireland

Forests cover 10.5% of the total land area of Ireland. This figure is 40% for most European countries. The forestry industry employs 16,000 people in jobs such as planting, harvesting and timber milling. The Irish government is aiming to increase forestry to 18% of the total land area of Ireland.

Trends			Challenges		
Government Incentives	→ More training programmes have helped those involved in the industry to learn new planting and harvesting methods. This has led to an increased output of timber and wood from Irish land.		**Disease**	→ Trees may be affected by diseases which can limit their growth or kill them. Forest owners must watch out for signs of disease and report concerns to the relevant authorities.	
Environmental Impact of Forestry	→ Businesses and consumers are more aware of the environmental impact of forestry. They want to ensure that the wood they purchase has been grown and harvested using sustainable methods.		**Brexit**	→ The possible reintroduction of tariffs between Ireland and the UK will make Irish exports more expensive. This may reduce timber sales and reduce forestry income.	

Unit 6

Trends		Challenges	
Increased Employment	→ An increased worldwide demand for timber has led to a rise in the number of people working in the industry, e.g. in sawmills and timber processing businesses.	**Landowners**	→ The government may have to offer more incentives to encourage landowners to plant forests. It can take up to 25 years for a forest to produce an output and some landowners are not prepared to wait that long to earn a profit.
Increased Investment	→ More people are using forests for sport and recreation. Forests require investment to develop family-friendly tracks and trails.	**Forest Certification**	→ It can be difficult to encourage forest owners to gain certification (e.g. the Forest Stewardship Council), due to the costs involved.

 DID YOU KNOW? *It is estimated that every 100 jobs in forestry create an additional 70 full-time jobs in other sectors of the Irish economy.*

Certification from the Forest Stewardship Council (FSC) indicates that the forest has been planted, maintained and harvested in an environmentally sustainable manner.

Activity 23.5

Choose the correct answers.

1 What percentage of the land in Ireland is covered in forest?
(a) 20.2 %   (b) 13.4%   (c) 10.5%

2 What percentage of Ireland's forest products are exported?
(a) 64%   (b) 78%   (c) 51%

3 How many people are directly employed in the forestry industry?
(a) 16,000   (b) 25,000   (c) 32,000

Answers: 1 (c); 2 (b); 3 (a)

2 Secondary Sector

The **secondary sector** involves the **transformation of raw materials into finished products**. This sector includes manufacturing, construction and agribusiness.

A Manufacturing

Manufacturing in Ireland is focused on the following areas:

- Pharmaceutical and chemical products
- Food and beverages
- Computer, electronic and electrical equipment.

Approximately 400,000 people are directly or indirectly employed in the manufacturing sector in Ireland. Manufacturing firms also source around €14 billion worth of materials and services from Irish businesses.

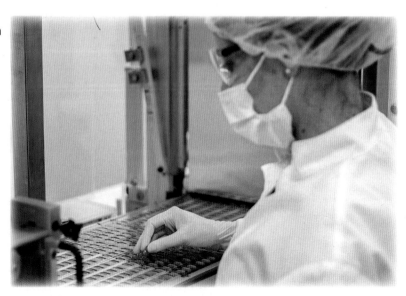

Manufacturing at Newbridge Silverware

Newbridge Silverware manufactures homeware, gifts and jewellery at its factory in Newbridge, Co. Kildare.

Skilled workers in the factory take raw materials such as copper, zinc and silver and transform them into finished products such as cutlery, clocks and photo frames. The company uses the excess materials from cutlery production to manufacture the jewellery range. Jewellery now accounts for 60% of total company sales.

Newbridge Silverware provides direct employment for around 90 workers in Kildare.

Trends and Challenges in the Manufacturing Industry in Ireland

Trends		Challenges	
Highly Educated Employees	→ Ireland is an attractive location for manufacturing businesses due to our highly educated workforce. The government must continue to invest in education to ensure that there is a supply of employees available to fill future vacancies.	**Low-cost Economies**	→ Irish manufacturing firms are under intense cost competition from manufacturers in low-cost economies such as China. Irish manufacturers need to find USPs for their products that enable them to compete in areas other than price.
Increased Consumer Demand	→ Increased consumer demand for manufactured products such as electronics and pharmaceuticals can create opportunities for Irish firms to export. This can help to increase business sales and profits.	**Job Losses**	→ Automated machinery allows businesses to manufacture products more efficiently. This has led to job losses in the manufacturing sector.
Environmental Sustainability	→ Irish manufacturing businesses can produce their products in an environmentally sustainable manner. This can help to attract more environmentally conscious consumers.	**Investment in Infrastructure**	→ Continued government investment is needed to develop infrastructure in Ireland, e.g. airports and motorways. This will help to attract foreign businesses to establish manufacturing plants in Ireland.
Growth of Pharmaceutical Firms	→ International pharmaceutical firms have paired with Irish third-level institutions to work on research projects. This encourages other pharmaceutical businesses to locate in Ireland.	**Brexit**	→ Irish manufacturing exports may become more expensive when the UK leaves the EU due to the reintroduction of tariffs. This will have a negative impact on sales and profits for Irish-based manufacturing firms.

Unit 6

DID YOU KNOW? *More than half (52%) of 25–34-year-olds in Ireland have a third-level qualification.*

B Construction

The construction sector consists of all individuals and businesses involved in the design and construction of buildings, e.g. houses and offices. It also includes the construction and maintenance of roads, bridges and tunnels.

The construction sector is sensitive to the economic activity of a country. When the economy is growing, the construction sector tends to grow too. When the economy experiences difficulty, activity in the construction sector tends to fall.

DID YOU KNOW? *The construction industry provides direct employment to 137,000 workers and indirect employment to 53,000 workers.*

CASE STUDY — PJ Hegarty & Sons

Hegarty Building & Civil Engineering Contractors was established in Cork in 1952. It is well known for constructing two of Ireland's tallest buildings: Cork County Hall in 1968 (67 metres) and the Elysian Building in 2008 (71 metres).

The company, now known as PJ Hegarty and Sons, has recently completed the **construction** of the €35 million Cork prison. This project provided **direct** and **indirect employment** for around 200 people. Construction industry experts estimated that the majority of the €35 million would be spent in the local economy, for buying raw materials and services, and employees spending their wages in the area. The company has survived the recent **economic recession** and now employs 250 staff. MD John Hegarty has said, 'Our goal now is to continue to grow the business in a sustainable way by taking advantage of the improving economy and with a construction industry at last emerging out of recession.'

Trends and Challenges in the Construction Sector in Ireland

Trends		Challenges	
Graduates	→ Government and business must work together to ensure that there are jobs available for construction sector graduates, e.g. engineers and architects. This will reduce the need for them to emigrate to find work.	**Shortage of Housing**	→ There is a shortage of housing around Ireland with many people unable to afford to rent or buy their own homes, especially in large urban areas such as Dublin, Cork and Galway.
Increased Disposable Income	→ Employees have more disposable income and greater job security. This has increased the demand for housing and created job opportunities for the construction sector building homes.	**Access to Finance**	→ Construction firms can find it difficult to obtain loans from banks. This has resulted in the delay of construction projects, e.g. private housing and office sites.

Trends		Challenges	
Employment	→ An improvement in the economy has led to an increase in direct employment, e.g. plumbers and bricklayers, and indirect employment, e.g. building suppliers and shops.	**Shortage of Skilled Employees**	→ There is a shortage of skilled employees in the sector, e.g. quantity surveyors and engineers. Businesses may need to recruit employees from abroad to fill the vacancies.
Brexit	→ Offices need to be built in advance of international firms moving to Ireland after Brexit.	**Protection of Migrant Workers**	→ Many migrant workers are unaware of their employment rights, e.g. the minimum wage. It is important that these workers are protected from exploitation.

Activity 23.6

Working in pairs, examine the infographic and answer the following questions.

1. Which area has the highest average price per home?

2. Which area has the lowest average price per home? Why, do you think, does this area have the lowest prices?

3. What is the largest percentage price increase?

4. In which county did the percentage price decrease? What was the average price per home in this county?

5. If the average price per home in Carlow increased by 9%, what was the average price of the home before the increase?

6. What is the average price of a home in your county?

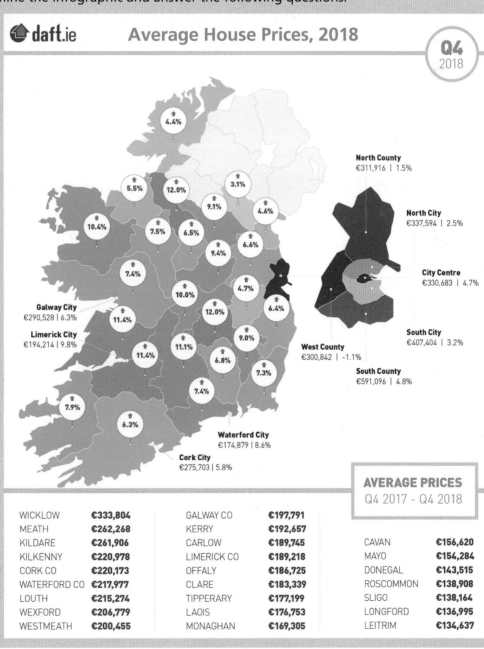

daft.ie — Average House Prices, 2018

Q4 2018

North County €311,916 | 1.5%
North City €337,594 | 2.5%
City Centre €330,683 | 4.7%
South City €407,404 | 3.2%
West County €300,842 | -1.1%
South County €591,096 | 4.8%

Galway City €290,528 | 6.3%
Limerick City €194,214 | 9.8%
Waterford City €174,879 | 8.6%
Cork City €275,703 | 5.8%

AVERAGE PRICES Q4 2017 – Q4 2018

WICKLOW	€333,804	GALWAY CO	€197,791
MEATH	€262,268	KERRY	€192,657
KILDARE	€261,906	CARLOW	€189,745
KILKENNY	€220,978	LIMERICK CO	€189,218
CORK CO	€220,173	OFFALY	€186,725
WATERFORD CO	€217,977	CLARE	€183,339
LOUTH	€215,274	TIPPERARY	€177,199
WEXFORD	€206,779	LAOIS	€176,753
WESTMEATH	€200,455	MONAGHAN	€169,305

CAVAN	€156,620
MAYO	€154,284
DONEGAL	€143,515
ROSCOMMON	€138,908
SLIGO	€138,164
LONGFORD	€136,995
LEITRIM	€134,637

Unit 6

C Agribusiness

Agribusiness refers to manufacturing businesses that make products using raw materials from the agricultural sector, e.g. cereals, meat, milk, fruit and vegetables. There are a number of large agribusinesses in Ireland, including Glanbia, Glenisk and the Kerry Group.

CASE STUDY — Glenisk

Glenisk is a second-generation family-owned **agribusiness** based in Killeigh, Co. Offaly. It produces a range of organic cow's milk and yoghurts and goat's milk and yoghurts. The company employs seventy people directly and sources organic milk from fifty small family farms around Ireland.

Seventy-five per cent of yoghurts consumed in Ireland are imported. Glenisk conducted **market research** to help it to create a yoghurt range for the Irish market. The twelve-month research included one-to-one **interviews** with consumers, **focus groups** and in-home tastings. This led to the development of the Glenisk high-protein Greek yoghurt range. The company also invested €1 million in **marketing** to promote this new product line.

Glenisk now sells two million servings of yoghurt per week and its share of the yoghurt market has increased from 4% to 14% over the past ten years. The company has a **sales turnover** of approximately €25 million.

The United Arab Emirates is the company's fastest-growing **export market** and its products are available in Bahrain, Saudi Arabia and Kuwait. Sales are increasing in the UK and the company has plans to develop more markets in Europe.

Trends and Challenges in Agribusiness in Ireland

Trends		Challenges	
New Products	→ Agribusinesses can develop new products to cater for the demand for a healthier lifestyle, e.g. Flahavan's microwaveable porridge oats. New products can increase a firm's sales and profits.	**Lower Prices for Suppliers**	→ Irish agribusinesses may have to accept lower prices for their produce from national supermarkets. This is particularly difficult for small to medium-sized producers that rely on the Irish market for their sales.
Mergers and Acquisitions	→ Smaller agribusinesses find it difficult to compete with larger competitors. Many have decided to merge with other firms or are acquired by larger firms.	**Extreme Weather Conditions**	→ Extreme weather has destroyed crops and limited global supply, e.g. lettuce, peppers and spinach. This has increased costs for agribusinesses and reduced their profits.

Example

Cloetta, a Swedish confectionery-manufacturing company, acquired a 75% stake in Aran Candy Ltd, based in Blanchardstown, which produces luxury jelly beans under the trade name the Jelly Bean Factory®. The company currently manufactures 12 million jelly beans each day, in 36 different flavours, using no artificial colours.

Trends			Challenges		
Food Waste	→ Agribusinesses have developed innovative packaging and products that allow consumers to reduce the amount of food going to landfill, e.g. individual portions.		Exports	→ Costs of Irish agri-exports to Britain will probably increase after Brexit. Irish agribusinesses may need to find new export markets to boost their sales and profits.	
Growth of Indigenous Irish Firms	→ There has been a growth in the number of Irish agribusinesses, e.g. Glenilen Farm. Government agencies need to encourage the growth of agribusinesses to provide employment in local areas.		Higher Operating Costs	→ Irish agribusinesses face increasing operating costs, e.g. higher wages. Irish firms must find ways to reduce costs to remain competitive.	

DID YOU KNOW? *Households in Ireland throw out almost 50% of salads and 20% of bread and bakery products purchased. Potatoes, apples and bananas are the most common fruit and vegetables thrown out.*

Activity 23.7

Each person in Ireland throws away 80kg of food per year. If an average tin of beans holds 421g, express the amount of food waste per person in terms of tins of beans.

3 Tertiary Sector

The tertiary or services sector includes firms that provide services to businesses and individual consumers. Examples of tertiary businesses include insurance, banking, tourism, education and health.

DID YOU KNOW? *Seventy-five per cent of the workforce in Ireland work in the services sector.*

An estimated 200,000 people are employed in the tourism sector in Ireland. The sector contributes over €7 billion to the Irish economy.

One in five people in Ireland are employed in a transnational company. This equates to 187,056 jobs.

Unit 6

Exam Tip!
Remember: the tertiary sector is also known as the services sector.

CASE STUDY

Laundrie

Dubliner Evan Gray found it difficult to deliver and collect his suits for dry cleaning, as most dry cleaning businesses operate during office hours. He realised that if he was experiencing this problem, there must be other consumers in the market with the same **frustration**.

Evan decided to create a website and app which would allow consumers to have their dry cleaning and laundry collected and delivered at a convenient time and place.

Consumers can log on to the Laundrie website or download the app and input their details. A driver collects the items to be cleaned from a location specified by the customer. Laundrie partners with quality cleaning professionals and the items are returned to the consumer within 48 hours. The service is offered seven days a

week from 9 a.m. to 10 p.m.

Evan identified young families and professionals as the natural **target market** for his app. They tend to have higher levels of disposable income but are also very time poor.

The company has partnered with Unilever, which supplies detergent products in return for anonymous **customer feedback**.

Laundrie currently has 5,000 customers in Dublin and is planning to launch the service in Europe, focusing on Milan, Amsterdam and Brussels.

Trends and Challenges in the Tertiary Sector in Ireland

Trends		Challenges	
Tourism	→ Increasing numbers of tourists are visiting Ireland. → Businesses in the tourism industry must ensure that tourists get value for money to protect Ireland's reputation as an attractive tourist destination.	**Consumer loyalty**	→ Competition in this sector is intense; therefore businesses need to find creative ways to increase consumer loyalty, e.g. special offers, loyalty cards and improved customer service.
Growth of e-business	→ A growing number of Irish firms use their website to market and sell their goods and services abroad to a larger consumer market.	**City centre locations**	→ Many tertiary businesses in city centre locations have closed down due to declining customer footfall. This can be as a result of rising car parking fees and the growth of suburban shopping centres, e.g. Liffey Valley.
Transnational companies (TNCs)	→ Many TNCs have established bases in Ireland, e.g. PayPal and Google. They are attracted to Ireland by our low corporation tax rates, highly skilled employees and EU membership.	**Access to finance**	→ Businesses in the tertiary sector may find it difficult to obtain finance. Banks may view the businesses as having a high risk of failure and refuse to provide loans.
Increased employment	→ Rising consumer income has increased demand for services in the tertiary sector, e.g. entertainment, gyms and restaurants, thus creating more jobs in the industry.	**Exploitation of workers**	→ Foreign workers in the tertiary sector may be unaware of their employment rights. These employees need to be protected from exploitation, e.g. being paid less than the minimum wage.

BENEFITS OF THE PRIMARY, SECONDARY AND TERTIARY SECTORS

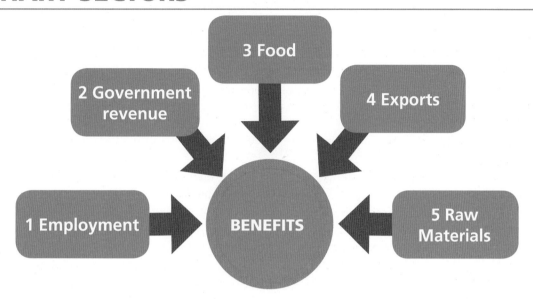

1 Employment

The three sectors provide direct and indirect employment for thousands of workers in Ireland. This increases the standard of living for people and reduces the amount of social welfare payments paid by the government.

2 Government Revenue

Low corporation tax rates in Ireland make it an attractive location to establish a business. The government uses the tax revenue collected to invest in schools, health and transport.

3 Food

The primary and secondary sectors provide food needed for Ireland's population. Local food production reduces CO_2 emissions and reduces Ireland's impact on global warming.

4 Exports

Ireland has a strong tradition of exports, particularly in the pharmaceutical, food and financial services sectors. Exports benefit the Irish economy as they bring foreign currency into the country, which can be used to pay for imports.

5 Raw Materials

The secondary sector uses raw materials from the primary sector to produce goods. This boosts sales for businesses operating in the primary sector and can help to increase their sales and profits.

KEY TERMS

Now you have completed this chapter, you should understand and be able to explain the following terms. In your copybook, write a definition of each term to build up your own glossary of terms.

- factors of production
- land
- labour
- capital
- enterprise
- primary sector
- secondary sector
- manufacturing
- construction
- agribusiness
- tertiary sector

Unit 6

 **PowerPoint Summary**

EXAM-STYLE QUESTIONS

Ordinary Level

Section 1 – Short Questions (10 marks each)

1 List the factors of production and the rewards earned by each factor.

2 Distinguish between land and labour as factors of production.

3 Review the list of items in the table below and identify, using a tick (✔) the factor of production to which each item belongs.

	Land	Labour	Capital	Enterprise
Climate				
Factory worker				
Mark Zuckerberg				
Motor vehicles				

4 List **three** challenges faced by the fishing industry in Ireland.

5 Describe **two** current trends in the Irish construction sector.

6 Describe **two** challenges faced by firms in the manufacturing sector in Ireland.

7 Explain the term *agribusiness*. State **one** example of an agribusiness in Ireland.

8 Indicate whether each of the following statements is true or false.

Statements		True or False
A	A solicitor works in the primary sector.	
B	A shop assistant works in the tertiary sector.	
C	A miner works in the secondary sector.	
D	Coca-Cola is an example of a business involved in the manufacturing industry.	
E	Snapchat is an example of a business involved in the tertiary sector.	

Section 2 – Long Questions

1 List and explain the **four** factors of production.	(20 marks)
2 Distinguish between the primary, secondary and tertiary sectors.	(15 marks)
3 Describe the challenges experienced by the forestry sector in Ireland.	(15 marks)
4 Farming is a difficult occupation. Discuss this statement with reference to the challenges facing the farming industry in Ireland.	(15 marks)
5 Describe **three** current trends in the manufacturing sector.	(15 marks)
6 A friend of yours is considering establishing a business in the construction sector and seeks your advice. Describe the current trends and challenges in this sector.	(20 marks)
7 Outline the trends faced by businesses in the services sector.	(15 marks)
8 Discuss **two** trends and **one** challenge faced by the tertiary sector in Ireland.	(20 marks)
9 Outline the benefits that each of the primary, secondary and services sectors bring to the Irish economy.	(15 marks)

Unit 6

Higher Level

Section 1 – Short Questions (10 marks each)

1 Distinguish between land and capital as factors of production.

2 Illustrate your understanding of the term *tertiary sector*. Outline **one** trend and **one** challenge in this sector

3 Name **two** industries in the secondary sector. Outline **one** trend and **one** challenge in this sector.

4 Distinguish between agribusiness and aquaculture.

5 What is Brexit? What impact could Brexit have on the Irish manufacturing sector?

6 Circle the correct answer in the following sentences.

   (i) Brexit is the withdrawal of **Brussels/the UK** from the European Union.

   (ii) Indigenous companies are **native to Ireland/foreign companies which establish in Ireland**.

   (iii) Agribusinesses use raw materials from the **primary/secondary** sector.

   (iv) The construction sector is currently experiencing a **skills shortage/over-supply of skilled workers**.

   (v) The tertiary sector is also known as the **suppliers sector/services sector**.

7 Write out and fill in the blanks in the following sentences relating to the factors of production.

   (i) L_____ describes anything that is extracted from nature. The economic return is r_____.

   (ii) E_____ combines all of the other factors of production to make a business. The economic return is p_____.

   (iii) Labour is the h_____ effort needed to provide goods and services. The economic return is w_____.

   (iv) C_____ refers to any items used to provide goods and services. The economic return is i_____.

8 The following companies operate in the primary, secondary or tertiary sectors. Identify the sector to which each business belongs: primary, secondary or tertiary.

	Sector
(i)	
(ii)	
(iii)	
(iv)	

Section 2 – Applied Business Question (80 marks)

Decisions at the Local Enterprise Office

Máiréad Mackey is a business development officer. She works for the local enterprise office and is responsible for allocating grants to local entrepreneurs. This month she has received two proposals requesting grants of €20,000. Máiréad must read these proposals and decide which business should receive the grant aid.

Proposal 1

Joanne Dunphy decided to open an agribusiness producing organic ice cream. Her company, BóPeep Ice Cream, was established seven years ago and employs three people. She sources her milk supplies from local farmers and has invested heavily in machinery that allows her to use batch production to produce her range of ice creams.

BóPeep Ice Cream is a small company and is under intense price competition from two main sources. There have been a number of mergers and acquisitions in the industry recently and these companies are able to charge lower prices for their products. The supermarkets that Joanne has approached to stock her ice cream have offered her very low prices for her products and she is frustrated with the situation.

Joanne exports 65% of her ice cream to the UK and she is particularly concerned about the withdrawal of the UK from the European Union. Joanne has conducted market research and has identified new markets for her organic ice cream in Sweden and Denmark. She would use the grant to purchase machinery to increase ice cream production for export.

Proposal 2

Aidan O'Neill is the owner of Café au Lait, a small café employing six people in the city centre. Business has improved over the past year as local employment levels have increased and local people appear to have more money to spend.

A local tourist attraction opened recently and this has had a positive impact on his sales and profits. Larger numbers of tourists are visiting each day and Aidan believes that his USP of providing food and drinks from local suppliers makes his café stand out among international coffee shop franchises.

Aidan is delighted that the government is investing €2 million in upgrading the roads and parking facilities around the city centre. This will make the café more accessible and hopefully boost sales and profits.

The €20,000 grant would help Aidan to set up his own company website. This would be a very useful marketing tool and consumers would be able to view menus and book tables in advance of their visit.

Máiréad Mackey has some difficult decisions to make in order to decide who should receive the €20,000 grant, as both businesses would bring benefits to the local and national economy.

A Describe the factors of production and the associated rewards relating to BóPeep Ice Cream. **(20 marks)**

B (i) Explain what is meant by the term *agribusiness*. Outline the trends and challenges currently affecting this industry. **(20 marks)**

    (ii) In which sector does the business in Proposal 2 operate? Define this sector and discuss the trends affecting it. **(20 marks)**

C Write a report on behalf of Máiréad Mackey, the business development officer, to her manager outlining the benefits these businesses would bring to the economy. **(20 marks)**

Section 3 – Long Questions

1 Define the term *primary sector*. Outline the current trends affecting the farming sector in Ireland. **(25 marks)**

2 Using a business of your choice, illustrate the factors of production that it uses to produce its goods or services. **(30 marks)**

3 Business is improving for the fishing industry in Ireland. Discuss this statement with reference to the trends in the industry. **(20 marks)**

4 Analyse the challenges affecting the Irish forestry industry. **(15 marks)**

5 Outline the challenges facing the construction sector in Ireland. **(15 marks)**

6 Contrast the trends faced by the manufacturing and construction sectors. **(25 marks)**

7 Evaluate the trends and challenges affecting the agribusiness sector in Ireland. **(20 marks)**

8 Evaluate the contribution that the primary, secondary and tertiary sectors make to the Irish economy. **(25 marks)**

PREVIOUS LEAVING CERTIFICATE EXAM QUESTIONS

Ordinary Level

Section A – Short Questions (10 marks each)

1 Complete the missing factors of production.

Land _____ Capital _____ [LC OL 2016]

2 Write TRUE or FALSE for each of these sentences:

Sentences		True or False
A	The Primary sector of the economy deals with manufacturing and construction.	
B	The Secondary sector of the economy deals with raw materials.	
C	The Tertiary sector provides a variety of services to the economy.	
D	Agribusiness processes the output of the Primary sector.	
E	The Extractive industries include agriculture, forestry, fishing and mining.	

[LC OL 2001]

3 Indicate, by means of a tick (✔) the category or sector of industry to which each of the five businesses listed belongs.

		Primary	Secondary	Tertiary/Services
A	A factory making candles			
B	A taxi company			
C	Insurance brokers			
D	A dairy farmer			
E	A coal mining company			

[LC OL 2010]

Section B

1

> Tourism initiatives such as the 'Wild Atlantic Way', 'The Ancient East' and 'The Gathering' have helped to boost business sales in Ireland. The Wild Atlantic Way has boosted the reputation of Ireland as a holiday destination. Communities throughout the West of Ireland have experienced increased visitor numbers. Local construction firms have been busy as new businesses such as hostels, restaurants and cafés have been established. Farmers and fishermen have experienced an increase in demand for their raw materials from local restaurants, cafés and bars.

  (i) From the information provided above, name the sector of the economy that tourism operates in. State **one** example of a business in the tourism industry. **(10 marks)**

  (ii) Explain the **two** other sectors of the economy and provide **one** example of a business in each sector from the information provided above. **(20 marks) [LC OL 2017]**

2 Explain the term *secondary sector*. Name **one** other sector in the economy. **(15 marks) [LC OL 2016]**

3

> *Google, Facebook, Twitter and many other large organisations in the Tertiary (Services) sector have set up European headquarters in Ireland. IDA Ireland is the state agency responsible for attracting Multinational Companies (MNCs) to Ireland.*

  (i) Name the **two** other sectors/categories of industry and state **one** example of each. **(15 marks)**

  (ii) List the **four** factors of production and explain **one** of them. **(15 marks) [LC OL 2015]**

Higher Level

Section A – Short Questions (10 marks each)

1 Name and give an example of each of the **three** types of industry. **[LC HL 2002]**

2 Define the term *primary sector*. Outline **two** current trends affecting this sector in Ireland. **[LC HL 2012]**

3 Write True or False for each of these sentences.

	Sentences	True or False
A	Factors of production refer to the resources required for the generation of goods and services.	
B	The secondary sector refers to the construction and manufacturing industries.	
C	Service industries manufacture physical products for sale to consumers.	
D	Industries such as agriculture, fishing and forestry are based on a country's natural resources.	
E	Indigenous firms are foreign-owned firms located in Ireland.	

[LC HL 2015]

Section B

1 Discuss current trends affecting businesses in the services sector of the Irish economy. Provide examples to support your answer. **(20 marks) [LC HL 2013]**

2 Discuss the importance of the categories of industry to the current Irish economy. **(20 marks) [LC HL 2007]**

 Solutions

24 TYPES OF BUSINESS ORGANISATION

When you have completed this chapter, you will be able to:

1 Identify different types of business organisation
2 Compare and contrast different types of business organisation
3 Explain why businesses change their organisational structure over time.

Literacy Link

Sole trader, partnership, private limited company, co-operative, public limited company, franchise, strategic alliance/joint venture

Numeracy Link

Addition, subtraction, percentages, statistics

Cross-curricular Link

Accounting – accounts of sole traders, public and private companies

 CASE STUDY

Dunnes Stores

Dunnes Stores is Ireland's largest retailer, selling fashion, food and homewares. The business was founded by Ben Dunne Sr, using **savings**, and it opened its first store on Patrick Street in Cork in 1944.

As a **sole trader**, Ben Dunne Sr personally ran all his stores. He established stores throughout Ireland, later grouping his stores together and changing the **business structure** to a **private limited company** limited by shares. The company had a **separate legal entity** from its shareholders, thereby giving the Dunne family **limited liability**.

As the firm continued to expand into Spain and Northern Ireland, Ben Dunne Sr was faced with the possibility of becoming a **public limited company**. Instead the business structure was changed to an **unlimited company**, and as a result the business no longer has to file detailed financial statements with the **Companies Registration Office (CRO)**.

The firm was at one point the subject of a **takeover** bid by US retailer Walmart, which already owns the supermarket chain Asda in the UK. However, no

sale was agreed, and the Dunne family retained **control** of the business.

The company **acquired** the Café Sol chain in 2015 and has plans for further **acquisitions** in the future. Dunnes Stores offers customers a wide range of locally sourced Irish produce, including products from Irish **co-operative** Ornua, which produces the Kerrygold line of products.

Dunnes Stores controls 22% of the Irish grocery stores market, and has estimated sales of over €3.6 billion per year.

PART 1: ORGANISATION STRUCTURES FOR NEW BUSINESSES

The most common business organisation structures for new businesses are:

1 Sole trader	2 Partnership	3 Private limited company	4 Co-operative	5 State-owned enterprise

Exam Tip!
Make sure that you can **contrast** *the different types of business organisation. This means that you must be able to show the* **differences** *between the types of business.*

Before we examine each of these types of business organisation there are a number of terms you need to understand.

Important Terms

Term	Explanation
Unlimited liability	→ The owner(s) of a business are personally liable for all business debts if the business becomes bankrupt. This means that the owners' private savings might have to be used or their property be sold to pay for the debts if the business fails, e.g. private car or home.
Limited liability	→ The owner(s) of a business are not personally liable for business debts if the business fails. They are responsible only for the amount they invested in the business. Personal assets cannot be taken to repay debt.
Separate legal entity	→ The business exists as a legal entity separate from its owners, i.e. it can sue and be sued in its own name.
Continuity of existence	→ A business that has its own legal entity will have continuity of existence – it continues to exist when the owner dies or retires.
Companies Registration Office (CRO)	→ The central register for Irish companies and business names. (You learned about the CRO in Chapter 21.)

1 Sole Trader

Formation

A sole trader is easy to set up as there are few legal requirements unless a licence is needed to trade, e.g. a taxi driver needs to obtain a taxi licence. The sole trader must register for self-assessment income tax and may also be required to register for VAT where sales exceed a certain value. If the business name differs from the sole trader's name, the name must be registered with the CRO, e.g. sole trader Ciaran Jones must register his business name Jones's Newsagent.

Definition: Sole trader
A business owned and run by one person. This person has sole responsibility for the business.

Example
Butchers, pharmacists, taxi drivers, florists and farmers

Unit 6

Features of a Sole Trader

Feature	Explanation
Finance	→ A sole trader can use personal savings, loans and grants to finance the business.
Liability	→ Liability is unlimited.
Control/Decision-making	→ Sole traders have complete control over how the business is run. → They make all the decisions, e.g. opening hours, what product to sell and who to employ.
Profits	→ A sole trader keeps all the profits, which are taxed at 20% or 40% under self-assessment income tax.
Dissolution	→ A sole trader ceases to exist if the owner: — Retires — Closes down the business — Dies. → There is no continuity of existence in a sole trader business, if there is nobody else to take over the business.

Advantages and Disadvantages of a Sole Trader
See Chapter 21.

Activity 24.1

First for Feet – A Sole Trader

As a result of company downsizing, Fred lost his job in the shoe section of a large department store in Tullamore, Co. Offaly. He used his redundancy money, together with a small loan, to set up his own shoe store. Fred called his business First for Feet and began trading.

Fred found working for himself very rewarding but found the hours demanding. He regularly worked 12- to 15-hour days selling to customers, dealing with suppliers and updating the shop's social media platforms.

Questions
1 Did Fred require a licence to set up his business? Explain your answer.
2 Outline **one** advantage and **one** disadvantage of a sole trader business, with reference to the text.
3 With which organisation did Fred have to register the business name 'First for Feet'?
4 Thinking of your own hobbies and interests, select **one** type of sole trader business you would consider setting up. Name your business and share your business idea with other students in your class.

Activity 24.2

In pairs, make a list of sole traders you are aware of in your local area. Create a questionnaire and arrange to interview a local sole trader to find out about their experience of running a business as a sole trader in Ireland.

Unit 6

2 Partnership

Formation

There are few legal requirements for setting up a business as a partnership. The partnership must register the business name with the CRO and with the Revenue Commissioners for taxation purposes. The partners do not have a separate legal entity from the business, i.e. they can sue and be sued in their own names.

Partnerships are formally set up by a written agreement drawn up by a solicitor. This is known as a **deed of partnership/partnership agreement** and it sets out details such as:

- Each partner's role in the running of the business
- How profits will be shared, e.g. equally or in proportion to the amount invested
- The procedure for admitting new partners and the procedure for partners who want to leave
- The salary for each partner.

Definition: **Partnership**

A business with between two and twenty partners who agree to run the business together.

Examples
Accountants, solicitors, doctors and dentists

To register as a sole trader or partnership in Ireland you must be a resident. If you are a resident but a non-EU national you will also need a letter of business permission from the Department of Justice in order to register a business name.

Features of a Partnership

Feature	Explanation
Finance	→ Partnerships are likely to have access to larger amounts of capital than a sole trader as each partner contributes finance to the business. → New partners can bring extra finance to help expand the business.
Liability	→ All partners have unlimited liability. → The partners become collectively responsible for each other's partnership debts.
Control/ Decision-making	→ Decision-making is shared among the partners. This can be effective as the partners have different skills and knowledge. → Differences of opinion may lead to delays in making decisions.
Profits	→ Profits are shared, equally or as set out in the deed of partnership. → Similar to sole traders, profits are taxed at 20% and 40% under each partner's self-assessment income tax.
Dissolution	→ A partnership ends if: — The partners agree to dissolve the partnership — One partner dies or becomes bankrupt – like a sole trader, partnerships do not have continuity of existence. → If a partner leaves, the partnership ends. If the remaining partners (provided there are more than two) wish to continue, a new deed of partnership must be drawn up.

Example

Wejchert Architects, based in Dublin, is a partnership with five partners that provides a range of design and planning-related services. The partnership has provided services on a range of projects, including Waterford Courthouse and the Helix at Dublin City University.

A partnership can also have a sleeping partner. This is someone who invests in the business but is not involved in the day-to-day running of the business.

Advantages and Disadvantages of a Partnership
See Chapter 21.

Activity 24.3

In pairs, use a graphic organiser (e.g. a fishbone diagram) to compare and contrast a sole trader and a partnership as types of business structure.

3 Private Limited Company

The rules and regulations of a private limited company are set out in the Companies Act 2014. Under this Act there are a number of different types of limited company, some of which are outlined below.

Definition: **Private limited company**
A business organisation owned by one or more shareholders.

Types of Limited Company

	Company Limited by Shares	Designated Activity Company (DAC)	Company Limited by Guarantee (CLG)	Unlimited Company (UC)
Name	→ Limited/Ltd after company name	→ DAC after company name	→ CLG after company name	→ UC/Unlimited Company after company name
Number of Shareholders	→ 1–149	→ 1–149	→ 1–unlimited	→ 1–unlimited
Governing Document	→ Constitution	→ Memorandum of Association → Articles of Association	→ Memorandum of Association → Articles of Association	→ Memorandum of Association → Articles of Association
Liability	→ Limited	→ Limited	→ Limited	→ Unlimited
AGM	→ Does not need to hold an AGM	→ Mandatory	→ Mandatory	→ Mandatory if there are more than two shareholders
Activity	→ Any commercial activity, e.g. a hotel or a bakery	→ Specific commercial activity, e.g. a bank	→ Used by charities and sports organisations	→ Commercial activity whose financial information owners want to keep confidential
Examples	→ Longridge Bakery Ltd	→ Ulster Bank DAC	→ Donegal Local Development Company CLG	→ Dunnes Stores Unlimited Company

Example
Keelings is an unlimited company with estimated sales of €330m. The company, which traces its roots back to 1926, supplies Dunnes Stores, Tesco, Musgraves and Marks & Spencer with both home-grown and internationally sourced fruit and vegetables from 42 countries.

Governing Documents

Constitution
This document outlines information including:
- The company name
- A statement that the company is a private limited company limited by shares
- Any other regulations the company wants to include.

> ### Memorandum of Association
> This document is used to form the company. It includes:
> - The company name
> - The objectives of the company, e.g. running a restaurant
> - The type of liability held by shareholders, e.g. limited liability.

> ### Articles of Association
> This document outlines the internal rules and regulations for running a company. It includes the procedures for:
> - Organising general meetings
> - Voting at general meetings
> - Company closure.

Formation

A private limited company is formed when one or more investors (shareholders) agree to form the business. It must be registered with the CRO and the Revenue Commissioners. A private limited company is more expensive to set up than a sole trader.

Steps in Setting up a Private Limited Company

1 **Document preparation:** The directors of the company prepare Form A1 (application to become a private limited company) and, depending on the company type, a constitution or a memorandum of association and articles of association.

2 **Submission:** These documents are sent to the CRO with the appropriate fee.

> **Examples**
> Dyson Ltd, GlaxoSmithKline (Ireland) Ltd and RSA Insurance DAC

3 **Certificate of incorporation:** The CRO examines the documents and, if all information is correct, issues a certificate of incorporation. This confirms that the business is a legal entity and allows it to begin trading with other firms.

Features of a Private Limited Company

Feature	Explanation
Finance	→ Equity finance can be raised by selling shares. → The company can also take out loans and receive grants.
Liability	→ Shareholders (owners) have limited liability.
Control/ Decision-making	→ Shareholders appoint a board of directors and a CEO (chief executive officer) or MD (managing director). → Shareholders can influence decision-making at shareholder meetings, as one share is equal to one vote.
Profits	→ The board of directors decide on the amount of dividend to be paid to shareholders from company profits. → The dividend received by shareholders is based on the number of shares held. → Companies pay corporation tax at a rate of 12.5% on company profits.
Dissolution	→ Shares can be sold or passed on to another person on the death of a shareholder. This means that a private limited company has continuity of existence. → The company can be wound up by the agreement of shareholders or by a court order in the event of bankruptcy.

Advantages and Disadvantages of a Private Limited Company
See Chapter 21.

Unit 6

Activity 24.4

In groups, prepare a poster or infographic to display in the classroom.
- Group 1 – outline the steps involved in setting up a private limited company.
- Group 2 – compare and contrast a company limited by shares and a DAC.
- Group 3 – using your phone or other suitable device, collect images of local private companies to create a collage.
- Group 4 – using newspapers, the Internet and/or other sources, collect images of other private companies operating in Ireland to create a collage.

4 Co-operative

Formation

> **Definition: Co-operative**
> A co-operative is owned and controlled by members rather than shareholders. It is run in a democratic manner and operates for the benefit of its members. Each member has an equal say in the running of the co-operative.

> **Definition: Registry of Friendly Societies**
> The Registry of Friendly Societies is part of the CRO. It is responsible for registering co-operatives and ensuring that they meet their statutory obligations, e.g. filing financial returns.

A co-operative must have a minimum of seven members and there is no maximum number of members. The co-operative must register with the Registry of Friendly Societies and the Revenue Commissioners. There are a number of different types of co-operative.

Worker Co-operative
The co-operative is owned and managed by people who work in the business. It often occurs as the result of worker buy-out, where employees buy out the existing owners of the firm. It can arise due to the retirement of the owners or if the business experiences financial difficulties and the workers want to safeguard their jobs.

Example
Bridge Street Co-operative, Co. Cork

Financial Co-operative
Credit unions are the most common example of a financial co-operative. They are owned and run by members who have a common bond, e.g. where they live or their occupation. Members save together and then lend to each other at a low rate of interest. Surplus income earned by the financial co-operative is given as a dividend to members or used to pay for improved services.

Example
Clearistown Credit Union

Producer Co-operative
This type of co-operative tends to be found in the agri-business sector. A group of producers form a co-operative and set up their own processing facility. For example, a group of dairy farmers sell their produce (milk) to the co-operative and it is processed into a finished product, e.g. yoghurt. This processing adds value to the milk and the farmers can sell it (in the form of yoghurt) at a higher price to supermarkets, thus increasing their income.

Example
Aurivo Co-operative Society Ltd

Unit 6

Consumer Co-operative

These are co-operatives owned and managed by consumers. They offer better choice and lower prices to consumers. They often take the form of retail outlets in the food sector but also feature in healthcare and education.

Example
Co-Op UK

Features of a Co-operative

Feature	Explanation
Finance	→ Equity finance is raised by issuing shares, which can be purchased by members of the co-operative. → There is no incentive for members to invest more capital as members have one vote per person rather than one vote per share.
Liability	→ Members are protected by limited liability.
Control/ Decision-making	→ Members own and control the co-operative. → They appoint a management committee to run the business day to day.
Profits	→ Profits are shared between the members in the form of a dividend. → Co-operatives pay corporation tax on profits at 12.5%.
Dissolution	→ A co-operative can be dissolved by: — Agreement — A court order due to bankruptcy.

Advantages and Disadvantages of a Co-operative
See Chapter 21.

Activity 24.5

Search on the Internet for a LifeinFocusIreland video 'The Story of the Bridge Street Co-op'. Watch this and answer the following questions.
1 How much capital was needed to get the project started?
2 Outline **two** reasons why the members decided to use the worker co-op model for their business.
3 Describe the advantages of this type of business to a community as identified by the speaker.

 DID YOU KNOW? *Over 100 million people are employed in co-ops around the world, 20% more than people employed in multinational companies (MNCs).*

Activity 24.6

If 100 million is 20% more than the number of people employed in multinational companies (MNCs), calculate the number of people employed by multinational companies.

5 State-owned Enterprise

Formation

A state-owned enterprise can be established in two ways:

1 By passing an Act of the Oireachtas (parliament, consisting of the president, Dáil Éireann and Seanad Éireann). These companies are known as statutory companies, e.g. RTÉ.

Definition: State-owned enterprise
A business organisation that is set up and run by the government. They can also be referred to as semi-state or state-sponsored bodies.

2 The government registers the company with the CRO and the government is a shareholder. One or more government minister posts hold shares in the company. For example, the Minister for Agriculture, Food and the Marine and the Minister for Public Expenditure and Reform hold shares in Coillte (Irish Forestry).

DID YOU KNOW? *There are approximately 100 state-sponsored bodies in Ireland and they employ around 75,000 people.*

Example
An Post, RTÉ, CIÉ (Dublin Bus, Irish Rail and Bus Éireann)

Features of a State-owned Enterprise

Feature	Explanation
Finance	→ Finance for start-up and running costs is supplied by the government.
Liability	→ Liability is limited.
Control/Decision-making	→ The relevant government minister appoints the board of directors. → The board appoints a CEO to run the business.
Profits	→ Profits (if any) are paid to the government in the form of dividends or reinvested in the business.
Dissolution	→ The government can sell a state enterprise. This is called privatisation, e.g. the Irish government sold its shareholding in Aer Lingus. → The government may decide to wind up the business.

STATE-OWNED ENTERPRISES

✓ Advantages	✗ Disadvantages
1 Provide Employment State-sponsored enterprises employ around 75,000 people in the economy, helping to reduce unemployment in Ireland.	**1 Lack of Profit Motive** There is no incentive for the business to be run efficiently as there may be no other competition in the market. State enterprises are often accused of wasting taxpayers' money.
2 Provide Essential Services They provide services that private enterprises may not provide because they are not commercially viable, e.g. rural bus routes operated by Bus Éireann.	**2 Loss-making** Many state-owned enterprises are loss-making and cost the government (the taxpayer) money to finance.
3 Income for the Government Profitable state enterprises such as ESB provide income for the government, which helps finance services, e.g. education and social welfare.	**3 Management** Directors who have no business expertise are often appointed. They may be appointed for political reasons rather than for their business knowledge.

Unit 6

PART 2: ORGANISATION STRUCTURES FOR EXPANDING BUSINESSES

The most common business organisation structures for expanding businesses are:

1 Public Limited Company

Formation

A public limited company is formed when a private limited company or other form of business, e.g. a co-operative, seeks a stock exchange listing or quotation. To be listed on the stock exchange the business must have a good trading history and meet the many rules and regulations of the stock exchange.

Under the Companies Act 2014:

- The name of the company must end in plc.
- A public limited company has a constitution of two documents: the memorandum of association and the articles of association.
- A public limited company must have at least seven shareholders, but there is no maximum. It must have at least two directors.
- The business must issue a prospectus setting out the company's history. It is used to invite and persuade people to buy shares in the company.

> **Definition: Public limited company**
> A business organisation whose shares (stocks) can be bought and sold by the general public.

> **Examples**
> Greencore plc, Glanbia plc and CRH plc

Features of a Public Limited Company

Feature	Explanation
Finance	→ A large amount of finance can be raised through issuing shares. → Shares are openly sold on the stock exchange, e.g. Irish businesses are listed on the ISEQ Index. (ISEQ is the Irish Stock Exchange Quotient.)
Liability	→ Liability of shareholders is limited.
Control/ Decision-making	→ At the AGM, shareholders appoint a board of directors to run the business. → The board of directors appoints a CEO to run the business.
Profits	→ Profits are shared among shareholders in the form of dividends. The greater the number of shares held, the larger the dividend received. → The amount of dividend paid is decided by the board of directors. → Public limited companies pay corporation tax at a rate of 12.5% on their profits.
Dissolution	→ A plc can be dissolved because of bankruptcy or based on a court order.

PUBLIC LIMITED COMPANY

✓ Advantages	✗ Disadvantages
1 Limited Liability Individual shareholders are liable for business debts only up to the amount they invested in the business. Their own private assets, such as their home and car, are not at risk.	**1 Difficult to Set Up** Setting up as a plc is time-consuming and expensive. The listing rules of the stock exchange are complex.
2 Finance A plc can raise a very large amount of capital through issuing shares on the stock exchange, e.g. the ISEQ Index (Ireland) or the Dow Jones (USA).	**2 Lack of Confidentiality** The company's financial records must be published in detail. Other information must also be made available to the public, e.g. a list of shareholders.
3 Business Reputation Having a stock exchange listing gives a business a good reputation, making it easy to attract top employees and managers.	**3 Profits** Profits must be shared between the shareholders. As there can be a large number of shareholders the dividend per share may be small. If the return is not adequate, shareholders may sell their shares, causing a fall in the value of the company.
4 Ability to Borrow A plc will find it relatively easy to borrow money, e.g. debenture. A public limited company often has a higher company credit rating than other business structures such as a partnership.	**4 Hostile Takeovers** Since shares are openly sold on the stock exchange, the company may become subject to a hostile takeover. This is when a company is taken over against the wishes of management.

Example

Tótal Próduce is an Irish public limited company that traces its origins back to a fruit and vegetable business in the 1850s. The company has sales of €4.3bn a year. It grows, imports and distributes over 300 lines of fresh fruits, vegetables and flowers. The company continues to grow its global operations using acquisitions. It acquired a 45% equity stake in US-based Dole Food Company. Dole is one of the world's largest fresh produce firms and a producer and marketer of high-quality fresh fruit and vegetables.

2 Franchise

Formation

A franchise is formed when a franchisee buys the rights to use a business idea from the franchisor through a franchise agreement. The franchisee agrees to comply with the rules and regulations set out by the franchisor.

Definition: Franchise

A business (the franchisor) agrees to let another business (the franchisee) use its business name, logo and business ideas in return for a fee and a percentage of profits. Examples of franchises include Subway and Supermac's.

Features of a Franchise

Feature	Explanation
Finance	→ The franchisee invests the amount required to obtain the franchise agreement, e.g. it costs approximately €100,000 to obtain a Subway franchise. The franchisee might source this finance from banks or savings, as well as friends and family.
Liability	→ Franchise agreements generally take the form of a private limited company, so liability is limited.
Control/ Decision-making	→ The franchisee runs and manages the franchise but must follow guidelines laid out by the franchisor.
Profits	→ An annual fee plus a share of the profits must be paid to the franchisor.
Dissolution	→ If the franchisee breaches any terms of the agreement, the franchisor can cancel the franchise agreement, e.g. if minimum sales are not reached. → The agreement can be dissolved by mutual consent.

Advantages and Disadvantages of a Franchise

See Chapter 22.

Activity 24.7

Search on the Internet for the WBEZ video 'How Franchising Works: An Illustrated Guide'. Watch this and answer the following questions.
1 Outline **two** reasons why a business might want to franchise its business model.
2 Explain the reasons why a person would want to run a franchisee.
3 Name **three** items commonly found in a franchise agreement.
4 Discuss the effects the franchise business model can have on an economy.
5 List **three** franchise businesses, apart from fast food restaurants, in your area.

3 Strategic Alliance/Joint Venture

Formation

An alliance is formed when all parties enter into a contract to work together on a business project. An alliance can be for a specified period of time or for a specific project. For example, ESB and Kingspan entered a joint venture to create Funded Solar. This enables a business to use its space, e.g. rooftops, to generate renewable electricity without needing to pay the capital costs for the equipment.

Definition: Strategic alliance/joint venture
Two or more businesses agree to work together on a common project which benefits both firms. The businesses agree to co-operate and share resources and expertise.

Features of a Strategic Alliance/Joint Venture

Feature	Explanation
Finance	→ Each business invests an agreed amount of money as negotiated between the firms.
Liability	→ Limited liability if formed between private/public limited companies, state-owned enterprises and co-operatives.
Control/ Decision-making	→ It is shared between all businesses in the strategic alliance as per the terms of the contract.
Profits	→ Profits are shared between all businesses as per the terms of the contract.
Dissolution	→ Ends after the completion of an agreed project or time frame.

Example

Tesco and Carrefour created a strategic alliance in order to reduce prices and increase their competitiveness. The alliance between the global grocery giants will include the joint purchasing of own-brand products. With combined annual sales of €147 billion, the alliance is designed to secure a better deal from suppliers such as Nestlé, Procter & Gamble, Unilever and Danone. The alliance is seen as a way for the supermarket giants to fight back against the rise of Amazon and discount retailers such as Lidl and Aldi.

Advantages and Disadvantages of a Strategic Alliance/Joint Venture
See Chapter 22.

Forms of Business Organisation: Summary

	Sole Trader	Partnership	Private Limited Company	Public Limited Company	Co-operative	State Enterprise
Number of Owners	→ 1	→ 1–20	→ 1–149	→ 7–unlimited	→ 7–unlimited	→ 1 (the government)
Register	→ None (business name only)	→ None (business name only)	→ CRO	→ CRO	→ Registry of Friendly Societies	→ CRO
Liability	→ Unlimited	→ Unlimited	→ Limited	→ Limited	→ Limited	→ Limited
Who Runs the Business	→ Owner	→ Partners	→ Board of directors	→ Board of directors	→ Management committee	→ Government minister
Share of Profits	→ All to the owner	→ As set out in the deed of partnership	→ Dividend per share	→ Dividend per share	→ Divided between members	→ Government income, i.e. Department of Finance
Examples	→ Pat Ryan, Farmer	→ Keenan Fitzgerald Solicitors	→ Dunnes Stores Ltd	→ Manchester United plc	→ Templeogue Credit Union	→ ESB

RECENT DEVELOPMENTS IN THE STRUCTURE OF BUSINESS ORGANISATIONS

In recent times there have been changes in the types of business organisations in operation in Ireland, including the following:

1 **Increase in franchising:** There has been an increase in franchising because people view it as having a greater chance of success as it uses a tried and tested business structure, e.g. Subway and Eason.

DID YOU KNOW?

There are approximately 4,000 franchises in operation in Ireland with over 43,000 full-time staff. The average initial franchise fee is €24,000.

2 **Emergence of Irish global businesses:** Many Irish firms have grown to become global companies, e.g. Kingspan and Glanbia. They do not rely solely on the domestic market in Ireland and spread their trading risk across a number of worldwide markets.

You will learn more about global businesses in Chapter 31.

3 **Privatisation:** There has been an increase in privatisation, i.e. the sale of state-owned enterprises to private individuals and businesses. For example, the Irish government sold Eircom (now called Eir) and Aer Lingus.

4 **Strategic alliances:** There has been an increase in the number of firms forming strategic alliances. This can result in access to a larger market and benefits from economies of scale, e.g. Tesco and Carrefour.

5 **Plcs delisting:** There has been an increase in the number of public limited companies which have decided to delist from the stock exchange and become private limited companies. This can enable the business to keep certain business information confidential.

CHANGING ORGANISATIONAL STRUCTURE

Over time, businesses change their organisational structure. For example, a business may begin as a sole trader and change ownership to become a private limited company, or a co-operative may become a public limited company.

A business may decide to change its structure for many reasons, including:

1 **To raise finance:**
  - **Equity capital:** If the business requires more capital for expansion or development it may need to change its structure to make it easier to raise capital, e.g. a sole trader may change to a private limited company to raise capital through issuing shares.
  - **Borrowing:** Some forms of business organisation find it easier to obtain loans from financial institutions, as they have a higher credit rating, e.g. private limited companies and public limited companies.

2 **To reduce risk:**
  - **Limited liability:** Businesses may change their organisational structure to benefit from limited liability. For example, a sole trader and partnership may become private limited companies.
  - **Separate legal entity:** Unlike a sole trader, a company, rather than the individuals who make up the organisation, can sue and be sued in law.

3 **To expand:** It can be easier to expand as a private or public limited company than as a sole trader or partnership. Businesses can expand through mergers, takeovers and franchise agreements. Larger businesses such as public limited companies find it easier to attract skilled employees to the business.

4 **To acquire skills:** A sole trader may join with others to form a partnership. The partners will have a greater range of skills and knowledge working together, thus helping to increase business sales and profits.

5 **Taxation:** Businesses may change structure to benefit from lower taxes on their profits. For example, a sole trader pays self-assessment income tax at 20% or 40%, whereas a private limited company pays corporation tax at 12.5%.

Indigenous Firms

An indigenous firm is an Irish business that has been established and is owned by Irish people or residents. The business produces goods or provides services in Ireland. The owners of the firm have a direct, personal interest in the survival and growth of the business.

Example
Smyths Toys, Steeltech Sheds and Eason.

Benefits of Indigenous Firms to the Irish Economy

1 **Loyalty:** Indigenous firms are loyal to the local area and their employees. They are more likely to remain in Ireland even in times of recession, which protects jobs in the local economy.

2 **Profit distribution:** Indigenous firms reinvest their profits in Ireland and spend money in the Irish economy, creating spin-off businesses and employment, e.g. in restaurants and shops.

3 **Entrepreneurship:** Successful indigenous firms can encourage local people to set up their own businesses. These firms can create a culture of enterprise in the local area.

4 **Foreign trade:** Many indigenous firms produce goods and services for the export market, improving Ireland's Balance of Payments.

5 **Tax Revenue:** Indigenous firms pay tax on their profits in the form of corporation tax, as well as employer's PRSI. Staff employed at these firms also contribute tax revenue in the form of PAYE income tax, PRSI and USC.

KEY TERMS

Now you have completed this chapter, you should understand and be able to explain the following terms. In your copybook, write a definition of each term to build up your own glossary of terms.

- unlimited liability
- limited liability
- separate legal entity
- continuity of existence
- Companies Registration Office (CRO)
- sole trader
- partnership
- deed of partnership/ partnership agreement
- private limited company
- company limited by shares

- designated activity company (DAC)
- company limited by guarantee (CLG)
- unlimited company (UC)
- constitution
- memorandum of association
- articles of association
- certificate of incorporation
- co-operative

- Registry of Friendly Societies
- worker co-operative
- producer co-operative
- consumer co-operative
- state-owned enterprise
- public limited company
- franchise
- strategic alliance/joint venture
- indigenous firms

PowerPoint Summary

EXAM-STYLE QUESTIONS

Ordinary Level

Section 1 – Short Questions (10 marks each)

1 Explain what is meant by the term *unlimited liability*.
2 Outline **one** advantage and **one** disadvantage of a sole trader as a type of business organisation.
3 Explain the term *partnership*. Name **one** example of a partnership.
4 Name **three** documents that must be completed when forming a private limited company.
5 What do the letters (i) plc and (ii) DAC stand for?
6 Name **three** types of co-operative. Describe **one** of these co-operatives in more detail.
7 Fill in the missing words in the following sentences.
 (i) When two or more people form a partnership they formally set out the rules in a d_____ of partnership.
 (ii) The constitution of a DAC has two documents: the m_____ of association; and the a_____ of association.
 (iii) A s_____-_____ e_____ is a business organisation set up and run by the government.
 (iv) A c_____ is a type of business organisation that is owned by its members and run in a democratic manner.
 (v) Any business which has its own legal entity will have c_____ of e_____.
8 Outline **one** reason why a business might change its organisation structure.

Unit 6

Section 2 – Long Questions

1

> **Megan's Muffins**
>
> Megan was always a keen baker. From an early age she baked cakes and muffins and entered local cookery competitions, winning many prizes. She recently won top prize at the 'Amazing Bake Awards' run in conjunction with Bord Bia. Megan set up her own business, Megan's Muffins, as a sole trader. She sells her cakes, muffins and pastries to local supermarkets, hotels and cafés.

   (i) Explain the term *sole trader*.
   (ii) Outline **two** advantages for Megan of operating as a sole trader.   **(15 marks)**

2 Describe the features of a partnership under the following headings: (i) formation;
   (ii) access to finance; and (iii) liability.   **(15 marks)**

3 Explain the term *private limited company*. Outline **two** disadvantages of a private limited
   company business structure.   **(15 marks)**

4 Describe the features of a co-operative under the following headings: (i) liability;
   (ii) decision-making; and (iii) profits.   **(15 marks)**

5 Outline the steps involved in setting up a private limited company.   **(15 marks)**

6 Kerry Foods is a public limited company. Explain **two** benefits of operating a business
   as a plc.   **(15 marks)**

7 Define the term *state-owned enterprise*. Outline the benefits and drawbacks of
   state-owned enterprises.   **(20 marks)**

8 Outline **two** recent developments in the structure of business organisations.   **(20 marks)**

Higher Level

Section 1 – Short Questions (10 marks each)

1 Explain the term *limited liability*.

2 (i) Outline the purpose of a company's constitution.
   (ii) Name **three** items of information found in it.

3 Distinguish between a memorandum of association and articles of association.

4 In the context of business organisations what do the following abbreviations stand for?
   (i) Plc   (ii) DAC   (iii) Ltd   (iv) CRO   (v) UC

5 Choose the correct answer in the following sentences:
   (i)   A sole trader business structure has **limited/unlimited** liability.
   (ii) A partnership is a business which is formed between two and **twenty/forty** people.
   (iii) A business set up by the government is called a **state/national** enterprise.
   (iv) A business which sells its shares on the stock exchange is called a **private/public** limited company.
   (v)   The sale of a state-owned enterprise is known as **nationalisation/privatisation**.

6 What is meant by the term *franchise*? Name **three** franchise businesses operating in Ireland.

7 Column 1 is a list of key business terms associated with business structures. Column 2 is a list of
   possible explanations for these terms. Match the two lists in your copybook by writing your answers in
   the form *number = letter* (e.g. 1 = A).

Terms		Explanations
1	Unlimited Liability	A	A business structure appropriate for non-profit companies such as charities and sports clubs.
2	Consumer Co-operative	B	A formal document drawn up by a solicitor when forming a business with unlimited liability that has between two and twenty owners.
3	Private Limited Company – DAC	C	When the owner(s) of a business are personally liable for all business debts if the business goes into bankruptcy.
4	Company Limited by Guarantee (CLG)	D	A business owned and managed by its customers.
5	Deed of Partnership	E	A type of company which has two documents (memorandum of association and articles of association) in its constitution.

8 Describe the features of public limited company under the headings (i) profits and (ii) control.

Section 2 – Applied Business Question (80 marks)

The Duncormick Co-operative

David Shiel has run his farm on his own for the past thirty years. Over the years he has used personal savings and loans to expand the farm. He enjoys making all business decisions but falling milk prices have made it difficult for farmers to make a living. Taxes on farm profits are high and farmers are wary of taking out large loans as they have unlimited liability. David is also concerned about the future of the farm as his children do not want to run it when he retires.

David knows that many local farmers are in the same position and he arranged a meeting to discuss his concerns. At the meeting the farmers decided that they needed to add value to their milk produce in order to earn higher farm incomes. The farmers agreed to set up a co-operative business structure manufacturing a range of dairy products including cheese and yoghurt. David was appointed managing director and they agreed on the name Duncormick Co-operative.

After two years of trading, the co-operative decided to expand its product line into ice cream. It formed a joint venture with an ice cream manufacturer in the local area. The co-operative received a number of enquiries from people interested in setting up ice cream shops using the co-operative's ice cream range. The co-operative declined this offer as the managing committee has longer-term plans for the business.

As managing director, David knows that the co-operative needs more capital to compete with larger dairy businesses. He wants Duncormick Co-operative to be world-renowned and to attract the best managers to run the business.

A meeting was arranged to discuss the future of the firm with the co-operative's members. During the discussions, David proposed that the co-operative should change structure to become a public limited company. David explained that limited liability would continue for shareholders, but some of the shareholders were worried that their share of the profits would be drastically reduced if the firm decided to change structure. Others were concerned about the large amount of money needed to fund the expansion and the length of time for it to be completed.

Duncormick Co-operative has a lot more to discuss before it makes any changes to its structure.

A There are a range of different business organisation structures operating in Ireland today. Describe these structures with reference to the text. **(20 marks)**

B David operates his farm as a sole trader. Outline the features of a sole trader. **(30 marks)**

C The Duncormick Co-operative is considering changing its organisation structure from a co-operative to a public limited company. Evaluate the benefits and risks of becoming a public limited company. **(30 marks)**

Section 3 – Long Questions

1 Distinguish between a sole trader and a partnership as forms of business ownership using the following headings:

   (i) **Formation**   (ii) **Liability**   (iii) **Finance**   (iv) **Control**

   Use an example of each in your answer. **(25 marks)**

2 Compare and contrast a private limited company with a designated activity company (DAC). **(15 marks)**

3 Outline the stages involved in the formation of a private limited company. **(20 marks)**

4 Contrast a sole trader with a public limited company as a form of business organisation. **(20 marks)**

5 Explain why you would recommend a co-operative as a type of business structure for a new business. **(15 marks)**

6 Outline the arguments for and against state-owned enterprises. **(20 marks)**

7 Discuss the recent developments in the structure of business organisations. Illustrate your answer with appropriate examples. **(15 marks)**

8 Describe why a business enterprise might change its organisational structure over time. Illustrate your answer using appropriate examples. **(20 marks)**

PREVIOUS LEAVING CERTIFICATE EXAM QUESTIONS

Ordinary Level

Section A – Short Questions (10 marks each)

1 Explain the term *limited liability*. **[LC OL 2015]**

2 Column 1 is a list of business terms. Column 2 is a list of explanations for these terms. (One explanation has no match.) Match the two lists in your copybook by writing your answers in the form *number = letter* (e.g. 1 = A). **[LC OL 2013]**

Business Terms		Explanations	
1	Certificate of Incorporation	**A**	Has 8 or more members with a common bond
2	Articles of Association	**B**	Has unlimited liability
3	Private Limited Company	**C**	It states the main objectives of a company
4	Sole Trader	**D**	Document proving the company legally exists
5	Memorandum of Association	**E**	Has the abbreviations LTD or DAC after its name
		F	Internal rules governing how a company operates

3 State **two** benefits of a partnership as a type of business. **[LC OL 2010]**

Section B

1
> Local Enterprise Offices (LEOs) across Ireland provide advice and assistance to potential start up businesses. This includes help in setting up the business, drawing up a business plan, accessing finance, marketing and the day-to-day running of the business. Mentors are provided for the new business owner, to offer independent advice in order to aid decision making.

Explain **two** differences between a Sole Trader and a Partnership as forms of business ownership.
(15 marks) [LC OL 2018]

2
> Kevin Fitzpatrick, MD, and his two brothers set up Solar Solutions Ltd in their home town of Kilduff to produce solar panels for private and commercial buildings. They identified an increased market demand for renewable energy sources. They received a Government grant of €90,000 to help set up the business. Kevin is a firm believer in running the business in an ethical manner and hopes this will ensure its success in this sector.

Limited Liability and Continuity of Existence are **two** advantages of a Private Limited Company. Explain these underlined terms. **(20 marks) [LC OL 2012]**

Higher Level

Section A – Short Questions (10 marks each)

1 State the correct option in the case of each of the following statements.
(i) A Sole Trader business has **continuity of existence/is affected by the death of the owner.**
(ii) The shares of a PLC **can be quoted on the stock exchange/cannot be quoted on the stock exchange.**
(iii) In a Franchise agreement, a fee is paid to the **franchisee/franchisor.**
(iv) In a Co-operative, the voting rights of members **depend on their share ownership/are equal.**
(v) A Partnership **is a separate legal entity/is not a separate legal entity.** **[LC HL 2017]**

2 (i) Outline the purpose of a company's Articles of Association.
(ii) List **three** items of information included in the 'Articles of Association'. **[LC HL 2010]**

Section B

1 Outline the reasons why a business may change its organisational structure from a *Sole Trader* to a *Private Limited Company*. **(20 marks) [LC HL 2010]**

2 Outline the advantages of a private limited company as a form of business ownership for a start-up business. **(20 marks) [LC HL 2015]**

3 Discuss Co-operatives and Private Limited Companies as forms of business ownership using the following headings

Formation   Liability   Finance   Control   **(25 marks) [LC HL 2012]**

Solutions

25 BUSINESS AND THE ECONOMY

 Learning Outcomes

When you have completed this chapter, you will be able to:

1 Outline the concept of an economy

2 Identify and illustrate the different types of economic system

3 Describe and illustrate the economic cycle

4 Outline the impact of economic variables on business and the economy

5 Discuss the impact of business on an economy.

 Literacy Link

Economy, economic system, economic growth, inflation, interest rates, exchange rates, unemployment, taxation

 Numeracy Link

Percentages, use of formulae, multiplication

 Cross-curricular Link

Accounting – budgeting, inflation, financial planning
Economics – economic variables
Geography – economic systems

CASE STUDY *Woodie's DIY*

Woodie's DIY is the market leader for DIY products in Ireland, with 35 branches nationwide. The business stocks over 30,000 products for all forms of home improvement.

Woodie's opened its first branch in Walkinstown, Dublin in 1987. At this time the Irish **economy** was recovering from the **recession** of the early 1980s. As **employment** levels increased, **disposable incomes** began to rise, and people began to spend more on home improvements.

With growing sales, Woodie's opened more stores around Ireland to cater for increased consumer demand. During the late 1990s, Ireland experienced an **economic boom** known as the **Celtic Tiger**. There was rapid growth in the construction sector

with the completion of houses, roads and hotels. **Growing employment** and increasing **consumer confidence** encouraged Woodie's to continue expanding. The firm opened its first superstore in Cork with a much extended product range.

Around 2007, Ireland began to experience an **economic recession**. During this stage of the **economic cycle**, the construction sector began to decline. **Unemployment** grew rapidly as consumers reduced expenditure in areas such as DIY. Many of Woodie's' competitors were forced to close stores to survive; some closed down their entire operation.

However, Woodie's DIY survived the recession. As **interest rates** set by the **European Central Bank (ECB)** fell to record lows, consumer confidence began to increase. During the **economic recovery**, consumers started to borrow money to renovate and extend their homes after years of postponing these plans.

Today Woodie's DIY is the largest chain of DIY stores in the country and has ambitious plans for the future.

THE ECONOMY

An economy is how businesses, consumers and governments trade and interact with each other in the production and distribution of goods and services in a country.

As we saw in Chapter 23, there are four main factors of production: land, labour, capital and enterprise. It is the management of these four factors that determines how the economy performs.

ECONOMIC SYSTEMS

There are three main economic systems in the world today.

Economic System	Explanation	Example	Benefits	Disadvantages
Free Enterprise	→ Little or no government involvement. Businesses provide goods and services to satisfy consumers' needs and wants.	→ USA	→ Consumers have a wide choice of goods and services at competitive prices.	→ A large gap can develop in the distribution of wealth between the rich and the poor.
Centrally Planned	→ The government makes all the decisions relating to the production of goods and services. It decides what will be made, how it will be made and who will use the goods and services.	→ North Korea	→ There is more equal distribution of wealth in the country.	→ Lack of profit motive makes firms inefficient. → Consumers do not have enough goods or services to satisfy their basic needs.
Mixed	→ Combines elements of the free enterprise and centrally planned systems. Decisions about the production and distribution of goods and services are made by businesses, consumers and the government.	→ Most developed economies, including Ireland, the UK and Japan	→ Consumers have a wide choice of goods and services. → The standard of living is high and more equally distributed among the population.	→ Private industry is encouraged but it is regulated by government. → Certain goods and services may be provided by government, e.g. health and education.

ECONOMIC ACTIVITY

The level of activity in an economy fluctuates over time, i.e. the demand for goods and services rises and falls. The government monitors economic activity by measuring economic growth.

Definition: Economic growth

An increase in the demand for goods and services in an economy. It is measured by gross national product (GNP) and gross domestic product (GDP).

Unit 6

The Difference between GDP and GNP

GDP measures the **value of goods and services produced in a country**, e.g. Ireland. It includes the goods and services produced by foreign-owned businesses that are located in that country. For example, the iMac desktop computers produced by Apple in Cork contribute to Ireland's GDP.

GNP measures the **value of goods and services produced by citizens and businesses of a country**, e.g. Ireland, whether they are in Ireland or abroad. It does not include economic activity from foreign-owned businesses based in Ireland. For example, Irish company Smurfit Kappa, which manufactures paper and cardboard products, has manufacturing facilities in Germany. The value of goods produced by Smurfit Kappa operations in Germany is included when calculating Ireland's GNP.

Activity 25.1

Search on the Internet for the video created by Zulkhairi Hj Nisa using PowToon and called 'GDP vs. GNP'. Watch this and then, in groups, create a PowToon (at www.powtoon.com) of your own to describe one of the economic systems you learned about earlier in this chapter.

THE ECONOMIC CYCLE

Economic activity in every country will rise and fall.

- An economic **boom** is when the level of activity in an economy rapidly rises.
- An economic **recession** is when the level of activity in an economy slows down.

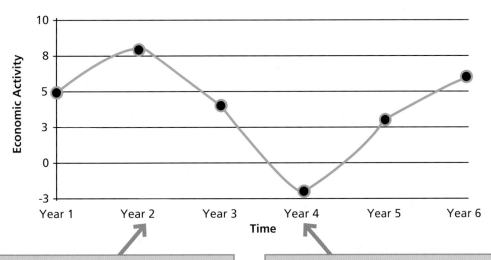

Economic boom

This occurs when economic activity is increasing rapidly, e.g. greater than 4% GDP growth. For example, Ireland's GDP growth in 2013 was 1.6%, whereas in 1999 GDP growth increased by 10.6%, reflecting the boom of the Celtic Tiger years.

During an economic boom:

- There is an increase in demand for goods and services
- Property prices rise
- Unemployment levels decline.

Economic recession

This is when GDP growth is negative and falls for two consecutive quarters, i.e. six months. For example, Ireland's GDP growth rate was −2.2% in 2008 and further decreased sharply by −6.4% in 2009, reflecting the economic recession that occurred after the boom of the Celtic Tiger years.

During an economic recession:

- The demand for goods and services falls
- Unemployment levels rise
- Consumer confidence falls.

> **Definition: The Celtic Tiger**
> The economic boom that took place in Ireland from the mid-1990s to 2007. Economic growth increased by an average of 9.4% annually from 1995 to 2000 and by almost 6% until 2007.

Economic Depression

If a period of recession is prolonged, a country could end up in an **economic depression**.

This results in a significant decline in economic activity (more than 10% from its peak) and sharply reduces the standard of living. Unemployment levels also increase. The level of credit (loans) available to businesses and consumers falls considerably.

The Great Depression and the Great Recession

The Great Depression	The Great Recession
→ This period was the longest global depression in history, lasting for almost ten years. Worldwide, GDP fell by around 15% from 1929 to 1932. International trade went into decline and in many countries unemployment rose to over 30% of the population.	→ The Great Recession, which started in 2008, began a five-year period of large-scale economic downturn across the USA and many European countries. In Ireland unemployment levels rose to 15% and income levels fell on average by 16%.

DID YOU KNOW? From 2009–2014, Greece was in a state of depression when GDP fell to levels 25% lower than its peak level.

Economic Recovery

An economy will, as part of the economic cycle, recover from the lows of a recessionary period. This is known as **recovery**. Governments use fiscal policy (government expenditure) to try to stimulate demand in the market to kick-start an economy.

Even though economists agree that an economy will always experience periods of boom and recession, a government should try to manage the impact so that an economy is more resilient in a downturn and doesn't increase too rapidly in a growth phase.

You will learn more about fiscal policy in Chapter 28.

Benefits of Economic Growth

The benefits of economic growth include:

1 **Higher employment:** An increase in demand for goods and services leads to a rise in employment levels. It becomes easier to find employment and unemployment levels decrease.

2 **Lower government expenditure:** The government spends less on social welfare payments, e.g. Jobseeker's Benefit, as more people are employed. It can allocate money previously spent on social welfare to other areas such as transport and education.

3 **Higher government revenue:** The government raises more tax revenue from the workforce, e.g. PAYE and USC. Consumers buy more items, resulting in more VAT revenue for the government.

4 **Higher business profits and sales:** Consumers buy more goods and services from businesses, which increases their sales and therefore profits.

5 **Confidence:** Economic growth creates confidence in the market, which encourages potential entrepreneurs to establish their own businesses and makes existing firms more likely to expand.

Activity 25.2

Study the bar chart, which illustrates a country's GNP and GDP from 2012 to 2017, and answer the following questions.

1 In which year was the level of economic growth highest?

2 In how many years was there GDP growth of less than 7%?

3 Find out Ireland's current rate of GNP and GDP.

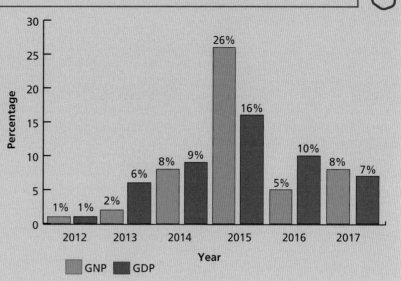

ECONOMIC VARIABLES

An economic variable measures how an economy functions. They are vulnerable to change and have major implications for the economy, businesses and consumers. The main economic variables are:

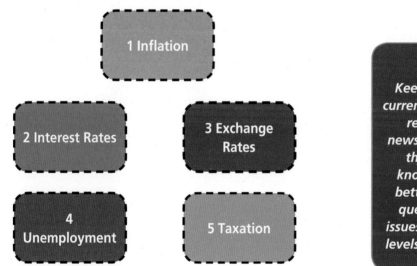

1 Inflation

2 Interest Rates

3 Exchange Rates

4 Unemployment

5 Taxation

Exam Tip!
Keep up to date with current business news by regularly reading newspapers and/or watching the news. Having prior knowledge will make you better prepared to answer questions in the exam on issues such as unemployment levels and taxation in Ireland.

Some economic variables can be influenced by the government through its fiscal policies, e.g. taxation. Others are influenced by market activity and the economic cycle, e.g. inflation.

1 Inflation

Inflation is the sustained percentage increase in the price of goods and services in an economy from one period to the next, usually for one year. It is measured by the Consumer Price Index (CPI).

Definition: Consumer Price Index (CPI)

The CSO (Central Statistics Office) records the price of a specific number of goods and services (referred to as a 'basket of goods') that an average consumer buys, e.g. bread, mortgage repayments, a litre of petrol. It then compares the price with the prices of the same products from the previous period. The percentage increase in prices between the periods is referred to as inflation.

DID YOU KNOW? *The European Central Bank aims to keep inflation in the eurozone countries at approximately 2%.*

In simple terms, inflation records the increase in prices and the fall in the purchasing power of money. For example, in 1994 a Cadbury Freddo bar cost the equivalent of 12.7c, whereas today the same bar costs 40c. The change in price level from 1994 to today reflects inflation.

Unit 6

Calculating the Rate of Inflation

Let us assume that a litre of milk cost 95c last year. It now costs €1.00. To calculate the rate of inflation, we use the following formula:

$$\frac{\text{Increase in Price} \times 100}{\text{Previous Price}} \qquad \frac{5c \times 100}{95c} \qquad = 5.3\%$$

Activity 25.3

The graph shows the cost of an average basket of goods in Ireland. Examine the graph and answer the following questions.

1. Calculate (i) the price difference and (ii) the percentage difference between the two baskets.
2. Identify a year when the price levels decreased rather than increased. Give a reason why this might have happened.
3. Visit the CSO's website (www.cso.ie) to find out:
   (i) Which items are typically included in the basket of goods and services used to measure inflation.
   (ii) Ireland's current rate of inflation.

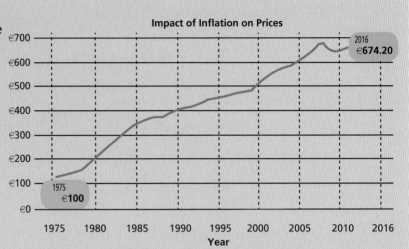

Impact of Inflation on Prices

1975 €100

2016 €674.20

Deflation

Deflation occurs when the rate of price increase (inflation) is less than zero. For example, if a protein bar cost €2 last year but retails at €1.80 this year, the rate of deflation is –10%.

This might seem positive from a consumer's point of view as products and services become cheaper. However, in the long term, if consumers expect prices to fall further they will postpone planned purchases. This erodes business confidence and can cause an economy to go into a recession.

Impact of Inflation

Impact on:	Deflation (Declining Inflation)	Rising Inflation
Government	→ The government receives less VAT revenue. Consumers postpone purchasing items as they believe that prices may fall further.	→ The government may need to increase tax credits to maintain the level of disposable income of individuals. This reduces the amount of income tax revenue received.
Business	→ The price of raw materials may fall and the business can pass on lower prices to consumers.	→ Falling sales as consumers may purchase goods and services at a cheaper price from suppliers outside Ireland.
Consumer	→ In the short term, consumers have more confidence as their purchasing power has increased. Therefore, they may spend more money in the Irish economy.	→ An increase in the price of goods and services may force consumers to demand pay rises.
Challenges/ Opportunities	→ Lower prices charged by firms reduces profit revenues. The firm may reduce staff numbers in order to cut costs.	→ There may be industrial action due to increased pay demands from employees. This can damage Ireland's international business reputation.

Unit 6

2 Interest Rates

Interest rates are expressed as a percentage of the amount borrowed or saved. They are set by a country's central bank, e.g. the Bank of England sets the interest rate in the UK. As Ireland is a member of the eurozone (19 countries that use the euro currency), interest rates here are set by the European Central Bank (ECB).

> **Definition: Interest rate**
> The cost in percentage terms of borrowing money from a financial institution, e.g. a bank or credit union. It is also a reward given by a financial institution for saving money over a period of time, e.g. a borrower pays 5% interest on a loan and a saver receives 2% interest on a deposit account.

Activity 25.4

Research the current interest rate set by the ECB and at least **two** other central banks in the world.

Impact of Interest Rates

Impact on:	Low Interest Rates	High Interest Rates
Government	→ Businesses decide to expand, leading to higher employment levels. This can increase tax revenue for the government, e.g. PAYE and PRSI.	→ A reduction in spending by consumers reduces VAT revenue.
Business	→ Consumers may borrow more money and purchase more goods and services. This increases business sales and profits.	→ Businesses may postpone expansion as the cost of borrowing has increased.
Consumer	→ The cost of mortgage repayments will reduce, if the ECB lowers interest rates.	→ If interest rates on deposit accounts increase, consumers may decide to save their money rather than spend it in the economy.
Challenges/ Opportunities	→ Businesses may take out too many loans. If there is an economic recession in the future, a business may be unable to make loan repayments as they fall due. This may lead to business failure.	→ People may be unable to repay mortgages and the financial institutions will repossess their homes.

3 Exchange Rates

An exchange rate is the price of one currency expressed in terms of another, e.g. €1 = £0.88 sterling. Exchange rates fluctuate daily, i.e. the value of a currency goes up and down.

Example

John Howlin's farm sells potatoes to a hotel chain in the UK. John invoices the company in pound sterling (£). John currently sells his potatoes on the Irish market for €9 per bag. If the exchange rate is €1 = £0.88, how much will John have to charge the hotel chain for a bag of potatoes?

$$9 \times 0.88 = £7.92$$

Suppose the exchange rate is €1 = £0.95. John would have to charge the hotel £8.55 per bag.

$$9 \times 0.95 = £8.55$$

This results in a higher cost for the hotel chain. The company may decide to source their supplies elsewhere at a cheaper price or John would have to lower his price in order to retain the contract.

> **Converting rules:**
> *When converting € to a foreign currency you multiply by the exchange rate.*
> *When converting foreign currency to € you divide by the exchange rate.*

DID YOU KNOW? *Before the 2016 Brexit referendum in the UK the exchange rate was €1 = £0.74. The euro subsequently increased in value relative to sterling, resulting in a dramatic change in the exchange rate to €1 = £0.92.*

Impact of Exchange Rates

Impact on:	Decrease in the Value of the Euro	Increase in the Value of the Euro
Government	→ An increase in the cost of essential imports for government organisations, e.g. medicines and medical equipment.	→ Sales may decline in export businesses, thus leading to lower corporation tax revenue for the government.
Business	→ Increased export sales may lead the business to recruit more staff.	→ The firm's products may be more expensive in foreign markets, which may lead to a decline in sales.
Consumer	→ Consumers may switch from buying imports as they become more expensive. Instead they may purchase cheaper domestic products.	→ Consumers will have greater spending power while on holiday/travelling in non-eurozone countries.
Challenges/ Opportunities	→ Businesses may take the opportunity to sell into new foreign markets, as their products may be more competitive.	→ Consumers may decide to purchase items from non-eurozone countries, e.g. Irish consumers could buy groceries at a lower price in Northern Ireland.

Stable Exchange Rates

Ideally, businesses, consumers and governments want a stable exchange rate, i.e. only small currency fluctuations. For firms, this makes business planning easier as they can estimate sales revenue and costs more accurately.

Activity 25.5

Look up the value of the euro against (i) £ sterling, (ii) US $, (iii) Japanese yen and (iv) Australian $ and make a note of the exchange rates. Then compare those exchange rates to what the rates were two years ago. Has the euro increased or decreased in value?

4 Unemployment

The unemployment rate is the percentage of people who are out of work but actively seeking employment. Unemployment rates are expressed as a percentage of the labour force.

Definition: Labour force
The total population of a country minus people under 18 and over 65, people in full-time education and people out of work who are suffering from a long-term illness.

Activity 25.6

In groups, research the unemployment rates for Ireland and **five** other EU countries. Discuss your findings in the group and answer the following questions:
1 Which country has the highest unemployment rate? Which has the lowest? Identify possible reasons.
2 In your opinion, what can a government do to increase employment levels?

Unit 6

Impact of Changes in Unemployment Rates

Impact on:	Decreasing Unemployment	Increasing Unemployment
Government	→ There is more tax revenue (e.g. PAYE income tax and PRSI) to spend on areas such as infrastructure and education.	→ Increased expenditure on social welfare payments, e.g. Jobseeker's Benefit.
Business	→ Increased sales can lead to business expansion, thus creating more jobs.	→ The business can find it easier to find suitable staff as there are more people out of work.
Consumer	→ People have more disposable income to spend on discretionary items, e.g. holidays.	→ Some consumers may find it difficult to repay their mortgage or to save money while they are unemployed.
Challenges/ Opportunities	→ As more people are employed, increased traffic congestion can have a negative environmental impact.	→ Increased social issues such as crime and anti-social behaviour.

5 Taxation

Taxation Policy

Governments use taxation to:

- Run the country, e.g. hospitals, transport, education
- Encourage individuals and businesses to change behaviour, e.g. carbon tax on fossil fuels to reduce pollution
- Ensure a more equal distribution of wealth, e.g. social welfare payments.

> *For more on taxation policy see Chapter 28.*

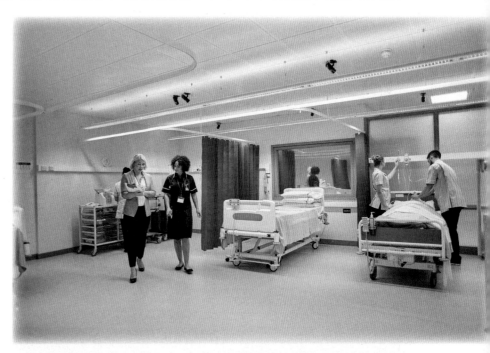

Impact of Taxation

Impact on:	Higher Taxes	Lower Taxes
Government	→ More tax revenue to spend in the economy on infrastructure and essential services.	→ Less tax revenue results in less spending on services such as health and education.
Business	→ Cost of doing business in Ireland increases, making businesses less competitive.	→ Lower taxes such as VAT lead to increased sales and profits, e.g. 13.5% VAT in the hospitality sector.
Consumer	→ Reduced levels of disposable income, resulting in less to spend on goods and services.	→ More disposable income gives consumers increased confidence to spend, especially on luxury items such as cars and holidays.
Challenges/ Opportunities	→ Employees may not work overtime as more wages are paid in tax and so businesses may find it difficult to meet production deadlines.	→ Businesses can use increased profits generated from higher levels of sales demand to expand the business or pay off existing debts.

Unit 6

CASE STUDY — *Nolan Transport*

Nolan Transport, based in New Ross, Co. Wexford, is one of the largest transport firms operating throughout Europe. The business was established over 50 years ago and today has more than 450 trucks and 1,200 trailers in its fleet.

With such a sizeable operation, one of the firm's largest costs is the price of fuel. Government **tax policy** includes actions to support national climate change commitments. Therefore, **excise duties**, **VAT** and **carbon taxes** all impact on the price of diesel. The impact of increased taxation on fuel prices is of great concern to Nolan Transport and other hauliers in the country.

Activity 25.7

1 Outline **three** reasons why the government would increase taxes on diesel.
2 What impact would an increase in diesel tax have on businesses like Nolan Transport?

Activity 25.8

MacDiarmada Coaches has three large coaches in its fleet. Each coach requires 120 litres of diesel. A litre of diesel costs €1.32. The government increases the excise duty on diesel by 5c in the budget.
1 Calculate the cost of filling the three coaches before the duty was increased.
2 Calculate the cost of filling the three coaches after the increase in duty.

THE IMPACT OF BUSINESS ON THE ECONOMY

We have seen in this chapter that different economic variables and the overall state of an economy have an impact on businesses.

Businesses have an impact on the economy in positive and negative ways, including the following:

Positive		Negative	
Standard of Living	→ Increased business activity brings improved services and facilities to an economy. This improves the standard of living for citizens.	**Inflation**	→ Businesses may continually increase prices to boost profits, e.g. Dublin hotel prices increase dramatically when there is a major event in the city such as a sports final or concert. This can lead to increased inflation.
Employment	→ Higher employment reduces social problems such as criminal activity and health issues.	**Infrastructure**	→ Rapid economic growth may put pressure on a country's infrastructure, e.g. traffic jams in large urban areas.

Positive			Negative		
Community Development	→ As businesses become more profitable they often sponsor local activities, e.g. SuperValu sponsors Tidy Towns.		Competition	→ Foreign competition from low-cost economies may enter the Irish market. As a result, Irish firms and particularly SMEs may become less competitive. Some businesses may be forced to close down, resulting in higher unemployment.	
Tax Revenue	→ As businesses become more profitable they pay more taxes to government. This results in more government expenditure on services such as agriculture and tourism.		Environment	→ Increased business activity can cause environmental damage if it is not managed properly. This could harm other sectors such as tourism.	

Activity 25.9

In pairs, create a revision quiz with ten questions and answers on economic variables. Swap your quiz with another pair of students. When completed, swap back the quiz and mark the answers out of ten.

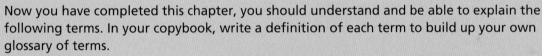

KEY TERMS

Now you have completed this chapter, you should understand and be able to explain the following terms. In your copybook, write a definition of each term to build up your own glossary of terms.

- economy
- economic system
- free enterprise
- centrally planned
- mixed economy
- economic cycle
- economic growth
- gross domestic product (GDP)

- gross national product (GNP)
- economic boom
- economic recession
- economic depression
- economic recovery
- inflation
- Consumer Price Index (CPI)

- deflation
- interest rates
- exchange rates
- unemployment
- labour force
- taxation

PowerPoint Summary

Unit 6

EXAM-STYLE QUESTIONS

Ordinary Level

Section 1 – Short Questions (10 marks each)

1 Name the **three** types of economic system. Give an example of each.
2 Explain the term *economic cycle*.
3 Complete the following sentence using the words below. (One word does not apply.)

        inflation   **deflation**   **CPI**   **standard of living**

The general rise in prices in an economy is referred to as _____ and is measured by the _____.
The opposite effect is called_____.

4 State whether each of these statements is true or false.

Statements		True or False
A	A free enterprise economy is one where the government is involved in all business decisions.	
B	Deflation is when prices are falling in an economy.	
C	Interest rates in Ireland are controlled by the European Central Bank.	
D	The exchange rate of the euro against sterling does not fluctuate in value.	
E	Rising taxation in an economy is always a benefit to consumers.	

5 List **four** economic variables that can impact on an economy.
6 Outline what is meant by the term *interest rates*.
7 Explain the term *exchange rate*.
8 What do the following letters stand for? (i) CPI, (ii) GDP, (iii) ECB.

Section 2 – Long Questions

1 Ireland is viewed as a mixed economy. Explain the term *mixed economy* and outline, using examples, other types of economic system. **(15 marks)**
2 Explain the term *inflation* and outline **two** benefits to Ireland of having low inflation. **(20 marks)**
3 What is the official measure of inflation? Outline briefly how it is calculated. **(15 marks)**
4 Discuss the impact of interest rates on the Irish economy. **(20 marks)**
5 Describe the effects of rising unemployment in the Irish economy. **(15 marks)**
6 The Irish government is considering increasing taxes in the upcoming budget. Describe **two** effects this increase in taxes might have on the Irish economy. **(15 marks)**
7 Read the information supplied and answer the questions which follow:
The following table shows the exchange rate of €1 to £1 over five months.

	Month 1	Month 2	Month 3	Month 4	Month 5
Exchange rate	€0.75	€0.80	€0.85	€0.80	€0.90

  (i) Draw a line graph to represent the above information. **(10 marks)**
  (ii) Outline **two** effects of fluctuating exchange rates on business. **(15 marks)**

Higher Level

Section 1 – Short Questions (10 marks each)

1 Identify **three** economic systems. Briefly describe **one** of these systems.

2 Explain what is meant by the term *economic growth*.

3 Illustrate your understanding of the term *economic recession*.

4 Name **four** economic variables that affect the Irish economy. Describe **one** of these variables in more detail.

5 Distinguish between inflation and deflation.

6 Column 1 is a list of economic terms. Column 2 is a list of possible explanations for these economic terms. Match the two lists in your copybook by writing your answers in the form *number = letter* (e.g. 1 = A).

Terms		Explanations	
1	Inflation	A	The main revenue-raising mechanism used by governments
2	Taxation	B	The price of one currency expressed in terms of another
3	Interest Rate	C	The general rise in prices in an economy measured by the CPI
4	Exchange Rate	D	The level of activity in an economy fluctuates over time from high to low
5	Economic Cycle	E	The cost of borrowing money

7 Explain what is meant by the term *exchange rate*. Outline **one** impact on an Irish business exporting to the US market if the euro increases in value relative to the US dollar.

8 Identify the correct answer in the following statements.

   (i) An increase in the value of the euro (€) against the dollar ($) is **good/bad** for Irish exporters to the USA.

   (ii) The general increase in prices in an economy is called **inflation/deflation** and is measured by **CPI/GDP**.

   (iii) The economic cycle is made up of periods of booms and recessions. A prolonged recessionary period is called a **depression/recovery**.

   (iv) The cost of borrowing money is the **interest/exchange** rate.

   (v) Interest rates in Ireland are regulated by the **Bank of Ireland/European Central Bank**.

Section 2 – Applied Business Question (80 marks)

Baldwinstown Hotel and Country Spa

Located just outside Glenbeigh, Co. Kerry, Baldwinstown Hotel is an award-winning five-star hotel and it employs 50 staff.

The owner of the hotel, Carina Baldwin, has seen many changes in the last few and running the hotel has not always been easy, due to the highs and lows of economic cycles.

In 2011 the hotel suffered a severe downturn in business, as Ireland was in the middle of its greatest recession. Carina found it difficult to attract customers to the hotel, whereas only the year before the hotel was fully booked up to nine months in advance. Carina made the difficult decision to make six staff redundant and cancel contracts with local suppliers.

Despite difficult trading conditions, Carina took a risk and obtained a loan from a local bank to upgrade the hotel's website. Interest rates were at an all-time low and this helped to reduce the cost of upgrading her online presence. Eventually bookings began to increase and Carina told her staff that 'green shoots are beginning to appear once again'.

Carina was delighted to see that online bookings were increasing. She believed that the fall in the value of the euro made Ireland a more attractive destination for tourists from the UK and the USA.

Section 2 – Applied Business Question (80 marks) *continued*

Business activity in the local area increased with the opening of a new supermarket, filling station and gym. Carina has also seen advertisements for the launch of a new boutique hotel in the town centre. To give back to the local community, Carina decided to sponsor the local GAA club, St Anne's.

Some local people have accused Carina of increasing prices when local events take place, such as the Seafood Festival and the Opera Festival. Carina has denied this claim and has said that she charges a fair price based on demand from customers.

A Outline the impact of Baldwinstown Hotel on the economy. **(25 marks)**

B (i) Explain the term *economic cycle* in relation to Baldwinstown Hotel.

   (ii) A recession is only one feature of an economic cycle. Illustrate the other elements of an economic cycle with reference to the text. **(25 marks)**

C Businesses are impacted on by economic variables. Identify **three** economic variables and describe how they impact on a business such as the Baldwinstown Hotel. **(30 marks)**

Section 3 – Long Questions

1 Explain the main economic systems that operate in the world today. **(15 marks)**

2 Define the term *economic growth*. Outline the benefits of economic growth to Ireland. **(20 marks)**

3 Illustrate the economic cycle using a suitable diagram. **(20 marks)**

4 Identify **three** economic variables and explain how they impact on business. **(20 marks)**

5 Outline the impact of taxation and interest rates on a business. **(15 marks)**

6 The unemployment rate in the Irish economy has decreased in recent years since its peak in 2011. Describe the impact of rising unemployment levels on (i) consumers, (ii) business and (iii) government. **(15 marks)**

7

> 'Rising rents drive Irish inflation to 18-month high of 0.9%.' *Irish Times 2018*

Discuss the impact of rising inflation on (i) the government, (ii) business and (iii) consumers. **(15 marks)**

8

> Irish businesses do not operate alone. The Irish economy interacts with Irish businesses.

Evaluate the impact that business activity has on the Irish economy. **(20 marks)**

PREVIOUS LEAVING CERTIFICATE EXAM QUESTIONS

Ordinary Level

Section A – Short Questions (10 marks each)

1 State **two** effects of high interest rates on business. **[LC OL 2010]**

2 Write True or False for each of the following statements.

	Statements	True or False
A	Inflation refers to an increase in general price from one year to the next.	
B	A recession leads to increased spending by consumers.	
C	Lower interest rates means that the cost of borrowing money is cheaper.	
D	Exchange rates refer to the price of one currency expressed in terms of another currency.	
E	High unemployment leads to an increase in government spending on social welfare.	

[LC OL 2016]

Section B

1 The following table shows Unemployment Rates from November 2007 to May 2009.

	November 2007	May 2008	November 2008	May 2009
Total persons on the Live Register	150,000	200,000	250,000	400,000

(A) (i) Draw a bar chart to represent the above information. **(10 marks)**

(ii) Outline **two** effects of increasing unemployment on business. **(20 marks)**

(B)

> In recent times there has been a large increase in the number of Irish consumers shopping in Northern Ireland.

State **two** effects of this situation for the Irish economy. **(15 marks) [LC OL 2010]**

2

> Unemployment in Ireland is less than 5% but some economists are concerned because interest rates have risen and are forecast to increase.

(i) Outline **three** benefits of low unemployment to the Irish economy. **(15 marks)**

(ii) Outline **three** effects of increasing interest rates on Irish business. **(15 marks) [LC OL 2007]**

Higher Level

Section A – Short Questions (10 marks each)

1 (i) Explain the term *exchange rate*.

(ii) Describe **two** possible risks which exchange rates could present for business in Ireland. **[LC HL 2015]**

2 (i) Explain the term *interest rate*.

(ii) Outline **two** possible economic impacts of low interest rates for Irish business. **[LC HL 2014]**

3 Write True or False for each of the following statements.

Statements		True or False
A	Inflation refers to the decrease in the cost of living from one year to the next.	
B	An increase in the value of the euro (€) against sterling (£) has a negative impact on Irish exports to the UK.	
C	Decrease in unemployment results in an increase in PAYE revenue for the Government.	
D	High interest rates stimulate business expansion.	
E	A recession represents an upturn in the economy and an increase in demand.	

[LC HL 2016]

Section B

1 Describe the impact of inflation and interest rates on business in Ireland. **(20 marks) [LC HL 2006]**

2 Outline the benefits and challenges of increasing employment for the Irish economy. **(25 marks) [LC HL 2018]**

3 Analyse how the economic variables (factors) in the Irish economy have an impact on a local economy. **(20 marks) [LC HL 2001]**

 Solutions

26 COMMUNITY DEVELOPMENT

When you have completed this chapter, you will be able to:

1 Describe the concept of community development

2 Identify and outline the services provided by community development organisations

3 Explain the importance of community initiatives for social and economic life in a local area.

Literacy Link

Community development, Local Enterprise Office (LEO), LEADER Programme, Area Partnership Companies (APCs), Pobal

Numeracy Link

Percentages, multiplication, calculating distances

Cross-curricular Link

Geography – economic development
Religion – belonging to a community

CASE STUDY **IRD Kiltimagh CLG**

Kiltimagh, Co. Mayo was for many years part of the 'Black Triangle' – areas in the west of Ireland with very **high levels of unemployment** and **low levels of investment**.

A survey identified that 75% of people between the ages of 17 and 25 years were forced to emigrate from the area to find work. Local people realised that they needed to take action to halt the decline of the area.

A committee of local people formed **IRD Kiltimagh CLG**, which is a rural development company. The aim of the company is to develop the **economic and social potential** of the area.

The first course of action was to improve the appearance of the town centre. The company employed the services of a local architect and set about refurbishing buildings and encouraging local people to do likewise with small **grants** from the **LEADER** Programme.

IRD Kiltimagh CLG understood the importance of developing tourism in the area. It helped to map and market local walking trails, provide access to local rivers and lakes to encourage fishing tourism, developed a Sculpture Park and Trail and built an outdoor and indoor children's play area with investment of €150,000.

INTEGRATED RESOURCE DEVELOPMENT KILTIMAGH

The most ambitious project undertaken was the development of the Cairn International Trade Centre at a cost of €7 million. The office building comprises 15 business suites with meeting rooms, a world-class broadband connection and a range of other business facilities. Finance for the project was raised from **Enterprise Ireland, commercial banks**, Western Development Commission and IRD company funds.

The work of the community through IRD Kiltimagh CLG has been socially and economically successful:

- There was a 28% growth in population.
- Many new facilities and amenities have been developed in the area.
- 715 jobs have been created in companies which had help from IRD.
- There was shown to be an annual 30.2% growth in economic activity.

IRD Kiltimagh CLG shows what a local community can achieve when they work together for the benefit of the area.

Activity 26.1

Visit www.ird-kiltimagh.ie to find out more about the work that is done in the local community.

Definition: CLG
A company limited by guarantee: it does not have share capital and its members have limited liability.

INDICATORS OF A VIBRANT OR DECLINING LOCAL COMMUNITY

	Vibrant Local Community	Declining Local Community
Employment	→ Plentiful supply of jobs in the local area. → Lower levels of unemployment. → Higher standard of living.	→ Few jobs available in the local area. → High levels of unemployment, with more people claiming social welfare payments. → Lower standard of living.
Infrastructure	→ High-speed broadband connection. → Good transport links. → Reliable water and energy supply.	→ Weak or inconsistent broadband connection. → Limited transport links. → Poor-quality water and energy supply.
Education and Training	→ Access to education and training programmes. → Access to a range of qualified third-level graduates. → Link with local third-level institutions for research and development.	→ Education centres located far from the local community. → High drop-out rates in second- and third-level education. → Low uptake of training programmes.
Sports and Recreation	→ Variety of sports and recreation facilities for all ages, e.g. sports pitches, gyms and social clubs.	→ Limited sports and recreation facilities.
Crime	→ Good relationship between the local community and the Gardaí. → Low levels of crime and anti-social behaviour. → Neighbourhood Watch schemes.	→ High levels of crime and anti-social behaviour. → Local people feel unsafe in their homes.
Local Goods and Services	→ New businesses opening in the local area. → Wide range of essential services, e.g. post office and banks.	→ Closure of local businesses. → Longer commute for goods and services, e.g. doctor's surgery, shops and cafés.

Unit 6

THE LOCAL COMMUNITY

The local community consists of people who interact with each other in a common area. Your local community may comprise people who live in your housing estate, your local village, town or city.

It is important that individuals, businesses and voluntary organisations, e.g. the GAA, work together to develop the local area socially and economically.

Activity 26.2

Examine the images below and answer the following questions.

1 Describe in detail what you can see in each photo.
2 Which image shows a vibrant local community? Give **two** reasons why you have chosen this image.
3 In the images representing a declining local community, suggest **two** ways to promote future economic growth.

CASE STUDY KiltyLive

FAMILIES WANTED

TIRED OF THE HUSTLE, BUSTLE AND EXPENSE OF CITY LIFE?
Raise your family in a safe, tranquil, **NORTH LEITRIM VILLAGE** steeped in culture and history.

AWARD WINNING NATIONAL SCHOOL - NOW ENROLLING -

☑ Small Classes ☑ Excellent Facilities
☑ Subsidised Activities

INTERESTED?
We would LOVE to hear from YOU!
RENT ALLOWANCE CONSIDERED
📘 Follow us @KiltyLive
Email: kiltylive@gmail.com

KiltyLive
Kiltyclogher awaits you!

📞 **083 048 5281**

Designed in Kiltyclogher by www.MyDesigner.ie

The village of Kiltyclogher in Co. Leitrim had a declining population, with only 233 residents. The two-teacher local school had 14 students registered and if numbers continued to fall, the school would close.

The local community worked together to set up the KiltyLive Facebook page. It advertised the village as an attractive place for people to live to escape the hustle and bustle of city life and encouraged families to move to the area.

The Facebook page received enquiries from families all over Ireland about moving to Kiltyclogher and within six weeks, six families had decided to move to the area.

The local school now has 30 pupils registered and the local community is actively promoting a range of activities such as drama, boxercise and pottery classes.

Activity 26.3

1 Search for Kiltyclogher, Co. Leitrim on Google Earth to see where the village is located. List the services and amenities that you can find in the area.

2 If you were to move to Kiltyclogher, what distance would you need to travel? Use a distance calculator such as www.theaa.ie/routes or Google Maps to find out how far Kiltyclogher is from your local area.

3 Visit the KiltyLive Facebook page to see the programmes and initiatives for people in the local area and report back to your class.

COMMUNITY DEVELOPMENT

Community development involves the local community coming together to identify and find solutions to economic and social problems in the area. Members of the community are in the best position to identify how to solve these issues.

Community Development Committee

In order to identify and solve local problems, local people often form a community development committee. Below are the steps required to form such a committee:

Step 1 Forming the Committee
A group of local people come together to form a committee. The group should be representative of the ages and interests of people in the local community, e.g. local business people, sports groups and active retirement groups.

Step 2 Structure
The committee may decide to form a CLG (company limited by guarantee). This type of structure gives the committee members limited liability.

Step 3 Planning
The committee undertakes a SWOT analysis to identify and analyse local problems, e.g. high unemployment. The committee then develops a plan and a strategy to solve these problems.

Step 4 Finance
The committee must obtain finance from a range of sources, for example:
- Local fundraising events, e.g. sponsored walks
- Loans, e.g. credit unions
- Grants, e.g. the LEADER programme.

Can you remember what the letters SWOT stand for in relation to planning?

Activity 26.4

In groups of three or four, identify any social or economic problems in your local area. What could you do to improve these problems? What types of support would you need?

We will learn more about the LEADER programme later in this chapter.

CASE STUDY

Kilmacthomas Social Enterprise Development Group

Kilmacthomas is a village of 800 residents located approximately 26km from Waterford city. During the **economic recession** many local businesses closed down and the community was hit by a further blow when the bank branch also shut its doors.

The community set up Kilmacthomas Social Enterprise Development Group to identify ways in which they could improve the **economic** and **social development** of the local area.

The group recognised the importance of opening the Waterford Greenway. At 46km, it is the longest off-road cycle route in Ireland. The group decided to focus on encouraging users of the Greenway to stop in Kilmacthomas. It organised fundraising events to build a pedestrian walkway from the Greenway to the

centre of the village and it erected signage with photographs of the village and named it the 'Heart of the Greenway'.

With the success of the Waterford Greenway, the group is now working on developing historical tourist trails featuring Daniel O'Connell (1775–1847), who spoke in the village square, a local business that sold tickets for the *Titanic*'s maiden voyage and the workhouse, dating from 1914. A café and whiskey distillery have also opened.

Helen Rigard, who is a member of the Kilmacthomas Social Enterprise Development Group, said, 'We are ready to play our part developing businesses and attracting tourists. We want Kilmacthomas to be a wonderful place to live and a bustling and thriving tourist village. We want it to be a destination of choice.'

Activity 26.5

Examine the infographic on the Waterford Greenway and answer the following questions.

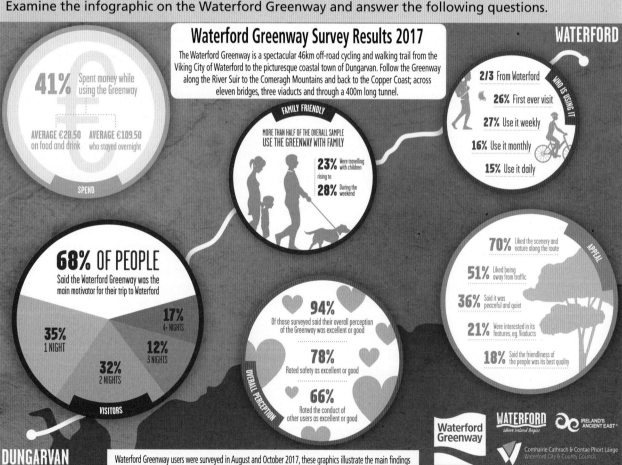

1 According to visitors, what was the main appeal of the Greenway?

2 What percentage of visitors were motivated to visit Waterford by the development of the Greenway?

3 How much money on average did people spend on food and drinks while using the Greenway?

4 How much money on average did visitors who stayed in the area overnight spend?

5 Based on your knowledge, what economic benefits can an initiative such as the Greenway have in a local area?

Unit 6

Activity 26.6

Conduct research online or in local newspapers to find out if there are any local community initiatives in your area. Use PicCollage to create an image gallery of any initiative you find.

Organisations that Support Community Development

There are a number of government agencies that support community development around Ireland. They include:

 **1 Local Enterprise Office (LEO)**

 **2 LEADER Programme**

3 Area Partnership Companies (APCs)

4 Pobal

1 Local Enterprise Office (LEO)

There are thirty-one Local Enterprise Offices in Ireland, offering a range of government supports to help entrepreneurs establish and grow their businesses.

A Training

Each LEO runs a range of training programmes to help entrepreneurs to increase their business knowledge and skills, e.g. financial management and social media.

B Mentoring

A business mentor is matched with the entrepreneur to help identify and solve business problems and implement solutions. This is often used when the entrepreneur needs extra support or advice.

C Financial Support

The LEOs offer a range of grants, e.g. start-up and feasibility studies. They also operate a small loan scheme, whereby entrepreneurs can borrow up to €25,000 at reduced interest rates.

> **Exam Tip!**
> Make sure that you can **list** the community development organisations and **outline** the services they provide to the local community.

Activity 26.7

Acheson Ltd receives a loan from its LEO for €20,000 at a rate of interest of 6.8%. How much interest will it have paid at the end of year 1?

D Food Academy Programme

This programme is run in conjunction with SuperValu. Entrepreneurs receive advice from industry experts on how to develop their products. SuperValu stores may trial products for twelve weeks and the producers receive direct customer feedback.

Activity 26.8

Visit www.supervalu.ie and search for the Food Academy Programme. Select your local area to find businesses that have benefited from the programme. Do you recognise any of the brands? What types of products have been developed?

Unit 6

CASE STUDY — LEO: Nobó

Nobó is an Irish company that produces dairy-free ice cream and chocolates. It received help from the Dublin City **Local Enterprise Office (LEO)** when establishing and expanding the business. The company took part in the **Food Academy Programme**, received **mentoring** support and also **grants**. Nobó is now stocked in over 400 stores in Ireland, the UK and the Middle East, and the company has plans for further expansion.

nobó

Activity 26.9

Search on the Internet for the LEO Dublin City video about Nobó ice cream. Watch it and answer the following questions.

1 What is the USP of Nobó?
2 What did the entrepreneurs do with the first grant they received from their LEO?
3 State **three** plans Nobó has for the future.

2 LEADER Programme

This is an EU-funded programme that aims to provide local communities with the resources needed to:

- Reduce poverty
- Increase social inclusion
- Promote economic development.

Projects	Local Action Groups	Funding
Specific types of project are funded by the LEADER programme to fulfil its aims, including: promoting rural tourism; improving broadband access; and rural youth schemes.	In order to receive funding, the area must set up a Local Action Group (LAG), which formulates a Local Development Strategy. These strategies may include the development of tourist walking trails and local festivals and events.	Local community groups submit project ideas to their Local Action Group (LAG). The LAG assesses the ideas and distributes grants to help the community group to develop their project, e.g. local playgrounds and training for youth in rural areas.

CASE STUDY

LEADER: Ardmore Open Farm and Mini Zoo

The owners received a **grant** from the **LEADER** programme to develop their farm into a family and tourist attraction in Ardmore, Co. Waterford. The family constructed a purpose-built premises to house animals, a café and an indoor play area for children. The farm has been highly successful and has added a mini zoo to its attractions.

3 Area Partnership Companies

Area Partnership Companies (APCs) support local communities to:

- Reduce local unemployment and poverty
- Encourage educational engagement
- Improve social inclusion.

APCs offer a number of services, including:

Education	→ APCs encourage local people to engage with education and learning. They provide up-to-date information on education and skills training. They may also work with local schools to combat early school leaving.
Enterprise	→ APCs encourage entrepreneurship in the local community. They offer training courses and workshops to support and encourage local people to become entrepreneurs.
Employment Support	→ APCs often operate in areas of high unemployment. They offer support services for people looking for work, including CV preparation and interview techniques.
Childcare and Family Support	→ Many APCs offer childcare and family support services. They may provide childcare facilities and parenting courses.

Unit 6

CASE STUDY: *Area Partnership Companies*

Northside Partnership

Northside Partnership in Dublin provides support services to over 130,000 people in the areas of education, enterprise and health. The partnership runs Healthy Food Made Easy, a six-week programme that shows people how to plan and budget healthy meals.

Dublin North West Area Partnership

This APC runs a specialised jobs club, which helps people searching for work with CV preparation and interview skills. It also operates adult education and training programmes to help local people access further education.

4 Pobal

Pobal works with organisations to improve the lives of people experiencing social exclusion and disadvantage. Pobal facilitates a number of programmes, including:

A Gateway

Gateway provides short-term employment opportunities for people who have been unemployed for more than two years. Participants are involved in work that benefits the local community, e.g. tourism ambassadors and landscaping.

B Dormant Accounts Fund

This scheme redistributes money from dormant accounts to social enterprises that provide employment in the local community, particularly for disadvantaged people in rural areas.

> **Definition: Dormant account**
> An account in which there have been no customer-led transactions in over 15 years.

> **!**

> **DID YOU KNOW?** The government has distributed over €40 million from dormant accounts to support projects that benefit disadvantaged areas of society.

Activity 26.10

Search online for 'Projects approved for Dormant Accounts Funding under the Social Enterprise Measure'. Find out:
1 Which project received the highest level of funding.
2 Which project received the lowest amount of funding.
3 Which county received the largest payment.

C European Refugee Fund

Pobal provides funding to organisations to develop and implement integration programmes for refugees. These programmes focus on areas such as education, health and the provision of information.

D Tús

Under this programme, people who are long-term unemployed complete a twelve-month work placement in the local community. Pobal manages the payroll function for this initiative.

Economic and Social Benefits of Community Development

Economic Benefits		Social Benefits	
Employment	→ Community development helps to create jobs in the local area. This reduces unemployment and increases the standard of living of local people.	**Community Spirit**	→ Community development programmes help to create community spirit. Local people work together to improve the physical appearance of the area to attract tourists, e.g. painting buildings and planting flowers.
Enterprise Culture	→ Growth in the local community encourages entrepreneurship in the area. This creates an enterprise culture and leads to the development of more local businesses.	**Reduces Emigration**	→ Community development helps to reduce emigration of people from the local area. Jobs, education and leisure facilities encourage people to stay in the local area.
Commercial Rates	→ A growth in the number of businesses in the area increases the amount of commercial rates collected by local authorities. This money can be reinvested into the local area, e.g. developing playgrounds and sports facilities.	**Less Anti-social Behaviour**	→ Local people take pride in their area. With increased employment and amenities, there is less anti-social behaviour.

KEY TERMS

Now you have completed this chapter, you should understand and be able to explain the following terms. In your copybook, write a definition of each term to build up your own glossary of terms.

- local community
- vibrant local community
- declining local community
- community development
- Local Enterprise Office (LEO)

- mentoring
- grants
- LEADER
- Area Partnership Companies (APCs)
- Pobal

 PowerPoint Summary

EXAM-STYLE QUESTIONS

Ordinary Level

Section 1 – Short Questions (10 marks each)

1 Describe what is meant by the term *local community*.
2 List **four** features of a vibrant local community.
3 Describe **two** features of a declining local community.
4 Outline what is meant by the term *community development*.
5 What do the following letters stand for? (i) APC (ii) LEO.
6 Describe **two** benefits of local community development.

Unit 6

Section 2 – Long Questions

1 Outline the features of a declining local community. **(15 marks)**

2 Describe the steps involved in setting up a local community development committee. **(20 marks)**

3 Describe the services of (i) mentoring and (ii) training that are provided by Local Enterprise Offices. **(15 marks)**

4 Discuss the ways in which Local Enterprise Offices help entrepreneurs. **(15 marks)**

5 Explain **two** of the services provided by Pobal to the local community. **(15 marks)**

6 Outline **two** economic benefits of community development to a local area. **(15 marks)**

Higher Level

Section 1 – Short Questions (10 marks each)

1 Outline the impact that a vibrant local community can have on (i) employment and (ii) infrastructure.

2 Complete this sentence: Community development is important _____

3 Illustrate the support provided by the Food Academy Programme at the Local Enterprise Office (LEO).

4 Describe **two** services provided by Area Partnership Companies (APCs).

5 What is the Dormant Accounts Fund?

6 Column 1 is a list of community development organisations. Column 2 is a list of services provided by these organisations. Match the organisation with the service in your copybook by writing your answers in the form *number = letter* (e.g. 1 = A).

Column 1		Column 2	
1	LEO	**A**	Provides childcare facilities and parenting courses.
2	APC	**B**	Redistributes money in dormant accounts to social enterprises, particularly in rural areas.
3	LEADER Programme	**C**	Provides a range of services to entrepreneurs, including training programmes, mentoring and the Food Academy.
4	Pobal	**D**	Provides funding for local community projects to reduce poverty, e.g. tourism and broadband initiatives.

Section 2 – Applied Business Question (80 marks)

Culmore Town

Anne Barrett owns a shop in the town of Culmore selling hand-made cakes and jams. Over the past ten years, Anne has noticed a number of positive and negative changes in the town. While high-speed broadband access has been introduced and a new motorway has been built, lots of shops have closed down, the local sports pitches have become overgrown and the town walls are covered in graffiti. Anne has noticed the lines of people queuing to collect their social welfare payments growing each week.

Anne cannot understand why businesses are not thriving in the local area. The town is located near an institute of technology, so there are lots of highly qualified graduates available for work.

Anne decided that something needed to be done to rejuvenate the local community. She organised a meeting in the town hall and a committee was formed to put plans in place to develop the town. The committee included representatives from local businesses, as well as sports and other voluntary clubs.

The committee reviewed all the suggestions made by local people and decided to concentrate on improving the appearance of the town by painting buildings and landscaping the town centre. Long-term planning will focus on attracting new businesses to the area. Land is available at reasonable rates and the local people are very supportive of new businesses in the community.

All this positivity has made Anne realise that she needs help to develop her own business. She has seen advertisements for the SuperValu Food Academy and wants her products to be stocked in stores around Ireland. Unfortunately Anne doesn't have the finance to purchase new machinery or undertake any market research. She knows that she needs help with budgeting and cash flow management. She would also like to get some advice from other business owners in the same industry.

Section 2 – Applied Business Question (80 marks) *continued*

A (i) Describe the features of a declining local community.

   (ii) With reference to the town of Culmore, what factors influence the decision by a
   business to locate in a local community? **(30 marks)**

B (i) What is meant by the term *community development*?

   (ii) Outline the steps needed to form a local community development committee in the
   town of Culmore. **(30 marks)**

C Identify a state agency that could help Anne develop her business. Describe the services
that Anne could access at this state agency. **(20 marks)**

Section 3 – Long Questions

1 Discuss the steps a local community should take to establish a community development
committee. **(15 marks)**

2 What do the letters APC stand for? Describe the role of an APC in the local community in
relation to (i) enterprise, (ii) education and (iii) employment support. **(20 marks)**

3 Name **two** organisations that support community development. Outline how **one** of these
organisations helps economic and social development in the local community. **(25 marks)**

4 Evaluate the features of the LEADER programme. **(20 marks)**

5 Discuss **two** services provided by Pobal in the local community. **(15 marks)**

PREVIOUS LEAVING CERTIFICATE EXAM QUESTIONS

Ordinary Level

Section A – Short Questions (10 marks each)

1 Outline **two** benefits which business can bring to a local community. **[LC OL 2007]**

Section B

1

Local community enterprise is important for the local economy.

Name **two** agencies which can help local community development and outline the role
of **one** of them. **(20 marks) [LC OL 2003]**

Higher Level

Section B

1

Business and community activities and structures must change and adapt to meet new challenges.
The planned interaction between business, the local community, government agencies and
society is the foundation on which the success of all sectors is based.

   (i) Define *community development*. **(10 marks)**

   (ii) Analyse how local communities and local businesses can benefit from each other's presence
   in an area. Use an example in each case to illustrate your answer. **(20 marks) [LC HL 2003]**

2 Name **three** examples of community development organisations and describe the
services provided by **one** of them. **(20 marks) [LC HL 2007]**

 Solutions

27 ETHICAL, SOCIAL AND ENVIRONMENTAL RESPONSIBILITY

When you have completed this chapter, you will be able to:

1 Understand and explain the concept of business ethics
2 Identify and describe the reasons why businesses act in an unethical manner
3 Outline the ways in which a business can encourage ethical behaviour
4 Discuss the social responsibilities of business
5 Identify and describe the ways in which a business can act in a socially responsible manner
6 Analyse the impact on business of environmental issues
7 Identify and describe the characteristics of an environmentally conscious business
8 Evaluate the benefits and costs of a firm meeting its social and environmental responsibilities.

Literacy Link

Business ethics, ethical audit, whistleblowing, social responsibility, corporate social responsibility (CSR), environmental responsibility

Numeracy Link

Subtraction, division, multiplication, percentages

Cross-curricular Link

Geography – renewable and non-renewable energy, environmental pollution, sustainable economic development, EPA
Religion – moral decision-making

CASE STUDY

Business Ethics at Volkswagen

The Volkswagen Group (VW) is one of the world's largest automobile manufacturers with twelve distinct brands including Volkswagen, Audi and Škoda.

Senior management at the company made a **strategic plan** to overtake Toyota as the world's largest car manufacturer. In order to achieve this goal, VW needed to increase the number of diesel cars it sold in the USA.

VW began working on a diesel engine to pass the strict US vehicle emissions test, but it soon became apparent that it would not be successful. Instead, the VW team took an **unethical** approach and developed a 'defeat device' that could cheat the test. Software installed in the car

could identify when the engine was being tested and lower its emissions to pass the test. In some cases, the actual emissions were 15–35 times higher than acceptable US standards.

The device was fitted to approximately 11 million cars across the VW brands, including 500,000 vehicles in the USA. After a number of government agency investigations, VW eventually admitted to installing the device on its vehicles and a number of staff were arrested by the FBI for defrauding the USA.

The fallout from this scandal has had a significant impact on the reputation and profits at the VW Group. It is estimated that the emissions scandal could cost the company over €4 billion to resolve. It negotiated a settlement of over €3 billion to US regulators and has agreed to be independently monitored in the USA for the next three years. The firm must also buy back or fix US vehicles that have been affected by the issue.

Individual **consumers** in Ireland and across Europe have sued VW for compensation over its admission that its technology had cheated emissions tests.

The company has also faced lawsuits from disgruntled **investors** who saw the value of the company decrease by one third after news of the emissions scandal was made public. Investors claim that Volkswagen Group failed to disclose the scale of the emissions scandal when they became aware of the issue.

VW has a long road ahead to show its stakeholders that it has become a more **ethical** and a more **socially and environmentally responsible** business.

PART 1: ETHICAL RESPONSIBILITY

Personal ethics relates to an individual's view of what is morally right and wrong. It can be influenced by our upbringing and life experiences.

The business must ensure that all employees take a common ethical approach in all business decisions.

Business ethics are the moral rules and standards that help people to make decisions in a business. Everybody in the business must be able to identify what is morally 'right' and 'wrong' in business situations and then choose the 'right' option, regardless of its impact on the firm's profits.

Many firms include information on ethical behaviour in the employee staff handbook or during induction training.

CASE STUDY — Turing Pharmaceuticals

Martin Shkreli, the founder and CEO of Turing Pharmaceuticals, caused outrage when he increased the price of a medicine, called Daraprim, manufactured by his company from €11.45 per tablet to €636 per tablet. Patients using the medicine could not swap to other brands, as there is no alternative in the market.

Questions

1 Do you think this was ethical behaviour by the business? Give a reason for your answer.
2 What impact did the price increase have on the firm's stakeholders, such as investors, consumers and employees?
3 If the price of the Daraprim tablet increased from €11.45 per tablet to €636 per tablet, what was the percentage price increase?

Activity 27.1

Search online for the Ted-Ed video lesson called 'Would you sacrifice one person to save five?' by Eleanor Nelsen.

1 Answer the 'Think' questions associated with the clip.
2 Discuss in groups how you would react to the two scenarios presented in the clip. Give reasons for your decision.

Unit 6

Reasons for Unethical Business Behaviour

While people may not act unethically in their daily lives, there are a number of reasons why employees might behave unethically in the workplace.

DID YOU KNOW?

A study by Ernst & Young found that 50% of senior managers in Ireland would act unethically to help their business grow during an economic downturn.

1 **Fear:** If there is a culture of fear in the business, employees may not report unethical behaviour. They may be afraid that their job security will be under threat, e.g. demotion or dismissal.

2 **Pressure from management:** Senior management may set unrealistic goals for employees to meet. Staff may feel that they have no option but to behave unethically in order to achieve these goals.

3 **Business culture:** If employees see senior management behaving in an unethical manner they may follow their example and behave unethically when making business decisions.

Example

Toshiba employees overstated the company's earnings by almost €2 billion over a seven-year period in order to reach unrealistic profit targets set by senior management at the company. The firm's president was forced to resign as he admitted that he had known about the financial irregularities.

4 **Greed:** Businesses may place an emphasis on making profit above everything else. Employees may want to help the business maximise its profits and resort to behaving in an unethical manner.

5 **Lack of legislation:** Lack of legislation can make it easier for businesses to behave unethically as there may be no consequences for their actions. Low fines and weak enforcement of laws may also enable businesses to act unethically.

Ways of Encouraging Ethical Business Behaviour

Businesses must work hard to encourage employees to act ethically in all business decisions. They can do this in the following ways:

1 **Ethical audit:** An independent firm completes an ethical audit in the business. It reviews how the business is run from an ethical perspective. The auditor compiles a report outlining to the business which areas require improvement.

2 **Lead by example:** Senior management must act in a highly ethical manner at all times. They set an example for employees to follow and employees will understand that they too must act ethically in all business situations.

3 **Whistleblowing:** Whistleblowing is when a person in the business reports unethical behaviour by co-workers or managers. The business must create a culture in which employees report unethical behaviour, regardless of who is responsible.

4 **Staff training:** During induction, employees should receive information on the firm's code of ethics. The business should also provide ethics training to remind employees of the importance of ethical behaviour.

| 1 Ethical audit |
| 2 Lead by example |
| 3 Whistleblowing |
| 4 Staff training |
| 5 Rewards |

Example

On a day in May 2018, 8,000 Starbucks stores throughout the USA closed early for staff training to promote inclusion and prevent discrimination. The company had been accused of racial bias after two African-American men were arrested at a Philadelphia store as they waited for another man for a business meeting but did not make any purchases. The closure is estimated to have cost the company over €10 million in lost profit.

5 **Rewards:** Rewards can be offered to employees who act in an ethical manner, e.g. bonus payments and promotion. Unethical behaviour should be punished to show employees that such behaviour will not be tolerated, e.g. dismissal.

Unit 6

Code of Ethics

A code of ethics is a formal written statement that outlines the type of behaviour expected by the business from all employees when dealing with stakeholders, e.g. investors and the local community. It can also be referred to as a code of business conduct.

A simplified code of ethics might include the following points:

CODE OF BUSINESS CONDUCT

All employees must obey the laws of the country in which the business operates.

Employees must keep all business information confidential.

Discrimination and harassment will not be tolerated.

Employees must comply with all health and safety rules in the organisation.

Example: Code of Ethics at Ford Motors

Ford Motors has an extensive code of ethics that applies to all employees. In relation to the receipt of gifts, employees are **not** allowed to:

- Ask for a gift or a favour from firms that do business with Ford

- Accept gifts over a certain value

- Receive discounts on goods or services from other businesses unless the discounts are offered to all employees in the company.

CODE OF ETHICS IN THE WORKPLACE

✓ Benefits	✗ Challenges
1 Ethical Behaviour It shows employees what ethical behaviour is expected of them in the workplace. This can prevent unethical decisions being made that would damage the firm's reputation.	**1 Decreased Productivity** Time and resources must be allocated by the business to develop and update the code of ethics. This may take time away from employees' day-to-day duties and reduce business productivity.
2 Marketing Businesses with a code of ethics can use this in their marketing material, e.g. on the firm's website. This can increase consumer awareness of the ethical beliefs of the firm and may increase sales and profits.	**2 Slow Decision-making** Employees may be afraid to make decisions in case they are judged to have acted unethically. This can slow down decision-making and result in missed business opportunities.
3 Management Time Employees are empowered to make decisions on behalf of the business in line with its code of ethics. This frees up management time to focus on other managerial issues, e.g. staff recruitment.	**3 Poor Industrial Relations** Employees may feel that the business has introduced a code of ethics because it does not trust them to make ethical decisions. This can lead to poor industrial relations between employer and employees.

Activity 27.2

Working in pairs, draw a noughts and crosses grid with three columns and three rows. Each student takes turns to add a key word related to business ethics in a box in the grid. The first student to get three in a row (horizontal, diagonal or vertical) wins.

Unit 6

PART 2: SOCIAL RESPONSIBILITY

Social responsibility, or corporate social responsibility (CSR), ensures that businesses take into account the impact of their decisions on stakeholders, e.g. the local community and employees.

CASE STUDY

Social Responsibility at Greyston Bakery

In 1982 Bernie Glassman opened Greyston Bakery to provide employment and training opportunities to local people in Yonkers, New York. Yonkers had a high unemployment rate and Glassman believed that he could create a successful business that would have a strong **social responsibility** to the local community. Bernie introduced the Open Hiring™ policy, which gives everybody the chance to get a job and training at the bakery regardless of their education, work experience and whether they have a criminal record. Potential employees are simply placed on a waiting list and as soon as a vacancy arises, the next person on the list gets the job. The bakery does not conduct any background checks on its employees. Greyston bakery produces 35,000 pounds of brownies per day and has supplied Ben & Jerry's ice cream since 1987. The profits from the bakery are used to fund the not-for-profit Greyston Foundation.

The Greyston Foundation has built apartments to provide housing for bakery workers. It has also developed a childcare centre, community garden and an environmental education programme. Greyston Bakery began as a small bakery but has grown to provide a wide range of services and it acts as a role model to show other firms that business can achieve more when it works with its local community.

Activity 27.3

Visit www.benjerry.ie and find the section 'Issues We Care About'. Make a list of the causes that Ben & Jerry's supports. Note **three** interesting facts to discuss with other students in your class.

Social Responsibility Towards Stakeholders

A business has a social responsibility towards its stakeholders in the following ways.

1 Investors

- The business provides honest and transparent financial information.
- It does not pay excessive salaries and bonuses to senior management.
- It rewards investors with a reasonable return when the business is profitable.

Innocent Drinks	**Enron**
The founders of Innocent Drinks provided open and honest financial information to potential investors. They received an investment of €280,000 from a private investor.	The US energy company Enron deliberately falsified company accounts. Senior managers sold their shares while encouraging investors to continue buying shares. The company went bankrupt and investors lost all the money they had invested.

2 Employees

- The business pays a fair wage based on the work performed.
- It provides healthy and safe working conditions.
- It makes it clear that bullying and discrimination will not be tolerated in the workplace.

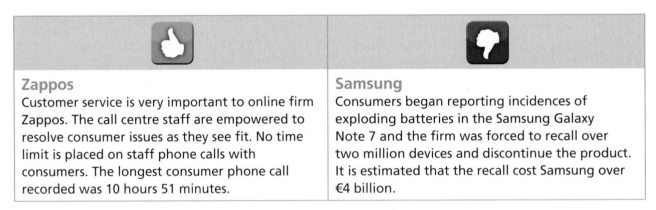

👍	👎
Google Employees at the company's headquarters in the USA receive a range of perks, including free meals, fitness classes and an on-site doctor.	**Nike** Nike has admitted that in the past there was widespread exploitation of workers in many of its manufacturing plants, e.g. exposure to toxic fumes, employees working up to 70 hours per week.

3 Consumers

- The business provides high-quality goods to consumers at a reasonable price.
- It manufactures products that are safe for consumers to use.
- It deals with complaints quickly and fairly.

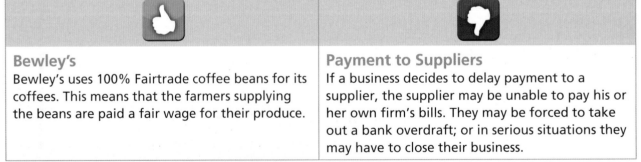

👍	👎
Zappos Customer service is very important to online firm Zappos. The call centre staff are empowered to resolve consumer issues as they see fit. No time limit is placed on staff phone calls with consumers. The longest consumer phone call recorded was 10 hours 51 minutes.	**Samsung** Consumers began reporting incidences of exploding batteries in the Samsung Galaxy Note 7 and the firm was forced to recall over two million devices and discontinue the product. It is estimated that the recall cost Samsung over €4 billion.

4 Suppliers

- The business pays a fair price for goods received from suppliers.
- It pays its suppliers in full and on time.
- It avoids using suppliers that pollute the environment or exploit workers.

👍	👎
Bewley's Bewley's uses 100% Fairtrade coffee beans for its coffees. This means that the farmers supplying the beans are paid a fair wage for their produce.	**Payment to Suppliers** If a business decides to delay payment to a supplier, the supplier may be unable to pay his or her own firm's bills. They may be forced to take out a bank overdraft; or in serious situations they may have to close their business.

> **Definition: Fairtrade**
> Fairtrade ensures that farmers and workers in developing countries get fair pay for the goods they produce, e.g. cocoa beans and bananas.

5 Government

- The business pays all taxes in full and on time.
- It complies with Irish laws.
- It uses grants received from government agencies as intended.

Keogh's	**Dunnes Stores**
Keogh's crisps received a grant of €92,000 from the LEADER programme to purchase equipment needed to expand the firm.	Dunnes Stores was forced to repay €36.5 million to the Revenue Commissioners because it had failed to pay the correct tax on the plastic bag levy over a four-year period.

6 Local Community

- The business provides employment to local people.
- It sources raw materials and other supplies from the local community.
- It invests money in the local community, e.g. sponsorship of local events and teams.

Xerox	**TEPCO**
Employees at Xerox are encouraged to get involved in local community projects. The firm's solicitors provide their services free of charge to charities in local areas.	A tsunami caused three nuclear reactors at the Tokyo Electric Power Company (TEPCO) energy plant in Fukushima, Japan to leak radiation into surrounding areas. As a result, 154,000 people were forced to evacuate their homes and many have been unable to return due to contamination in the area.

Activity 27.4

Examine the two images and answer the following questions.

1 Describe what is happening in each image.
2 Where, do you think, are these workplaces are located?
3 In which sectors do these businesses operate?
4 Is the employer socially responsible to the people featured in each image? Give reasons for your answer.
5 What steps could the employers take to be more socially responsible?

Unit 6

PART 3: ENVIRONMENTAL RESPONSIBILITY

CASE STUDY: BP Deepwater Horizon Environmental Disaster

In 2010 the Deepwater Horizon oil rig owned by BP exploded, killing eleven workers and leaking oil into the Gulf of Mexico.

Company officials informed the public that 1,000–5,000 gallons of oil per day were leaking into the sea. It later emerged that the real figure was ten times higher than the company's estimates.

The oil spill continued for 87 days and it is estimated that 4.9 million gallons of oil leaked into the Gulf. It caused catastrophic damage to plant and animal life along the US coastline. The oil spill was the worst in US history and the company agreed to pay **investors** €148 million to settle claims that it had deceived shareholders by downplaying the severity of the spill.

During a court case relating to the spill, an expert witness outlined that BP had an **unethical corporate culture**, which had **placed pressure on supervisors** on the Deepwater Horizon rig to increase the speed of drilling and keep costs down. The engineering expert believed that BP **placed profit ahead of the health and safety of its workers and the environment**.

Questions

1 Use Google Earth (www.google.com/earth) to locate the Gulf of Mexico. Name **two** US states and **one** country that border the Gulf of Mexico.

2 Which stakeholders in the area were affected by the oil spill?

3 What characteristics, do you think, should an environmentally conscious business possess?

Environmental Responsibilities of a Business

Businesses have a responsibility to conduct their business activities without damaging the environment, i.e. they should not damage the air, sea or land.

There are a number of ways in which a business can protect the environment, including the following.

1 Energy

Many businesses use energy sourced from non-renewable fossil fuels such as oil, gas and coal. Environmentally responsible firms should reduce the amount of this type of energy they use and try to source renewable energy, e.g. wind and solar power.

DID YOU KNOW? *A joint venture between ESB and Bord na Móna plans to develop four large solar farms in County Roscommon, County Offaly and County Kildare. It is estimated that the farms will provide electricity to power up to 150,000 homes.*

2 Waste

If waste is not disposed of appropriately, it can contaminate soil, water and air. Businesses should reduce the waste they create by reducing, reusing and recycling, e.g. putting recycling bins in offices to encourage staff to recycle.

3 Pollution

Businesses should take steps to reduce or eliminate the harmful substances they produce and emit into the atmosphere, e.g. install filtration systems and use biodegradable raw materials where possible.

> **Definition: Pollution**
> Pollution occurs when harmful or poisonous substances are released into the environment. There are many different types of pollution, including air, noise, soil and water pollution.

4 Deforestation

Deforestation occurs when trees are permanently removed from land. This can cause flooding, and loss of natural habitat for plants and animals.

Businesses should ensure that the wood products they use are sourced from sustainably managed forests or use recycled wood where possible.

DID YOU KNOW? *Palm oil is found in 40–50% of household products, including food, cosmetics and detergents. According to the World Wildlife Fund (WWF), an area equivalent to 300 football fields of rainforest is cleared every hour for palm oil production.*

5 Water Scarcity

Many parts of the world suffer from water shortages due to climate change. Businesses should reduce their water usage and find ways to conserve water supplies, e.g. harvesting rainwater and purchasing water-efficient machinery.

Example: LEGO

The LEGO group has undertaken a number of measures to reduce the company's impact on the environment:

- Ninety per cent of production waste is recycled – the equivalent of 5.25 billion LEGO bricks.
- It has reduced the size of packaging, saving 6,000 tonnes of cardboard, equivalent to the weight of 1,800 elephants.
- All of the energy used for operating the business comes from renewable sources.
- It has released the first LEGO pieces made from a plant-based plastic – they are made from sugar cane.

Characteristics of an Environmentally Responsible Business

Environmentally responsible businesses have a number of common characteristics, including the following.

1 Honest Communication

If the business discovers that it has damaged the environment, it works with the authorities to rectify the problem and put measures in place to ensure that the damage does not happen again.

2 Environmental Awareness

The business creates a culture of environmental awareness among staff by providing training through workshops, seminars and workplace programmes.

Example

Google uses 0.001% of the world's energy and wanted to find ways to reduce its energy consumption. It has used AI (artificial intelligence) to reduce its data centres' energy use by 15%, as machine-learned algorithms can make more informed decisions than humans on energy usage.

Unit 6

3 Product Design
Businesses use new technology to design and manufacture more durable and recyclable products. This reduces the amount of waste that ends up in landfill.

Example
Nestlé UK and Ireland was the first large-scale confectioner to introduce 100% recyclable packaging for its Easter eggs. Within two years of its introduction, over 150 tonnes of plastic and 175 tonnes of packaging were saved from going to landfill.

4 Compliance with Environmental Laws
The business complies with all relevant environmental laws, including waste disposal, pollution and recycling. If the firm needs additional advice or training on environmental law it contacts the Environmental Protection Agency (EPA) for assistance.

Definition: **Environmental Protection Agency (EPA)**
An independent state body that is responsible for environmental protection and monitoring in Ireland. Its head office is at Johnstown Castle, Co. Wexford.

5 Sustainable Development
Sustainable development means that businesses take into account future generations when using natural resources, e.g. coal and wood. For example, a business that uses wood products will plant trees for each tree used.

CASE STUDY

Lidl

Lidl is the first supermarket in Ireland to stop using black plastic packaging, which can't be recycled, for fruit and vegetables. This will remove over 65 tonnes of black plastic waste each year from fruits and vegetables alone. The supermarket chain has replaced single-use plastic items such as cups and cutlery with biodegradable alternatives. The firm also intends to reduce plastic packaging by 20% by 2022. By 2025, Lidl plans to make 100% of its own brand packaging recyclable, refillable, reusable or renewable. A spokesperson from Lidl has said, 'Sustainability is core to our business and we are proud to continue leading the retail sector in implementing ambitious measures which will deliver real and lasting benefits for everyone.'

MEETING ETHICAL, SOCIAL AND ENVIRONMENTAL RESPONSIBILITIES

✓ Benefits	✗ Costs
1 Access to Finance Businesses may find it easier to raise finance, as some investors will invest only in firms that meet their ethical, social and environmental responsibilities.	**1 Investors** Ethical businesses are open and honest about all aspects of the firm. This may reduce the amount of money that investors are willing to invest in the business.
2 Recruitment and Retention Employees who are treated fairly and believe that the business behaves in an ethical manner tend to remain in their jobs longer. This helps to reduce recruitment, selection and induction training costs for the business.	**2 Higher Production Costs** Production costs for socially and environmentally conscious businesses may be higher as they tend to: • Pay employees a higher wage • Pay suppliers a fair price for their raw materials.

Unit 6

MEETING ETHICAL, SOCIAL AND ENVIRONMENTAL RESPONSIBILITIES *continued*

✓ Benefits	✗ Costs
3 Marketing Businesses can use awards for socially or environmentally responsible behaviour in their marketing material, e.g. Green Awards Ireland. This can increase consumer loyalty to their brand.	**3 Staff Training** Staff training should be provided to ensure that employees understand their ethical, social and environmental responsibilities. This may reduce workplace productivity as it takes staff away from their day-to-day jobs.
4 New Products Changes in legislation may open up new markets for products or services, e.g. energy-efficient light bulbs. This can lead to increased sales and profits for the firm.	**4 Different Ethical Standards** The business may lose out on business opportunities, sales and profits by refusing to lower its ethical standards. Competitors with lower standards may increase their sales and market share.

KEY TERMS

Now you have completed this chapter, you should understand and be able to explain the following terms. In your copybook, write a definition of each term to build up your own glossary of terms.

- business ethics
- ethical audit
- whistleblowing
- code of ethics

- social responsibility
- environmental responsibility
- pollution

- deforestation
- Environmental Protection Agency (EPA)
- sustainable development

 **PowerPoint Summary**

EXAM-STYLE QUESTIONS

Ordinary Level

Section 1 – Short Questions (10 marks each)

1 What is meant by the term *business ethics*?
2 State and explain **two** reasons why employees may behave in an unethical manner.
3 Outline **three** ways in which a business can encourage employees to act ethically.
4 What is a code of ethics?
5 Explain the term *social responsibility*.
6 Name **five** stakeholders to whom a business should be socially responsible.
7 Name **three** environmental issues facing businesses today. Explain **one** of these issues in detail.
8 Column 1 is a list of business terms; column 2 is a list of explanations of these terms. Match the two lists in your copybook by writing your answers in the form *number = letter* (e.g. 1 = A).

Terms			Explanation
1	Business Ethics	**A**	This occurs when a person in the business reports unethical behaviour of co-workers or management.
2	Whistleblowing	**B**	When businesses take into consideration the impact their decisions will have on stakeholders.
3	Code of Ethics	**C**	The use of resources that meet current needs but do not compromise the needs of future generations.
4	Corporate Social Responsibility (CSR)	**D**	The moral standards that help people make ethical decisions in business.
5	Sustainable Development	**E**	A formal written statement that outlines the behaviour expected by the business of its employees.

Section 2 – Long Questions

1 A business culture of fear and greed can prompt both employees and managers to act unethically. Do you agree with this statement? Outline your reasons. **(15 marks)**

2 It can be difficult for a business to encourage employees to act ethically. Outline **two** methods a business can use to encourage ethical behaviour in the workplace. **(15 marks)**

3 Describe **three** benefits of introducing a code of ethics into a business. **(15 marks)**

4 Outline the difficulties a business may experience when it introduces a code of ethics. **(15 marks)**

5 Describe how a business can behave in a socially responsible manner towards (i) its investors and (ii) the local community. **(20 marks)**

6 Outline the ways in which a business can be socially responsible towards (i) employees and (ii) suppliers. **(20 marks)**

7 Describe **three** environmental responsibilities of a business. **(20 marks)**

8 Discuss the ways in which a business could encourage employees to become more environmentally responsible. **(15 marks)**

9 Describe **two** benefits to a firm of meeting its social, ethical and environmental responsibilities. **(20 marks)**

Higher Level

Section 1 – Short Questions (10 marks each)

1 Outline the reasons why an employee may act unethically in the workplace.

2 What is meant by the term *whistleblower*?

3 Complete the sentence: A code of ethics can bring many challenges to a business including …

4 Explain what is meant by the term *corporate social responsibility*.

5 Describe how a business can show its social responsibility to **two** stakeholders of your choice.

6 List **four** environmental issues facing businesses.

7 What do the following letters stand for?

(i) EPA   (ii) CSR

8 Outline the characteristics of an environmentally conscious business.

Section 2 – Applied Business Question (80 marks)

Aileen's Irish Foods

Aileen Dawson owns Aileen's Irish Foods, which manufactures a range of traditional Irish food products. An employee informed Aileen that a colleague in the finance department intended to bribe a local authority official to grant permission for a plant extension. Aileen was shocked at this behaviour, as she believed that her employees knew the difference between 'right' and 'wrong' behaviour.

Aileen employed Marian Dunphy, an ethical auditor, to investigate the issue. She wanted to introduce measures to ensure that this type of behaviour would never happen.

Employees admitted that the finance manager had threatened them with dismissal if they didn't bribe the local official and they felt that they had nobody to tell. The finance manager told staff that crimes such as bribery are never punished in Ireland, so they didn't need to worry about the Gardaí.

Marian has encouraged Aileen to introduce a code of ethics and offer staff training so that all employees know the type of ethical behaviour that is expected of them. She hopes that this will stop employees leaving the business for jobs with competitors.

Aileen was also disappointed to read an article in a national newspaper about a fine her business received for breaches of environmental legislation. She knows that investors will be angry when they read about this scandal and may not be willing to invest more capital to fund the plant's expansion.

Section 2 – Applied Business Question (80 marks) *continued*

The business was found guilty of polluting a local river, which had wiped out all fish stocks. The newspaper article also referenced that the business did not purchase its wood products from ethically certified sources. This has been a PR disaster for the company and Aileen is determined to make the firm more environmentally conscious.

Aileen plans to introduce environmental awareness training for employees as soon as possible. She thinks that the business should try to achieve 'green' awards to show consumers that the firm has become more environmentally aware.

Aileen thinks there must be an opportunity to develop 'green' products that will appeal to new markets and consumers. She firmly believes that the business will meet its social, environmental and ethical responsibilities and the firm will once more be successful.

A (i) With reference to the text above, discuss the reasons why employees behave in an unethical manner. **(15 marks)**

(ii) What would you recommend that Aileen should do to prevent unethical behaviour at Aileen's Irish Foods? **(15 marks)**

B (i) What is meant by the term *environmental responsibility*?

(ii) Outline the ways in which a business can become more environmentally conscious. **(25 marks)**

C Evaluate the merits of a business meeting its ethical, social and environmental responsibilities. **(25 marks)**

Section 3 – Long Questions

1 'Employees simply don't care about doing the right thing any more.'
Describe the reasons why employees might not act ethically. **(20 marks)**

2 Outline the difficulties a business may experience when it attempts to introduce a code of ethics into the business. **(15 marks)**

3 Outline the ways in which a business could develop a culture of ethical behaviour in the workplace. **(20 marks)**

4 Businesses must act in a socially responsible manner to their stakeholders, particularly towards their <u>employees</u>, the <u>local community</u> and the <u>government</u>.
(i) Illustrate what is meant by the term *social responsibility*.
(ii) Describe how a business acts in a socially responsible manner to the underlined stakeholders.
(20 marks)

5 Outline how a business should act in a socially responsible manner towards its investors and consumers. **(15 marks)**

6 Environmentally conscious businesses must be aware of environmental issues such as water scarcity, deforestation, pollution and energy usage.
Choose **three** of these issues and discuss in detail. **(15 marks)**

7 Describe the characteristics of an environmentally responsible business. **(20 marks)**

8 Evaluate the benefits of a firm meeting its social, ethical and environmental responsibilities. **(20 marks)**

9 Describe how a business may experience challenges when trying to meet its social, environmental and ethical responsibilities. **(15 marks)**

Unit 6

PREVIOUS LEAVING CERTIFICATE EXAM QUESTIONS

Ordinary Level

Section A – Short Questions (10 marks each)

1 Outline **two** environmental responsibilities of business. [LC OL 2009]

2 Outline **two** ways in which a business could become more environmentally friendly. [LC OL 2016]

3 The ice cream manufacturer Ben & Jerry's is considered to be an ethical business. Explain the term *ethical business*. [LC OL 2014]

Section B

1

Goodfoods Ltd is an indigenous company set up by sisters Una and Jane O'Sullivan and it has 14 full-time employees. As a company, it benefits from limited liability. The company prepares readymade meals for the home market and is currently considering exporting to foreign markets. The owners have drafted a code of ethics for the business, believing that decisions made should be guided by what is morally right, honest and fair.

(i) Describe **two** environmental responsibilities of Goodfoods Ltd. **(20 marks)**

(ii) Using examples, describe how Goodfoods Ltd can behave ethically towards (a) its employees and (b) its customers. **(20 marks) [LC OL 2007]**

Higher Level

Section A – Short Questions (10 marks each)

1 Define *ethical business practice*. [LC HL 2006]

Section B

1 (i) Define the term *business ethics*.

(ii) Outline how ethical behaviour in business can be encouraged. **(20 marks) [LC HL 2012]**

2 (i) Explain the term *code of ethics*.

(ii) Outline the benefits and challenges for a business of introducing a code of ethics. **(20 marks) [LC HL 2017]**

3

Corporate Social Responsibility refers to how businesses interact with their stakeholders on a daily basis including investors, employees, suppliers, customers, and government.

Discuss the social responsibilities of a business to any **four** stakeholders referred to above.

(20 marks) [LC HL 2016]

4

'Protecting and managing Ireland's environment is a shared responsibility. It involves Government and public bodies; businesses and industry; as well as members of the public, working in partnership.'

Environmental Protection Agency (EPA)

Discuss how a business could operate in an environmentally conscious way. **(20 marks) [LC HL 2015]**

 Solutions

Unit 6

28 THE GOVERNMENT AND BUSINESS

 When you have completed this chapter, you will be able to:

1. Identify and describe the ways in which the government creates a suitable climate for business by using:
   - Government income and expenditure (fiscal policy)
   - State agencies
   - Taxation
   - Laws and regulations
2. Outline the ways in which the government affects the labour force
3. Describe the opportunities and challenges of privatisation
4. Outline the benefits and drawbacks of nationalisation.

 Literacy Link

Government, fiscal policy, Enterprise Ireland, IDA Ireland, public sector, civil service, private sector, state-owned companies, public–private partnership, privatisation, nationalisation

 Numeracy Link

Multiplication, division, percentages

 Cross-curricular Link

Accounting – taxation
Economics – fiscal policy, national debt, national budget, state intervention in the economy
Home Economics – social welfare assistance, consumer protection

 CASE STUDY — *Córas Iompair Éireann (CIÉ)*

Córas Iompair Éireann (CIÉ) is a **commercial state-owned company** formed by the Irish government in 1944 to provide the essential service of public transport for the citizens of Ireland. CIÉ is now a **holding company** with four subsidiaries: Dublin Bus, Irish Rail, Bus Éireann and CIÉ Tours International.

Each year CIÉ receives a budget allocation in the **national budget**. This is used to pay for **current expenditure** such as the salaries of CIÉ staff, and **capital expenditure** such as the purchase of new bus fleets and rail carriages. The company is currently operating at a deficit of over €40 million.

To **improve efficiency** at the firm, pay cuts for non-drivers, voluntary redundancies and changes to driver rosters have been implemented. The firm has also **won the tender** to provide a bus service in Waterford city, which will require the purchase of 17 new buses.

In 2018, 10% of Dublin Bus routes were **privatised** with the contract awarded to a UK private operator, Go-Ahead. The contract is valued at €172 million over a five-year contract and will employ 425 staff.

Customers make 263.5 million journeys per year using CIÉ services and the firm has an overall customer satisfaction rating of 95%.

REASONS FOR GOVERNMENT INVOLVEMENT IN BUSINESS AND THE ECONOMY

Ireland operates in a mixed economic system (see Chapter 25). This is when the government and private businesses provide goods and services.

The Irish government is involved in business and the economy for several reasons, including:

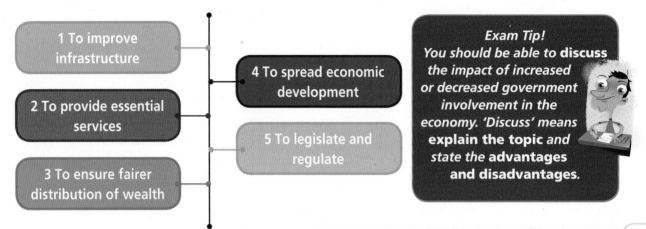

Exam Tip!
You should be able to **discuss** *the impact of increased or decreased government involvement in the economy. 'Discuss' means* **explain the topic** *and state the* **advantages and disadvantages.**

1 **To improve infrastructure:** To develop and improve essential infrastructure, e.g. roads, water supply and hospitals. These projects would be too expensive for private enterprise to build and operate.

Definition: **Infrastructure**
Basic services and systems such as transport and power supplies that are necessary for a country to run effectively.

2 **To provide essential services:** The government provides essential services that private enterprise would not supply as they are unprofitable, e.g. electricity and transport services in rural areas.

3 **To ensure a fairer distribution of wealth:** It is undesirable to have a large wealth gap in a society. The government imposes higher taxes on those with greater wealth and redistributes it through the social welfare system to those in greater need.

4 **To spread economic development:** To ensure that all parts of the country benefit from business growth, not just major cities such as Dublin and Cork. This is done through various regional policies such as the Regional Enterprise Development Fund.

5 **To legislate and regulate:** The government introduces and enforces laws to encourage the development of businesses, protect employees and consumers, e.g. the Employment Equality Acts 1998–2015 and the Consumer Protection Act 2007.

THE GOVERNMENT'S ROLE IN CREATING A POSITIVE CLIMATE FOR BUSINESS

The government plays a key role in creating a positive business environment that encourages businesses to establish and operate in Ireland. It does this through various policies, including:

1 Government income and expenditure (fiscal policy)
2 State agencies
3 Taxation
4 Laws and regulations.

1 Government Income and Expenditure (Fiscal Policy)

Each year the Minister for Finance presents the national budget to Dáil Éireann. It shows the government's planned income and expenditure for the following year. Government income comes from a range of sources, including tax revenue, EU grants and government bonds.

Definition: **Fiscal policy**
The government's policy for raising revenue (mainly taxation) and prioritising expenditure in order to influence the economy of the country.

Unit 6

Government expenditure is used to run government departments such as the Department of Education and Skills and the Department of Health. All government departments require **current** and **capital** expenditure.

> **Definition: Current expenditure**
> Money spent on the day-to-day running of the country, e.g. wages and salaries of teachers and nurses, social welfare payments.

> **Definition: Capital expenditure**
> Money required for long-term projects, e.g. new schools and hospital medical equipment.

The national budget can have three possible balances:

- **Surplus** – income is greater than expenditure
- **Deficit** – expenditure is greater than income
- **Balanced** – income and expenditure are equal.

How Does the Government Deal with a National Budget Deficit?

It can:

- Increase taxes – either increase the tax rates or introduce new taxes, e.g. a sugar tax
- Reduce expenditure – decrease the amount each government department has to spend, e.g. a wage cut for government employees
- Borrow – it can borrow money on the international money market by issuing government bonds.

> **Definition: Government bond**
> A government issues bonds in order to raise money to help run the country. A bond is similar to an interest-only loan, in that the government promises to repay the holder of the bond (known as the bondholder) at some point in the future. Until the bond is repaid, the government only makes interest payments on the bond. Government bonds are bought by, for example, corporations, pension funds and insurance funds. Irish government bonds are issued by the National Treasury Management Agency (NTMA).

 DID YOU KNOW?

The Irish government has borrowed over €130 billion in the form of bonds.

Activity 28.1

Working in pairs, visit www.whereyourmoneygoes.gov.ie.
1 Which government department receives the largest budget allocation?
2 What percentage of the national budget is spent on current expenditure?
3 In which years did government expenditure fall to its lowest level? Suggest a reason for this reduction in expenditure.

Unit 6

CASE STUDY *Project Ireland 2040*

The Irish government has launched Project Ireland 2040. This is a €116 billion plan which aims to prepare and develop Ireland for the future. Some elements of the plan include:

- Developing a second runway at Dublin airport
- Building a new hospital in Cork
- Allocating €8.4 billion for building new schools around Ireland.

Activity 28.2

1 Calculate the percentage of money from the Project Ireland 2040 fund allocated to building new schools.
2 Search the Internet for the clip 'Project Ireland 2040'. Watch it and note **two** interesting facts from the clip and share them with other students in your class.

The Impact of Government Expenditure on the Business Climate

Increase in Government Expenditure		Decrease in Government Expenditure
→ **Sales increase** as government departments and agencies buy more goods and services from Irish firms, e.g. Garda uniforms and hospital medicines.	Sales	→ A reduction in social welfare payments or in the pay of public sector workers reduces disposable income. People buy fewer goods and services, thus **reducing business sales**.
→ Increased expenditure on infrastructure (e.g. roads and ports) **reduces business costs** as transporting goods becomes faster and more efficient.	Costs	→ If the government spends less on education, there will be less skilled labour available for business. **Business costs may increase** as firms may have to pay higher wages to attract employees from abroad to fill vacancies.
→ Higher government spending creates confidence in the economy and may **encourage entrepreneurs to start or expand their businesses**.	Outlook	→ Businesses may be unsure about the future of the business and decide to **delay expansion or hiring new staff**.

2 State Agencies

Government agencies play a very important role in creating a positive business climate. They offer a range of services, including grants and advice, to help create an environment that encourages enterprise.

Area of Business/Services	State Agencies
→ Communications	→ An Post → RTÉ
→ Enterprise and business development	→ Enterprise Ireland → IDA Ireland → Local Enterprise Offices (LEOs)
→ Industrial relations	→ Workplace Relations Commission (WRC) → Labour Court
→ Transport	→ CIÉ (includes Irish Rail, Dublin Bus, Bus Éireann and CIÉ Tours International) → Dublin Airport Authority (DAA)
→ Laws and regulations	→ Competition and Consumer Protection Commission (CCPC) → Companies Registration Office (CRO)
→ Production	→ ESB Group (Electric Ireland) → Bord Gáis Energy
→ Infrastructural development	→ Transport Infrastructure Ireland (TII) → Ervia (gas and water infrastructure)

Area of Business/Services	State Agencies
→ Marketing	→ Fáilte Ireland → Bord Bia
→ Training and education	→ Solas
→ Community development	→ LEADER → Area Partnership Companies (APCs)

Activity 28.3

Working in pairs, create a mind map to record the various state agencies. You could draw this mind map or use an online tool such as Canva or Coggle.

The government encourages and promotes enterprise through the distribution of grants and venture capital investments. The three main bodies that encourage enterprise are:

- Enterprise Ireland
- IDA Ireland
- Local Enterprise Office.

> See Chapter 26 for more details on Local Enterprise Offices.

Enterprise Ireland

Enterprise Ireland helps indigenous Irish businesses export their goods and services. It focuses on Irish-owned enterprises with ten or more employees that want to grow their export sales.

Enterprise Ireland assists businesses in the following ways:

- **Funding:** Provides funding to businesses that want to start or increase international sales. It usually provides equity capital and takes a share in the business.
- **International offices:** Operates over thirty international offices worldwide. They help Irish businesses by providing marketing services and organising introductions with potential clients abroad.
- **Encouraging R&D:** Encourages businesses to invest in R&D (research and development) and to develop new products, thus increasing the likelihood of long-term business success.
- **Market research centres:** Provides business with a range of up-to-date information, including market size, key competitors and country statistics. This information is available online and at the Market Research Centre in Dublin.
- **Events:** Organises trade missions and trade fairs, often in co-ordination with country visits by government ministers. These trade missions build links with other countries and give Irish businesses the opportunity to meet with heads of government and consumers.

CASE STUDY **Nūdest**

Fiona Keane spotted a **gap in the market** for a healthy snack that consumers could eat on the go. She called her company Nūdest and developed a range of healthy fruit grain and yoghurt based snacks in resealable squeezy packets.

Fiona received **funding** of €100,000 from **Enterprise Ireland** and took part in its Foodworks programme to develop her products for the **export market**. Nūdest products are now stocked in Ireland, the UK and Belgium, as well as selling online, with plans for further expansion.

nüdest
good energy - good day!

IDA Ireland

IDA Ireland aims to attract foreign direct investment (FDI) into Ireland by providing advice and financial support.

IDA Ireland attracts and assists foreign businesses to set up in Ireland in a range of ways, including:

- **Information and statistics:** It compiles information on key business sectors and locations around Ireland.
- **Assistance:** It provides support to businesses that want to set up in Ireland by helping to find the ideal location for their business, e.g. IDA business parks.
- **Links:** It creates networks between international businesses, third-level institutions and research centres. This ensures that the correct skills and R&D facilities are in place to support these clients.
- **Grants and funding:** It provides financial assistance through capital and training grants.

DID YOU KNOW?

Over 1,150 international businesses, including Google, Facebook and PayPal, have chosen Ireland as their strategic location.

Google and Apple have received €25m in grant assistance from IDA Ireland.

Definition: **Foreign direct investment (FDI)**
This is when a business invests money in a foreign country by establishing operations there, e.g. Google is an American company but has set up operations in Ireland.

Activity 28.4

Watch the online clip 'STATS makes Limerick home for their European HQ 2018' and answer the following questions.

1 In which sector of the economy does STATS operate?
2 STATS provides sports information to businesses around the world. Name **two** of the businesses mentioned in the clip.
3 List **two** ways in which IDA Ireland provided assistance to STATS.

The Impact of State Agencies on the Business Climate

Increased Assistance from State Agencies		Reduced Assistance from State Agencies
→ Grants can help businesses develop and launch new products into the market. This can **increase business sales** and profits.	**Sales**	→ Less grant aid can discourage entrepreneurs from entering new markets either in Ireland or abroad, thus **reducing business sales**.
→ Grants can help a business to pay for market research and feasibility studies, thus **reducing its costs**.	**Costs**	→ Less grant funding may result in the business obtaining additional loans, which must be repaid with interest. This **increases business costs**.
→ Greater availability of grants can attract foreign direct investment (FDI) and **increase employment** in the Irish economy.	**Outlook**	→ Lower amounts of funding may **discourage existing businesses from expanding**. It could also mean that businesses postpone hiring new staff.

3 Taxation

A tax is a payment made to the government that funds public services such as healthcare and education. Taxation is used to regulate the level of spending in an economy. The rate of taxation influences how people spend their money and this has an impact on the demand for goods and services.

You learned about the types of taxes the government imposes on businesses in Chapter 16.

Activity 28.5

Working in pairs, use sticky notes to write down all the taxes that you can remember from Chapter 16. Place your sticky notes on the classroom wall. Compare your list with those of other students in your class. Write a brief summary of each tax in your copybook.

CASE STUDY: VAT Rate Changes in the Tourism and Hospitality Sectors

The standard rate of VAT on goods and services sold in Ireland is 23%. In order to protect and encourage growth in the tourism and hospitality sector, the government introduced a temporary VAT rate of 9% in 2011, which applied to items and services including hotel accommodation, hairdressing, restaurant meals and cinema tickets.

The Restaurants Association of Ireland set up a website to emphasise the advantages associated with retaining the 9% VAT rate, including:

- The creation of 37,800 direct jobs and 17,388 indirect jobs in Ireland
- A reduction of €765 million in the government's social welfare expenditure.

The Restaurants Association of Ireland wanted the 9% VAT rate to be extended to ensure that the tourism and hospitality sectors remain competitive.

Despite the campaign, the government increased the VAT rate from 9% to 13.5% in Budget 2019.

Questions

1 What does VAT stand for?
2 What type of organisation is the Restaurants Association of Ireland?
3 Which stakeholders are affected by VAT in the tourism and hospitality sectors?
4 What techniques, do you think, did the Restaurants Association of Ireland use to try to influence decision- makers to keep the VAT rate at 9%?
5 Discuss the impact the VAT rate increase to 13.5% will have on businesses in the sector.

Activity 28.6

1 If the cost of a hotel room in Dublin is €120 per night before 9% VAT is applied, how much would the hotel room have cost inclusive of VAT at this rate?
2 How much will the room cost after the change to the VAT rate in Budget 2019?

The Impact of Taxation on the Business Climate

Increased Taxation		Reduced Taxation
→ An increase in taxes such as VAT increases the price of goods and services. This reduces consumer demand and can lead to a **decrease in business sales**.	Sales	→ A decrease in employee taxes such as PAYE and PRSI increases consumers' disposable income and can increase demand for goods and services. This **increases business sales**.
→ Businesses act as a tax collector for the government. If taxes increase, this can **increase business administration costs**.	Costs	→ A decrease in employer's PRSI contributions **reduces wage costs** for the business.
→ An increase in taxes such as corporation tax reduces business profits. This may **discourage businesses from establishing or expanding in Ireland**.	Outlook	→ A reduction in taxation would **encourage more people to set up their own business**.

4 Laws and Regulations

The government influences the business climate through laws and regulations that control how a business can operate in Ireland. The aim of such legislation is to protect consumers and businesses. Government legislation on how a business can operate takes many forms, including:

1 **Employment laws** to protect employees from unfair practices, e.g. Industrial Relations Act 1990 (see Chapter 3).

2 **Consumer laws** to protect consumers from unfair business practices, e.g. Consumer Protection Act 2007 (see Chapter 2).

3 **Data protection laws** to protect people against businesses incorrectly using their personal details, e.g. General Data Protection Regulation (GDPR) 2018 (see Chapter 9).

4 **Company law** to control how businesses are established and monitored, e.g. Companies Act 2014 (see Chapter 21).

5 **Competition law** to protect the consumer from unfair competition in the marketplace, e.g. ComReg and CCPC (see Chapter 22).

6 **Environmental laws** to make sure that businesses do not harm the environment, e.g. the Environment Protection Agency (EPA) (see Chapter 27).

Definition: ComReg
The statutory body responsible for regulating the electronic communications sector (telecommunications, radio communications and broadcasting transmission) and the postal sector.

Example
Eir (formerly known as Eircom) was awarded the contract to provide rural telephone boxes, print telephone directories and provide an affordable telephone service in remote areas of Ireland. ComReg fined Eir €3m for breaching a number of targets relating to the connection and repair of phone lines. This is one of the largest fines ever issued by ComReg.

The Impact of Laws and Regulations on the Business Climate

Increased Laws and Regulations		Reduced Laws and Regulations
→ Increased laws regarding product safety encourages consumers to buy more products, thus **increasing business sales**.	Sales	→ Fewer competition laws can allow larger firms to dominate the market and **reduce sales** for smaller businesses.
→ More product safety laws mean that better-quality products are produced. This leads to **fewer returns** of faulty products and **reduces business costs**.	Costs	→ Fewer business laws may make it more difficult for businesses to collect debts owed from customers. This can increase their bad debts and **increase business costs**.
→ Increased regulations may create new **business opportunities** for businesses, e.g. new products or services such as hands-free kits for using mobile phones while driving.	Outlook	→ A reduction in product safety laws may result in lower-quality products. This may make firms **less competitive** than businesses from other countries that operate to higher standards.

THE PUBLIC SECTOR

Goods and services are provided in Ireland by both the public and private sectors. **The public sector refers to businesses and organisations owned and run by the state.**

It includes:

- The civil service
- Local authorities, e.g. Louth County Council
- State-owned companies, e.g. Dublin Bus
- State agencies, e.g. Fáilte Ireland.

All employees who work in the public sector are paid by the government.

Definition: Civil service
Public officials who advise and support the government ministers in running their departments, e.g. Department of Education and Skills. Roles in the civil service can range from administrative duties to managerial positions.

Public–Private Partnership (PPP)

The private sector relates to business activity that is not owned or funded by the state. In some cases, the public and private sector may work together on a project. This is known as public–private partnership (PPP). It usually involves providing infrastructure and services that in the past would have been provided by the public sector. A PPP stays in place until the contract is completed.

Some examples of PPPs are:

* M1 Dundalk
* Skibbereen Community College
* Dublin Criminal Courts of Justice.

DID YOU KNOW?

It cost €140 million to build the Criminal Courts of Justice. This was the largest court developed since 1796 when the Four Courts was built in Dublin. It took 20 years to build the Four Courts, but only 31 months to build the Criminal Courts of Justice.

PUBLIC–PRIVATE PARTNERSHIP (PPP)

✓ Advantages	✗ Disadvantages
1 Expertise Expertise and experience from the private sector is used in PPP projects, which may lead to better results.	**1 Cost** The project could be more expensive in the long term as private enterprises will earn a profit from the PPP contract.
2 Finance It enables the government to raise finance from the private sector for a project that it would not be able to fund by itself.	**2 Quality** The firm awarded the PPP contract may apply lower standards in constructing and maintaining infrastructure projects. This can have a negative impact for users of these services, e.g. hospitals and schools.
3 Speed Projects are completed faster and on time. There is often a penalty imposed if the contract is completed behind schedule.	**3 Risk** Many PPP contracts are awarded to the same firm. If the firm files for bankruptcy, it will be unable to complete existing projects and maintain completed projects.

DID YOU KNOW?

Carillion was awarded a number of PPP projects to construct schools in Ireland. It collapsed in 2018 with debts of €8 billion.

DID YOU KNOW?

Forty-two schools built by Western Building Systems underwent testing for structural defects.

Unit 6

453

THE GOVERNMENT AND THE LABOUR FORCE

The public sector is the largest single employer in the state. Government policies can affect the number of people who make up the labour force.

You learned about the labour force in Chapter 25.

Impact of Government on the Labour Force

1 **Taxation:** The government sets the PAYE, PRSI and USC rates. Increasing these rates may discourage people from working, as more of their pay will be deducted as taxes. Reducing taxes has the opposite effect and increases the supply of labour for employers.

2 **Employment:** The government is Ireland's largest employer. It employs people directly in the public sector, civil service and semi-state companies. This reduces social welfare payments and provides tax revenue for the government.

3 **Government expenditure:** The government buys goods and services from Irish firms as part of its current and capital expenditure, e.g. medical supplies, Garda vehicles. This creates indirect employment.

4 **Education and training:** Government investment in third-level institutions ensures a supply of highly skilled labour. Training agencies such as Solas help the unemployed to upskill and enter the labour force.

5 **Regulations:** Many laws protect employees, e.g. the Unfair Dismissals Acts 1977–2015. These regulations give employees more protection and security in the workplace.

Activity 28.7

Working in pairs, research the following information:
1 How many people were in the labour force when Census 2016 was taken?
2 How many people work in the public sector?
3 What is the current minimum wage rate in Ireland for (i) an adult worker and (ii) a worker under 18?

Privatisation

A state-owned company or state-sponsored body is an organisation that is owned, financed and operated by the government.

There are two types of state-owned company:

- **Commercial** – provides services to the public for a fee, e.g. Bus Éireann, RTÉ.
- **Non-commercial** – provides services but do not generally charge a fee, e.g. IDA Ireland, Bord Bia.

In these businesses the government is the shareholder, i.e. the owner. Sometimes the government may decide that it is in the best interests of the country to sell all or part of these businesses to private shareholders. This is referred to as **privatisation**.

Privatisation happens for two main reasons:

- To generate finance, e.g. the sale of Aer Lingus
- To enable the government to spend more time on regulation rather than providing goods and services, e.g. the sale of the National Lottery Company.

Definition: Privatisation
The sale of a state-owned company, whereby ownership is transferred from the government (public sector) to the private sector.

Unit 6

Benefits of Privatisation for the Irish Economy

Benefit	Reason
Government Revenue	→ The sale of a state-owned company gives the government a lump sum of money. This can be used to build infrastructure, e.g. roads and schools, or to repay the national debt.
Efficiency	→ Private firms are profit-driven and are usually run in a more efficient and cost-effective way than state-owned companies.
Access to Finance	→ Privatised companies have greater access to sources of finance than state companies, e.g. they can take out loans and sell shares. This makes it easier for businesses to expand, thus increasing employment in the economy.
Competition	→ Privatisation can encourage other businesses to enter into the market and lead to greater choice and lower prices for consumers, e.g. Aer Lingus, Eir.

Challenges of Privatisation for the Irish Economy

Challenge	Reason
Loss of State Assets	→ Privatisation may mean the loss of state assets that have strategic importance to the country, e.g. water supply and transport networks.
Increased Unemployment	→ Privatised businesses often run the firm more efficiently than state-owned businesses, which may result in employee redundancies. This increases social welfare costs for the government.
Social Isolation	→ Essential services that are not profit-making, e.g. transport and postal services in rural areas, may be discontinued when a state enterprise is privatised. This may lead to social isolation.
Increased Prices	→ Privatised businesses aim to make a profit for their shareholders. This may lead to increased prices for consumers.

Examples of Privatised Companies

State Company	Private Company
→ British and Irish Steam Packet Company (B&I Line)	→ Irish Continental Group plc (Irish Ferries)
→ Bord Telecom Éireann plc	→ Eir plc
→ ACC Bank	→ Rabobank
→ Aer Lingus	→ IAG

Nationalisation

Nationalisation occurs when a private sector industry is taken over by the government (public sector). It can happen for a number of reasons, including:

- **Owning strategically important industries:** The state wants to gain control of valuable natural resources, e.g. water and electricity, which are considered too important to be owned and run by private industries.
- **Protecting employment:** Private firms that are profit-motivated may reduce the number of employees to cut costs.
- **Taking over an important private industry that is in danger of financial collapse,** e.g. financial institutions such as banks.

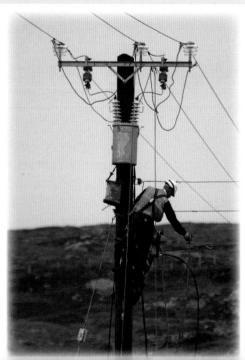

Unit 6

Private industries that have been nationalised in Ireland:

1 Anglo Irish Bank
2 Quinn Insurance
3 Allied Irish Banks (AIB)
4 Educational Building Society (EBS).

The railways were nationalised in 1944 to form CIÉ

Benefits of Nationalisation

1 **Protects essential services:** Provides services that might not be profitable for private enterprise to provide, e.g. post and transport services in remote rural regions.
2 **Protects industries:** It protects essential industries such as communications, water and electricity.
3 **Profit:** The government can turn a poorly performing business into a profitable firm, e.g. AIB has now returned to profit.

Drawbacks of Nationalisation

1 **Cost:** The cost of buying out the private sector business is an additional cost to the taxpayer.
2 **Inefficiencies:** Government ownership may not solve problems in the industry as government businesses are sometimes inefficient due to a lack of profit motive.
3 **Shareholders:** In certain circumstances, shareholders lose the money that they have invested in the firm once it has been nationalised.

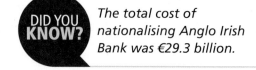

DID YOU KNOW? *The total cost of nationalising Anglo Irish Bank was €29.3 billion.*

KEY TERMS

Now you have completed this chapter, you should understand and be able to explain the following terms. In your copybook, write a definition of each term to build up your own glossary of terms.

- government
- infrastructure
- fiscal policy
- government bond
- national budget
- current expenditure
- capital expenditure
- national budget surplus
- national budget deficit

- balanced national budget
- state agencies
- Enterprise Ireland
- IDA Ireland
- foreign direct investment (FDI)
- ComReg
- public sector
- civil service

- private sector
- state-owned companies
- public–private partnership (PPP)
- labour force
- privatisation
- nationalisation

PowerPoint Summary

EXAM-STYLE QUESTIONS

Ordinary Level

Section A – Short Questions (10 marks each)

1 List **three** reasons for government involvement in business and the economy.
2 Distinguish between current and capital expenditure. Give **one** example of each type of expenditure.
3 Name a state agency responsible for (i) transport (ii), communications and (iii) industrial relations.
4 Outline what is meant by the term *public–private partnership*.
5 What is the public sector?
6 Name **one** state-owned company in Ireland that was privatised. Outline **one** advantage that privatisation can bring to an economy.

Section A – Short Questions (10 marks each) *continued*

7 Column 1 is a list of terms associated with the government and business. Column 2 is a list of possible explanations for these terms. Match the two lists in your copybook by writing your answers in the form *number = letter* (e.g. 1 = A).

Business Terms			Explanations
1	IDA Ireland	A	Public officials who advise and support the government ministers in running their departments.
2	Capital expenditure	B	The public and private sector come together to work on a project.
3	Civil service	C	Money used for long-term projects, e.g. new schools.
4	Public–private partnership (PPP)	D	An organisation that is owned, financed and operated by the government.
5	State-sponsored body	E	A state agency established to attract foreign direct investment (FDI) into Ireland.

8 What does FDI stand for? Name the state agency that attracts FDI to Ireland.

Section 2 – Long Questions

1 Outline **three** reasons why the government intervenes in business. **(15 marks)**

2 What is a national budget deficit? Describe **three** ways in which a government can overcome a national budget deficit. **(20 marks)**

3 Describe **two** ways in which an increase in taxation can impact on business. **(15 marks)**

4 Outline the impact of government legislation on business. **(20 marks)**

5 Define the term *labour force*. Describe **two** ways in which the government affects the labour force. **(20 marks)**

6 Describe the services provided by Enterprise Ireland. **(15 marks)**

7 What is meant by the term *privatisation*? Outline **two** advantages and **one** disadvantage of privatisation. **(20 marks)**

8 Outline **two** reasons why a government may nationalise certain businesses. Describe **two** advantages of nationalisation. **(20 marks)**

Section 1 – Short Questions (10 marks each)

1 What is meant by the term *fiscal policy*? If the government decides to increase spending as part of its fiscal policy, explain **one** effect this could have on the business climate.

2 Explain the term *government bond*.

3 Name **one** state agency in each of the following areas: (i) production; (ii) marketing; (iii) community development; (iv) training and education.

4 Outline **two** ways in which state agencies have an impact on businesses in Ireland.

5 List **four** government rules and regulations which have an impact on Irish businesses.

6 Describe the impact that increased laws and regulations have on business in terms of (i) sales and (ii) costs.

7 Distinguish between the public sector and the civil service.

8 What do the letters PPP stand for? Outline the positive and negative effects that PPP can have on the economy.

9 Fill in the appropriate words to complete each of the following statements.

   (i)   How the government raises revenue and spends that money to influence the economy is called
        f_____ p_____

   (ii) N_____ is when a private sector industry is taken over by the government.

   (iii) Aer Lingus was p_____ by the government when it was sold to IAG.

   (iv) Teachers and nurses are employed in the p_____ s_____

   (v)   The statutory body responsible for the regulation of the electronic communications sector is
        C_____.

Section 2 – Applied Business Question (80 marks)

Enterprise in Rural Ireland

Fiona Lanigan is a TD for the Galway West constituency. She is part of a committee investigating the possibility of privatising rural bus routes. A presentation from the Department of Finance has indicated that it is in favour of privatising rural routes. It believes that the service will be run more profitably by a private operator and customers will benefit from a greater choice of routes. Fiona knows that many of her constituents will be worried about the possibility that unprofitable routes will be cancelled.

Fiona is also preparing for a political clinic that she holds once a month in her constituency office. She has received emails from concerned constituents regarding the impact on their businesses of the introduction of GDPR in 2018 and the recent increase in the minimum wage. Other business owners are concerned about the lack of support for new product development. Fiona knows that increased environmental laws and product quality legislation have also impacted on costs for local firms. She is aware of how important local businesses are to rural areas and is determined to increase entrepreneurship in the Galway West region.

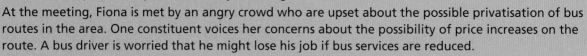

At the meeting, Fiona is met by an angry crowd who are upset about the possible privatisation of bus routes in the area. One constituent voices her concerns about the possibility of price increases on the route. A bus driver is worried that he might lose his job if bus services are reduced.

Once the matter of the bus route has been discussed, another constituent raises concerns about the lack of assistance for businesses in the area that want to expand into foreign markets. They are experiencing difficulty raising finance from local banks, as well as accessing information on foreign markets and meeting with buyers from foreign countries. Fiona informs the business people in the area that she will contact Enterprise Ireland to arrange meetings regarding events to promote their products abroad.

Fiona acknowledges that lots more work needs to be done to protect rural life and returns to Dublin to plan ways to further help her constituents.

A 'The Department of Finance has indicated that it is in favour of privatising rural routes.' Outline the benefits and drawbacks of privatising a rural bus route in an area such as County Galway. **(30 marks)**

B Discuss the impact that government laws and regulations have on businesses in Ireland. **(25 marks)**

C Describe the services provided by Enterprise Ireland that could help businesses in Galway expand abroad. **(25 marks)**

Section 3 – Long Questions

1 The government plays a pivotal role in creating a positive business climate. Outline reasons why the government chooses to get involved in the business environment. **(25 marks)**

2 The national budget, government bonds and capital expenditure are all important aspects of government planning. Describe the **three** underlined terms. **(15 marks)**

3 Outline the impact that government spending has on business. **(15 marks)**

4 Name **five** state agencies. Explain the impact that these agencies have on business. **(20 marks)**

5 Evaluate the role of IDA Ireland in encouraging business in Ireland. **(20 marks)**

6 Explain how the government uses legislation to support businesses that operate in Ireland. **(20 marks)**

7 Evaluate the privatisation of state-owned companies. **(15 marks)**

8 Describe the positive and negative impact of nationalisation. **(15 marks)**

PREVIOUS LEAVING CERTIFICATE EXAM QUESTIONS

Ordinary Level

Section A – Short Questions (10 marks each)

1. Indicate which government body is responsible for further education and training. Place a tick (✔) in the correct box.

   Solas (Formerly known as FÁS)

   IDA (Industrial Development Authority) **[LC OL 2016]**

2 Identify **three** Semi-State organisations that help Irish businesses. **[LC OL 2005]**

3 Name **one** state-owned enterprise/state agency involved in each of the following areas.

		Name of state-owned enterprise/state agency
(i)	Production	
(ii)	Transport	
(iii)	Training	
(iv)	Marketing	

[LC OL 2008]

4 The Irish government privatised Bord Gáis in 2014. Explain the term *privatisation*. **[LC OL 2018]**

Section B

1 Outline **two** ways the Government assists businesses in Ireland. **(20 marks) [LC OL 2014]**

2 Explain **one** service provided by IDA Ireland to foreign multinational companies (MNCs). **(10 marks) [LC OL 2015]**

Higher Level

Section A – Short Questions (10 marks each)

1 Explain the term *privatisation*. Illustrate its impact on the development of the Irish economy. **[LC HL 2006]**

2 Name a state-owned enterprise in the production category. Explain **two** reasons for state involvement in this category. **[LC HL 2007]**

Section B

1

> In the Government's Budget 2016, the national minimum wage was increased from €8.65 to €9.15, an increase of 50 cent per hour.

Discuss the different ways in which the Irish Government affects the labour force in Ireland. **(20 marks) [LC HL 2016]**

2 Outline the role of the Irish Government in encouraging **and** in regulating business in Ireland. **(20 marks) [LC HL 2013]**

3 Outline the opportunities **and** challenges for the Irish economy of the privatisation of state-owned enterprises. **(20 marks) [LC HL 2014]**

Unit 6

Solutions

459

CHAPTER 29 · INTERNATIONAL TRADE

 Learning Outcomes

When you have completed this chapter, you will be able to:

1. Distinguish between imports and exports
2. Calculate and interpret the balance of trade and balance of payments
3. Describe the changing nature of the international economy and its impact on Irish business
4. Identify and describe the barriers to free trade
5. Explain the role of ICT in international trade
6. Describe the opportunities and challenges for Irish businesses in international trade.

 Literacy Link

International trade, open economy, import, export, trading bloc, World Trade Organization (WTO), protectionism, tariff, quota, embargo, subsidy

 Numeracy Link

Addition, subtraction

 Cross-curricular Link

Geography – economic geography
History – international agreements and alliances
Maths – interpretation of graphs

CASE STUDY · *Glanbia plc*

As Ireland has an **open economy**, many firms based in the country choose to become involved in **international trade**. One such company is Glanbia plc. The firm owns brands such as Avonmore, Kilmeaden cheese and Glanbia Performance Nutrition. It **exports** its high-quality dairy and agri-ingredients as well as branded products to over sixty countries worldwide.

Glanbia plc benefits from its location in Ireland as it has access to **free trade** within the EU. This means that it can sell its products to a potential market of over 500 million people, without the imposition of any **trade barriers** such as **tariffs** or **quotas**.

The USA is the fifth largest market for dairy and Glanbia has taken part in a **trade mission** with Bord Bia to network and build relationships with customers and suppliers there. The company is closely monitoring **protectionist** measures introduced by the US government, such as tariffs on Chinese imports. There have been warnings from the head of the **WTO** outlining the damage these **trade disputes** can have on international trade.

China is a growing market for Glanbia plc, particularly in the area of sports nutrition. The firm is currently ranked fourth in the market in terms of sales volume, but it has ambitious plans to be the number-one leader in the market. The Irish government is keen to support the agribusiness sector, including businesses such as Glanbia plc, because this sector accounts for 10% of total Irish exports. These exports help to create a **surplus** on the **balance of payments**, which benefits the Irish economy.

INTERNATIONAL TRADE

International trade is the exchange of goods and services between countries, i.e. importing and exporting products. Countries engage in international trade for many reasons, for example to obtain raw materials to manufacture products. Some countries limit international trade, while others such as Ireland have an open economy.

Definition: Open economy
An economy that engages in international trade, i.e. goods and services are traded between countries.

DID YOU KNOW? *Ireland is ranked as the fifth most open economy in the world.*

IMPORTS AND EXPORTS

Imports are goods and services that are bought from other countries, e.g. Sheehy Motors, based in Kildare, buys Audi and Volkswagen cars from Germany.

Exports are goods and services that are sold to other countries, e.g. O'Shea Farms in Ireland sells potatoes to Brazil.

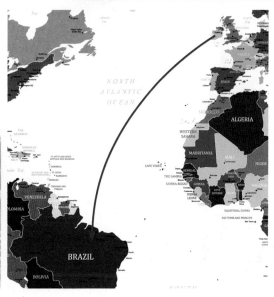

Ireland's Main Imports and Exports

Imports

Example: Japan

Exports

Example: USA

Ireland's main imports include:	Ireland's main imports come from:
→ Machinery	→ UK
→ Cars	→ USA
→ Chemicals (medical and pharmaceuticals)	→ Germany
→ Food	→ China
→ Oil	→ Japan
Ireland's main exports include:	**Ireland's main exports go to:**
→ Pharmaceutical products	→ USA
→ Food and drink products	→ UK
→ Optical and photo apparatus	→ Belgium
→ Electronics	→ Germany
→ Perfumes, cosmetics and toiletries	→ Switzerland

Unit 7

Classification of Imports and Exports

Definition: Visible and Invisible Trade !
Visible trade = buying and selling physical goods.
Invisible trade = buying and selling services.

Definition: Import/Export !
Import = money leaves Ireland.
Export = money comes into Ireland.

	Explanation	Examples
Visible Imports	→ Physical goods (those you can see or touch) that Irish businesses and individuals buy from foreign countries. → Imports cause money to leave Ireland.	→ Cars → Fruit → Clothing → Oil
Invisible Imports	→ Services that Irish businesses and individuals buy from foreign countries. → Imports cause money to leave Ireland.	→ An Irish tourist travels to the USA with American Airlines → An Irish person attends a concert by UK performer Adele in the 3Arena
Visible Exports	→ Physical goods that Irish businesses and individuals sell to foreign countries. → Exports bring money into Ireland.	→ Beef → Medicines → Computer equipment → Dairy products
Invisible Exports	→ Irish services sold to customers in foreign countries. → Exports bring money into Ireland.	→ A German tourist travels to Ireland on a Ryanair flight → U2 play a concert in the USA

DID YOU KNOW? *Ireland imported €77 billion worth of goods and services in 2017.*

DID YOU KNOW? *Ireland exported €112 billion worth of goods and services in 2017. This is equivalent to €22,336 for each resident of Ireland.*

Activity 29.1

Study the pie chart, which illustrates the main countries from which Ireland imports goods and services. Answer the following questions.

1 What percentage of Ireland's imports come from:
   (i) the USA?
   (ii) the UK?
2 Thirty-eight per cent of Ireland's imports come from the rest of the world. Find out **three** other countries in the rest of the world from which Ireland imports goods and services.
3 Research **two** products that Ireland imports from the Netherlands. Compare your research with other students in your class.

Ireland's main imports come from:

24%
38%
20%
3%
6%
9%

■ UK ■ USA □ Germany ■ China
■ Netherlands ■ Rest of World

Activity 29.2

Study the bar chart, which illustrates the main countries to which Ireland exports goods and services. Answer the following questions.

1 What is the combined percentage of exports to the USA and the UK?
2 Research **three** 'Rest of World' countries to which Ireland exports goods and services.
3 Research the types of goods and services that Ireland exports to:
   (i) Belgium
   (ii) Switzerland.

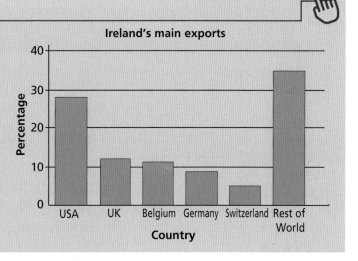

Ireland's main exports

REASONS FOR IRISH BUSINESSES' INVOLVEMENT IN INTERNATIONAL TRADE

As a small open economy we are heavily reliant on international trade for a number of reasons, including:

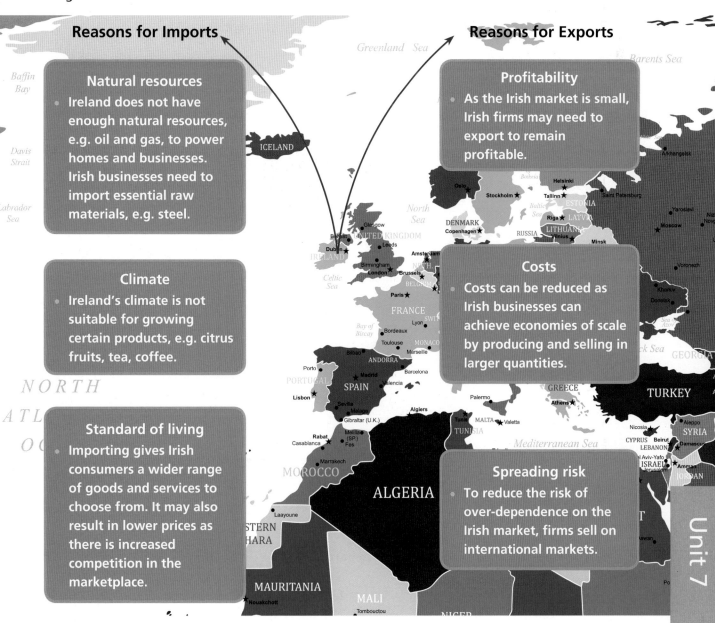

Reasons for Imports

Natural resources
- Ireland does not have enough natural resources, e.g. oil and gas, to power homes and businesses. Irish businesses need to import essential raw materials, e.g. steel.

Climate
- Ireland's climate is not suitable for growing certain products, e.g. citrus fruits, tea, coffee.

Standard of living
- Importing gives Irish consumers a wider range of goods and services to choose from. It may also result in lower prices as there is increased competition in the marketplace.

Reasons for Exports

Profitability
- As the Irish market is small, Irish firms may need to export to remain profitable.

Costs
- Costs can be reduced as Irish businesses can achieve economies of scale by producing and selling in larger quantities.

Spreading risk
- To reduce the risk of over-dependence on the Irish market, firms sell on international markets.

Unit 7

CASE STUDY | Kerrygold Butter

Irish dairy **co-operative** Ornua owns the Kerrygold range of products. Kerrygold butter is an example of a **visible Irish export**. The company sells over 350 million blocks of butter worldwide annually and Kerrygold is the second most popular butter brand in the USA. The Kerrygold brand has sales of almost €900 million per year. Kerrygold butter is bought by more than 50% of German households and it is the number-one selling butter there, selling more than German or imported butters.

Ornua has begun to export Kerrygold butter to Asian and African countries. The firm has established a packaging plant in Nigeria and

Kerrygold butter was recently launched during a **trade mission** to South Korea. The company hopes that the demand for dairy products in Asian markets will help to create a **global dairy brand** worth in excess of €1 billion.

MEASURING INTERNATIONAL TRADE

The level of imports and exports in a country is measured in two ways:

1 Balance of trade (BoT)
2 Balance of payments (BoP).

1 Balance of Trade

BoT measures the difference between visible exports and visible imports. Remember, visible trade refers to physical goods that are imported and exported to and from Ireland.

When visible exports are greater than visible imports, there is a balance of trade surplus. When visible exports are less than visible imports, there is a balance of trade deficit.

> Visible Exports > Visible Imports = Surplus
> Visible Exports < Visible Imports = Deficit

2 Balance of Payments

BoP measures the difference between total exports (visible and invisible) and total imports (visible and invisible). When total exports are greater than total imports, there is a balance of payments surplus. If total exports are less than total imports, a country experiences a balance of payments deficit.

> Total Exports > Total Imports = Surplus
> Total Exports < Total Imports = Deficit

Sample Question

The following information relates to trade in a country for one year:

	€ million		€ million
Visible Exports	204	Visible Imports	216
Invisible Exports	156	Invisible Imports	134

From the above information, calculate (i) the balance of trade and (ii) the balance of payments. State in each case whether the balance is a surplus or a deficit.

(i) Balance of Trade = Visible Exports – Visible Imports

	€m
Visible Exports	204
Less Visible Imports	–216
Deficit	**–€12m**

(ii) Balance of Payments = Total Exports – Total Imports

	€m	€m
Visible Exports	204	
Invisible Exports	+156	360
Less:		
Visible Imports	216	
Invisible Imports	+134	–350
Surplus		**€10m**

Activity 29.3

Find out Ireland's balance of trade and balance of payments for the most recent year available.

Impact of the Balance of Trade

Deficit	Surplus
→ More money is leaving the country.	→ More money is coming into the country.
→ Government may have to increase taxes, e.g. VAT, to raise income.	→ Government may be able to reduce taxes, e.g. PAYE income tax and corporation tax.
→ People lose jobs as Irish businesses need fewer employees.	→ Higher employment levels. People have more disposable income. This improves the standard of living.

How to Overcome a Balance of Trade Deficit

- **Increase exports:** Sell more goods and services abroad in existing and new markets, e.g. developing economies.
- **Reduce imports:** Encourage consumers to buy more Irish products and services, e.g. import substitution.

> **Definition: Import substitution**
> This occurs when foreign imports are replaced with domestically produced goods and services.

- **Raw materials:** Try to adapt products to use more raw materials available from the domestic market, e.g. a soft drinks manufacturer could make fewer lemon-flavoured drinks and more strawberry-flavoured drinks as strawberries can be grown in Ireland.

Activity 29.4

Working in pairs, create a quiz with eight questions about the balance of trade and balance of payments. Swap the questions with another pair of students and receive a new quiz for you and your partner to answer. Return your answers to the pair of students who created the quiz and receive your score out of eight.

IMPORTANCE OF INTERNATIONAL TRADE TO IRELAND

International trade is important to businesses, consumers and the economy of a country.

Business	Consumer	Economy
→ **Larger market:** Irish businesses can sell their goods to more customers. This results in increased sales and profits, e.g. Ornua exports Kerrygold butter to the USA.	→ **Wider variety of goods:** Irish consumers have a wider choice when buying goods and services, e.g. they can buy Irish toothpaste or an international brand.	→ **Foreign exchange:** Exports bring in foreign currency, which helps to pay for imported goods.

Unit 7

Business	Consumer	Economy
→ **Lower costs:** Producing goods in larger quantities leads to a reduction in business costs. Firms can achieve economies of scale. This can result in larger profits.	→ **Better-quality goods:** Some countries have better skills when manufacturing certain goods, which results in higher-quality products, e.g. Japanese electronics.	→ **Balance of payments:** Having a surplus balance of payments helps a country to repay loans and invest overseas.
→ **Growth of TNCs:** With increased profits, a business can afford to expand further and become a transnational company (TNC) (see Chapter 31).	→ **Lower prices:** As a result of competition in the market, the price of goods and services may fall, e.g. Dunnes Stores has had to reduce prices because of competition from Aldi and Lidl.	→ **Higher employment:** Increased exports creates more jobs in Ireland. This reduces social welfare payments paid by the government and increases tax revenue, e.g. PAYE income tax and USC.
→ **Raw materials:** International trade enables firms to purchase raw materials that are unavailable in the domestic market, e.g. Fruitfield imports oranges to produce its Irish marmalade.	→ **Infrastructure:** International trade requires good transport and communication links. Developing modern roads, railways and communication networks also benefits consumers, e.g. the Enniscorthy bypass.	→ **International recognition:** International trade helps to build relationships between countries. This results in more co-operation and less conflict between trading countries, e.g. Ireland and the USA.

FREE TRADE

International trade between countries can often be complex and difficult. To overcome these issues, many countries engage in free trade.

In order to encourage free trade, some countries have created trading blocs. **The countries in a trading bloc create a free trade area and agree to reduce or eliminate barriers to trade between member countries.** The trading bloc also agrees a common set of tariffs on imports from countries outside the trading bloc.

> **Definition: Free trade**
> Free trade enables countries to buy and sell each other's goods and services without barriers to trade such as tariffs, quotas or embargoes.

> **Definition: World Trade Organization (WTO)**
> An international agency that aims to promote free trade. It does this by negotiating with governments to remove taxes and other barriers that prevent free trade. It monitors free trade agreements and helps settle disputes between governments, e.g. if the USA and Europe were in a dispute over car imports.

Examples of trading blocs include:

- European Union – the European Single Market (see Chapter 30)
- USMCA – the United States–Mexico–Canada Agreement.

Free trade has also developed due to deregulation in worldwide markets.

Deregulation occurs when trade barriers are reduced or removed from a market, which enables firms to enter and trade in the market. It may result in an increase in competition, leading to lower prices for consumers. For example, the EU deregulated the airline industry, allowing more competition and choice for consumers. This has led to the emergence of low-cost airline carriers such as Ryanair and easyJet.

Activity 29.5

Watch the online clip 'The World Trade Organization (WTO) Explained in One Minute' and answer the following questions:

1 When was the WTO set up?
2 How many countries are members of the WTO?
3 How does the WTO try to solve any disputes that arise?
4 Identify **one** criticism of the WTO.
5 Search online to find out whether Ireland is a member of the WTO.

BARRIERS TO TRADE (PROTECTIONISM)

Protectionism occurs when governments introduce barriers to trade such as tariffs, quotas and embargoes to protect domestic industries from foreign competition. There are a number of reasons a government may impose barriers to trade, including:

1 **New industries:** Protectionism gives new industries time to grow and benefit from economies of scale, so that they can compete in the future with foreign firms.

2 **Domestic jobs:** Protectionism helps to protect jobs that might be under threat from increased competition from foreign firms.

3 **Raise revenue:** A government can raise tax revenue by imposing tariffs on foreign imports. This increases government income and can be used to invest in the country's infrastructure, e.g. healthcare and education.

4 **National security:** Barriers to trade can protect industries that are of strategic importance, such as electricity and steel supplies. These industries become important in times of conflict and crisis and governments want to protect them from foreign competition.

5 **Consumer protection:** Governments may introduce measures to protect consumers from unsafe products. For example, the EU restricted poultry imports after an outbreak of avian flu.

Protectionist measures can be used by a single country or by trading blocs such as the EU. These reduce imports or make them more expensive. This helps to protect jobs and specific industries in the domestic market and improves the balance of payments.

The main protectionist measures include:

Barrier to Trade	Explanation	Example
Tariff	→ A tax placed on imported goods. This makes the imported item more expensive. It encourages consumers to buy goods from domestic producers.	→ A tax on cars imported from Japan into Ireland makes them more expensive than cars imported from France.
Quota	→ A limit on the number of products that may be imported. Quotas discourage imports and encourage more sales of domestically produced products.	→ The EU placed a quota on how many clothing items could be imported from China.
Embargo	→ A complete ban on all imports from or exports to a particular country. It is often imposed for political, economic or environmental reasons.	→ The USA has an import and export ban against Cuba and Syria.
Subsidy	→ A government gives financial support to a domestic industry. This can make the firm's products cheaper than those of foreign competitors.	→ The EU has subsidised agricultural products to protect them from non-EU competition.
Administrative Regulations	→ Creating customs delays or demanding excessive paperwork to make importing as difficult as possible.	→ A country might insist that detailed documentation is completed for each product imported.

DID YOU KNOW?

In 2018, the USA launched the largest trade war in economic history. As part of its 'America First' agenda it:
- *Placed 25% tariffs on over €173 billion worth of Chinese export goods*
- *Imposed a 25% tariff on steel and 10% on aluminium from the EU, Canada and Mexico.*

The EU retaliated with tariffs on American goods such as blue jeans and motorbikes.

Activity 29.6

Watch the online clip 'Protectionism easily explained' and answer the following questions.
1 What is the president's main objective?
2 How does protectionism initially help home countries?
3 Name **two** drawbacks of protectionism for consumers.
4 What would be the outcome of a protectionism spiral?

TRENDS IN INTERNATIONAL TRADE

As an open economy, Ireland is impacted by changes and trends in international trade. These include:

1 **Globalisation:** There has been an increase in the number of global firms operating around the world, e.g. Starbucks, Coca-Cola. These businesses use a global marketing mix to increase consumer awareness of their product ranges.

2 **Transport:** Improvements in international transport infrastructure enable trade to take place faster and more efficiently, e.g. Terminal 2 at Dublin Airport and improvements at Dublin Port.

3 **Developments in ICT:** Developments in ICT mean that it is easier and more cost-effective for home industries to engage in international trade. For example, the Internet enables businesses to engage in e-commerce. Firms can sell their goods and services on their own website to customers all over the world.

4 **Trade agreements:** There has been an increase in trade agreements and the creation of trading blocs. This enables trade to take place between countries without barriers to trade, e.g. the EU–Japan trade deal and the United States–Mexico–Canada Agreement (USMCA).

5 **New markets:** There has been growth in new markets such as Brazil, Russia, India, China and South Africa (the BRICS countries). This gives Irish business greater opportunities to sell their products internationally.

6 **Increased competition:** Irish businesses face increasing competition from low-cost economies. Businesses from these countries can sell their products more cheaply because of their lower cost base, e.g. low wages in countries such as the Philippines and Latvia.

Impact of ICT on International Trade

Advances in ICT have enabled firms to engage in international trade. The benefits of ICT include the following.

Faster Communication

Businesses can use ICT such as email to communicate with stakeholders, including suppliers and customers, around the world. The business can send promotional emails outlining special offers or discounts to multiple customers. It is a cheap and fast form of communication.

Improved Decision-making

The business can use the Internet to research information from a variety of sources. This can help the firm to make better and faster decisions, which benefits the business.

Increased Sales

Many firms have set up interactive business websites to promote and sell their goods and services to consumers all over the world. This helps to increase the firm's sales, without the need to establish shops or employ staff in each country to which it sells.

Unit 7

Lower Costs

ICT can be used to reduce business costs. Firms can use video conferencing to hold virtual meetings with people in different locations. This can reduce time spent travelling and cut transport and accommodation costs.

Marketing

Businesses can use company websites as well as social media platforms such as Facebook and Instagram to promote their products to consumers worldwide. A firm can interact with consumers in the website's comments section and build brand loyalty.

OPPORTUNITIES FOR IRISH BUSINESSES IN INTERNATIONAL TRADE

As the Irish domestic market is relatively small, with just over 4.5 million people, many businesses choose to take advantage of the opportunities available in international markets.

Access to larger markets – by selling to a larger number of potential consumers, Irish businesses can increase sales and profits.

EU membership – foreign firms have established in Ireland to gain access to the EU free market. These firms buy goods and services from Irish businesses, which increases employment in Ireland.

Educated workforce – Ireland has a highly educated workforce, which is recognised worldwide by international businesses. This is a key reason why high-tech firms such as Google and PayPal have set up business in Ireland.

OPPORTUNITIES

Language – English is a key international business language, so the workforce in Ireland can communicate with other businesses worldwide.

Government aid – Advice and support from state agencies such as Enterprise Ireland encourages Irish firms to export to foreign markets.

Green image – Ireland has a 'green' image, which is a USP when selling Irish food and drink products abroad. This helps to increase the sales and profits of Irish food and drinks firms.

CHALLENGES FOR IRISH BUSINESSES IN INTERNATIONAL TRADE

Irish firms may face challenges when engaging in international trade. They must overcome these obstacles in order to succeed on the international market. These challenges include:

- **High costs:** It is expensive to run a business in Ireland, e.g. wage and insurance costs. This can make Irish goods and services more expensive than those of competitors based in low-cost economies such as Poland.
- **Languages:** Irish firms must translate their websites, product packaging and advertising into a range of foreign languages. This can be time-consuming and expensive.
- **Location:** As Ireland is an island, goods must be transported by air and sea, which is expensive for Irish firms. It can also slow down distribution of goods to customers around the world and make Irish firms less competitive.
- **Cultural differences:** Irish firms must understand the cultural differences of countries around the world to avoid the risk of offending foreign customers.

Example
Using the image of a cow on Irish butter sold in India could offend Indian customers as cows are regarded as sacred in Hinduism.

Unit 7

- **Exchange rates:** As the euro strengthens against foreign currencies such as the US dollar, Irish exports become more expensive, leading to a decline in sales in international markets.
- **Payment difficulties:** It can be difficult for Irish firms to collect debts from foreign customers due to physical distance or differences in the legal system.

KEY TERMS

Now you have completed this chapter, you should understand and be able to explain the following terms. In your copybook, write a definition of each term to build up your own glossary of terms.

- international trade
- open economy
- imports (visible and invisible)
- exports (visible and invisible)
- balance of trade
- balance of payments

- surplus
- deficit
- import substitution
- free trade
- trading bloc
- deregulation
- World Trade Organisation (WTO)

- protectionism
- tariff
- quota
- embargo
- subsidy
- administrative regulations
- trade agreements

 **PowerPoint Summary**

EXAM-STYLE QUESTIONS

Ordinary Level

Section 1 – Short Questions (10 marks each)

1 Explain what is meant by the term *international trade*.
2 Distinguish between a visible export and an invisible export. Give **one** example of each.
3 Outline **two** reasons why goods are imported into Ireland. Give **two** example of goods imported into Ireland.
4 The following information relates to the trade figures for a country for the past 12 months:

Visible Exports	€2,800m
Visible Imports	€2,400m

Calculate the balance of trade (show your workings). State whether it is a surplus or a deficit.
5 What do the following initials stand for? (i) WTO (ii) EU (iii) BoP
6 Outline **two** reasons why a government would introduce protectionist measures.
7 Name and explain any **two** protectionist measures that governments use to restrict international trade.
8 Fill in the blanks for the following sentences.
   (i)   The European Union is an example of a trading _____
   (ii) Buying goods from other countries is called _____
   (iii) A _____ is a tax placed on imported goods that makes the imported good more expensive.
   (iv) When we purchase an Irish-made product rather than a similar imported item, this is referred to as import _____.

Section 2 – Long Questions

1 Outline **two** reasons why Ireland is involved in international trade. **(15 marks)**
2 Explain the difference between visible and invisible trade. Give examples in each case. **(15 marks)**
3 Explain what is meant by protectionism. Identify and explain **three** protectionist measures. **(20 marks)**
4 Explain the following terms: (i) *free trade*, (ii) *balance of trade*, (iii) *trading bloc*. **(15 marks)**
5 Outline the benefits of international trade to Irish businesses. **(15 marks)**
6 Describe the benefits that consumers receive from international trade. **(15 marks)**
7 Describe **two** opportunities for Irish business involved in international trade. **(15 marks)**
8 Discuss **three** challenges faced by Irish business involved in international trade. **(15 marks)**

Higher Level

Section 1 – Short Questions (10 marks each)

1 Illustrate what is meant by the term *open economy*. Give **two** examples of countries with an open economy.
2 Distinguish between invisible imports and visible imports. State **one** example of each type of import.
3 Using the following information, calculate both the balance of trade and the balance of payments. In each case clearly indicate if it is a surplus or a deficit. (Show your workings.)

Visible Exports	€100bn	Invisible Imports	€80bn
Visible Imports	€60bn	Invisible Exports	€70bn

4 Using the following information, calculate both the balance of trade and the balance of payments.

Total Imports	€32bn	Invisible Exports	€22bn
Total Exports	€38bn	Invisible Imports	€18bn

5 Illustrate what is meant by the term *trading bloc*. Name **one** trading bloc currently in existence.
6 Explain what is meant by the term *protectionism*. Name **two** methods that governments can use to reduce or eliminate the amount of international trade.
7 Indicate whether each of the following statements is true or false.

Statements		True or False
A	Your friend buys a new BMW car. This is an example of a visible import.	
B	When an Irish business exports to a foreign country, foreign money comes into Ireland.	
C	An embargo limits the quantity of goods that a country can import.	
D	Protectionism is often used by governments to encourage foreign trade.	
E	The European Union is an example of a trading bloc.	

8 Choose the correct word in each of the following sentences.
   (i) An invisible import is when a business or individual buys a **product/service** from outside Ireland.
   (ii) Protectionism is when **businesses/governments** use measures to **reduce/increase** the volume of international trade.
   (iii) The balance of trade measures the amount of **visible/invisible** goods coming into and going out of a country.
   (iv) The World Trade Organization is an **Irish/international** organisation which aims to establish free trade agreements between **European/global** countries.
   (v) Subsidies are amounts of money paid by governments to help businesses **increase/decrease** their operating costs in order to make them **more/less** competitive on international markets.

Section 2 – Applied Business Question (80 marks)

Here 2 There Ltd

Richie and Claire Farrell established a courier business, Here 2 There Ltd, 15 years ago. The business became a national success and the firm has decided to expand into the UK and Europe. This would give it a potential market of over 500 million people.

Although Ireland is an island, increased investment by the government has improved transport links. This will enable Here 2 There Ltd to transport goods quickly across the world.

Expansion was supported by a government grant from Enterprise Ireland, which the company used to invest in technology. Vehicle GPS tracking enables Claire to keep in contact with employees at all times. The firm has recruited highly educated and skilled IT staff to create a new online payment system, which reduces the costs and risks associated with foreign payments.

Richie and Claire want to expand their business to new markets in Russia and Turkey. Even though these countries impose higher taxes on foreign imports, they believe that the market has great potential. However, they have found it difficult to find staff to translate relevant documents into Russian and Turkish. Richie does not want to cause offence to local customers by using inappropriate language and has decided to use a recruitment company to find qualified staff.

With growing distribution outside the EU, Claire has noticed a significant increase in the amount of paperwork and documentation that must be completed. Richie has examined the running costs of their fleet of vehicles. He is concerned about rising costs such as driver wages, as these are higher than wages paid to drivers in low-cost economies such as Poland.

While population numbers offer an enormous potential market for Here 2 There Ltd, Claire and Richie are concerned about recent political turmoil in both Turkey and Russia. Irish media outlets have indicated that the Russian government may impose a limit on foreign imports and the EU may retaliate by banning Russian imports.

A Discuss the opportunities and challenges for Here 2 There Ltd when selling their service in other countries. **(30 marks)**

B Outline the barriers to trade that Here 2 There Ltd might experience when they expand into the Russian and Turkish markets. **(20 marks)**

C Evaluate how changing trends in the international business environment could impact on the development of Here 2 There Ltd. **(30 marks)**

Section 3 – Long Questions

1 Describe the reasons why the Irish economy is involved in international trade. **(15 marks)**

2 Read the information below and answer the questions that follow.

	2020	2021
Visible trade €m	€20,008	€13,780
Invisible trade €m	€19,320	€18,384

(i) What is meant by the terms *balance of trade* and *balance of payments*?

(ii) Calculate the balance of trade and the balance of payments for 2021.

(iii) Illustrate your understanding of the term *visible imports* with reference to Ireland.

(iv) Outline the importance of international trade to a small open economy such as Ireland. **(20 marks)**

3 Explain the following terms in relation to international trade:

(i) Deregulation

(ii) Subsidy

(iii) Free trade

(iv) Open economy. **(20 marks)**

4 Identify and explain the current trends in international trade. **(20 marks)**

Section 3 – Long Questions *continued*

5

> Governments use strategies such as protectionism to place barriers to free trade.

Discuss, using examples, the different protectionism methods used to restrict free trade between countries. **(20 marks)**

6 Describe the ways in which ICT can impact on businesses engaged in international trade. **(15 marks)**

7

> When a domestic business begins to trade on the international market it can be presented with many opportunities and challenges that do not exist on the home market.

Discuss the opportunities that may arise for a domestic company if it operates internationally. **(25 marks)**

PREVIOUS LEAVING CERTIFICATE EXAM QUESTIONS

Ordinary Level

Section A – Short Questions (10 marks each)

1 Column 1 is a list of terms used in international trade. Column 2 is a list of the explanations of these terms. Match the two lists in your copybook by writing your answers in the form *number = letter* (e.g. 1 = A). One explanation has no match.

Business Terms		Explanations	
1	Trading bloc	**A**	A European Union law which must be implemented in each EU country immediately.
2	Regulation	**B**	A limit to the amount of a particular product which can be imported into a country.
3	Embargo	**C**	The treatment of the world as one single market by global firms.
4	Quota	**D**	A tax on imported goods and services.
5	Tariff	**E**	A group of countries that freely trade with each other – there are no barriers to trade between these countries.
		F	A ban on a particular product being imported into a country.

[LC OL 2018]

2 (i) Explain the term *Visible Imports*.

(ii) Explain the term *Invisible Exports*. **[LC OL 2017]**

3 (i) Calculate the Balance of Trade, using the following information. (Show your workings.)

Visible Imports	€1,500 m
Visible Exports	€1,300 m
Balance of trade	_____

(ii) Tick (✔) the correct box to state if the Balance of Trade is a surplus or a deficit.

☐ Surplus   ☐ Deficit   **[LC OL 2014]**

Section B

1 Read the information supplied and answer the questions which follow.

Irish International Trade	The World's Biggest Exporters
The value of **total exports** for the month of March 2017 rose to **€11 billion**. At the same time, the value of total imports for the month of March fell to **€5.8 billion**.	
Source 1 – www.irishtimes.com	Source 2 – www.independent.ie

(A) (i) From the information provided in **Source 1** calculate the Balance of Payments for March.

(ii) State whether it is a surplus or a deficit. Show your workings. **(15 marks)**

(B) Explain, using an example in each case, the difference between visible exports and visible imports. **(15 marks)**

(C) From the information provided in **Source 2**,

(i) Identify the country that has the largest percentage share of global exports.

(ii) Identify what percentage share of global exports the EU accounts for. **(15 marks)**

(D) Outline **two** challenges for Irish businesses exporting to China. **(15 marks) [LC OL 2018]**

2

In June 2016, the UK voted to leave the European Union (EU). This became widely known as 'Brexit'. More than €1.2 billion of goods and services are traded between the UK and Ireland every week. Brexit could result in trade barriers such as tariffs being imposed.

(i) Explain the term *tariff*.

(ii) Name **two** other trade barriers. **(15 marks) [LC OL 2017]**

3

Irish agricultural based exports have increased by almost 12%, highlighting the importance of this sector to the Irish economy.

Visible Exports €1,400 million

Visible Imports €1,200 million

(A) (i) Using the above information calculate the Balance of Trade. (Show your workings.)

(ii) State whether it is a surplus or a deficit. **(15 marks)**

(B) (i) Explain the term *visible export*.

(ii) Name **two** examples of Irish agricultural visible exports. **(15 marks)**

(C) Outline **two** benefits for Irish business engaged in international trade. **(15 marks) [LC OL 2012]**

Higher Level

Section A – Short Questions (10 marks each)

1 Study the bar chart below, which illustrates a country's visible trade from May to August 2017.

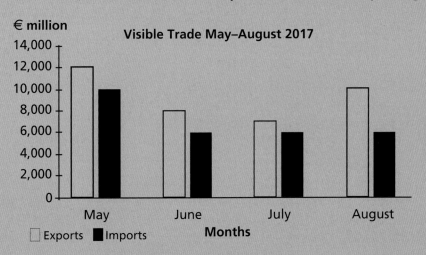

€ million

Visible Trade May–August 2017

☐ Exports ■ Imports

Months

(i)   Name the month which has the highest level of visible exports.

(ii) Name the month which has the largest balance of trade.

(iii) Explain the term *import substitution*.   **[LC HL 2018]**

2 (i) Calculate the missing figures in the **three** unshaded areas in the table below.

Visible Exports €bn	Visible Imports €bn	Balance of Trade €bn
€70	€105	
€90		€25 surplus
	€110	€30 deficit

(ii) Explain the term *visible exports* and provide **one** example with reference to Ireland. **[LC HL 2016]**

3 'The goal of the World Trade Organization (WTO) is to reduce <u>protectionism</u> and allow free trade.'
Illustrate your understanding of the underlined term.   **[LC HL 2014]**

Section B

1 Explain the following terms in relation to international trade: Trading Bloc, Tariffs,
Embargoes, Subsidies.   **(20 marks) [LC HL 2018]**

2

'The Irish economy is "Performing well" but Brexit poses a threat.'

Source: *Financial Times, December 2016*

Invisible Exports	€101,750 million	Invisible Imports	€109,376 million
Total Exports	€194,366 million	Total imports	€171,543 million

(i)   Calculate the Balance of Trade using the figures above. (Show your workings.)

(ii) Define the term *tariff* and explain the possible effect on the Irish economy if the UK Government
were to impose a tariff on Irish goods in the future.   **(25 marks) [LC HL 2017]**

 Solutions

Unit 7

CHAPTER 30 | THE EUROPEAN UNION

Learning Outcomes

When you have completed this chapter, you will be able to:

1 Identify and explain the main European Union institutions and policies

2 Outline the impact that the main European Union institutions and policies have on Irish businesses

3 Describe the decision-making process in the main European Union institutions

4 Identify and explain the role of special interest groups in the European Union

5 Discuss the benefits and challenges for Ireland as a member of the European Union

6 Identify and explain the opportunities and challenges of the European Union.

Literacy Link

European Union (EU), EU institutions, EU policies, deregulation, co-decision, directive, regulation, special interest group

Numeracy Link

Exchange rates, addition, multiplication, percentages, analysis of charts

Cross-curricular Link

Economics – exchange rates, EU, European Central Bank (ECB), European Investment Bank (EIB), economic policies, impact of Brexit

Geography – impact of categories of industry on European regions, economic developments in European countries, trading patterns between EU countries, influence of the EU on the Irish economy

CASE STUDY | The European Union

After the end of the Second World War, many European countries began to formulate plans to prevent further wars on the continent. It was agreed that the materials needed for war, e.g. steel and energy, needed to be jointly controlled. In 1951 six countries – Germany, France, Belgium, the Netherlands, Italy and Luxembourg – decided to establish the European Coal and Steel Community (ECSC) to unite their coal and steel industries. This co-operative approach was very successful. In 1958 these countries set up the European Economic Community (EEC) to create a **common market** between European countries. This allowed free trade between **member states** and removed **barriers to trade** such as **tariffs** and **quotas**.

Ireland joined the EEC in 1973 and as a member agrees to adhere to **common economic and political policies** which benefit all EU states. In 1995, the EEC became known as the **European Union (EU)**.

The EU has many aims, including:

- Promoting peace
- Ensuring freedom, security and justice
- Promoting economic and social progress
- Combating social exclusion and discrimination.

In 2002, the **euro** was introduced as a **common currency** and is now used in 19 member states.

Change is on the horizon in the EU as, in a 2016 referendum, 51.9% of UK voters chose to leave the EU, dubbed **Brexit** (merging the words 'Britain' and 'exit') by the media. Negotiations about how the UK will leave are ongoing and are expected to continue for the foreseeable future.

DID YOU KNOW? *Since Ireland joined the EU, an estimated 700,000 jobs have been created and foreign direct investment (FDI) has increased from €16 million to €30 billion.*

 DID YOU KNOW? *The European Union has an anthem. It is an excerpt from Beethoven's Ninth Symphony. Why not listen to it? Just search for 'Anthem of Europe'.*

Activity 30.1

Working in pairs, can you name:
- All the countries of the EU?
- The EU countries that use the euro?
- The currencies of the EU countries that do not use the euro?

You may need to search online to help you complete this activity.

EU INSTITUTIONS

There are a number of EU institutions that: decide on the direction of the EU; create and enforce legislation; and represent the interests of the citizens of the member states. These include:

1. European Commission
2. European Parliament
3. Council of the European Union
4. European Court of Auditors
5. Court of Justice of the European Union (CJEU)
6. European Investment Bank (EIB).

1 European Commission

The European Commission **is responsible for the day-to-day management of the EU**. It consists of one commissioner from each EU member state, appointed by their own government. Each commissioner is assigned a Directorate-General (DG), which relates to an area of responsibility, e.g. trade, energy, agriculture. The commissioners meet once a week in Brussels or Strasbourg.

 DID YOU KNOW? *Approximately 33,000 people work at the European Commission.*

Functions of the European Commission

A **Proposes new laws:** It consults experts, interest groups and the public to identify new laws that are needed to protect the EU and its citizens. It proposes these laws to the European Parliament and the Council of the EU.

B **Enforces EU laws:** It enforces EU laws and can bring cases of breaches of these laws to the Court of Justice of the European Union (CJEU).

C **Represents the EU internationally:** It represents all EU member states when negotiating international agreements on behalf of the EU, e.g. trade agreements with Japan.

D **Formulates and monitors the EU's budget:** It draws up the annual budget for approval by the European Parliament and the Council of the EU. The Commission also monitors the EU budget to ensure that it is used appropriately.

Activity 30.2

Find out the name of Ireland's current EU Commissioner. Which directorate-general does he/she hold?

Unit 7

2 European Parliament

The European Parliament is the **only directly elected EU institution**, with elections held every five years. The Parliament, which is based in Strasbourg, consists of 751 MEPs (Members of the European Parliament). The number of seats allocated per country is based on the population of each member state.

Debates in the European Parliament are translated into the twenty-four officially recognised EU languages.

The President of the European Parliament is elected for a renewable two and a half-year term and acts as a representative of the EU to other EU institutions and with institutions around the world.

Activity 30.3

Visit the European Parliament website (www.europarl.europa.eu) to see how many MEPs represent Ireland in the European Parliament.

Functions of the European Parliament

A **Passing laws:** It debates laws proposed by the European Commission. It can accept, reject or amend these proposals. Using a process known as co-decision, the European Parliament and the Council of the EU work together to examine the proposals and turn them into laws.

B **Supervisory powers:** It supervises the work of the European Commission. The Commission must submit regular reports to the European Parliament, e.g. on the implementation of the annual budget.

C **Appointments:** It appoints the President of the European Commission and auditors to the EU Court of Auditors.

D **Preparation and approval of the EU budget:** It helps to prepare the EU's annual budget. The budget is agreed between the European Parliament and the Council of the European Union. The Parliament monitors the EU budget to ensure that funds are spent appropriately.

Activity 30.4

Watch the online clip 'The European Parliament in 40 Seconds'. Name **one** sector for which the European Parliament proposes laws on behalf of EU citizens.

Activity 30.5

Analyse the EU budget summary for 2018 and answer the following questions.

A Summary of the EU Budget for 2018	
Expenditure	*Billion €*
Smart and Inclusive Growth	77.534
Sustainable Growth	59.285
Security and Citizenship	3.493
Global Europe	9.569
Administrative Expenditure (for all EU institutions)	9.666
Special Instruments	567
Total	

1 What was the total budget for the EU in 2018?
2 What percentage of the budget was spent on security and citizenship?
3 What percentage of the budget was spent on administrative expenditure in all EU institutions?
4 Research the current year's EU budget total.

Ireland has held the presidency of the Council of the European Union seven times, most recently in 2013. The presidency brought more than 24,000 visitors to Ireland. Ninety-seven per cent of EU representatives who came to Ireland during the presidency rated their experience as good or very good.

Unit 7

3 Council of the European Union

The Council of the European Union and the European Parliament make up the main decision-making body in the EU. The Council consists of ministers from EU member states, who meet regularly. The topic to be discussed at the meetings of the Council determines which government ministers attend. For example, if foreign trade is to be discussed, the minister responsible for foreign trade in each EU country attends. The ministers have the authority to vote on behalf of their country on topics discussed at the meetings. The presidency is held by each member country in turn, rotating every six months.

Activity 30.6

(i) Who is the current president of the Council of the European Union? Which country will hold the presidency next?

(ii) When did Ireland last hold the presidency of the Council of the European Union? When is Ireland next due to hold the presidency?

Functions of the Council of the European Union

A **EU laws:** Through a process known as co-decision, the Council of the European Union and the European Parliament negotiate and adopt EU laws proposed by the European Commission.

B **EU budget:** It agrees the EU budget with the European Parliament. The budget is usually approved in December and begins on 1 January the following year.

C **EU common policies:** It is responsible for creating common policies across the EU, e.g. security, defence and humanitarian aid.

D **International agreements:** It gives the European Commission permission to negotiate agreements on behalf of the EU with non-EU countries and international organisations. These agreements can cover a range of areas, including transport, trade and technology.

Activity 30.7

Read the infographic and answer the following questions.

1 What was the value of goods exported from EU countries to Japan in 2019?

2 What percentage customs duties was charged on beef?

3 Why was selling fruit in Japan difficult?

4 Name **two** improvements that will arise once trade barriers are reduced or removed.

DID YOU KNOW? *660,000 EU jobs are linked to exports to Japan.*

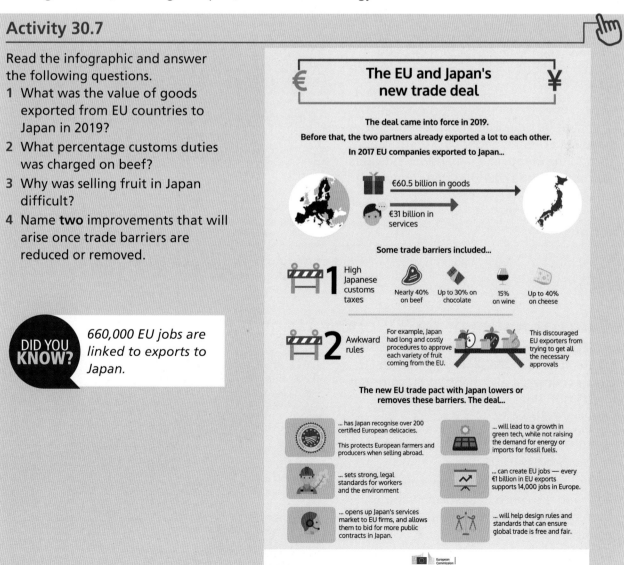

The EU and Japan's new trade deal

The deal came into force in 2019.
Before that, the two partners already exported a lot to each other.
In 2017 EU companies exported to Japan...

€60.5 billion in goods

€31 billion in services

Some trade barriers included...

1 High Japanese customs taxes

Nearly 40% on beef

Up to 30% on chocolate

15% on wine

Up to 40% on cheese

2 Awkward rules — For example, Japan had long and costly procedures to approve each variety of fruit coming from the EU.

This discouraged EU exporters from trying to get all the necessary approvals

The new EU trade pact with Japan lowers or removes these barriers. The deal...

... has Japan recognise over 200 certified European delicacies. This protects European farmers and producers when selling abroad.

... will lead to a growth in green tech, while not raising the demand for energy or imports for fossil fuels.

... sets strong, legal standards for workers and the environment

... can create EU jobs — every €1 billion in EU exports supports 14,000 jobs in Europe.

... opens up Japan's services market to EU firms, and allows them to bid for more public contracts in Japan.

... will help design rules and standards that can ensure global trade is free and fair.

European Commission

Unit 7

479

Activity 30.8

In pairs, complete a revision clock template. Fill in the template using both text and colourful drawings to summarise the workings of the European Commission, the European Parliament and the Council of the European Union. There will be four parts of the clock template for each institution. Your teacher will set a time for you to complete this task. Once completed, check back to ensure that you have covered all the details relating to the institutions.

4 European Court of Auditors

The European Court of Auditors is responsible for ensuring that EU funds are raised and used correctly. It also aims to improve management of EU finances. Each member state has one representative in the the European Court of Auditors.

> **Definition: Auditor**
> An auditor independently examines financial accounts, e.g. the balance sheet and cash flow forecasts of an organisation. The auditor ensures that information contained in the financial accounts gives a true and fair view of the financial position of the organisation.

Functions of the European Court of Auditors

A **Audits:** It conducts audits to ensure that money collected and spent in the EU is done so appropriately and gives the best value for money to EU citizens.

B **Reports:** It publishes audit reports with findings and recommendations for national governments and the European Commission. It also produces an annual report for the European Parliament and the Council of the EU.

C **Fraud:** It reports any suspicions of fraud and corruption to the European Anti-Fraud Office (OLAF).

D **Spot checks:** It conducts spot checks on any organisation or individual responsible for handling EU funds, including EU institutions such as the European Commission, individual EU countries and countries that receive EU aid.

Example
In 2012, the European Court of Auditors identified that €6.8 billion of the EU's budget was spent in error on fraudulent or ineligible projects. In one case a farmer had received over €80,000 per year to maintain 350 acres of grassland for endangered birds, when he should have received just over €11,000.

Activity 30.9

On the Internet, watch the clip 'European Court of Auditors – Guardians of EU Finances' to revise its role in the EU.

5 Court of Justice of the European Union (CJEU)

The CJEU is responsible for ensuring that EU laws are applied in the same way in each EU member country. It also monitors EU countries and EU institutions to ensure that they are abiding by EU laws.

Functions of the Court of Justice of the European Union

A **Advice to member countries:** It can provide advice to the courts in member countries if they are unsure how EU laws should be applied.

B **Enforces EU laws:** It can force EU member

Unit 7

states to comply with EU laws. If an EU member is found to have broken EU laws, it must resolve the issue immediately. If a second case is brought against the country, it can be fined.

C **Cancels EU laws:** It can cancel EU laws if it finds that these laws breach fundamental human rights. Cases to cancel laws can be brought by the European Commission, member country governments and individual EU citizens.

Example

The European Commission is taking Ireland to the CJEU for failing to stop raw sewage being discharged into Irish waters. Ireland was warned at least three times that it would face prosecution if it did not introduce waste water treatment plants in a number of locations around the country. If found guilty, the CJEU could impose a fixed fine of €10 million as well as a daily fine of up to €20,000 until Ireland complies with the law.

DID YOU KNOW? *If you were to lay out the 24,000 books at the law library at the CJEU, they would stretch for 10km.*

6 European Investment Bank (EIB)

The European Investment Bank (EIB) is jointly owned by EU member states and is based in Luxembourg. **The EIB is responsible for providing funding to projects that help to achieve the aims and objectives of the European Union.**

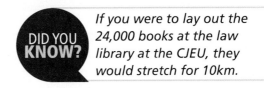

The EIB aims to:

- Improve opportunities for jobs and growth in the EU
- Support projects which help to reduce climate change
- Promote EU policies around the world.

The EIB provides three main services.

A **Lending:** The EIB lends money to clients, e.g. local authorities and universities, for projects that aim to increase growth and jobs in the EU.

Example

University College Cork (UCC) received €100 million in funding from the EIB to upgrade student accommodation and build a range of facilities, including a research centre, a hospital and outdoor sports facilities. Approximately 500 jobs will be created in the construction phase of these works.

B **Guarantor:** It acts as a guarantor on loans for EU projects and this may encourage other investors to invest in projects.

C **Advising:** The EIB offers advice and technical assistance to clients to ensure that the borrower gets the best value for the money borrowed.

Example

The EIB is helping to finance the construction of a new power plant in Kiel, Germany. The EIB is providing a €105 million loan, as the plant will emit 70% less carbon dioxide than the coal plant which it is replacing.

Activity 30.10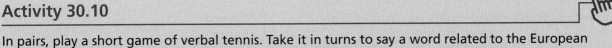

In pairs, play a short game of verbal tennis. Take it in turns to say a word related to the European Court of Auditors, the Court of Justice of the European Union or the European Investment Bank. Players score a point for each relevant term. The game ends when one player can no longer think of any terms.

Unit 7

THE DECISION-MAKING PROCESS IN THE EUROPEAN UNION

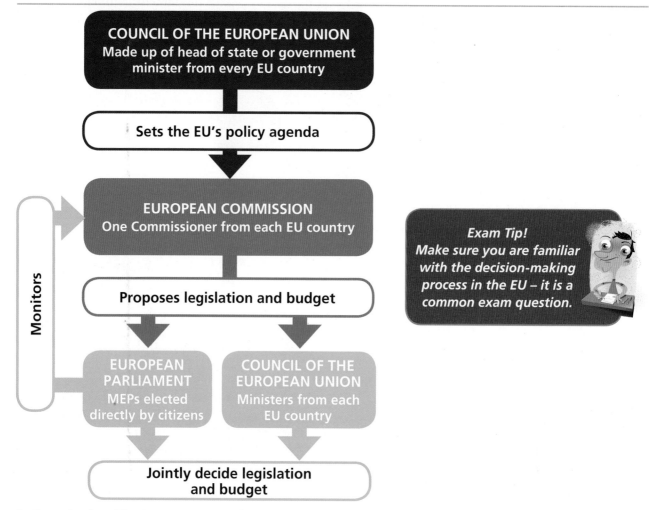

COUNCIL OF THE EUROPEAN UNION
Made up of head of state or government minister from every EU country

Sets the EU's policy agenda

EUROPEAN COMMISSION
One Commissioner from each EU country

Monitors

Proposes legislation and budget

EUROPEAN PARLIAMENT
MEPs elected directly by citizens

COUNCIL OF THE EUROPEAN UNION
Ministers from each EU country

Jointly decide legislation and budget

> **Exam Tip!**
> Make sure you are familiar with the decision-making process in the EU – it is a common exam question.

1 **Consultation:** The European Commission proposes laws to be introduced in the EU. The Commission consults with interest groups, experts and citizens to find out their views on what legislation is needed in the European Union.

2 **Legislation proposal – first reading:** The European Parliament and the Council of the European Union review the proposed laws sent by the Commission. At this stage the proposals can be accepted, rejected or amended. If the Council and the Parliament agree on the proposals, the legislation is adopted.

3 **Legislation proposal – second reading:** A second reading takes place if the European Parliament and the Council of the European Union cannot agree on the proposed legislation. At this stage both bodies can suggest amendments to the proposals. If the Council and the Parliament agree on the proposals at the second reading, the legislation is adopted.

4 **Conciliation committee:** If an agreement cannot be reached on the proposed legislation after the second reading, the issue is referred to a conciliation committee. If the committee cannot help the European Parliament and the Council of the European Union to reach agreement, the proposed legislation is not adopted.

> **Note!**
> Referral to the conciliation committee is generally reserved for very difficult proposals and is not commonly used.

5 **Third and final reading:** There are no further amendments allowed at this reading. Both the European Parliament and the Council of the European Commission may give the final draft their approval. The law is adopted and becomes a piece of EU legislation.

Activity 30.11

Watch the online clip 'Council animation decision making (EN)' to help you revise this topic. Draw a diagram to show how the decision-making process takes place in the EU.

Problems with Decision-Making in the EU

Problem	Reason
Slow	→ Decision-making in the EU is a very complex. This means that it is slow to make decisions and react to problems, e.g. dealing with refugees fleeing from war-torn countries.
Centralised	→ Decisions that affect all EU citizens are often made in central European countries such as Belgium. The decisions may not fully consider the needs of citizens in peripheral countries such as Ireland.
Over-regulated	→ Many people believe that there are too many rules and policies in the EU, which has led to higher costs for businesses and higher prices for consumers.
Democratic Deficit	→ Members of the European Parliament are directly elected by EU citizens and they do not have the ability to make decisions by themselves in the EU. This is known as democratic deficit. The MEPs cannot propose laws and must pass or reject laws in conjunction with the Council of the European Union.

EU Legislation

There are a number of ways in which new legislation can be implemented into EU member states. The most common are:

1 Directive   2 Regulation

3 Recommendation   4 Decision.

1 Directive

A directive is a law that **applies to all EU member states**, and which must be implemented within a specified time limit. Each member state can choose how they will implement the directive in their own country.

Example: Consumer Rights Directive
When consumers buy goods and services online they are entitled to a 14-day cooling-off period from the day they receive the goods. The consumer can cancel their purchase without giving the seller a reason and without incurring any additional penalties.

Example: WEEE Directive
This directive forces manufacturers of products with a battery or a plug to take back and recycle their own equipment. It aims to reduce the number of electrical appliances that end up in landfill.

Activity 30.12

Examine the infographic from WEEE Ireland and answer the following questions.

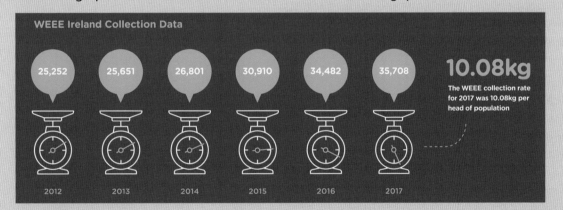

WEEE Ireland Collection Data

2012	2013	2014	2015	2016	2017
25,252	25,651	26,801	30,910	34,482	35,708

10.08kg
The WEEE collection rate for 2017 was 10.08kg per head of population

1 What was the percentage increase in WEEE collection from 2012 to 2017?

2 Why, do you think, was there an increase in collections from 2012 to 2017?

3 What could WEEE Ireland do to continue to increase collection amounts?

2 Regulation

This means that **laws are introduced and enforced in the same way** across all EU member states. EU regulations take precedence over national laws.

Example: Vacuum cleaners

Manufacturers of vacuum cleaners must label their products in terms of energy efficiency. Studies have shown that more efficient vacuum cleaners would save the equivalent amount of energy needed to keep the London Underground running for up to twenty years.

Example: General Data Protection Regulation (GDPR) 2018

This regulation improves data protection rights for data subjects. It also places greater responsibility on organisations that process personal data. Large fines can be imposed on organisations that breach this regulation.

3 Recommendation

EU recommendations are not legally binding but give **EU institutions** the opportunity to **make their views known** on particular issues or concerns.

Example: Video conferencing

The European Commission issued a recommendation that member states should improve their use of video conferencing to assist the judicial services to work more effectively across borders.

4 Decision

Decisions can be given to individuals, businesses and member states. These decisions can be made by the **Council of the European Union and the European Commission.** Decisions are **binding** and are often used for rulings on proposed business mergers.

Example: Ireland and Apple

The European Commission issued a decision which ruled that the Irish government had given the company Apple two special tax deals in 1991 and 2007. The Commission has stated that the Irish government must collect €13 billion of unpaid taxes from Apple.

Example: Google

Google was fined €2.42 billion by the European Commission for abusing its dominant position in the search engine market. The firm placed its own comparison shopping service higher than its rivals' in search results. This limited consumer choice and prevented rival companies competing in a fair market. Google faced fines of 5% per day of its daily sales if it did not stop its illegal action.

SPECIAL INTEREST GROUPS

EU laws have a significant impact on individuals, organisations and businesses across the EU member states. This has led to the establishment of special interest groups.

- **Aim:** Interest groups aim to influence the political and decision-making process in the EU. They have greater strength in numbers and possess more capital and resources than individuals, so they are more likely to be listened to by decision-makers.
- **Techniques:** They use a range of techniques to get decision-makers to listen to their opinion, e.g. lobbying, publicity campaigns and public protests.
- **Consultation:** They are also consulted by the European Commission when the Commission is proposing new legislation.

Special interest groups include:
- Trade unions, e.g. SIPTU
- Employer organisations, e.g. Ibec
- Transnational companies, e.g. Microsoft
- National governments, e.g. the Irish government
- Consumer protection bodies, e.g. Consumer Association of Ireland (CAI)
- Environmental protection organisations, e.g. Greenpeace.

Methods Used to Influence Decision-makers

| 1 Lobbying | 2 Establishing offices | 3 Publicity campaigns |

1 Lobbying

The interest group tries to influence decision-makers by outlining the views of the group on particular issues. The interest group wants their position to be taken into consideration by decision-makers when they draft policies and propose legislation.

Example
Google has spent almost €5 million on EU lobbying. It has lobbied EU commissioners, MEPs and other officials on issues such as cyber security and the future of the Internet.

2 Establishing Offices

Some interest groups establish a permanent office in Brussels and/or Strasbourg so that staff can monitor developments in the European Parliament and the European Commission. This enables the interest group to react quickly to any developments that may affect its members.

Example
The Irish Farmers' Association (IFA) established an office in Brussels in 1973 in order to create a direct link with decision-makers in the EU. They hold formal and informal meetings with the commissioners and officials responsible for formulating agriculture policy.

3 Publicity Campaigns

These campaigns aim to increase public awareness of the issue concerning the interest group and to influence the decision-makers. Campaigns can include petitions and events.

Example
Greenpeace activists unveiled a sun-shaped banner outside a meeting of the European Parliament and European Commission. Greenpeace wants the EU to improve EU citizens' rights to produce and share their own renewable energy.

EU POLICIES

The EU has formulated a number of important policies on areas of concern in the EU, including free trade, the environment, economic development and competition in the marketplace.
The policies include:

1 Common Agricultural Policy (CAP)	2 Common Fisheries Policy (CFP)	3 Competition Policy
4 European Single Market (ESM)	5 European Monetary Union (EMU)	6 EU Social Charter
	7 EU Regional Policy	

Unit 7

1 Common Agricultural Policy (CAP)

This policy aims to:

- Ensure that high-quality, safe and affordable food is available in the EU
- Provide a decent standard of living for farmers
- Protect the environment and preserve natural resources.

Advantages of the CAP

A **Food supply:**

- It ensures that EU countries have access to a secure and stable supply of food at reasonable prices.
- Consumers are not reliant on food imports with fluctuating prices.

B **Farm incomes:**

- Farm incomes have increased since the introduction of CAP.
- The EU uses a system of direct payments, subsidies and market supports to ensure that farmers receive a stable income.

> **Definition: Farm subsidy**
> A payment made to farmers by the government to support farm incomes.

C **Improved farming methods:** CAP has provided farmers with access to new farming methods to enable them to make the best use of their land and improve their agricultural yields.

D **Environmental protection:** CAP helps to protect rural environments. Farmers receive higher payments if they follow environmentally friendly practices, e.g. use fewer chemicals and protect wildlife.

Disadvantages of the CAP

A **Unemployment:** EU grants have enabled farmers to improve the efficiency of their farms, using modern machinery. This has reduced the need for farm labourers, thus increasing unemployment in rural areas.

B **Unequal distribution of funds:** Large farm owners receive higher CAP payments than smaller farmers. This can lead to an unequal distribution of wealth among farmers.

C **Loss of small farms:** Small farmers are unable to compete with larger farms that benefit from higher CAP payments and economies of scale, e.g. buying stock at lower prices. This has led to the loss of small farms and has had a negative impact on rural life.

D **Cost to the taxpayer:** CAP is the most expensive EU policy. Many EU taxpayers feel that too much of their taxes are spent on CAP and want the money collected to be spent on other areas such as transport and healthcare.

Activity 30.13

Search online for the clip 'EU Agriculture-CAP-Produce Food' to learn about how the CAP supports EU farmers.

2 Common Fisheries Policy (CFP)

The CFP is a set of rules governing the management of European fishing fleets and the conservation of European fish stocks.

The CFP aims to:

- Give people working in the fishing industry a fair standard of living
- Provide a stable source of food for EU citizens
- Ensure that fishing and aquaculture is done in an environmentally sustainable manner.

Advantages of the CFP

A **Protection of fish stocks:** A TAC (total allowable catch) is allocated to each member state. Once the quota has been fished, the country must close the fishery. There are also rules regarding net mesh sizes to prevent the overfishing of young fish.

> **Definition: Total allowable catch (TAC)**
> A limit placed on catches of fish species such as cod and sea bass. The TAC is usually set for a year or a fishing season.

B **Quality and price:** The CFP has enabled workers in the fishing industry to get a fair price for their produce and ensure that consumers get high-quality products.

DID YOU KNOW? *The aquaculture industry now provides direct and indirect employment for over 85,000 people in the EU.*

C **Aquaculture industry:** The CFP helps this industry to grow by providing funding, which has made the sector more competitive on international markets.

D **Targeted funding:** The CFP provides funding for local, low-impact fishing fleets. This is important for providing employment in local areas.

Disadvantages of the CFP

A **Centralised decision-making:** Officials in Brussels make decisions about the entire EU fishing industry. They may not take into consideration local issues faced by fishermen, who often know best what is needed to improve the industry at local level.

B **Decline of fish stocks:** Despite numerous policies, fish stocks have continued to decline in EU waters.

C **Food waste:** Fishermen dump millions of dead fish back into the sea if the catches are too small or the wrong species. This process, known as discarding, wastes fish catches and can further reduce fish stocks.

D **Policing:** It is not possible to ensure that certain fishing boats do not fish more than the TAC. This can result in overfishing and further damage fish stocks.

Activity 30.14

In pairs, create ten statements on the CAP and the CFP that can be answered True or False. Swap your statements with another pair of students, complete each other's quizzes and mark them.

3 Competition Policy

The Competition Policy was introduced to ensure that markets in the EU remain competitive. The policy has allowed consumers to benefit from greater choice, lower prices and higher-quality goods and services. It prevents businesses behaving in an anti-competitive manner, which can harm consumers.

To ensure that there is fair competition in the EU member states, the European Commission monitors the following areas:

- Mergers and takeovers
- Deregulation
- Companies that abuse their dominant market position
- Cartels
- State aid.

Mergers and Takeovers

Certain mergers and takeovers must be examined and approved by the EU Commission. The merger or takeover may be denied if the Commission finds that it would have a negative impact on consumers, e.g. higher prices or lower-quality goods and services.

Example
- The EU Commission approved the €715 million takeover of Irish fruit distributor Fyffes by Japanese firm Sumitomo.
- The EU Commission prevented the proposed Ryanair takeover of Aer Lingus, as it would have made Ryanair a dominant company in a market and restricted consumer choice.

Unit 7

Deregulation

Deregulation reduces or removes state involvement in certain industries, e.g. transport and telecommunications. It allows private companies to enter the market and it usually leads to greater consumer choice and lower prices.

Example

For many years, the ESB (Electricity Supply Board) was a state-run monopoly in the energy market in Ireland. Since 1998, the market has undergone deregulation and in 2004 the market was completely opened to competitors. The energy market now contains a number of competitors, including ESB Electric Ireland, SSE Airtricity, Energia and Bord Gáis Energy.

Abuse of Dominant Position

This policy prevents dominant businesses pushing smaller firms out of the market, e.g. using a predatory pricing strategy to make it very difficult for smaller companies to compete on price.

Example

Pharmaceutical company AstraZeneca was fined €52.5 million for abusing its dominant position in the market for medication to treat ulcers. It was found guilty of preventing lower-priced competitors entering the market.

Cartels

A cartel is a group of firms in the same industry that agree to restrict the market for consumers, e.g. by fixing prices or limiting production levels. As the cartel members agree to behave in the same way, consumers pay higher prices for lower-quality goods and services.

Example

The EU Commission imposed a fine of almost €3 billion on truck manufacturers MAN, Volvo/Renault, Daimler, Iveco and DAF. They had run a cartel for fourteen years and had colluded on pricing.

State Aid

The EU's Competition Policy does not allow EU governments to provide state aid to businesses, e.g. subsidies. This would give some companies an unfair advantage over similar businesses in the EU.

Example

Ryanair has been ordered to repay €2 million to the Austrian government. The EU Commission ruled that agreements made relating to airport services and marketing gave Ryanair an unfair competitive advantage and breached state aid rules.

Advantages of the EU Competition Policy

A **Lower prices:** There is intense competition between firms in the EU market. To increase market share, businesses offer lower prices to consumers.

B **Improved quality:** Competition in the market can encourage businesses to improve the quality of their products for consumers, e.g. a longer battery life for electronic goods.

C **Greater consumer choice:** Consumers can purchase goods and services from businesses throughout Europe. This gives consumers greater choice and allows them to buy goods and services that offer the best price, quality and choice.

D **Innovative products:** Competition encourages businesses to develop new and creative products. Consumers benefit from innovations in product design, packaging and production techniques.

Disadvantages of the EU Competition Policy

A **Small business closure:** Smaller businesses may be unable to compete on price or quality. They may have to close down, leading to job losses.

B **Reduced expansion:** The EU can deny certain mergers and acquisitions. This can reduce firms' ability to expand in order to increase sales and profits.

C **High fines:** Businesses that have been found guilty of breaking laws in relation to competition may face large fines. These fines reduce business profits.

Activity 30.15

In your copybook, create a bingo grid with nine squares. Each student fills in the squares using key terms related to EU Competition Policy. Your teacher will describe aspects of the policy and if they describe a key term that you have chosen, cross it off on your bingo grid. The first student to fill in all nine squares calls out 'Bingo' and ends the game.

4 European Single Market (ESM)

The European Single Market (ESM) views the EU as one single territory without any borders. It allows for the freedom of movement of people, goods and services between EU member states.

Advantages of the European Single Market (ESM)

A **Free trade:** The ESM allows free trade between EU member states. EU businesses are protected from competition from non-EU countries by common protectionist measures such as tariffs and quotas.

B **Free movement of capital:** Irish businesses and citizens have the opportunity to use financial services across the EU, e.g. obtain loans from German banks.

C **Simplified documentation:** The ESM has simplified the documentation needed to move goods and services across EU states. This has lowered costs for businesses operating in the EU.

D **Improved quality:** The ESM has helped to increase the quality of products sold in EU member states. The CE mark was introduced to show that a product meets EU health and safety requirements. This protects consumers from low-quality and potentially dangerous goods.

Disadvantages of the European Single Market (ESM)

A **Government contracts:** Governments cannot favour firms from their own country when awarding contracts for tenders, e.g. building a school or hospital.

B **Competition:** Large firms from other EU member states can sell their goods and services in Ireland. This may make it difficult for small Irish firms to compete on price, quality and quantity and many may be forced to close down.

> **Definition: Tender**
> A bid by a firm or group of businesses to complete a government contract, e.g. building a road or a school. The bid includes details of costs and a timeline for completion.

C **Free movement of labour:** EU citizens can move freely to work in any EU country. This can lead to increased competition for jobs as businesses in Ireland recruit employees from other EU countries. This may result in higher unemployment levels among Irish workers.

Activity 30.16

In your opinion, what is the biggest advantage or disadvantage of the European Single Market (ESM)? Use the website http://breakyourownnews.com to create a breaking news headline with your chosen advantage or disadvantage. Download it and show it to your classmates. Vote on the best one.

Unit 7

IRISH BUSINESSES IN THE EUROPEAN SINGLE MARKET (ESM)

✓ Opportunities	✗ Challenges
1 Free Movement of Labour Workers from other member states can move freely and work in Ireland. This means that businesses based in Ireland have a greater choice of job applicants for vacancies.	**1 Free Movement of Labour** Irish people can move to work in other EU countries. Businesses in Ireland may find it difficult to find suitable staff to fill job vacancies.
2 Government Tenders Irish businesses can tender for government projects in all member states. This gives Irish firms the opportunity to increase their sales and profits.	**2 Government Tenders** Government tenders may be awarded to firms from other EU states rather than to Irish firms. This can lead to a loss of jobs for Irish workers and money paid to employees of foreign firms will leave the Irish economy.
3 Documentation Simpler documentation has been introduced for trade between countries. This has reduced business costs, time and resources.	**3 Bureaucracy** Critics of the ESM believe there is too much bureaucracy, form-filling and processes to be adhered to in order to trade freely in the EU. This can lead to firms missing out on market opportunities, e.g. increased demand for their products.
4 Economies of Scale Increased production levels can result in economies of scale for Irish firms. This can help to reduce business costs, which can be passed on to the consumer as lower prices.	**4 Competition** Irish businesses may be unable to compete with larger EU firms that have a wider range of products or can sell at lower prices. Irish firms may be forced to close, leading to redundancies.

5 European Monetary Union (EMU)

The EMU policy involves co-ordinating common economic, monetary and currency policy among the EU member states. All EU countries operate in the economic union, but 19 countries have adopted the euro as the common currency. The currency area that uses the euro is known as the eurozone.

DID YOU KNOW? *Ireland chose the image of the harp for the country side of the euro coins. This was the same symbol that had been used on the IR£1 coins. Ireland is the only eurozone country that uses one symbol for all its coins.*

You have already learned about exchange rate calculations in Chapter 25.

Activity 30.17

Look at the one euro coins below. Can you name which European countries they are from?

1  2  3  4  5

Advantages of the European Monetary Union

A **Price comparisons:** A common currency allows consumers to compare the price of goods and services across the EU. This means that they can shop around and get the best value for their money.

B **Increased tourism:** Tourism has increased, as people do not have to change currency when they travel between eurozone countries. This has helped to increase sales and profits in the tourist industry.

C **Foreign exchange:** Businesses do not have to pay currency conversion rates or deal with currency fluctuations when making payments to other businesses. This reduces business costs.

D **European Central Bank (ECB):** The ECB sets interest rates, which impact on inflation rates. This helps to ensure that businesses do not experience rapidly increasing prices for goods and services.

Disadvantages of the European Monetary Union

A **Export partners:** Ireland's main export partners, the UK and the USA, are not members of the eurozone. If the euro increases in value against the pound sterling or the US dollar, it makes Irish exports more expensive. This may result in a loss of sales and profits.

B **Reduced independence:** Eurozone countries must adhere to strict rules relating to government spending, borrowing and inflation. This reduces the ability of national governments to make decisions that may be in the best interests of the country, e.g. increasing or decreasing interest rates.

C **Increased supervision:** Since the recession, the Irish government has been forced to make difficult economic decisions, e.g. reducing government spending based on advice given by the European Union. These decisions have been unpopular with many Irish citizens.

Activity 30.18

Duff Ltd purchases raw materials from a UK company. This month the raw materials cost £2,500. How much will the raw materials cost in euro?

	Bank Sells	Bank Buys
Currency	1.045	1.120

---

6 EU Social Charter

The European Social Charter guarantees certain social and economic rights to all EU citizens, e.g. in housing, employment, education and health. It also places specific emphasis on protecting the rights of certain vulnerable groups, including elderly people, children, people with disabilities and migrants.

Advantages of the EU Social Charter

A **Employment:** It has helped to improve pay and working conditions for employees throughout the EU. Employees have the right to healthy and safe working conditions and a minimum of four weeks' annual holiday with pay.

B **European Social Fund (ESF):** The ESF was established to help prevent unemployment in the EU. It invests in education and skills, e.g. training for young people and people with disabilities.

DID YOU KNOW? *Ireland has received over €7 billion in funding from the European Social Fund since 1973.*

C **Equality in the workplace:** All workers have the right to equal treatment in the workplace, e.g. access to training and promotion. Male and female employees have the right to receive equal pay for equal work.

D **Social assistance:** The Social Charter ensures that people in EU member states are provided with medical and social assistance if they do not have the resources themselves.

Disadvantages of the EU Social Charter

A **Increased costs:** The EU Social Charter has increased business costs, as firms must comply with more rules and regulations relating to pay and working conditions for employees.

B **Social welfare tourism:** Some EU citizens may claim to be living in one country to obtain social welfare but work in another state, e.g. claiming Jobseeker's Benefit in Ireland but working in the UK. This social welfare tourism has led to increased costs for EU governments.

Activity 30.19

On the Internet watch the European Parliament video 'Free Movement of Workers' to help you to revise the EU Social Charter.

Unit 7

7 EU Regional Policy

The EU regional policy focuses on urban and rural areas across the member states of the EU. It aims to encourage job creation, businesses' competitiveness and sustainable development and to improve the quality of life of EU citizens.

The regional policy is delivered through two main funds:

- European Regional Development Fund (ERDF)
- Cohesion Fund.

Fund Name	Description	Programmes Funded	Examples
European Regional Development Fund (ERDF)	→ Aims to reduce the gap between wealthy and poorer regions in Europe.	→ Investment in high-speed broadband for all citizens and businesses. → Financial support and training for small and medium enterprises.	→ Family business Goatsbridge Trout Farm experienced a fall in the sale of fresh trout due to increased imports. The company received ERDF funding to develop a range of smoked trout, which created a new market for the firm.
Cohesion Fund	→ Aims to reduce economic and social imbalance and encourage sustainable development. It applies to certain countries, e.g. Malta and Greece.	→ Flood relief projects. → Railway line upgrades. → Waste water treatment projects.	→ A national flood relief project in Malta received €44.9 million in funding from the Cohesion Fund. The funding was used to construct a network of underground tunnels, canals and bridges, reducing the negative impact of flash floods.

Advantages of the EU Regional Policy

A **Distribution of wealth:** All member states contribute to this fund. Money is given to countries that need assistance to improve areas such as infrastructure. The EU wants all its countries and citizens to have the same social and economic standards.

B **Long-term unemployment:** It supports schemes that invest in education and training programmes to prevent long-term unemployment in the EU.

C **Entrepreneurship:** Funding to small and medium-sized businesses helps to encourage entrepreneurship in the EU. This creates direct and indirect employment in local areas and may encourage others to establish their own businesses.

Disadvantages of the EU Regional Policy

A **Tension:** Some countries may resent contributing money to less-developed countries, e.g. Estonia and Cyprus. This can lead to tension and discontent between member states.

B **Complexity:** Some critics believe that it is difficult for businesses and organisations to obtain funding from the various funds, e.g. Cohesion Fund and ERDF. Some countries and programmes may miss out on available funds for their projects.

BENEFITS OF EU MEMBERSHIP FOR IRELAND

Since joining the EU, Ireland has received a range of benefits from membership, including:

1 **Single market:** The single market has helped Irish businesses recruit workers, obtain goods and services at more competitive prices and enabled Irish citizens to travel freely within EU countries.

2 **Agriculture:** Agricultural methods in Ireland have improved due to funding from the CAP. Irish farmers have been guaranteed prices for their produce, which has led to a higher standard of living.

3 **Education:** Funding from the EU has increased the number of students in Ireland attending third-level institutions. EU study schemes such as Erasmus have allowed Irish students to study at other EU third-level institutions.

DID YOU KNOW?

Over the past thirty years, the Erasmus programme has provided support and grants to 3.3 million students to study, train and work in EU countries.

4 **Larger market:** Free trade has enabled Irish businesses to sell to a large market of EU customers. This can help to increase a firm's sales and profits.

5 **Consumers:** Irish consumers benefit from access to a wider range of goods and services at lower prices because of our membership of the EU. Products are also safer due to EU legislation relating to product safety.

DID YOU KNOW?

Fifteen thousand free InterRail tickets have been made available for 18-year-olds in the EU as part of a programme to increase young people's connection with the EU.

DRAWBACKS OF EU MEMBERSHIP FOR IRELAND

1 **Decision-making:** Some EU decisions benefit the majority of member states but may not be in the best interests of Ireland.

2 **Business closure:** A significant number of small Irish businesses have been unable to compete with larger and more efficient EU firms. This has led to business closures and job losses.

3 **The euro:** As part of the eurozone, Ireland can be impacted by an increase in the value of the euro. This can make Irish exports more expensive and lead to a decrease in sales and profits for Irish firms.

4 **Brexit:** The Irish export market is closely linked to the UK and there are concerns that after Brexit the UK will reintroduce tariffs and other protectionist measures. These will make Irish exports more expensive and could lead to a fall in sales and profits for Irish firms.

OPPORTUNITIES FACING THE EUROPEAN UNION

Despite the uncertainty of Brexit and political instability in some member states, the European Union still offers many opportunities:

1 **Enlargement:** A number of countries want to join the EU. This would increase the potential market size for businesses and help to increase business sales and profits.

2 **Improve institutions:** EU institutions are known for their complex procedures and slow decision-making. The EU has the opportunity to simplify these procedures and give its institutions the ability to react faster to changes in the EU.

3 **EMU expansion:** An increase in the number of eurozone countries would help consumers to compare prices across member states and increase tourism, as tourists would not have to change currency.

4 **Budgetary reform:** Many member states have criticised the amount of money allocated to agriculture in the EU budget. Some critics believe that budgetary reform is needed to reallocate funding to other areas such as transport, education and employment.

CHALLENGES FACING THE EU

- **Countries leaving the EU:** The exit of the UK from the EU could encourage other member states to leave. This could result in the reintroduction across Europe of trade barriers such as tariffs.

 It is estimated that it will cost the UK €45 billion to leave the EU, taking into account its unpaid debts and other costs.

- **Corporation tax:** Pressure has been placed on the Irish government to increase corporation tax in line with other EU countries. If this happens it would reduce the country's competitive advantage and transnational companies might locate in other countries instead of Ireland.

- **Refugees:** The EU needs to develop a better common policy to deal with the large number of refugees, so that individual countries are not overwhelmed by a mass influx of migrants.

 Almost 11 million refugees have left their homes since the outbreak of civil war in Syria in 2011. Many have travelled in boats to European countries such as Greece and Italy.

- **Climate change:** The EU needs to increase its commitment to the European Climate Change Programme to ensure that all member states are working together to reduce their impact on climate change for future generations.

Activity 30.20

Create a mind ma p to summarise the opportunities and challenges facing the European Union. You can draw this or use mind map websites such as www.coggle.ie or www.popplet.com.

KEY TERMS

Now you have completed this chapter, you should understand and be able to explain the following terms. In your copybook, write a definition of each term to build up your own glossary of terms.

- European Union
- European Commission
- European Parliament
- Member of the European Parliament (MEP)
- co-decision
- Council of the European Union
- European Court of Auditors
- Court of Justice of the European Union (CJEU)
- European Investment Bank (EIB)

- EU directive
- EU regulation
- EU recommendation
- EU decision
- democratic deficit
- special interest groups
- Common Agricultural Policy (CAP)
- Common Fisheries Policy (CFP)
- EU Competition Policy
- deregulation
- cartel

- European Single Market (ESM)
- government tender
- European Monetary Union (EMU)
- eurozone
- EU Social Charter
- European Regional Development Fund (ERDF)
- European Social Fund (ESF)
- Cohesion Fund

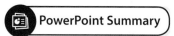 PowerPoint Summary

EXAM-STYLE QUESTIONS

Ordinary Level

Section 1 – Short Questions (10 marks each)

1 Name **three** European Union institutions.

2 Name **two** functions of the European Parliament.

3 What do the following letters stand for? (i) EU (ii) ESM (iii) EMU

4 What do the following letters stand for? (i) CAP (ii) CFP (iii) MEP

5 Complete the following sentences using the correct policy from the list.

EU Competition Policy   EU Social Charter   Common Fisheries Policy

European Single Market   Common Agricultural Policy

  (i)   The _____ sets a limit on the quantity and species of fish that can be caught by EU boats.

 (ii)   The _____ ensures that employees have safe and healthy working conditions and receive four weeks' paid holidays a year.

(iii) The _____ allows for free trade between EU member states.

(iv) The _____ ensures that businesses do not abuse their dominant position in the market.

 (v)   The _____ ensures that there is a sustainable supply of food in Europe and that agricultural incomes are protected.

6 Outline **one** benefit of the Common Fisheries Policy.

7 Name **three** EU policies.

8 Distinguish between an EU directive and an EU regulation.

9 Outline **two** advantages of EU membership for Ireland.

10 State whether each of the following statements is true or false.

	Statements	True or False
A	Special interest groups use lobbying to influence decision-makers in the EU.	
B	The Competition Policy can prevent certain mergers taking place.	
C	The European Single Market (ESM) does not allow freedom of movement of people between EU countries.	
D	The countries that use the euro are known as Euroland.	
E	The EU budget is prepared by the Court of Auditors.	

Section 2 – Long Questions

1 The European Commission is responsible for <u>proposing new laws</u> and <u>enforcing EU laws</u>. Explain the underlined terms. **(15 marks)**

2

> The Council of the European Union can sign agreements on behalf of all EU countries.

  (i)   What is an international agreement? Name **one** agreement that the Council of the European Union has signed.

 (ii)   Describe **one** other function of the Council of the European Union. **(15 marks)**

3 Outline the role of the European Court of Auditors. **(20 marks)**

4 Describe the role of the Court of Justice of the European Union. **(15 marks)**

5 Discuss the methods used by special interest groups to influence decision-makers in the European Union. **(15 marks)**

6 Distinguish between an EU decision and a recommendation. **(15 marks)**

7 Discuss **two** advantages and **one** disadvantage of the EU Social Charter. **(15 marks)**

8 The European Single Market (ESM) allows for <u>free trade</u> between member states and <u>freedom of movement of capital</u>. Explain the underlined terms in relation to the ESM. **(15 marks)**

Section 2 – Long Questions *continued*

9 What is the name of the common currency used in 19 EU member states? Explain **two** advantages of Ireland using this currency. **(15 marks)**

10 Discuss **two** opportunities and **one** challenge for Irish firms operating in the EU. **(20 marks)**

Higher Level

Section 1 – Short Questions (10 marks each)

1 Outline **two** functions of the European Commission.

2 Outline **two** functions of the European Parliament.

3 Distinguish between an EU directive and an EU decision.

4 List **three** special interest groups who aim to influence decision-making in the EU. Outline **one** method used by the interest group.

5 Name **four** EU policies. Outline **one** of these policies.

6 What do the following letters stand for? (i) EMU (ii) ESM (iii) EU (iv) CJEU

7 Outline the disadvantages of the Common Fisheries Policy.

8 'The European Social Charter helps to protect EU citizens.' Discuss this statement.

9 What is meant by the term *deregulation*?

10 Indicate by means of a tick (✔) the EU policy described in each sentence.

Statements		Common Agricultural Policy	Common Fisheries Policy	Social Charter	European Single Market	Competition Policy
A	This policy ensures that cartels cannot be formed among businesses.					
B	This policy provides funding for training courses for young people to prevent unemployment.					
C	This policy aims to protect rural environments by providing higher payments for commitment to environmentally friendly farming practices.					
D	This policy supports the growth of the aquaculture industry.					
E	This policy imposes common tariffs on imported goods and services from outside the EU.					

Section 2 – Applied Business Question (80 marks)

The Curran Family and the European Union

The Curran family has a long association with the EU and recently Louise Curran moved to Brussels to take up her position as a Member of the European Parliament.

There is a lot for her to learn about her new role and she wants to make sure that she represents her constituents to the best of her ability. Her first duty is to review some new legislative proposals regarding farming regulations. A representative from the Irish Farmers' Association (IFA) has already scheduled a meeting with Louise. The representative is based in the Brussels office of the IFA and wants to discuss a new social media campaign to support rural employment. Louise has also received documentation concerning the EU budget which she must review and consider the impact it will have on Ireland. This morning Louise received a report from the EU Commission relating to the implementation of the EU budget. Louise has a number of questions that she would like to pose to the Commission and gets to work to ensure that she has all the relevant information.

In Brussels Louise's sister, Lily Curran has started working at a local engineering firm. Lily is a recent engineering graduate but struggled to find work in Ireland. In conversation with fellow engineering graduates in Ireland, she has found that some Irish businesses are offering lower rates of pay for women performing the same duties as men. She decided to take up a position in Brussels as the wages were far higher than offered in Ireland. Lily has spent some time today researching her employment rights in Belgium, particularly in relation to leave entitlements. Lily wants to visit friends in Berlin and as she is so busy with her new job, she is relieved that she will be able to use euro there as she doesn't have time to go to the bank. She has booked her flights and found it very easy to compare prices as they were all given in euro.

Back in Ireland, Louise and Lily's father, Joe, is working on his farm. He grows wheat and barley which will be used in the food sector. Joe has seen many changes in farming over the years, particularly in the area of technology – lots of new machinery and methods to improve crop and animal yields. Today is a busy day for Joe as he must plant some new hedgerows in a number of his fields to provide more natural protection for animals and wildlife. On his way to the fields, Joe meets a local man who farmed the land for many years. Times have been difficult for this family and the farm has ceased production as it was simply too small to survive. Joe thinks this is a shame as small local farms are vital to maintaining rural life in Ireland.

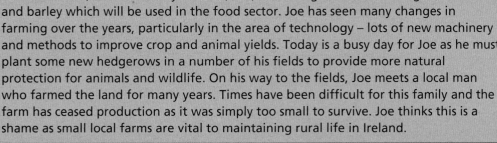

A Louise Curran is a recently elected MEP in the European Parliament. What do the letters MEP stand for? Outline the role of the European Parliament. **(15 marks)**

B The introduction of EU policies has had a significant impact on EU citizens.

  (i) Evaluate the impact of the EU Social Charter and the European Monetary Union (EMU) on the life of Lily Curran. **(25 marks)**

  (ii) Discuss the impact of the Common Agricultural Policy on Joe Curran. **(20 marks)**

C Define the term *special interest groups*. Discuss the methods used by special interest groups to influence MEPs such as Louise Curran. **(20 marks)**

Section 3 – Long Questions

1 Explain the role of any **two** of the following European institutions.
  - The European Commission
  - The Court of Justice of the European Union (CJEU)
  - The Council of the European Union. **(20 marks)**

2 Contrast the role of the Court of Justice of the European Union and the Court of Auditors. **(25 marks)**

3 Evaluate the methods used by special interest groups to influence decision-makers in the EU. **(20 marks)**

4 Evaluate the benefits and drawbacks of the EU Social Charter on business. **(20 marks)**

Section 3 – Long Questions continued

5
> Small farming communities are becoming a rare sight in the Irish countryside.

Outline the impact the Common Agricultural Policy has had on Irish farmers. **(15 marks)**

6
> 'Irish seafood industry to achieve €1 bn sales by 2020.' *Irish Examiner*

Outline the impact the Common Fisheries Policy has had on the fishing industry in Ireland. **(20 marks)**

7 Evaluate the impact of the following policies on Irish businesses:
- European Single Market
- European Competition Policy **(20 marks)**

8 Describe the benefits and drawbacks of the EU Regional Policy. **(15 marks)**

9 Discuss the benefits to Irish firms of membership of the EU. **(20 marks)**

10
> International activity has allowed a small country like Ireland to obtain a greater range of goods and services.

Explain the opportunities and challenges facing the European Union. **(25 marks)**

PREVIOUS LEAVING CERTIFICATE EXAM QUESTIONS

Ordinary Level

Section A – Short Questions (10 marks each)

1 Name **two** EU institutions. [LC OL 2017]

2 Name **two** European Union (EU) policies. [LC OL 2016]

3 State **two** benefits of EU membership for Irish business. [LC OL 2010]

Section B

1 Name **two** EU institutions and explain the role of **one** of them. **(20 marks) [LC OL 2013]**

2 List **three** EU policies and explain the role of **one** of them. **(20 marks) [LC OL 2000]**

3
> In June 2016, the UK voted to leave the European Union (EU). This became widely known as 'Brexit'. More than €1.2 billion of goods and services are traded between the UK and Ireland every week. Brexit could result in trade barriers such as tariffs being imposed.

(i) Outline **two** advantages for Ireland of membership of the EU.

(ii) Outline **one** disadvantage for Ireland of membership of the EU. **(20 marks) [LC OL 2017]**

Higher Level

Section A – Short Questions (10 marks each)

1 Write True or False for each of the following statements.

Statements		True or False
A	The EU Commission is directly elected by EU citizens.	
B	Membership of the eurozone is essential for the free movement of goods, services, people and capital between EU member states.	
C	A 'Directive' is a law applicable to all EU member states with immediate effect.	
D	The Council of the European Union is the main decision-making body of the EU.	
E	In the co-decision procedure the European Parliament shares legislative power with the Council of the European Union.	

[LC HL 2018]

Section A – Short Questions (10 marks each) *continued*

2 Column 1 is a list of EU institutions. Column 2 is a list of possible explanations of these institutions. *(One explanation does not relate to any of the institutions.)*

Match the two lists in your copybook by writing your answers in the form *number = letter* (e.g. 1 = A).

Terms		Explanations	
1	European Parliament	A	Draws up proposals for new EU law.
2	European Commission	B	Most important decision-making body in the EU.
3	European Court of Justice (Court of Justice of the European Union)	C	Ensures the EU budget is spent efficiently.
4	European Court of Auditors	D	Is responsible for ensuring the correct interpretation and application of EU laws by member states.
5	Council of the European Union (Council of Ministers)	E	Is responsible for managing the euro currency and the EU's monetary policy.
		F	Directly elected by EU citizens.

[LC HL 2010]

3 The flow chart states the role of the institutions involved in the EU decision-making process. Fill in the names of the **three** different European Union institutions at (A), (B) and (C).

(A)	(B)	(C)	Legislation applied in member states.
Drafts a proposal.	Approves or rejects a proposal.	Adopts a proposal, making it law.	

[LC HL 2016]

4 (i) Explain the role of the European Commission.

(ii) Name the **two** other main decision-making institutions of the European Union. [LC HL 2017]

Section B

1

Examples of an EU Directive and a Regulation affecting Ireland

Waste Framework Directive 2008/98/EC requires member states to adopt waste management plans and waste prevention programmes.

Regulation (EU) No.1169/2011, which came into effect on 14 December 2014, includes new requirements for the way in which allergen information must be displayed in restaurants, delis, canteens, takeaways, cafés and retail outlets.

Outline how EU directives and regulations are formulated and implemented. **(20 marks)** [LC HL 2015]

2 In the context of the European Union (EU), distinguish between a Directive and a Regulation. Choose **one** example of either and describe its purpose. **(15 marks)** [LC HL 2008]

3 Evaluate the impact that any **two** of the following EU policies have on Irish businesses:

(i) European Monetary Union (EMU)

(ii) European Union Competition Policy

(iii) European Social Charter. **(20 marks)** [LC HL 2014]

4 Should Ireland leave the European Union? Outline reasons for your answer. **(20 marks)** [LC HL 2017]

Solutions

Unit 7

CHAPTER 31
GLOBAL BUSINESS

Literacy Link

Transnational company (TNC), globalisation, global business, global marketing, standardised marketing mix, adapted marketing mix

Numeracy Link

Percentages, addition, multiplication, currency conversion

Cross-curricular Link

Geography – globalisation, multinational companies
Languages – global communication
Religion – global citizenship

CASE STUDY

The Coca-Cola Company

Formed in 1886, the Coca-Cola Company has grown from a business primarily based in the United States to a **transnational company** and then expanded into a **global business** with **brands** that are recognised all over the world. In addition to the iconic Coca-Cola drinks range, other **global products** owned by the firm include Fanta, Sprite and Powerade. As the world's largest drinks company, it has operations in over 200 countries and its distinctive red and white logo is recognised by 94% of the world's population. The **brand name** alone is valued at over €61 billion.

In 2016, the company announced that three Coca-Cola brands – original Coke, Diet Coke and Coke Zero – would be united under a **global marketing mix** with the slogan 'Taste the Feeling'. The company has always used **global promotion** methods such as **sponsorship** and has supported every Olympic Games since 1928.

The Coca-Cola Company uses **computer-aided design (CAD)** to create different bottles and cans for its product ranges. Redesigning packaging helps the company save money and reduce packaging waste. The firm has a global ambition to make all its packaging recyclable by 2030.

Coca-Cola arrived in Ireland in 1952 and was produced under **licence** by Munster Bottlers of Cork. As a client of **IDA Ireland**, the company announced an investment of €26 million in its operations in Ballina, Co. Mayo. This investment led to the creation of twenty-five new jobs at the plant.

The firm employs 1,700 people in Ireland at facilities in Antrim, Dublin, Kildare, Louth, Mayo and Wexford. In addition to the **foreign direct investment (FDI)** made by Coca-Cola in Ireland, the company also partners with **Enterprise Ireland** to mentor fast-growth food and drink entrepreneurs in Ireland. The Thrive project has helped **indigenous businesses acquire knowledge and skills** from global businesses such as Coca-Cola.

The Coca-Cola Company continues to expand globally and recently acquired the Costa Coffee chain for over €4 billion.

TRANSNATIONAL COMPANIES

Many businesses expand by selling their products in different countries. This gives the business the opportunity to increase sales and profits by selling to a larger, more diverse market of consumers. Some businesses expand to become transnational companies.

A transnational company produces and markets goods in more than one country. It moves operations from one country to another in response to changing market conditions, e.g. cheaper raw materials or changing political systems such as the UK planning to leave the European Union.

> **Definition: Transnational company (TNC)**
> A business with headquarters in one country and branches of the firm in other countries, e.g. Glanbia, Circle K and Smurfit Kappa Group. TNCs are also referred to as multinational companies (MNCs).

Reasons for the Development of Transnational Companies

1 **Improvements in transport:** Transport vehicles, e.g. ships and aeroplanes, are now capable of carrying larger loads and can travel at faster speeds. This allows more goods to be transported faster to supply markets worldwide.

2 **Free trade:** Free trade agreements allow goods and services to move between countries with fewer trade barriers. For example, the European Single Market enables Irish firms to sell goods and services to other EU states without the imposition of protectionist measures such tariffs or quotas.

3 **Developments in ICT:** Advances in communications technology such as email have made it easier and faster for businesses to send and receive information around the world. This enables firms to make quicker and often better business decisions.

4 **Economies of scale:** Expanding abroad helps firms to achieve economies of scale, e.g. discounts received from bulk buying materials. This enables TNCs to compete more effectively with larger competitors.

5 **Larger markets:** Many businesses find that the home market is too small and offers little scope for expansion. By selling overseas, a business can maximise sales and therefore profits. This also helps to spread the risk of selling only in the home market.

Reasons why TNCs Locate in Ireland

Ireland has become a popular location for many transnational companies for a number of reasons, including:

1 **Corporation tax:** Ireland's low corporation tax rate of 12.5% means that businesses get to keep more of their profits.

2 **Ireland's reputation:** Many TNCs, such as Intel and PayPal, are based in Ireland. This has earned Ireland a reputation that it is a good place to do business and this encourages other businesses to locate here, e.g. Facebook and eBay.

3 **Skilled labour:** Ireland has a highly skilled and well-educated workforce. TNCs employ skilled graduates, many of whom work in research and development (R&D). R&D is a very important area in these businesses, e.g. Google.

1 Corporation tax

2 Ireland's reputation

3 Skilled labour

4 IDA Ireland

5 European Single Market

6 English language

Unit 7

501

4 **IDA Ireland:** This state agency is responsible for attracting foreign direct investment (FDI) to Ireland. Businesses such as Apple, Microsoft and Facebook have set up here with support from IDA Ireland.

You learned about IDA Ireland in Chapter 28.

5 **European Single Market:** The ESM allows free movement of goods, services, labour and capital between member states. Transnational companies located in Ireland have access to the EU market of over 500 million people.

6 **English language:** English is the main international business language and since Ireland is an English-speaking country it helps attract TNCs. The growing number of people living in Ireland who speak different languages is also a key factor in attracting TNCs to locate in Ireland.

DID YOU KNOW? *Ireland is the European hub of over 1,000 leading transnational companies.*

IMPACT OF TRANSNATIONAL COMPANIES ON THE IRISH ECONOMY

✓ Opportunities	✗ Challenges
1 Direct Employment TNCs provide jobs for thousands of workers in Ireland. Many employ staff in a wide range of roles such as computer programmers, customer services, marketing and administration.	**1 Footloose** Some TNCs are not loyal to Ireland and leave the country to move to low-cost economies, e.g. developing countries with lower wage costs. For example, Dell moved its production plant from Limerick to Poland, resulting in a loss of 2,500 direct jobs and almost 7,000 indirect jobs.
2 Spin-off Businesses TNCs buy goods and services from other businesses in Ireland, thus increasing employment in these firms, e.g. restaurants and taxi firms. This can encourage people to set up their own businesses to cater for the needs of employees in TNCs.	**2 Repatriation of Profits** While the government earns corporation tax on the profits earned by TNCs in Ireland, most of the money earned returns to the country where the firm's headquarters are located.
3 Reputation When TNCs choose Ireland as a location for their business, it gives the country a positive international reputation and may attract other TNCs to locate here.	**3 Tax Avoidance** Some TNCs use loopholes in the tax system to pay less tax to the Irish government. Therefore, the actual tax revenue earned by the government is less than expected.
4 Knowledge TNCs bring modern business knowledge and expertise to Ireland. Irish managers gain experience and learn from these foreign business managers.	**4 Over-reliance on TNCs** The Irish economy is over-reliant on TNCs to provide employment. People need to be encouraged to develop more indigenous businesses. These tend to remain loyal to Ireland even during difficult economic times and try to keep jobs in the Irish economy.
5 Balance of Payments Many of the TNCs export their products, which can help Ireland achieve a surplus on its balance of payments.	**5 Irish Firms** Small Irish firms may be unable to compete with larger TNCs, as they may not benefit from economies of scale. This can lead to the closure of Irish firms.

Valeo Foods Group

Valeo Foods is an Irish **transnational company** formed through a number of **mergers and acquisitions**. The firm owns brands such as Jacob's confectionery, Batchelor's, Kelkin and Odlums and sells more than 600 million units from its manufacturing facilities in Ireland, the UK and other parts of Europe. Valeo Foods sells its products into 92 international markets and has annual sales of over €870 million. It employs 2,000 staff and since 2010 has developed over 170 new products.

Activity 31.1

Working in pairs, research a transitional company operating in Ireland. Create a video presentation of this company using a presentation package such as Adobe Spark or Emaze.

GLOBAL BUSINESS

Globalisation is the integration of societies, cultures and economies around the world. This has occurred due to an increase in trade, communication, migration and transportation between countries. Globalisation has led to an increase in the number of global businesses operating worldwide.

> **Definition: Global business**
> A global business sells its goods and services all over the world. It views the world as one large market.

Global businesses produce goods anywhere in the world where they can avail of the cheapest labour and finance, i.e. they pay the minimum wage and borrow from banks that offer the lowest interest rates. They use a **global marketing strategy**, which can include a **standardised global marketing mix** (product, price, place, promotion) or an **adapted global marketing mix**. This helps to build a global brand. (You will learn more about the global marketing mix later in this chapter.) Examples of global businesses include Disney, Nike and Audi.

Activity 31.2

Search online for the video 'HSBC UK: Global Citizen' to see the impact of global businesses on the economy and society.

Reasons for the Development of Global Businesses

Global businesses have developed for a number of reasons, including:

1 **To spread risk:** When a business operates in multiple countries, it is not dependent on one market for its sales. Therefore, a fall in sales in one market can be offset by sales growth in another market. This reduces the risk of business failure.

2 **Economies of scale:** Savings can be made by operating on a larger scale, e.g. discounts for bulk purchasing raw materials. The business can pass on these lower costs to consumers in the form of lower prices.

3 **Deregulation:** A number of free trade agreements, e.g. the European Single Market, have led to a reduction in the barriers to international trade. This has allowed businesses easier access to foreign markets.

4 **Communication:** Advances in information and communications technology (ICT) has made communication between a business and its stakeholders such as consumers and suppliers easier, quicker and cheaper, e.g. email.

5 **E-commerce:** Goods can be sold worldwide via the internet, i.e. there is no need to set up stores in other countries, thus reducing business costs.

Unit 7

BEING A GLOBAL BUSINESS

✓ Benefits	✗ Risks
1 Increased Sales Global firms have access to larger markets all over the world. This gives them the opportunity to increase their sales and profit.	**1 Local Customers** Consumers might not purchase a standardised product, so the business must adapt the product to suit local tastes. This customisation increases business costs.
2 Economies of Scale As many global businesses buy raw materials in larger quantities, they benefit from economies of scale, e.g. discounts for bulk purchases.	**2 Local Customs** The global business must be aware of local customs to ensure that its product range or marketing mix does not offend local customs or cultures.
3 Marketing A standardised global marketing campaign can increase brand awareness among consumers in global markets. The business can find it easier to expand into new markets or launch new products as consumers recognise the global brand name, e.g. Nike, Pepsi, Chanel and Ford.	**3 Laws** New laws can make it difficult to trade globally. Some governments may introduce restrictions or bans on the products sold by the global firm. For example, some governments are considering restrictions on Airbnb rentals in city centre locations to make housing more affordable for local people.
4 Spreading Risk By operating in several global markets, the firm spreads its risk of failure. Sales in one market can compensate for falling sales in another market. This helps to reduce the likelihood of business failure.	**4 Complex Structure** Global firms can have a complex organisation structure. Communication and decision-making can slow down and the firm may not be able to react quickly to changes in the market.

Irish Global Businesses

Many Irish firms have grown to become global businesses. Some of these businesses have received advice and financial support from Enterprise Ireland.

> *You learned about Enterprise Ireland in Chapter 28.*

Some of the main global Irish businesses are:

- **CRH (Cement Roadstone Holdings):** A global market leader in building materials with over 80,000 employees in 32 countries worldwide.

- **Kerry Group:** An international leader in the ingredients market, its products include household names such as Dairygold, Denny and Charleville. It has over 24,000 employees and an annual turnover of €5.8 billion.

- **Smurfit Kappa:** Founded in 1934, making cardboard boxes and packaging boxes for the Irish market, it is now a global leader in paper packaging. It employs over 45,000 people in 350 production sites across 33 countries and has an annual turnover of over €8 billion.

IMPACT OF TECHNOLOGY ON THE GROWTH OF GLOBALISATION

Impact	Reason
Design	→ Computer-aided design (CAD) has made the design process faster and easier. This allows global businesses to react quickly to changes in global markets. For example, car manufacturers use CAD to develop car models faster at a lower cost.
Production	→ Global firms use computer-aided manufacturing (CAM) to control equipment and machinery using computers. This can enable global firms to mass produce their products. For example, battery manufacturer Duracell uses CAM to mass produce its range of batteries for worldwide markets.
Decision-making	→ Global businesses use the Internet to research information about competitors, markets and consumers. The business can visit competitors' websites and consumer forums and access government reports to aid decision-making, e.g. new product development or entering into new markets.
Stock Management	→ Electronic data interchange (EDI) can be used by global firms to manage stock levels around the world. EDI ensures that stores around the world have sufficient stock levels to meet consumer demand.
Marketing	→ Businesses can use social media platforms such as Facebook and Instagram to advertise their products and increase consumer awareness of their brand. Regular social media interaction with the brand can increase consumer loyalty.
Distribution	→ Container transport as well as computer software programs have helped business to distribute and transport their products at a lower cost to markets all over the world.

EFFECTS OF GLOBALISATION ON THE IRISH ECONOMY

Globalisation affects the Irish economy in many ways, including:

Positive Effects

1 **Economic growth:** Irish businesses can sell their products to much larger markets abroad. Since more goods are produced, this leads to economic growth for the Irish economy, e.g. Kerry Group.

It is estimated that American companies alone employ 115,000 people in Ireland, e.g. Microsoft and Intel.

2 **Labour force:** Demand for labour increases as global businesses fill job vacancies. This means that more Irish people stay in Ireland (less emigration) and people who left Ireland come back because there are more jobs here (immigration).

3 **Employment:** Global businesses provide direct and indirect employment in the economy. With more disposable income, consumer demand for services in areas such as health and wellbeing has increased, e.g. gyms, healthier food outlets, thus leading to job creation in these areas.

4 **Consumer choice:** Irish consumers have a greater range of products to choose from as more goods and services are available at competitive prices.

Negative Effects

1 **Competitiveness:** Globalisation may be viewed as a threat to Irish firms. It can result in an increased demand for foreign products and could lead to the closure of Irish firms unless they reduce costs and increase efficiency.

2 **Power:** In some cases, global businesses may hold too much power over local governments and can exert pressure on the government to make or change laws to suit the business. They may threaten to pull out of the country if their demands are not met.

3 **Profit repatriation:** Similar to TNCs, most of the profits earned by global businesses leave Ireland and are repatriated to the country where the firm's headquarters are located.

4 **Taxes:** Some global businesses locate in Ireland to pay less tax than they would pay in other countries. Such businesses may establish small-scale operations in Ireland, resulting in few jobs being created, and at the same time pay minimal corporation tax here.

Activity 31.3

Using your phone or similar device, take pictures of global branded products in your home, e.g. food, drinks, technology products. Share your pictures with your classmates and compile a Top Ten list of global brands. Make a poster or infographic of the top ten brands to display on the classroom wall.

GLOBAL MARKETING

Global businesses use a global marketing strategy. This involves marketing the firm's products worldwide using a standardised or adapted marketing mix, i.e. product, price, promotion and place.

> **Exam Tip!**
> You should be able to **explain** the 4Ps of global marketing and **describe** the changes that need to be made when using an adapted marketing mix.

Standardised Marketing Mix

This occurs when a business uses **the same marketing mix in all markets**, i.e. the **same product, price, promotion and place**. Firms such as Nike and Superdry use this approach when selling their products. This results in lower costs for the business and increased profits.

Adapted Marketing Mix

A global business may **change some element(s) of the marketing mix**, e.g. product or promotion. The changes are made to reflect differences in the market, such as differences in languages, cultures and economies. For example, car manufacturers produce right-hand-drive models for sale in Ireland and the UK.

The Global Marketing Mix

The global marketing mix consists of:

1 Global product

2 Global price

3 Global place

4 Global promotion.

1 Global Product

Global businesses aim to sell an undifferentiated product in all markets, e.g. Coca-Cola, Adidas. The product (i.e. the same product) is designed in a way that appeals to as many consumers as possible.

However, in some cases the product, including the brand name and packaging, may need to be adjusted to take into consideration:

- Language, e.g. product instructions and ingredients must be translated into the local language
- Cultural, e.g. Nike has created a range of hijabs for Muslim women
- Tastes, e.g. KitKat sells soy sauce-flavoured bars in Japan.

In some cases a business may need to adapt the brand name of the product when selling on the global market. For example, the Galaxy chocolate bar is sold with the brand name Dove in other countries.

DID YOU KNOW?

Starbucks adjusts its menu to reflect local tastes. In Hong Kong it sells dragon dumplings, while omelettes feature on the menu in France.

Activity 31.4

Study the image and then answer the following questions.

1 Identify **five** global brands that you recognise from this image.

2 List **two** products sold by each of your chosen brands.

3 Working in pairs, create a picture collage showing the development of the brand logo for one of the global brands that you have chosen. You could use PicCollage or a similar application to prepare your presentation.

Activity 31.5

The table below contains a number of global brand names found in Ireland. In pairs, find the name and logo used for these well-known brands in the countries listed in the right-hand column.

Brand name in Ireland	Countries where a different brand name is used
1 TK Maxx	USA
2 Opel Corsa	UK
3 Lynx	USA
4 HB ice cream	Bolivia
5 Flash cleaner	Germany

2 Global Price

The global business aims to charge the same price to consumers around the world, e.g. the Apple Watch.

Activity 31.6

In pairs, find out the price of an Apple Watch in Ireland, USA and the UK (make sure you select the same model for each country). Write down the price and the local currency. Using an app or website, e.g. An Post, convert the US and UK prices to euros. Based on your research, do you think Apple tries to charge a global price?

It is not always possible for a global business to charge the same price. The following factors affect the price that can be charged to customers in different markets.

Price Factor	Explanation
Cost of Living and Disposable Income	→ The price must reflect the cost of living and income levels in different countries. For example, a brand could charge a higher price in countries with a higher cost of living and larger disposable income.
Taxes	→ Different levels of taxation, e.g. VAT, affect the final price charged to consumers. For example, the price of an iPad is subject to VAT at 23% in Ireland, while in New York sales tax is 8.75%.
Local Price Levels	→ A global business will have to charge a price that is in line with local competitors in the market.
Exchange Rates	→ Exchange rates fluctuate and may increase the cost of manufacturing the product for the business. The firm then passes on these costs to the consumer in the form of higher prices.
Costs	→ Production, distribution, transport and marketing costs may be different in countries around the globe, thus impacting on the price charged to consumers. For example, transport costs for diesel and petrol are higher in Europe than in the USA.

Activity 31.7

The cost of making a McDonald's Big Mac includes the cost of ingredients, e.g. meat, vegetables, cheese, bread, as well as the cost of rent, equipment and labour. The selling price of a Big Mac is lower in countries with a lower cost of living. Here are some examples (converted into euro):

Argentina	€3.11	Germany	€4.00
Belgium	€4.20	India	€2.30
China	€2.70	Ireland	€4.20
Mexico	€2.20	Norway	€5.17

1 Calculate the difference in both amount and percentage terms between the highest and lowest prices in the countries listed above.

2 Why, do you think, does a Big Mac cost €2.20 in Mexico and €4.20 in Ireland?

3 Divide students into groups. Each group is assigned a particular item to research, e.g. a cup of coffee, a cinema ticket or a litre of petrol. The group must find out the price of the assigned item in five countries. You could use websites such as www.globalprice.info/en to help you with your research as well as the foreign exchange calculator on www.anpost.ie. Present your findings in chart format and share with the rest of the class.

3 Global Place

Goods and services are distributed from the producer to the consumer through various channels of distribution.

Global channels of distribution tend to be long, due to the distance between where the goods are produced and where the consumers are located. It often involves more intermediaries such as exporters and agents.

> *You learned about channels of distribution in Chapter 20.*

The channels available include:

- **Direct export:** The business can set up its own website and sell direct to customers. The firm does not need to set up shops or employ staff in each country into which it sells, thus reducing business costs.

- **Agent:** This is an independent person or business who sells the product in the local market in return for a commission payment. For example, Mercedes-Benz sells its cars through local car dealers in different countries, e.g. Sheehy Motors' Carlow.

- **Manufacturing abroad:** The business establishes a manufacturing plant in another country to produce the goods. This may reduce transport costs, as the products are made closer to the target market.

- **Licensing:** The firm gives a local business permission to produce or distribute the product in a particular market, in return for a fee. For example, Britvic produces 7UP in Ireland under a licence agreement with PepsiCo.

- **Joint venture:** The firm sets up a joint venture with a local firm to produce for a local market. For example, Volkswagen entered the Chinese market through a 50:50 joint venture with Shanghai Automotive Industry Corporation.

4 Global Promotion

Global businesses tend to use the same methods of promotion to market their products worldwide, i.e. they use a standardised promotional mix. This helps to keep costs low, but minor changes may need to be made in different markets, e.g. the language used in television and magazine advertisements may need to change in different countries.

Unit 7

Global businesses promote their products through:

Promotion Channel	Explanation	Example
Advertising	→ Global businesses may use the same advertisements worldwide but will have to consider differences in language, culture and advertising laws around the globe.	→ Coca-Cola advertising uses high-quality imagery and few words or phrases. These standardised advertisements can be used all over the world, with few changes to be made when shown in different markets.
Public Relations	→ Global businesses sponsor global events to increase consumer awareness and exposure of the brand and its products.	→ Nike sponsors sports events such as the Olympic Games and the FIFA World Cup.
Sales Promotion	→ Global firms run worldwide competitions and provide free samples to increase sales of their products.	→ Coca-Cola has run competitions where consumers can win holidays in locations around the world. The firm has also given away free samples of Coca-Cola Zero Sugar to promote the range.
Personal Selling	→ Global businesses train salespeople to share their knowledge and expertise with consumers. This can help to increase brand loyalty.	→ Apple trains its store employees to be able to explain the functionality and features of Apple products to consumers.

CASE STUDY — Global Marketing

Successful Global Marketing

Domino's Pizza is one of the largest pizza sellers in the world. It uses a standardised product in global markets, i.e. bread, sauce and cheese. Over half of the pizza toppings offered by Domino's are standard worldwide, but it offers different toppings to cater for local tastes in international markets, e.g. fish in Asia and curry in India.

Unsuccessful Global Marketing

Car manufacturer American Motors launched a model called the Matador. However, in Puerto Rico the name didn't have the intended meaning of courage and strength. In Spanish, 'matador' means 'killer', which, in a country with many hazardous roads, didn't give the drivers confidence in the car.

Activity 31.8

Working in pairs, complete a fishbone graphic organiser, summarising **two** elements of the global marketing mix assigned by your teacher, e.g. product and place. Swap your graphic organiser with another pair of students who have completed the other two elements of the marketing mix. Evaluate and add any missing information to the graphic organiser you have received.

Importance of Global Marketing

1 **Increased sales:** Global marketing increases consumer awareness of the brand. When the business launches new products, consumers recognise the brand name and are willing to try new products launched by the firm. This increases sales and profits for the global business.

2 **Lower costs:** A global business can sell a standardised product all over the world. It can benefit from economies of scale achieved through bulk buying and discounts received from suppliers. This reduces business costs and enables the firm to sell the product at competitive prices.

3 **Improved quality:** Global businesses invest heavily in R&D to produce high-quality products for consumers. As they also produce large quantities of the same product, they develop high quality standards, resulting in better-quality products for consumers.

Unit 7

4 **Adapted marketing mix:** Most successful global businesses are aware that certain elements of the marketing mix will need to be changed to meet consumer demand in all markets. It changes elements to appeal to consumers in the market, thus increasing sales.

Example
Ben & Jerry's ice cream launched a new flavour, exclusively for the Japanese market, called Lemont Fuji. It uses lemons and apples grown in Japan to appeal to Japanese consumers.

KEY TERMS

Now you have completed this chapter, you should understand and be able to explain the following terms. In your copybook, write a definition of each term to build up your own glossary of terms.

- transnational company (TNC)
- foreign direct investment (FDI)
- repatriation of profits
- globalisation

- global business
- Enterprise Ireland
- global marketing
- standardised marketing mix
- adapted marketing mix

- global product
- global price
- global place
- agent
- global promotion

 **PowerPoint Summary**

EXAM-STYLE QUESTIONS

Ordinary Level

Section 1 – Short Questions (10 marks each)

1 What is a transnational company? State **two** examples.
2 List **two** reasons why transnational companies have developed.
3 List **two** advantages and **one** disadvantage of transnational companies to the Irish economy.
4 Name the 4Ps of the global marketing mix.
5 Using your knowledge of global brands, identify the brands below from their logos.

Logo		Brand Name/Business
(i)		
(ii)		
(iii)		
(iv)		
(v)		

6 Describe **two** reasons why a global business might need to change the price of its product in different global markets.

7 Outline **two** ways in which a global business can sell its products into global markets.

8 In your copybook write the correct words to complete each of the following statements.

(i) The 4Ps of the global marketing mix are product, global p_____, global price and global p_____.

(ii) A global business is one that views the world as one s_____ marketplace.

(iii) E_____ _____ is a state agency that helps Irish businesses to expand into overseas markets.

(iv) An independent a_____ sells goods or supplies services in a local market in return for a commission.

(v) F_____ d_____ i_____ is used to encourage TNCs and global businesses to locate in Ireland. This funding is provided by IDA Ireland.

Section 2 – Long Questions

1 Explain **three** reasons why a transnational company would locate in Ireland.	**(15 marks)**
2 Describe **three** advantages for the Irish economy of the growth of TNCs.	**(15 marks)**
3 Distinguish between a standardised marketing mix and an adapted marketing mix.	**(15 marks)**
4 Describe the changes a business may need to make to its product, before selling it into a global market.	**(15 marks)**
5 A global business can use (i) *an agent*, (ii) *direct export* or (iii) *licensing to sell its products on the global market*. Outline **two** of the three terms relating to global marketing.	**(15 marks)**
6 Outline the benefits and risks for a firm operating as a global business.	**(20 marks)**

Higher Level

Section 1 – Short Questions (10 marks each)

1 Describe the positive impact that transnational companies (TNCs) have had on the Irish economy.

2 What is meant by the terms (i) *TNC* and (ii) *FDI*? Explain **one** of these terms.

3 Identify **two** reasons for the development of global companies.

4 Outline **two** changes in technology which have aided the growth of global firms.

5 Define *global marketing* and name **two** businesses that use global marketing.

6 CRH is a leading Irish global company operating in many countries around the world. Outline **two** benefits for CRH of operating globally.

7 Describe **two** risks for a business operating in a global market.

8 Column 1 is a list of key business terms associated with global business. Column 2 is a list of possible explanations for these terms. Match the two lists in your copybook by writing your answers in the form *number = letter* (e.g. 1 = A).

Terms		Explanations	
1	Agent	**A**	The use of the same 4Ps in all countries around the globe.
2	Enterprise Ireland	**B**	A business that views the world as one single marketplace.
3	Standardised Marketing Mix	**C**	When a business adjusts the marketing mix to suit local market conditions.
4	Global Business	**D**	An independent business that sells a company's products in a foreign market, for which it is paid a commission.
5	Adapted Marketing Mix	**E**	A state-owned organisation that provides financial assistance to Irish firms that want to export to foreign markets.

Unit 7

Section 2 – Applied Business Question (80 marks)

Kilchip Technology

Patrick Kilmartin established his computer chip manufacturing company, Kilchip Technology, in California 15 years ago. He wanted to expand the business by becoming a transnational company and planned to establish a high-tech manufacturing plant, using CAM, in Europe in order to sell into the EU market. As this was a very important decision, Patrick spent a lot of time researching online, examining where other large global businesses had established their European operations and the laws imposed on businesses in these countries. The market information for Ireland was positive, as it imposed relatively low taxes on company profits, as well as the fact that potential staff spoke English. After meeting with an IDA representative, Patrick chose Mayo as the location for his manufacturing facility, as it had good transport links and was located in close proximity to Galway–Mayo IT, which would provide a range of qualified staff.

Over the years, Patrick has established other manufacturing plants across Europe and he now wants the firm to become a global business. Patrick knows that there could be difficulties if the business grows too large but is aware that the company cannot remain competitive at its current size. Even with improvements in the firm's use of CAD, global competitors such as Intel produce in such large quantities that Patrick's firm is unable to compete on price.

In order to operate as a global business, Patrick wants to introduce an expensive stock management system to ensure that the firm operates as efficiently as possible. He knows that operating in a range of global markets will stop the firm becoming dependent on a small number of markets in the EU and increase the firm's sales and profits. Patrick also plans to invest in software programs to manage the distribution of the chips from factories around the world.

A   What is meant by the term *transnational company*? Outline the reasons why Patrick Kilmartin decided to base his transnational company in Ireland.   **(30 marks)**

B   Describe the benefits and risks that Kilchip Technology may experience operating as a global business.   **(30 marks)**

C   Evaluate the types of technology which have helped Kilchip Technology to become a global business.   **(20 marks)**

Section 3 – Long Questions

1 Describe the opportunities and challenges that a transnational company (TNC) can bring to the Irish economy.   **(20 marks)**

2 The number of global companies operating around the world has greatly increased over the past decade. Outline the factors which have led to the growth of global businesses.   **(20 marks)**

3 Explain what is meant by the term *adapted marketing mix*. Illustrate your answer with appropriate examples.   **(20 marks)**

4 Discuss the factors a global business might have to consider when setting the price of its product on the global market.   **(20 marks)**

5 Identify the benefits and risks for a business seeking to operate globally.   **(15 marks)**

6

> Vincent O'Rourke established his street food business in Co. Kildare in early 2000. Since then his business has become a nationwide success with over thirty branches. Vincent recognises the many opportunities for his business to expand by bringing Irish street food to markets in Europe and the USA.

The international environment offers Irish businesses such as Vincent's street food business many opportunities and challenges. Evaluate the importance of global marketing for a business such as Vincent's.   **(25 marks)**

PREVIOUS LEAVING CERTIFICATE EXAM QUESTIONS

Ordinary Level

Section A – Short Questions (10 marks each)

1 Describe, using an example, what is meant by a multinational company. **[LC OL 2018]**

2 Choose the appropriate words to complete the sentence below (one word does not apply).

    Standardised   **Strategic**   **Single**

    Global businesses view the world as one _____ market and use a global adapted marketing mix to sell a _____ product. **[LC OL 2015]**

3 Explain the term *global marketing*. **[LC OL 2008]**

4 What is a global product? Give **two** examples of global products. **[LC OL 2009]**

Section B

1 | Transnational companies, Irish-owned firms and the agricultural industry have an important role to play in the recovery of the Irish economy.

    Explain **two** reasons why transnational companies (multinational companies) locate in Ireland. **(15 marks) [LC OL 2011]**

2 (i) Explain the term *global business*.

   (ii) Name **two** global businesses. **(20 marks) [LC OL 2017]**

3 | **Glanbia**

    Glanbia plc, one of Ireland's top agribusinesses, produces food products for the Irish and international markets. It is based in Kilkenny, employs over 3,500 people in 14 countries, and had an annual turnover of €2.9 billion in 2012.

    Outline **two** benefits to Glanbia plc of being located in 14 different countries. **(15 marks) [LC OL 2014]**

Higher Level

Section A – Short Questions (10 marks each)

1 Explain the term *global business*. Name **two** examples of global businesses. **[LC HL 2017]**

Section B

1 Discuss reasons why multinational companies (MNCs) may choose to locate in Ireland. Provide examples to support your answer. **(20 marks) [LC HL 2015]**

2 Illustrate your understanding of the terms *standardised marketing mix* and *adapted marketing mix* in relation to global marketing. **(20 marks) [LC HL 2015]**

3 Discuss the different channels of distribution that Irish businesses may consider when introducing their products to international markets. **(15 marks) [LC HL 2017]**

4 (i) Explain the term *global marketing* and name **two** global businesses.

   (ii) A business involved in global markets faces additional marketing challenges. Discuss these challenges, using examples to support your answer. **(30 marks) [LC HL 2009]**

 Solutions

INDEX

NOTES

NOTES

NOTES